The sources of social power

VOLUME 4

Globalizations, 1945–2011

Distinguishing four sources of power – ideological, economic, military, and political – this series traces their interrelations throughout human history. This fourth volume of Michael Mann's analytical history of social power covers the period from 1945 to the present, focusing on the three major pillars of postwar global order: capitalism, the nation-state system, and the sole remaining empire of the world, the United States. In the course of this period, capitalism, nation-states, and empires interacted with one another and were transformed. Mann's key argument is that globalization is not just a single process, because there are globalizations of all four sources of social power, each of which has a different rhythm of development. Topics include the rise and beginnings of decline of the American empire, the fall or transformation of communism (respectively, the Soviet Union and China), the shift from neo-Keynesianism to neoliberalism, and the three great crises emerging in this period – nuclear weapons, the great recession, and climate change.

Michael Mann is Distinguished Professor of Sociology at the University of California, Los Angeles. He is the author of *Power in the 21st Century: Conversations with John Hall* (2011), *Incoherent Empire* (2003), and *Fascists* (Cambridge 2004). His book *The Dark Side of Democracy* (Cambridge 2004) was awarded the Barrington Moore Award of the American Sociological Association for the best book in comparative and historical sociology in 2006.

The sources of social power

VOLUME 4
Globalizations, 1945–2011

MICHAEL MANN

University of California, Los Angeles

CAMBRIDGE
UNIVERSITY PRESS

CAMBRIDGE UNIVERSITY PRESS
Cambridge, New York, Melbourne, Madrid, Cape Town,
Singapore, São Paulo, Delhi, Mexico City

Cambridge University Press
32 Avenue of the Americas, New York, NY 10013-2473, USA

www.cambridge.org
Information on this title: www.cambridge.org/9781107610415

First published 2013

Printed in the United States of America

A catalog record for this publication is available from the British Library.

Library of Congress Cataloging in Publication data
Mann, Michael, 1942–
    The sources of social power / Michael Mann.
        v.   cm.
    Contents: v. 1. A history of power from the beginning to AD 1760 – v. 2. The rise of
    classes and nation-states, 1760–1914 – v. 3. Global empires and revolution, 1890–1945 –
    v. 4. Globalizations, 1945–2011.
    Includes bibliographical references and index.
    ISBN 978-1-107-03117-3 (hardback : v. 1) – ISBN 978-1-107-63597-5 (pbk. : v. 1) –
    ISBN 978-1-107-03118-0 (hardback : v. 2) – ISBN 978-1-107-67064-8 (pbk. : v. 2) –
    ISBN 978-1-107-02865-4 (hardback : v. 3) – ISBN 978-1-107-65547-8 (pbk. : v. 3) –
    ISBN 978-1-107-02867-8 (hardback : v. 4) – ISBN 978-1-107-61041-5 (pbk. : v. 4)
    1. Social history.   2. Power (Social sciences)   I. Title.
    HN8.M28   2012
    306.09–dc23   2012028452

ISBN 978-1-107-02867-8 Hardback
ISBN 978-1-107-61041-5 Paperback

Contents

1   Globalizations

This fourth and final volume of my study of the history of power in human societies covers the period since 1945. It will focus on the three major pillars of postwar global order: capitalism (and the fate of the Soviet and Chinese alternatives to capitalism), the nation-state system, and the sole remaining empire of the world, the United States. The most obvious characteristic of all three in this period is their expansion over the globe, a process universally called globalization. Yet in my third volume I pluraled this term to indicate that more than one process of globalization was under way. As I have argued throughout my volumes, human societies form around four distinct power sources – ideological, economic, military, and political – which have a relative degree of autonomy from each other (this is my IEMP model of power). Their globalizations have also been relatively autonomous and remain so in this period. But the power sources are ideal types. They do not exist in pure form in the real world. Instead, they congeal around the major macroinstitutions of society – in this case, capitalism, the nation-state, and empires. The major novel ideologies of the period emanate from human attempts to understand the entwining of these three.

Let me first give a short definition of the four power sources. More detailed exposition can be found in the first chapters of my other three volumes. Power is the capacity to get others to do things that otherwise they would not do. In order to achieve our goals, whatever they are, we enter into power relations involving both cooperation and conflict with other people, and these relations generate societies. So power may be collective, embodying cooperation to achieve shared goals – power through others– and distributive, wielded by some over others. There are four main sources of both powers.

(1) **Ideological power** derives from the human need to find ultimate meaning in life, to share norms and values, and to participate in aesthetic and ritual practices with others. Ideologies change as the problems we face change. The power of ideological movements derives from our inability to attain certainty in our knowledge of the world. We fill in the gaps and the uncertainties with beliefs that are not in themselves scientifically testable but that embody our hopes and our fears. No one can prove the existence of a god or the viability of a socialist or an Islamist future. Ideologies become especially necessary in crises where the old institutionalized ideologies and practices no longer seem to work and where alternatives offered have as yet no track record. That is when we are most susceptible to the power of ideologists who offer us plausible but untestable theories of the world. Ideological power is generally a response to

developments in the other three power sources, but it then develops an emergent power of its own. It tends to be very uneven, suddenly important when we have to grapple with unexpected crisis, much less so at other times. Revived religious meaning systems will figure in this period, as will secular ideologies like patriarchy, liberalism, socialism, nationalism, racism, and environmentalism.

(2) **Economic power** derives from the human need to extract, transform, distribute, and consume the produce of nature. Economic relations are powerful because they combine the intensive mobilization of labor with more extensive networks of exchange. Contemporary capitalism has made global its circuits of capital, trade, and production chains, yet at the same time its power relations are those that penetrate most routinely into most peoples' lives, taking up about one-half of our waking hours. The social change economies produce is rarely swift or dramatic, unlike military power. It is slow, cumulative, and eventually profound. The main organization of economic power in modern times has been industrial capitalism, whose global development is central to this volume. Capitalism treats all the means of production, including labor, as commodities. All four main forms of market – for capital, for labor, for production, and for consumption – are traded against each other. Capitalism has been the most consistently dynamic power organization in recent times, responsible for most technological innovation – and most environmental degradation.

(3) **Military power**. I define military power as the social organization of concentrated and lethal violence. "Concentrated" means mobilized and focused; "lethal" means deadly. *Webster's Dictionary* defines "violence" as exertion of physical force so as to injure or abuse, or intense, turbulent, or furious and often destructive action or force. Thus military force is focused, physical, furious, and above all lethal. It kills. Military power holders say if you resist, you die. Since a lethal threat is terrifying, military power evokes distinctive psychological emotions and physiological symptoms of fear, as we confront the possibility of pain, dismemberment, or death. Military power is most lethally wielded by the armed forces of states in interstate wars, though paramilitaries, guerrillas, and terrorists will all figure in this volume. Here is an obvious overlap with political power, though militaries always remain separately organized, often as a distinct caste in society.

(4) **Political power** is the centralized and territorial regulation of social life. The basic function of government is the provision of order over a given territory. Here I deviate not only from Max Weber, who located political power (or "parties") in any organization, not just states, but also from political scientists' notion of governance administered by diverse entities, including corporations, nongovernmental organizations (NGOs), and social movements. I prefer to reserve the term "political" for the state – including local and regional as well as national-level government. States and not NGOs or corporations have the centralized-territorial form, which makes their rule authoritative over persons residing in their territories. I can resign membership of an NGO or a corporation and so flaunt its rules. I must obey the rules of the state in whose territory I reside or suffer punishment. Networks of political power are routinely regulated and coordinated in a centralized and territorial fashion. So political power is more geographically bounded than the other three sources. States also normally cover smaller, tighter areas than do ideologies

So what is generally called globalization involved the extension of distinct relations of ideological, economic, military, and political power across the world.

Concretely, in the period after 1945 this means the diffusion of ideologies like liberalism and socialism, the spread of the capitalist mode of production, the extension of military striking ranges, and the extension of nation-states across the world, at first with two empires and then with just one surviving. The relations among such phenomena form the subject matter of this volume.

Most discussions of globalization are not particularly interesting. In itself globalization has no distinctive content other than its range. Globalization does not *do* anything – with one exception to be discussed in a moment. Globalization in itself cannot be praised or blamed for the state of human society, for it is merely the product of expansions of the sources of social power. This is reflected in the fact that globalization has not generated innovative theories of society; theories previously used in the days when social scientists equated societies with nation-states have for the most part simply had their range expanded geographically, although this is often concealed by the desire of theorists to claim fame by unearthing fundamental transformations of society. Hyperglobalizers claim that globalization has led to a fundamentally different kind of society. More pejoratively, one might call this globaloney. Yet one aspect of globalization is intrinsically transformative: where human actions expand until they fill up the earth and rebound back on us. This is a boomerang effect whereby actions launched by human beings hit up against the limits of the earth and then return to hit them hard and change them. We can already see two ways this might occur. The first is that weapons of war have become so deadly that a nuclear or biological war might actually destroy human civilization. We already live under this threat, and I discuss it in Chapter 2. The second threat has not yet materialized but is predictable: economic expansion increases the harmful emissions produced by burning fossil fuels, and this too might eventually make human civilization insupportable. I discuss this in Chapter 12. Marxists identify a third possible boomerang. They argue that the expansion of capitalist markets might eventually fill up the earth, making further economic expansion impossible and generating major crisis. But to analyze these particular scenarios we must give content to globalization in terms of economic or military power relations. They, not globalization itself, produce the boomerang effect.

The most popular way of giving content to globalization has been to identify capitalism as its essential driver. Materialists see globalization as driven by economic pressures powered by capitalists' drive for profit, which in this period has generated revolutions in communications technology allowing the global extension of production chains and markets. No one can doubt that this has helped produce a remarkable expansion of capitalism across the globe. Only China now lies half-outside its sway (I discuss this in Chapter 8). Economists measure globalization by the increasing ratio of international trade to gross domestic product (GDP), or by global convergence of commodity prices, with indices of labor migration sometimes added. On these measures, we can see that economic globalization was proceeding gradually through the seventeenth, eighteenth, and early nineteenth centuries, but then between 1860 and 1914 came a surge. This was followed by stagnation mixed with depression and wars up until 1950, followed by recovery and then a second surge beginning about 1960 (O'Rourke & Williamson, 1999). This produced the most global economy there has ever been. Though trade-to-GDP ratios and migration flows are now only a little higher than in the period before 1914, much of the real economic product could not then be measured and included in calculations, whereas international trade flows were much easier to measure. The resulting ratio was biased upward. During the second surge finance capital flows have become almost instantaneous across the world, while manufacturing chains now also spread globally. All this is discussed in Chapters 6 and 11.

Economists actually define globalization as the global integration of markets, though this neglects the other main drivers, wars, political institutions, and ideologies. They also imply that globalization occurs only when the economy grows. Yet as my volumes show, recessions go global too. It is conventional to regard the period 1914 to 1945 as one in which globalization receded. International trade as a proportion of world GDP certainly did decline. I can agree that economic integration declined in the period, but economic disintegration globalized. There was a surge in the global diffusion of socialist and fascist ideologies, plus the only two wars we call world wars, as well as a depression so great that it dislocated almost all the countries of the world. This was a period of disintegrating globalizations. Similarly, the stalling of expansion from the 1970s led to neoliberal policies that brought about the global recession of 2008. And now we are faced with an even more global economic crisis – climate change. Growth has been increasingly global, but so too have its crises. This has not been simply an onward and upward story, for every human success story has entailed severe problems while every major disaster has had a silver lining. Economic growth destroys the environment and depletes natural resources; world wars yielded greater citizen rights.

Economic expansion has also varied geographically and has so far been less than global. Its late nineteenth-century surge tended to integrate western and northern Europe and its settler colonies into an Atlantic economy, while intensifying a great divergence from the rest of the world. The second surge from the 1960s drew in southern Europe and East Asia, and then much of Asia too – but not yet Africa or central Asia. We cannot generalize about globalization without regard for its varied geography or its precise temporality. Exactly where and when it expands are always important.

Economists try to explain global expansion through growth in total factor productivity (TFP), divided into capital, labor, and land productivity, with the residual assigned to technological innovation. Unfortunately, this residual is usually large; that means that to explain growth we need an explanation of technological change, which we lack. Economic historians narrow down the decisive nineteenth-century technological innovations to transport technologies – railroads and especially shipping – and in the early twentieth century to general-purpose technologies applicable across many industries, like electricity and the internal combustion engine. In the second surge period they have emphasized microelectronics and biotechnology. They also emphasize that the initial invention matters less than its subsequent diffusion. But to explain invention and diffusion takes economists away from their customary variables into social institutions in general. Consider the economic stagnation after World War I. There was no loss of technology; indeed communications technology was still developing. Instead, economists say, there was a failure of political institutions, with inadequate regulation of banking and currency practices and too ready a recourse to protection. Conversely, after World War II, they say that growth at first resulted more from better government policies and more open markets than from new technology. Even when the Internet and other microelectronic and microbiological products later kicked in, they produced much less growth than hyperglobalizers expected. Economists are still scratching their heads about growth and looking for help from historians, sociologists, and political scientists.

Unfortunately, we do not offer them much help. Most scholars prefer to describe rather than explain globalization. Scholte (2000: 89–110) has a go, trying to explain globalization in terms of two structural forces, capitalist production and rationalist knowledge, both in turn propelled forward by what he calls "actor initiatives" like technological innovations and governance regulation. This, however, is rather vague. My own view is that globalization results as human groups have sought to expand their collective and distributive powers to achieve their goals, and this has involved all four types of power source. It might be thought that this is a little vague, too, but much more content will be provided in the course of this volume.

Many sociologists also see globalization as primarily economic. Harvey (1989) sees it as produced in spurts by the overaccumulation of capital, and he does demonstrate the importance of this aspect. Castells is a hyperglobalizer, identifying a global "network society" modeled on the information technology revolution and its consequent restructuring of the capitalist enterprise. He says this produces changes in every aspect of life, from our material existence to our notions of civil society, nation, and self. It transforms, he declares poetically, the foundations of life, space, and time, through the constitution of a space of flows and of timeless time (1997:1). Capitalism is the new global empire, say the hyperglobalizers Hardt and Negri (2000). They see the order traditionally provided by nation-states as having been unraveled by the impact of transnational capitalism and replaced by an acephelous supranational capitalist order too complex to be monitored by any authoritative center. Sklair declares that capitalist forces are "the dominant driving force of the global system" – "a transnational capitalist class based on the transnational corporation is emerging that is more or less in control of the processes of globalization" (2000: 5; cf. Robinson & Harris, 2000). World systems theorists identify a capitalist world system embodying a division of labor between capital-intensive production in the core countries and low-skilled labor and raw materials in the global periphery, with a semiperiphery zone lying in between. This global structure is integrated at its higher levels by capitalism, though with cultural and political pluralism surviving lower down. In the world system, they say, "the basic linkage between its parts is economic," operating "on the primacy of the endless accumulation of capital via the eventual commodification of everything" (Wallerstein, 1974a: 390; 1974b: 15). They qualify this with a dose of geopolitics, saying that the world system developed most in periods when one single imperial state was hegemonic. First the Dutch, then the British, and most recently the Americans became hegemonic, setting the rules of the world system. As each state's hegemony faltered, so did globalization (Arrighi, 1994; Arrighi & Silver, 1999). Yet the emergence of hegemony is attributed to the functional needs of the capitalist world system – economic power transforms geopolitical power. I critiqued this argument in Volume 3. All these models see globalization as driven by the capitalist economy, which is partly true . Yet the economy is not the only driver of human societies.

Note the relative absence in these paragraphs of the working or middle classes. In Volume 3 I argued that in the advanced countries the masses were leaping onstage in the theater of power – concentrated in cities and factories, demanding citizen rights, conscripted into mass armies, mobilized by demotic ideologies and mass parties. Yet this contrasted with the colonies, where the masses were only just beginning to stir. Now in this volume we see a partially reversed contrast. In the former colonies, nowadays styled as the South of the world, we see the masses leaping onstage in the theater of power. In the advanced countries, now styled the North of the world, we initially see the deepening of mass rights of civil, political, and social citizenship. But then we see something of a regress in the North. Of course, there is considerable variability in both the North and the South. But since most writers on the globalization of capitalism tend to focus on recent decades and on the Anglophone countries, they tend to be pessimistic about the capacity of working- and middle-class people to resist the power of capitalism, and they are alarmed by the rising inequality there among the classes. These are issues I will explore in this volume.

Materialists have been challenged by idealists, their traditional adversary, arguing that globalization is essentially ideological. Robertson says globalization is the compression of the world through the intensification of consciousness of a singular world. The world is becoming one – we apprehend it and then will it into existence (1992: 8). Waters says, "Material exchanges localize; political exchanges internationalize; and symbolic exchanges globalize.... We can expect the economy and the polity to be globalized to the extent that they are culturalized" – an ideologically powered theory of globalization (1995: 7–9). Meyer and his collaborators (1997, 1999) believe globalization is driven by a world culture. Since the nineteenth century a rationalized world cultural order has emerged, embodying universal models shaping states, institutions, and individual identities. After World War II this became pervasive across the globe. States at all levels of economic development have adopted common models and institutions, generating what they call global "isomorphism." States are not themselves the drivers of globalization. Their structure and authority derive from a broader "world polity" consisting of common legitimating models shared also by countless nongovernmental organizations like scientific associations, feminist groups, standard-setting bodies, and environmental movements. Meyer has not spent much time on explaining why this world polity/culture emerges, but he seems to say that it is driven primarily by ideological forces. We shall see once again that this model has some truth but is grossly exaggerated.

Giddens (1990), Beck (1992), and Lash and Urry (1994) do not offer such one-dimensional theories, but they suggest that recent globalization embodies a distinctive ideological "reflexivity," by which we become aware of our impact upon the globe and then orient our actions toward devising new global rules of conduct. This, they suggest, involves a different recursive role for ideas in human conduct in our times. We monitor the impact of changes on our lives and identify our own position in relation to the larger process. No one can feel comfortably at home anymore, they say. I am not sure that this is true. Have not human beings always possessed reflexivity, and is this really a novel age of anxiety? However, we are in need of reflexivity to comprehend the boomerang effect of potential nuclear war and environmental destruction. All these arguments suffer from the traditional weakness of idealism, a tendency to see ideologies and human consciousness as flowing above societies. I prefer to see ideologies as the search for ultimate meaning in the interplay of military, political, and economic power relations.

Many materialists and idealists alike see globalization as a singular process. As the economic or cultural order fills up the planet, it generates a single world order, world society, world polity, world culture, or world system. In addition to those scholars already discussed, Albrow (1996) defines globalization as "those processes by which the peoples of the world are incorporated into a single world society, global society," while Tomlinson (1999: 10) notes that the world is becoming one place, subject to the same forces, connected in what he calls a "unicity." Holton does say globalizations are plural, but he sees them as comprising "one single world of human society in which all elements are tied together in one interdependent whole" (1998: 2). The notion of a single emerging global system stretches back into the nineteenth century, to St.-Simon, Comte, Spencer, and Marx and Engels's *Communist Manifesto*, which remains the boldest statement of economic globalization. Giddens rejects this, noting that globalization "is a process of uneven development that fragments as it coordinates" (1990: 175). I agree with him.

A few have deployed Max Weber's three-dimensional model of cultural, economic, and political forces (Osterhammel & Petersson, 2005; Waters, 1995), and this is the closest to my own approach, though I separate military from political power relations. Postmodernists go further and reject all "master narratives," arguing that society is infinitely complex and inexplicable. They sometimes add a tweak toward chaos theory or relativism, emphasizing global incoherence, hybridity, and fragmentation. Appadurai (1990) enumerates varied "ethnoscapes," "mediascapes," "technoscapes," "finanscapes," and "ideoscapes," which comprise "the fluid, irregular landscapes" and "disjunctures" of globalization. Pietersee (1995) sees globalization as hybrid, involving "inherent fluidity, indeterminacy and open-endedness." Baumann (2000), a hyperglobalizer, prefers the term "liquid modernity," which he explains means a modernity composed of uncertain ethics, the doubting of expert belief systems, flexible organizational forms, informational war, and deterritorialized politics and economics. He declares boldly that liquid modernity has changed all aspects of the human condition. While accepting that globalization is hybrid, I resist a giddy descent into liquidity, fragmentation, and indeterminacy, preferring to see globalization as driven by a few networks that are far more powerfully structuring than others, and that have a relatively hard and durable reality. They have new forms but old pedigrees. General narratives are possible, if rendered plural and a little less grand.

The theories noted so far have not mentioned military power relations. They do mention political power relations, but usually to argue that globalization is undermining the nation-state. Ironically, until the 1990s most sociologists had ignored the nation-state. Their master concept was industrial society or capitalism, both seen as transnational. Though in practice almost all sociologists confined themselves to studying their own nation-state, they did not theorize it, for they viewed it as merely an instance of a broader industrial or capitalist society. Then suddenly they recognized the nation-state – at the supposed moment of its decline! The belief that globalization is undermining the nation-state is very widespread (e.g., Harvey, 1989; Robinson & Harris, 2000; Albrow, 1996: 91; Baumann, 1998: 55–76; Giddens, 1990; Lash & Urry, 1994: 280–1; Waters, 1995). Beck (2001: 21) says that globalization is "denationalization." He critiques what he calls "methodological nationalism," which relies on the "container theory" of society – mea culpa, though my metaphor is a cage. But he says that these containers have sprung leaks, global fluidity and mobility are now rampant, and "the unity of the national state and national society comes unstuck." Geographers coined the term "glocalization" to indicate that the nation-state was being undermined from both above and below, for global economic forces also strengthen local networks like world cities and Silicon Valleys, connected more to the global than the national economy (e.g., Swyngedouw, 1997).

All this is greatly exaggerated, as we shall see. It is a very Western-centric view, tending to see market capitalism as universal. Yet as we shall see, much of the world lives under politicized versions of capitalism in which one acquires access to economic resources through connections to the state. Moreover, even in the West the state is not so much declining as changing. The global economy still needs regulation by states, and nation-states have acquired a whole range of new functions, from providing welfare to interfering in family and sexual life (Hirst and Thompson, 1999; Mann, 1997). Osterhammel and Petersson (2005) reject what they call the liberal determinism of much globalization research. They see no single global social structure at work, and the nation-state remains strong, still involved in tariff wars, trade disputes, and stricter migration controls. Holton (1998: 108–34) stresses the staying power of states, which have been reinforced by stronger notions of ethnicity, and their combination can mount vigorous resistance to the forces of global capitalism. Scholte (2000) disagrees, seeing state and nation decoupling amid a proliferation of cosmopolitan and hybrid identities. He says globalization involves "deterritorialization," although this does not mean the end of the state. Rather, he says, governance becomes more multilayered as regulation is divided among substate, state, and suprastate agencies. Weiss (1999) observes that when states retreat, they initiate the action, as, for example, when they implement neoliberal policies. They could as easily initiate a resurgence of their powers. International relations (IR) theorists are divided over the nation-state. Some accept that in a postnuclear age states do not behave as if they live in a simple Westphalian world (they never did, of course). Some accept that transnational forces are undermining states, producing more varied governance structures. In the 1980s IR theorists split between realists, clinging to the state as an actor, and interdependence theorists, stressing economic and normative ties across the globe carried by transnational capitalism, global civil society, and global governance.

When did the nation-state supposedly dominate and when did it decline? Pietersee says that from the 1840s to the 1960s "the nation-state was the single dominant organizational option" for human society. This is both exaggerated and Eurocentric. Western Europe did move somewhat in that period toward nation-states; Eastern Europe moved back and forth between them and empires. But the rest of the world remained dominated by empires. Even in Europe nation-states did rather little until after World War I, for before then states had few economic policies beyond tariffs and currencies and almost no social policies. Their intensive power over their territories was usually rather limited: the lives of most people were dominated by local power networks, while some elites were fairly transnational. We saw in Volume 3 that a sense of nationhood did diffuse but that it rarely dominated peoples' consciousness. Then the planning pretensions that states had acquired in World War I were exposed as hollow by the Great Depression. So they briefly returned to what they had always done best, making war.

After World War II, however, most of their swords were turned into plow-shares and their economic and social policies deepened. So it was only in the short period after 1945 that states developed much greater infrastructural power among their citizens. Only then might it seem that nation-states were becoming the world's common political form. In this short period all but two empires collapsed, while the number of self-styled nation-states kept rising. There are now more than 190 member states of the United Nations, though many of them have very limited powers over their supposed territories. Moreover, alongside the transnational elements of modern globalization are international elements composed of relations among the representatives of states – like the UN, the IMF, the G-20. Geopolitics have gone more global and more pacific – "soft geopolitics" is the conventional label for this new external realm of nation-states. But they still involve the relations among states.

The nation-state and globalization have not been rivals in a zero-sum game with one undermining the other. They rose together in a first phase, discussed in Volumes 2 and 3, when the motherlands of empires became nation-states. Osterhammel and Petersson (2005) note that while the emergence of imperialism and the Atlantic economy created networks of traffic, communication, migration, and commerce, amid the growth of these global networks, nation-states and nationalist movements also strengthened. In a second phase, discussed in this volume, nation-states emerged globally out of the colonial ashes, and the more advanced nation-states acquired much greater powers over, and responsibility for, the lives of their citizens. As my second volume argued, the last two or three centuries have seen the entwined growth of nation-states and capitalism. The European Union is a more complex political form, embodying both Europe-wide political institutions and autonomous nation-states. But it is ultimately driven by the interests of the most powerful member states. The Soviet and American empires constituted more fundamental exceptions, and the latter endures as the only global empire the world has ever seen. So current globalization is driven by capitalism, nation-states, and American empire, which are the major power institutions discussed in this volume.

The entwining of these three major power organizations has generated globally diffusing ideologies. In Volume 3 we saw the influence of communism and fascism. In this one we will see the importance of social and Christian democracy, liberalism and neoliberalism, and religious fundamentalism. And although interstate wars have declined greatly since World War II, they have been replaced by a cold war, civil wars, and American militarism. Thus this period of globalizations requires explanation in terms of all the four sources of social power. Globalization is universal but polymorphous. Human groups need meaning systems; they need to extract resources from nature for their subsistence; they need defense and perhaps offense as long as the world remains dangerous; and they need law and order over defined, controlled territories. Societies – networks of interaction at the boundaries of which exists a certain degree of cleavage – involve ideological, economic, military, and political power organizations. These contain different logics operating over different spaces, all in principle of equal causal significance. Sometimes they reinforce each other, sometimes they contradict each other, mostly they are just orthogonal to each other, different and disjunctive, creating unintended problems for each other, preventing coherence and singular integration in the expansion process, as we will see in the following chapters.

I begin in Chapter 2 by discussing the postwar global order (although it also contained disorder in some parts of the world). Its three pillars were neo-Keynesian economic policies, both domestic and international; a cold war that intensified an ideological power struggle yet also stabilized geopolitical relations and cemented order among most of the advanced countries of the world; and American empire. Given the importance of the United States, I then spend two chapters analyzing the development of American society up to the 1960s. Chapter 5 analyzes American imperialism across the world, stressing its variety – in some regions it has been rather militaristic, in others only hegemonic; in some regions successful in its goals, in others misguided and unsuccessful, leaving unfinished business for the new century (discussed in Chapter 10). Chapter 6 begins by analyzing the ability of postwar liberals, social democrats, and Christian Democrats to humanize capitalism by achieving greater citizen rights and neo-Keynesian mass consumption economic policies, but it ends by charting the faltering of this brief golden age and the rise of harsher neoliberal regimes. Chapter 7 discusses the failure of the Soviet communist alternative as well as the relative failure of the post-Soviet countries to effect the desired transition to democratic capitalism. Chapter 8 discusses the second major communist regime, China, and its pioneering a much more effective economic transition toward a hybrid of the party-state and market capitalism, though with no pretense of moving toward democracy. Chapter 9 develops a theory of modern revolution drawing from material from Volume 3 as well as this one.

Chapter 10 contrasts the enduring success of American economic imperialism with its abject failure in seeking a resurgence of military imperialism. Chapter 11 discusses the paradox of neoliberalism: on the one hand, its harmful economic policies led not to an increase in collective power but to the Great Recession of 2008; on the other hand, this only seemed to intensify its distributive power among the advanced countries. These two chapters conclude by focusing on the relative decline of the West in face of the rise of the Rest. Chapter 12 discusses the looming disaster of climate change and emphasizes just how massive is the task of combating it. Climate change ironically results from the three great success stories of the twentieth century: capitalist pursuit of profit, nation-states' commitment to economic growth, and citizens' pursuit of mass consumption rights. To challenge them is to challenge the three most powerful institutions of recent years. Finally, Chapter 13 attempts conclusions at two levels, offering generalizations on the global trajectory of modern society, as well as on the debate within sociological theory on the question of ultimate primacy – what is it that ultimately drives society forward?

2 The postwar global order

World War II radically changed geopolitical power relations in the world. It delivered a mortal blow to the European and Japanese empires, which now fell either immediately or after a decade or two. The war also ensured two communist triumphs: the stabilization and expansion of the Soviet Union over Eastern Europe, and communist seizure of power in China (which I discussed in Volume 3). These two regimes now had a major ideological impact on the world; they intermittently sent military support to sympathetic regimes and movements abroad; their economies were largely autarchic, somewhat separated from most of the rest of the world. Together these war-induced changes left the United States astride most of the rest of the world. Its domination rested on two main pillars, a new and much more effective international economic order whose rules it set, and a geopolitical stability ensured by American military power and by what is called the "cold war" – though it was actually hot in Asia. I begin with the decline and fall of empires.

The end of colonialism

Though I will argue in Chapters 5 and 10 that the United States since World War II has been an empire, it has not had colonies. A case could be made that the Eastern bloc countries were colonies of the USSR, but they were unlike all others. For one thing, the USSR did not bleed the economies of these countries: quite the reverse – it subsidized them. Only Soviet rule over the three small Baltic states might be considered "colonial," since it involved both exploitation and Russian settlers. But the other empires and colonies fell. The war delivered a swift coup de grace to the German, Italian, and Japanese empires. The devastation of Germany and Japan was such that they struggled for a decade to regain political autonomy and economic recovery. More permanent was their demilitarization, which became accepted as desirable by most of their peoples. Germany and Japan became great economic powers but without wielding military muscle. For them, soft replaced hard geopolitics.

The war also undermined the other European empires. As our period began, they were tottering, on their last legs. Colonial native elites did not intend to be fooled a second time, seduced into fighting for their empire as in World War I by vague and broken promises of more postwar political rights. Many were emboldened by colonial weaknesses that the war, and in Asia the Japanese, had exposed. France, Belgium, and the Netherlands had been conquered by

Germany in 1940. Japan had rapidly seized and occupied most of Britain's Asian colonies, along with those of France and the Netherlands. The rapid seizure of Malaya by Japanese forces culminated in the fall of supposedly impregnable Singapore and the surrender of British forces more than twice the size of the Japanese forces. This was humiliation enough for the British. But the fall also involved a shocking degree of complicity by Malay nationalists. "We have suffered the greatest disaster in our history," declared Churchill to Roosevelt (Clarke, 2008: 19). It shattered the myth of white and British invulnerability and immediately deprived Britain of its enormous profits in rubber and tin. Though Britain was to win the war, its empire in Asia was never to regain its former power and prestige.

The Asian colonies before the arrival of the Europeans either had possessed their own states (as in Vietnam) or had possessed a core state among multiple political entities (as in Indonesia). Elites and perhaps some of the people had some sense of belonging to a single political entity and perhaps even a single community. The colonists introduced modernization involving better communications infrastructures, educational institutions, plantations, and factories, but these tended to foster a sense of nationhood, just as comparable processes had in nineteenth-century Europe. The more the colonists developed their lands, the more nationalism surfaced. Even before the war nationalists were petitioning, demonstrating, and rioting for political autonomies – and some were even demanding independence. But these protonationalist movements had been usually divided by class and ethnicity, and the colonists still possessed overwhelming power. The war bit into the latter.

Britain's major Asian colony, India, already had quite a powerful nationalist movement, and it was not conquered. But with typical imperial arrogance, the British Raj had declared war on the Japanese without consulting Indian leaders, and these were livid. Gandhi opposed entry into the war; other nationalists would support it if they received ironclad guarantees of political rights afterward. In the event most Indian soldiers, two million of them, proved loyal and fought with great valor in both Africa and Burma. Yet another Indian army of forty-five thousand men fought with the Japanese against the British and one of thirty-five hundred even fought with the Germans. Nazism plus Japanese militarism aimed against whites paradoxically attracted freedom fighters across Asia. Churchill's racism did not help. The secretary of state for India, Leo Amery, remembered a wartime conversation: "During my talk with Winston he burst out with: 'I hate Indians. They are a beastly people with a beastly religion.'" Churchill refused to aid "the next worst people in the world after the Germans.... The Indians would starve to death as a result of their own folly and viciousness" (Bayly & Harper, 2004: 286). Churchill had Gandhi and Nehru imprisoned to weaken Indian opposition, but that did no good. So instead Stafford Cripps, a Labour minister in the cabinet, was sent off to India to make concessions in return for Indian cooperation in the war effort. On the way he stopped off in the Sudan, where university graduates unexpectedly handed him a document demanding self-rule. The natives were stirring in more than one continent.

In India Cripps promised Indian nationalist participation in the viceroy's wartime Executive Council, though not in military affairs. The nationalists responded by demanding a share in devising military strategy, while Jinnah's Muslim League was moving toward demanding its own independent state after the war. Churchill refused both demands and clearly intended the immensely popular Cripps (a potential rival to be prime minister) to fail. He did fail and there was no agreement. But the Indian nationalists took Cripps's mission as a sign that there would be independence after the war and they then split, many supporting the war effort. The Indian army under British commanders and helped by Burmese hill tribes fought on in Burma, to no great effect in 1942 and 1943, but then in early 1944 halting and then comprehensively defeating the overstretched Japanese. This was the first great military reverse suffered by the Japanese on land, and it saved India, the only good British news from Asia (Bayly & Harper, 2004: chap. 7; Clarke, 2008: 19–23). In contrast, the Japanese advance had conquered all of the French and Dutch empires in Asia.

Divisions in the British political elite, especially in the Labour Party, were surfacing. The Labour Left recognized that the Indian Raj should and would end when the war ended. Conservatives were united in resisting this. Had Churchill won the 1945 election, he would have sought to stave off Indian independence, though the rising Congress Party and Muslim League would have made his life difficult. But Labour comprehensively won the election. Though the new prime minister Major Clement Attlee and Stafford Cripps (now in charge of the British economy) still believed in the white man's burden and sought to hold on to India, resilient Indian opposition complicated by conflicts between Hindus and Muslims forced the government to yield independence in the form of the creation in 1947 of two new states, India and Pakistan. What had become clear was that the British no longer had the military resources to provide order across the subcontinent. There was not only fierce resistance to British rule but also disorder among various nationalist factions. The Indian army was catching the bug of factionalism and could no longer be reliably used for repression. The war had made independence in the subcontinent inevitable.

The problem was different in the other countries of Southeast Asia. The Japanese had destroyed British, French, and Dutch rule there, yet had signally failed to deliver on their promise of freedom to the colonized peoples. Their rule was more terrible than European rule had been. But local resistance to the Japanese had generated guerrilla movements, while the Japanese themselves had created some local militias to assist their war effort. These paramilitaries were of various political and ethnic hues. Nationalism, say Bayly and Harper (2007: 16), was given a new face – "a youthful militaristic one." The returning colonialists had to cope with bands of armed rebels who were claiming independence while also sometimes fighting each other. This again strained the resources of the colonial powers. In fact, in 1945 Britain was the only colonial power with an intact and formidable army in the region. Its core up to about 1946 was the Indian army, stiffened by British, West African, and Australian regiments. Its power meant that Britain easily regained Burma, Malaya, and Singapore, all of which had resources valuable to the empire. The great crescent of empire across Asia could still be anchored in the Southeast, reasoned the British. The French and the Dutch could not do this. But Britain sent its forces onward to help restore French and Dutch rule in Indochina and Indonesia. The British Empire suddenly seemed to dominate the whole region. Yet in reality British military resources were stretched, and in both Indonesia and Vietnam the British resorted to rearming Japanese troops who had surrendered there to assist in the crushing of nationalist rebels, an extraordinary demonstration of colonial solidarity. In Vietnam this pushed the rebel nationalist Viet Minh leftward toward communism while enabling France to regain the South of the country, so precipitating a terrible thirty years of civil war. The Dutch were the weakest, and they were kicked out after only two years of civil war, with the approval of the Americans. They had realized that to prop up the Dutch would likely turn Indonesian nationalism toward communism – a rare instance of good sense in Washington. U.S. policy in the French and British Empires differed, for they saw these empires as fighting communism.

But as Indian independence loomed, using the Indian army for deployment abroad became problematic and then impossible (apart from the formidable but privately recruited Gurkha regiments). British military power in the region weakened. But Japanese repression had prevented nationalists' developing stable, institutionalized parties on the model of the Indian Congress Party or the Muslim League. Ethnic and political factionalism weakened the overall power of movements for independence while also increasing disorder. The British could continue ruling in a rather minimal sense for a while yet, though only through gun barrels and summary executions. In Burma they decided to strengthen the Burmese military – with a terrible legacy of military despotism lasting until today. In Malaya the British divided-and-ruled, moving to indirect rule through a federation of Malay aristocratic rulers, privileging them and the British planter and the Chinese merchant elite. But this disprivileged most of the large Chinese minority, who now supported communist guerrilla forces that had earlier led resistance against the Japanese. A bloody ten-year civil war, the so-called Malayan Emergency, was finally won by British forces using scorched earth tactics, including the invention of forcible relocation of villages into areas controlled by British forces. This was to be the only Western military victory against communism during the so-called cold war in the region. In Asia, therefore, hot wars transitioned almost seamlessly from wars against the Japanese empire to wars against the European and then the American empires. The travails and the terrors of empire continued, even though the writing had seemed in 1945 to be on the wall (Bayly & Harper, 2004, 2007; Douglas, 2002: 37–57).

In Africa, nationalists had been less powerful before the war. Unlike in Asia nationalism could not usually grow out from an existing sense of political community, for colonial boundaries did not usually correspond to precolonial political entities. Yet the war assisted them while leading them down less violent paths. There were no independent militias here. Africans fought for their colonial masters, against their neighbors. But fighting alongside British or German soldiers often involved de facto equality and even shared comradeship in the field. Africans also spent several years legitimately killing white men, eroding any imperial claims to racial superiority. More than a million African soldiers were recruited into the British armies. Such immense mobilization required new infrastructures of communication, more macroeconomic planning, and even some public welfare in the colonies. Two official reports on the African colonies by Lord Hailey made clear the failure of indirect rule in Africa and the need for more economic development. Yet the British remained reluctant to grant representative government. Colonial Secretary Lord Cranborne declared, "If we want the British Empire to endure … far from teaching Colonial people to govern themselves, we should do the contrary, and welcome their participation in our administration" (Nugent, 2004: 26).

Developmental policies continued after the war, focused on building more roads, railroads, and schools. Four African and one West Indian university were founded. There was an influx of British medics, agronomists, vets, and teachers (White, 1999: 49; Kirk-Greene, 2000: 51–2; Lewis, 2000: 6; Hyam, 2006: 84–92). African elites were introduced into most local governments, and in the Gold Coast (soon to be Ghana) they participated in colony-wide government. Britain had two main motives in its new development strategy: to head off independence movements and to derive economic benefit for Britain. African exports of raw materials to the United States were recognized as especially useful in alleviating Britain's chronic postwar shortage of dollars. Thus increasing them would be good for Britain too. By 1952 the African colonies contributed more than 20 percent of the sterling area's dollar reserves. African development was expected by British politicians to prolong the imperial life span by increasing non-European stakeholders in the imperial enterprise (Nugent, 2004: 26–7; White, 1999: 9–10, 35, 49).

It did not. Economic development in the 1940s expanded the number of urban workers, teachers, lawyers, and civil servants. Hundreds of thousands of soldiers returned home, emboldened and demanding. The war and the development strategy had greatly expanded the core constituencies of nationalism (Cooper, 1996: part II). In Ghana whereas the colonial government had avoided dealing with unions and they had suppressed strikes since the 1920s, in 1941 the war led to the recognition of the legitimacy of unions and strikes. The government needed class cooperation not class conflict in wartime. Labor unrest rocketed upward in the 1940s, more substantially than it had after World War I, its core being in mining and transportation. This led to the recognition of union rights and the regulation of collective bargaining. Unions and farmers' organizations and urban demonstrations converted elite dissent against colonialism into a mass movement. As Kwame Nkrumah, first president of Ghana, said, "A middle class elite, without the battering ram of the illiterate masses could never hope to smash the forces of colonialism" (Silver, 2003: 145–8). However, the nationalist leadership did manage to harness and tame the leftism of the trade unions, for they too needed national solidarity not class conflict.

This was a peculiar nationalism, however, since there was little sense of attachment to a nation. Nationalism was a by-product of the fact that colonialism had to be attacked at the political level of the individual colony. But the Ghanaian or Nigerian nations were really projects for the future, stored in the minds of a few elites. The present reality was that African nationalism, as its name suggests, was really a racial category, a claim to unity among Africans against their exploitation by whites (and in the north of the continent of Arabs and Muslims exploited by white Christians). This and the Asian equivalent, which has been called Occidentalism, were responses to the racism and Orientalism of the West, and they bore the same tenuous relationship to reality. Nationalism had been created in Asia by both racial and national attachments, while in Africa, race had to do the work alone. That is why Asia was ahead of Africa in achieving independence. Yet the emergence of racial anticolonialism made race a contested concept, and when these movements succeeded in expelling the whites, the racial ideology of white superiority could not be plausibly maintained. Thus the racial challenge paradoxically produced a decline in the ideological power of racism – as it was also doing in the domestic politics of the United States at this time. What had been perhaps the most powerful ideology of the last two centuries was now in serious decline.

Ironically, the natives who transmitted imperial rule most benefited from it yet were the most likely to become nationalist agitators. In the Sudan they were "colonialism's intimate enemies, making colonial rule a reality while hoping to see it undone" (says Sharkey, 2003: 1, 119). They first demanded autonomy within the empire, but expanding political parties, some controlling municipal governments, made independence unstoppable through the 1950s. Though the British envisaged gradually yielding Dominion status to African colonies, and the French arrived later at a similar view, neither power would yield to demands for equal social citizenship for Africans. Neither white settlers nor the homeland's taxpayers would support incorporating natives into the citizen body, with the same social rights as whites, so independence became inevitable. Racism had always mattered in the European empires, as I stressed in Volume 3. Now it mattered in decolonization, on both sides.

Liberals and socialists were generally the first to recognize the inevitability of independence, and they moved toward assisting decolonization, collaborating with the nationalists (Wilson, 1994: 21, 39, 77–8, 149–50, 201). The United States added a little pressure for decolonization, goaded on to match the anticolonial rhetoric of the Soviet Union, though it backed off whenever it needed British or French support in the cold war. The newly established United Nations (UN) sniped against imperialism on the sidelines, but this was more a consequence than a cause of decolonization, since countries acquiring independence joined the UN, steadily increasing its anticolonial majority. In the 1950s the perception grew that the development programs for Africa were failing while Britain's recovery meant less need for dollars. When Prime Minister Macmillan commissioned a cost-benefit analysis of empire in 1957, this concluded that though the colonies did generate some profit, decolonization would involve no significant loss for Britain. This had also been true when the American colonies had secured their independence almost two hundred years previously, and the Dutch had recently had the same experience after they left Indonesia. The American empire now avoided colonialism altogether; they discovered other ways to control the natives. But British governments were prodded all along the way by assertive native nationalists, though these usually operated through strikes and demonstrations, not guerrilla wars, and there was little threat of communism in the continent, unlike in Asia (McIntyre, 1998; cf. Douglas, 2002: 160; Cooper, 1996: part IV).

Historians have given varied explanations of the fall of the British Empire. Hyam (2006: xiii) lists four possible explanations: national liberation movements, imperial overstretch, a failure of British will, and international pressure. In a study of the British "official mind," he concludes that international pressure was the most important of all. I would rate this one the least important factor (except for the Japanese military pressures). That pressure depended on large nationalist movements' in the colonies continuing forcibly to demand the rights to which the United States and the United Nations were formally committed. "Overstretch" was obviously important in a military sense, though only if native resistance had to be countered by military force. This in turn involved some fiscal overstretch. But the empire remained moderately profitable, even though Macmillan's report trumped this by concluding that profit could continue without formal empire. Military overstretch and failure of will were connected, though the British had decided some years earlier that development, not repression, would preserve empire. They were wrong because it led to more nationalism. But they were unlikely to move back to severe repression once embarked on the development strategy – especially given the dramatic failures of French repression in Vietnam and Algeria. The British departed earlier from Africa and Asia than the French. But this should not be described as leaving more gracefully, as is often claimed. The British were pushed out, but they showed greater realism earlier in Africa before serious repression became necessary. I noted in Volume 3 that the British Empire was not only the largest empire, it was also the most profitable, and success had resulted from greater

political and geopolitical sagacity. Perhaps they were still the smartest imperialists as they departed. They perceived that war and development had strengthened native resistance to a point where all the other three factors mentioned by
Hyam came into play. Continuing native resistance was ultimately decisive.

But there was another kind of international pressure too. Like revolution in
the twentieth century, and like the breakup of empires in Europe after World
War I, decolonization occurred in waves. India set off a cascade of independence among the bigger Asian colonies, essentially complete by 1957 though
Malaysia and Singapore were tidied up in 1963. Independence spread to Africa
in 1956 with Tunisia, Morocco, and the Sudan, though this was an unusual
case where a joint British-Egyptian mandate fell apart. The major African spur
was the next year as the Gold Coast became independent Ghana. It had the
most developed economy apart from colonies with extensive settler populations, and it had the largest and best-led urban nationalist movement. African
colonial governors (including some in French West Africa) were now com-
plaining that Ghana was "infecting" their natives. Indeed it was. As Prime
Minister Macmillan declared in 1960, first to a delighted Ghanaian audience,
then more famously to a hostile South African white audience, "The wind of
change is blowing through this continent. Whether we like it or not, this growth
of national consciousness is a political fact. We must all accept it as a fact,
and our national policies must take account of it." He was detecting a great
gust of ideological power, empowering group after group of nationalists across
the empires. It did not calm down. The winning of independence continued
through the 1960s, the bigger colonies like Nigeria and Kenya tending to pre-
cede the smaller ones. White settlers successfully delayed a handover of power
in proportion to their relative numbers. South Africa was the extreme example,
in which the largest white settler population (appalled by Macmillan's speech)
broke free of Britain but intensified racial exploitation through apartheid. That
major remnant of the British Empire lasted until the 1990s.

The final British departure ceremonies were graceful since the British political elite chose not to interpret departure as defeat. This was unlike the French,
who saw departure as defeat and so resisted longer until their armies were
actually defeated in Vietnam and Algeria. There was no equivalent British case
for the British left well before this point. Having models to hand from the grant
of self-government to the white Dominions, British politicians interpreted the
handover of power as generous British policy, not forced by native agitation.
Some politicians believed exit would mean "the preservation of post-colonial
'influence.'" Britain's "Commonwealth of Nations" could be a "third way," a
union of first and third worlds, unlike the two superpowers – so said British
politicians in the 1950s and 1960s (White, 1999: 35, 98–100; Heinlein, 2002).
And to a limited extent, it was.

In the long run the British Empire had become more benign. Having started
out as the pillaging, enslaving, and killing enterprise I described in Volume 3,

it settled into indirect empire, with freer labor relations and a more open international economy. This drew colonies into the globalizing economy though development had remained minimal until World War II. In indirect rule native elites were conceded some political power and British administrators had tried to damp down racism in the public sphere. But though native clients often admired their imperial overlords, they were held at arms' length by racial contempt in the private sphere. Economic development contributed to imperial collapse when it finally appeared across the mid-twentieth century for it broadened native nationalist movements. The world wars broke the military but not the economic power of the Europeans for it was in this period of war and postwar austerity that they put most resources into their empires. But it did not do empire much good, since development increased anti-imperialism. The first two waves of twentieth-century imperial collapse had in common two assassins, rival warring empires and native liberation movements. It was the end of the era of segmented globalization. Soon only two empires were left.

Postcolonial postscript

On independence educated middle-class elites claimed power, not the gentry or chiefs. But their power base was limited for there was no "nation" to mobilize. Democracy did not usually last long (India was different). Yet economic growth continued at about the level of the world economy, mainly in response to its demand for raw materials. This lasted until the general economic crisis of the early 1970s initiated a downturn in demand for African products, worsened by the secular decline in prices for raw materials relative to manufactured goods. Dependence on the export of a single agricultural or mineral commodity made economies vulnerable when demand slackened and prices fell. Contrary to popular belief, decolonization made no big economic impact either way. The most appropriate periodization is one by phases of the world economy, not the nature of the political regime (Cooper, 2002: 85–7). But the narrow sectoral economy also reinforced the narrow power base and autocracy of political elites. Their corruption led to vast sums of money being taken abroad instead of being invested in the country. It was estimated in 1999 that almost 40 percent of African private wealth was held abroad, compared to 10 percent in Latin America and 6 percent in East Asia (Maddison, 2007: 234). Political failure gravely compounded African problems.

What if any are the enduring legacies of colonialism? Everyday life has been greatly changed. Diets, languages, music, racial attitudes were transformed, for better or worse. The English language increasingly dominated, latterly helped on by the United States. British sports were exported. Football was spread globally by the British informal empire, whereas cricket and rugby were largely restricted to its direct empire. American baseball and basketball are still spreading across its informal empire while Hollywood dominates the world. But there are no great enduring cultural artifacts, the equivalent of Mayan temples, Roman arenas, or the Great Wall of China. European empires removed the surplus and replaced it with cheap goods and cheap buildings. Shoddy empires leave few traces.

Scholars have attempted to quantify colonial economic and political legacies. Their economic conclusions have been mostly negative. The less sovereign a country was in the colonial period, the greater in 1960 and 1980 was its integration into the world economy (measured by its trade to gross domestic product [GDP] ratio), but the lower the proportion of manufacturing industry in its GDP, the lower were its adult literacy rates, years of schooling, and overall rate of economic growth since 1870. Had colonies been sovereign countries their growth rates would have been on average higher by 1.6 percent (Alam, 2000: chap. 6). Krieckhaus (2006) concurs: "By far, the most effective route to economic success over the last forty years" was avoidance of European colonialism.

The highest growth was in the former white settler colonies, like the United States, Canada, and Australia. These European settlers, having "mastered the art of sustained increase in per capita GDP," set up a capitalist system guaranteeing property rights, a liberal state, and investment in human capacity. The "Neo-Europes" partially settled by Europeans, like South Africa, Brazil, and Algeria, grew more than the extractive colonies, whose benefits went disproportionately to European elites. Least growth occurred in Africa and Asia where Europeans' interests were to "conquer, plunder, and proselytize." Acemoglu et al. (2001) say that in the Tropics where colonizers suffered high mortality rates, they established a narrow extractive exploitation that persisted after independence. Where they could settle permanently, they established more development-minded institutions. They conclude with the euphemism that "institutions matter." In reality the policy of killing off the natives and replacing them with Europeans and their institutions was what had made the difference. Genocide yielded development, though not for the natives, and not a policy to be recommended. It seems that most of the world would have been economically better off without empires. There was one very different case, for the Japanese Empire produced considerable economic benefit in its colonies, though alongside atrocities in other spheres (as we saw in Volume 3).

There is less consensus on the effects of colonialism on representative government. Some say that colonial despotism and the suppression of civil society movements left a bad legacy for postcolonial regimes (e.g., Young, 1994: chap. 7; Chirot, 1986: 112–18). Quantitative research shows that all other types of historical regime were more likely to generate stable democracy than nonwhite colonies, though it is difficult to separate out the effects here of economic backwardness (Bernhard et al., 2004). There was long felt to be a "British legacy" making for better chances for representative government after empire (Rueschemeyer et al., 1992). More recently, the failure of democracy in many former British colonies has lessened this effect, though former British colonies remain slightly more likely to generate democracy, alongside former American colonies (Bernhard et al., 2004: 241). But the effects of colonialism do not seem very strong. We should not attribute everything to empires. Countries and regions have their own indigenous cultures and institutions, often with greater impacts on development. Europe and the white United States and Dominions continued to boom. Latin America has half-stagnated, half-developed – as indeed its population proportions (half-indigenous, half-European, plus African slaves) might suggest. Its indigenous populations are only now acquiring full citizenship. Sub-Saharan Africa is the great failure, with signs of regress. In contrast, East and South Asia are now booming.

So if a country possessed a high level of civilization before the Europeans arrived, and then managed to hold onto it after the colonists departed, it could adapt its own forms of advanced economy and government. This fits India, China (under communism), South Korea, and most of Southeast Asia, the countries that have had the highest growth rates. In more backward Africa the Europeans throttled nineteenth-century movements toward centralization in the Zulu, Sokoto, Mahdist, and Ashanti empires and ended the chances that indigenous African economies might have been actors in the world economy (Austin, 2004; Vandervort, 1998: 1–25). After the destruction of these weaker civilizations, the departure of empires left infrastructures better suited to remove raw materials abroad than to integrate the territories of the new countries. Africa was too damaged to recover quickly from the ravages of empires. On balance modern empires had not been good news for the rest of the world. But growth did eventually occur in many of them in the twenty-first century, as we shall see.

American Empire in the cold war

The year 1945 marked the end of a two-hundred-year period in which Europe dominated the world through a process of segmented and conflictual globalization. Now America acquired near-global dominance as the Soviet Union and China turned inward into autarchy. Fifty years later American dominance was helped by the fall of the Soviet Union. A modus vivendi was established with China, securing its entry to the American-led global economy. American dominance is now beginning to weaken. By the time it ends, it will have probably lasted about eighty years. American empire has been one of the three main pillars of today's globalizations alongside transnational capitalism and the nation-state system.

Lacking colonies or settlers, America has not had direct or indirect empire but has instead run the rest of the imperial gamut from a conquest-withdrawal sequence engendering strictly temporary colonies, through informal empire, to mere hegemony. Hegemony, it will be remembered from Volume 3, is not imperial since it does not kill. The United States has intermittently waged major wars of conquest, not to found colonies but to defend or install client regimes and then leave, usually retaining local military bases. The United States possesses such massive military power that it has been able to pursue scorched earth tactics, inflicting devastation on enemies, effective in preventing unfriendly behavior but not very effective at inducing positive behavior. But since the United States has also led the global capitalist economy, it could instead confer economic benefit on itself and on conquered countries, integrating them into the global economy. Informal empire and hegemony involve less political and ideological intervention in the periphery than do colonies, but colonies were impossible for the United States since it lacked settlers. Americans have been too comfortable at home. So though America has had more *extensive* power than any other empire and has more potential military power and more actual economic power, its domination was in some ways less *intensive* than some previous empires. It tended to stay offshore and to dominate through proxies.

Views on American empire have differed enormously. Most Americans deny they have ever had an empire. This chapter, like chapter 3 of Volume 3, will prove them wrong. Some claim that American militarism and capitalism have produced exploitation and suffering in the world; others say they yield peace, stability, freedom, and prosperity, and so are legitimate. Such variety results partly from a tendency for both Left and Right to exaggerate American power but also partly from the sheer variety of forms of domination the United States has deployed. In the West the United States has been merely hegemonic. In East Asia it began with indirect empire imposed by military interventions but later lightened this to hegemony. In Latin America and the Middle East it tried heavier methods of informal empire with gunboats and through proxies, with very different outcomes. I will discuss these regions later. I regret leaving out other regions, but no more than the United States can I master the whole world.

Yet World War II had suddenly left the United States as the dominant world power. In 1945 U.S. armed forces totaled 8 million. Major demobilization still left 3.5 million spread through a global network of military bases, spending half the world's military budget. The United States also had almost half the world's GDP and manufacturing industries, and it held the world's reserve currency. Though the Soviet bloc and China were no-go zones, the other leading states were near-bankrupted by war. For the first time State Department desks, Pentagon command centers, and American corporations spanned the globe. Except for the communist bloc and its clients, this was now a global empire. The troops might have all gone home, the United States might have turned inward upon itself, but this was never very likely since enough politicians and corporations saw American prosperity as tied to the fortunes of the global economy, one that also needed military defense against communism. Thus emerged the distinctive sense of responsibility that American leaders have felt for the world and that is still dominant inside Washington's Beltway. This has always involved a willingness to intervene militarily and economically across the world in defense of freedom, a concept that does not only imply political freedom (which virtually the whole world has valued) but also economic freedom in the sense of free enterprise – that is, capitalism (which has been more contested). The two combined constitute the American form of the mission statement that as we saw in Volume 3 every empire has had. As we shall see, however, American defense of capitalism has been much more consistent than its support of democracy.

Though American economic power had grown steadily through the twentieth century, global dominance had been acquired suddenly, through a world war that the United States had not caused and with armed forces it had not wished so enlarged. In fact, neither superpower had sought empire. They had been quite inward-looking until attacked in World War II, but as with many empires their suddenly enlarged armed forces could be deployed amid a postwar power vacuum.

Yet American dominance was not entirely accidental. Woodrow Wilson and Franklin Roosevelt had seen the world wars as opportunities to defeat enemies and subordinate allies. Wilson's liberal internationalism was not only idealism. It was also an attempt to undermine imperial rivals. Roosevelt was no naive idealist either. From 1939, before the United States joined in the war, the American Council on Foreign Relations saw that with Europe dominated by Nazi Germany, the United States must integrate the remaining economies of the Western Hemisphere, the British Empire, and much of Asia, in what was called a grand area strategy. In return for aiding Britain during the war, the United States would get an open door into its empire. Massive British purchases of American food and war materials between 1939 and 1941 were paid for in dollars or gold. By 1941 the British were running out of both, forced to sell off their U.S. assets. When the United States was forced into the war, a Lend-Lease program enabled the British to get their supplies on credit, but the repayment terms included a postwar open door (Domhoff, 1990: 113–32, 162–4). Pearl Harbor also made clear that security was now a global problem. Though the United States favored a world economy based upon equal commercial opportunity, its leaders believed free trade needed buttressing by collective American-led security institutions. American economic and military power, market and territorial sway, were mutually reinforcing (Hearden, 2002: chap. 2, quote from p. 39).

The United States hoped to win from the war the grander area of a Nazi-free Europe plus an Asia ensured by the defeat of Japan and the expected victory of the Chinese Nationalists, plus secure access to Middle East oil. No one called this empire, since there would be no colonies, once temporary colonies like Germany and Japan were restructured. It would be a free world of capitalism and independent states, if protected by a global network of bases. Isaiah Bowman, a Roosevelt confidant, said, "Hitler would get a lebensraum, but not the one he expected, an American economic lebensraum. No line can be established anywhere in the world that confines the interests of the United States because no line can prevent the remote from becoming the near danger." This he called "nationalist globalism" and "global open access without colonies," which would be coupled with "necessary military bases around the globe both to protect global economic interests and to restrain any further belligerence" (Smith, 2003: 27–8, 184). The Philippines, for example, gained independence disciplined by bases (Hearden, 2002: 202–12, 313–14). This was global informal empire, using bases and more technologically advanced versions of gunboats. The United States assumed its own strength backed by a concert of powers would provide a global security framework that Moscow would have to accept (Hearden, 2002: chap. 6).The political notion of exporting democracy was not yet emphasized. American leaders thought in terms of military and economic power, though their geographic sway was called ideologically the free world.

The economic pillar: The Bretton Woods System

Two economists, Harry Dexter White for the United States (who, bizarrely, was passing U.S. documents to Soviet spy contacts) and John Maynard Keynes, the famous economist, for Britain, led discussions of the new economic order. Keynes argued that if the United States wanted an open trading system, it had to help postwar reconstruction by providing cash for war-ravaged countries. The Roosevelt and Truman administrations agreed, seeing this as also being in American interests. To prevent recession, exports would replace war production as the American engine of growth, but the Europeans were currently too poor to buy American goods. Keynes proposed an International Clearing Union to deliver American funds to them. Both governments wanted to avoid the instability of the interwar economy, and they favored relatively stable exchange rates and low tariffs encouraging trade flows. Keynes wanted some repression of capital flows preventing them leaping rapidly between countries in search of speculative profit. This would also make it easier for European governments to use progressive taxation to finance desired unemployment benefits, social programs, and public goods, without fear of capital flight. For some of them the avoidance of the severe class conflict that had marred the interwar period was the main priority. The British also wanted flexible institutions that could force creditor countries (i.e., the United States) to assist debtors (e.g., Britain). The Americans wanted institutions that could pressure debtors (i.e., foreigners). Other countries were only allowed a brief say, at the final meeting at Bretton Woods in July 1944 (Block, 1977: 32–52).

The consequent Bretton Woods Agreement led to the International Monetary Fund (IMF), the World Bank, and the first formal system of global financial regulation (the old gold standard had been informal). Currencies were pegged against the dollar, while allowing for periodic regulated adjustments, and the dollar was fixed against gold. Financiers could only move funds across the world to further trade or productive investment. This was Keynesian but also reflected American power. "It was a case of brains pitted against power," says Skidelsky; "Churchill fought to preserve Britain and its Empire against Nazi Germany, Keynes fought to preserve Britain as a Great Power against the United States. The war against Germany was won; but, in helping to win it, Britain lost both Empire and greatness" (2000: 449, xv; Cesarano, 2006). But when the United States forced Britain to waive its right to devalue its currency or protect its sterling area, the resulting sterling crisis of 1947 shook the global economy and persuaded the United States to slow its market-opening policies. Washington now lived with a monetary compromise, recognizing that European barriers against currency convertibility were necessary, though they hurt short-term American business (Eichengreen, 1996: 96–104). The United States was accepting more pragmatic global responsibilities.

Bretton Woods ensured international economic stability through multilateral cooperation among nation-states under U.S. leadership. It was in effect a compromise of nation-states, American empire, and transnational capitalism. Ruggie (1982), drawing from Polanyi, called this embedded liberalism. After the depression, said Ruggie, the interwar tendency had been to make international monetary policy conform to domestic social and economic policy, rather than vice versa. Yet after the war, under American leadership, most of the world became economically more interdependent, and an international currency mechanism for the multilateral exchange of goods and services was more than ever needed. In the interwar period governments had failed to find a system of international currency relations compatible with domestic stability. At Bretton Woods they succeeded: governments would collectively act to facilitate balance-of-payments equilibrium and relatively open trade, both geared to providing full employment plus whatever social security and labor relations might be pursued by individual nation-states. It was on this basis that a more humane form of capitalism was reached in the advanced countries, one where almost everyone had social citizenship rights, which helped the development of a high consumer demand economy to forge capitalism's Golden Age.

There remained a tension, however, between an increasingly transnational financial sector and the national needs of states. Suspicious New York bankers and conservative Republicans also weakened the compromise by leaving the IMF undercapitalized, while a projected International Trade Organization proved dead on arrival in the protectionist Congress (Aaronson, 1996). Instead, an interim General Agreement on Tariffs and Trade (GATT) began in 1947, gradually negotiating ad hoc tariff reductions over the next decades. But since the United States did not abandon tariffs for goods that the Europeans could produce more cheaply, a trade imbalance resulted, with more American exports than imports. The Europeans had to pay the balance in gold, and by

1949 the United States had almost all their gold. Europe retaliated with currency depreciations and tariffs, which had been counterproductive before the war. The consequence was recession and then the United States recognized that for everyone's sake loans to Europe were necessary.

The Marshall Plan was mutual self-interest, the United States providing the Europeans with dollars so they could buy American goods and be integrated into the American realm (Skidelsky, 2000; Domhoff, 1990: 164–81; Domhoff, forthcoming; Schild, 1995: 131). Receiving governments signed pacts to balance budgets, restore financial stability, maintain market economies, and stabilize exchange rates to encourage international trade. Yet they could use monetary policy to reduce unemployment, and they were free to nationalize industries, repress finance capital, and develop progressive welfare and social insurance programs. Most of the Europeans sought full employment by manipulating effective demand, delivering more egalitarian distribution of income, welfare benefits, and economic growth. This was decidedly Keynesian (or Swedish school), though Keynes was blended into national and macroregional practices ranging from social democratic, through Christian Democratic and lib-lab (an alliance of liberals and labor), to the commercial Keynesianism of the United States. These were state-regulated capitalist economies, which meant that though they shared certain practices, there were national cages separating economic interactions. This was more an international than a transnational economy.

Most developing countries had capitalist economies that were more statist than those of the developed countries. They had experienced capitalism in its colonial forms and had not much liked it. Most of the bigger capitalist enterprises operating within their territories remained foreign, while the indigenous capitalist class was usually small and not very powerful. These countries could borrow a range of techniques from communist countries, like five-year plans and nationalized enterprises, for communism seemed at this time seemed to be successful at economic development. State-led development was widely assumed to be the best way of catching up. Since they were sovereign states they had a measure of autonomy through which the state could steer domestic capitalist markets in desired directions. They had sometimes to bargain with more powerful countries. For example, they could pursue import substitution industrialization (ISI), so long as multinational firms (almost all American) could open up branches there. The United States might not like such policies but it lumped them. Economic globalization was dual: American global rules but implemented with some autonomy by a world of nation-states. What was to become the golden age saw a high-production, high-consumption capitalism regulated by nation-states. It was only from 1970 onward that it began to fray (Chang, 2003: 19–24).

Thus the golden age was not just a phenomenon of the global North. Some developing countries also saw the highest growth rates ever recorded. In the economic boom at the end of the nineteenth century the highest growth rate had been that of Norway, around 2 percent growth per annum. In the more difficult interwar period, Japan and its colonies and the Soviet Union had achieved growth rates of around 4 percent. Yet in the golden age and after, the highest growth rates, of Japan, South Korea, Taiwan, China, and India, were between 6 percent and 10 percent. They were all in Asia. These growth rates were much higher than those of the more advanced economies. Why were they so high? The first precondition was that all the postwar record breakers were firmly sovereign over their territories. None was a colony or even economically dependent on more powerful states. They could devise their own growth-oriented policies. Second, as a benefit of the cold war, they were either allies of the United States so that the United States practiced a policy of benign neglect of their domestic economies; or in the cases of China and India they were just too powerful to allow interference. In fact, the United States actually helped its allies export their goods to the United States. Third, they all benefited from having had long-lived Asian civilizations whose effects lived on in the form of social and ethnic (religious, in the case of India) cohesion and high literacy rates. Fourth, as Rodrik (2011: 72) has shown, their growth policies were not based on their supposed comparative advantages in primary products, which was how previous developing economies had sought growth, but on the improvement of their industrial capabilities, in direct competition with the advanced countries. More specifically they practiced

(1) explicit industrial policies in support of new economic activities – trade protection, subsidies, tax and credit incentives, and special government attention;
(2) undervalued currencies to promote tradables;
(3) a certain degree of repression of finance, to enable subsidized credit, development banking, and currency undervaluation.

Underlying this were two novelties: the emergence of real sovereignty among poorer nations – that is, the dawning of an age of nation-states – and the pragmatic acceptance of this by the United States, pressured by its cold war needs. American domination was not total, and the United States accepted this, ensuring that its dominance in Asia would eventually become hegemonic rather than imperial.

This was also so with its European allies. The Truman administration, backed by corporate moderates, tried to sell the Marshall Plan for Europe to business as a way of remedying inadequate domestic demand. Congress, unaccustomed to giving money to foreigners, demurred. Yet when the Soviet Union refused to join the plan and marched into Czechoslovakia, Congress accepted Marshall Aid as part of the defense of Europe against communism (Bonds, 2002; Block, 1977: 86–92). It was not a turning point for Europe, whose growth had already begun, but it was a boost. Bretton Woods plus the Marshall Plan benefited the whole West, enhancing growth, though financial markets required constant fine tuning by governments and central banks (Aldcroft, 2001: 111–17; Kunz, 1997: 29–56; Rosenberg, 2003; Block, 1977; Eichengreen, 1996: 123, 134). Though the United States dominated the new system, it was multilateral and mutually beneficial, less empire than hegemony. The other advanced states grumbled but recognized the benefits.

The imperial and ideological pillar: The cold war

Roosevelt had expected a benign postwar geopolitical order, and both emerging superpowers substantially cut their military forces as the war ended. The United Nations was set up to help keep the peace. It was first designed to have a Security Council of the United States, Britain, the Soviet Union, and Nationalist China, but Stalin opposed this since it was thought at the time that this would be a three to one majority against him. The more complex UN structure of today, involving veto powers by the permanent members of the Security Council, emerged instead. Until decolonization the new UN was mainly composed of Western European and Latin American states and so had a secure American majority (Hoopes & Brinkley, 1997; Schild, 1995: 153–61). China unexpectedly became communist in 1949, but its seat in the UN was occupied by the Chinese Nationalist government in exile in Taiwan until 1971. Thus the USSR had to use its veto in the Security Council repeatedly to block security decisions; that has meant that though UN institutions have greatly helped economic development, health, education, and refugees, the security of the world is rarely negotiated at the UN. This chapter will contain numerous instances of U.S. military intervention abroad, but only one of them, Korea in 1950, was authorized by the UN, and only because it occurred during a brief period during which the Soviet Union had withdrawn from the UN. Instead, world security turned on bilateral negotiations between the United States and the Soviets, heading rival military blocs.

Underlying the cold war was a geopolitical clash intensified by a clash of ideological power on a global scale. Each side believed its own ideological model, capitalist or communist, should rule the world, and these diametrically opposed models played into each other's worst fears. Stalin perceived U.S. liberal internationalism, global strike power, and control of the UN as capitalism trying to strangle the communist bloc, an accurate perception of the American empire by someone who did not want to be in it (recalling Japanese fears of the 1930s). Stalin was alarmed by the Marshall Plan and by American rebuilding of West Germany, which seemed like grabs for his Western neighbors (Mastny, 1996). We know that Soviet intelligence agencies exaggerated fears that the Americans might use their nuclear superiority to launch a surprise first strike, since they thought this was what their masters wished to hear (Andrew & Mitrokhin, 1999). This was reinforced by Soviet Marxism-Leninism's assumption that there would be a final culminating war between capitalism and socialism – until Khrushchev realized that nuclear war would produce mutually assured destruction (appropriately abbreviated to MAD) to the world.

Stalin's fears would have been confirmed had he read NSC-68, the secret U.S. policy document signed by Truman in 1950. This is often said to favor containment rather than rollback of the Soviets, but it actually declared "the fundamental purpose of the US is to assure the integrity and vitality of our free society, which is founded upon the dignity and worth of the individual.... The Soviet Union, unlike previous aspirants to hegemony, is animated by a new fanatic faith, antithetical to our own, and seeks to impose its absolute authority over the rest of the world." It is "inescapably militant because it possesses and is possessed by a world-wide revolutionary movement." Thus the United States must use all its power to defeat it, with overwhelming military superiority, preparations for offensive operations, and "intensification of affirmative and timely measures and operations by covert means in the fields of economic warfare and political and psychological warfare with a view to fomenting and supporting unrest and revolt in selected strategic satellite countries.... We should take dynamic steps to reduce the power and influence of the Kremlin inside the Soviet Union and other areas under its control" (National Security Council, 1950: 3–5, 13–14). This sounds more like rollback to me, though without outright war. Stalin may have been paranoid, but a superpower was out to get him. Soviet leaders believed they could not be safe until they had their own atom and hydrogen bombs, and helped by spies they poured massive resources into acquiring them (Holloway, 1994). Soviet rejection of nuclear negotiations then in turn fueled American fears.

Americans also exaggerated Stalin's aggressive intent. If there was a power vacuum, Stalin (like Truman) would expand into it. But in a world most of which was dominated by the United States, the Soviets and communist Chinese were not very expansionist. They were not like French revolutionaries of the 1790s who had tried to export revolution by war (pace Goldstone, 2009). Americans did not appreciate the traumas induced by the level of war devastation inflicted on the Soviet Union. It was unable to launch another war. Far from sponsoring world revolution, Stalin was terrified Germany would rise again. He declared, "**I hate the Germans.** It's impossible to destroy the Germans for good, they will still be around.... That is why we, the Slavs, must be ready in case the Germans can get back on their feet and launch another attack against the Slavs" (Leffler, 2007: 30–1, Stalin's emphasis). Having acquired Eastern Europe, he wanted it as a security belt, an autarchic fortress of buffer states, initially of friendly and then of communist regimes, with some limited autonomy from Moscow (Mastny, 1996; Pearson, 1998: 40; Service, 1997: 269). But this escalation from indirect to half-direct empire caused consternation in the West, as did Stalin's probes into power vacuums in Iran, Turkey, and Northeast Asia. The West probed a little in Eastern Europe and more in Asia. Fear led both sides to develop the defensive justification of aggression we have seen to be normal in imperial expansion, leading to the paradoxical conclusion that the bigger the empire, the more insecurity it feels. Objectively it might seem to have been possible for the two sides to agree to let peaceful competition decide the winner. But given these actors and their fears, this was impossible. Cold warriors were in control on both sides (Leffler, 2007; Zubok & Pleshakov, 1996).

Yet the cold war conferred some stability on regions like Europe that now lacked severe class conflict (unlike East Asia). Around Europe the United States practiced a containment milder than that advocated by Kennan. Except for Khrushchev in the Cuban missile crisis, the USSR also proved risk-averse. Maintaining bloc security was the first priority, as interventions in Hungary (1956) and Czechoslovakia (1968) and pressures on Poland (1981) revealed. In forty years the only direct Soviet intervention outside the bloc was in 1979 in neighboring Afghanistan. The cold war therefore aided stability between nation-states, and in the West it aided capitalist stability. That is why it was a pillar enabling postwar globalization. As ideology the cold war became more important domestically than in determining relations between the superpowers, where its intensity was reduced by pragmatism.

The USSR was a repressive dictatorship with its empire held down by force in Eastern Europe, unlike American domination in Western Europe. It was benign in one economic respect, for the Soviet center was subsidizing the imperial periphery. Both U.S. and Soviet elites now saw their rival as the main source of exploitation in the world. How much of this fear penetrated the masses is difficult to say. I doubt many Soviet citizens thought much about Marxism-Leninism in their off-duty hours, though they did accept the official line that their country was threatened by foreigners. Most Americans feared foreigners too, though the notion of freedom as our cause was also built into political rhetoric, into the material prosperity of everyday life, and into American pride in the country's strength and constitutional liberties. Anticommunism became the main ideological meaning system filling the gaps in knowledge about the outside world. More pacific pressure groups could make little headway. Defensive aggression had majority support.

So the conflict underlying the cold war was real, though amplified by ideologies and emotions. Conflict was not merely cognitive, based on mutual misunderstanding, as Gaddis (1972) first suggested. Nor did it correspond to Gaddis's (1997) revised view of ideology plus Stalin. If Stalin was paranoid, so was Truman. Leffler says he was "the prisoner of his own rhetoric" – an apt characterization of both the American and the Soviet leaders. American presidents saw their own actions as defensive, but they seemed offensive to Moscow; ditto when Soviet leaders sought to shore up their position in Berlin or Afghanistan. To withdraw from some foreign venture, and after 1950 to reduce defense spending, seemed to both sides like backing down, which superpowers do not do. Status mattered as well, until Gorbachev and Reagan broke the pattern (Leffler, 1999, 2007: 71; Mastny, 1996).

The difference from earlier imperial rivalries was that the threat was global. The defensive aggression that had always accompanied imperial rivalries had gone global. If the two superpowers could not agree on a multilateral process of disarmament, it would be madness for one of them to disarm unilaterally, for then the other one would have expanded its sway, believing that this was only self-defense. The USSR would have extended protectorates or client states over Greece, Turkey, Iran, and Afghanistan, and perhaps Finland and Austria too. They would have been foolish to try the same with Western Europe, but the temptation would have been strong. The United States would have expanded into Eastern Europe. Similar expansions did happen in Asia. So given that neither side would back down, the cold war was necessary. And in turn this meant that the United States protected its sphere of interest from communist or Soviet domination, and the USSR protected its sphere from capitalism. With this precondition they acted as rival global sheriffs, with ultimate responsibility for order and defense in their own zone of dominance.

MAD and the decline of war

Unusually for rival empires, these two did not fight each other. At first they were war-weary and then they inadvertently devised mutually assured destruction (MAD) – the nuclear balance of terror. This induced fear and intermittent panic on both sides. But they were careful to escalate only to indirect wars, sending troops only into their own spheres of influence, elsewhere intervening covertly or through proxies, so that their forces did not directly clash. This was reason triumphing over ideology, though the leaders still saw their ideologies as involving such high ends that they justified dubious means. Covert operations required plausible deniability. We will see numerous American examples in Chapter 5, while the Soviets used their own soldiers only as advisers and Cuban soldiers as proxies. Four thousand Cubans died in African battles (Halliday, 1999: 116–24). By 1980 Soviet leaders claimed that thirty-one states were orienting themselves in one way or another toward socialism. They were deluding themselves, since these were backward countries with oppressive military regimes, a million miles from socialist ideals. But the claim scared Americans (Halliday, 2010). So the United States expanded the Central Intelligence Agency (CIA), trained foreign military forces, and distinguished between merely authoritarian regimes – our allies – and totalitarian regimes – the enemy's allies. In reality there was no difference between them. The authoritarian Guatemalan military dictatorship, murdering more than 200,000 of its citizens, was far worse than the supposedly totalitarian Castro. Westad (2006) sees the cold war as a joint U.S.-Soviet successor to colonial exploitation. Though Third World countries could sometimes play off the two empires against each other, outcomes were often tragic. The cold war was in fact often hot, generating wars and about twenty million dead across the world.

But then it did cool. The term "postwar period" began to have another meaning as interstate wars virtually disappeared from the world. The Correlates of War (COW) project has compiled a dataset of all wars fought in the world since 1816, distinguishing civil war, interstate war, and extrastate (i.e., colonial) war.[1] About 60 percent of all conflicts in the period 1816 to the 1940s were interstate wars, but this fell in the 1950s to 45 percent, in the 1970s to 26 percent, and by the 1990s to 5 percent. Civil wars now became the main problem and so armies shifted from pointing outward to pointing inward, repressing their own citizens. Only three of the fifty-seven major armed conflicts occurring during 1990–2001 were interstate: Iraq versus Kuwait, India versus Pakistan, and Ethiopia versus Eritrea. The period 2001 to 2012 saw about fifty civil wars and only two full-scale interstate wars, the American invasions of Afghanistan and Iraq. Apart from the two American interventions, wars were low-intensity with relatively few casualties. Wars in the 1950s had nine times the casualty rates of wars in the 2000s.

Civil wars became less about class versus class, socialism against capitalism. Most were instead disputes over the dominant political ideal of the contemporary period, the nation-state – a state ruling over defined, bordered territories in the name of the people. The problem was, Who was to constitute the people when more than one large ethnic group inhabited the same territories of a state? Most civil wars had an ethnic, religious, or regional basis, in which one group claimed to be the true nation. Were others to be full citizens in the state, or second-class citizens, or worse? Most reluctantly accepted some discrimination because they felt they lacked the power to do otherwise. But empowered minorities, especially those helped by coethnics from abroad, resisted and so began civil wars (I make these arguments at greater length in Mann, 2005). For a time Collier's memorable summary of civil wars held sway. Wars, he declared, were about greed not need or creed – loot, not objective grievances or ideologies. Later Collier (2000, 2003) moderated his view, and subsequent research has shown that greed and lootable resources were not usually causes of the outbreak of rebellions though obviously rebels needed to seize material resources to sustain their struggle. Political grievances and distinct identities are the main causes of civil wars (Arnson & Zartman, 2005). Advanced nation-states learned the very hard way not to make war, while one hopes that developing countries are learning that the desirable nation-state is multicultural.

In the past Europeans had fought far more wars than anyone else. Gleditsch (2004) says that up to the 1950s Europeans contributed 68 percent of them, though serious COW undercounting of colonial wars means that the real figure

---

[1] COW data are available at http://cow2.pss.la.psu. They have been updated by the Department of Peace and Conflict Research at Uppsala University (see Eriksson et al., 2003). Some revisions have also been made by Skrede and Ward (1999).

was probably greater than 80 percent. Europe led, followed by Asia, then the Middle East, with Latin America and Africa lagging well behind. Lemke calculates that Africa's number of wars and its ratio of wars to state-years are three to five times less than the global average. His tables indicate that the Latin American ratio must be about the same (Lemke, 2002: 167–71, 181; cf. Centeno, 2002: 38–43). Then the aftermath of World War II produced a reversal. Since then Europeans, like Africans and Latin Americans, fought almost no wars, while the Middle East, Asia, and the United States took over martial leadership. Wimmer and Min (2006) found two waves of modern war, the first in the nineteenth century, the product of colonial wars, the second in the mid-twentieth century composed of anticolonial wars of liberation. Modern wars were largely due to the rise and fall of empires. When the Europeans lost their empires and stopped fighting, so largely did the world.

These data show that war making is not due to invariant human nature but to certain types of society. The hopeful message is that it can be abolished. A second hopeful sign for human reason is that so far nuclear weapons have restrained the powers who acquired them: the United States after 1945 and the Soviet Union, Britain and France, China, India, and Pakistan. Nuclear weapons do not guarantee peace but have produced just enough restraint by state elites to avoid their actual use. Cooler reason emerged among American and Soviet leaders. When their confrontation intensified, it terrified them and they deescalated: first Kennedy and Khrushchev during the Cuban missile crisis, then Reagan and Gorbachev after the Soviet panicky reaction to the North Atlantic Treaty Organization's (NATO's) "Able Archer" wargame in 1983. MAD was the global crisis that did not engulf us, a somewhat precarious success for human rationality to be contrasted to two world wars, the Great Depression, and the Great Recession. It was easier to solve because only two great nuclear powers were directly confronting each other, making the consequences of action easier to predict. It lacked the dislocating sequences of action and reaction among multiple powers that had started both world wars. Other countries acquiring nuclear weapons have also moderated their foreign policies, including India and Pakistan – another dual confrontation.

MAD also had knock-on effects. That the superpowers must avoid at all costs warring with each other made for implicit understandings between them. They might use whatever provocative rhetoric they liked, but they would not actually intervene militarily (except in niggling little ways) in each other's spheres of interest. They would fight only indirectly through much less powerful intermediaries who could do less damage to the world. Each superpower kept the peace across its own sphere, at least in the areas it felt were most strategic. The Soviets stopped any potential wars in Eastern Europe, while, since the American sphere comprised much of the world, the United States began to see itself in the role of a global sheriff. The Washington political establishment grew to believe that the United States had a global responsibility to preserve the peace and order of the world, and this became deeply embedded in American thinking. Both Republicans and Democrats believe that the United States has kept the peace, though today they worry that U.S. decline might lead the world into chaos (e.g., Kagan, 2012; Brzezinski, 2012). Without U.S. hegemony, they say, the world would be chaotic and conflict-ridden.

I will be a little skeptical of this idea in this volume. It is difficult to find cases in which either the United States or the Soviets prevented other states from making war. The United States did stop short the Anglo-French invasion of Egypt in the Suez crisis of 1956. In 1983 it saber rattled to prevent Libyan attacks on the Sudan and Egypt. It has protected Taiwan from possible invasion by China. In 1990–1 it tried to stop Iraqi attacks on Saudi Arabia and Kuwait, but this attempt failed and led to war. It intervened in Bosnia in 1993, stalling a Serb invasion. But that seems to be all. It is not an impressive list. There have been far more interventions in the internal affairs of countries to support one faction against another, and many of these create at least as much disorder as order, as we see in Chapter 5. Moreover, since the year 2000 wars have been launched only by the United States, the only empire left. I find it difficult to see the United States as a global sheriff. Given the number of armed interventions it has made in other countries' affairs (discussed in Chapter 5) it seems more like a global warlord.

Unfortunately, despite U.S. hegemony, nuclear proliferation has slowly continued. When a power has felt threatened by an enemy armed with nuclear weapons, it has acquired them as well – North Korea and perhaps Iran are current examples. So far this has not ended nuclear deterrence since it has simply increased the number of pairs of powers glaring at each other. However, danger is now resurfacing in cases where ideology might potentially trump reason, as might be the case with the weapons of Pakistan, Iran, and Israel. I will explain this in Chapter 10. Yet with just a few exceptions only third-rate powers have made war in the postwar period, and the exceptions were waged by major against minor powers (van Creveld, 2008: chap. 5). The backbone of advanced states except the United States is no longer the fiscal-military nexus. To revise Charles Tilly's famous dictum, wars used to make states, and states used to make wars – but no longer. Military power relations have played much lesser roles in recent advanced countries. The best news emerging from the second half of the twentieth century was the extension of a zone of peace across the North and some of the South of the world. Wars continued, but they were mainly civil or American wars. However, this did not happen all at once; nor was it evenly spread across the world. Some regions were much hotter than others. Thus I will deal separately with several regions of the world in Chapter 4. But first I will examine American life at home during the cold war.

3   America in war and cold war, 1945–1970: Class conflicts

Since the United States was the leading superpower, its domestic economy and politics became of great significance for the world. Since my general method in these volumes is to focus on the "leading edge" of power in any period, I give most attention now to the United States. In the postwar period, compared to other Western countries, the United States became much more conservative at home in terms of class politics, while becoming more liberal in terms of protecting personal identities. Neither process was steady or continuous. Class politics were closely contested both in the immediate postwar period and in the 1960s, after which conservatism racheted upward. But identity liberalism tended to surge later. In this chapter I will take both stories up to about 1970.

The impact of World War II

To explain postwar developments we must start during the war. The United States did not declare war until the end of 1941 and for two full years before then had profited from selling war material to Britain and mobilizing for a possible war amid a recovering economy. There was military-led growth. Unused industrial capacity and unexploited technological improvements were brought onstream, aided by an increased labor supply (especially women), a decline in low-productivity sectors, and a modest increase in hours worked. Manufacturing production continued to rise as the United States fought across the Pacific and Europe. The share of military expenses in gross national product (GNP) rose from 1.4 percent in 1939 to an astonishing 45 percent in 1944, shattering conceptions of fiscal rectitude. Neither balancing the books nor encouraging private investment mattered anymore. Since the United States was receiving the world's gold to pay for supplies sent to its allies, it could also run large deficits without adverse monetary effects. Real GNP rose a phenomenal 55 percent during 1939–44, due to an across-the-board mobilization of resources (Rockoff, 1998: 82). Economically, it was a very good war for Americans. For everyone else it was bad. The difference meant the United States dominated the world economy afterward.

Few Americans suffered. There was no bombing, no dire food or housing shortages, only some restrictions of consumption goods. A grand total of six people died in the continental United States as a result of enemy action, members of a church group who chanced on a parcel attached to a large colorful balloon while picnicking on the Oregon coast. The Japanese had launched it with the help of prevailing winds toward America, perhaps the only one that actually reached the country. When the picnickers opened the parcel, the bomb inside exploded. Other Americans benefited from war. Unemployment fell from 17 percent in 1939 to below 2 percent by 1943 and stayed there for the rest of the war. Since wages rose faster than prices, consumption and real incomes rose. Manufacturing workers did best, white and black, male and female. The taxes and war bonds to pay for the war fell mostly on the wealthy. Most Americans got butter while the troops got guns. Only Japanese Americans did badly. African Americans were beginning to do better under the horizon. They were flooding into manufacturing employment and receiving higher wages, and as soldiers they were experiencing the same emboldening (amid deeply racist armed forces) as colonial soldiers were elsewhere.

Unlike in other combatant countries, actually under attack, electoral politics could continue as usual. As shown in Volume 3, chapter 8, the New Deal lib-lab offensive had already lost much of its steam, though politics remained balanced, with potential to break either left- or rightward. A Democratic president headed the administration, balanced by a Republican/southern Democrat majority in Congress. New Deal relief programs ended as unemployment fell. The Wagner-Murray-Dingell Bills of 1943 and 1945 would have expanded social insurance, added national health insurance, and replaced the patchwork of federal/state programs for the needy with a federal program. But they were defeated in Congress, with southern Democrats playing the pivotal role. Roosevelt did not expend much energy supporting them since he saw this as being a losing fight. He was in any case focused on the war effort. The welfare state retained the dual, divisive benefit structure described in Chapter 8. There was no drift toward a universal welfare state, as in other Anglophone countries. The leftward surge of the 1930s was halted. Yet wartime low unemployment, stabilized wages, and progressive taxes meant inequality fell substantially through the 1940s. Hours worked equalized and paid holidays were extended (Goldin & Margo, 1992; Brinkley, 1996: 225). The 1940s was the only decade of the century in which inequality of both income and wealth fell in America, and they fell substantially (Piketty & Saez, 2003). The Anglophone countries now had the most equal income distributions in the world. In this respect the war was good for the American working class. It was especially good for African Americans, raising their wages from 40 percent to 60 percent of white incomes. Military power had in these respects solidified the New Deal achievement.

The war state also continued expanding in size and regulatory scope. To pay for the war, the government relied largely on the federal income tax and on bonds, so that more of the assets of individuals and financial institutions became invested in the federal government. This "nationalization" of finance endured until the 1970s, when it became more transnational (Sparrow, 1996: 275). State-sponsored industrial investment rose from less than 5 percent of capital investment in 1940 to a massive 67 percent in 1943 (Hooks, 1991: 127). The demands of war were still not as heavy as in Britain, Germany, or the Soviet Union. In response they had set up supreme war councils intervening anywhere in society. There was no American equivalent. The United States did not sacrifice the needs of civilians at the altar of war. Instead, ad hoc wartime corporate planning agencies were set up and nudged America's vast economic resources into war. These agencies would not rival Roosevelt's authority, would leave the economy mainly in private hands, and might be dismantled at the end of the war.

The agencies were run by politicians, civil servants, military officers, a few trade unionists, but above all by big business executives, the "dollar-a-day men" seconded from their corporations and still receiving salaries from them. Under them, federal civilian employees rose from 830,000 in 1938 (itself a historic peak) to 2.9 million by war's end. This enlarged state has occasioned a muted reprise of the argument between state autonomy and class theorists which I discussed in chapter 8 of Volume 3. But there were differences this time. Since this was war, military officers were the major statist faction, and since the main purpose was to fight a war, class conflict was not as important as during the New Deal. It figured little in the War, Navy, or highest-level production boards, where labor had no significant presence and where the main conflicts were among the military, the corporate executives, and the New Deal officials.

There is general agreement on the outcomes of these struggles, though with some differences of emphasis among the main scholars (Hooks, 1991; Sparrow 1996; Domhoff, 1996: chap. 6; Waddell, 2001; Koistinen, 2004). They all accept some version of what Sparrow calls "resource dependency theory," meaning that the state agencies remained dependent on those who supplied their resources, especially big business and (with less consensus) the military. Hooks offers a compromise between a state autonomy and class theory. The enhanced powers of the American state, he says, were being redirected away from New Deal social objectives toward the more conservative goals of a military-industrial alliance. This comprised, on the one hand, semiautonomous military bureaucrats and, on the other, monopoly-sector corporations emerging from the war in joint possession of the state, though the military also controlled its own productive resources. War produced big-state conservatism, not leftist but led by business corporations and the military.

From the beginning of 1947 the cold war allowed the military to consolidate its powers, while the corporations regained their autonomy as a more market-oriented economy returned. A sector comprising aircraft, defense electronics, and shipbuilding remained under joint Pentagon-corporate control – what President Eisenhower later called the "military-industrial complex" – and this was the main site of industrial planning in the United States. During the next half-century presidents and Congress intermittently sought to clip its wings by creating civilian agencies independent of the Pentagon – like the Atomic Energy Commission, the National Aeronautics and Space Administration, the Arms Control and Disarmament Agency, and the Department of Energy. But most of their resources ended up directed to military ends and subordinate to the complex. Domhoff emphasizes the power of the corporations; Hooks emphasizes military power in industries like the fledgling aircraft industry. In more established industries he agrees that the main corporate contractors "gained the economic resources and political authority to coordinate entire economic sectors" (Hooks, 1991: 150, 161). This was the context in which C. Wright Mills (1956) devised his famous theory of the "power elite," fused joint rule over America by economic, military, and political elites. In the context of war and cold war it made sense, though of course it was not fusion to the extent found in fascist or state socialist regimes, and it was to some extent balanced by the political institutions of democracy.

Officers and businessmen, supported by Congress, overcame the New Dealers, who favored more liberalism than business or Congress wanted, and more civilian control than the military wanted (Hooks, 1991; Brinkley, 1996: chap. 8; Waddell, 2001). Roosevelt and Truman needed business and congressional support, while the New Dealers had nowhere else to go. Business and the military arrived at a modus vivendi, as Koistinen (2004: 503) describes: "The military remained acutely aware that its long-run interests rested with the corporate structure. ... Industry reciprocated since the army and navy negotiated and let contracts. Consequently, more often than not, the armed services and corporate America stood together on mobilization policy even though, at times, their immediate interest differed." New Dealers lost their jobs as agencies trying to protect themselves from congressional committees sought the protection of more conservative bosses. Roosevelt still sometimes talked New Deal, but he did not often walk it.

Liberal designs for postwar government-led reconversion to aid small business and labor and for a full Keynesian policy were stymied. As Waddell (2001) noted, wartime mobilization had developed a warfare not a welfare model for expanding state power, and this was acceptable to major corporations and congressional conservatives. In the cold war this endured, though now it needed more civilian support, especially in Congress. Senators and representatives were generally supportive once military bases or industries were placed in their constituencies. By the end of the cold war there was one in every congressional district. Everyone knows of Eisenhower's speech at the end of his presidency, warning Americans of the rise of the "military-industrial complex." Yet Eugene Jarecki, director of the documentary film *Why We Fight*, says the president's children told him that the penultimate draft of their father's speech had referred to the "military-industrial-congressional complex." Eisenhower had removed the word "congressional" when advisers said it would cause political difficulties (BBC, "Storyville," March 3, 2005). The tripartite version was more accurate, and it was food for Mills's "power elite" theory – an alliance of economic, military, and political elites. But the complex (sometimes called the national security state) did not dominate the whole state. Most industry was not supplying the military after 1945, and its lobbyists often urged butter rather than guns. Congress had to worry about both. Their relationships would depend on the perception of threat from abroad, and this fluctuated through the cold war. But in general wars were to help steer big government, big business, and Congress down conservative paths.

Wartime labor relations: Corporatism and union growth

However, not all wartime agencies were controlled by business or the military. The Office of Price Administration, setting consumer prices and rents across the economy from January 1942, was a bastion of consumer democracy under New Dealer leadership. An army of women checked up on prices across the country, ensuring they were kept at the specified level. At the peak, it froze almost 90 percent of retail food prices. It was popular – though the National Association of Manufacturers (NAM) unsuccessfully attacked it as "petty bureaucratic dictatorship." It was a lib-lab triumph, but with a limited shelf life, for it was unlikely that a radical interference with markets would survive in a peacetime America. It was abolished in 1947, revived during the Korean War, and then abolished for good.

The war needed corporatist labor relations, as had happened in World War I. Labor had to be co-opted to eliminate disruptions to essential materials caused by strikes and go-slows. In 1941 Roosevelt repeatedly sent the troops in to break up strikes and enforce settlements, but he did not like doing this (Sparrow, 1996: 72–83). Business opposed a labor presence in planning boards, yet neither the NAM nor the U.S. Chamber of Commerce could draw up an alternative plan; nor were they empowered to reach agreements on behalf of all business. The American Federation of Labor (AFL) and Congress of Industrial Organizations (CIO) union federations did represent labor but they squabbled. The AFL remained suspicious of involvement with government, and both had difficulties disciplining shop-floor militants, among whom there were many communists. CIO president John L. Lewis also rejected corporatism. Roosevelt persisted and was prepared to make concessions to the unions and ride roughshod over business intransigence. But conservative Republicans and southern Democrats opposed any increase in union power (Katznelson et al., 1993). Southerners, chairing half the Senate committees at the time, defended their own racial capitalism, without unions (Korstad, 2003). After a 1941 strike wave the House, urged on by business, passed a bill to restrict union rights that would rescind the Wagner Act. The Senate was set on passing it and Roosevelt was unsure whether his veto would stick. He knew that if it became law, it would only lead to more strikes.

But the Japanese now attacked Pearl Harbor, and Roosevelt could play the patriotic card. Isolationism was finished and congressional opposition faltered. Roosevelt used a small group of corporate moderates plus New Dealers and CIO allies to agree on a plan, which he steamrollered through the business peak associations who lacked an alternative plan. Still fearing Congress, he did it by executive order, setting up a National War Labor Board with much greater regulatory powers than the old NRLB discussed in Volume 3, Chapter 8. The unions entered the board's agencies as the only representatives of labor, sitting alongside business and government representatives as formal equals in a tripartite corporatist structure. They received institutional privileges, especially a "maintenance- of-membership" rule, which allowed unions already recognized by the employer to recruit all new employees there. Employers anticipated flouting this rule but then saw this might lose them federal contracts, and this also pressured other employers into conceding union shops. Union membership rose by 40 percent, from 25 percent of the nonagricultural workforce in 1939 to more than 35 percent in 1945. The board set national wage policy, and under norms of equal wartime sacrifice, it was more egalitarian. Unskilled workers' wages rose faster than skilled, black rose faster than white, female faster than male, low-wage faster than high-wage industries. Labor leaders were now inside a major wartime administrative agency, while more members meant more funds, more grievance procedures, and more benefits and paid holidays, encouraged by the board as stabilizing influences on employment relations. In the late 1940s the United States was no longer in comparative terms a union laggard. Its membership rates were in the middle of the range of industrial democracies.

In the South the board empowered black workers: "From the perspective of the South, and especially southern black workers, a federally imposed system ... known as 'industrial jurisprudence' was quite simply indispensable.... [It] ... was anything but a legalistic barrier to militancy ... it offered their only conceivable route to power" (Korstad, 2003: 223–5). Voting in board elections was the first time most black workers at R. J. Reynolds had ever voted. They voted for union representation. The white workers of the Harriet and Henderson mills set up their CIO union affiliate in 1943. The grievance procedures licensed by the board helped them defend pay levels and established rules for job security, transfers between jobs, extra shift working, and lateness and absenteeism. These rules prevented management from arbitrarily increasing workloads, hitherto the main source of conflict. Women workers valued regulations allowing them to combine work with family responsibilities and so exert greater control over their lives. These workers *wanted* to be regulated, unlike employers (Clark, 1997: 100, 104, 4, 147). These two studies make clear that southern workers wanted unions – and regulation.

Regulation cut both ways, however. The board wanted responsible unions, and unions traded no-strike pledges for employer recognition and institutional gains. Communist unions were especially compliant, told by Moscow to sacrifice for the war effort (Zieger, 1995: 172–7). The fixed term contract became normal, confining conflict to the end of the contract period, when the board's arbitration procedures helped regulate it. Bargaining became ritualized. Sparrow (1996: 274–5) concludes, "Labor unions went from being risk-takers in the 1930s and early 1940s to becoming risk-averse actors in the mid- and late 1940s, anxious to protect the status quo."

Union leaders had hoped for a corporatism in which labor was an equal partner in industry "councils." At the shop-floor level they wanted participation in production decisions and hiring and firing, plus the right to inspect companies' books. They failed to get any of this. Roosevelt was not interested, and even the unions were divided, so business simply refused to yield managerial prerogatives. Union leaders were now required to take action against shop-floor militants, and so the CIO made new demands of local officials. They must be "capable of administering contracts on a relatively peaceful basis." Where they would not toe this line, they were purged. Lichtenstein comments, "Instead of fighting for each grievance until they satisfied rank and file members, union committeemen were now expected to process only those grievances supported by the language of the contracts" (2003: 23; cf. Cohen, 1990: 357–60).

Grievances were supposed to go through the NLRB arbitration procedures. Yet by early 1943 the board was receiving ten thousand to fifteen thousand cases a month and the backlog was growing. Dissatisfied workers responded with wildcat strikes in 1943 and 1944, fewer, however, than in wartime Britain. Some AFL unions, warier of political regulation, were more supportive of the strikes and increased their membership at the expense of the CIO. Inter- and intraunion struggles continued (Brinkley, 1996: chap. 9; Lichtenstein, 2003: introduction; Zieger, 1995; Stepan-Norris & Zeitlin, 2003; Sparrow, 1996: chap. 3). This was not a simple "sellout" by the leaders. The pressures worked both ways. Militants got rank-and-file support when workers had a strong sense of grievance, yet labor leaders felt the pressure of wartime patriotism, amplified by biased mass media and electoral trends. Wildcat strikes were unpopular among the general public. Militants who caused trouble were widely regarded as unpatriotic, and this helped electoral trends unfavorable to unions and to communism, since many militants were communists. The main problem was the way the United States participated in the war. Civilians were not making great sacrifices for which they could expect to be rewarded afterward. There was no great reservoir of sympathy for striking workers. This war, like the first war, and despite the growth in labor unions, was on balance a slide backward for American labor, increasing their visibility as a sectional rather than a national interest group. In America the working class would not be elided into the nation, as in some other countries.

In contrast, British factory districts were being pulverized from the air, and the British worked longer hours in more dangerous conditions. Food rationing created a "black market culture" in which the rich were believed to prosper while the workers suffered. British unions felt forced to make the same deals as American ones did, and Ernest Bevin, the minister of labour, was a prominent trade union leader. But when the British wildcat strikes occurred, they evoked more sentiments of sympathy from the general public. During the war British opinion moved leftward as the notion deepended that the people's sacrifices must be rewarded with reforms. This produced Labour's sweeping electoral victory of 1945, surprising and for Churchill devastating. In the United States opinion moved somewhat rightward, as wartime elections showed. Nonetheless, by the end of the war the unions remained hopeful that they could consolidate wartime gains.

Postwar planning: Commercial Keynesianism, military-industrial complex

After the war New Deal monetary and fiscal policy was maintained and a macroeconomic consensus emerged from wartime experience that government should assist and regulate market forces. U.S. business now depended heavily on government planning and the large corporations recognized this and embraced what was called "commercial Keynesianism." Government fiscal and monetary policy eased the cycles of a capitalist economy, increasing employment, stabilizing prices, and steadying economic growth. There were political differences: under Democrats growth tended to be stressed, under Republicans price stability. Under both, agricultural subsidies and government expenditures, especially on the military, helped maintain aggregate demand and stimulated growth. Now a national economy could be "measured" by government collection of systematic economic statistics, and the United States was the first to capitalize on economic tools developed in the 1930s and especially in the war to establish in 1947 national macroeconomic accounts. But the United States also had global responsibilities, not only to withstand communism but also to boost global prosperity. American growth depended upon the economic revival of Western Europe and Japan, and government policy was designed to aid that. This new phase of a national-cum-global economy was to prove Marx wrong. Capitalism could generate collective organization to protect itself from the worst effects of unfettered competition, both domestic and international – partly through a militarism that Marx had associated with feudalism, not with capitalism. Military power was not withering away with capitalist development.

Domhoff (forthcoming) shows that the Committee for Economic Development (CED), the think tank of the "corporate liberal" wing of business, acted as a moderating force between lib-labs and the free-market conservatism of the NAM and the U.S. Chamber of Commerce. While strongly opposing (as all business did) lib-lab pressures for unions, redistribution, the welfare state, and regulation of business, the CED welcomed government fiscal and monetary policy to stimulate growth and employment, and so preserve stability, both for the intrinsic merits of such policies and for heading off more radical lib-lab planning schemes. From 1946 presidents got advice from the new Council of Economic Advisors, Keynes-influenced economists of whom the majority had also worked for the CED. The CED was also willing to support economic aid to Europe and some limited deficit financing of growth. The CED often battled with the balanced-budget orientation of rival business organizations for the votes of the conservative majority in Congress formed by Republicans and southern Democrats.

The last lib-lab attempt at adding an explicit commitment to full employment had been in 1944, with a Full Employment Bill designed to ensure "maximum employment, production and purchasing power." Yet it was so watered down in its passage by conservative insistence that "incentives" should remain for low-paid workers that neither New Dealers nor Keynesians could recognize the final Employment Act (no "Full") as their child. It involved tax adjustments to stimulate growth but not investment in direct job creation, as they had wanted (Rosenberg, 2003: 43–63; Barber, 1985: 165–8; Brinkley, 1996: 260–4; Domhoff, forthcoming).

Nonetheless, low unemployment of around 4 percent lasted for twenty-five years after the war, and the living standards of the large majority steadily improved. The years between 1950 and 1973 are generally seen as a golden age, the period of the most rapid economic growth the world has ever seen. It was as off the scale as the Great Depression and it was led by the United States (Maddison, 1982). As with the Great Depression, economists have difficulty explaining this singular growth event. Neither neoclassical steady-state growth models nor the model of a "natural rate of growth" could apply. These models were also undermined by the appearance of large variations in technological innovation, in investment, and in the labor supply, which now spurted through one-off boosts like migration from the countryside and the baby boom (Bombach, 1985). Conservatives remained committed to "free markets," and they understood the boom in simpler terms: capitalism worked. In 1953 the U.S. economy had 45 percent of the manufacturing output of the entire world and American techniques were adapted globally, assisting growth through "catch-up" (Abramowitz, 1979).

The war had increased productive capacity, but by government restraint of prices and supply of consumer durables. Americans had been forced to save. Thus the postwar period saw a burst of spending as durables came back onstream. By 1950 80 percent of Americans had a refrigerator and 60 percent a car. Most owned their own homes, assisted by the mortgage reforms of the New Deal and the GI Bill of Rights. Suburban tract development was in full flow. The American way of life materialized as a consumer boom, as "consumer citizenship" (Cohen, 2003). Then it spread first to Europe, then to Japan and East Asia and to large parts of China and India. The growth continued after adequate living standards were reached. New technologies, new gimmicks, new needs were created, repeatedly. Automobiles, televisions, laptop computers, VCRs, DVDs, Blu-Ray, cell phones, I-pads, with new models every year, plus ever-changing desirable logos on everything. The mass of citizens became addicted to everyday capitalist commodity gadgets. Advertising increasingly adorned the media, the streets, and human clothing. Not only in production did people reproduce capitalism; they did so more concretely through their consumption. The capitalist economy had solved the interwar combination of high productivity of manufacturing goods and failure to boost consumer demand. This had brought on crisis. Now the United States balanced high productivity and high consumer demand, and boom resulted across the world. The golden age of capitalism, called in France *les trente glorieuses* (thirty glorious years), lasted from 1945 to 1975 and economically benefited most people across the world (Hobsbawm, 1994; Maddison, 1982). American capitalism had not found the solution on its own. It had been boosted to this end first by Roosevelt's New Deal and then by military Keynesianism. In this case Schumpeter's "creative destruction" had not resulted from the logic of capitalism per se, but from entwined economic, political, and military power relations. This generates the sobering thought that capitalism might not possess the means of its own salvation and that market forces are not self-correcting.

The combination of market forces, government planning, and progressive taxes generated a new consumer citizenship. Though business and many Republicans would have liked tax changes, Republican leaders knew how unpopular more regressive taxes would be. Electoral considerations constrained the Right as well as the Left. The income tax, deducted almost invisibly at source, constituted two-thirds of total revenue by 1950. Though other taxes tended to be somewhat regressive, they were not large enough to counterbalance the income tax. Yet consumption was not actually a universal right but a privilege, dependent on unevenly distributed purchasing power within markets. Full employment and progressive taxes helped, but the poor were left outside.

Yet for the large majority of Americans, this was a world away from the 1930s. Unemployment and inequality were combated by the seemingly impersonal forces of the market nudged discreetly along by government officials and the demand of the military-industrial complex (Sparrow, 1996: chap. 4). The interstate highway system and the contemporary research university boosted the economy but were mostly developed for military reasons. The United States had the big state decried by conservatives. Government spending was 20 percent of GNP in 1940, 31 percent by 1962, and 40 percent by 1990 (Campbell, 1995: 34). The highest marginal income tax rates were around 90 percent in the 1940s and dropped to about 70 percent in the 1950s and 1960s, before dropping again to around 50 percent under President Reagan. But unlike the

New Deal, state planning and bigness lacked popular mobilization or indeed any connection with the Left. Carefully ignoring the military-industrial state and agricultural subsidies, conservatives proclaimed the virtues of free markets and denounced big states as fascist or communist. The corporations earlier denounced as evil trusts now seemed benign. They were secure places of employment, offering their own social security provisions, run by managers with Wall Street only a distant presence, for the corporations were basically self-financing. Around 1950 less than one in ten American families held company shares. The word "capitalism" was rarely used: the economy was free enterprise, as if corporations, the military-industrial-congressional complex, and agricultural subsidies freed people. This was a big state with big corporations, but conservatives pretended otherwise.

The pretense had important consequences. Commercial Keynesian was administered by the Washington elite. It was abstract, removed from the lives of most people, whose work and whose consumption seemed dominated by markets. That the politicians preached free markets to them, while the Keynesians did not preach at all, meant that free markets were more embedded and resonant in American ideology. This was a Keynesianism that dared not speak its name. So the myth arose later that the period of the golden age in America was dominated by markets and low taxes, whereas the big state and high taxes were a product of more recent years – and caused lower growth. The ideology was not true, but it was powerful.

The big state was cemented after the Soviets acquired the A-bomb and during the Korean War, which I discuss in the next chapter. Recognizing from near-defeat in Korea that U.S. armies could not be as large as communist ones, the military pursued capital-intensive, high-tech warfare. Military R&D expenditure rose five and a half times in real terms in the 1950s and corporations like General Electric and General Motors remained the major defense contractors they had become during the world war. From the 1950s to the 1980s military R&D expenditure varied between 40 percent and 65 percent of all R&D expenditure (Hooks, 1991: 27–8). This proved good for the economy, for it provided a stable industrial sector boosting secure employment and limiting market downturns. Military R&D produced civilian spin-offs, like computers and semiconductors (Alic, 2007). This was less commercial than military Keynesianism, less economic policy than the unintended consequences of global military power. The military-industrial complex of the 1950s was then succeeded by what Linda Weiss (2008) calls a development-procurement complex, a $450 billion federal defense procurement budget ($1 trillion if we include all levels of government) plus sponsorship of many public-private joint ventures. Its cultivation of dual-use (military and civilian) technologies like ICT (computers, semiconductors, and software), biotechnology, and nanotechnology blurred the line between state and business, and between civilian and military needs – deliberately, for the U.S. government recognizes that its military and security needs depend on maintaining a high-tech lead. In this sector this is a big state. Military-economic linkages are also found on a smaller scale in other military powers including Russia, China, Britain, and France.

In the United States economic success seemed to obviate the need for direct state relief or redistribution. This was not true in many other countries, as we saw in Volume 3, chapter 9. The high stable incomes of workers in federally funded defense industries and in an automobile industry helped by cheap gas and federal spending on highways, plus the boom in exports provided by European recovery boosted by the Marshall Plan, provided the core of consumer prosperity for almost all. New Deal relief programs were disbanded: no need to expand welfare, and even veterans' programs were transferred from federal to state agencies (Brinkley, 1996: 224–6, 268–9; Maier, 1987a). Consumption, corporate welfare, and state-run welfare targeted specifically at the poor generated not universal rights but particular privileges, not shared by all. For the majority, however, it seemed that there was no need for the European pursuit of social citizenship through universal welfare programs and active labor market policies. In the United States whether under Democratic or Republican presidents and congresses, lib-lab policies faltered. Voter turnout was down to 53 percent in 1948, and from there on, its highest point was 63 percent in 1953. Few of the poor were now voting. America commenced its long, though not entirely steady, march rightward through the rest of the century, the product of both domestic and geopolitical forces.

After Roosevelt's death, in 1946 the Republicans took control of House and Senate, helped by reaction against a national strike wave, and by the southern Democrats. The move rightward continued into the cold war, as conservatives mobilized antitotalitarian rhetoric against big-state New Dealers and "socialist" and "communist" labor unions. Communists had long been demonized in the United States. A 1938 Gallup Poll reported that though 97 percent of Americans interviewed said they believed in freedom of speech, only 38 percent believed in free speech for communists. In a 1941 poll 69 percent said they favored prison or other repressive measures for communists (White, 1997: 30). Before the cold war this did not mean much. If asked fixed-choice questions about communists, respondents replied negatively, but they did not really care about communists. Now communists were the main enemy, trying to enslave us. This was the beginning of an unusual period in American politics, when domestic and foreign policy reinforced each other strongly through the national security state. As always, foreign policy in so-called democracies was formulated by tiny elites, but this time it was genuinely popular, rooted in shared anticommunism.

The Democrats tried to compete. "Scare Hell out of 'Em Harry" became Truman's motto when provoked in 1946 by Republican propaganda that the choice was between Communism and Republicanism. Truman introduced public service loyalty programs that Senator McCarthy was later able to exploit.

There really were Soviet spy networks in the administration though they were soon dismantled. Years later Clark Clifford, counsel to President Truman, said, "It was a political problem.... We never had a serious discussion about a real loyalty problem ... the president did not attach fundamental importance to the so-called communist scare. He thought it was a lot of baloney. But political pressures were such that he had to recognize it. A problem was being manufactured" (White, 1997: 60) Foreign aid programs were now sold this way (more than 90 percent of their cost was military anyway).

Southern Democrats and the military-industrial complex were particularly keen on emphasizing anticommunism and the cold war. Other Republicans had been initially hesitant about the taxes the cold war required, but they soon came around, perceiving that anticommunism gave them a unifying theme across both domestic and foreign policy. Liberals were denounced as favoring socialistic policies and being soft on communism at home and abroad. Dulles, Eisenhower's secretary of state, acknowledged in private that he cultivated domestic anticommunism to legitimate the expensive brinkmanship he pursued abroad (Gaddis, 1982: 136, 145). Geopolitical scares were important in steering America rightward. Employers denounced unions as socialist or communist – and some of them were. The president of General Motors declared in 1946, "The problems of the United States can be captiously summed up in two words: Russia abroad and labor at home" (White, 1997: 31).

The Labor Movement: Stagnation and decline

In such a hostile climate the unions had to respond or decline. In 1946 the CIO had tried to turn the tide by cracking the South. In Operation Dixie it sent 150 union organizers south. But Dixie failed within six months. Its organizational model was based on large northern corporations rather than on the small enterprises of the South, and it was beset by factionalism. Many communist organizers were prevented from participating, thus weakening the drive, and the CIO failed to establish its legitimacy in southern culture (Griffith, 1988; Honey, 1993). Anticommunism was deployed against anyone favoring racial integration, as many union organizers did. Dixie was destroyed by the intransigence of southern employers, backed by police, state troopers, and politicians. It proved counterproductive, eroding existing southern unions. The CIO tobacco workers of R. J. Reynolds in Winston-Salem failed to unionize other firms and then in 1949–50 lost their own NLRB election. Reynolds fired the activists and the union disintegrated. Nonfarm unionization in the South fell between 1940 and 1960 from more than 20 percent to less than 10 percent (Korstad, 2003: chap. 15; Zieger, 1995: 227–41; Lichtenstein, 2002: 112).

There had also been a national strike wave in 1946; 4.6 million workers had gone on strike, the highest annual American figure in the twentieth century. The solidarity and restraint of the strikers were impressive, and employers were forced to yield some wage increases (Zieger, 1995: 212–27). But for the first time, a strike wave failed to attract more union members, suggesting a mixture of a declining reservoir of sympathy and more fatalism among workers at the rightward political drift. The strike wave hardened conservatives and alienated much of the middle class. Congress, egged on by business, passed onto the offensive, convinced that recent events proved unions had too much power. Business spent heavily on propaganda against "communist" unions, and the unions lacked the financial resources or unity to counter effectively. There was no moderate business stance on this issue. All business wanted to destroy the unions and felt it had a chance to achieve it (Rosenberg, 2003: 71; Domhoff, forthcoming).

The result was the Taft/Hartley Act of 1947 (Plotke, 1996: chap. 8). It outlawed unfair labor practices, banning jurisdictional strikes (over which union should organize a given body of workers), secondary boycotts (where unions strike, picket, or refuse to handle the goods of another company with which they are not in direct dispute), and closed shops (agreements requiring an employer to hire only union members). Union shops (where new recruits were required to join the union under a collective bargaining agreement) were permitted only after a vote of a majority of employees, and states were allowed to pass right-to-work laws that outlawed them. The right to work shifted from meaning the right to a job to the right not to join a union. The act also banned supervisors and foremen from joining unions, which was claimed to be both treasonous and harmful to property rights, and these were fast-growing occupations. The federal government could get a strikebreaking injunction if a strike "imperiled the national health or safety," which the courts interpreted broadly. To use NLRB services a union must declare under oath that its officers were not communists, and unions could not contribute to political campaigns. These last two clauses were later rescinded as unconstitutional – after union leftists had virtually disappeared. The act still stands as the bedrock of U.S. labor relations, making life very difficult for unions.

The expulsion of communists deprived the unions of many activists. Relations between communists and other unionists had never been good, but communist backing for a new Progressive Party in the 1948 election had also alienated the CIO leaders. Some were happy to use the law to get rid of the communists; others looked the other way. Harry Bridges, leftist (though not communist) leader of the longshoremen, spoke against the expulsion of the electrical workers union (the UE) at the 1949 CIO convention. He observed, "I don't find a single charge that says that the UE has not done a good job for its members. Not a single economic charge is leveled. So now we reach the point where a trade union is expelled because it disagrees with the CIO on political matters." He then posed a question: "My union did not support the Marshall Plan ... [or]... the Atlantic Pact, either, so will you expel us too?" "Yes," shouted back delegates in unison. The convention proceeded to throw out nine unions who provided 25 percent of CIO members. The communist unions were actually the most democratic ones (Stepan-Norris & Zeitlin, 2003: quote from p. 271; cf. Goldfield, 1997). Perhaps they were more democratic because they were the opposition in most unions. Yet expelling them was fratricidal folly, reducing the organizational capacity of unions. But they were no longer considered brothers.

Infighting was bad news for southern union locals. In Winston-Salem tobacco workers were threatened by hostile employers and mechanization, and the black union local collapsed under the pressure of the Red Scare (Korstad, 2003). In Memphis interracial unionism was "virtually crippled" by the purge of the Left, who had been its main activists. Here anticommunism, segregation, and sound business principles were virtually interchangeable in the minds of the employers, and of white skilled workers who benefited from segregation (Honey, 1993: 8).

Industrial relations now contained a contradiction (Gross, 1995): on the one hand, Taft-Hartley proclaimed adherence to "the practice and procedure of collective bargaining," but, on the other, it was slanted toward protecting individual, not collective, rights and especially those of property owners. This has allowed employers to oppose unionization by interfering in the electoral process laid out in the act. During a strike permitted under the act, employers can hire permanent replacements and dismiss the strikers, formidable restrictions on workers' power to withdraw their labor. The members of the NLRB are also political appointees. Whereas Democratic appointees tended to preserve but not advance labor's rights, Republicans trimmed them back, beginning with Eisenhower, continuing through Nixon, Reagan, and Bush the Younger, with stalemate under Obama and a Republican House majority. The NLRB became less and less supportive of workers' collective rights. A new era of judicial repression turned back the progress of the New Deal. And again, American unions were being organizationally outflanked by American business, which was being organized into larger corporations and trade associations.

The notion that labor might be an equal partner in a corporatist system was gone. Individual free riders could get the benefits secured by unions to which they did not belong, reducing the incentives to pay union dues. Right to work laws were passed by twenty-two states and the strikebreaking business became very profitable. Taft-Hartley condemned the unions to "a roughly static geographic and demographic terrain, an archipelago that skipped from one blue-collar community to another" (Lichtenstein, 2002: 114–22). This was largely confined to the Northeast and the Midwest, less of a national than a regional movement (Goldfield, 1987: 235). Bargaining became firm-centered and segmental, and the legal basis of unionism again rested on individual not collective rights, a denial of any class basis. Unions never fully recovered from the interrelated blows of 1946–7. The year 1945 remained the high-water mark of union membership, while strike rates declined under the Taft-Hartley restrictions (Wallace et al., 1988). Unions held on to around 30 percent of the nonagricultural labor force until the early 1960s, but by then they were gradually but continuously declining across most private industry (unlike in other countries), a trend that was only partially offset by gains in the public sector (as was also occurring in other countries). Since unions in other countries were gaining overall members, by 1960 the United States was a union laggard among the advanced democracies, though it did not become wholly deviant until later. Goldfield (1987) is quite clear about the causes of decline. It was not due to occupational or industrial shifts, or to race, sex, or age. It was more political, he says, resulting from, first, postwar domination by the Republican/southern alliance able to pass antiunion legislation and steer the NLRB rightward; second, the increasing intransigence of business in creating new ways of destroying unions; and third, the feeble and unimaginative tactics of labor itself.

Under pressure and without the political power or interest provided in other countries by Socialist and Labour Parties, CIO leaders moved rightward, settling for whatever deals they could get. With the leftists expelled, there was no longer an ideological divide between the AFL and CIO so they merged in 1955 and embraced AFL economism focused on wage and benefit bargaining, leaving managerial prerogatives alone (Lichtenstein, 2002: chaps. 3 & 4). Since this business unionism was so geared to profit, it also generated illegitimate business practices – corruption and Mafia links, especially in the Teamsters, Longshoremen, and mining unions. Their vices allowed the conservative authors of the Landrum-Griffin Act of 1959 to restrict unions' rights further on the grounds of combating crime (Fitch, 2006). There were material gains from economism and it did compel some nonunion firms to grant benefits to avert the entry of unions. Unions entrenched themselves in older sectors of corporate America, ensuring they got their cut from capitalist prosperity. They turned inward, away from broader social goals toward the material interests of their own members. But since their industries then began to decline, so did membership. This was the end of the lib-lab New Deal in America. The battered labor movement could no longer provide one-half of the deal.

In most other prosperous countries the early 1950s saw further extension of welfare provision toward universal coverage of all citizens, and institutionalization of corporatist institutions of collaboration among business, unions, and the state. These extensions were positively correlated with the level of unionization (Hicks, 1999: chap. 5). Since the United States lagged in union power, so it did too in universal citizen benefits and corporatist power sharing. Nor were unions in the forefront of the next progressive struggles, for civil, gender, or sexual rights, or for environmental protections (Lichtenstein, 2002: chaps. 3 & 4; Zieger, 1995: 327). The unions had tacitly agreed to forget about broader issues of social citizenship and focused instead on their members, predominantly white males enjoying employment and corporate welfare – citizenship by privilege not by right.

Unions did not lose all influence; 20 percent of Americans were members, and the AFL-CIO remained the nation's largest voluntary association. The New Deal and the war had established close relations between the unions and the Democratic Party, especially in liberal states and cities. Unions remained key to the Democratic coalition. They failed to redistribute either wealth or power, but they had secured for their members their cut of economic growth, and this in turn boosted aggregate demand. Though they failed to turn back the tide of labor relations policy, on other social and economic issues they had some influence, as part of a broader coalition for a rather top-down liberalism, lacking the bite supplied by mass mobilization. Their influence was also regionally specific, so many Democratic politicians did not have to please the unions, but were electorally beholden to other parts of the Democrat coalition. Unions had helped achieve a postwar consensus, but they were incorporated into it in a subordinate capacity, unable to go further. That was the key part of America's march rightward. The research cited in chapter 9 of Volume 3 showed that union strength was the single greatest predictor of the extent of social citizenship. That strength was now lacking in the United States, with predictable results.

Anticommunist ideology

Soviet defense rested on mass armies, which were also needed to keep down its buffer states. Thus Soviet society remained substantially militarized (Odom, 1998). In contrast, the high-tech American military and the fact that the Iron Curtain was a long way from American territory meant that its militarism remained somewhat abstracted from the lives of most Americans. Sherry (1995: xi) describes America as militarized but means by this "the process by which war and national security became consuming anxieties and provided the memories, models and metaphors that shaped broad areas of social life." This is rather abstract. The success of military Keynesianism meant that Americans got guns *and* butter, and prosperity and defense were built in to the experience of "freedom." "Defense" was of a whole "way of life" and that was experienced in more everyday terms (Kunz, 1997).

Radicals and liberals were often smeared as "communists," harried during the cold war by loyalty oaths, the FBI, Senator McCarthy's Committee on Un-American Activities, and judicial interpretations of sedition laws. The attack was on "fellow travelers," "dupes," and those "soft on communism" or "influenced by communism." Added to the end of many such lists of enemies was the word "etc." – just in case any leftist had been omitted. Such a broad target was easy to smear. Of course, punishment was nowhere near as severe as dissidents faced in the Soviet Union. Accusations of communist influence, especially in the federal government, in colleges and universities, and in Hollywood and television, merely resulted in thousands being denied security clearances, fired from their jobs, and sometimes imprisoned. Many were blacklisted because they had once, years before, been associated with liberal and leftist causes. Millions of Americans had to take loyalty oaths to get or keep employment. If discovered to have leftist ties, they were fired and liable for criminal prosecution. That was all. It was not terror but it destroyed careers and it was politically disabling.

Schrecker estimates that ten thousand to twelve thousand Americans lost their jobs this way, including her own sixth-grade teacher. She concludes, "McCarthyism destroyed the left" (1998: 369). This is overstated, but it did weaken it. Anyone labeled as a communist found resistance difficult. The persecutors were helped by two celebrated spy trials, in which Alger Hiss and the Rosenbergs were (correctly) found guilty of spying for the Soviets. Liberals were damaged by this since many had publically proclaimed their innocence. Stone shows that only during wartime – in the Civil War, the two world wars, the cold war, the Vietnam War, and the recent wars in the Middle East – has the U.S. government seriously attempted to suppress criticism of government officials or policies. But, he adds, the early years of the cold war were "one of the most repressive periods in American history" (Stone, 2004: 312). In the fog of war one can accomplish other goals – in this case, the disabling of labor and liberalism.

Alas, academe cooperated with the witch hunt. In 1949 the president of the American Historical Association urged his colleagues to "assume a militant attitude," because neutrality had no place during a period of "total war, whether it be hot or cold." Anticommunism became central to the national culture and intellectual life (Whitfield, 1996: chap. 3, quote from p. 58). Loyalty and patriotism meant respect for authority, from the military and the FBI to the idealized nuclear family. Popular novels, films, and television series portrayed the military and the FBI as champions of democracy, and yet respect for authority was also constantly stressed. Filmmakers were reluctant to make war or spy films without Pentagon approval, and television series like *The FBI* and *I Led Three Lives* were submitted to Hoover for his approval. Hoover's own anticommunist tract, *The Masters of Deceit*, was a best seller.

Some cold war culture reads horrendously today. In Mickey Spillane's novel *One Lonely Night* (1951) the hero, Mike Hammer, boasts, "I killed more people tonight than I have fingers on my hand. I shot them in cold blood and enjoyed every minute of it.... They were commies.... They were red sons-of-bitches who should have died long ago." Spillane was America's best-selling author in the 1950s. A *Screen Guide for Americans* was distributed by Hollywood studio and union bosses, who included the young Ronald Reagan. It laid down a list of don'ts for movies. Here are a few of them.

Don't Smear the Free Enterprise System

Don't Deify the Common Man

Don't Show That Poverty Is a Virtue ... and Failure Is Noble. (White, 1997: 32)

Almost all American religion was strongly opposed to godless communism and identified with Americanism – just as in the Red Scare of the 1920s. The religious celebrities of the period – Billy Graham, Fulton J. Sheen, Norman Vincent Peale, Cardinal Spellman – blended their spiritual mission with national defense against communism, while anticommunist political rhetoric reciprocated, full of allusions to religion.

Most Americans were convinced. In 1949 70 percent of Americans rejected Truman's pledge of no first strike of nuclear weapons. In 1950, 59 percent said the Soviet Union should be told "we will immediately go to war against her with all our power, if any communist army attacks any other country." In 1951, 51 percent were in favor of using nuclear bombs in Korea. In 1951 and 1952, when asked to choose between preventing communism from spreading or staying out of another war, two-thirds chose war. In 1954, 72 percent thought we would have to fight it out with the Russians. In 1952, 81 percent agreed there had been "a lot of communists or disloyal people in the State Department." The objects of their venom were in reality liberals. In 1954, 87 percent said it was impossible for a man to be a communist and a loyal American. Even in 1989, 47 percent of Americans preferred to fight an all-out nuclear war rather than live under communist rule (White, 1997, 4, 10, 28, 67–6; Whitfield 1996: 5; Wittkopf & McCormick, 1990: 631, 634; though Filene, 2001: 159, is more skeptical). The slogan "Better Dead than Red" is powerful testimony to the demonization of communism – worse than being dead was the night of the living dead. Better to fight them abroad than at home was also a popular refrain – as it was to be in the case of a different enemy in the first decade of the new millennium. Cold war anticommunism was a powerful ideology, one that was immanent in the sense that it reinforced the cohesion and sense of solidarity of the nation – and the same was true on the other side of the Curtain.

The State Department and the CIA always contained people who did not believe that the Soviet threat was monolithic and who thought that more conciliatory policies might induce splits inside the Soviet elite and bloc. However, they did not dare say this publicly, given the hysterical climate of the country. Nor did politicians dare openly oppose Senator McCarthy, despite often despising him. Liberals were quick to distance themselves from any association with left-wing ideology. They sought to reorient "left-of-center political debate around the twin themes of individual freedom, or 'civil rights', at home and anti-communism abroad" (Bell, 2004: 145, 150). The contrasting of individual rights in America versus the collectivism of Soviet communism was the positive side of cold war culture. Yet, ironically, this was done by liberals who were themselves being persecuted. Many conservatives had forgotten what individual rights should be. By 1950 the range of permissible debate on Left-Right issues had narrowed. There were censorship and curtailment of the liberties of the few dissenters, yet self-censorship was more important in Hollywood and among publishers and writers of history textbooks. Producers and editors anticipated pressure and persecution by cutting down what they would permit their directors and writers to say. In turn most directors and writers did not want to be persecuted and complied (Fousek, 2000: 161; Whitfield, 1996). There were open debates about how big the military budget should be, and whether the cold war had produced a too powerful state, but in the end Congress always passed bills on military and security spending that maintained the warrior consensus (Hogan, 1999).

The postwar welfare state

There was no frontal attack on welfare provision, however. Nothing much happened in this sphere during or soon after the war. Sparrow (1996) says this situation confounds expectations, since Americans were not rewarded for wartime sacrifice. Similarly, Amenta and Skocpol (1988; cf. Amenta, 1998), attacking the notion that war necessarily led to the extension of the welfare state, say it did in Britain, but not in the United States. They then try to explain this in terms of different political institutions in the two countries. In stressing political power relations they are attacking what they conceive to be an obsession with class and the economy in modern social science. They say America now had a less democratic political system than Britain, that the U.S. polity was more fragmented, that the British state had more capacity, and that wartime collaboration among the parties and classes was greater in Britain. The last of these differences did make it more likely that Britain would develop a postwar welfare state, yet this reflected their different war experience. War does not "necessarily" lead to any particular outcome. That leading sociologists like Skocpol and Amenta argue against that straw man shows their naivete when confronting military power relations. Stated simply, different kinds of war have different impacts on society.

In World War II the British sacrificed; the Americans did not. Amenta and Skocpol (1988: 101; cf. Amenta, 1998: 232) try to deny this by claiming that Britain was relatively unscathed by the war. They admit that there were sixty thousand British civilian deaths (remember, six Americans died!), but they ignore the fact that broader destruction caused by bombing raids plus the very realistic fear of a German invasion exacerbated a sense of common anxiety and suffering. The Labour Party and union leaders were immediately invited into wartime government because the very survival of Britain was threatened. This was never true of the United States. Neither Germany nor Japan could hurt the continental United States. The alternative in Britain to intense class cooperation was probably Nazi rule. Churchill's distinctive belligerency also mattered, for he was fighting not only to protect the country but also the Empire (always capitalized). Thus he wanted the conduct of the war to remain in safe proimperial Tory hands. This meant that he had to give most civilian ministries to the Labour and Liberal Parties.

Labour and the unions then made sure they would not be betrayed again, as in the first war, when most of the promises of postwar reform made to the British people had been broken afterward. So cabinet ministers developed the plans leading to the postwar welfare state, and Liberal intellectuals like Keynes and Beveridge helped them. As we saw in Chapter 2, Britain's colonial nationalists made a similar judgment about sacrifices and rewards, and India promptly gained independence after the war. Britain itself got a welfare state, a National Health Service, 800,000 public housing units, and nationalized industries. American experience of war was different: no great sacrifice, no deep class collaboration, no increased power to the Left, and so no substantial increase in social citizenship.

What proves this hypothesis is that one group of Americans – the armed forces – did sacrifice during the war, and they did get their own welfare state. Under the GI Bill of Rights of 1944 military veterans received bonus payments, national unemployment benefits, free medical care, low-interest housing mortgages with no down payment, loans to start businesses, and fully funded job-training and college education. Almost $100 billion was poured into these programs. For the first time unemployment benefits also covered agricultural and domestic workers, and all programs were in theory open to all, regardless of class, race, age, or gender, though Congress – always vigilant against unions – refused to grant unemployment benefits to veterans who participated in strikes. The GI Bill of Rights created the most privileged generation in American history. Nine million people received twenty dollars a week unemployment benefit; eight million received educational benefits, of whom 2.3 million went to universities; and 3.7 million got 100 percent mortgages (Keene, 2001). It was a genuine welfare state, though only for Americans who had earned it through sacrifice in the face of danger. Welfare for a privileged segment, separately administered by the Veterans Administration, helped stymie the chances for universal welfare (Amenta, 1998: 213).

Many officers might have gone to college or obtained mortgages anyway, but for the ordinary soldiers, sailors, and aircrews this was a tremendous opportunity. Fully funded GIs provided a big boost to the universities, whose size now began to swell toward their present levels. The first phase of American leadership in global education had been the nineteenth-century growth of public elementary education, the second the early twentieth-century growth of the public high schools, and now over the next three decades was the third phase, of universities. But the program with the greatest impact on the American landscape was the GI mortgage scheme, which boosted suburban tract housing development across the nation. Few blue-collar workers had been able to afford the payment terms of the New Deal mortgage program. Now working-class GIs could become property owners and join the consumer suburban society. As with the universities, this boost was amplified by postwar social trends. Rising prosperity allowed other working-class Americans to purchase their own houses, generally with only 10 percent down payment (usually 50 percent before the New Deal), assisted by federal programs.

Though all benefits were in principle available to African Americans, the bill had been crafted so that in practice they rarely were. Few white universities would accept blacks, and there were few accredited black colleges. Blacks found it difficult to get mortgages or to find a realtor who would sell them a house except in largely black inner city areas where FHA officials often refused to insure their mortgages. Blacks were excluded from suburban society. Residential racial segregation increased, geographically and in terms of housing tenure. By 1984, 70 percent of whites owned their own homes, but only 25 percent of blacks – and their average home was worth only three-fifths the value of a white house (Katznelson, 2005). The GI Bill was another separate but unequal welfare program, reinforcing the drift toward a two-tier social citizenship.

Yet New Deal welfare legislation was not cut back. It was too popular and Congress dared only stall extensions of programs. The Social Security Act became institutionalized, accepted by most Americans as a part of life, making them feel secure, especially in old age. As the programs came into maturity, more drew benefits. Though the real value of the benefits eroded during the 1940s, this meant a growth of coverage that did not cause fiscal pain. Most Republican leaders preferred quiet erosion of the value of benefits and ignored business urging to dismantle the system. They had elections to win. Truman's Fair Deal program after his unexpected electoral victory in 1948 was intended to include national health insurance, but Congress scaled it back to old-age insurance extensions, paid for by the growth in the trust fund that the economic boom had produced, plus a 1 percent increase in Social Security payroll taxes. Old age and survivor insurance now reached 75 percent of Americans. The weighting of social security toward the aged became an enduring feature of American welfare. In 1952 Eisenhower moderate Republicans triumphed over Taft-McCarthy conservatives within the party, and even business began grudgingly to accept it. It was an achievement, yet it was also truncated (Brown, 1999: 112–34), beginning to lag behind other welfare states.

Employers wishing to retain their workforce amid low unemployment began to add private schemes. Welfare capitalism had almost died during the New Deal but it now revived. Unions developed their own benefit schemes. Private health insurance, which had formerly covered 12 million Americans, now covered 76 million. Growth in both public and private pensions continued through the 1950s as relatively secure full employment put more within the coverage of social security and more firms saw the desirability of having their own schemes. Employers and workers received considerable tax breaks for these programs. These plus tax relief on housing mortgages yielded what Howard (1997) calls America's hidden welfare state, which he calculates amounts to about half the value of the visible welfare state. But it redistributes not to the poor but to the middle class, including securely employed white male workers, exacerbating the dual-track tendencies of New Deal welfare provisions. Women, blacks, and low-paid whites mostly had to depend on stingier public assistance. American welfare provision became a privilege of the relatively well-off, not a universal citizen right. Its recipients viewed it as a self-insurance system – I have earned my benefits through my own efforts – so beginning the ideological consigning of the word "welfare" to the poor, who had not proved themselves worthy.

Company pension and health programs grew over the 1950s and 1960s, their terms increasingly set by employers and insurance companies. Workers had to accept cash indemnity programs with fewer services, exclusion of preexisting medical conditions, and heavier users paying higher premiums, which discouraged those in greatest need from seeking medical care. Insurers paid a portion of whatever doctors and hospitals charged but could not judge whether this was value for money, so there was a shift to fee-for-service plans providing fewer services than the prepaid plans that unions preferred. Up to the late 1970s the programs worked quite well for most workers – though not for the poor. But this was the costliest system of health care of all advanced countries, and fiscal pressures then significantly reduced the extent and quality of coverage (Klein, 2003; Sparrow, 1996: chap. 2; Gordon, 2003; Lichtenstein, 2002) Yet in other welfare areas the maturing of welfare programs did gradually extend benefits to groups or problems not initially covered, as in other countries. The major surge in citizenship rights was to occur elsewhere, with the distinctively American problem, race. I discuss this in Chapter 4. But in the meantime race harmed the Left.

Racial conflict in the cities

Racism could no longer be simply defined as a southern problem. It had become national and predominantly urban. I consider three cities in diverse regions, the North, the West, and the South. The first city is Detroit. Interviews conducted there in 1951 found that blacks and whites both saw race relations as improving, yet most whites wanted to retain some segregation. Workers especially wanted this. Seventy-nine (79) percent of those who had not graduated from high school, 61 percent of those with only a high school diploma, 65 percent of CIO members, and 58 percent of other union members favored segregation. Having migrated there from the South in the 1950s and 1960s, blacks did get jobs, though the unions made sure they were low-skill, and so work remained informally segregated.

But the greatest problem, whites said, was "Negroes moving into white neighborhoods" (Kornhauser, 1952: 82–105). This issue had surfaced in Detroit before the civil rights period and endured afterward, and it continued to undermine anything resembling working-class consciousness. White workers battled to protect their neighborhoods from an invasion of blacks escaping the ghetto.

Whites saw themselves as protecting the value of their family's investment, for house prices would decline if many blacks moved into a neighborhood. They also feared pollution from the racial Other. Community solidarity to preserve housing values meant adding racial covenants to house deeds and the complicity of real estate brokers, mortgage lenders, and FHA and VA officials in refusing to cooperate with black purchasers. Neighborhood associations pressured politicians to stop building multiracial housing in white areas. Blacks fought back through civil rights and Black Power movements. They infiltrated neighborhoods once real estate agents broke ranks to make money out of "block busting." Violence flickered, especially in blue-collar areas. Mere ethnicity no longer much divided white workers – only race mattered. Between 1945 and the 1960s more than two hundred acts of violence were committed in Detroit against blacks moving into white neighborhoods. Militant blacks fought back. Black Power was small in numbers but large in its capacity to frighten whites (Sugrue, 1996: 233, 265–6). The white workers, mostly union members, lost faith in liberals urging integration. They voted mainly for Wallace, the southern Democrat with a national campaign, and then for Nixon.

Workers and employers had the option of exit. Employers migrated to the low wages and absent unions of the South. Workers went westward, where the economic opportunities lay. The working-class suburbs of my second city, Los Angeles, were built on home ownership, helped by New Deal and GI mortgages. Local industry was boosted by military contracts. Workers became proud patriots, flying the flag, loving parades. Their initial working-class identity was subsumed into a "public culture centered around patriotism and Americanism, led by veterans and divorced from any association with labor." Memorial Day, not Labor Day, was commemorated with picnics, speakers, and entertainment in the park. Then blacks arrived from the South. At first they moved into their own areas, then some sought to move up into white areas. They faced the same ferocious response as in Detroit, the same discriminatory housing practices, and similar violence. White workers now embraced more of a racial than a class identity. Almost half voted for Goldwater in 1964 and more than half later voted for Nixon and Reagan (Nicolaides, 2002: chap. 7, 251). Since LA had plenty of space, the solution was white flight, leaving blacks to take over most of South Central LA. All Los Angeles became informally segregated, exacerbated by the relocation of aerospace industries into the new white suburbs (Sides, 2004).

In Atlanta, my third city, racism was subtler. In the 1960s many whites facing civil rights legislation against housing discrimination turned to the Ku Klux Klan and vigilante violence. But when federal pressure was put on the city, the mayor (busy attracting new business) led a coalition of business progressives, moderate politicians, and black community leaders to desegregate parks, schools, and other public facilities. The mayor boasted Atlanta was "a city too busy moving to hate" and clamped down on violence. The city boomed and plenty of new jobs were created for both races. But white flight to the suburbs occurred just the same. The city became informally segregated despite compliance with the Civil Rights Acts, and white politics shifted rightward as all classes embraced ideologies of "rights, freedoms, and individualism," often code words for racism (Kruse, 2005: 6, 234).

Informal segregation was practiced in all three cities. It became national even as blacks achieved civil rights. Between 1930 and 1970 the neighborhood in which the average African American lived rose from 32 percent to 74 percent black. Outside the South, residential segregation of ethnic groups was much greater than ever recorded (Massey & Denton, 1993: 45–51, 63–7; Katz et al., 2005). Most black children went to schools that were in practice segregated, while the quality of education in white areas was far superior (Patterson, 2001: 185–90). Blacks and whites had equal rights but lived at a greater geographical and cultural distance from each other – like Protestants and Catholics in Northern Ireland. The solution to racial/religious strife in both places was informal apartheid, separate though a little more equal. And in both places working-class identity was stymied.

The last lib-lab offensive

In the 1960s a Democratic revival began with Kennedy and continued with Johnson's "Great Society." Pressured by the civil rights movement, the only mass mobilization of the period, liberals renewed their drive to expand welfare. Many had assumed in the 1940s and 1950s that economic growth was solving the problem of unemployment and poverty. An "affluent society" would take care of all material needs. Yet by 1962 Michael Harrington's *The Other America* publicized what social scientists already knew: amid continuing affluence, many Americans lived in dire poverty. In 1964 the Council of Economic Advisors reported that a fifth of families were living below the poverty level. Of them 78 percent were white, though they included an astonishing 80 percent of all nonwhites. Poverty tended to be inherited, passed down through the generations. The children of the poor received substandard education and often faced lengthy unemployment. Some Democrats and Republicans began to feel that the postwar compromise had not worked. They had a half-structural sense of poverty, though they saw it as located in pockets.

There was again a spin-off from the cold war. America presented an image of a future better than communism, yet this was stained by poverty and race. Kennedy and Johnson felt this strongly, and so did many southern Democrats, who now saw poverty as the root of their racial troubles. If blacks and whites could be raised out of poverty, strife in the South would lessen. The Council of Economic Advisors became convinced by sociologists that mere tax cuts (accepted as the way to lower unemployment) would do little to alleviate the pockets of poverty across the nation and so recommended programs targeted at the poor. They recognized that income transfers to the poor, especially the black poor, would be politically difficult and thought the provision of services would occasion less hostility (Brauer, 1982). Expert social scientists did play a role here, mainly as muckrakers exposing the seamy side of America.

Some of the new legislation merely filled in the gaps between existing programs. The Food Stamp Program of 1964 was to "help lower-income Americans maintain a nutritious diet." In 1972 the Federal Supplementary Security Income made small cash grants to the needy poor, based on a means test. In 1965 Medicare and Medicaid – health care for the elderly and the poor – were more substantial steps. Medicare was a universal benefit, paid for on the self-insurance principle but with a redistributive element. Social Security pensions were extended to cover almost everyone in the paid labor force, with a benefit formula by which the working poor received proportionately more back than did the working rich. This was a quite progressive welfare state. The Civil Rights Act of 1964 outlawed gender as well as race discrimination. Feminists had been able to piggyback on the efforts of the civil rights movement, and the combination greatly extended the coverage of welfare programs. Between 1960 and 1980 social welfare as a proportion of GNP more than doubled, from 4.9 percent to 11.5 percent (Campbell, 1995: 113).

Yet Medicare and Medicaid were feeble compromises in a cold war environment where insurance and medical companies and physicians, backed by Republicans and southern Democrats, labeled any comprehensive health system as socialism. Though Medicare was popular, the special interests had to be bought off with inflated hospital, drug, and doctor payments, and so costs rocketed. But Medicare did lower the chances of the elderly falling into poverty. Further additions extended coverage to about 40 percent of Americans – to the elderly, public employees, military and veterans' families, and many poor people. About 70 percent are today also covered to one degree or another by private programs, leaving about a quarter of the nation outside any effective health coverage. Some see the patchwork of additions as preventing more comprehensive reform (e.g., Gordon, 2003), but without them outcomes might have been worse.

Few reformers now thought of poverty as being produced by the structural inequalities of capitalism. Instead it was seen as the problem of particular needy groups – single parents, inner-city blacks, poor children, et cetera. "Medical models" and the "culture of poverty" required individual programs of correction. "Defective families," especially black families (Mittelstadt, 2005: 52–76), needed "rehabilitation." Debate concerned the responsibilities of individuals and families, not of government. Conservative ideology revived, combining traditional anticommunism, an onslaught on big government, a racism gone covert, and repugnance at the supposed moral laxity of liberals. Antistatist libertarians allied with social conservatives, with members of evangelical religious sects and denominations figuring large (McGirr, 2002). Class voting was cross-cut by moral or cultural voting, as we see later.

The end result, given advances in other countries at this time, was and still is the worst health care system of any advanced democracy. The combination of the highest health costs and an elevated mortality rate among advanced countries makes the U.S. health system hard to defend, except of course by the private interests to whom it is finely attuned. Overall, however, the social security system did become more extensive though maintaining its dual-tier characteristics. Welfare carried on along its uneven combination of progressive taxation, social insurance supplemented by private welfare schemes for the majority, and patchy, reluctant, and racially tinged assistance for the needy, generous only for the elderly.

For Lyndon Johnson the core of his Great Society, the last lib-lab offensive in America, was the War on Poverty, targeting education, job training, and community development programs to the poor. The best way of overcoming the "culture of poverty," it was believed, was to involve community action, participatory democracy, the involvement of the poor themselves in designing and implementing poverty programs. This was a coded way of having benefits distributed to black Americans, and it was much cheaper than a universal welfare program (Brown, 1999: 266). One of the leading participants, Daniel Patrick Moynihan (1969), blamed the defects of the programs mainly on the speculative theories of sociologists and criminologists, practitioners of what he called an "occult ... highly uncertain art." This was bizarre since as usual economists and lawyers dominated the agencies involved.

A genuine war on poverty would have been much bigger. The Vietnam War cost $128 billion, compared to the War on Poverty's $15 billion, which was only 15 percent of what a smaller number of veterans had received under the GI Bill. The National Association of Manufacturers noted the dilemma for the program: "You seem to have a choice between a program which is so small as to be ineffective, and one so large as to be damaging" (Andrew, 1998: 67). Johnson chose the former, and so the programs were limited by fiscal conservatism. In a desire to retain business confidence, he sought to lower taxes and give incentives to companies to create jobs in poor areas. Later deficit spending would then increase federal program spending. These were the same kinds of structural constraint that liberals under Roosevelt and Truman had also faced. Fiscal conservatism, not civil rights pressure, produced the targeting that was to prove so damaging. Brown (1999) notes that civil rights leaders favored universal, not targeted programs. But Johnson also had a political strategy. He knew there might be only a brief window of opportunity created by his big victory over Goldwater in 1964, and he focused on immediate legislation to set the programs rolling, hoping Congress would finance them once they were under way. Yet Congress cut back most programs. They remained underfinanced – especially after the Vietnam War began to suck away federal funds, just as the cold war had sucked away Truman's Fair Deal.

The money was spread through programs to improve the skills of the poor. But Congress shifted funding away from 69 targeted areas of high poverty to 780 areas spread through all their constituencies. So almost every project was underfinanced and some were rather disorganized. *Maximum Feasible Misunderstanding* was how Moynihan (1969) titled his book. It was easy to blame top-heavy bureaucracy, as conservatives did. Yet some programs like Operation Head Start for preschool education and the Jobs Corps providing employment for young people worked quite well. The War on Poverty did raise people out of poverty at quite low cost. Between 1965 and 1969 the number of people officially defined as living in poverty declined from 17 percent to 12 percent, mostly as a result of the program (Andrew, 1998: 187). It was a success.

But programs that did not work so well got most media attention. The Community Action Program channeled federal funds to neighborhood-run programs, often antagonizing local party elites, especially big city mayors. A few programs were run by the poor themselves or by black militants. The civil rights movement split and declined and was succeeded by urban race riots – 164 in the first nine months of 1967. This helped racialize the issue of poverty (Andrew, 1998: 73, 83–5; Katz, 2001). Most of the American poor were (and still are) white, and they received most of the funds. Yet blacks were receiving serious federal aid for the first time and were encouraged to be active, both trends evoking negative reactions among whites. Bad publicity focused on black recipients – especially on those few programs involving black militants. The Aid to (Families of) Dependent Children was also seen as disproportionately benefiting African Americans and white opinion turned against it (Brown, 1999: 134–64, 184–5; Mittelstadt, 2005: 82–91). Quadagno's (1994) study of four Great Society programs under Johnson and Nixon – community action, housing reform, welfare reform, and child-care proposals – concludes that racial conflict stymied all four. White backlash against any proposal that seemed to threaten the racial hierarchy stopped them short of significant achievements. She suggests an American exceptionalism paradigm driven by the politics of racial inequality – and America's domestic racism was indeed exceptional among the advanced countries.

Images of lazy, feckless blacks dominated white perceptions. In national magazines blacks were 20 percent of the poor people depicted in the 1950s. But between 1967 and 1992, this rose to 57 percent. In reality blacks were only 25 percent of the poor, so "racial stereotypes play a central role in generating opposition to welfare in America" (says Gilens, 1999: 3, 68, 114). The War on Poverty generated an electoral backlash at the end of the 1960s. Though Nixon continued some programs, he did so quietly. In any case, the expanded middle class, now including relatively secure blue-collar workers, received proportionately more benefits than the poor. Yet blue-collar allegiance to reform weakened (Gordon, 1993: 294–303; Mettler, 1999: 223–7). White working-class people had been raised into middle-class America by the New Deal and GI welfare states and by the warfare full employment state. They then fought

against the extension of those benefits to blacks. Racial conflict over housing and welfare was bad news for liberals because it undermined a traditional
constituency of support. Fear of the black community played a role out of
all proportion to its size in undermining the last lib-lab surge toward social
citizenship. The legacy of slavery endured. Politicians and the mass media no
longer purveyed it openly, but it had become more covert and more national.

Conclusion: Death by a thousand cuts

World War II, transitioning into the cold war, had fractured the New Deal. Its
moves toward more equality in income and wealth were furthered by mass
mobilization warfare and a postwar phase of a capitalism of high employment
and mass consumption. Along with the other Anglophone countries the United
States was now as equal as almost any European country, except that profound
racial inequality endured (for the Europeans this existed in their empires). New
Deal welfare policies were gradually extended, but their original inequities
were not corrected, as they were in most countries in this period. Racism and
sexism still permeated America's two-tier welfare state. State regulatory powers and macroeconomic planning grew but had no popular base and were appropriated by the military-industrial-congressional complex. Unlike in continental
Europe midcentury mass movements failed to entrench their power inside the
American state. The labor union movement, critical for working-class organization, suffered death from a thousand cuts and lib-lab sentiments generally
declined. The failure of Operation Dixie, a war that only empowered veterans, the Taft-Hartley Act, labor union splits over communism, the cold war,
McCarthyism, a Keynesianism that dared not speak its name, judicial repression, growing employer intransigence, the growth of private rather than public welfare, and continuing divisive racism – none of these was individually
decisive, but cumulatively they cascaded toward the Right. Politics lacked progressive pressure until the rise of the civil rights movement (discussed in the
next chapter). Though this was successful, it helped produced a white backlash
that virtually finished off the slight lib-lab surge of the 1960s.

   With the exception of declining inequality, this was a conservative drift
(with a bleep in the 1960s). There was an anticommunist consensus in both
domestic and foreign policy. The result was to make the United States extreme
among the advanced countries since up to the 1970s or 1980s they were moving in the opposite direction, toward the center-Left. Though also anticommunist in foreign policy, domestically they fused social democracy and/or
Christian Democracy plus corporatism in a grand class compromise embed-
ding universal social citizenship within democratic capitalism. In contrast the
United States was retreating from New Deal universalism, its social citizen
rights becoming more a question of privilege through corporate and private
welfare and consumerism among those who could afford them, with residual,

targeted handouts for those who could not. Yet progressive taxation remained (until the administrations of Reagan and Bush the Younger), the one solace for the poor during this period.

What had ultimately caused the conservative drift? The New Deal had lost some steam just before the war. Racism, whose political resonance was at first mainly in the South, meant that lib-labs could not now find a majority in Congress. The world war gave a short-lived boost to labor unions and a more enduring boost to equality. But on balance war followed by cold war gave to America (and only to America) a big military-industrial state. This damaged the American Left, subjecting it to judicial repression and exacerbating its internal splits. Its labor union core retreated in self-defense into sectional and segmental rather than class organization, pressing for social privileges for its members rather than universal social rights. Conservatism was not yet set in stone, but a liberal revival in the 1960s was electorally stymied by a backlash of covert racism and a costly and unpopular war. Conservatives and capitalists were then able to turn back some of the gains of the previous period. In turn this impacted on foreign relations, giving American imperialism its distinctive rightist slant (as we see in the next chapter). When the next economic crisis arose – the collapse of Bretton Woods and Keynesianism and the rise of neoliberalism – there would be few defenses left. This proved a global crisis in which all the advanced countries felt the cold winds of neoliberalism (as we see later), yet American winds were already colder.

4   U.S. civil rights and identity struggles

The American civil rights movement influenced globally the struggles of ethnic and religious minorities, of women, of people with disabilities, and later of
people with unconventional sexual identities. These can all be viewed as identity politics, concerning rights held by people because of who they fundamentally are, not because of their position in a class structure. So the movement
was important in shifting the political left away from class politics toward
identity politics, and this shift was especially marked in the United States since
it was the only major country in which racial oppression occurred at home
rather than in colonies.

Social movements theory

Most sociologists have analyzed the civil rights movement as the paradigm
case for other recent social movements. They have tried to generate concepts
applicable to them all, including environmental, gay, sexual preference, and
disability movements. The main concepts of this social movements theory
are "resource mobilization" (McCarthy & Zald, 1977), "political opportunity structures" (Meyer, 2004), "framing theory" (Benford & Snow, 2000),
and finally "political process" theory – a catch-all model embodying all the
others. Political process involves three main components of social movement
formation: the buildup of insurgent consciousness, organizational strength, and
political opportunity structures. These concepts are obviously abstract and universal, applicable to all movements everywhere – at least their practitioners
see them in this way. Nonetheless, this school of sociology has a certain narrowness. It tends to focus on progressive protesters, neglecting those favoring
the status quo or reactionaries seeking to restore conditions as they were in the
past. They also tend to see opportunity structures as only political, neglecting the economic, military, or ideological opportunities I will discuss here.
Resource mobilization theorists identify the main resources as money, political influence, access to mass media, and committed militants – revealing a
concern with movements in advanced democratic countries. For subsistence
peasants, monetary and media resources might be less relevant, while weapons do not figure as a resource. These sociologists prefer to study rather nice
pacific groups, not fascists or ethnic cleansers or peasant revolutionaries. Thus
some of their accounts of the civil rights movement focus on its nonviolence,
especially neglecting the violence of their segregationist opponents. This is

67

business as usual in modern sociology, which systematically neglects the role of organized violence in society.

Most theory has also been rather rationalistic, portraying militants weighing up their options and power resources, developing what is called a repertoire of contention of strategies and tactics. Indeed, some within the field have criticized these approaches as overstrategic and overrationalistic (McAdam et al., 2001: 14–20). Is insurgency rational at all? Is it not better to free ride on the energy and risk taking of others? Better to sit back and watch others taking risks, and hope they win, than it is to join in. But if everyone takes this rational decision, no one will take the risk and new social movements will not form. Yet they do form. Why? The answer, say some, is to add to social movement theory "framing." Successful social movements frame grievances inside a wider mobilizing appeal, usually developing an injustice frame, ideas, and symbols that evoke the salience of exploitation and of the movement's cultural legitimacy in seeking redress (Ryan & Gamson, 2006: 14). Yet the notion of framing strategies still seems too rationalistic, neglecting the raw emotional power of ideological commitment we already saw in the twentieth-century in my third volume among many thousands of Bolshevik, fascist, and Chinese revolutionaries. This will be true of the civil rights protesters too.

The faltering of the Jim Crow system

The civil rights protesters needed an unusual degree of commitment if they were to break the Jim Crow system of racial segregation, unmatched in its capacity as a system of repression in the twentieth century. It had long mobilized overwhelming ideological, economic, political, and military power against blacks in the southern states, and it held back opportunities for black Americans everywhere in the United States. As Omi and Winant (1994) say, white racism has been fundamental to American life (though it was to the European empires as well). Its southern economic core first lay in cotton sharecropping but was then industrialized through northern mills moving South, drawn by low wages and no unions, generating high profits for local white planter-merchant-business elites. Racial capitalism was buttressed by political power relations that disenfranchised blacks and poor whites and allowed white elites to control elections, constitutionally supported by states rights and federally supported by disproportionate southern power in Congress. I noted in Volume 3 when discussing the New Deal how political traditions of uncontested elections and the seniority system on the Hill gave southern senators and congressmen far more power than their numbers or the economic power of the South should warrant. Southern racism had a political lock on the country.

It was also buttressed by ideological power. Whites genuinely believed that blacks were racially inferior and that their bodily presence was morally and physically polluting. Very strong emotions kept less privileged whites loyal to

Jim Crow. Ideology was entrenched in everyday practices – separate toilets, washrooms, lunch counters, seats on buses, and so on. If blacks strayed into white personal space, whites felt a physical sense of shock and outrage, often rooted in sexual fears, especially of black men violating the bodies of white women. Racism was a true ideology of the strongest kind, for it operated at levels deeper than human reason and it intensified the immanent solidarity of each community. Of course, blacks did not believe they were inferior. This notion contradicted both the Bible and the American Constitution, both of which had a vibrant presence in Negro culture. Like the Chinese peasants discussed in Volume 3, they knew they were exploited, but they had usually seen this as grim, unchangeable reality and so they had adapted psychologically in order to make this reality minimally tolerable. They showed deference to "quality folks," saying, "yes sir, no sir," showing they "knew their place," humbly petitioning rather than demanding, emphasizing their distance from "niggahs [who] don't know how to talk or act at a decent dance" (Bloom, 1987: 122–8). These were ideological self-restraints – as long as redress seemed impossible. Among the Chinese peasants discussed in Volume 3, this pessimism about redress was what the communists were finally able to overcome, and this had opened the floodgates of revolution.

But Jim Crow rested finally on military power. Protest and resistance were intermittent but ubiquitous, yet were met with brutality by police, state troopers, and white paramilitaries like the Ku Klux Klan, and with everyday acts of impromptu violence, like kicking a black man off the sidewalk or beating him for looking at a white woman. Resistance was not advisable. It had been tried many times but had not worked. This power was military rather than political, for though some of it was committed by local authorities, they were acting against the law of the land. But the law was helpless. Of more than five thousand lynchings committed between 1882 and 1940, only forty resulted in legal action, and that was usually minor. There was, however, a decline in the number of lynchings from World War I onward, due first to the substitution of more draconian institutions disprivileging African Americans, and then from the 1940s in growing sentiment that lynchings were outdated and ineffective – which was a sign of progress (Belknap, 1995: chap. 1).

This formidable power structure put all blacks in the same boat, while all whites could enjoy the kicking. Race not class dominated the South and some of its features spread nationally. Segregated beaches fringed the shining seas, though in California there were precious few beaches open to blacks at all (only two in Los Angeles and blacks lost one of those in the 1920s). Most American whites continued to express racist views openly well into the 1950s.

Yet broad destabilizing social changes were also in motion. Two world wars and restricted immigration from abroad had increased the demand for labor. Together with the forcing of blacks off the land and the decline of cotton, this produced the Great Migration of blacks from the rural South into cities across the country. The cities had more jobs and better education, since the Jim Crow system there was less pervasive. Urban blacks lived in segregated neighborhoods, but these gave more autonomy from everyday white control. Black colleges, churches, and workplaces could mobilize collective action. Teachers, union organizers, lawyers, and ministers emerged to lead the black community, and more students followed. The National Association for the Advancement of Colored People (NAACP) seeking equal civil rights attained respectable national prominence, and black leaders were received sympathetically in Washington by New Dealers. Black voters made their presence felt in the North in the late 1940s. All these forces gradually increased black collective action (McAdam, 1982: chap. 5).[1]

Economic changes impacted on labor unions, though in different ways. Leftist CIO unions tried harder to combat racism than did other unions. Socialism is in principle antiracist, committed to universal human values while also seeing racism more practically as preventing working-class unity (Stepan-Norris & Zeitlin, 2003; Cohen, 1991: 337). Yet even so most antiracist officials and militants felt they had to defer to rank-and-file racism. A survey of Detroit in the early 1950s found 85 percent of white workers supporting racial segregation, with CIO members no less racist (Kornhauser, 1952: 82–105; Nelson, 2003). Yet since most of the more conservative AFL locals were segregated, this paradoxically enabled black AFL workers to develop their own collective action at the shop-floor level, even in the South (Honey, 1993). Economic opportunity structures were opening and black unionists gradually grew in confidence.

World War II opened up a new military opportunity structure, as it had for colonial natives (in Chapter 2). Bloom (1987: 128) says it "was the single most important catalytic event: it opened up jobs for blacks, took them off the farms, and set them in the cities; it put guns in their hands and trained them to use them, it exposed blacks to education and to the world and made them more cosmopolitan. As a result by the war's end blacks were becoming more self-assertive." Segregation continued in the armed forces, but this also increased a shared sense of comradeship among black soldiers. Thus black veterans were active in postwar civil rights agitation. Attempts at postwar organization in the South were greeted by a spate of lynchings. Yet one incident, in Columbia, Tennessee, in 1946 unfolded differently. A black veteran knocked a white man through a plate-glass window after the white man had slapped his mother. As was the custom, a white lynch mob immediately formed and surged into his neighborhood to get him. But it met determined resistance by 150 black veterans aided by black CIO activists from a local chemical plant. There was a sporadic exchange of gunfire and four policemen were wounded. But the whites were driven back. A black participant said, "No, there ain't gonna

---

[1] McAdam's book is easily the best general account of the civil rights movement. I am only skeptical of some of the social movement theory that he espouses.

be no more trouble. Thats the one thing I learned from 1946. They know now that negroes have guts.... Blood was shed, but it paid off. A colored man used not to have the chance of a sheep-killing dog. But 1946 changed that" (Bloom, 1987: 129).

The lynchings also put pressure on President Truman. Faced with potential electoral defections from blacks and liberals considering a third-party option in the next election in 1948, he created a President's Committee of Civil Rights at the end of 1946. Next year he addressed the NAACP in terms favorable to civil rights. He put civil rights in his 1948 electoral platform and issued executive orders to desegregate the military. Black leaders duly supported him in the election. But afterward, he eased off further commitment to civil rights. White votes were more important than black ones. There was no more direct help for years from the White House.[2]

The NAACP focused on voting registration drives and legal suits against segregated education and transport. These campaigns stayed strictly within the law and involved few demonstrations. Seeking implementation of existing constitutional rights, they were regarded with sympathy by northern white liberals. Northern elites began to look down on the South as a rustic, backward social order. In Volume 3 I stressed the regional diversity of the United States. This was the beginning of a new regional divergence, the isolation of a South that seemed to contradict the freedom that the United States supposedly represented in the world. This loomed larger as the cold war intensified in nonwhite continents. The Soviets were quick to denounce American racism, and they played up the lynchings in their appeals to Africans. The Truman administration could not deny the charge but tried to frame racism in a narrative of national democratic redemption that would eventually overcome it. This required U.S. presidents to pursue civil rights reforms, which they found easier to do rhetorically than in reality (Dudziak, 2000: 49, 77). If the cold war helped American blacks, it did not help them much.

The political door remained locked. The southern Democrats ran segregationist "Dixiecrat" candidates in the election of 1948, and they got more votes than did the liberals. For fear of the South neither Congress nor the president would sponsor civil rights legislation. To preempt the Dixiecrats, the liberal Adlai Stevenson chose as his running mate in the 1952 presidential election the Alabama Senator Sparkman, a leading segregationist. Even so the Democrats lost the election and they also lost five southern states. Neither Eisenhower nor Stevenson mentioned segregation in the 1952 or the 1956 presidential campaign. They had elections to win and were more worried about alienating whites than blacks.

In contrast, the judicial opportunity structure was creaking ajar. The Supreme Court had decided in 1896 in *Plessy v. Ferguson* that segregation was not

---

[2] I am indebted to Joshua Bloom for this paragraph.

unconstitutional since separate education could be equal. Through the 1930s and 1940s NAACP lawyers then successfully pressed cases forcing school districts to live up to that requirement (Patterson, 2001: 14–20), with the unexpected consequence of strengthening black colleges as southern states were forced to spend more to improve and extend black education (McAdam, 1982: 102–3). The Supreme Court – hitherto a conservative body – was shifting. It had ruled in 1944 that the white primary, disenfranchising blacks from selecting a party's candidate, was unconstitutional. Between 1945 and 1950, the NAACP won more than 90 percent of the cases it brought before the Supreme Court. Then in 1954 in the *Brown v. the Board of Education* (of Topeka, Kansas) ruling, the Court unanimously declared segregated schools unconstitutional since their practices would be inherently unequal.

World War II had changed the ideological climate, with its "democratic ideology, the civil rights consciousness it fostered among blacks, the unprecedented political and economic opportunities it created for blacks, and the Cold War imperative for racial change that followed." The ideological assumptions of the educated social circles in which judges moved had shifted. Polls showed the Court decision was approved by 73 percent of college graduates but only 45 percent of high school dropouts. Even conservative justices were moving. Justice Reed thought segregation was constitutionally permissible and supported school segregation if black schools could be brought up to scratch. He also opposed desegregation of restaurants, since a "nigra" might come in "and sit down and eat at the table right next to Mrs. Reed." Yet he acknowledged that "segregation is gradually disappearing" and "that 'of course' there was no 'inferior race.'" Klarman comments that the "of course" "speaks volumes that an upper-crust Kentuckian ... would have said such a thing. Most white southerners – less well educated, less affluent, and less exposed to the nation's cultural elite – would have demurred." The justices, he says, were now "culturally biased" (2004: 173, 308–10, 444; Patterson, 2001: chap. 3). The South was isolated from elite culture. The *Brown* decision was recognized at the time as a landmark, though further Court decisions allowed desegregation to proceed very slowly. It did encourage blacks and led to some school desegregation in border states. This was progress, but it did not penetrate the South proper.

White and black reactions in the south: Citizens Councils, the civil rights movement

Southern whites reacted with fury to the court's "communistic attempt to mongrelize the races." Eisenhower tried to explain their feelings to Chief Justice Earl Warren. White southerners, he said, "are not bad people. All they are concerned about is to see that their sweet little girls are not required to sit in schools alongside some big black bucks." But it was not just southerners. In a 1958 poll only 1 percent of white southerners and only 5 percent of whites elsewhere approved of interracial marriage. In 1959 twenty-nine states criminalized interracial marriages; however, by 1967 only sixteen did (Romano, 2003: 45, 148; 168, 186). Racist emotions swayed white Americans.

White Citizens' Councils appeared across the South, determined to resist desegregation and to isolate the few civil rights agitators by exploiting the economic vulnerability of sharecroppers, clients, and employees. This use of economic power silenced all but the brave or economically independent (Bloom, 1987: 93–101; Moye, 2004: 64–73; Payne, 1995: 34–46; Thornton, 2002: 392–413). They denounced the civil rights movement as part of a foreign, Communist-inspired conspiracy threatening the "southern way of life." Most were sincere enough in these beliefs. Violence was generally left to the reviving Ku Klux Klan, which until about 1964 enjoyed the sympathy and support of police authorities and juries, though not of southern politicians (at least not openly). Between 1960 and 1965 at least twenty-six black and white civil rights workers, mostly students, were killed by southern racists and hundreds received severe beatings (Belknap, 1995: 121). The councils also silenced southern politicians who preferred to focus on class rather than racial issues, as well as white liberals and churchmen who hoped for gradual reform. They were asked, "Do you support the white race against black and communist outside agitators?" Few dared reply "no" or say that this was the wrong question (Klarman, 2004: 318–20, 389–421; Bloom, 1987: 91–3). So the struggle would be racial, whites against blacks.

Black activists organized themselves into the civil rights movement, which Morris (1986) defines as a loose-knit federation of local movement centers. Middle-class ministers, church elders, teachers, trade union leaders, businessmen, and other professionals initially led these. Their vitality, activists, and most of their funds were from the community. Unions contributed alongside more ad hoc mobilizations of workers and farmers, but the churches could mobilize more diverse support and were less vulnerable to personal violence (Morris, 1986: 54). This ensured that movement demands would remain integrationist, for civil and political citizenship. Economic demands for social citizenship were sidelined and black nationalism rejected.

Its self-righteous Christian religiosity set this movement apart from most other modern social movements, including revolutionary ones. Its Christian fervor was not without resonance in white religion. White ministers traveled south to help, local Catholic hospitals helped, and a rhetoric of forgiveness and redemption helped shift white attitudes. Religiosity involved the mobilization of emotional commitment from all classes and age groups. Women did most of the behind-the scenes organizing, mostly middle-aged, experienced in churches and neighborhood networks (Morris, 1986; Payne, 1995: chap. 9). Robnett (1997:17–23) calls them "bridge organizers" and "door-to-door mobilizers." Militants risking life and limb in the streets were mostly students. But moderates and radicals alike felt emotionally empowered by an ideology that combined religiosity with core American values, with frequent invocations of Abraham Lincoln and his defense of the Union. In a 1963 poll 47 percent of blacks and 58 percent of their leaders said they were willing to go to jail for their cause. McAdam (1982: 163) asks, "Can one imagine 47 percent of the American population professing a willingness to go to jail for **any** contemporary cause?"

The churches produced the charismatic interplay between preacher and audience that the world came to know through the political speeches of Martin Luther King, which was common across the Southern Christian Leadership Conference (SCLC). This charisma was neither an innate personality trait nor truly spontaneous; it was honed in church services long before it was put to political uses. By then, however, it had become the preachers' natural form of rhetoric and it was rather disconcerting for whites (Morris, 1986: 7–11). Righteousness was not a self-conscious framing of the issues calculated for maximal effect, for this was how the religious leaders of the black community routinely spoke in church.

The SCLC was moderate, but it was pressured by more radical voices when northern activists, white and black, began to join in, spurred by the ferment in the universities during the 1960s over the Vietnam War. The Congress of Racial Equality (CORE) and the Student Non-Violent Co-Ordinating Committee (SNCC) introduced more militancy, especially the Freedom Rides, busloads traveling across the South invading white-only transport and restaurant facilities, provoking violent backlash from whites. Two-thirds of the riders were college students, three-quarters were male, and a little more than half were black (lessening later). This infusion of younger blood and broader ideology was the most important white aid to the movement. Like the students in the Russian and Chinese Revolutions, these militants had fewer material interests at stake and were predominantly ideologically motivated. They were less cautious, more impatient, immediately leading sit-ins at whites-only facilities across the South. Though they lacked a mass base, their "fierce independence and defiance of local law and custom" inspired southern blacks to believe that "they, too, could take control over their lives" (Dittmer, 1994: 424–5, 95, 244–5). The leaders were well aware that the death of a single white student at the hands of racist southerners was worth more in national publicity than the death of ten blacks. That is why they often put them in harm's way.

The movement now had a more organized radical wing paying more attention to economic grievances, with some support from lower-class blacks, spreading out from the cities into rural regions. In the Mississippi Delta the SNCC and CORE helped the rural poor, small farmers, and illiterate sharecroppers organize themselves. They focused on voter registration, though behind that lay demands for black empowerment and economic justice (Moye, 2004: 90–104). They were paralleled in the North by Malcolm X and an emerging black nationalism. The NAACP and the SCLC leaders who led the movement in most southern cities tended to be more genteel blacks. For a time, while confronting an unyielding white power structure, the varying strands of the movement worked well together.

Battle is joined

The civil rights movement endorsed nonviolence. After having initially bought himself a pistol, King began to see that blacks, being a minority, would lose any violent confrontation. Revolution was impossible. Nonviolent but often illegal protest was then refined as a way to provoke southern white violence, in the hope of provoking intervention from a federal agency. This became the dominant tactic, and it was highly calculating. It was provocative and designed to split the ruling race, but it was hardly revolutionary. It merely manipulated the constitutional division of powers between state and federal authority, for it was believed (or hoped) that the federal government would have to step in and implement reform if violence in the streets continued. In the meantime nonviolence would give moral legitimacy to the movement, enabling it to win more black recruits and more sympathy from whites. Nonviolence is particularly suited to contexts (as in British India) where insurgents are confronted by superior force that nonetheless wishes to be seen as exercised within constitutional restraints. This was only true in a special sense here. Many southern whites cared not at all for restraint, though some did and it was hoped that the feds did. Though some activists endorsed nonviolence for tactical utility, others did for its congruence with their religious beliefs and drew analogies with Christ's kicking the moneylenders out of the temple.

The first great success was the year-long Montgomery bus boycott begun in 1955, after Rosa Parks was again thrown off a bus (a movement veteran, she had tried it twice before). The local civil rights leaders settled on her as the ideal victim because of her spotless reputation, after their first choice, a fifteen-year-old unmarried girl, was discovered to be pregnant! The boycott involved a mass action that could not be repressed by force since the black community merely avoided the buses. Since blacks constituted two-thirds of the passengers, the bus companies lost big money. The Supreme Court then ruled that segregated public buses were unconstitutional. But the federal government was still wary of the political power of the white South and did not enforce the ruling.

There followed an upward spiral of boycotts, freedom rides, sit-ins, voter registration drives, and marches – nonviolent, but seeking to provoke mob violence by whites or mass arrests by the authorities (McAdam, 1982). Its success depended on a quasi-military discipline of restraint in the face of violence and on the choreographed simultaneity of sitting down, singing, chanting, letting the body go limp, and so forth. Success or failure resulted from the interaction of these tactics with those of the authorities, whose responses varied from heavy repression to evasion, either to crush the protest or to sit it out, hoping it would lose momentum. The former had more support from white activists, though the latter tended to work better, since the movement could not rely on local people to continue making mass sacrifices over long periods. The police chief of Albany, Georgia, Laurie Pritchett, inflicted a damaging defeat in 1962. Defying white extremist fervor, he showed due respect for demonstrators' rights during arrests. If they knelt to pray, he would kneel and pray with them. Then he dispersed them to jails across the county, while conspicuously keeping empty space in Albany jail available for any more protesters. He outlasted the protest. Even the KKK in Mississippi sent out leaflets urging people to avoid violence since that was what the agitators wanted (Bloom, 1987: 181).

Not all white leaders agreed. Knowing full well that the hold of racism over the South was ultimately maintained by paramilitary violence, they believed that letting go of it was dangerous. To have to defend segregation only by legal means was clearly a retreat, perhaps the thin end of a wedge that would soon destroy the system. From their perspective this was not an unreasonable belief – except that they underestimated the changing pressures on northern politicians. Birmingham sheriff Bull Conner was not simply stupid when in 1963, playing to his electorate, the vocal white constituency, he turned fire hoses and dogs on high school demonstrators in front of national television cameras. This was despite being warned by Chief Pritchett that police brutality was what King wanted. This "revealed to the world what Birmingham's blacks already knew, that for men like Connor, the core of white supremacy was violence" (says Thornton, 2002: 311; cf. Lewis, 2006: 146–50). Selma, Alabama, saw similar events in 1965, when a mass march was met by violence led by Sheriff Clark, also captured on national television. Such white violence proved self-destructive. It inflamed black communities, drawing more support to the movement. If publicized – and it was great television – it generated national sympathy and horror. This eventually led to federal intervention if the local authorities were unwilling to stop white atrocities and unable to stop black disruption. A series of constitutional minicrises followed, as state and local governments failed to fulfill their primary duty, the preservation of order. The tactics of the civil rights movement and the obduracy of many white racists had now brought about a tripartite struggle, between the two of them and the federal government.

The federal government remained reluctant to intervene. The Kennedy administration still did not want to antagonize white southerners, and it was particularly difficult to find allies in the Senate. Attorney General Bobby Kennedy urged CORE and SNCC leaders, "Why don't you guys cut out all that shit, Freedom Riding and sitting-in shit, and concentrate on voter education.... If you do that I'll get you a tax exemption" (Morris, 1986: 234–5). When they ignored this rather crass advice and carried on the Freedom Rides, he was forced to protect them with federal marshals – otherwise many would have been killed. In the televised demonstrations it seemed that the southern authorities, not the demonstrators, were the main threat to order. This allowed King's charisma to flourish, for his speeches identified the movement with the eternal moral values of the nation. The context and the rhetoric allow the triumph of this appeal to civil rights – but not demands for economic equality (Thornton, 2002: 567, 570).

It did not everywhere culminate in violence. Most southern whites became appalled at the escalating violence and began to desert the segregationists. Violence by the KKK and police and state troopers declined. Parents grew unhappy at school confrontations, for white school boards responded by closing the schools so that no child was being educated. Some integration was already under way by 1960. Urban businesses recognized that unless the violence stopped, no one would invest in their communities. Though most shared many of the views of the Klansmen and the Bull Conners, and they offered peace terms that were insufficient, they did favor a deal so that they could resume normal business life, and be free of strife, federal intervention, and economic loss. New Orleans business leaders did not want integration, but they formed a Committee for a Better Louisiana to resolve racial issues, since they "were not so obtuse that they failed to see that continuing turmoil over integration would badly hurt the city's economy" (says Fairclough, 1995: 254; cf. Kirk, 2002: 139; Belknap, 1995; Jacoway, 1982; Dittmer, 1994: 248). Nationally, corporate capitalism, the CED, and moderate Republicans were wanting an end to disorder and beginning to favor limited civil rights. Capitalist desire for profit was turning away from racial capitalism. But few southern whites favored full equality of civil and political rights.

McAdam's (1982) careful research on event sequences during the civil rights era showed that causality usually went from the rising power of the southern civil rights movement and its confrontation with white racism, to political changes at the national level. Though macrosocial forces across the nation also exercised a diffuse causality in increasing black sense of empowerment during this period, the direct influence of white liberals, white money, and national political elites was small, except in reaction to increasing black power. Though the *Brown* decision had been part of a widening judicial opportunity structure, there was little widening of the political opportunity structure, except what the movement itself could wrest. Politicians above all favor their own reelection, and it had not seemed that black votes would be more helpful to them than white ones.

In the end the White House and Congress were pressured by disorder into legislation. The Civil Rights Act of 1964 banned discrimination in employment and public accommodation. The Voting Rights Act of 1965 suspended poll taxes, literacy tests, and other voter tests and authorized the attorney general to replace local election registrars with federal officials if necessary. These acts produced a spike in white violence, which further alienated northern political elites. A Civil Rights Act of 1968 banned discrimination in housing. All three acts had effective enforcement mechanisms. They passed because northern Republicans had stopped supporting southern filibusters. Johnson remarked that in signing the 1965 bill he had lost the South for the Democratic Party. He was right. Though blacks turned out in large numbers to vote Democrat, out-migration had made them a minority in every state, and southern whites now voted solidly Republican in protest. Though they had conceded more than anticipated, this way they retained political control of the South and some economic privilege.

The achievements of the movement widened its internal divisions. Neither the old Negro leadership class nor the middle-class NAACP nor most of the SCLC would work with the sharecroppers, maids, and day laborers of radical factions demanding economic equality. This fissure was paralleled in the North in the rise of black nationalism and Black Power. This plus the anti–Vietnam War stance of King and most civil rights leaders, and the riots that swept through many major U.S. cities, generated a national white backlash. As we see later, the Johnson administration associated the radicals with disorder and began backing away. Federal government help lessened. In cities where radicals had been prominent, like Birmingham, they were displaced by "bourgeois accommodationists" trading away economic for political gains (says Eskew, 1997; cf. Thornton, 2002: 571–3). Radicals shifted into protesting the Vietnam War, and the economic needs of poor blacks were sacrificed in the pursuit of universal civil and political rights and economic advancement for the black middle class (Payne, 1995: chap. 13; Dittmer, 1994: 429; Eskew, 1997: 331–4). Perhaps this was all that could be realistically attained in a United States that in other respects was becoming quite conservative. Even some radical SNCC leaders, later to become mayors and congressmen, came to believe so in their middle age. But of course they were part of the shift away from class toward identity politics.

Conclusion: Explaining the civil rights movement

The movement was essentially over. It had achieved its integrationist goals mainly through African Americans' growing collective confidence, nurtured inside their segregated communities and then mobilized by leaders who were integral to the community's moral solidarity. They began with a strong perception of injustice, but the vital change was their belief that redress could be secured. This was both ideological and political. Their growing power had been encouraged by diffuse social forces – interregional economic power shifts plus wars, hot and cold. This had generated a growing division between North and South ensuring that white southerners ultimately lost northern support. Yet blacks had to make the political system unworkable before this happened, and they did not receive much direct help from whites. Particular boosts had come from the

Supreme Court and from Truman, Kennedy, and Johnson. Labor unions and northern liberals gave some money, and the growth of liberal sentiments among elites and the universities gave more national resonance for black rhetoric. In the end, however, the most important whites were the northern conservative politicians and the southern capitalists (plus many ordinary southerners) who realized that the best way to stem an unacceptable level of disorder was to yield civil and political rights. As I emphasized in Volume 3, if protest movements, especially in democracies, can threaten not so much revolution as a moderate level of chaos that destabilizes labor relations or politics, the more sagacious forces of order will react with concessions. As usual, this had the added advantage of dividing the civil rights protest movement and heading off more radical social citizenship demands. In this respect it was similar to the New Deal.

In some ways my account also resembles the political process variant of social movement theory, emphasizing the buildup of insurgent consciousness, organizational strength, and widening opportunities for action. Yet I have not restricted my analysis to *political* opportunities, and I have attempted to give the enemy equal treatment – if inadequately because the segregationists have been underresearched. In the end white politics reinforced the middle-class African American ideology of integration, ensuring that black economic demands and the Black Panthers would lose their support. President Nixon finished them off by offering affirmative action. The Black Panthers now split asunder, its remnants repressed by paramilitary police forces – rather like ultraleftist class movements of the past.

Ideology also played a much larger role than mere strategic framing. This movement had a religious-cum-American nationalist soul, rooted in churches, generating self-righteous emotions. It also had a radical boost from the ideological leftism sweeping American universities in the 1960s, intensified by the Vietnam War. Thus both sets of civil rights militants, locals and outside agitators, developed a reckless courage that enabled them to risk life and liberties. In Weberian terms they were driven by value rationality – commitment to ultimate values – much more than by instrumental rationality. Though their tactics revealed instrumental reasoning, their ability to confront superior paramilitary power was value-driven. On the other side, segregationist "massive resistance" also had a very emotional ideology grounded in regional nationalism, desperate fear of miscegenation, and ferocious anticommunism. If in contrast the emphasis on culture and cultural frames of social movement theory seems a little bloodless, that is because most of the movements it studies *are* bloodless. They do not shed blood only bruises. This demonstrates that we need to be wary of abstract universal models supposedly capable of explaining all kinds of social dissent, and that we need to entwine economic, ideological, military, and political power relations, using the four to explain the rise and partial success of the mass civil rights movement, and the decline and partial failure of mass white resistance.

So rather than compare the civil rights movement to gays or greens, better to place it within the range of revolution/reform class movements discussed in this volume. A 10 percent minority population could not achieve revolution, but this was a movement for major reform, it involved mass demonstrations provoking mass violence, and it succeeded in a racial version of Lenin's explanation of revolutions. That is, it occurred when the dominated race no longer wished to carry on in the old way, and the dominant race could not do so. But my analysis most resembles my account of reformist not revolutionary class struggle, for faced with the civil rights movement the old regime split and government began to intervene, introduce reforms, and compromise the struggle. Broad social shifts enhanced the power of African Americans/ the working class to resist to the point where some within the ruling race/class and especially within the state recognized that the preservation of social order required reforms. This then in turn undermined the radical/revolutionary wing of the movement. The main difference from class movements is that though blacks occupied different class positions, they were forcibly and collectively sentenced to being black and suffering racial oppression. This also meant that during its main period of struggle the black community showed more unity, more moral fervor, and so more bravery than most working-class movements – certainly in America. Race trumped class, though success further exacerbated black class divisions.

Racial aftermath

The civil rights movement had yielded enduring gains. Racial violence was vanishing, civil and political rights of citizenship were acquired, and there were even some economic improvements for most blacks. School desegregation improved black education, and job prospects improved through desegregation in public employment and in private businesses seeking federal contracts. Minchin (1999, 2001) shows that in southern textile and paper mills the proportion of black mill hands rose greatly, primarily because newly emboldened blacks flooded the Equal Employment Opportunity Commission with class action suits alleging discrimination. Some firms were forced to hire blacks by the courts; others acted first to preclude lawsuits. Managers preferred hiring lighter-skinned, overqualified African Americans and then giving them the worst jobs, while white managers and workers continued to hold racist views. But black workers improved their wages, benefits, and access to bathrooms and cafeterias – indeed, the paper workers got sole use of these, since white workers quit them when the blacks moved in!

The national gap between white and black education and wage levels narrowed. Employment and wages increased for blacks, and they made gains against white pay levels across various industries, especially in the South. But the black middle class gained more than black workers, and black women, except for single mothers, did better than black males in employment rates, wages, and educational and occupational attainment. By 2000 little difference remained between black and white women, except for the much larger proportion of black single mothers. Among black men earnings had by 1980 reached up to between 70 percent and 80 percent of comparable white occupations – they had been only 40 percent to 50 percent in 1950. But they stayed there, with no further improvements. At the bottom the African American experience even got worse. Only 9 percent of black men had not been in the labor force in 1940, but by 2000 the figure had risen to 34 percent. From the 1980s black imprisonment rates, mostly for drug offenses, were contributing alarmingly to this. Half the nation's prisoners in 2000 were black – though blacks were only 13 percent of the national population (Katz et al., 2005; Massey, 2007; Western, 2006). More of this in Chapter 6. So racial issues remained very important but only when reinforced by class. Class politics and race politics became conjoined, but only for lower-class blacks.

Overall racism was not ended but it was reduced. Most importantly black people had won a war and no longer felt they had to bow down to whites. Quite the reverse. Whether black dignity was expressed through educational and occupational success, black style, rap music, or ghetto slang or violence, whites knew that intimidation was no longer theirs alone. The downside remained: inner-city ghettos that were deprived, casually employed, non-voting, violent, ringed by armed police, cut off from the black middle class and labor unions. Race remains a visible national disgrace, but mainly in class pockets. By recalling that this period of the 1950s, 1960s, and 1970s also saw the collapse of the European empires, we can see that racism was by 1980 no longer the dominant ideology of the world. It had dominated my Volume 3. It will not dominate the rest of Volume 4. And that is a decided blessing for the world.

The liberal rhetoric of the civil rights movement then became the national rhetoric. Since racism could not be expressed overtly, it went covert. Discrimination is informal, but usually less than previously, with imprisonment rates as the exception. Most whites still harbor negative feelings toward blacks but are wary of expressing them openly. Surveys reveal half of whites think blacks are prone to violence and are less intelligent than whites and three-quarters think blacks prefer welfare to work. Most whites will accept the presence of a few blacks as neighbors but not a majority. Race and class reinforce one another as the characteristics of poor, unemployed, and criminal blacks are imputed to the whole black community (Massey, 2007: 65–112). Republicans have exploited such sentiments among whites, especially racializing crime (Western, 2006). In 1981 Lee Atwater, the Republican Party strategist, was candid:

You start out in 1954 by saying, "Nigger, nigger, nigger." By 1968, you can't say "nigger" – that hurts you. Backfires. So you say stuff like forced busing, states' rights, and all that stuff. You're getting so abstract now you're talking about cutting taxes, and all these things you're talking about are totally economic things, and a byproduct of them is blacks get hurt worse than whites. (Bob Herbert, *New York Times*, October 6, 2005)

Identity politics

The influence of the civil rights movement was global. Its protest songs were sung all over the world. Its sit-down strikes, its appeal to values that were simultaneously universal and core to the sense of national identity, were all widely adapted to the conditions of foreign protest movements. This was immediately evident, for example, in the late 1960s and early 1970s in Northern Ireland, where the first phase of a thirty-year struggle against a sectarian (Protestant) state was dominated by rhetoric and tactics consciously borrowed from the U.S. civil rights movement. This was later swept away as the Protestant Unionist community managed to manipulate the British government into intervention on its behalf – the opposite of what had happened in the United States. In South Africa Nelson Mandela fully realized the importance of taking the moral high ground and of provoking violence in order to secure outside intervention, in this case of foreign economic intervention, which as in the American South eventually impacted on the self-interest of the white business community, inducing them to pressure the apartheid government into negotiations.

The civil rights movement was also influential as part of a new liberalism focused on the politics of identity more than class. What are generally called the new social movements – feminism and other recent identity politics movements, plus environmentalism – embodied a discourse of individual rights. This emerged out of class-based struggles for full citizen rights, but most of the new movements then broke with class politics. The rights revolution first secured rights for African Americans, then for other racial minorities.

Second-wave feminism arose at the same time as the civil rights movement and was influenced by it. However, women already freely exercised the vote, and so the movement focused on civil and especially social rights. Postwar social transformations were important in its rise, especially those affecting labor markets. When World War II ended, women's employment declined sharply, but from 1950 it was rising again amid the labor shortages of the golden age. By 1956, 35 percent of all adult women were in the formal labor market and a quarter of married women were. Women were particularly useful in white-collar work for by now they were being well educated. In employment women experienced a combination of more independence yet persistent discrimination. Then from the 1970s the rising wages of the golden age were squeezing capitalist profits, as I discuss in Chapter 6. One of the ways employers reacted to this was to employ more female labor, sometimes in full-time positions, but more often part-time and casual, and always with lower wage costs than employing men. This offered the employer the option of a lower wage bill and more flexibility. Now not boom but recession increased female labor force participation. Over the next decades men's wages were static and increasing household income depended on women's wages. This tended to give more equality to male-female relations within the family, though this was lessened for several decades by the double burden of formal employment and housework that was imposed on married women. But the ideology of patriarchy was weakening.

At the same time traditional gender and sexual norms were being challenged, while better contraceptives were enabling more women to choose whether and how frequently to bear children. Separation and divorce become more frequent, allowing women (and men) to decide whether they wanted to stay married. However, this freedom had a negative aspect for women, since it increased substantially the number of single mothers, women left to raise children on their own, and this increased their poverty and sense of exclusion from society.

As in the first wave feminists had to struggle to attain their rights, but they did to a lesser degree than had either male workers or ethnic minorities in their struggles. Almost no organized violence was required. Moreover, some triggering events in the United States were rather top-down, like President Kennedy's influential Commission on the Status of Women of 1963, which led to the formation of many women's pressure groups, to the Equal Pay Act of 1963, and to the addition of Title VII concerning women's rights to the Civil Rights Act of 1964. U.S. feminism benefited by piggybacking on the struggle of African Americans. Successful court cases were also distinctively important, since the law of the land asserted formal equality of civil and political rights for all, and there were no Jim Crow–like structures blocking women's rights. Feminist movements emerged as in most countries from within existing leftist pressure groups, though often reacting sharply against the gender discrimination practiced within those groups, as was the case with the New Left movements of the 1960s. The reason for the relative ease with which women attained equal rights may be that males and females are not segregated – indeed their relations are intimate – so that discontented women can exert pressure on their partners, family members, work mates, and political comrades from the inside. Once women began to organize in substantial numbers, the struggle did not organize all or most women against all or most men.

The pressures were being felt at the same time across most advanced countries, indicating that the most important causes of second-wave feminism resulted from broad global trends, not from specifically American trends. However, the demands of this feminism were greatly influenced by the institutional traditions of each macroregion and nation-state, producing considerable variations in the kinds of women's rights that followed.

Macroregional trends tended to fit quite well into Esping-Andersen's tripartite model (discussed in Chapter 6), as he has noted (Esping-Andersen, 1999). The liberal Anglophone countries tended to accord women equality of formal civil citizenship rights but less generous social rights. Theirs is a "gender same-ness" model giving the same rights to women as to men, especially in the labor market. They encouraged women to work while retaining the male breadwin-ner model of the household, whereby welfare was geared more to supporting the living standards of the primary male in the household than to supporting women as the bearers and caregivers of children. They also encouraged private welfare schemes while the public schemes required long-term formal employ-ment in order for men or women to gain eligibility. There were of course varia-tions among the Anglophone countries: Canada veered slightly and Britain more substantially toward social rights than the United States, while Australia combined the citizenship rights of women with recognition of women's role as caregivers. And whereas Britain and Australia have been more successful in reducing the gender wage gap than Canada and the United States, the latter pair have been more successful in weakening occupation segregation between men and women (O'Connor, Orloff, & Shaver, 1999).

The conservative continental countries, which I call the Euros, were in many ways the reverse. They did not like intervening in market capitalism yet they would help anyone falling out of markets. They maintained and even reinforced gender differences in civil citizenship rights; they discouraged women from labor force participation, seeking to preserve the autonomy of the family from the encroachments of capitalist markets; but they granted considerable transfer benefits to women as the bearers of children and the caregivers of the house-hold. Conversely, there was very little public provision of services, especially of child care. Here the family and not the individual was the unit of welfare. This balance of rights was very much influenced by social Catholicism, and so the Netherlands and France had less of it. The Netherlands was rather closer to the Anglophone model while France was distinctive in both encouraging women to work and providing generous family allowances for the care of children, which in effect socialized the cost of this benefit (van Keesbergen, 1995; Pedersen, 1993). This was a consequence of weaker labor unions and stronger pronatalism for reasons of national security, as I explained in Volume 3, Chapter 9.

The social democratic Nordic countries combined both civil and social rights. Here pronatalist movements had strongly encouraged women toward labor force participation in order to correct labor shortages, and this was backed by generous public provision of child care facilities. This model largely abandoned the male breadwinner/female caregiver household model in favor of a dual-earner model (Sainsbury, 1996). Yet, especially in Sweden it is not a woman's right to choose employment or not. The tax and contributory insur-ance schemes mean that women virtually have to work in order to live ade-quately. And though there is plenty of work available for women, it tends to be segregated in the public sector, leaving the private sector for men.

Women have still not achieved full equality and the feminist movement remains split between those advocating gender sameness and complete equality of rights versus those emphasizing gender difference (with the consequence that women should be rewarded for their distinctive roles in society). Yet in the last half-century feminism has triumphed in many of its goals, country by country, in the process becoming institutionalized at both the national and inter-national levels (most recently through the United Nations and international feminist NGOs). As I have just implied, the United States has generally lagged behind the Nordic countries in winning social rights, but in the sphere of civil rights it has been among the leaders. This momentum has spun off into the demands of the gay, sexual, and disability rights movements that followed. The United States has also been distinctive in spearheading the conservative addition to identity politics, the rights of the unborn fetus. Struggles over sexuality rights versus traditional family values, and between a woman's right to choose (abortion) and the rights of the unborn child (anti-abortion) now create more political emotion in the United States than do class struggles, and this is not so in any other advanced country, not even Catholic ones. Some of these civil rights struggles have been essentially won. This is true of disability and women's rights, and rights are being rapidly won by gays. In 2012 the majority of Americans supported the legalization of gay marriage, a remarkable turnaround in only a few years. In America the new liberalism pioneered a major leap forward in citizen rights and a major decline in patriarchy.

Yet once rights were achieved, class divisions reared up. The victory of the civil rights movement weakened the solidarity of the African American community and increased class inequalities within it. So too with feminist successes, which in some respects (discussed in Volume 3, chapter 9) increased inequalities among women. We can expect the same sequence as gays achieve their victory. In the United States these movements had received rather little input from labor and a divide emerged between the old Left and the new liberals. In George McGovern's unsuccessful 1972 campaign for the presidency many union leaders were unhappy with the racial, feminist, sexual diversity, and countercultural tone of his core support. It was at this point that the Democrats began widely to lose white worker support. Nixon's southern strategy contained racial undertones aimed at securing white worker votes, while he portrayed himself nationally as the champion of oppressed taxpayers victimized by the worthless (and black) poor and by privileged counterculturals (Lichtenstein, 2002: chap. 5; Cowie, 2010). American liberalism had bifurcated into class and identity struggles, the former declining, the latter surging, a rather mixed blessing whose weakness in matters economic was soon to be exposed fully. For labor this would mean fewer allies at a time when the economic balance of power was tilting away from labor toward capital. Business – corporate moderates as well as small business – was becoming restive at inflationary trends and lower profit rates evident at the end of the 1960s. Lowering wage costs seemed part of the answer, as we see in Chapter 10.

5   American empire during the cold war, 1945–1980

The world is a very varied place. Though in the post–World War II period it has experienced globalization, all three of the main pillars of globalization – capitalist expansion, the adoption of the nation-state form, and American empire – have entwined with very different social structures and development opportunities across the world. U.S. policy was dominated everywhere by the cold war and fear of communist advances, but different parts of the world were situated differently in relation to the cold war. So I discuss separately four macroregions, the West, East and Southeast Asia, Latin America, and the Middle East. I will do this through the narrative lens of American empire, though this should not be taken as indicating that I believe American policy was decisive in determining their patterns of development.

It is useful to begin by recapitulating the main varieties of empire that I distinguished in Volume 3.

Direct Empire occurs where conquered territories are incorporated into the realm of the core, as in the Roman and Chinese Empires at their height. The sovereign of the core also becomes sovereign over the periphery. The United States has never attempted this.

Indirect Empire: a claim of political sovereignty by the imperial core, but with rulers in the periphery retaining some autonomy and in practice negotiating the rules of the game with the imperial authorities. There is continuing military intimidation, though not usually repeated conquest, and the imperial state rules more lightly, possessing lesser despotic and infrastructural powers. Americans attempted this in the Philippines in 1898 but massive resistance forced a partial climb down. The United States did not subsequently attempt indirect empire other than in temporary circumstances.

These first two types involve territorially delimited occupation, *colonies,* unlike the other ones.

Informal Empire occurs where peripheral rulers retain full formal sovereignty, but their autonomy is significantly constrained by intimidation from the imperial core, which combines varying degrees of military and economic power. This has become the predominant form in modern empires, since capitalism can add considerable economic coercion. But since uses of the term "informal empire" are often imprecise about the nature of coercion, I distinguish three subtypes, involving differing forms of coercion.

> (3a) *Informal Gunboat Empire*: Military power is deployed in short, sharp military interventions. The gunboat and its more modern equivalents cannot conquer

a country, but they can administer pain by shelling ports (more recently by bombing) and landing troops for brief incursions. American "Dollar Diplomacy" at the beginning of the twentieth century had been an example of direct military intimidation, but without colonies.

(3b) *Informal Empire through Proxies:* This arrangement uses local proxies to do the coercion. In the 1930s the United States had shifted toward subcontracting coercion to local despots who supported U.S. foreign policy, giving them economic and military aid in return. Then in the post–World War II period, the United States added covert military operations to aid its local clients, mainly through the newly formed Central Intelligence Agency (CIA). This is indirect military intimidation in which the authoritative power is not directly commanded from the core.

(3c) *Economic Imperialism:* Here military is replaced by economic coercion. The United States has intervened inside peripheral economies through international banking organizations that it leads. In such "structural adjustment" the peripheral country is free to say no, but the deterrents are powerful – the denial of foreign investment and trade. Since there is little or no military force or indeed authoritative power of any sort, under my definition of empire used in Volume 3 this is not strictly imperialism, yet the term "economic imperialism" is widely used and I will continue using it.

(4) *Hegemony:* I use this term in the Gramscian sense of routinized leadership by a dominant power over others, which is regarded by the latter as being "legitimate" or at least "normal." Hegemony is built into the everyday social practices of the periphery and so needs little overt coercion. Whereas in indirect and informal empires peripheral regimes feel constrained to serve the imperial master, under hegemony they defer voluntarily to the hegemony's rules of the game, which are seen as normal, natural. The rule of the U.S. dollar has involved economic "seigniorage," whereby other countries buy dollars at low rates of interest, benefiting Americans more than themselves. But this has been seen by foreigners as simply what one does with one's export surpluses. It is diffuse, not authoritative power. No one is directly commanded. Weaker states may also pay for a hegemonic state to establish military bases in their territories to defend them from others – as the Europeans have invited in the United States.

These types involve descending levels of military and ascending levels of political, economic, and ideological power as we move from direct to indirect, through the informal subtypes of empire, to hegemony. In fact, mere hegemony is not empire at all since it is not experienced as coercion. Since these are "ideal types," no actual empire fits neatly within any one of them. Indeed, empires typically combine several of these forms of domination. This has also been true of American domination. In some places the United States exercises indirect empire, in others informal empire, while all these have muted into hegemony (without employment of military power) in many parts of the world. I start with the West.

Hegemony in the West

The West comprises the United States, Western Europe, and the former white dominions of Britain. The West contained most of the world's industrial capitalism and its most effective nation-states. As a result of the war all were now committed to capitalism and political democracy. Obviously American domination here would be limited. It did not need to be more. But Western Europe was the key strategic region, abutting directly onto the Iron Curtain, containing a few large communist parties and advanced economies essential for the prosperity of American capitalism. Here the United States was defending allied capitalist countries from Soviet communism. Since they wanted to be protected, they often requested even more defense from the Americans. This was American hegemony, legitimate domination. After a short debate within his administration, Truman rejected advice to punish (West) Germany by depriving it of industrial resources, deciding instead to help rebuild it as a prosperous bastion against the Soviets (Hogan, 1987; Beschloss, 2002). European and American governments recognized their mutual economic and military interdependence, and the United States encouraged plans for unity in Europe, seeing this as better containing the Soviets while also tying Germany peacefully into Europe. The process of integration into the eventual European Union began, though during this period it was more a free association of autonomous nation-states than a supranational body.

The United States required only that Europe not seek to become a "Third Force," and that any European rearmament fit into a "larger Atlantic framework" led by the United States, though with Britain as its loyal Anglophone retainer. Conversely, the Europeans understood that they paid for their defense by subsidizing the dollar. They gained much from the Bretton Woods system. They could pursue a development strategy of an undervalued currency, controls on capital flows and trade, and accumulation of reserves. They used the United States as a financial intermediary that lent credibility to their own financial systems, while the United States lent long term to them, generally through foreign direct investment (Dooley et al., 2003). American hegemony was the necessary price paid for economic growth and military protection. This was also true for Australia and New Zealand, who in the war had been protected from the Japanese by the United States, not by Britain.

Lundestad (1998) aptly calls this "Empire by Invitation." It became lighter too. When European economic recovery was complete, fixed currency rates were no longer needed, especially since the United States was reaping large transfer payment receipts for its financial services. In 1965 de Gaulle denounced "this signal privilege, this signal advantage" of the dollar. Next year he pulled France out of the NATO command structure. But he failed to dislodge American financial dominance. Despite grumbling, the Europeans accepted hegemony just as the United States accepted them as economic rivals.

Britain and the United States used their military power to suppress communism in Greece and the two allies supported the existing dictators in Spain and Portugal. No democratic mission here – that was subordinated to keeping communism at bay. Of course, the United States did not have a democratic mission in the rest of Europe since it did not need one. The locals either already had democracy or were now mostly adopting it. The United States did not have much power over European domestic politics. It had bases, but they were not designed for local intervention. They pointed outward, eastward. These countries were allies, and the United States had no settlers. The center-Right was helped a little against fascists, the center-Left against the communists, which was important in France and Italy. West Germany was only a "temporary colony," getting its own autonomous government in 1949. Indeed, the British and French persuaded the United States to back-pedal on its anticolonialism for the United States needed their support, just as it needed the support of Europe's socialist parties and unions. Though it urged them to focus on productivity not redistribution, the ensuing growth allowed both. Most labor leaders accepted wage restraint and higher productivity in return for welfare states and growth (Maier, 1987a & b; Hogan, 1987).

So the United States had to accept policies that would have been anathema at home, such as German codetermination (unions sharing in the management of corporations), nationalization, and Keynesian planning for full employment. The Marshall Plan fostered national solutions based on bargaining among local political forces. This helped provide a more human face of capitalism, redefining the historic competition between capitalism and socialism (Cronin, 2001). Continental Europe made the massive step forward of finding the Christian Democrat/Social Democrat compromise it had failed to achieve in the first half of the century. The national governments decided themselves how to use the Marshall funds. The French used them to finance colonial wars! U.S. governments needed Europe almost as much as Europe needed them. It helped that Europeans were seen as from the same racial stock and so were considered civilized (Katzenstein, 2005: 57–8). Racism was not quite gone yet.

All this ensured the deepening of political and social citizen rights, as described in Volume 3, chapter 9, coupled to Europe-wide economic growth, which resulted from class compromise, pent-up technological dynamism, the rapid diffusion of technology across borders, migration of labor from agriculture, and a high, sustained level of demand. Trade grew faster than production, since this was the only source of dollars for clearing accounts, then because of trade liberalization and the Bretton Woods financial regime in which states were free to steer investment into domestic industry. Growth produced inflation, but central banks were relaxed about this since there was no pressure on exchange rates. Investment remained high, since Keynesian demand management proved successful. Unprecedented economic growth and full employment lasted more than two decades, an economic miracle (Aldcroft, 2001: 128–62; Eichengreen, 1996; Eichengreen, ed., 1995). Growth was coupled with political stability, greater social citizenship, and an absence of domestic militarism to generate a golden age of capitalism coupled with democratic nation-states (Hobsbawm,

1994). U.S. hegemony worked, both for Americans and for Europeans. It was a successful, rational, and very light form of domination, limited to foreign policy, including international finance.

The European nation-states remained allies. U.S. presidents often consulted their leaders and American empire was invisible to most Europeans. Ikenberry (2001: chap. 6) notes that to maintain American dominance, revitalize the world economy, and contain the communist bloc, Europe, Japan, and the United States were bound together in an open, multilateral economic order. Potential conflicts among the allies were "captured and domesticated in an iron cage of multilateral rules, standards, safeguards, and dispute resolution procedures." He sees the United States as a reluctant hegemon trading power for cooperation, transparent in its goals, its allies wanting to bind in American economic and military security. His model of institutional binding works well for the West, though not elsewhere. The fundamental difference between Western and Eastern Europe was that the West consented to some subordination; the East did not. That was the justified part of the West's claim to constitute the free world. In the West there was no American empire. But in the rest of the world the United States began more forcibly.

East and Southeast Asia, phase A: Imperial wars

For the United States East Asia was strategically second only to Europe, since it was adjacent to the two major communist states, and there were active communist and leftist nationalist movements all around. It also contained a very large population and tremendous economic potential. The main ongoing transformation was decolonization. These were mostly already national states; that is, most of them had long been sovereign states with moderate infrastructural powers and cohesive elite cultures, and the colonial empires had preserved (and strengthened) their boundaries. Their emerging nationalisms were not artificial and in reality racial, as in Africa, though they were now more populist than anything previously seen in the region. They soon finished off the European empires, established sovereign states ruling in the name of the people, and made even indirect empire more difficult to achieve. Everywhere the nation-state became the hegemonic political ideal, and it was inherently anti-imperial. Yet rival claims to represent the emerging nation were made by leftists and rightists. Their severe conflicts, appearing as class conflicts, posed both problems and opportunities for American imperialism.

In Europe the superpowers had quickly agreed how to divide up the continent, but East Asia was still being fought over. From 1949, however, China and Japan were securely within, respectively, the communist and capitalist camps. The Soviet Union also had Pacific shores. Yet outcomes elsewhere remained unclear. Superpowers could roll back each other if their local allies won across the region. Both sides began the period as anticolonial. Both wanted a more informal empire, acquiring independent but client states. The United States wanted also to free up trade, redirect it toward its own economy, and push back Soviet and Chinese attempted expansion through local revolutionaries (McMahon, 1999: 218–21).

Japan was the most important nation-state for the United States, since it had already been an advanced industrial power and was accustomed to having an infrastructurally powerful state and ideological cohesion. General MacArthur, Supreme Commander of Allied Powers (SCAP) in the East, decided to retain the emperor as the legitimacy symbol of the new regime despite Emperor Hirihito's implication in Japanese aggression. MacArthur's view of the Japanese was decidedly racist, as he later revealed to a congressional committee:

If the Anglo-Saxon was say 45 years of age in his development, in the sciences, the arts, divinity, culture, the Germans were quite as mature. The Japanese, however, in spite of their antiquity measured by time, were in a very tuitionary condition. Measured by the standards of modern civilization, they would be like a boy of 12 as compared with our development of 45 years.

This from a man who almost never met any Japanese people while in Tokyo (Dower, 1999: 550)! But MacArthur wanted to make an impression back home as a man of action (he hoped to become president) and declared he would remake Japan, purging the regime and dismantling the corporate conglomerates, the zaibatsu. But this was more easily said than done, since these were entrenched institutions. Then, as U.S. allies in China and Korea began to look wobbly, and as Japanese economic stagnation generated popular discontent, other American policy makers advocated subordinating reform to economic growth to avert its becoming communist. Threatened Japanese elites entrenched in the state and capitalism played skillfully on this fear, and this view won out.

So reform weakened. MacArthur's arrogance managed to alienate almost everyone, and his enemies denounced his reforms as socialistic, now the kiss of death in Washington. George Kennan, the brains of the State Department, urged reconciliation with Japanese elites – unity in the face of communism. From 1947 purges were stopped, the dismantling of the zaibatsus lessened, reparations ceased, and economic aid kick-started Japanese growth and redirected it toward America. Land reform had already gone ahead, pushed by MacArthur and popular among the Japanese. But a threatened general strike by workers in 1947 worsened American fears and so SCAP now purged the Left instead. The United States would go with a conservative elite-dominated quasi-democracy. Japan's new constitution guaranteed individual rights, trimmed military institutions, and reduced the emperor's role, but a top-down corporatism developed in which contending interests were compromised within authoritative organizations rather than through conflict played out in public. Elections produced one-party rule, by the Liberal Democratic Party, while labor unions were incorporated inside the zaibatsu. This revealed a blending of traditional Japanese institutions with democratizing desires encouraged to a limited extent by the United States. American empire did not have the power to roll over the world's institutions. But the United States got essentially what it wanted, an orderly society and a growing American-oriented economy, though with a patriarchal corporatist version of democracy that was inside the purportedly free world (Rotter, 1987: 35–43; Schaller, 1985, 1997: chap. 1; Dower, 1999; Shoichi, 1998; Forsberg, 2000; Katzenstein, 2005).

It is common to view Japanese institutions as being traditional, representing cultural continuity with the past. Yet we saw in Volume 3 prewar Japan had contained diverse tendencies and conflicts. The diversity lessened as the war finished off the extreme Right and SCAP repressed the center-Left. But as in Germany, U.S. military government then transitioned into hegemony. From 1952 Japan enjoyed the rights of an independent nation-state except that it had been pressured as Germany had to renounce making war. Its military developed as almost entirely defensive, kept below 1 percent of its GDP until 1986. Japan actually got the better of the economic deal, acquiring American technology while protecting its own economy more than the United States did. Like Europe, it became an economic rival, the result of both Americans underestimating Japanese growth potential and their rather naïve expectation that growth would lead naturally to an open market economy (Forsberg, 2000: 6–9, 187–97). Most Americans did not realize that more statist and social varieties of national capitalism might be as efficient as their own liberal version (and had been in their own past). Yet, as with Western Europe, the United States accepted the economic rivalry as the price for securing Japan within its sphere of influence. Again it had bases but could not use them to coerce the Japanese while the communists were rattling the gates. And it had no settlers. Japan had been effectively a colony for the years immediately following 1945, but thereafter America ruled only as a hegemon.

It was otherwise elsewhere in the region. Two political issues dominated: throwing out the colonialists and resolving struggles between landlord and peasant classes – and sometimes between ethnic groups – over which nation was to possess the state. The fall of the European and Japanese Empires had delegitimized the capitalists and landlords who had collaborated with them. The communists had won in China by attracting peasant support through land reform and by posing as the true nationalists against the Japanese. This Chinese model of revolution seemed applicable elsewhere. In civil wars in Korea and Vietnam the United States supported the conservative landlord/capitalist side, against Left nationalists mobilizing the lower classes. The United States defined as "enemies" anyone who allied with the USSR or China or who pursued "revolution" within. The converse was true for the Soviets and Chinese. In this region neither side represented a free world.

The Korean crisis erupted first. At the end of the war it was divided in two. Soviet troops had entered against the Japanese from the north and had panicked the United States into invading from the south. The imperial game had begun. They both advanced to the 38th parallel and stopped there by agreement. In the North the Soviets were helped by the Korean army of Kim Il-Sung, already fighting alongside Chinese communist forces in the war against Japan. Southern guerrillas were led by the independent communist Pak Hun-yung. The Soviets soon left, handing government of the North to Kim Il-Sung, who imposed land reform and nationalized the factories, which were popular measures. He was a national liberation hero and his policies were attractive to many in the South, which badly needed land reform. The U.S. military government had imposed martial law. Worker and peasant unions and local people's committees then sprang up, demanding land reform and self-rule. Leftists had led the struggle against the Japanese, while most of the Right was tainted with collaboration.

A debate now raged among the Americans between those favoring a UN trusteeship over the whole of Korea, including the Soviets, ranged against those hostile to the Soviets and the people's movement in the South. They doubted Koreans' capacity for self-rule, on racial grounds again (Hunt, 1987: 162–4; Katzenstein, 2005: 55–8). Fear of chaos leading to revolution had again surfaced. Hard-liners won this debate, and though internal Soviet debates were more evenly balanced, each superpower grew to prefer secure control over its half of the country to the risk that the other might be able to take over the trusteeship of a united Korea. From their soundings, the Americans also feared free elections might result in a leftist victory (Matray, 1998). So the United States suppressed the leftist movements and allied with the elites, even though most of them had collaborated with the Japanese. Of the higher civilian and police officials in the new government 70 percent had been Japanese collaborators. So had more than twenty thousand policemen, who now assisted U.S. forces to suppress the guerrillas, labor and peasant unions, and peoples committees. About one thousand Koreans were killed and thirty thousand imprisoned. Few of these were communists and almost none had collaborated with the Soviets, as the American governor claimed. Popular uprisings in 1946 and 1948 were harshly repressed. By 1948 the government of Syngman Rhee had managed to achieve a wider basis of support, though his regime was still authoritarian.

Korea was divided between repressive communists facing repressive capitalists, each holding phony elections, with a high level of tension between them. Rhee was not liked by most Americans (they would have preferred a less autocratic ruler) and in January 1950 Secretary of State Dean Acheson unwisely remarked that the Korean Peninsula and Taiwan lay outside the "defense perimeter" of the United States. This was interpreted locally to mean that the United States would not defend the South against communism. The guerrilla leader Pak Hun-yung now assured Kim Il-Sung, who in turn assured

Mao and Stalin that southerners would welcome a northern invasion. Stalin had been resisting Kim's requests to invade, but now he consented, though he told Kim that if it went wrong he would not bail him out.

When the invasion occurred, many southern peasant families did help northern troops drive back the Americans southward. The whole of Korea might now go communist! The United States felt compelled to demonstrate to Japan and other allies that the United States would defend them too, come what may. The policy would be conquest and temporary direct imperialism followed by withdrawal, while retaining bases from which informal empire might be maintained. Stalin had withdrawn from the UN in protest at its refusal to give membership to communist China, and so Truman gained UN backing for a counterattack. At that time a UN without the Soviets was a Western creature. Truman regained the territory of the South and then ordered his forces led by MacArthur to continue beyond the 38th parallel. MacArthur, always the loose cannon, then spectacularly exceeded his orders by sending his soldiers as far north as the Chinese border. Perhaps a united Korea might be ruled by an American client state after all.

But Mao could not accept a hostile American imperialism at his very border. He was already contemplating intervention, and he hoped that revolutionary nationalism might reestablish China's imperial Central Kingdom status in Asia, that the Chinese revolution might serve as a model for Asia, and that the Chinese people might be mobilized through war to maintain the momentum of their own revolution (Jian, 1994; Zhang, 1995: 253–4). He had hesitated, however, until the sight of American soldiers massing on China's border, urinating provocatively in the Yalu River, seemed to give him little choice. A Chinese invasion followed. Again the Americans were driven back in headlong retreat. MacArthur was fired and Ridgeway, his successor, managed a naval landing at Inchon behind communist lines, supported by massive air power. In turn the Chinese had to retreat. Presidents Truman and Eisenhower both rejected military requests to deploy atomic weapons. The U.S. military managed to stabilize the front where it had all begun, on the 38th parallel – which still divides the two Koreas.

Some call this a limited war necessary to contain communism. It did contain communism, yet it was neither limited nor necessary. It killed four million Koreans, one million Chinese, and fifty-two thousand Americans. American bombing was scorched earth policy, devastating the North not only to win the war but also to demonstrate to other countries that communism would generate only suffering. Mao was also extremely callous in sacrificing the lives of a million of his underequipped soldiers,[1] while Stalin obstructed peace

---

[1] My account is drawn from Armstrong, 2003; Cumings, 1981 & 1990, 2004; Lowe, 2000; Putzel, 2000; Stueck, 1995; essays in Stueck, 2004; Weintraub, 1999; and Zhang, 1995.

negotiations since the war tied down both the United States and China and kept China dependent on Soviet military supplies (Mastny, 1996; Weathersby, 1998). The war was only necessary once the Americans and Soviets had failed to agree on a trusteeship, and once the United States had failed to reconstruct South Korea in a way acceptable to its people. This had encouraged insurrections, which in turn brought on invasion from the North. Then the war became necessary. But the South could have been won without a war, with reforms and a transition to democracy. In this mistake, lack of attention had played a part, for the Americans lacked accurate knowledge of the political situation in the Peninsula. This was a sideshow and a very conservative military governor was given a free hand. But Korea also revealed a preference for authoritarianism, a fear of reform that might become leftist, and a racist view of lesser peoples who might produce chaos, not progress. As we saw in Volume 3, this had been a familiar story in the earlier phase of American imperialism.

Seen in China as a success, the war solidified Mao's rule and intensified North Korea's militarized version of socialism. In the South it froze in place authoritarianism and the chaebol corporations, though together they provided an effective state and capitalism. But the war's main beneficent consequence was to persuade the United States and Syngman Rhee to initiate land reform, which increased equality, productivity, and regime popularity. This could have been a model for American imperial practice elsewhere, but alas it was not. Large American forces remained in Korea, but, as in Japan, they did not intervene in local politics. Massive American economic aid also helped growth and economic integration into the American-led global economy. Between 1953 and 1960 U.S. aid was 10 percent of total GDP and 74 percent of total investment. South Korea became a viable and largely independent nation-state. With hindsight we know that South Koreans were much better off under capitalist mild despotism than they would have been under the local highly despotic and repressive version of communism.

The war did show that the United States would fight to defend its client states. National Security Council document 68 (NSC-68) became policy in 1950, committing the United States to a "perimeter" defense all around the world since "a defeat of free institutions anywhere is a defeat everywhere" (Gaddis, 1982: 90–2). This stimulated more global base building. In the United States the war quadrupled the defense budget, introduced the doctrine of a first-strike resort to nuclear weapons if necessary, and produced the national security state and paranoid anticommunism. For Japan the Korean War, said the governor of the Bank of Japan, generated "divine aid" from the United States, the "equivalent of the Marshall Plan in Europe" (Forsberg, 2000: 84–5). Japan was the supply base for U.S. forces and the war revitalized its economy. With Japan integrated into the Western rather than the Chinese economy, the United States ended formal occupation in 1952. U.S.–Japanese relations had shifted from temporary colonialism to hegemony. The openness of the

American economy remained its main virtue, providing trading partners were advanced enough to compete with American goods. The Korean War had produced major effects.

The United States also sought to secure Japan's raw materials procurement across the region, which required further client states. Taiwan had not had a prior national history, having been formerly under minimal Chinese control, then much tighter Japanese control, and from 1949 it was occupied by Chiang Kai-shek's nationalist administration and armies fleeing from the mainland, occupying the island as a new ruling class, with considerable cohesion and a one-party Kuomintang (KMT) state until the 1980s. They put down rebellions by the indigenous peoples, but they also learned from their mistakes in China and from the Korean War to introduce land reform, increasing their legitimacy (Putzel, 2000). Massive American aid in the 1950s and 1960s greatly assisted development. Taiwan's industrial development was led by an authoritarian state disciplining capitalism by keeping control over finance. The state could allocate capital as well as subsidies to tariff-protected export industries (Wade, 1990). Taiwan was safe for the free world, and it was beginning to prosper, but it was not yet free itself.

U.S. policy had already shifted from anticolonialism to neutrality in liberation struggles, but after the Korean War neutrality was subordinated to fighting communism. British and French colonies in the region would do fine as allies, though not the Dutch, whose days in Indonesia were clearly numbered (McMahon, 1999: 27, 36–45). Authoritarian Asian regimes were acceptable as bulwarks against communism. There was no democratic mission, whatever American politicians said back home.

In Vietnam the United States was reluctantly sucked into aiding France's colonial war against the Viet Minh insurgents. Most Viet Minh leaders were members of the Communist Party though their main concern was national independence. This goal was widely accepted among the Vietnamese people since Vietnam had historically been an autonomous kingdom. Now, as Ho Chi Minh put it, before one could practice Communism one had to have a country to practice it in. He invited all Vietnamese political factions to join the struggle against foreign rule, and he admired the American Revolution as a model for his own independence struggle. The Viet Minh tried hard to make friends with the Americans (Schulzinger, 1997: 18–19; Hunt, 1996). But the Americans had already plumped for France during the war, and they distrusted the Vietnamese racially. U.S. World War II planning documents had said the Vietnamese "had no organizing abilities or initiatives"; "they are quite incapable of developing an organization of any kind, certainly not an underground"; "they will do anything for money"; they were thought to need twenty-five years of tutelage in Western values before attaining independence (Bradley, 2000: 44, 73–106). Lyndon Johnson later called the ancient civilizations of the region "young and unsophisticated," needing guidance from a more mature America (Sherry, 1995: 251). The United States also distrusted a nationalism accompanied by any social program. As Acheson said in a cable to the Hanoi embassy: "Question whether Ho [Chi Min] as much nationalist as Commie is irrelevant, all Stalinists in colonial areas are nationalists. With achievement of national aims (i.e. independence) their objective necessarily becomes subordination of state to Commie purposes" (Gaddis, 1997: 156–7). The United States accepted rightist nationalists in Indonesia and the Philippines, but leftist nationalists were "commies," unable to provide order, likely to ally with the Soviets or Chinese. Such misperception was the persistent error of American imperialism, creating more not fewer communists – just as later it was to create more not fewer terrorists (see Chapter 10).

The Vietnamese defeated the French in 1954, but the United States took over, setting up a client regime. But even repeated increases in U.S. troops could not win the war. The Soviets and China reluctantly entered to support a troublesome revolutionary ally, since it was assailed by the United States. After their breach with China, the Soviets sought a negotiated end to the conflict but were frustrated by North Vietnamese and American intransigence (Gaiduk, 1996: 2003). Both of the great communist powers mistakenly believed American power was declining, but whereas Khrushchev generally believed this increased the chance of peaceful coexistence, Mao believed the "high tide of socialism" could now frontally defeat American imperialism. He was also unwilling to accept the position of younger brother that the Soviets accorded him (Westad, 1998; Zhang, 1998; Chen & Yang, 1998). But Chinese involvement plus fear of Soviet nuclear weapons and MAD ensured that the United States did not use its entire firepower to devastate North Vietnam as it had North Korea. Though American conservatives urged this policy, U.S. administrations showed more sense.

U.S. policy in Vietnam was built on three delusions: the war was against international communism not anticolonial nationalism; it must be fought primarily in military not political terms; and the United States must persist in "the impossible task of creating a separate state and society in the southern part of a single land" (Schulzinger, 1997: 327, 96; Mann, 2001: 3). The struggle was between two different versions of Vietnamese nationalism, one communist and populist, the other more elitist with its nationalist credentials harmed by support from what was identified as being the new colonial power, the United States. Inside the United States the antiwar movement generated by the introduction of conscription could not at first overcome cold war anticommunism, nor the normalcy of using overwhelming military power to secure U.S. goals, nor the domino theory (whereby if one country fell others would topple over too), nor the need to defend national prestige in the eyes of the world.[2]

---

[2] Aware that Vietnam might break him, Johnson still felt he could not be the first American president to lose a war. When journalists asked him why the United States was in Vietnam, he "unzipped his fly, drew out his substantial organ, and declared, 'This is why!'" (Dallek, 1998: 491; cf. Hunt, 1996: 106; Logevall, 1999: 389–93). War was still little boys in the playground, as I remarked in Volume III.

Americans hoped that their South Vietnamese client state, if politically reformed, could defeat the communists, but the ally would not play ball. The North had the edge in nationalism, since it had defeated the French, was more independent, and had a more popular program. Communists redistributed power to the peasants and imposed more equitable taxes and more open local government. The South Vietnamese sought military security, leaving power relations largely unchanged, while its local government was more authoritarian and corrupt (Race, 1972).

Elliott (2003) conducted interviews with four hundred communist prisoners and defectors. They said that poorer peasants had benefited from communist land programs, but once this made them grow into middle peasants, they did not want to hand over their property to communal farms. They saw the Communist Party as authoritarian and were horrified by the torturing and killing of those suspected of being South Vietnamese sympathizers. Yet they added that U.S. firepower killed far more innocent people than the communists could. Though their commitment to the communists was not whole-hearted, their nationalism made them hate the Americans and the southern government more. They saw them as merely the new colonial exploiters and their clients. Northern and Vietcong soldiers were thus better supported by the locals and had higher morale, while corruption undermined southern military performance.

Military escalation by Nixon and Kissinger did force North Vietnam to the negotiating table, securing what was then seen as a face-saving withdrawal by U.S. forces. But the peace accords let northern forces remain in parts of the South. The North waited a year, until March 1975, before striking. It expected a two-year campaign, but a month later its soldiers marched into Saigon, brushing aside the fourth largest army in the world lavishly provided with American tanks, artillery, and aircraft. Superior morale, ideological power, had won the war (Long, 1998; Nagl, 2002; Willbanks, 2004).[3]

Was the war worth it? Most Americans say no, since it was a defeat and led to serious divisions within American society. This was the only episode in the cold war when popular opposition at home grew sufficiently large to limit U.S. policy options and make withdrawal likely. This was probably due to conscription, putting ordinary young Americans at risk of having to fight in a distant land against people who had not been attacking them, and for a rather abstract cause. Even virulent anticommunists paused at that prospect. Some who did not have to fight nevertheless call Vietnam a necessary war in terms

---

[3] Nixon and Kissinger later blamed Congress and antiwar protesters for the defeat by not letting them escalate further and weakening the U.S. bargaining position by not offering them support. Most scholars see the political – and ultimately the military – weakness of the South Vietnamese government as irredeemable. For contending viewpoints, see Kissinger, 2003: 100–1, 561; Asselin, 2002: 187–90; Berman, 2001; Schulzinger, 1997; Willbanks, 2004.

of the broader cold war struggle, for it showed that the price of victory for other communists would be too high (Lynd, 1999). Asselin (2002: 165) sees Nixon's escalation as a cruel necessity, leading to the final peace negotiations. But negotiations achieved nothing that a voluntary U.S. withdrawal could not have achieved earlier. Was the war worth two million dead Vietnamese, plus perhaps near half a million dead in neighboring Laos and Cambodia – and 58,000 dead Americans? Was Nixon's escalation worth an extra 300,000 dead Vietnamese and 20,000 dead Americans? This was again scorched earth tactics. Aerial bombing through World War II, Korea and Vietnam, to Iraq and Afghanistan has been a great stain on the country.

America lost the war but no dominos fell. Scorched earth in Korea and Vietnam had undoubtedly helped ensure this but the major factor was that conditions differed elsewhere. In Korea and Vietnam anticolonialism and class struggle had blended together into the revolutionary leftist nationalism characterizing the second phase of twentieth-century revolutions (see Chapter 9). The Philippines was different. The sense of nationhood centered on the stability of rule on the ground of the *illustrados*, a solidaristic class of notables, through both the Spanish and American colonial periods. As we saw in Volume 3, chapter 3, the United States had stabilized rule by this landholding elite in formally democratic but highly clientelistic political institutions. World War II led to full independence but also continuity of elite rule afterward, and the regime unthreatened by more populist nationalism felt strong enough to survive without land reform. Though reform remains much needed, it has been only minimally implemented (Putzel, 2000). But given the Filipino elite's stability and power, the United States had no need of reform or military intervention to keep the country in the free world.

Indonesia had never been ruled by a single state, but its core island, Java, had seen dominant kingdoms, and Islam added a dose of social cohesion through the period of Dutch rule. After the defeat of the Japanese a nationalist military drawn from Java and the central islands had defeated the Dutch and their native allies, who were mainly from the peripheral islands. The postindependence government imposed what was in effect a "Javanese imperialism" over the islands, but it was a development-oriented regime with center-Left populist tinges. The United States did not like it. The CIA tried and failed over an eight-year period to destabilize the government of General Sukarno. But in 1965 a failed coup by leftist officers led to his overthrow by the rightist General Suharto. The new regime devastated the Javanese region in which the communist movement had its headquarters. At least 500,000 people died in atrocious massacres of the population. The CIA had wanted to be rid of Sukarno and was implicated in drawing up lists of people for death, yet this was largely an Indonesian atrocity. But the United States welcomed this anticommunist regime and even approved of its invasion of East Timor in 1985. Democracy lagged way behind antileftism in the driving of American foreign policy in Indonesia.

Just as Vietnam was sacrificed to broader cold war interests, so were other countries. Thailand was never colonized. It was a kingdom of rather limited power until 1932, and then it remained under military rule. Its conservatism made it suitable for U.S. military bases, and American administrations were more concerned to preserve a government of order rather than democratization or land reform and sided with military and authoritarian factions in Thai politics: "American policy aims were incompatible with Thai democracy" (says Fineman, 1997: 261). Laos had a recent history of disunity and remained divided, riven by a class-cum-ethnic civil war won by the leftist Pathet Lao, who were clients of the Vietnamese communists. Their rule was then destabilized by CIA aid to the minority Hmong people, used as guerrillas against both the Vietcong and the Pathet Lao (Warner, 1996). However, President Kennedy secured a U.S. withdrawal, recognizing a quagmire when he saw one. In these wars ethnic minorities were often used by the United States to attack its enemies even though they were not numerous enough to win. When the United States withdrew, their lives became threatened. Still, the remnants of the Hmong people are today living quite prosperous lives in Fresno and Los Angeles!

Cambodia had been both a dominant and then a subordinate state in the region, subject before the French arrived to Vietnamese domination. After the French departed, the country suffered a terrible fate. Technically a neutral country during the Vietnam War, it was bombed by the United States to interdict North Vietnamese supply lines into South Vietnam. Many thousands of Cambodians perished, weakening Cambodia's government while strengthening the Khmer Rouge peasant guerrillas whose main bases were in the bombed regions. This was not the main cause of the growing strength of the communist Khmer Rouge, but the bombing strengthened support for its anticolonial nationalism. In 1975 it conquered the whole country and then perpetrated its terrible "classicide," slaughtering around 1.8 million people whom it defined as "bourgeois" counterrevolutionaries. The Khmer Rouge were crushed in 1979 by an invasion from Vietnam provoked by their wholesale killing of the Vietnamese minority in Cambodia, followed by foolish military incursions over the Vietnamese border. The Khmer Rouge were not only murderous but also suicidal (Mann, 2005: 339–50). Their fall remains the most successful case of "humanitarian interventionism," ironically achieved by a communist army.

The U.S. military record in Asia might not seem very good. The U.S.-backed side lost the civil wars in China and Vietnam and fought a draw in Korea. It failed in covert wars and coups in Laos and Northern Burma. It did harm in Cambodia and Thailand. These results were in proportion to the cohesion of the states and societies of the region. However, the United States began to define "success" differently, for the ferocity of its bombing did deter communism. Its scorched earth tactics made communist regimes unable to prosper or induce others in the region to follow their example. In Indonesia, the Philippines, and

Thailand U.S. administrations turned a blind eye to the human rights violations of allies. They would have done a lot better had they pushed for land reform, as in Korea. True, the United States did not have much power inside Southeast Asian countries. Their states and peoples had varying degrees of cohesion but were receptive to anticolonial nationalism. The region was a long way from America, it contained few Americans, and not much of its trade was with the United States. American military strength had helped keep communism at bay in the region, though this success was mainly due to repression by local elites seeking to avoid land reform, independent labor unions, and democracy. Both sides of the cold war were perverting their original ideals when they operated abroad. The chief difference was that the Soviets and Chinese did so at home as well, but that was irrelevant if you were Vietnamese or Cambodian.

The United States was a largely noncolonial power and could have behaved differently. It would have benefited from a more reform-oriented strategy with less militarism. Yet it was difficult for those in Washington to stand up to the virulent anticommunism rampant in the United States. Being soft on supposed communists was not a political option back home, for it threatened one's reelection. Domestic politics trumped political realities in far-off countries. Yet it was not just communist-leaning groups who were cold-shouldered but any left of center groups seeking land reform or workers' rights. It seems that Americans were also sucked into the militaristic strategy by their close ties with local upper-class conservatives. This was path dependency: first choice of friends determined allies and enemies in later wars. It is difficult to weigh the relative strength of two main American motives: global great power rivalry with communist powers versus support for capitalists and landlords in the interests of American capitalists. U.S. administrations probably preferred local regimes to be more democratic, but if that was not an option, then authoritarianism would do – and it did produce order, or so it was believed. Yet Americans' relative indifference to regime type meant that the decisive actors were not they but the local Asian elites, few of whom would yield an ounce of their power. Though American administrations gave military backing to authoritarians, the decisive actors producing authoritarian regimes were local elites.

East and Southeast Asia, phase B: Toward hegemony

Yet America's wars did stabilize Asian borders between the communist and capitalist worlds, and after Vietnam this enabled the United States to play to its real economic strength of trade and investment rather than its delusional military preponderance geared to knee-jerk anticommunism (McMahon, 1999: 210). From 1976 onward the United States gradually shifted toward hegemony. Capitalist development led by the U.S./Japanese condominium, aided by the vibrant overseas Chinese diaspora, increasingly contrasted with the more stagnant autarchic economies of the communist zone. Japan's economic miracle was followed by that of the East Asian Little Tigers and then later by development across the whole macroregion. Most nation-states chose the same strategy as postwar Europe and Japan. They undervalued their exchange rates, managed foreign exchange interventions, imposed capital controls, accumulated reserves, and promoted export-led growth, sending goods to the core countries, especially to the United States (Dooley et al., 2003). This was the developmental state model, accepted a little reluctantly by the United States since it was unthinkable back home. America's economic power strategy achieved far more in tandem with autonomous nation-states than had military power. One of its particular achievements was to encourage a decline of racism toward and within Asians.

It should be clear by now that American policy in the region was not driven by a democratic mission. Huntington's second wave of democratization, from 1944 to 1957, barely affected this region.[4] Comparative studies of democratization across the nineteenth and twentieth centuries find that landlords have been the most antidemocratic class, followed by capitalists, with other classes having more varied tendencies. In the West, Latin America, and the Caribbean the middle classes, despite being trumpeted as democrats by a tradition of theory stretching from Aristotle to Lipset (1960) and Huntington (1991: 66–8), sometimes favored, sometimes opposed democracy. The most prodemocratic force since the late nineteenth century was actually the organized working class, followed by small peasants. Labor and peasant parties and unions have most persistently pressed for democracy (Rueschemeyer et al., 1992), for the rather obvious reason that once democracy is defined as universal suffrage, they are the most numerous classes. For most of the modern period the Aristotle-Lipset middle-class theory was in general wrong.

Yet postwar Asia differed. South Korea is perhaps the last country to have experienced a broad-based industrial development that generated a large, organized working class. In Taiwan, the other relatively early developer in the region, firms were smaller and family-run and so generated less trade unionism – industrialization without an organized working class. Elsewhere in the region (and in other regions of the world) industrialization has tended to occur in smallish enclaves whose workers have not been representative of the popular classes as a whole. Their unions tend to be sectionally not class-oriented. Young women's agile fingers have been preferred for textile stitching or microelectronic assembly, and they are not usually good union material. Subcontracting chains and international competition to attract manufacturing jobs weaken labor unions and government interest in protecting workers' rights. They enable employers to control the lives of workers, who are often migrants from distant areas in debt bondage to recruiting agencies, subject to deportation if they cause trouble

---

[4] I have followed Doreenspleet's (2000) modifications of Huntington's (1991) wave theory.

and forced to use much of their wages in repaying the inflated costs of their transportation. The work is in small factories with low profit margins competing for the contracts of bigger Western or Japanese corporations who disclaim all responsibility for their work conditions. These are all factors making for less collective organization by workers, including less working-class pressure for democracy. This might be expected to change slowly as a country becomes industrialized. Wallerstein (2003) sees a gradual exhaustion of capitalism's ability to migrate to zones of cheap, highly exploited labor. He estimates that there is a lag of about thirty years between the entry of capital into a formerly rural country and the time when workers become organized, and this process then continues across the world as capital moves offshore to find cheaper labor zones. Africa will be the last to be industrialized and organized, he says. But in the meantime labor organization lags, and so working-class pressure for democracy is less than in the past.

Wallerstein emphasizes the power of capitalist markets, but Kohli believes as I do that late developing states have had some leeway in the industrialization process. Kohli calls the successful ones "capitalist-cohesive states." They encourage production-oriented alliances between the state and dominant business classes with "single-minded and unyielding political commitment to growth." Sometimes regimes attempt to get the prices right (as neoclassical economists urge); more often they practice deliberate price distortions, undervaluing exchange rates, subsidizing exports, and holding wages behind productivity gains. This usually involves some repression of workers and peasants, again delaying their collective organization (Kohli, 2004: 10–14; cf. Rodrik, 2011). For Kohli, the paradigmatic case is South Korea. In 1961, with military support, Premier Park Chung Hee offered state subsidies to export-oriented chaebols. Labor demands were repressed and military disciplinary practices introduced in factories. Workers had low wages, though with good job security, and some had lifetime contracts. With profits high and wages and consumption low, technology transfers could be bought with domestic capital, permitting industrial upgrading without depending on foreign capital. Business was rewarded with tax breaks according to export targets set them, creating incentives for the most productive (Amsden, 2001; Wade, 1990). This, Kohli concludes, was a "militarized, top-down, repressive, growth-oriented state" (2004: 88, 98–101). There was some corruption, but most countries were not cases of politicized capitalism in which access to the state confers the right to dispose of its resources, sometimes as your own private property. In terms of collective economic power, these arrangements worked. The downside was in terms of political and military power, for the semiauthoritarian fusing of economic and political power over workers led to military repression rather than political citizenship.

Despite these obstacles capitalist development had mildly positive effects on civil citizenship (Marshall, 1963; Zakaria, 2003). Laws protecting private capitalist property tended to spin off into rights of individual equality before the law, and individual freedom of speech, association, and religion. This encourages liberalization – individual more than collective rights – which is the American conception of democracy. U.S. willingness to transfer technology and open its doors to imports was extremely beneficial and helpful to liberalization as it extended from Japan to Hong Kong, South Korea, Taiwan, Indonesia, Malaysia, Singapore, and Thailand (McCauley, 1998: 103). These countries also had competent states guaranteeing public order and (to some extent) the rule of law. The payoff occurred at the end of the cold war in Huntington's third wave of democratization beginning in 1987. Nonetheless democratization was not simply the product of industrialization and it was also taking longer. From the 1960s to the mid-1990s in East and Southeast Asia there was no overall correlation between economic development and democratization. Intervening factors such as statist economic development, racial-ethnic divisions, the strength of anticommunism, and repression by elites and the United States caused the differences (Laothamatas, 1997). American fear of communism led to its support for repression of peasant and worker movements and this slowed democratization until after the fall of the Soviet Union.

So South Korean democracy had genuine elections only in the 1990s. Before then, the government and the chaebols repressed labor unions, denouncing militants as communists. Yet their development model was based on an educated, high-skill workforce, and on a limited development of social citizen rights, with a compressed wage structure and public education and housing programs. Exploiting their associational rights, students, professionals, and religious voluntary associations demonstrated for democracy from the 1960s onward (Oh, 1999: 70). Across East and Southeast Asia, in the absence of much working-class pressure, middle-class groups became more prominent in prodemocratic dissent (Laothamatas, 1997). This seems to offer some support for the Aristotle-Lipset middle-class theory of democracy. But without much effective support from worker and peasant organizations their gains were limited. When broader explosions of protest occurred, the pattern changed. In the Kwangju uprising of 1980 most of the initial dissident leaders were college educated, experienced in earlier struggles, yet factory workers did most of the actual fighting (Ahn, 2003: 16–20). This was the turning point, not least because Reagan's support for the dictator Chun and for his deployment of the Korean military units that suppressed the uprising produced a surge of anti-Americanism. This scared the Americans, who shifted into supporting democratization. The cross-class alliance of students and workers reappeared in 1987, when democratic political rights were consolidated. Finally, after the fall of communism, the United States relaxed and became a mildly prodemocratic force in the region. Before then, the mission had been anticommunism, but that had not included democracy.

American imperialism eventually did a disappearing act in this region, replaced by a lighter hegemony allowing nation-states to determine their own policies. They mostly chose democracy, though sometimes it was a pale imitation of democracy. The natives eventually benefited, though they had suffered along the way when the United States had failed to engage with the region's center-Left nationalism. We will see that this was a failure of American policy in other regions too. But luckily this was outweighed by the greater failure of nationalist movements pushed leftward toward communism, who failed to produce a desirable form of society in the region. Thus Asians acquired their own blend of citizen rights and their own version of capitalism. By the end of the cold war, American empire no longer dominated East and Southeast Asia – but nor did communism.

Gunboats in the American hemisphere

The hemisphere was America's backyard, but it was a lower-priority area – with a wary eye kept on Venezuelan oil and the Panama Canal – since it had few communists and was already safely within the American informal empire. This was reflected in the meager sums spent on the region. Most apologists and critics of American empire alike exaggerate its power in the hemisphere, praising or blaming the United States for many developments for which it was not responsible. This was a region of long-established sovereign nation-states, which contained social conflicts too intense to be solved by the United States (and still less by the USSR). The United States had to continue relying on the low-cost "sons-of-bitches" proxies and covert operations that I discussed in Volume 3 (Cordell Hull had famously said of a Latin American dictator of the 1930s, "He may be a son-of-a-bitch but he's our son-of-a-bitch"). It had limited ability to influence social forces on the ground and the locals were mostly responsible for their own fate. Leftists knew that the slightest hint of communism would reap American retribution, but this should not have been much of a problem since there were very few communists there. Only two small countries, Cuba and Nicaragua, had revolutions over the whole period and only the Cuban one endured.

The region contained more class and regional inequality, often buttressed by ethnic cleavages, than any other macroregion of the world, and many movements demanding radical change arose. Some of these were socialist; a few espoused violence. Yet they failed. Latin America was not involved in the world wars and saw very few interstate wars, so any would-be revolutionaries had to face ruling regimes determined to yield nothing to social pressures whose strength was not weakened nor their attention span diverted by war. The main problems in Latin America, as everywhere, were domestic. U.S. assistance to repressive regimes did not help matters, for it emboldened repression, fueled anti-Americanism, and pushed protest movements leftward and some to violence. But all this was exacerbation of already rampant conflicts. As Brands (2010: 1–2) says, "Superpower rivalry, foreign intervention, and inter-American diplomatic strife dominated Latin America's external relations; ideological polarization, rapid swings between dictatorship and democracy, and acute internal violence constituted the essential features of domestic politics." Thus it was "a period of intense and often bloody upheaval." This was not cold, but rather warm war. U.S. influence was also much greater in Central than South America, whose countries were farther away, and generally bigger.

World War II had produced the economic boom customary among those neutral countries that did not suffer blockades. Latin America in this period depended on the export of foodstuffs and raw materials and so developed the economic policies known as import-substitution industrialization (ISI). State-aided, tariff-protected industrialization was hoped to stimulate local manufacturing industry and lower dependence on manufactured imports. Though ISI infringed U.S. free trade policies, the United States accepted this, provided American corporations were not discriminated against and could set up branches there. ISI was aided by the worldwide boom and it generated higher growth during the 1950s and 1960s than in any other decade of the twentieth century (until the 2000s, in fact). It increased the size and living standards of the industrial working class and the middle class, though massive urban growth created much social disruption. According to Kutznets's simple theorem, inequality widens with initial industrialization and then narrows. But Latin American inequality did not narrow, in most countries mainly because the lower classes were divided by ethnic-racial and regional divisions. The culturally cohesive upper classes plus their clients extracted rents from land and the state and launched repression or military coups when faced with radical reformers. Public sector workers, being strategically quite powerful within the state, were sometimes admitted into this rent seeking oligarchy in a subordinate role. However, when the global boom ended, ISI worsened balance of payments difficulties and indebtedness, and the protected industries remained inefficient. Economic difficulties mounted from the 1970s (Bulmer-Thomas, 1994; Bethell, 1991; Cardenas et al., 2000).

The hemisphere saw a distinctive pattern of oscillation between military-backed dictators and (imperfect) democratic regimes, neither of whom produced much success for their countries in this period. Huntington's second wave of democratization, begun in 1944, affected Latin America, encouraged by the New Deal, a world war won by democracies, and wartime growth. Parties mobilized around unions and middle-class associations to urge democratization. Center-Left parties in Costa Rica, Venezuela, and Peru also demanded social reforms. This was probably the most vibrant period of democracy up until the 2000s. But U.S. policy makers were divided between cold war liberals wanting to jettison the "sons-of-bitches" dictators and democratize in order to head off communism and cold war conservatives favoring the dictators as the guarantors of order. The conservatives were generally supported by the CIA and by U.S. business interests involved in extractive industries, seeking the lowest possible labor costs. The common element between them was that both factions fiercely defended capitalist freedoms. The liberal Spruille Brady pressed for elections across the hemisphere but declared, "The institution of private property ranks with those of religion and family as a bulwark of civilization. To tamper with private enterprise will precipitate a disintegration of life and liberty as we conceive and treasure them." Americans denounced as communists the economists of the UN Commission for Latin America (ECLA) who advocated some central planning of national economies. The United States also rejected local requests for economic aid on the grounds that this would interfere with natural market forces – though it was also reluctant to waste dollars on a low-priority region.

The liberals lost these battles. By early 1948 U.S. democratizing pressure ceased and the oligarchies were hitting back. In 1946 more than two-thirds of Latin American countries had constitutional governments; by 1954 more than two-thirds had dictators. This was not primarily the fault of the United States, for the local oligarchs needed little prompting from outside, while the U.S. attitude was more one of indifference than interventionism. But after the coups, the United States regarded the dictatorships as bulwarks against communism. In 1954 Eisenhower awarded Perez Jimenez, the repressive Venezuelan dictator, the Legion of Merit for "special meritorious conduct in the fulfillment of his high functions and anti-communist attitudes." World War II surplus armaments were delivered to the dictators, indicating support for internal repression but on the cheap (Bethell & Roxborough, 1988; Bethell, 1991: 53–4, 67; Coatsworth, 1994: chap. 3, espec. 53; Ewell, 1996: 160; Leonard, 1991: chap. 7; Roorda, 1998: chap. 8; Rouquié, 1987: 24; Gambone, 1997; Schwartzberg, 2003).

Intervention was easier in Central America. In 1954 the U.S. reacted sharply against the constitutional government of Arbenz in Guatemala when it implemented land reform amid an upsurge of labor and peasant unions and center-Left parties. Unused land was confiscated from the dominant families and from the U.S. United Fruit Company (UFCO) and distributed to landless peasants, with compensation paid at current market prices for unimproved land. Arbenz's government contained a small Communist Party presence comprising four of his fifty-one votes in the Assembly and one communist in the leadership. The oligarchical families, the Catholic Church, UFCO, and the United States all became unhappy. Local reactionaries were the prime movers, but U.S. ambassador Peurifoy encouraged the Guatemalan Army to intervene and the CIA financed and armed a 1954 invasion by Guatemalan opposition forces. When this stalled, CIA planes bombed the Guatemalan Army and the United States asked senior army officers to turn their weapons against Arbenz. They did so, fearing that otherwise Eisenhower would send in the marines (Cullather, 1999: vii–xv, 97–110).

Arbenz was deposed. In the 1955 elections the U.S. client Castillo Armas received 99 percent of the vote – a Soviet-style election! He returned to UFCO its confiscated lands, reduced trade and investment barriers with the United States, and banned unions and Left of center parties. This radicalized the opposition and pushed them toward violent resistance. The economy grew a little, mostly benefiting the oligarch families while the incomes of three-quarters of the population declined. The growing opposition was repressed with arms supplied by the United States, which was grateful, said the State Department, for a "strong counterinsurgency state." Peasants and indigenous peoples stirred up by the Arbenz reforms proved tough opposition, including some insurgency. In 1965 a State Department security expert, John Longan, arrived to organize Operation Cleanup by the first of the Guatemalan death squads. It killed the leaders of trade unions and peasant federations. Green Berets and CIA operatives were sent to train the Guatemalan military and security police in counterinsurgency methods, and some were involved in the death squads' activities. Over the next twenty years at least 200,000 dissidents and indigenous peoples were killed, while another 40,000 disappeared. This would not have happened without persistent U.S. support, training, and weapons. This lessened under Carter only to intensify under Reagan. CIA and diplomats' reports critical of the atrocities and U.S. complicity were buried. Reagan flouted State Department norms on human rights in delivering arms to the military to accomplish their dreadful work (Streeter, 2000: 108–36, 239–48; Grandin, 2004: 12). In 1999 President Clinton was to issue a formal apology to the people of Guatemala. They were at the receiving end of what was probably the worst sequence of U.S. covert operations in the hemisphere

U.S. officials said they had intervened to forestall communism. But as the CIA-authorized history later revealed, there were no links between Arbenz or the small Guatemalan Communist Party and the Soviet Union, though the CIA had been fabricating them (Cullather, 1999). The subsequent insurgencies, mostly in the rural hinterlands, showed no trace of either Soviet or indigenous communist links. Marxist ideas had influenced Arbenz's land reform program, though blended into the ECLA Keynesian model of national economic development that aimed at turning landless peasants into property owners to make them consumers of national manufactures. The theory was that planters, previously made somnolent by cheap labor and land, would be forced to invest in new technology, improving their efficiency (Gleijeses, 1991: 3–7, 361–87; Grandin, 2004). Mahoney (2001: 212–16) says the land policy was ironically similar to that in the Kennedy administration's subsequent Alliance for Progress. It would not have led to revolution.

Land reform was the sticking point for the United States, yet this was a precondition for democracy across much of the hemisphere, for rule by landed oligarchs was oppressing the poor and stymieing economic growth. A CIA official denounced land reform as making "land available to the Guatemalans on the communist pattern." The State Department declared it strengthened "political and Communist control over the rural population" (U.S. Department of State, 2003: 20, 70–1). The land was transferred to 100,000 peasant families, many of them oppressed Mayans. It had empowered them, and they formed civil society institutions demanding further citizen rights. The oligarchy was horrified and resisted, blessed by the church hierarchy, armed by the officer corps, and with UFCO lobbying effectively in Washington. Both Dulles brothers, then secretary of state and director of the CIA, were former employees and present shareholders of UFCO (Grandin, 2004). Though it is not likely that the company determined U.S. policy, its informal influence seems important. Ambassador Peurifoy invited to embassy functions educated English-speaking Guatemalans and American businessmen, not center-Left intellectuals or Quechua-speaking Mayans. The Americans were influenced by their local friends.

Communism was seen as a global virus. If Guatemalan land reform was a success, it could spread elsewhere. Though some U.S. officials privately conceded that the reform was a "long-overdue measure," they still opposed it, seeing it as "fomenting destructive unrest among the rural people of the other American republics." A State Department official declared, "It is a powerful propaganda weapon; its broad social program of aiding the workers and peasants in a victorious struggle against the upper classes and large foreign enterprises has a strong appeal to the populations of Central American neighbors where similar conditions prevail" (Streeter, 2000: 17–23; Gleijeses, 1991: 365). The coup and the subsequent counterinsurgency assistance were traditional imperial policy: doses of exemplary repression, an example of what would happen to others if they attempted the same. It worked. It did scare them and it emboldened the dictators.

The Eisenhower administration had begun arms transfer and training programs across the hemisphere. By 1957 training existed in forty-two countries, mostly Latin American. NSC Document 5509 of 1955 said this guaranteed "the security of Latin America and the availability of raw materials there from with a minimum of US forces" (Gambone, 1997: 85). Trained local soldiers would do the job. Sixty thousand soldiers and police were trained at the School of the Americas in counterinsurgency techniques, including most of the notorious violators of human rights across the hemisphere (Gill, 2004). The sons-of-bitches were back in favor, given cheap military aid to overwhelm their dissidents (Lieuwen, 1961: 226–34; Holden, 2004: part II; Rabe, 1988: 77–83). On the other hand, as Brands (2010: 48) laconically puts it, "No Latin American officer needed to be told to be anticommunist" even if they gratefully received U.S. military aid.

The late 1950s saw more pressure from below for democracy. Between 1956 and 1960 ten military rulers in the hemisphere were deposed by movements promising political and social reform. The United States had supported most of the dictators until the last moment. A Democrat majority in Congress pressed for a more liberal policy. Yet only days before Kennedy took office, the United States thwarted a coup by reformists in Honduras, replacing them with conservatives. Note that the interventions and repressions mentioned so far were aimed at the reformist Left. Their successful repression discredited peaceful dissent and led to more recourse on the Left to violence, guerrilla movements. It was only tit for tat once the Right had initiated the violence. These interventions and repressions occurred *before* Castro turned leftward after his seizure of power. Though Castro's Cuba and the Soviet Union did then offer direct military aid to numerous guerrilla movements, bloody repression of the Left was already normal and not the consequence of Castro or the Soviets. The specter of Castroism did exacerbate rightist paranoia (as Brands, 2010, emphasizes), but why did they not respond by conciliating centrist and center-Leftist peaceful reformers and so undercut the violent Left? The answer is that most ruling oligarchical regimes had already been refusing to yield any of their privileges for most of the postwar period.

But U.S. policy was now in ferment over Cuba, traumatized by Castro's seizure of power in 1959 from the son-of-a-bitch Batista. Castro initially hoped to be nonaligned in foreign policy while pursuing economic nationalism and redistribution at home. When it became clear that nonalignment meant playing off the United States against the Soviet Union – for example, taking most of his oil from the Soviets – the United States turned nasty, inducing American and British oil companies to refuse to refine the Soviet oil. Congress then terminated the Cuban sugar quota, and the CIA began training Cuban exiles. In response Castro nationalized oil and some other U.S. companies and accepted military aid from the Soviets, who now dared to think that other revolutions might be brewing (and might be assisted) across the hemisphere (Brands, 2010: 31–3). In response, the United States imposed a trade embargo, and Eisenhower authorized the CIA to plan an invasion. Kennedy had opportunistically lambasted Eisenhower during his election campaign for being soft on communism. Now he felt he had to be tough.

For the first and only time in the hemisphere a leftist regime became allied to the Soviet Union and Cuban nationalism gave Castro a David versus Goliath boost at home (Welsch, 1985). The escalation was mutually stupid. U.S. policy escalated Soviet interest in Cuba and produced an anti-American backlash across the hemisphere. Yet Castro's folly was the greater. Given the U.S. track record, why did he not see that an alliance with the Soviet Union only ninety miles from Florida would yield political isolation and economic strangulation? The Soviets were taken by surprise, astonished at their good luck, in contrast to lack of influence elsewhere in the hemisphere. The by-now cynical Soviet leaders were also charmed by Castro's new-convert naive enthusiasm for revolution (Miller, 1989). The Cuban Revolution and Soviet aid encouraged extreme leftists elsewhere to turn to the path of violence, but in turn this encouraged the far Right to violence as well, and they had considerably greater military power. Cuba was counterproductive for all.

But since other allied dictators seemed vulnerable, Castro would be made an example. Some in Washington sensibly argued that the U.S. case would be strengthened if we persuaded the other dictators to make reforms. Indeed Eisenhower had in 1959 sought to nudge Trujillo from office in the Dominican Republic, but the dictator had too many friends on Capitol Hill. Kennedy expressed his own feelings: "There are three possibilities in descending order of preference: a decent democratic regime, a continuation of the Trujillo regime, or a Castro regime. We ought to aim at the first but we cannot renounce the second until we are sure we can avoid the third" (Smith, 2000: 143). This statement might be applied to most American policy across the less developed countries of the world. Kennedy did approve the assassination of Trujillo in 1961. But he still lacked a policy to bring about his preferred first option.

During his campaign speeches Kennedy had declared that he would work with Third World nationalism to meet a global revolution of rising expectations. He found the supposed new policy in the Alliance for Progress, begun in 1961. It accepted the argument that economic development and land reforms were the necessary infrastructure on which democracy might be built. It provided $20 billion in economic aid, designed to head off communism by economic means, though it was buttressed by the modernization theory of the sociologist Talcott Parsons and the economist Walt Rostow, who perceived common stages of growth and development across the world. The most modern society, the United States, could assist more backward societies by inducing them to apply its model of development (Latham, 2000; Smith, 2000: 146–8).

Unfortunately, it did not work very well. The money went in, but much was siphoned off by corrupt elites. U.S. officials were often reluctant to work with local reformers, since land reform intensified class conflict and this might threaten stability, the main U.S. objective in the region. Funds were also purloined by administration officials who thought the money was better spent on counterinsurgency measures, termed by Bobby Kennedy "social reform under pressure." The Peace Corps was the best program, staffed by idealistic volunteers. Most returned to the United States with a greater awareness of Latin American reality, though disillusioned with their own government (Fischer, 1998). It proved more Alliance than Progress, for it had turned into the bribing of governments to remain pro-American and defeat the Left. The president, torn between anticommunism and progressive goals, became disillusioned with the Alliance. Opinions are divided as to whether it was always doomed or whether more determination might have seen it through to modestly progressive results (Dallek, 2003: 222–3, 436–7, 519; Levinson & de Onis, 1970; Kunz, 1997: 120–48; Smith, 1991: 71–89; Leonard, 1991: 146–52). But its failure discredited land reform, most urgently needed in the region. Indeed, says Brands (2010: 63), it actually worsened class conflict by enabling an increase in large-scale commercial agriculture at the expense of poor tenant farmers.

Kennedy's pressure on Cuba led the Soviets to believe he was about to invade, which was a factor in the missile crisis. But in the crisis itself his conduct was firm yet restrained, allowing Khrushchev a way out without losing face, which Khrushchev gratefully seized (since by now he regretted his adventurism). The defusing of a nuclear crisis was their mutual achievement (Gaddis, 1997: chap. 9; Stern, 2003: 14, 82, 127, 424–6; White, 1997). Kennedy wavered elsewhere. In Venezuela, Peru, Chile, and Costa Rica he supported centrist politicians, but elsewhere he launched covert operations to overthrow centrists. He undermined constitutional regimes in Argentina and Guatemala. He misidentified Joao Goulart, president of Brazil, as a dangerous leftist and told Brazilian generals he would support a coup if they believed he was "giving the damn country away to the Communists." He helped overthrow Cheddi Jagan in a Guyana transitioning from British rule. The British assured him Jagan was not a communist but were not believed. Kennedy approved more covert operations in the hemisphere than any other cold war president, though they were small-scale (Rabe, 1999: 63–70; 197–9; Dallek, 2003: 401, 520–2).

Lyndon Johnson helped finish off Goulart and Jagan. In the Dominican Republic Trujillo had been succeeded by the reformer Juan Bosch, resented by the military after he cut its budget and identified by the United States as a potential communist. After the Dominican military failed to overthrow him, in 1965 this was achieved by a U.S. marine invasion, a very big affair in a small country. Six thousand Dominicans died in the turmoil (Lowenthal, 1995; Atkins & Wilson, 1998: 119–49). Kennedy and Johnson both saw dictatorship as strong and stable, while democracy though more ideal was in practice susceptible to communist subversion (Wiarda, 1995: 69). The "specter of communism haunting the US" prevented a more rational, prodemocracy foreign policy, says Dominguez (1999: 33–4, 49). The United States seemed to share Che Guevara's view that Latin America was ripe for revolution. But it was nonsense. Guevara's belief in a homogeneous, revolution-inclined peasantry that could be stirred into revolutionary resistance by violence led up a blind alley that sent guerrilla movements isolated from the masses to speedy defeat and him to his miserable death. Brands (2010: 52–5) summarizes Che's strategy as "better suited to radicalizing the Right than radicalizing the masses."

Nixon mirrored the far Left with his policies. After the leftist Salvador Allende won the Chilean election of 1970, the economic mistakes of his government caused much discontent among the upper and middle classes and divisions within his own coalition. Coup plotting began, and led by General Pinochet the military seized power. But Allende had also faced unrelenting hostility from the United States. Nixon instructed the CIA to "leave no stone unturned ... to block Allende's confirmation." Kissinger oversaw a CIA $8 million economic sabotage program "to make the economy scream," reasoning, "I don't see why we should let a country go Marxist just because the people are irresponsible." Nixon reasoned, "If we let the potential leaders in South America think they can move like Chile and have it both ways, we will be in trouble. ... No impression should be permitted in Latin America that they can get away with this, that it's safe to go this way" (Brands, 2010: 116–20; Miller, 1989: 128–30; Gaddis, 1982: 320; White House, National Security Meeting on Chile, Memorandum, Nov. 7, 1970). Exemplary destabilization was the plan in what was the most extensive covert operations program in South America. It was in the short term successful. In the 1960s ten new military governments were installed across the hemisphere, primarily by local forces though with U.S. approval secured in advance. By 1979 only four Latin American countries were not dictatorships.

U.S. policy makers had generally been careful before an intervention to secure local allies on the ground able to form a viable regime. This was the key to success, and it enabled the United States to play only a supporting and often a covert role in most of these coups. In Chile, for example, local opposition to Allende became broadly based as the government floundered amid its own divisions. The Soviets did not offer Allende help because they saw him as a loser. The Bay of Pigs intervention in Cuba was the only true exception, when the United States pressed ahead with an invasion without securing local support. Some in the CIA and in State predicted the fiasco that followed (Karabell, 1999: 173–205). The United States was then reduced to sponsoring eight assassination attempts on Castro between 1960 and 1965 (Dallek, 2003: 439). All failed; Castro remained – but in the meat grinder of sanctions, depending on a Soviet alliance that brought Cuba little gain. The United States learned to live with Castro, grinding him down, using him as a permanent warning to others of what might happen if they invited in the Soviets. This was exemplary repression, and at least in an economic sense it was also scorched earth. Other countries, other insurgencies took note.

But once again repression caused resistance. In the 1980s the cycle swung again, toward democratization, mainly the product of local forces assisted by a Catholic Church embracing more socially conscious doctrines and urging land reform. President Carter had seemed sympathetic. Declaring, "We are now free of that inordinate fear of communism," he sought "moderate paths of change," pursuing "new global questions of justice, equity and human rights." He said he would even negotiate deals with unfriendly regimes if they wished to trade with the United States (Skidmore, 1996: 26–51; Smith, 1986; Muravchik, 1986). The ensuing Reagan administration sent out mixed signals, sometimes supporting military regimes, sometimes declaring verbally for democracy but doing little to help it. Carrothers (1991) calls the latter a policy of "democracy by applause" (cf. Wiarda, 1995: 73–5; Muravchik, 1986). Yet on the ground policies varied. In Nicaragua and Grenada the United States intervened militarily against leftist civilian governments, and in Nicaragua this was a democratically elected one. In El Salvador, Guatemala, and Honduras the United States preferred civilian governments and encouraged them with economic and military aid, though in El Salvador and Guatemala human rights violations increased, committed by a military on which the United States also showered aid and counterinsurgency training. In the Central American republics policy was dictated by the perceived need to combat the Sandinista virus originating in Nicaragua. But in Chile, Paraguay, Panama, and Haiti, the second Reagan administration did pressure for elections. The administration now saw from the hemispheric trend that democracies too could be stable (Carrothers, 1991; Leonard, 1991: 167–91). The shifts by both the United States and the papacy were parts of that broader third wave of democracy identified by Huntington.

Nonetheless, the cold war period ended with major intervention in Nicaragua, killing more than thirty thousand Nicaraguans, undermining its economy and its regime, and destabilizing neighbors. Carter had tried to replace the dictator Somoza discreetly with conservative parties dominated by businessmen. But this policy was overwhelmed as worker and peasant demonstrations, aided by middle-class liberals and even some planter families, propelled the Sandinistas into power. Similar forces in El Salvador next door could not quite seize power and a civil war broke out (Paige, 1997). Carter vacillated, under cold war pressure at home, yet sensibly not wanting to push the Sandinistas down the Cuban road. The Reagan administration then ferociously undermined this small country through a policy of indirect exemplary repression. The United States would so devastate the Nicaraguan economy and civil society that Sandinista legitimacy would be destroyed, demonstrating what would happen to other countries attempting revolution. Economic sanctions caused hardship since the country's natural trading partner was the United States. The United States opposed attempts by Nicaragua's neighbors to negotiate a solution. The Arias peace plan that did end the war was signed by all the parties except the United States.

Opinion polls revealed that most Americans opposed the use of U.S. forces and the administration recognized that an invasion might create a quagmire (as had previous invasions there). Instead, Reagan deployed as proxies the Contra paramilitaries, former Somoza Guardsmen augmented by disaffected peasants and unemployed young men. The Argentine military government had begun training them in dirty war techniques, including torture and murder, and had developed a network of officers across the hemisphere, a "sort of secret foreign legion whose job was rooting out Communists wherever they happened to be." By 1982 the Argentines commanded twenty-five hundred Nicaraguan Contras (Armony 1997: chaps. 1 & 2). Then the United States took over and expanded them. The Contras were proxies who would not have survived without massive U.S. aid. Lacking much domestic support, they could not win the war. For Reagan to describe the Contras as freedom fighters was one of the more ludicrous uses of language of the period. Their tactics were to spread terror and destroy. U.S. sponsorship of the Contras, leading into the Iran-Contra scandal, did encourage the repression of leftists in El Salvador and Guatemala, but this damaged the United States over most of the hemisphere and elsewhere (Coatsworth, 1994: chaps. 5 & 6; Carrothers, 1991; Brands, 2010: chaps. 6 & 7).

Some Americans deplored such excesses but still regarded the war as necessary to keep communism at bay. Secretary of State Haig told the Senate Nicaragua was part of "worldwide Soviet interventionism that poses an unprecedented challenge to the free world." This was false. The Sandinistas wanted good relations with everyone, the United States, the Soviets, and Europe. The Soviets, burned by the Cuban missile crisis and now entering crisis at home, were reluctant, but after two years in which the United States organized Contra attacks on Nicaraguan oil fields and harbors, they gave the Sandinistas aid. Perceiving that the Contras could not win the war, they wanted to tie down the United States in Nicaragua. But Gorbachev then signaled that he wanted out. For the Soviets, this was never a Cuba (Miller, 1989: 188–216).

So Reagan administration rhetoric switched away from the Soviet threat to the threat of indigenous communism, declaring that the Sandinistas provided an undesirable model of revolution to the hemisphere. The Sandinistas wanted national economic development, social reform, and popular mobilization, and these were the goals of many Latin American leftists. National development was broadly supported among the middle class too, and even among some planter families. The extent of support for reform depended on how far the Sandinistas would go, while the popular mobilization program alienated the middle class. But aware of the power of the planters, the Sandinistas compromised. They started off well, doubling literacy and introducing a health service that slashed infant mortality rates. They began land reform by expropriating unused land (the standard Latin American program). Nationalizations were almost all of Somoza family property. Between 1979 and 1983 GDP per capita rose 7 percent while that of Central America as a whole declined 15 percent. They encouraged mass participation in grassroots organizations. In 1984 they held the first free elections the country had known and won 63 percent of the vote (Walker, 1997).

What would have happened had the United States not then devastated the country? Coatsworth (1994) suggests the Sandinistas might have resembled the Mexican PRI, with a fairly mild one-party rule. The Sandinistas would have lost the support of the planters anyway, but the scorched earth war lost them far more support, forcing them to pour resources into war not development, and to centralize and militarize. They became dependent on the more extreme parts of their popular base, which were providing most of their fighters. The planter class transferred its support to the Contras; the middle class preferred peace (Paige, 1997: 37–41, 305–12). In the closely fought election of

1990 a center-Right coalition just won, helped over the finish line by a generous American aid program promised only to them. The Reagan policy was successful for it removed the Sandinistas from power (today they once again form
the government, but a moderate one). But the Sandinista legacy was that mass
organizations of workers, peasants, and women continued to play important
roles (Walker, 1997).

In between sporadic interventions, life in the hemisphere went on. The United
States was viewed positively in other ways. Its popular culture was embraced
through Hollywood, rock music, and baseball, and many Latin Americans emi-
grated to the United States. The saying went "Yankee go home – and take me
with you." Trade and investment relations were pursued through negotiation,
not intimidation. Aid programs increased in the 1950s and again in the 1980s,
though their absolute level was low and they were subordinated to political
purposes (Griffin, 1991). U.S. business did not act as a single bloc. Firms seeking cheap labor, as did agrobusiness, supported more conservative regimes
than did more capital-intensive business. Latin America remained basically
a source of raw materials and foodstuffs. But some internationally oriented
U.S. corporations had supported ISI policies, which could help them export
capital goods for local industries or set up factories in the hemisphere behind
ISI tariff walls. They also lobbied the United States to reduce its tariffs, so that
they could export their goods back home, but this was denied (Cox, 1994).
Capitalist interests were usually united in opposing redistributive reforms.
Then the debt crisis brought another harsh phase of American economic policies to the hemisphere from the 1980s, though eventually with some democratizing benefits, as we see in Chapter 6. Though America's strategic interests in
Central and especially South America were low, business lobbies were more
important here than in many parts of the world, and they were dominated by
short-term profit concerns. This is why Marxists offer a quite good analysis of
U.S. foreign policy in the Americas.

Latin American conclusion

Throughout the period the United States had practiced informal empire laced
with covert operations, proxies, and gunboats, especially in nearby Central
America. It managed to install and maintain client regimes because its power
tipped over a local balance of power that favored the dominant economic
classes, the officer corps, and the church hierarchy – the oligarchs – against
centrists and leftists. Knight (2008: 36) says elite support made American
empire "a species of 'empire by invitation,'" but this is overstretching the term
for nobody asked the people. In the hemisphere the United States won not
because it represented more attractive ideals (as Gaddis, 1997, suggests) but
because it put more economic and military power in its clients' hands. This
worked better here than in East and Southeast Asia because the elites' powers

had not been weakened by war or anticolonialism. U.S. policy was dictated by its perception of a blend of cold war and capitalist needs. American leaders said the policy succeeded in keeping the Soviets out of the hemisphere. But since the locals did not want the Soviets anyway, this could have been attained by more humane means. One may eat garlic to keep the vampires away, and they do not come. But that is because vampires do not exist. Business interests, especially in extractive industries, believed the policy succeeded because it kept profits high. But a more progressive American policy would almost certainly have boosted the economic development of the hemisphere – and so American profits too.

U.S. claims to be introducing democracy to the hemisphere, trumpeted at home, were specious. In reality authoritarian stability was preferred. It trumped a democracy that was seen to carry the risk of instability. The United States feared democracy because it knew that movements seeking democracy also had social citizenship goals, and it feared the combination might lead to communism. U.S. business that had labor intensive operations in the hemisphere (above all, plantations) had an interest in suppressing leftists in order to keep wages down. Since this was the capitalist fraction that lobbied hardest in Washington, it is difficult to separate out politicians' paranoia from its interests. Of course, Americans did not see this as paranoia. Seeing reform as risky, they reasoned, Why take risks if we have the military power to ensure stability? That is why capitalism alone is not the explanation. American military power in the region gave both the motive and the method of intervention. At relatively low cost, U.S. policy makers felt they could make sure that leftists did not accede to or remain in power. And they were right, even if it was not the best policy on either practical or moral grounds. So this part of American informal empire had two necessary causes, and in combination they constituted a sufficient cause: a drive for short-term profit and avoidance of instability/communism whose paranoid element was masked by confidence in military power. Note the continuity from American imperialism in this hemisphere at the beginning of the twentieth century, described in Volume 3, chapter 3. The main change was that fears of instability had previously had more of a racist than a communist sense.

There were always policy dissidents. The State Department and the CIA sometimes divided over policy. Congress in the 1950s was a bastion of fanatic anticommunism but later became keener on promoting democracy. Some Democratic administrations were a little more progressive – Truman's early years, Kennedy with reservations, and Carter. There were also regional differences. The South was the most conservative region and the Southwest had most defense industries. Both favored aggressive internationalism (Trubowitz, 1998: chap. 4). But nationally the climate of anticommunist patriotism combined with public indifference (low cost, no conscription, little knowledge) to stifle debate. The costs of intervention were paid for by taxpayers without their knowledge, not by politicians at election times (Dominguez, 1999: 48). When nasty covert operations were exposed, like those in Guatemala and Nicaragua, the publicity they received was limited, no one was fired, and politicians were little harmed. Men like Oliver North got away with murder.

The effect was felt down the bureaucratic hierarchy. Embassies were instructed to spend an inordinate amount of time chronicling the activities of the few local communists and other leftists, and they wrote reports tailored to the hierarchy's expectations. If they reported that local communists were pitifully few and disorganized, they feared they would lose career credit (Lowenthal, 1995: 154–5). American politicians did not understand a local political climate that differed from the United States. Reform of all stripes and simple anti-Americanism were often proclaimed by their authors as revolutionary, but this was the empty rhetoric of factions that were often little more than networks of local families or caudillos, with very little ideological ballast.

The United States was not all-powerful, however, and it was often deceived by its Latino friends. U.S. military aid and training programs did not involve the United States' subverting Latin American militaries (as Huggins, 1998, and Gill, 2004, suggest). Local militaries realized the utility of telling U.S. military attaches, arms suppliers, and friends acquired at the School of the Americas that their political opponents were communists (Atkins & Wilson, 1998: 128–36). Embassy Americans met socially with wealthy educated elites, imbibing their political analysis. A conservative slant calling all leftists communists was then forced into the simple dichotomy of the cold war for consumption back in Washington (Gambone, 2001; Miller, 1989: 49). Latin American elites were finishing off their education at American universities, the Bolivian ambassador to Washington played golf with the Eisenhower family, Trujillo had his friends on Capitol Hill. Class solidarity undergirded informal American imperialism in the hemisphere. This had one progressive implication for it undermined race prejudice. The racism that had pervaded State Department documents in earlier periods (seen in Volume 3, chapter 3) disappeared – aided by the success of the civil rights movement in the United States.

U.S. politics now fueled not racism but anticommunism in the hemisphere. From 1959 administrations feared another Cuba more than they did overreaction – as in Johnson's sending the marines into the Dominican Republic. An imaginary missile gap between the United States and the Soviet Union was exploited by Kennedy to win the election of 1960. Johnson's fear of being the first U.S. president to lose a major war in Vietnam helped overcome his perception that the war was futile. Carter was blamed for losing countries over which the United States actually had no power, like Afghanistan, Mozambique, or South Yemen. But contrary to the fear revealed in American public opinion polls at the time, the Soviets were not making global gains. For them, Cuba briefly flickered and then became a drag. Rising nationalism hurt the Soviets just as much as the United States. Neither could control it around the globe. Yet blaming changes in Afghanistan or South Yemen or Iran on Carter seemed plausible to many Americans, especially given his botched attempt to rescue the American hostages in Teheran (Wiarda, 1995: 70–3).

Those with imperial strike power think they do not need to take risks. The drive for imperial security and the guarantee seemingly provided by military power were primary. But the guarantee was delusory. U.S. control was less than apologists or critics assert. The proxy regimes were not puppets, and they manipulated American fears of communism. The sanctions available to the United States were military intervention and economic blockade. These could block and destroy more than they could build. The United States could block the entry into government of leftists. If leftists did reach power, the United States could destabilize them. If all this failed, from a distance they could launch proxy militaries or economic blockades to devastate the country, as they did in Cuba and Nicaragua. But exemplary repression was unlikely to fulfill positive goals. Whereas American policy in the West had broadly conformed to the American mission statement of conferring peace, development, and democracy, and policy in East Asia was eventually reaching toward a similar end, in the Americas this was not so. On balance American empire continued to hinder peace, development, and democracy in this hemisphere. The policy was irrational, driving centrists in the hemisphere to the Left, worsening instability and weakening economies. The farther away a country was from the United States, the better it did. In its own hemisphere only local oligarchies and labor-intensive American business benefited much from American empire. By the end of the century, says Brands (2010: 268), the sway of democracy in the hemisphere "was only slightly greater than during the late 1950s and its quality was probably less than it had been in the wake of World War II." Latin American progress did not really begin until the first decade of the twenty-first century, by which time democracy, a moderate Left, and a moderate Right were ascendant and the attention of the United States was elsewhere. Though the travails of Latin America were mainly the responsibility of the locals, the United States had persistently made them worse. The American empire was negative in the Americas – and so too was the Soviet empire.

Frustrating proxies in the Middle East

This region was very strategic, was close to the Soviet Union, and had most of the world's oil, the only major commodity truly indispensable for advanced economies and especially for militaries. World War II had shown the United States just how crucial Middle East oil would be. Of the allies' oil supplies 80 percent had come from within the United States, but domestic supplies were dwindling while Saudi reserves were known to be enormous. In 1945 the State Department advised President Truman that Saudi oil was "a stupendous source of strategic power, and one of the greatest material prizes in human history" (Klare, 2004: 30–2). Though the United States might have left oil to purely market forces, since those who possess it need to sell it, the United States has never done so, preferring the supposed security provided by military and political methods of control. Oil had already attracted Britain and France, and their imperialism had not left a helpful legacy for the region. They had carved up Ottoman provinces between them in the period 1916–20. Iran was also a British Protectorate, providing oil for Britain but little benefit for the locals. In both world wars Arabs fought for the British in return for promised independence. Both times they were betrayed. This was in contrast to the Jews, Arabs noted, who had not fought for the British but were nonetheless given a state carved out of Arab lands. After 1945 the United States replaced Britain as the main imperial power, but it remained offshore, focused on acquiring oil through allies. The similar involvement of the Soviets in the region deterred actual imperial conquest (by either superpower). The maximal power attainable would be informal empire, through offshore balancing and proxies. In fact, the United States gradually evolved to an explicit doctrine of direct intervention only when there was a real threat of disruption of the oil supply.

During the cold war the United States mostly allied with tribal monarchies, while the Soviets allied with urban nationalists who had more progressive goals. But since they lacked mass support, these regimes turned toward despotism. Only in Turkey and Iran did agrarian smallholders, petty urban traders, and workers develop much collective mobilization. The "socialist" regimes of Nasser in Egypt and Ba'athists in Iraq and Syria were in reality rule by military officers attempting development but degenerating into despotism. Monarchies possessed most of the oil, becoming rich rentier states, acquiring and dispensing oil wealth without need to tax their subjects. In the West, democracy had been propelled by resistance to taxation, but this propulsion was lacking here. When we control for intervening variables, not Islam but oil and large landholdings are correlated with authoritarian regimes (Bromley, 1997). For most Arabs, oil was a curse, "the devil's excrement," generating corrupt despots and grotesque inequality.

Neither the United States nor the Soviet Union could easily find proxy allies who would be useful across the whole region. The United States acquired Turkey as an ally, having protected it in 1946 from Stalin's attempt to convert Turkish border provinces into a client Kurdish state. In return Turkey became a NATO member, hosting U.S. bases positioned against the Soviets. But Turkey was not an oil producer; nor would it agree to be used as a proxy against other Muslim countries. Saudi Arabia was an ally since a 1945 deal in which Roosevelt had promised military protection in return for access to its oil – and the Saudis had more oil than anyone else. The Saudi Wahhabi form of Islam was also fiercely anticommunist. The deal provided the United States with one-sixth of its crude oil imports, yielded profits to a web of U.S. and Saudi oil businesses, and committed the Saudis to invest oil profits in the United States. Once this was done, Saudi investments became tied to the health of the American economy, and this plus the more than $50 billion the Saudi monarchy has received in U.S. military aid made it willing to pump more or less oil according to the state of the market in order to maintain the stability of oil prices (Klare, 2004). Saudi Arabia has been America's most useful ally in the Middle East. But their relationship has one problem: its extent must remain hidden from the two peoples. If revealed, it would be embarrassing for both. So the United States cannot openly influence Saudi domestic politics or openly use the kingdom in regional ventures, though the Saudis were heavily involved in the covert Iran-Contra affair and in funneling aid to the Islamist rebels in Afghanistan. But this has been interdependence not empire. Each side gained the one thing it wanted, oil at stable prices in return for protection (O'Reilly, 2008: 70).

The United States tried to increase its influence by backing coups. In 1949 in Syria and 1952 in Egypt their clients seized power but were then overthrown in turn by nationalist officers. Greater success occurred in Iran in 1953. The elected premier Mosaddeq headed a rather fragile nationalist coalition of diverse political groups. They were united in their desire to nationalize the Anglo-Iranian Oil Company, which they did in 1951, but on little else. He was then trying to negotiate a better oil deal than the British would accept. The British played hardball and would not compromise. They organized a boycott of Iranian oil and relied on their control of Iraqi and Kuwaiti oil fields to pump more oil. Iranian oil production fell dramatically, as did Mosaddeq's popularity, even among his base support in sections of the middle echelons of the bazaaris (merchants, shopkeepers, and artisans), workers, and the new state-dependent middle class. His main enemies were the shah, landowners, and conservative politicians, while Mosaddeq's liberalism and secularism antagonized the army and the clergy too. As the situation polarized, he became more dependent on leftists, especially the Tudeh communist party, and seemed intent on establishing a republic. This further alienated monarchists, landowners, and much of the middle class. It also turned the Eisenhower administration against him. To let his rule continue might lead to economic difficulties and then (reasoned Americans) to chaos, opening the door to a communist coup – the usual American nightmare. This fear grew as Eisenhower succeeded Truman and Churchill succeeded Attlee. Conservatives feared that nationalist reforms led to communism, with China and Korea invoked as analogous cases. Churchill played on this, feeding Washington false information about Tudeh strength and Mosaddeq's supposed communist leanings (Kandil, 2012; Parsa, 1989: 41–5; Marsh, 2005; Bill, 1988: 85).

As the situation polarized, Mosaddeq rightly felt threatened by looming coups. His response was to dissolve parliament, but according to the constitution only the shah could do this. By this move he lost much of his legitimacy except on the Left. Violent crowds were mobilized by conservatives, landowners, and the ayatollahs, helped by the CIA distribution of large bribes to the rioters, ignoring administration vacillation back in Washington (Kinzer, 2004; Gasiorowski & Byrne, 2004). The police and army were paralyzed: did they support the constitutional prime minister or the equally constitutional monarch and Parliament? They did nothing until after Mosaddeq had been hounded out, and then they merely ratified the outcome. This was not a military coup or an American initiative. It was mainly an internal civilian affair launched against a man who had lost the support of most of the forces that had put him in power. The American (and British) contribution says Kandil (2012) was merely "pushing open an unlatched door."

The Tudeh Party was now destroyed and there were purges in the army, police, and civil administration. The monarch, Mohammad Reza Shah Pahlavi, returned with enhanced power. The coup had stifled the chances of democracy and national autonomy, thereby alienating the growing new middle and working classes, and the opposition always viewed the shah as an American puppet (Kian-Thiébaut, 1999: 99–119). While bogged down in Vietnam, the United States relied on the shah and the Saudis to protect its regional interests (O'Reilly, 2008). For a time the shah was the only loyal ally the United States ever found in the area, aiding pro-American forces across the region, though this alliance weakened through time. Yet Iran was neither Arab nor Sunni, which meant it could not influence other oil producers into a pro-American line. Nor did the shah last forever. I deal with the revolution that in 1979 overthrew him in Chapter 9.

U.S. administrations focused on the free flow of oil, excluding Soviet influence (as stated in policy documents NSC 5401 and NSC 5820/1), and at first protecting Western oil companies against a rising tide of economic nationalism. This had already succeeded in passing UN resolutions against concessions of sovereign natural resources to foreign companies, and nationalization was beginning to attract all the oil-producing regimes, whether of the Right or the Left. Eisenhower and Dulles hoped moderate Arab nationalists might become allies yet undercut this by viewing their declared stance of "positive neutralism" as a tool of communism. They preferred conservatives, but since these seemed vulnerable to revolt, they urged them to introduce reforms, though with scant success. Eisenhower, Kennedy, and Johnson also had little success in dealing with Arab–Israeli conflict. This was due more to Israeli intransigence and Nasser's ambition than American failings. Israel would not yield on its security concerns nor its nuclear weapons program, while Nasser spurned tentative American advances and would not wean Egypt off Soviet weapons (American cancellation of aid to his Aswan Dam project did not help). The United States failed to isolate Egypt and was reduced to defending its friends with unpopular interventions in Lebanon, Syria, and Jordan. In 1958 Syria joined in a union with Egypt. Matters looked bad for the United States, but luckily in 1962 Nasser went off to his

Vietnam. Forty thousand Egyptian troops intervened against Saudi-backed conservatives in the Yemeni civil war but failed and withdrew (O'Reilly, 2008: 71–4).

This was accompanied by strengthening ties with Israel, buttressed by a religious-cum-racial preference for Jews over Arabs. In Hollywood's "American Orientalism" Jews were increasingly portrayed as brave settlers, surrogate Americans, founding a new and democratic nation beset by more primitive indigenous peoples (Little, 2002; Mart, 2006). But there were also electoral concerns. American politicians soon came to believe that two major states, New York and then also Florida, could not be won without placating highly organized and well-funded Jewish pro-Israel lobbies. U.S. administrations became beset by competing strategic goals. They wanted Islamic support against the Soviets, but their oil dependence on the Saudis left them supporting a reactionary regime that was trying to subvert more leftist Arab regimes, while the unpopular concessions of the oil companies and U.S. support for Israel alienated all the Arabs. The lobbying from the oil companies favored oil-producing states and restraint of the Israelis. While U.S. administrations did try to restrain the Israelis, they failed, since the Israelis knew that ultimately the United States would not desert them. Thus, despite his doubts, Kennedy sold Israel state-of-the-art Hawk missiles since the Soviets had supplied tanks and planes to Egypt. Johnson then ended pressure on Israel to abandon its nuclear program or submit to nuclear inspections. Hopes of an Israeli–Palestinian deal now receded and American influence among Arabs weakened further. The Ba'athist coup d'état in Iraq in 1963 then made oil nationalization there inevitable. The United States, recognizing the writing on the wall, ignored the demands of the oil companies for forceful intervention and attempted to mediate the dispute. But the Iraqis and Libyans, buoyed by Soviet promises of assistance and by separate deals made with France and other countries, rejected this and went ahead with nationalization. At the end of the 1960s and beginning of the 1970s the formation of the OPEC cartel was also cutting back Western power in the region. This episode had revealed the divergence of interests between the U.S. government and the oil companies, as well as the limits of both their power. The ideology of nationalism continued to trim back economic and political imperialism.

Luckily the decline of Nasser and the degeneration of Arab socialism into military dictatorship also weakened Soviet influence. Only in Iraq had the Soviets had any chance of having an oil producer as an ally (Bass, 2003; Ben-Zvi, 1998; Yaqub, 2003; Hahn, 2004). Soviet activities then focused on Afghanistan and the Horn of Africa, which might look strategic on a map of the world but contained little of value. Two of the strategic goals of the United States (ensuring an oil supply and keeping the Soviets out) were achieved, despite Israel. There were few hints of an American democratic mission. This would not have been realistic given the nature of the allied regimes.

In 1980, responding to Soviet pressure on Afghanistan, the Carter Doctrine was enunciated. He declared: "Let our position be absolutely clear: an attempt by any outside force to gain control of the Persian Gulf region will be regarded as an assault on the vital interests of the United States of America. And such an assault will be repelled by any means necessary, including military force." Oil was too valuable to be left to market forces. The United States would stay off-shore until an actual crisis occurred, its navy in a threatening posture, relying on a balance of power among local states to keep the peace – "offshore balancing." In 1981 Reagan added explicit defense of the House of Saud, declaring, "We will not permit it to be an Iran," and he expanded Carter's military deployments into Centcom, a separate U.S. Middle East Command. The American military stance was toughening (Klare, 2004). But Reagan's intervention in the Lebanese civil war was a disaster, resulting in the deaths of 241 U.S. Marines in the first major postwar suicide bombing in the region. The force withdrew – as did French marines, also taking casualties from terrorist bombs. This led to the formation of Hezbollah and the spread of suicide bombing. However, punitive air raids on Libya in 1986 made Colonel Qaddafi more pliant. These interventions were not mainly driven by the cold war but by the conflict between American imperialism and three distinct expressions of anti-imperialism – the nationalism of a single state, pan-Arab nationalism, and a nascent Islamism.

The United States moved into ever-closer relations with Israel. Eisenhower had threatened Israel, Carter was even-handed in his attempts to draw Israel and Palestine to the negotiating table, and later presidents all urged the Israelis toward the conference table. Yet the Israelis knew that practically anything they did would not cause the United States to desert them – or even lessen its aid to them – for electoral reasons. Israel had the United States over a barrel, not of oil but of votes. This was not to the liking of the oil companies, who by now did not want to alienate the oil countries. In the 1973 war they urged the Nixon administration not to rush to Israel's support by airlifting it military supplies, but Nixon replied that his first obligation was to Israel. The airlift went ahead, revealing once again that American imperialism was not simply pursued at the behest of capitalism (Kelly, forthcoming). Kissinger made his own damaging contribution, encouraging Israeli militarism and settlement policies and rejecting Soviet overtures for broader peace negotiations. A pro-Israel bias then characterized American policy, helping frustrate a peace deal and alienating Arab states. This has lasted right up to the present (Tyler, 2009; Khalidi, 2009). Of course, Israel was a useful ally in covert operations in the cold war, but so too were both Iran and the Saudis. The decisive pressures were from the Jewish pro-Israel lobby in the United States and the emerging military-industrial complex of the two countries. Israel has even been the dominant partner in this alliance, able to call the American bluff whenever it wishes – the tail wagging the dog. American foreign policy in the Middle East has contained a gigantic contradiction. America's most vital interest in the region is to secure oil, yet its

closest ally by far is Israel, the one country that most angers all the oil producing countries. Not realpolitik but confusion is in the driving seat in U.S. policy
toward the Middle East.

The OPEC oil cartel of the early 1970s drove up oil prices. This was the
only time that the oil producers acted collectively to restructure market forces.
Since the cartel was led by American allies, such as Saudi Arabia and Iran
(still under the shah), the United States was not going to intervene, revealing
the pointlessness of using military power to secure oil supplies. One does not
invade one's friends, yet they are the ones putting on the economic screws.
The sensible oil policy is to let market forces rule while accepting the market
manipulations of one's friends.

The United States passed on the price hikes to its citizens, who now paid
much more for their gas. Price increases also lowered GDP and raised unemployment. Yet the oil companies quite liked the embargo since it drove up
prices and their profits – once again their interests were not the same as those
of the state. The administration now struck a deal with the oil producing countries. They could make more profit, but they would invest it in the West, recycling their petrodollars. The oil producers could also use their profits to buy
arms abroad. Half their purchases were from the United States, a policy that
made another major American industry happy. Of course, the consequences
were also felt by the Europeans: pain for the citizens, profit for their oil companies and armaments industries.

Then there were two deployments of sons-of-bitches. The first were the
Islamists deployed against the Soviets in Afghanistan; the second was Saddam
Hussein deployed against Islamist Iran. Both received military aid and were useful until they turned against America. Though the United States was increasing
its military pressure on the region, it had still not found reliable, useful clients.
Some inside the Beltway fretted about the insecurity of their interests since
the United States seemed stuck with shaky oil sheikhs and unpopular Israel
as allies. The fall of the Soviet Union greatly eased the situation, but informal
American imperialism was still mainly relying on unreliable proxies. There
was no high-minded mission whatever the rhetoric. The oil was flowing but
many Americans felt this to be unfinished business and Soviet collapse seemed
to create an apparent opportunity. This was to be delusory, however, for the
main enemy of American empire in the region had never been the Soviet Union
but local anti-imperialism. I discuss the disasters that ensued at the beginning
of the next century in Chapter 10.

Conclusion

I have emphasized variations among four macroregions within the American
sphere of influence. By being geographically and historically selective, we
might describe American policies in very different ways, and this is regularly

done. Apologists and empire deniers focus on the West or contemporary Asia; Marxian critics of an imperialism subordinated to capitalism focus on the Americas; other critics of imperialism focus on the earlier period in Asia and on the whole period in the Middle East. In the West American power was not imperial but hegemonic, accepted by countries bound together in a dense network of institutions under U.S. leadership, prospering mainly through their own efforts, though assisted by economic interdependence and mutual defense led by the United States. In Asia successful development and some eventual democratization were achieved by distinctive developmental states aided by American economic generosity. This was light American hegemony reached after a period of largely unsuccessful series of U.S. military interventions.

In the American hemisphere social and political conflicts remained perennial, not enough to cause many wars or civil wars, but enough to stymie much economic or democratic development. Here some American militarism persisted throughout the cold war period in the shape of informal empire backed by gunboats, covert operations, and proxies. Gunboats were deployed against small countries in Central America, weaker, closer, and easier to invade. In the South of the continent covert operations and proxies predominated, yielding less American control. U.S. interventions did not help the region, and a policy of supporting center-Left reform initiatives would have done better. Yet U.S. administrations were reasonably content with the results in their own hemisphere. Was not communism kept out? they reasoned.

Finally, imperialism in the Middle East remained unfinished business. The region suffered in terms of both economic and democratic development from the curse of oil, while interstate conflict and the worsened Israeli-Palestinian conflict compromised American policy. Washington remained less happy here (though the Soviet Union did no better) with its combination of informal off-shore empire, military threats, and allies of limited utility or reliability. The oil did flow, but it would have flowed anyway.

Where the United States felt it could influence domestic political outcomes – and it could not do this in Europe or Japan after about 1950 – it was normally in support of conservative elites against more popular forces. There were five reasons for this. First, paranoid anticommunism, electorally popular at home, exaggerated the communist threat and misleadingly identified centrist and leftist reformers with communism. This revealed the power of ideology to trump instrumental reason. This was not so in Europe, where the United States could see the difference between communists and social democrats, probably because it needed more allies against the nearby Soviet threat. But the Soviet threat rarely materialized anywhere. In no other country did a member party of the Soviet Comintern ever gain power. Trotsky in exile had accused the Soviet Union of containing not spreading revolution, and he was largely correct (Halliday, 1999: 110–16). Second, as cold war paranoia wound down, the drift toward conservatism in America, revealed in the last chapter, substituted for fear of the Soviet Union in dampening down interest in reform abroad. Third, there was an American profit motive in interventions, stressed by Marxist writers, to permit American business to extract maximal profit abroad. This was short-sighted, however. Keeping wages low also held down consumption, economic growth, and ultimately profit. The American economy would have benefited more from reform policies in Latin America and Southeast Asia resembling those initiated by the Europeans or the East Asians. Fourth, policy was often driven more by security fears than by profit. Giving military assistance to foreign regimes to repress the Left, however exploitative they were, seemed less risky than aiding a transition to political and social citizenship. America had enough military power to avoid economic and political risk – or that was how U.S. policy makers saw it. Fifth, where links did exist between local movements and Soviet or Chinese communists, U.S. scorched earth tactics did deter others from flirting with communism. This was as savage a strategy as had been followed by earlier empires – the rationality of the grim reaper.

These motives overwhelmed most of the nobler mission statements that American leaders declaimed at home. In practice U.S. administrations valued regime stability over political freedom, and they identified authoritarian regimes with stability, and democracy with risk. The United States supported elections if its local allies won them, but projects of land reform or redistribution almost always had it reaching for the gun, usually the gun of a proxy. Some Americans advocated more progressive policies, and these briefly prevailed in 1945, in Kennedy's Alliance for Progress, and in Carter's proclamations about human rights – meaning that Democratic administrations were slightly more benign than Republican ones. As democratization spread across the world, popular pressures intensified American democratic rhetoric but not its practice. When the Soviet Union fell, American politicians finally shifted into action, though their reluctance remained palpable and lasted right through the Arab revolts of 2011. The United States also gave helpful economic assistance provided there were also strategic reasons for this. In East Asia, where the United States had realistic fears of communist advances, Japan, South Korea, and Taiwan were helped to prosperity within the American-led global economy.

The lesson that should have been drawn from Europe and East Asia was that civil, political, and social citizenship plus state-aided and American-aided economic growth was good for foreign and American economies alike. Such capitalism worked well in Europe, but the United States limited it at home and only permitted it elsewhere where it desperately needed cooperation from the locals against communism. In the end, therefore, U.S. imperialism was neither very beneficent nor very rational, except where communism did loom large. The overall conclusion should be that U.S. imperialism/hegemony could have done better by aiding instead of repressing reformers. In that respect it was more like the British and Japanese empires than Americans have cared to acknowledge.

Nonetheless, the imperial yoke had lightened through time as Americans saw communist threats receding. American power on foreign soil became less than either apologists or critics assert (as had also been so with the British Empire). The United States had far more power to destroy or to block than to induce positive change abroad. It probably had less than most previous empires since it sent out no settlers and since the global rise of the nation-state and nationalism produced stiffer anti-imperial resistance. American dominance became more hegemony than empire, global but fairly shallow. In the new millennium the United States was to attempt to buck this trend, as we will see in Chapter 10.

Finally the Soviet enemy was seen off. As the weapons of war became more and more expensive, the Soviets had to sacrifice economic growth to military strength, and once nuclear weapons made war irrational and economic competition became the main thrust of the cold war, the West had a big advantage. After 1951 China did not even try to rival the West in military terms, though it was later to achieve comparable economic success by blending socialism with capitalism. The end of communism is generally seen in the United States as an American triumph, and it partially was. But we shall see that communism essentially perished because of its own contradictions, principally political and economic, leading also to ideological disintegration.

6 Neoliberalism, rise and faltering, 1970–2000

Introduction: Neoliberalism

Here I will chart the shift in the dominant form of political economy from neo-Keynesianism to neoliberalism before moving onto neoliberal tribulations as the century ended. Chapter 11 will follow up by analyzing what I call the Great Neoliberal Recession of 2008. I already introduced neo-Keynesianism in Chapters 2 and 5, so I only need to recapitulate it briefly here The postwar political economy was not actually Keynesian but a synthesis between it and classical market economics, labeled variously as neo-Keynesianism (the term I will use), commercial Keynesianism, or embedded liberalism. The synthesis resulted from introducing Keynesian mechanisms into neoclassical general equilibrium models. This aimed at full employment through mildly inflationary stimulation though within budgets that were near balance.

Neo-Keynesianism was not merely economic policy. It was also the product of a broader ideology of reformism that embodied some pragmatic compromise of the class struggle that swept across the Western world as a result of World War II. This war, like the Great War, had a radicalizing effect on the world. The explosion of labor unrest after the war resembled that after World War I though it was less in the advanced countries and a lot higher in the colonies (Silver, 2003: 125–30). And whereas unrest in the colonial world led on to political revolutions, the outcome in the advanced world was consistently reformist, essentially because the victors were by now themselves reformist – even the United States – and because they occupied and reconstructed the vanquished powers. Across almost the whole West and in Japan this intensified social citizenship in the sense of the pursuit of full employment, state redistribution through the tax system, full recognition of the rights of labor unions and of free collective bargaining, and the welfare state. This was the golden age of capitalism.

The neoliberal turn began in the late 1970s as a reaction against not just neo-Keynesianism, but also import substitution industrialization (ISI) in less developed economies, as well as the Bretton Woods system of the repression of capital movements. These had all emphasized the role of the state in promoting capitalist development. Implementing more market-oriented neoliberal policies began in earnest after 1980. In this chapter I chart their rise, successes, and failures. I try to disentangle neoliberalism from other contemporary pressures on states and from the conservatism with which neoliberalism allied. I distinguish between neoliberalism's collective and distributive powers. As we shall see, its collective power – its efficiency – has been low. Neoliberalism has endured more because of its distributive power, which has been exercised on behalf of powerful classes and nations over the less powerful. Yet neoliberalism's penetration of the world has been uneven. I reject the tendency of some to credit it with enormous global power (e.g., Harvey, 2005; Wacquant, 2002). Only in the Anglophone countries has it possessed overwhelming power, and then only in alliance with a conservative revival.

Neoliberalism involves market fundamentalism. Its "efficient market hypothesis" suggests that markets always maximize welfare, while the pursuit of short-term shareholder value ensures maximal efficiency by enterprises (Davis, 2009). Let economic power relations rip, unobstructed by the state or collective organizations, and they will produce the optimal result. Such a sentiment permeated the neoclassical economics dominant in the Anglophone countries since the 1970s and it permeates many business journals, notably the *Wall Street Journal* and the *Economist*. Neoliberalism urges freeing up commodity markets and international capital flows, deregulating labor markets, balancing state budgets, and generally reducing state intervention in the economy. In the South of the world these policies have been implemented in structural adjustment programs imposed on countries in debt by the IMF, the World Bank, and other international banks. In the North neoliberals seek the deregulation of finance and privatization. Everywhere they advocated rolling back labor unions and welfare states. Neoliberalism has a vision of capitalism freed from the state – economic dominating political power, the transnational dominating the national.

Neoliberal economics is embedded in an ideology seeing markets as natural and guaranteeing individual freedom, as in the title of Milton Friedman's famous book *Capitalism and Freedom* (1962). All-embracing, it is a genuine ideology, like socialism or Christianity, perceiving the active presence of good and evil in society – it was not just that Keynesian policies were considered to be inefficient, but also that they would lead to serfdom. Neoliberalism departs from nineteenth-century liberalism in two respects: it sees no problem with large corporations and it is very conscious of the horrors of early twentieth-century socialist and fascist statism, hence the title of Friedrich Hayek's *The Road to Serfdom* (1944). As a refugee in Britain, convinced it would introduce socialist policies after the war, he claimed this would again lead to serfdom. Hayek did not resist all state regulation but favored limiting it to securing the rule of law and equal access for all to the market and providing a minimal level of social insurance for the needy.

Neoliberalism has four theoretical weaknesses. First, markets are not in fact natural. As Polanyi put it when writing about nineteenth-century laissez-faire, "There was nothing natural about *laissez-faire*; free markets could never have come into being merely by allowing things to take their course. Just as cotton manufactures were created by the help of protective tariffs, export bounties, and indirect wage subsidies, *laissez-faire* was enforced by the state" (1957 edition: 139). Markets require rules and norms diffused through society, enforced by governments. These guarantee property rights, rules of exchange, and forms of legitimate control that make markets predictable and efficient. States are not antithetical to markets; they are necessary to them. Moreover, Polanyi noted that even in the "self-regulating market" of nineteenth-century laissez-faire counterembedding movements had emerged, securing government interventions as diverse as labor laws, land laws, tariff protection, central banking regulation, and international monetary coordination. Through these mechanisms diverse classes – workers, landlords, and capitalists – engaged in self-protection against the disruptions of markets. What Polanyi could not see was that after his own time there might be another countermovement toward further disembedding – neoliberalism.

Second, neoliberalism is a utopian ideology, just like socialism. A self-regulating market could never rule a real society. Just like socialism, real-world neoliberalism needs to make compromises with reality and with other power actors; that means that it has varied guises, some moderate, others more extreme – reformists and revolutionaries. There are those who want to cut back the state mildly or selectively, and there are others who want root-and-branch change. In the real world neoliberalism often is captured and used by distinct interest groups who then undermine its principles, as we see in the case of corrupted privatizations. As Harvey notes, neoliberalism as theory and as practice pull in different directions. Seeing practice as primary, he says neoliberalism is less "a utopian project to realize a theoretical design for the reorganization of international capitalism" than "a political project . . . to restore the power of economic elites." I partially agree, as will become clear later. Neoliberalism has also in practice been aligned with conservative politicians seeking to further the "national interest" against other nations, and to enforce morality, big defense budgets, and zero tolerance police and prison policies – all paradoxically characteristics of powerful states. Harvey sees these as necessary for market dominance, since markets alone would produce chaos (2005: 19, 82). But this is too functionalist and gives no autonomy to conservatives. Furthermore, neoliberalism is inherently transnational and should have no truck with nationalism. If neoliberals endorse statism or nationalism it is either because their conservatism undermines their neoliberalism or because they see an alliance with conservatives as being their best means of getting some of their desired reforms. Neoliberals, like socialists, must compromise with power realities to achieve any of their goals. So within what is often called the neoliberal movement I distinguish four tendencies: principled neoliberalism elevating markets and individualism, the interests of capitalists, the interests of political elites, and a conservatism that uses the state to enforce morality, law and order, nationalism, and militarism. Though there is overlap among all these, it is useful analytically to separate them.

Third, markets do not abolish power, as neoliberals claim; they distribute it differently. To give more power to markets increases the power of those who already possess more market resources (like property or scarce skills) and reduces the power of those with fewer market resources. The tendency of some neoliberals to oppose antitrust laws (they believe large corporations embody efficiencies of scale) encourages even more concentration of power in markets, which in turn gives large corporations greater power (Crouch, 2011). By reducing political power it also denies the people the use of state power to effect radical change. Thus it has a tendency to emasculate political democracy. As Streeck (2011) emphasizes, there is an inherent tension between capitalism and democracy that is at the fore in neoliberalism.

So the economists' view of efficiency – collective power – must be supplemented by the distributive power question, Who benefits? Like all economic programs, neoliberalism benefits some more than others and provokes resistance among those it harms. Here I focus on which classes and nations were winners and losers, and which losers had the power to resist. Neoliberalism's policies benefit investors over workers, the rich over the poor. Neoliberals agree in the short run, arguing that this is necessary to provide incentives for investment, but they add that in the medium term the resulting economic growth will trickle down to all. Since markets are natural, they are best left alone. If government tries to regulate them, this will distort market prices and worsen the economy for all. So I assess whether benefit has trickled down to the citizens. For nations its partiality differs. It appears to favor the home-base nations of its core sectors, especially finance capital, but ultimately it harms nations, rich or poor, that have relatively little economic sovereignty.

Fourth, the neoliberal connection between markets and freedom is only contingent. Other factors being equal, decentralized markets do protect against authoritarianism, while market capitalism has proved its overall economic superiority to state-run economies. However, in the contemporary world a minimal state dominated by the market may endanger democratic freedoms. I have argued in my volumes that freedom requires a pluralist balance among the sources of social power. The Soviet Union destroyed freedom because all four power sources were fused in the hands of a single party-state elite. Neoliberalism is not nearly that bad, but by subordinating political to economic power in a context where economic power has become highly concentrated, it restricts human freedom. We do not live in that idealized eighteenth-century English society in which economic power was widely distributed among tenant farmers, artisans, merchants, and manufacturers. Today's giant corporations and banks are not democratic but authoritarian, ruled by a board of directors, legally responsible only to shareholders, among whom authoritarian financial institutions also dominate. There are strong tendencies to oligopoly and monopoly, as well as to encroachments on political democracy. Milton Friedman proclaimed that capitalism "promotes political freedom because it separates economic power from political power" (1962: 9). In the past it might have, but not today. Most advanced states today are much more democratic than are giant corporations, and it is important to keep them that way, and to preserve them free of corporate corruption. There cannot be genuine democracy without pluralist political checks against economic authoritarianism.

The triumph and travails of Neo-Keynesianism

As we shall see, the neoliberal turn was caused by changes in economic, political, and ideological power relations. Though postwar capitalism also presupposed the global pacification provided by American military power (Chapters 2 and 5), by the 1970s this was largely invisible, and so military power plays only a marginal role in this chapter. Explanations of the neoliberal turn generally focus on the problems of Keynesianism, ISI, and Bretton Woods.

I resume discussion of the advanced countries in terms of a classification into three basic types, the Anglophone (Anglo for short), Nordic, and continental European (Euro) countries. World War II had a radical effect on most of the Anglos as the people were repaid for greater sacrifices than during the first war. The term "welfare state" was first used in a positive sense in 1941 by Archbishop Temple, who saw it as the ideal for which Britain was fighting against the warfare state of the Axis powers. British wage levels rose in the war, and the income tax became more progressive. In 1939, the standard rate had been 29 percent with surtax at 41 percent on incomes above £50,000. Ten million people were liable for tax. By 1944–5 the standard rate was 50 percent, with surtax at 48 percent for incomes above £20,000, and there were 14 million taxpayers. An excess profits tax raised more until 1946. The United States experienced even bigger shifts. Reductions in exemption levels left taxpayers with incomes of only $500 taxed at the bottom rate of 23 percent; those with incomes greater than $1 million faced a top rate of 94 percent. The number of taxpayers rose from 4 million in 1939 to 43 million in 1945.

Progressive taxes became difficult to change afterward since they now had a mass constituency of support. Though the war, followed immediately by the cold war, ultimately hindered welfare reform in the United States, conservatives could not undo previous achievements in social security nor alter the framework of progressive taxation. Instead, congressmen of both parties wrote in all manner of special exemptions and incentives. The tax code became very complex, and this reduced but did not eliminate its overall progressive direction (Steinmo, 1993: 136–44; McKibbin, 1998: 118–9). World War II also boosted progressive taxes and welfare states in the United Kingdom, Australia, Canada, and New Zealand. Baldwin (1990: 116–33) emphasizes the role of middle-class pressure in this period, and the war had increased the solidarity of the people, an alliance of working and middle classes disenchanted with the old regime elites who led them into the war.

Britain emerged from World War II with the most developed welfare state – a free health service paid out of progressive income and wealth taxes, the biggest subsidized public housing program, and (somewhat basic) old age and widows' pensions. In 1950 Britain had the highest proportion of government expenditures to GNP of the nine European countries for which data were available (Kohl, 1981: 315). From the 1950s the Anglos spent less on social policies (Iversen & Soskice, 2009: 472–3), but introducing taxation changes the picture. The taxes raised by the Nordics and Euros were more regressive than those of the Anglos from the 1950s to the 1980s (Cusack & Fuchs, 2002). The combination of spending and taxes meant that Britain and the Nordic countries formed the most progressive group from 1950 to about 1970 (Castles & Obinger, 2008). In 1965 Britain, Australia, and New Zealand were more redistributive than France, Germany, Italy, and Japan, while the United States was in the middle. The Anglos still get more revenue from progressive taxes on incomes and businesses than do the Nordics or Euros. They rely on more regressive sales and payroll taxes (Tanzi, 1969; Prasad, 2006: 25–9; Kato, 2003; OECD, 2008). Moreover, until the 1970s Canada and the United States led in measures of mass education (Lindert, 2004). The Anglos did not correspond to their stingy, inegalitarian stereotype during this period.

For the Nordics World War II brought Nazi occupation or difficult neutrality and an increase in national solidarity. For Finland the end of the war meant the discrediting of the rightist government that had allied with Hitler, and a surge in leftism. Though each Nordic country had its peculiarities, all moved toward a corporatist social democracy, helped by institutions supervised by the Nordic Council of Ministers. About thirty trans-Nordic institutions coordinate regional activities ranging from folklore to energy needs to statistics gathering – a vast store of shared information about best practices. The Swedish Social Democrats headed a national coalition government during the war. The ethos was that all classes and interest groups would sacrifice for the common good and be rewarded afterward. There were no sharp hikes in progressive taxes during the war, unlike for the Anglos, and after the war they continued focusing on transfer programs, which were more popular than taxes.

In Sweden 1946 had a large increase in the uniform flat-rate people's pension. Health legislation followed in 1953, a universal program resembling the British one, initially financed by a mixture of payroll taxes and income and inheritance taxes, and later by consumption taxes. Active labor market policy followed in the 1950s in Sweden, Denmark, and Norway, taking until the 1960s to mature into a comprehensive program, intervening in markets, redistributing between the classes and from men to women, all within corporatist structures – though Norway's maturation began earlier while Finland's started later (Steinmo, 1993: 91–3; Huber & Stephens, 2001; Klausen, 1999: chap. 5; Flora, 1983). In all four countries corporatist elements had been present early, but the wars and the depression had reinforced them.

After the defeat of fascism the Euros moved toward a social compromise model already pioneered before the war by Belgium and Holland. Helped by American and British military reconstruction policies, a grand Red-Black compromise emerged between reformist Socialists and the Social Catholicism of new Christian Democratic Parties. This compromise had eluded them during the interwar period when socialists had been anticlerical and Catholics had associated socialism with the devil. But with the extreme Right discredited and communists weakened except in France and Italy (where they had led resistance movements during the war), the Christian Democrats moved into the political center and were kept there by their Christian labor union wings. Under that compromise they matured their blend of status- and family-conscious social transfer programs. Their status and familial aspects owed more to the Christian Democrats, while their slightly redistributive drift owed more to the Left. France embodied a similar compromise though without formal Christian parties (Bradley et al., 2003: 225–6). In most of these countries the compromise was embedded inside the state in power-sharing corporatism – that is, the representatives of capital, labor, and the state hammered out compromises in government offices, unlike in the Anglo countries. The parties believed that in the interwar period laissez-faire capitalism had helped deepen the conflicts that had led toward fascism. Since the corporatist compromise seemed to guarantee social peace, it was popular. Proportional representation (PR) helped secure the compromise within parliaments, since no single interest group could dominate all others. But PR had failed to prevent fascism in the interwar period. If it worked now, it was because the major interest groups *wanted* compromise. It was achieved by political will, not by mere techniques of representation.

The Euros spoke many languages and were culturally diverse. Nonetheless, their politics tended to revolve around quasi-socialist and quasi-confessional parties, both with strong transnational links. Both major religions entered the compromise. Italy, France, Spain, Luxembourg, and Austria are overwhelmingly Catholic, while Germany, the Netherlands, and Belgium are divided between Catholics and Protestants. Moderate socialists and Social Christians, both Catholic and Protestant, supported class conciliation, though redistribution was undercut by religious support for traditional social statuses. Catholic economic and welfare policies were especially influenced by the male breadwinner model of the household, encouraging mothers' staying at home. France was a partial exception. French conservative parties bore relatively little imprint of Catholicism and so lacked the male breadwinner model (though they did subsidize mothers with children). While Social Catholics legitimated moderate levels of inequality, they were uneasy about leaving these to the capitalist market.

Overall in this period the labor movement moved toward becoming a movement of the popular classes in general, ensuring a trend toward social citizenship. However, the impact of the two wars and the depression on social citizenship had been variable, reducing the power of models predicting welfare outcomes on the basis of timeless variables like industrialization, union density, center-Left governments, and so forth. It redirected paths among the Euros and reduced path dependency among the Anglos. Though there was some continuity in lib-lab politics, large boosts and smaller reverses had come through depression and wars. Thus military power relations had also been important, while all three disasters revealed the important role of human folly. They also encourage counterfactuals – what would have transpired had the wars not occurred or had the victors been the vanquished?

The economic growth of the postwar period saw convergence around the sustained growth of welfare states and neo-Keynesian macroeconomic policies. Rising prosperity meant that social programs could be better afforded – as logic of industrialism theorists argue. But democracy was also deepening. Boosted by the sacrifices and cohesion of mass mobilization war, citizens believed they also had basic economic rights, while governments assumed they could sustain growth through full employment and mass consumption. Centrist governments sponsored welfare state extensions, while rightist governments rarely dared repeal them. All welfare states redistributed between the classes, though to varying extents principally determined for each country by its years of center-Left government and its density of union membership (Bradley et al., 2003: 226). This was the golden age of capitalism, a regulated form of capitalism, which spread social as well as civil and political citizenship across the population as a whole. Domestic state-regulated and state-aided capitalism was complemented by Bretton Woods repression of global flows of capital abroad, allowing states the autonomy to develop their own social and economic policies. Though capitalism now became more global, it was not more uniform, since autonomy encouraged different varieties of capitalism, welfare states, and tax systems, enabling different versions of Keynesianism and social citizenship to be implemented at the national level.

In 1930 average expenditure on social insurance programs had been less than 3 percent of GDP. By 1950 it was 5 percent, and by 1990 20 percent. The state share in GDP rose similarly from about 25 percent in 1950 to 45 percent by the mid-1970s (Flora, 1983: introduction). More of social life was being caged nationally, first during the war in the Anglo and Nordic countries and more universally in the OECD countries afterward. Most welfare programs also had expansion built into them. A new social insurance program would typically first grant low benefits to a few recipients. Then, as entitlements spread, more would become eligible with higher rates of benefit required from the state, since the recipient had also contributed more. This maturation factor produced inexorable increases in costs that later worsened fiscal crisis, as we see in Chapter 11.

This was not an unalloyed posthumous triumph for Keynes. Economics became dominated by a synthesis of his ideas and classical economics usually called the neoclassical synthesis or neo-Keynesianism – though I remember Joan Robinson fulminating against what she called bastard Keynesianism. Keynes's theories had been adapted to static equilibrium theory by economists like Hicks, Modigliani, and Samuelson. Hicks's investment–saving/liquidity preference–money supply model (IS/LM model) related aggregate demand and employment to three exogenous elements: the amount of money circulating, the size of the government budget, and business expectations. The Phillips curve appeared to show that increased employment implied higher nominal wages and therefore higher inflation: so unemployment and inflation were inversely related. An economist using the ISL-M model could predict that an increase in the money supply would raise output and employment and then use the Phillips curve to predict an increase in inflation. The positive message was that a high employment equilibrium could be maintained by tolerating a mild level of inflation. Governments reached the same conclusion more pragmatically. Faced with more powerful and apparently popular labor unions whom they did not want to alienate, they tolerated wage increases secured through free collective bargaining by mildly inflating their economies. Fairly full employment and prosperity spread across the West, and then into Asia, and with it more equality than had existed in the prewar period. In this sense there was some global convergence.

Yet national and macroregional differences also appeared. The Anglos saw a burst of welfare and progressive tax expansion in the 1940s, consolidated over the 1950s and 1960s, though without adding major new programs. Means testing ensured that costs grew less than in other countries since fewer citizens benefited. Conservative or center-Right government predominated in these countries in the 1950s, and the expansion now petered out. Canada deviated, with expansion in the late 1960s of both means-tested and universal programs. Ireland's programs also grew later because of later economic development. The Anglos and Nordics were maintaining their joint leadership in social citizenship. Esping-Andersen (1999: 87–90) later conceded that if he had started his analysis in 1960 and not 1980, Britain, Australia, and New Zealand would have to be added to the most progressive cases. Britain, he said, was a stalled social democracy, while Australia and New Zealand were at first fully social democratic welfare regimes.

Dylan Riley and I (2007) investigated Gini coefficients of inequality, which provide a rough measure of overall inequality within a country. Among Western countries we distinguished Esping-Anderson's three regimes. We also found adequate data on eighteen Latin American countries and several East and South Asian countries. In all regions we found that intraregional variations in inequality were considerably less than interregional variations. Thus macroregions provided shared ideologies that were then institutionally reinforced at the national level through political parties, elections, and the state. The ex-Soviet countries are another distinctive group (Castles & Obinger, 2008: 336–7). We found that Esping-Andersen's typology worked quite well after 1980, but the Anglos were until the 1960s more equal than the others. The United States was the most unequal among the Anglophones but was about level with the average for the Nordic countries. Then in the 1970s the Nordic countries became more equal than the liberals, and in the 1980s and 1990s the Euros also achieved this. These movements up and down were not merely national but "macroregional," for they involved most of the countries in each group.

Atkinson and colleagues (2007: chap. 13) examine the proportion of gross incomes contributed by the rich (the top 10 percent, 1 percent, or 0.1 percent of taxpayers) through the twentieth century in the six Anglo countries, France, Germany, the Netherlands, and Switzerland. They were all similar up to the 1970s, with high inequality in the early century, followed by descent until just before World War II. Up till then the Anglos (except for the United States) had been slightly more equal. Inequality declined further in World War II, largely due to the impact of progressive wealth and inheritance taxes on capital holdings. The rentier class was hit by the Great Depression and then by progressive wartime taxes. It did not recover after the war. In Canada, the United States, and Germany there was little change during 1955–75, but inequality continued to fall in Australia, New Zealand, the United Kingdom, Ireland, France, the Netherlands, and Switzerland. The Anglos were a little more equal than the Euros but global economic growth lifted all boats. Combined with progressive taxation, this lifted the incomes of the bottom fifth of the population most, even in the United States and Canada. Poverty rates sank everywhere.

The Nordic countries, with Finland lagging, gradually developed a panoply of more costly universal programs. The Swedish tax take as a proportion of GDP overtook the U.S. level around 1950 and the British level around 1955 and kept on going up (Steinmo, 1993: 28). As the welfare programs matured and more people were entitled to benefits, their redistributive effect increased. The Euros also expanded welfare though with less redistribution. In all these phases some path dependency was evident as earlier choices were institutionalized, generating relatively coherent varieties of welfare state. The differences between Bismarckian and Beveridge pension schemes became more entrenched – only the Netherlands shifted, from Bismarck to Beveridge. Bismarckian schemes could be easily extended gradually to more groups, so that virtually everyone became covered by public pensions. In contrast, Beveridge schemes took two different paths. In the Nordic countries second-tier earnings-related state pensions were introduced, a compromise between the two schemes. Only a pale imitation of this was introduced in Britain, whose middle classes reacted to the low level of Beveridge pensions by developing private pensions (Ebbinghaus & Gronwald, 2009). This became characteristic of the Anglos and reinforced their later drift toward widening inequality.

The Anglos had financed earlier welfare programs through taxes made possible by the war. But defeated and neutral countries could not do this and it was politically difficult to raise income taxes in peacetime. The Nordics and Euros turned to value-added taxes on consumption and social security taxes, more regressive but less unpopular. But as the burden of taxation grew, all countries resisted new taxes. A fiscal crisis now loomed, after the Nordics and Euros had boosted their welfare states but at a point where the Anglos would not be able to catch up, since their peoples would not accept higher taxes. This helped entrench the differences among the three varieties.

I have analyzed the development of social citizenship in the North of the world from 1945 up to about 1970. The big picture was of some convergence, though limited by national and macroregional differences. All the OECD countries became capitalist, industrial, and then postindustrial, and they all compromised class conflict, partly by macroeconomic planning aimed at full employment, partly by development of social citizenship rights offering self-protection in Polanyi's sense from the vagaries of capitalist markets and from the absolute power of capitalists. By lodging economic rights more broadly among the population, and by lodging their administration within democratic states, this was trimming the concentration of economic power in the advanced countries, ensuring that they were a little more pluralistic. Marshall was right in declaring that the twentieth century would be the century of social citizenship – at least in the North of the world. The most macro measure of this growth is the share of government spending in national income. In the OECD countries this was less than 10 percent at the beginning of the century, above 20 percent just before World War II, and more than 40 percent by 1970. This reformed half-national, half-global capitalism was the crowning achievement of the North, inaugurating an unprecedented period of social cohesion, stability, and prosperity – its golden age. This development was broadly caused by the conjunction of capitalist forces and relations of production in Marx's sense, though with an outcome of reform, not revolution, and with some help from the outcome of world wars.

Yet we have seen that there was never only a single version of social citizenship. Notions of best practices were influenced by the specific blends of power sources configured in each nation-state, and here ideological, military, and especially political power relations were important. In the course of their self-protection, citizens became more caged within their nation-state, while nationally regulated economies erected defenses against the insecurities produced by capitalism. Yet individual nation-states were also influenced by the macroregional cultures in which they were imbricated. National and macroregional varieties of capitalism and welfare regimes both had increasing analytical utility in the post–World War II period. Esping-Andersen's model of three welfare regimes, which I have relabeled as Anglo, Nordic, and Euro, became more apposite as the century progressed. National and macroregional trajectories also surged or stalled by three of the century's great crises: two world wars and the Great Depression. At the end of the period movement was still occurring. The Anglo countries had shown high levels of social citizenship up to that point but were now faltering, overtaken by the Nordic countries and even by some of the Euros. All of these achievements occurred after prolonged struggles in which outcomes were not set in advance by path dependency. Traditions were not unimportant, but they encountered crises that pushed collective actors into devising new paths of development.

In explaining both the overall growth of social citizenship and variations between countries I deployed what is called a power resources model, stressing classes, cross-class political alliances, center-Left governments, and labor unions, though it was also sometimes necessary to add churches and other sources of social cleavage. Alliances among such groups also enhanced the solidarity of the common people. The sense of belonging to a single nation was an ideological precondition for establishing much social citizenship in the countries I have considered. Thus the power resources involved were mainly political and ideological, though the politics derived from pressures from within civil society more than from the state itself.

Yet in explaining variation I stressed macroregional differences in corporatist versus voluntarist institutions, a distinction visible early in the century but later becoming more important – and about to become even more important when facing the neoliberal challenge. Some apparent support for a political institutionalist model of majoritarian versus PR electoral systems was largely explicable in terms of Anglophone countries versus the rest, and this difference I mainly attributed to the different periods in which electoral systems became institutionalized – plus multiple social cleavages that generated multiple parties, as stressed by Lipset and Rokkan. However, once institutionalized, these differences did matter. But the autonomous role of bureaucratic or expert elites was only occasionally significant. In the first half of the century military power relations expressed in wars had especially changed the trajectories of the Euro countries. The result of the second war allowed the grand compromise between socialism and Christianity to consolidate the distinctive social citizenship of most of the Euros. The two wars also consolidated Anglo social citizenship and eventually furthered it everywhere. This is obviously a rather multicausal explanation, with the common aspects of social citizenship largely powered by economic power relations, while the international and macroregional differences were caused by all the four power sources.

The rise of financialization

The neo-Keynesian economy began to experience crisis in the 1970s, as the economy slowed and inflation mounted. The United States, Britain, Australia, and New Zealand had economic difficulties a little earlier, in the late 1960s, leading to stop-go sequences of policy that could neither reverse previous welfare gains nor much extend them (Steinmo, 1993: 145–55). This opened a neoliberal door. Though most see neoliberalism as a response to this crisis (e.g., Arrighi, 1994), it first gathered strength through the neo-Keynesian period of success in spreading prosperity through full employment, progressive taxes, and generous welfare states. Prosperity diffused shareholding, home ownership, pensions, and insurance among the middle class and even workers, who also entered middling tax brackets for the first time. It also meant a more globally competitive capitalism, more transnational corporations, more international trade, and mildly debt-driven development. All of this expanded somewhat the financial services sector, which was to become the leading edge of neoliberalism. To enlist a metaphor of Marx's, which he used to predict the demise of the bourgeoisie, neo-Keynesianism produced its grave diggers through its very successes.

Krippner (2005: 174) defines financialization as "a pattern of accumulation in which profits accrue primarily through financial channels rather than through trade and commodity production." Stocks and other financial instruments had long enabled collective pooling of savings or profits for investment in trade or production. But postwar stock exchanges became dominated by investors holding paper financial wealth more liquid, transnational, and transferable than the fixed assets of manufacturing firms. Economic globalization and improved communications meant ownership title transfers could be instantaneous and frictionless across the world since they transferred electronic symbols, not physical goods or services. But the interstitial emergence of transnational financial flows strained the Bretton Woods repression of international capital flows.

Financialization had two main home-base states, the two Anglophone nations, which had provided the world's reserve currencies and so already had the biggest financial sectors. The U.S. dollar was the current reserve currency, most traded internationally, while its government and consumer debt were ballooning. Yet since American financial flows had been tightly regulated since the New Deal, the City of London, the main home of currency trading, was the first institution to liberate finance from the state. The City–Bank of England –Treasury power nexus had long subordinated the interests of British manufacturing industry to finance through deflationary policies designed to preserve an overvalued pound sterling (Ingham, 1984). This priority had been recently challenged by Keynesian concerns about unemployment. Oscillation between the two produced stop-go policies in which Keynesian stimuli alternated with deflation at any sign of overheating. In the 1970s this unsteady combination generated higher inflation, budget deficits, and speculator runs on the pound. This was the opening for a City-led neoliberalism backed by conservative think tanks and the financial press (Fourcade-Gourinchas & Babb, 2002: 549–56).

American financial markets became much bigger (Krippner, 2005: 178–9). The 1950s also saw the interstitial emergence of Eurodollars, dollars held and traded abroad by non-U.S. residents. They grew because of the dollar's role as reserve currency, plus the tight regulation within the United States. People holding dollars wanted to profit from them elsewhere. London seized the opportunity to attract them, and in the 1960s they supplanted sterling as the City's primary trading currency. The City was reestablishing itself as an offshore enclave (Shafer, 1995: 124) – one of the sturdiest grave diggers of Keynes.

Even sturdier ones were from America. In the 1960s the cost of Johnson's "Great Society" and the Vietnam War produced domestic overheating and large American debts and deficits. Those with export surpluses to the United States were left holding dollars, but they could cash them in for gold and so empty Fort Knox of its gold. So in 1971 President Nixon took the dollar off gold and let it float, and by 1973 this had forced the other major countries also to float. Bretton Woods had collapsed, less because it had intrinsic weaknesses than because pressure from both the United States and finance capital had destroyed it. This was part of a new movement once more, in Polanyi's term, to disembed the market from state control – though the workings of this market would favor one particular state, the United States. Increased capital mobility, coupled with an economic opportunity for American economic imperialism (discussed in Chapter 10), made it difficult for governments to continue pursuing neo-Keynesian policies. This was contingently reinforced in 1973 when the OPEC oil cartel's hikings of oil prices began, giving petroleum states massive export surpluses and petrodollars (for America was the military protector of most of them). This was the origin of global imbalances, the uneven distribution of debts and surpluses across the world that also gave an impetus to finance capital.

In the early 1970s American banks, fleeing U.S. regulation, streamed into the City of London, now rediscovering its historic role during sterling's reign (Burn, 2006). The Bank of England's embrace of monetarist targets in 1973 and 1976 was a further neoliberal step. So that its banks could compete, the United States abolished international capital controls in 1974–5, though domestic capital remained regulated. Yet when Paul Volcker curbed inflation with very high interest rates, this action sucked masses of capital into the United States. Global imbalances grew. There was a knock-on effect of financialization to Germany and Switzerland, which also possessed major currencies. Their bankers, hurt by Anglo-American offshore competition, wanted to join a sector already generating higher profits than domestic bank lending. Most countries in the 1970s were increasing their capital controls, trying to combat the volatility unleashed by floating currencies. But it was mostly proving a losing battle against speculation.

The neoliberal period since then has not been an economic success. It did not manage to restore real growth to the Western economy. It also generated problems of its own. Its financial epicenter has been volatile and susceptible to crises. All the eighteen financial crises occurring since 1945 have erupted since 1973 (say Reinhart & Rogoff, 2009). High unemployment, speculative short-term investment, and sluggish aggregate demand yielded lower growth in the real economy in the neoliberal period than in the neo-Keynesian period, and it became less and less (Brenner, 2002). Yet financialization did not need to demonstrate success. It fed upon the power conferred by its own expansion. Increased volatility in interest rates made bond trading more lucrative while surplus petrodollars added to banking strength. In the late 1970s the manufacturing share of American GDP and profits declined, while the financial services share increased. In the 1980s their profits exceeded those of manufacturing, as increasingly manufacturing jobs and plants were exported to the global South. We might see this as another phase of Schumpeter's "creative destruction" – manufacturing destroyed, finance creatively expanding – and that is what its boosters said, but this shift did not prove beneficial to capitalism as a whole.

In 1986 Mrs. Thatcher authorized the Big Bang, a radical deregulation of the British stock market, allowing the merging of commercial and investment banks, and opening up to foreign capital flows, the first country to deregulate finance fully. But Britain's pioneering role was now over. U.S. banks now dominated the City while U.S. manufacturers, faced with declining profits and greater international competition, withdrew capital from production and invested it in financial instruments instead. They also downsized their research and development (R&D) laboratories. By the 1980s almost all R&D was being done in government and university labs, a reversal of the 1950s (Block & Keller, 2011). Thus financialization was infiltrating the real economy (Krippner, 2005; Arrighi, 1994). Today General Electric, traditional symbol of corporate America, derives more profit from financial than manufacturing activities.

The financial sector benefits investors and their fund managers, disproportionately rich people. It privileges fighting inflation over fighting unemployment, and it seeks to keep wages low. This is its class bias. The financial sector itself contains little class conflict, and its predominantly white-collar workforce is rarely unionized. Its shareholders are rarely organized, and it is highly cartelized, dominated by a few big banks in each country. In theory insurance companies and pension funds might act as popular counterweights, for they represent the savings of millions of ordinary people (though not the poor). Half America's households now own shares, mostly through mutual funds. But a system of interlocking directorships between these funds and the banks ensures that financial elites share common, not conflicting interests. Banks set their executives' pay as advised by outsiders drawn from insurance and pensions funds and management consultants. In return, bankers sit on their compensation committees. So they scratch each other's backs and ratchet up salaries and stock options. The workings of finance have also become abstract, beyond popular understandings. Though leftist governments saw that financialization threatened their goals, there was no significant popular pressure from below on them to resist. And social democratic parties did not have a real answer to the economic crisis. Neo-Keynesianism had apparently failed, there was an apparently zero-sum conflict between the classes, and labor's attempts to protect wages at the expense of capital were defeated in a series of losing strikes and elections.

In the late 1980s and early 1990s almost all OECD governments abandoned controls on international capital flows. Some (e.g., Mudge, 2008) see this as simply the diffusion of neoliberal ideas, but it involved coercion too. There was firstly a struggle about how petrodollars resulting from OPEC's five price hikes should be recycled into productive investment in the rest of the world. The Europeans and Japanese favored doing this through central banks and the IMF, but the United States and Britain insisted that private banks handle it. The United States had more influence with the oil sheikhs and won the power struggle. Then as each government embraced deregulation, it became more difficult for others to resist the protests of their own bankers that there was unfair competition from foreign banks. Governments faced with greater international capital flows were now less able to control both their exchange rates and their domestic interest rates. If a country wanted to keep interest rates below prevailing global rates (to stimulate its economy), speculation would now likely depreciate its currency, with inflationary consequences, a powerful deterrent against trying it at all. This was a definite loss of sovereignty, though we saw in chapter 7 of Volume 3 that financial speculators had also possessed such powers in the 1920s. Speculators were now regaining strength. They now had an ambiguous identity, transnational but also disproportionately American. The financial managers profiting from their business were mainly located in Wall Street and the City of London and so were mostly Anglophone.

The German Bundesbank had been the financial driving force of the European Economic Community (the EEC). Though not neoliberal, it too privileged fighting inflation over fighting unemployment, a result of faulty German understandings of the failure of the Weimar Republic and the rise of Hitler (which had been due more to unemployment than to inflation!). Then there was an unexpected push from French technocratic socialists who had become leading figures in the EEC. Men like Jacques Delors and Pascal Lamy became advocates of free capital movement in the 1980s, for they had seen from the inside the failure of President Mitterand's 1981 attempt to impose draconian capital controls in France. The Reagan administration had also attacked France through high dollar and interest rates, and this plus a big trade deficit had forced three currency devaluations on the French government. This had taken France outside the rules of the (then) European Economic Community. In 1983 Mitterand abandoned capital controls, pressured by the other Europeans and having lost his struggle against the speculators. The rich had evaded his restrictions and the burden had fallen mostly on middle-class people with limited savings. Given the power of transnational capital, controls were ineffective and regressive, concluded these socialists. They felt they had to adjust to new power realities – the first of many socialist capitulations. Euro officials achieved free capital mobility within the EEC in 1988, and this was reinforced by the deflationary monetary policy of the Maastricht Treaty of 1992. Like all deepening of the Union, this resulted not from popular or democratic pressures but from those of elites. Japan's shift away from capital controls was mostly completed by 1990 and the OECD followed in 1992 (Abdelal, 2007).

This concerned only the financial sector. The EEC/EU and Japan have not otherwise been very neoliberal. Of the EEC total budget 60 percent went on subsidizing agriculture, and today after several reforms the EU's proportion is still 40 percent. It is otherwise a free market within, but highly protected externally by tariffs and other regulations from outside competition. Similarly Japan. Calling whole economies neoliberal is not appropriate. The United States also has many protective tariffs.

But as financial flows increased, so did stock markets. About fifty countries acquired their own after 1980, and a more global organization of finance aided more portfolio investment spread across emerging markets as well as the OECD countries, a positive aspect of financialization – though often undermined by increased volatility (Davis, 2009: 37). Central banks were also granted more autonomy, a product also of politicians' reluctance to be held responsible for economic policy amid recession. As economies stagnated, political power relations came more into play. Politicians shifted from claiming credit for the economy to seeking to avoid blame for the enduring crisis (Weaver, 1986; Krippner, 2007, 2011). No one could be blamed for austerity programs, it was argued. The impersonal forces of the market could coerce the necessary changes.

Nonetheless, government policy still mattered. To restore profitability, fighting inflation rather than unemployment spread. In the 1970s inflation rates averaged 10 percent per annum, but by the 1990s they averaged less than 3 percent, with fewer differences between countries (Syklos, 2002: 64). When the banks raised interest rates to fight inflation, this led to lower economic growth and rising unemployment. Instead of risking inflation by compromising with labor and allowing wages to rise, governments and central banks preferred to regulate the economy through adjusting the money supply and interest rates. Class inequality widened.

Yet many southern countries did not deregulate capital movements. Receiving less foreign capital, they were under less pressure to open up – unlike on trade matters, as we see later (Shafer, 1995). The most successful developing countries, India and China, received relatively little foreign capital until the twenty-first century. In 1995–7 the IMF was moving toward embracing free capital mobility, but in 1997 the Asian financial crisis revealed the downside of unrestricted short-term capital flows and the IMF drew back. There was no global victory, for the stronger states of the South held onto more of their sovereignty and resisted. This was a rare case in which the South (or rather parts of the South) did better than the North. But in the North financialization was rampant. This was the greatest neoliberal triumph. It was also to be its greatest disaster, as we see in Chapter 11.

The crisis of Neo-Keynesianism

Neo-Keynesian success had increased the power of finance capital, and then its failure gave neoliberals their chance to impose their policies. The early 1970s saw a serious economic downturn in the North, linked to greater global competition and overcapacity. Europe had fully recovered from the war and Japan and East Asia were picking up growth (Brenner, 2002). It was not a global crisis, as is often asserted, for East Asia was actually booming – and so were the oil producers. But traditional heavy industries in the North, such as mining, shipbuilding, and iron and steel, now largely collapsed. There was a sharp fall in the rate of profit, especially in the international manufacturing sector, which induced a slowdown in growth and an overaccumulation of capital, which was now placed more into financial instruments than manufacturing investment. Keynesian demand management through countercyclical deficit spending was the main policy response to the crisis, but this stimulation only increased manufacturing overcapacity, debts, and financialization. Stagflation, whereby inflation and unemployment rose simultaneously, resulted in the North, confounding those neo-Keynesians who had relied on the Phillips curve, which claimed that the two were alternatives. Inflation was wiping out profit levels, and business became convinced that profit could be best restored by cutting labor costs.

Stagflation intensified class conflict in the North. Since capital and labor were both suffering, each strove to retain its economic returns amid a stagnant economy. Hitherto redistribution and more social citizenship had been financed out of growth and mild inflation. Therefore, as growth faded, inflation grew. This was the first phase of the crisis. Governments then began to attack inflation, but at first only by raising interest rates and deficit spending. Deficit spending was the second attempted solution to the crisis, but no more than inflation could it be sustained. This was now becoming revealed as a zero-sum class conflict: for one class to gain, another must lose (Streeck, 2011; Krippner, 2011). The prior period of full employment and Fordist mass production had put skilled and semiskilled workers together and so strengthened labor unions (except in the United States). This had enabled workers to achieve relatively high wages. In the 1960s the political Left seemed to be increasing in strength in most countries, feeding on workers' discontent overlapping with new social movements based on students and identity politics. But workers' power was deceptive, for their main sectors of strength in manufacturing were being exported to the global South and their unity was faltering. Capital hit back, and the class compromise of the golden age disintegrated in the Anglophone countries along with the high productivity/high demand economy in which it had been embedded in the postwar period. In the United States hitherto-moderate corporations behind the Committee for Economic Development (discussed in Chapter 3) blamed unions for inflation and determined to cut down their powers (Domhoff, In press). They succeeded.

Neoliberals argued that austerity would trim high-cost, low-profit manufacturing production and reduce inflation to improve international competitiveness. The simplest way of deflating was to reduce the money supply, the monetarist solution offered by Milton Friedman. Budgets must be balanced, deficits prevented. Financial deregulation and dismantling of capital controls would produce financial growth. Labor unions and states should be downsized. Markets should be restored to their natural transnational condition, and unemployment should rise to its natural level. Corporations sought economies through drastic cost reductions, reducing wages and corporate welfare programs where they could, though subcontracting to smaller firms employing casual, low-wage, nonunionized labor saved even more. Less efficient corporations suffered hostile takeovers in the great merger wave of the 1980s, encouraged by the deregulation policies of the Reagan administration. To preclude this prospect, corporations tried to maximize shareholder value (Fligstein & Shin, 2007).

Antitrust legislation to restrict corporate mergers had hitherto been a feature of American political economy. Capitalism tends to encourage mergers and monopolies in established markets, and these had been thought to lessen competition. But neoliberals departed from classical liberals to argue that the bigger the corporation, the greater its efficiency and the better the service offered to consumers. They recognized that actual monopoly should be avoided, for it would lessen competition, but they said that competition would survive even if there were only three giant corporations in any economic sector (Crouch, 2011). At the same time, the ending of restrictions on banking across state lines was producing giant banks in the United States. Multidivision conglomerate corporations were especially vulnerable to takeover for each of the specialized divisions could be sold separately to its competitors to yield immediate profit for the seller and to reduce competitive pressure for the buyer. Only workers and consumers lost out, as redundancies and higher prices resulted (Fligstein & Shin, 2007). Thus unemployment rose, making the sack an effective deterrent against strikes; labor flexibility increased; and wages fell. This was intended to restore profitability, and after that, general growth would supposedly resume, benefiting all. But in the short run there was a confluence of neoliberalism and business interests, a class offensive at the expense of workers (Harvey, 2005: 15; Davis, 2009: 84–94).

None of this applied in East Asia, whose heavy and consumer durable industries were now expanding, undercutting those of the West. Japan first and then the Little Tigers (South Korea, Taiwan, Singapore, and Hong Kong) pioneered a new developmental statism based neither on "getting the prices right" within free markets nor on protecting domestic industry through ISI policies, but on subsidizing exports through credit and export incentives backed by close government monitoring of performance (Amsden, 2001). Neoliberalism initially passed them by. It was most at home in the Anglophone countries since in most European countries manufacturing corporations had close relations with more traditional banks and relied on worker welfare provided by the state. Neoliberalism's rise was not global outside the financial sector, and its seizure of political power centered on Britain and the United States. So we must return to these two countries.

The alliance with conservatism: Thatcher and Reagan

When Margaret Thatcher and Ronald Reagan rose to power in 1979 and 1980, respectively, they implemented much of the neoliberal agenda. In Britain class conflict exacerbated by economic crisis was the major cause of the conservative-neoliberal offensive. Two national miners' strikes in 1972 and 1974 over wage issues slashed energy supplies, created power shortages, and forced the Conservative government of Ted Heath to declare a three-day work-week. During the second strike Heath called a general election but narrowly lost, as slightly more of the electorate blamed him rather than the miners. The incoming Labour government settled the strike and tried to counter stagflation by negotiating corporatist policies of wage restraint. Yet this fell victim to British voluntarism as neither unions nor employers could be held to agreements made. We saw in Volume III that voluntarism was a traditional feature of the liberal, Anglophone countries. At the same time the Labour Left, newly strengthened by the 1960s and by the crisis, proposed a more radical economic policy, challenging the party leadership. This frightened business, and capital flight produced a rapid 12 percent fall in the value of the pound. The Labour government now felt it had to go cap in hand to the IMF for a loan, a humiliation that had electoral consequences.

In came Margaret Thatcher. Macroeconomic failure and inability to generate corporatism to handle class conflict had led to the Conservative victory (King & Wood, 1999). The crisis had made Conservatives and business favor union bashing, and this was now more popular, given recent class discord. Thatcher brandished neoliberalism with ideological certainty, banging down a copy of Hayek's book *The Constitution of Liberty* on the table at a shadow cabinet session, declaring, "**This** is what we believe." Yet it was not the attractions of neoliberalism but Britain's dismal economic record under Labour that brought her victory in 1979.

The reasons for Reagan's victory in 1980 were more varied. True, the United States had suffered low growth and high inflation during the 1970s, and Nixon, like Callaghan, had tried and failed to make price and wage controls work amid a voluntarist tradition. Yet as we saw in Chapter 3 American "lib-labs" had already stalled and conservatism was rising again. Labor union decline continued, reducing workers' pressure. Unlike in Britain, this economic crisis produced asymmetric class struggle in which the capitalist class was highly organized but labor was not. Indeed Democrats were facing worker disaffection, expressed in coded racism in the cities over forced busing, affirmative action, and crime. Stagflation also stymied Democrats' usual policy of redistribution through economic growth, splitting them between liberals still seeking redistribution and a larger center, fearful of alienating the middle classes. Resistance to taxes grew. California's Proposition 13 occurred in 1978, a demand for lower taxes with no reduction in public services, an absurd combination that has dominated Californian politics ever since. Government indebtedness steadily increased, to be later paralleled at the household and individual levels by easier mortgages and credit cards – a nation growing through debt.

Conservatism also benefited from economic and ideological discontent. From above, corporations and the CED backed Reagan's attack on unions and his promises to deregulate and took advantage of more relaxed campaign financing laws to shovel money his way. From below came an ideological backlash against what was seen as the excesses of the 1960s, demanding a return to true American moral values. The rights revolution and identity politics championed by highly educated liberals, feminists, and African Americans were more leftist, but they had moved away from the preoccupations of white workers. In this context new conservative think tanks like the American Enterprise Institute and the Heritage Foundation supplied neoliberalism while the Christian Right supplied morality. A conservative-neoliberal ideological alternative emerged, offering a plausible solution to America's woes.

In his 1980 presidential campaign Reagan stressed peace through strength against the Soviet Union. He ridiculed Jimmy Carter's botched attempt to liberate the U.S. embassy hostages in Iran. Reagan battled against big government in traditional Republican style, famously declaring, "Government is the problem, not the solution," and he supported states' rights, with its coded appeal to white racism. Finally, he promised good times ahead – 30 percent lower taxes and a balanced budget within three years, since tax cuts for business would supposedly promote growth and revenue alike. His sunny persona matched his positive message. The Republicans also benefited from recent campaign finance legislation enabling them to solicit contributions from rich Americans and corporations. Business support gave Reagan a significant financial and media edge in the campaign (Berman, 1998: 70–2; Edsall, 1984: chap. 3). This was a class as well as a conservative offensive, and a weakened labor movement could not counter it.

In the 1980 election, the poor voted less, disillusioned by Carter, while the rich voted solidly for Reagan, who also poached traditional Democrat constituencies, gaining a majority among white workers, Catholics, and evangelical

Protestants, revealing the salience of conservative moral and racial issues. On the other hand, for the first time a majority of women voted Democrat. Reagan won more votes in the South, maintaining Nixon's southern strategy. Republicans gained in both houses of Congress and in governorships. Conservatism allied with neoliberalism had advanced and the shift rightward of both parties continued (Busch, 2005; Wilentz, 2009; Berman, 1998; Edsall,1984).

The new administration pursued what was later called Reaganomics, a neoliberal agenda reducing government spending and business taxes, deregulating, and tightening the money supply. It deregulated less through new legislation than by reducing the number of regulations made by government agencies – especially the National Labor Relations Board (against labor interests) and the Environmental Protection Agency (against environmentalists' interests; see Chapter 12). Deregulation to protect consumers became probusiness under Reagan, disastrously so with respect to savings and loans institutions, which crashed in the late 1980s, a miniversion of the Great Neoliberal Recession of 2008.

Fiscal policies were regressive. This was the first postwar administration not to increase the minimum wage. Capital gains, inheritance taxes, and the highest rates of income tax were all slashed and $50 billion was cut from welfare programs. The top income tax rate fell from 70 percent to 28 percent within seven years. The rich got richer; the poor got poorer. Though wage inequality was beginning to widen, the surging inequality of the 1980s was mainly due to Reagan's tax policies (Edsall, 1984: 204–13; Massey, 2007). The unions in the shape of the air traffic controllers were defeated. This was all neoliberal in both its principled and class versions.

Yet despite Reagan's promises to reduce government, federal spending actually rose relative to GDP because of increased military spending. Beset by Japanese and European competition, the government was also pouring money into high-tech projects. Indeed, though always cast as liberal or neoliberal, the United States is actually rather uneven in its political economy. In some spheres it is rather statist. It has long highly state-subsidized agriculture, defense, and aerospace industries, and high-tech industries more generally. High-tech is seen as part of the national security state, as vital to compete with other nations at the cutting edge of new technologies. Hence high-tech firms are subsidized, network-connected with government and university laboratories, and kept rather secret – both for reasons of national security and because politicians, especially Republicans, claim publicly to be market fundamentalists, not statists. Thus neoliberalism among politicians is always somewhat hypocritical (Block, 2008). OECD statistics, used by many researchers, habitually distort the American picture because they exclude its military sector. Indeed, almost everyone neglects military power relations. As I have argued, states are not unitary but polymorphous, their multiple institutions crystallizing in different ways according to their different activities and the constituencies for these (Mann, 1986 & 1993: chap. 3). In its agrarian crystallization, the United States decommodifies much more than does its crystallization as a welfare state. Its agricultural subsidies resemble those of Japan, France, and Germany more than they do fellow Anglophone countries. Its military crystallization is unique and, of course, not remotely liberal. The consistent element, I cynically note, is that the United States sponsors redistribution, but to the rich, not to the poor!

Under Reagan the deficit soared, the result of an electoral alliance between incompatible small and big state ideals. In international political economy, far from letting currency markets rule, the administration pursued two major interventions, strong-arming foreign governments. The Plaza Agreement devalued the dollar in 1985 and the Louvre Agreement ended this revaluation two years later, at American convenience – nationalism predominating over neoliberalism. Neoliberals nonetheless proclaimed Reagan as their standard bearer, since their alliance with cold war conservatism was too electorally useful to be jettisoned. Reagan also pursued other conservative agendas, blocking civil rights and acquired immunodeficiency syndrome (AIDS) policies and stuffing the judiciary with conservatives (Wilentz, 2009: 180–94).

Neoliberalism suggested that people be forced off welfare rolls onto "workfare," which provided time-limited benefits only if they sought work. This would restore market incentives to the unemployed. Wacquant (2002, 2009) then sees a logical progression from neoliberalism to workfare and then on to what he calls "prisonfare," a growth in punitive policing and incarceration. Peck and Tickell (2002) similarly distinguish between rollback neoliberalism (rolling back regulations) and rollout neoliberalism, in which problems caused by rollback are remedied by new government activism, their main example also the progression from workfare to prisonfare.

Wacquant writes convincingly about workfare and incarceration. Yet he is too functionalist when he ties the two together and claims that rising incarceration rates were caused by neoliberalism. By failing to generate sustained growth and by prioritizing inflation, neoliberalism kept unemployment high, and workfare was a neoliberal response to this, as Wacquant argues. But higher unemployment was not correlated with higher crime since the supposedly higher crime rate of the period was a myth, a moral panic, not reality. Crime was actually falling, mainly because of demography – the number of young males was decreasing. So Wacquant focuses on the higher incarceration rate, which zoomed upward from the mid-1980s to the early 1990s. Yet in that period the number of those on welfare programs was static. The main thrust of tougher welfare requirements only occurred later, after Clinton's welfare reforms, and then the prison population grew only slightly. African Americans became the majority of the prison population in the 1980s, though they were less than 13 percent of the national population (they fell back slightly to 45 percent of the prison population in the 1990s). This rise was dominated by arrests for drug offenses. Yet surveys indicate that most of those who took or dealt in drugs were not in fact black. It was because young working-class blacks had a very visible street life that they were most easily caught – and because the cops were racist. But the War on Drugs plus racism were less a consequence of neoliberalism than of the moral panic over drugs turned in a racist direction. This was a distinctively American rather than a neoliberal concern, and, as we have seen, racism had long been part of American conservatism. Most of those who became unemployed as a result of neoliberal policies were white, yet few of them were imprisoned.

Lacy (2010) adds further criticisms of Wacquant. She notes the enormous differences in incarceration rates among American states. Louisiana's rates in the mid-2000s were five times Maine's, while those in the whole southern region were almost twice as high as those of the Northeast. Again, these differences seem due more to the influence of racial conservatism than to neoliberalism. Lacy notes, as I do, that neoliberalism only acquired much purchase in the liberal (Anglo) countries. She also notes how exceptional was the steep rise in the U.S. rate, reaching up to almost four times as high as that in the next country in her sample (Poland). Most countries' rates are much lower and have been static or rising only slightly. Britain saw a more substantial rise to having the highest rate among the Western Europeans. In the United Kingdom drug offenders are about a third of the prison population and the rate of black incarceration is three times the white rate, further suggesting that race, immigration, and drug scares were fueling the increase, not neoliberalism (Bewley-Taylor et al., 2009). Wacquant (2009: chap. 9) suggests that neoliberalism also permeated French penal policy, yet the evidence he produces concerns only the floating of neoliberal ideas by some pressure groups and not any changes in policy. Lacy shows that French incarceration rates have remained low and static. Wacquant says that the Commonwealth Anglophone countries also shared high incarceration rates and neoliberalism (2009: 305), yet in fact Australian, Canadian, and New Zealand incarceration rates have remained quite low. It seems that only the land of Thatcher follows the land of Reagan in penal policy. But the two countries shared racial conservatism as well as neoliberalism, and it seems that the former had the greater influence on penal policy.

Thatcher and Reagan remained in power until, respectively, 1990 and 1988. They reduced taxes on the rich. Reagan deregulated, and his judicial appointees, notably the neoliberals Robert Bork and Richard Posner, shredded the antitrust laws (Crouch, 2011). Thatcher privatized, liberalized capital flows, introduced legislation hamstringing unions, and introduced more competition and more capitalistic metrics (value for money, the bottom line, etc.) into the allocation of government funding. What became known as audit governance sought proxies for market mechanisms in public and nonprofit administrations, which had the paradoxical effect of making them more centralized and hierarchical, controlled by accountant substitutes (Peck & Tickell, 2002: 387). Introducing business accountancy into the provision of citizen social services is also a step in subordinating political to economic power. Both politicians helped engineer a temporary economic boom that then petered out, and both increased inequality, a victory for capital over labor. Thatcher had slightly downsized the British state. Public expenditure had been 43 percent of GDP when she came to power. It had fallen to 39 percent when she fell in 1990, mainly because of big sales of public industry and housing. But by 1995 it was back to the 1979 level. Of course, the proportion actually rose in the United States under Reagan because of large increases in military expenditure. These two cold warriors were also helped by their military victories. Americans believed that Reagan defeated the evil empire, while the Iron Lady led Britain to victory in the 1982 Falklands/ Malvinas War, both indirect military power boosts to neoliberalism. In terms of political power, their opposition parties proved incapable of mounting a coherent alternative. In Britain the Labour Party split, and a separate Social Democratic Party hived off in 1981. This plus Thatcher's military victory made Labour unelectable for a decade.

Neoliberalism made lesser progress in most other countries. Yet one of its policies, the privatization of publicly owned companies, did spread globally. This was partly due to political power relations. Nationalized industries constituted 12 percent–15 percent of GDP across Europe. Some were inefficiently run and they did exhibit some of the weaknesses of large bureaucracies. Yet their sale could also raise revenue to ease troubled government budgets in the phase of deficit spending. When this began, Harold Macmillan, the British prime minister, who was from an upper-class family, called it "selling off the family silver." Thatcher also reasoned that privatization would weaken labor unions and make ordinary people into shareholders, leading them to support capitalism and the Conservative Party. Republican strategists reasoned likewise. Other governments of the Right shared these motives and followed suit, but then leftist ones joined in, welcoming the new revenue stream in a period of deficits. France and the Nordic countries became especially prolific in privatizations. By the new century Europe's public enterprises were only 7–8 percent of its GDP.

The first privatizations in the South had been in General Pinochet's Chile in 1973–4, though it was at first mostly of companies nationalized by the previous Socialist government of Allende. With the help of his "Chicago Boys" Pinochet then privatized Social Security in 1981 and more public companies in the mid-1980s. In the 1990s, a wave of privatization engulfed Latin America and the former Soviet bloc, with lesser waves spreading across parts of Asia and Africa. Economists say that privatization usually generated more efficiency, but in the South, and especially in Muslim countries and in the former Soviet Union, it was often not really neoliberal at all, not the handing over of power to the market, but rather the handing over of hitherto public resources to the client networks of the ruling regime. This was not free market capitalism but "politicized capitalism," in which access to the state conferred possession of private corporations. Foreign companies also acquired many of these assets. For these reasons privatization was rarely popular across the South, and the global spread of democracy tended to dry it up. After 2000 public companies still accounted for about 20 percent of global investment (López de Silanes & Chong, 2004; Sheshinski & López-Calva, 2003). Yet the privatization drive was generally acclaimed as a neoliberal success, and it certainly did roll back state intervention across the world, even if it only sometimes led to competitive market efficiencies. However, one cannot blame neoliberals for the perversions of their ideas in practice.

Financialization, privatization, and central bank independence were the parts of the neoliberal offensive from which few countries were immune. States lost control of their interest rates and the power to devalue their currencies periodically (for most of the Europeans this was also a consequence of their joining the Euro common currency). However, in other spheres neoliberal achievements were much less complete. In 1994 the OECD first committed to reducing employment rights in order to increase labor market flexibility but then backed away from this. The European Union committed itself to a compromise, balancing increased competition against a charter guaranteeing social rights.

Comparative analysis of welfare regimes and inequality

Low growth and productivity plus rising unemployment caused recession, while the export of manufacturing jobs to poorer countries deepened unemployment, whose insurance costs became insupportable. Demographic trends also raised government expenses as higher education expanded and as the population aged, forcing up pension and medical costs. These forces acted as a generational scissors, as fewer workers had to support more nonproductive young and elderly persons. Germany had seven workers supporting one pensioner in 1980, but this was down to three by 2010. As welfare states matured, more people become eligible for more benefits. These pressures did not result from either neoliberalism or globalization, and only some were even economic in origin. But they strained the neo-Keynesian state, causing fiscal crisis right across the North during the 1980s (Pierson, 1998, 2001; Angresano, 2011). If governments were to avoid a crushing debt burden, they either had to cut government spending or to raise more revenue from taxes. Tax increases were usually deemed politically impossible. Thus spending had to be cut and social security items were the biggest part of government budgets. Pressure was on the welfare state and on the center-Left parties who had spearheaded it. Some cuts were made everywhere (Huber & Stephens, 2001). This gave neoliberals the impression that their time had come. The collapse of the Soviet Union and the move of China toward market reforms only increased this belief.

The Left weakened in most advanced countries. It was greatly hurt by declining unionization occurring from the 1980s, mirrored in some developing countries in the 1990s. Women's union membership rates increased, but men's and young people's membership declined more. Public sector unions held steady but private sector unions greatly declined. Militancy also declined and strikes virtually disappeared in some countries. Deindustrialization in the North was the main cause, motivated by employers' desire to lower costs by lowering wages and avoid labor unions by moving to less developed countries, in what David Harvey and Beverly Silver have called the spatial fix to class conflict. This left fewer workers in sectors of traditional union strength in the North. Conversely, these jobs expanded in developing countries, but worker resistance to their harsh forms of labor exploitation took time to develop. We see in Chapter 8 that this resistance is currently deepening in what has become the world's premier industrial country, China.

In the North, however, though workers in expanding sectors like transport and public services held on to or increased their collective powers, the new high-tech revolution centered in electronic communications industries was not labor-intensive, while the expanding private service sector had smaller establishments, more casual and flexible employment, and so lower unionization. The expansion has been of two quite different types of work: well-educated workers in offices, especially in financial services, and low-level, often casual workers in the personal service sector. The collective laborer identified by Marx as the bearer of revolution, the interdependent workforce of the large factory, was giving way in the North of the world to the individualized workstation of the office and the isolated personal service worker. The export of manufacturing sector jobs and labor-saving technologies in newer industries also meant that unemployment, especially long-term unemployment, went up, while inflation went down. Both trends further weakened unions (Silver, 2003: 97–123, 130; Ebbinghaus & Visser, 1999; Visser, 2006). Politicians concluded that there was less need to placate the unions. With the collapse of communism there was also less electoral pressure on socialists from the far Left. Pressure seemed to be only from the Right, and so ostensibly leftist parties moved into the center, as the British and American parties had. In fact, Mudge (2011) shows that they adopted a great deal of neoliberal rhetoric, though less than conservative parties were doing. Socialism in all its guises was in crisis everywhere, its offensive stopped by these structural changes.

Public opinion also shifted, though in a different way. Polling data for twenty developed countries reveal no decline in support for leftist economic programs, but greater salience of conservative moral and nationalist rhetoric, a sign of a broader malaise in the North. Rightist parties advocated nationalism, conservative morality, and law and order, and this attracted many workers. European antiimmigrant sentiments entwined with cultural nationalism, and double-edged views of the welfare state emerged. Though most still favored economic redistribution in principle, many also saw welfare as transferring wealth from hardworking ordinary people like them to welfare scroungers (often immigrants) supported by unproductive government bureaucrats. Overall, the correlation between class and voting did not decline (Houtman et al., 2008: chaps. 4 & 7; Manza et al., 1995), but rightist populism strengthened, and Left parties moved into the center, making further progressive taxes or welfare programs unlikely.

This was the end of the long postwar period of the grand class compromise spearheaded by the center-Left. Power within capitalism was becoming more asymmetric, as working-class organization remained at the level of the individual nation-state, and also declined, while the capitalist class became more globally organized. This asymmetry emboldened neoliberals, capitalists, and conservatives alike. It seemed like the last days of the working class. Indeed, inequality began to widen in most advanced countries. In the period from 1980 to 2000 Gini coefficients of inequality increased in about 70 percent of the twenty-four OECD countries. This was the high point of neoliberalism. They rose most in the Anglophone countries, as we shall see, but few countries were wholly immune. Then over the period from the mid-1990s to the mid-2000s there was no overall pattern. There was no significant change in half the countries while Ginis rose in a quarter of the countries and fell in a quarter (OECD, 2008). Perhaps the neoliberal offensive had peaked.

There had not been a uniform response to the crisis, as Prasad's (2006) comparison of the United Kingdom, the United States, France, and West Germany reveals. The two Anglo countries (as we saw in Volume 3, chapter 9) had combined progressive taxes with means-tested welfare benefits targeted at the poor. The rich paid most for the welfare of the poor, but the employed working and lower middle classes paid something too. Since ordinary people had believed misfortune might strike them too, they had to a degree empathized with welfare recipients. Popular solidarity, which the Left called class solidarity, underpinned welfare states. But the very success of neo-Keynesianism through the 1950s and 1960s raised middling-income groups into higher tax brackets and spread the fiscal burden lower down the class structure. When recession hit in the 1970s, the burden increased. Now people became more receptive to conservative views of "welfare dependency" by "worthless scroungers" – in the United States with racial tinges. Prasad notes that the main electoral base of the Thatcher/Reagan ascent was among skilled manual and lower white-collar workers, the most likely to switch their votes rightward in the elections of 1979 and 1980. The working class was split down the middle. In the United States white male workers were increasingly abandoning labor unions and the Democratic Party. It was not so much that France and Germany retained a more powerful working class, but they had less progressive taxes and less targeted welfare benefits. Thus the middle classes received equal or more benefits than workers and so also had a stake in the welfare state. So despite immigrant and racist-tinged attitudes to "scroungers," to slash the welfare state would attack most people, not just the poor. There was less incentive for politicians to call for it. Popular rather than class solidarity mattered here.

This might be seen as merely delaying the outcome. At the beginning of the twenty-first century German Social Democratic politicians, seeking to solve the fiscal crisis of deficits, did defy hostile public opinion and introduce major welfare reforms, which on balance liberalized by reducing benefits, especially for the unemployed and the elderly, though this was partially offset by more generous benefits for families. Hinrichs (2010) says the reforms combined elements of both the Nordic and Anglophone welfare models, in effect ending Germany's traditional Bismarckian model. But he adds that from 2008 there was resistance to further liberalization. A further reform program was abandoned, and benefits for the unemployed were increased. This was due to the pressure of public opinion and the rise of a Left party challenging the Social Democrats in some of their heartlands. The struggle over welfare is ongoing.

Yet Streeck (2009) sees a process of liberalization, "a decline in centralized control and authoritative coordination," sweeping across German industry in five major sectors of economic activity: collective bargaining, unions and employers' associations, welfare corporatism, public finance, and corporate governance. One result, he says, is wage stagnation with widening inequality. He says the process began before German unification and was not primarily due to global pressures or to neoliberal ideas. It is mainly has to do with fiscal pressures plus the inability of the old German corporatist model to deal with structural changes in the economy, as the growth of a service sector overtakes in size Germany's traditional manufacturing strength, as industries need more flexible production and labor methods, and as the sheer diversity of the German economy increases. He thinks this is a process of institutional exhaustion – of corporatist institutions eventually undermining themselves. But there is a downside, and not only for the poor who lose by them. Wage stagnation and rising unemployment and inequality have the effect of reducing aggregate demand in the economy, as well as adding fiscal problems, since welfare contributions largely depend on the level of employment and wages. Since there is a lively Left in Germany offering more Keynesian policies, the country may not continue down this liberalizing path.

France is a different case. Under various pressures, including neoliberalism, it had abandoned capital controls, then radically denationalized industries, introduced more labor market flexibility, and made firing workers easier. Yet both socialist and Gaullist governments also introduced measures to compensate those likely to suffer from such policies, in the form of extensive job retraining, early retirement programs, and the expansion of health care, child care, and housing subsidies. At the end of the century France was spending 30 percent of GDP on social programs, higher than any country except the Nordics, double the level of U.S. spending, and its level of inequality had not widened at all (Evans & Sewell, 2011; Levy, 2005; Palier, 2005). In the early 2000s Nicholas Sarkozy briefly advocated Anglo-Saxon remedies for France, but when elected president he could only nibble at the fringes of France's highly cushioning welfare state. When the Great Neoliberal Recession struck, he began to attack "the Anglo Saxon economic model."

The notion of *solidarité* still dominates French welfare policy – we are all in this together. In 2004 the government became sufficiently concerned about the depletion of funds for public pensions that they added one day without pay for all employed persons, their salary being paid instead into the national pension fund. This day is called *la journée de solidarité*, the day of solidarity, people working harder for the benefit of the sick and elderly. France has still not introduced the reforms that are probably necessary to solve its fiscal and unemployment crises (Angresano, 2011: chap. 5), but popular disenchantment in France and elsewhere with what is seen as EU neoliberalism restricts options. Though national parliaments continue to ratify its deepening treaties, all but one of the popular referenda held from 2002 to 2008 rejected them – in France, Holland, Ireland, Denmark, and Sweden (Spain was the deviant case) – and five further referenda were called off by the politicians for fear of "no" votes. Elites favored a deepening of the EU but the people did not. The main reason for this was the fear of ordinary people that whereas they could exercise some degree of democratic control over their own nation-state, the EU seemed distant and beyond their control. Two rather different policy areas had brought this about, the supposed economic neoliberalism of the European Union and the increasing immigration of foreigners from newly admitted countries and elsewhere which the widening of the European Union had brought.

If we widen our perspective to all the advanced countries, Esping-Andersen's three welfare regimes – which I renamed as Anglo, Nordic, and Euro – help us make some sense of international differences, though they are not static but have trajectories of development or decay. Under fiscal pressure, they all shifted. All countries ran deflationary fiscal policies when hit by recession. All found ways to trim government budgets, including welfare cuts. But easily the biggest cuts were in the Anglos. The two Antipodean welfare systems were especially torn apart in the 1980s and 1990s (Huber & Stephens, 2001; Swank, 2002: chap. 6; International Government Office [ILO], 2008; Kato, 2003: 133–56; Starke, 2008).[1] The Anglos had liberal traditions of classical economics and moral individualism. In contrast, neoliberalism in continental Europe was muted by the postwar Christian Democrat/Social Democrat

---

[1] Australia and New Zealand depend heavily on raw material and semifinished exports. They were hit when Britain entered the EU and by a downturn in raw materials prices. Unemployment rocketed, and there were serious fiscal crises. Hence they engaged in the first major cuts in welfare budgets (Castles, 1998: 32–4; Starke, 2008). The pressure on the Antipodeans ended when Chinese economic growth increased demand for their raw materials.

compromise. Its milder neoliberalism, "ordo-liberalism," or the social market, was quite pragmatic and usually maintained state protections (Mudge,
2008: 710–18). Prasad dismisses such cultural explanations by noting that
supply-side economics were not influential among the politicians. But neoliberalism lies deeper than economics. To Thatcher, cutting back the state and
labor unions, selling off nationalized industries, reducing taxes, and enabling
tenants in public housing to buy their houses, all represented a freer society.
Anglo political leaders said they privatized, attacked unions, and tinkered with
tax codes to achieve freedom. This ideology resonated powerfully in countries
with liberal traditions, less so among the Nordics or Euros.

It spread across the Anglophone political spectrum. Blair's New Labour
embraced market-friendly policies, as did Clinton's New Democrats. Their
"third ways" declared that individual citizens had responsibilities as well as
rights – rights were conditional, not universal. In Clinton's welfare reform,
work was made compulsory even for single parents in return for temporary
cash assistance, which could not last longer than two years (five years during one's lifetime). This plus stringent eligibility requirements halved the welfare rolls, though most pushed off them remained in poverty, beset by chronic
problems of child care, access to health care, low-wage casualization, and
hasty classification by overworked case workers into worthy and unworthy
cases (Handler, 2004). Blair's New Labour depoliticized state regulation so
that new rules seemed to result from market pressures. The Bank of England
set high interest rates and high sterling values to please the markets, and the
government could not be blamed for the consequent downward pressure on
wages, while the public sector was run by impersonal cost-accounting methods
(Burnham, 2001). The Australian and New Zealand Labour Parties introduced
market-conforming policies in trade, privatization, and welfare reform (Swank,
2002: chap. 6; Starke, 2008: chap. 4). Blair was influenced by the Australian
Premier Paul Keating and New Zealand's Rogernomics. New notions of best
practices diffused freely among the Anglos. Political elites in Australia and
New Zealand often receive their higher education in the United Kingdom,
while Canadians go to both the United States and the United Kingdom.

If neoliberal theory is correct, bigger cuts would be needed in the more
expensive welfare states. Yet the reverse happened. The biggest slashers were
the already-measly Anglos. Others cut only at the margins, with little regressive impact. The Nordic countries did not abandon universal benefit rights;
the Euros did move a little from their systems of universal but status-unequal
rights. A comparative study among them (Palier, 2010) reveals some liberalizing reforms, including more benefits targeted specifically at the poor like
noncontributory safety-net pensions. These save them money, as does raising the retirement age, and people are also encouraged to join private pension schemes. More have moved a little toward dualism or, as one of Palier's
authors puts it, "selective universalism." Like Germany most Euro countries

have borrowed Nordic as well as Anglo programs, such as health services based on citizen rather than employment entitlement (though this is the British pattern too). Apart from saving money, there does not seem much of a general pattern among the Euros (Palier, 2010). Angresano (2011) shows that relatively successful reform programs in Sweden and the Netherlands achieved consensus through introducing pragmatic, piecemeal reforms that did not threaten the fundamentals of their programs (he says that New Zealand reforms did this also, though at the cost of greater inequality and poverty). Neoliberal ambitions did emerge in most countries but were scaled down in the face of popular opposition. French and Italian reformers have been stymied in this way. The Swedish Moderaterna Party gained power in 1991 but had already abandoned most of its neoliberal program, having realized just how popular was the welfare state. The Social Democrats then returned to power and made minor cuts to balance the budget. When the neoliberals returned to power in 2006, they cut programs and taxes slightly and they claim to be committed to lower taxes in the long run, but if the welfare state remains inviolable, it is difficult to see how. Like the Danish neoliberal Venstre Party, they turned instead to a *Kulturkampf* focused on moral decline, nationalism, and immigrant bashing to win votes (Lindbom, 2008). The Nordics and Euros perceive a welfare crisis and are no longer moving forward. The fiscal pressures remain, and if the unemployment levels of the Great Recession continue, they will intensify.

The European equivalent of workfare was the activation program, in which welfare claimants had to enter individual contracts agreed with case managers: workers would seek employment, while case managers would help them and provide interim benefits. More jobs were also created with government subsidies. Similar case overload to that in U.S. workfare pushed case managers to hasty classification of the unemployed in order to devote more time to worthy cases (Peck, 2001; Handler, 2004). The Swedish system provided the template for the 1998 EU Employment Strategy, which imposed the duty on the unemployed to participate in labor market programs after a given length of unemployment. But unlike the United States, European countries paid higher short-term unemployment benefit, plus lesser social assistance with much longer duration than American programs. The Euro experience is that activation programs lowered unemployment rates, though at the cost of reinforcing dualism, for the jobs created in this way usually had low wages and benefits (Palier, 2010: 380–3). But again, if the Great Recession lasts much longer, these programs will be under greater pressure.

The Nordics and the more northerly Euros differed in having corporatist states inside of which capital and labor had reached binding agreements. Once such structures are institutionalized, big corporations often favor universal employment-related benefits and active labor market policies since they reduce the pressure from competition from low-wage industries – though we have seen German corporatism weakening. Under the Ghent system operating in several countries unions participated in the disbursement of work-related benefits. Here union membership held up 20 percent–30 percent better than among the Anglos, where benefits are distributed by civil servants and unions are confined to decentralized market bargaining (Western, 1993; Scruggs & Lange, 2002; Ebbinghaus & Visser, 1999; ILO, 2008; Huber & Stephens, 2001; Pontusson, 2005). This produced greater infrastructural powers in the form of binding agreements to cope with economic and fiscal difficulties. It entrenched conflict resolution inside the state and allowed the *defense* of welfare benefits, not their extension.

A conservatism of the Left was digging in, trying to freeze most of the existing welfare system, bending somewhat to fiscal pressures, unable to advance it further. The major regress was a new one. Immigrants from outside Western Europe experienced more unemployment, casualization, and restricted welfare benefits. Germany and Sweden also lacked minimum wage laws, which had not been a problem in times of full employment, but now this put further pressure on the poor. This was part of the drift toward the emergence of a dual labor market in corporatist countries. Native-born skilled and unionized workers maintained their defenses, but a growing casual labor market for less-skilled and immigrant workers meant fewer rights for them. This trend seemed especially strong – or perhaps just especially shocking – in Germany. Defensive racism and dual labor markets obviously weakened working-class movements.

The Anglos had very few protections. Since the participation of Anglo employers, unions, and the state in bargaining institutions remained voluntary, they could freely withdraw from them. When Mrs. Thatcher refused to invite union leaders into 10 Downing Street, she ended one bargaining institution at a stroke. Her predecessors had often solved industrial disputes over beer and sandwiches at No. 10. She then passed legislation restricting union rights to strike. Yet collective bargaining agreements did not decline in Euro countries, with the notable exception of Germany, and they expanded in the Nordic countries, the Netherlands, and France, where they rose to cover 90 percent of the labor force by 2000.[2] This was occurring at the same time as neoliberal advances in financialization and privatization, revealing how uneven neoliberal pressure was. In contrast, bargaining coverage declined in all the Anglos – precipitously in the United Kingdom and New Zealand, from (respectively) 70 percent and 60 percent in 1980 to 30 percent and 25 percent in 2000. By 2005 Australian and Irish union density had also fallen precipitously (Pontusson, 2005: 99; ILO, 2008: table 3.2, p. 82). Conservative governments abolished New Zealand's labor arbitration courts between 1987 and 1991 and emasculated Australia's

---

[2] Several sociologists claim French unions are weak because of low membership density (e.g., Prasad, 2006; Wilensky, 2002; Kato, 2005). This is misleading. In France only militants tend to be union members, but union bargaining covers almost all workers, and when a strike is called, members and nonmembers alike come out.

in 2006. This greatly reduced earlier Antipodean distinctiveness and made the Anglophone countries more similar to each other. In all the Anglo countries conservatives could relaunch class conflicts that had been thought settled.

These macroregional differences were reflected in inequality levels. The Anglophones had been among the most egalitarian countries in the 1950s, but the Nordics shot ahead of them in the late 1960s and the Euros in the 1980s. From the 1970s inequality widened most among the Anglos, especially in the United States. Though it widened in some Euros too, their collective Gini changed very little. Luxemburg Income Study data reveal big increases in wage inequality since the 1980s in the United States, United Kingdom, and New Zealand, with less change in most European countries. One new trend emerged in Europe. Three Mediterranean countries, Greece, Italy, and Spain, were reaching up toward the Anglos in their level of inequality (Mann & Riley, 2007; Smeeding, 2002; Kenworthy, 2004; Pontusson, 2005: chap. 3; Alesina & Glaeser, 2005: chap. 4).[3] So these macroregions should not be reified. They changed through time. Yet Anglophone enterprises also became dominated by the goal of maximizing shareholder value and giving equity stakes to top managers. Thus income and wealth for the top 1 percent rocketed. The managerial revolution, predicted by Berle and Means in the 1940s, had finally half-arrived. Top managers in Anglo capitalist enterprises were now paying themselves salaries equivalent to the wealth of their rentier predecessors. But what Berle and Means had not anticipated was that big shareholders were in league with them, owners and controllers of capital united (ILO, 2008: chaps. 1 & 2; OECD, 2008: figures 1.1, 1.2 & chap. 8; Castles & Obinger, 2008; Atkinson et al., 2007).[4]

One component of rising class inequality is increasing gender equality. This has gone further in higher income occupations, where it is accompanied by more intraclass mating. High-income men marry or cohabit with high-income women, greatly increasing their household income. Lower down the income scale, working women earn less than their men, often in part-time and/or casual jobs. Thus their household incomes have barely risen at all. Moreover, the divorce patterns of the feminist revolution have been unhelpful to the poor. Instead of divorce being more common among higher occupations, as in the past, it is now more common among lower levels. Single mothers are now concentrated among the poor, and their difficulties in combining work with

---

[3] Once the 15-state European Union was enlarged to cover Eastern European countries, inequality between EU countries widened since some were now much poorer.

[4] Neoliberals sometimes argue that growing inequality, especially tax cuts for the wealthy, results in their paying a higher proportion of U.S. taxes. This is true but only in a negative sense. The wealthy have paid more taxes because lower tax rates for them increased their numbers. The rich paid more tax because they made more, the poor paid less tax because they made less, and the number of the wealthy remains less than 1 percent of the population.

child care make them even poorer. But there are differences between the two main locations of mature feminism, the Nordic and the Anglo countries. In both more than 75 percent of women work full-time through most of their adult lives but only the Nordics provide free child-care facilities so single mothers can work full-time, normally in the public sector for decent wages. Thus female inequality is higher among the Anglos than the Nordics. In this respect the Euros are not a coherent group, since female participation rates are lower, while the Mediterranean countries have not yet experienced rocketing divorce rates among the poor. But maybe they will adopt the same feminist routes as the Anglo and Nordic pioneers (Esping-Andersen, 2011).

More generally, income inequality widened more where unions weakened more and where wage bargaining was most decentralized. Nordic and northerly Euro corporatism protected a little. The limits imposed by business confidence were greater in some countries than others. Anglo taxes also became much more regressive as the top brackets of income and corporation taxes were reduced. Redistribution was no longer such a high priority of their tax systems. In Britain "the tax system has come to be considered a source instead of a remedy for market distortions," while social security became a problem for economic efficiency more than a solution to poverty (says Kato, 2003: 85, 89; cf. Starke, 2008: 87). Since the Anglos had relied more on taxes to effect redistribution, their posttax and posttransfers inequality level rose most. In the Nordic and northerly Social Christian countries, posttax and transfer inequality widened less than labor market income inequalities (ILO, 2008: table 2.2, p. 53, 136–9; Castles & Obinger, 2008; Kato, 2003; Mahler & Jesuit, 2006; OECD, 2008: figure 4.4). Steinmo (2010) emphasizes the contrast between posttax transfers in Sweden and the United States. Overall social spending is a third higher in Sweden than in the United States. But posttax transfers are more than twice as high in Sweden. The Swedish tax system is simple: it taxes everybody (including welfare recipients) yet redistributes to the poor. In contrast, American taxes are complex, involving numerous allowances and exemptions whose effect is to redistribute in a hidden way to the middle and upper classes.

We have seen macroregional differences remained important throughout the period, though to a diminishing extent. Since I have persistently noted that one country or another does not conform to its macroregional type, nation-states also remain distinctive. Though Harvey is correct that the period of greatest neoliberal power saw redistribution toward the highest social classes, this was not quite universal. Most Anglophone scholars (who dominate these debates) tend to think their local experience is typical of the world. It is not – at least not yet. And so the fourth trend was that United States became truly extreme within the North – though paralleled in the world in terms of inequality by former communist countries. I discuss U.S. inequality further in Chapter 11, since it played such a large part in the Great Neoliberal Crisis of 2008.

Efficiency and equality

Growing inequality might, however, be a good thing. Neoliberals see trade-offs between efficiency and equality: too much equality reduces incentives, too much regulation and collective bargaining is a drain on employers, too much state expenditure crowds out private investment. Pessimistic leftists agree, gloomily seeing a race to the bottom as governments slash spending and regulation to attract investment. Both see capitalist efficiency, and especially "business confidence," imposing strict limits on states. Markets do best, neoliberals claim, and business confidence will be higher where markets are liberated. The world will converge on the liberal – usually the American – model, or it will fail, so this argument goes.

In this efficiency scenario, there should be trickle-down effects from neoliberal programs that after a time begin to reduce the incidence of poverty. Brady (2009) has examined data on eighteen OECD countries. Like many others, he finds that welfare generosity is correlated with the strength of the political Left. He shows, not unexpectedly, that there is a small effect of economic growth on the poverty rate: growth reduces poverty. But this effect is much less than that of government intervention in markets, especially through welfare programs, which reduce poverty much more. He also shows that labor productivity and human capital resources have almost no impact on the poverty level. It seems that if you want to reduce poverty, you do not rely on market forces; government must tackle it directly and Left governments do.

In the neoliberal scenario, the growth rate of countries with more equality and larger welfare states should also be lower. But this is not the case, either in the West, in Asia, or in Latin America (Amsden, 2001). Lindert (2004: chaps. 10–14) showed higher social spending and taxes did not lead to lower growth, provided the taxes were universal, simple, and designed to foster growth. Swank (1992) showed that higher welfare spending did not lead to lower investment. Garrett (1998) showed it did not make an economy less competitive. Pontusson (2005) confirmed all of this on more recent data. In Volume III I discussed varieties of capitalism models, finding them to be of some utility, despite many variations among individual countries. Between 1960 and 1980 the Social Market Economies (SMEs) of Europe did better economically than the Liberal Market Economies (LME Anglos), while between 1980 and 2000 there was no significant difference between them. In this study the United States only kept pace by increasing the number of hours people work – Americans endure more stress and less leisure for equal growth, not the most desirable option!

Iverson believes that each of the two systems has comparative advantages. The SMEs' higher level of investment in technical education and their active labor market policies gave young people at the lower educational end incentives to work hard to get into good vocational schools and apprenticeships, giving "a comparative advantage to companies that compete in markets where there is a premium on the ability to develop deep competencies within established technologies and to upgrade and diversify existing product lines continuously." In contrast, says Iverson, American bifurcated education gave companies a comparative advantage in low-skill services and high-skill, high-tech products, with more hiring and firing flexibility and "high responsiveness to new business opportunities and ... rapid product innovation strategies" (Iverson, 2005: 14–15). Yet Streeck (2009) sees a blend of the two as being more suited to the current German economy.

Bradley and Stephens (2007) analyze employment rates in seventeen advanced countries between 1974 and 1999. They find that high short-term unemployment replacement rates (i.e., high unemployment pay), active labor market policies, and neocorporatist bargaining structures (Nordic policies) are better at boosting employment levels, though long-term unemployment replacement rates, high social security taxes, and strict employment protection laws depress aggregate employment. But in educational performance Anglo inferiority is clear. Nelson and Stephens (2009) show that the Anglos perform much worse than the Nordics, with most of the Euros positioned between them. Whereas in the 1950s Canada and the United States had led the world in public education, by the 1990s they lagged. Particularly damning is a measure of "information age literacy" considered necessary by the OECD for future economic growth. Here the Anglos lag greatly (though Canada and Australia less so). Those world-class American and British elite universities are mostly for the elites rather than the masses (cf. Iversen & Stephens, 2008; Hall & Soskice, 2001: 38–44; Estevez-Abe et al., 2001). Human capital inequalities reinforce material inequalities – and the OECD considers that this limits growth potential. Is it possible to have economic growth while depriving 30 percent of the population of social citizenship? Such a model would have considerable costs.

Panic (2007) analyzes the performance of seven countries over the periods 1989–98 and 1999–2004. Overall, the Anglos were outperformed. Norway and Sweden ranked highest on his aggregate score, which combined five components of economic health (GDP growth, unemployment, consumer prices, Gini coefficient of inequality, and trade balances). Then came the Netherlands and Germany, then France, then at the bottom the United Kingdom and the United States. But, says Panic, social well-being not economic growth should be the goal. He assembles eleven measures of well-being: three measures of inequality, the poverty rate, mortality rates, obesity, illiteracy, economic security, size of the prison population, and perceptions of corruption and trust. On nine of the eleven the United States ranked the worst. The United Kingdom ranked next to the last on eight of the eleven measures. Sweden and Norway were best on all but one (Swedes were surprisingly obese), followed by the Netherlands and Germany. Panic sees a connection between economic and social well-being: the more shared is the good life, the greater the social cohesion, and the more effectively people will work – a social democratic and not a neoliberal view of efficiency.

Kangas (2010) uses an even more direct measure of well-being: life expectancy. Collecting data for seventeen OECD countries he shows that the higher the GDP per capita, the longer the lives of the citizens. This is not unexpected, though the effect tapers off at the highest standards of living. But he finds a stronger relationship between life expectancy and universal welfare state coverage. Universal rights to welfare are more important than the overall size of welfare spending – though that too improves life expectancy, he finds. It is better to have broader coverage or universal access to care than to have more generous benefits channeled only to some citizens. Welfare states are good for you, whatever neoliberals say.

So in the North of the world the neoliberal turn had variable impacts on welfare and inequality. It had major effects on the Anglos, where it resonated amid old liberal ideologies and voluntaristic institutions and where it could ally with conservatives and profit from shifts in the middle of the class structure and the decline of labor unions. Elsewhere neoliberal pressures were not the most important ones forcing budget cuts, and the outcomes were only partially neoliberal. Social and Christian Democrats sought to retain their historic compromise while bending somewhat to new fiscal pressures. On the whole neoliberalism was less efficient as well as being less humane. But for the most infrastructurally powerful states of the world, varied choices remained possible. There is more than one way to run capitalism. The rich do better in the Anglo-American model; ordinary people do better in European models. Business confidence is obviously very important, but it might go either way: economic elites might wish to see their own immediate incomes increase, or they might prefer their businesses to do well out of higher mass demand. Since norms are influenced by one's environment, each macroregion thought its own model was the natural version of capitalism and so maintained its own institutional practices (Hall & Gingerich, 2003: 22). But what about the supposedly less powerful states of the world?

The South: I. Structural adjustment programs and after

So far I have discussed within-country inequalities inside the global North. Since these countries all have quite similar standards of living, between-country inequality in the North is not great. Of course, the really big global inequality is between the North and the South. Economic development in the South has not yet changed this degree of inequality. Take India and China, the countries seeing the greatest growth. The average person in the top 5 percent of India's population makes about the same as the average person in the bottom 5 percent of Americans, an incredible statistic. For China the absolute gap in welfare between an average American and an average Chinese has widened significantly since China's growth spurt. The richest 10 percent of the world's population (almost all in the North) have 56 percent of global income, while the poorest 10 percent have only 0.7 percent (Milanovic, 2010: chap. 2). Part of the problem was that the growth of China, India, and others was occurring at the high tide of neoliberalism when it was widely thought that such inequality was good for growth. Yet in the South the countries with the least internal inequality actually had the most growth since this produced a more homogeneous, cohesive nation offering more support to government policies of export subsidies and picking winners (Amsden, 2001).

The full force of neoliberalism in the South was felt on countries falling into debt in the 1970s and 1980s. The OPEC oil price rise of 1973 made European and American banks awash with petrodollars and U.S. banks had been newly freed from investing in Treasury notes. This generated overaccumulation, a mass of liquid wealth unable to find sufficient avenues of productive investment (finally the Hobson/Lenin explanation of imperialism might work!). Now the banks wanted to lend to less developed countries, offering them low interest rates, enabling them to borrow massively to finance their sagging economies without having to prove themselves credit-worthy. Then in 1979 Fed Chairman Paul Volcker suddenly tripled U.S. interest rates, mainly to fight inflation at home. Other countries had to follow U.S. rates upward. The cost of repaying loans increased and a debt crisis ensued. When a country is heavily indebted, the limits imposed by investor confidence become much tighter, corresponding closely to the Marxian notion that modern states are dominated by capitalism. Here, indeed, they are.

The World Bank and the IMF now shifted their focus from the North to the South. Their structural adjustment programs became the cutting edge of an economic imperialism all the more effective because its practitioners sincerely believed it was rational economics, good for everyone, encouraging freedom. The neoliberal Washington Consensus resulted: the banks would bail out indebted countries, agreeing to restructure their loans in return for an austerity program of cutting government spending, imposing high interest rates, stabilizing the currency, privatizing state-owned enterprises, abolishing tariffs, freeing labor markets from union restrictions, and opening up domestic capital markets and business ownership to foreigners.

This was massive curtailing of the sovereignty of poorer countries. Enforcement of the loan terms would weaken government infrastructures in health, education, and transport and increase their dependence on the North. The peripheral state remained formally sovereign and so could in principle reject the loan offer, though the consequence might be bankruptcy, future higher interest rates, and even possible exclusion from the international economy. It was an offer that most southern governments felt they could not refuse. Indebtedness had weakened them.

Though led by the United States, and benefiting its business interests, this offensive was by global finance capital backed by most northern states. The IMF and the World Bank are international not transnational organizations. Their governing boards are composed of representatives of states whose influence depends on their geopolitical and geoeconomic power. The European representatives were endorsing policies abroad quite at odds with their domestic political economy. But they were also bankers, economists, and corporate lawyers protecting the interests of their friends and relations. The policy would get their loans repaid and they could acquire foreign assets at bargain prices. Geopolitics were also involved. IMF and World Bank loans were more likely to be given, and loan conditions were less likely to be enforced, where states were heavily indebted to U.S. banks, received U.S. aid, or voted at the UN with the United States – or indeed with France (Oatley & Yackee, 2004; Stone, 2004). The United States was the leader, but all northern finance benefited.

The programs contained elements with different effects. Better-off countries were able to pay their debts off – and this was the main goal of the programs. They also furthered countries' integration into the global economy, shrank budget deficits, and ended hyperinflation – all beneficial effects. The ending of hyperinflation in Brazil in the 1990s under President Cardoso was an important precondition for later economic growth. Where the local state was incompetent or corrupt, cutting it back might also do good. Existing Latin American welfare state benefits were not universal but reserved for a privileged public sector and the patron-client networks of ruling regimes. Cutting them back may have cleared the way for the later development of more universal programs. Neoliberalism had virtues and at first many southern elites believed they were necessary.

Yet the destruction of unions, the encouragement of more flexible labor markets, and the elimination of tariffs protecting domestic industries increased imports, unemployment, and poverty, all reducing demand, redistributing from the poor to the rich, from labor to capital, and from local to foreign capital. Some did well out of neoliberalism, but not the masses. Vreeland (2003; cf. Morley, 2001) calculated that the share of labor in the national income dropped an average of 7 percent where IMF structural adjustment programs were implemented. The financial reforms also increased inflows of short-term foreign capital, which tended to destabilize the local economy while allowing northern businesses and banks to buy up assets at bargain prices. Structural adjustment programs and level of debt servicing have particularly hurt labor unions in less developed countries, reducing their membership substantially (Martin & Brady, 2007). This was fully intended, of course. This was a shift in power from the people to capitalists.

The bottom line was supposed to be economic growth, which might in the long run justify what neoliberals admitted were short-term side effects. Yet growth rarely materialized. Vreeland examined 135 countries that between

1952 and 1990 were subjected to the equivalent of one thousand years of IMF programs. Controlling for intervening variables, the more IMF assistance they received, the worse they did. The cost of tutelage was on average 1.6 percent less economic growth per annum, a sizeble amount. When he repeated the analysis on a 1990s dataset, he got 1.4 percent less growth (2003: 123–30). Then Kose et al. (2006) found no relationship between growth and capital account openness up to the mid-2000s, while Prasad et al. (2007) and Gourinchas and Jeanne (2007) found productivity growth was highest in countries that shunned foreign capital! It seems foreign loans are not good for your economy, perhaps because they are used more for short-term boosting of consumer demand (often to win elections) than for long-term growth (Rodrik & Subramanian, 2008). Finally, the countries that did best in the 1980s and 1990s, when developing countries as a whole averaged exactly zero growth, were those that most ignored IMF and World Bank norms. China, India, South Korea, Taiwan, Botswana, Mauritius, Poland, Malaysia, and Vietnam blended existing local practices with both neoliberal and heterodox economic reforms (Roberts & Parks, 2007: 51; Lim, 2010). These data suggest that neoliberalism and lower growth were not just correlated – unalloyed neoliberalism *caused* low growth.

Given such a poor record, southern support for structural adjustment reforms declined sharply. Nonetheless, some states persisted with IMF programs. Many poor countries felt coerced by debt. The alternative to compliance was default and the complete flight of capital. Some were not doing much better than this, paying 20 percent–25 percent of their export earnings in debt interest (Sassen, 2010). But some local elites welcomed the programs since they could now introduce reforms that benefited them while deflecting criticism onto the IMF. Elites benefited from the redistribution from labor to capital. Vreeland calculates that while the share of labor in national income dropped on average 7 percent, capital made a net gain, despite overall GDP slowdown (2003: 126, 153; cf. Hutchinson, 2001; Biersteker, 1992: 114–16). Politicians were happy too. From a period in which little foreign capital had been available, they now had access to riches. Accepting loans enabled them to distribute benefits to their clients, a form of politicized capitalism. In democracies it helped them win elections by boosting immediate consumer demand and imports, rarely a recipe for long-term growth. Now neoliberals lamented their inability to implement the programs themselves and railed at corrupt politicians.

The crisis was later in East Asia. These countries' high domestic savings had kept them out of debt and in control of the inflow of foreign capital. At the time when neoliberalism was having its biggest impact on the West, East Asia remained statist. Export-subsidizing industrialization from the 1970s had generated economic success. But in the early 1990s, following current economic wisdom and pressure from international agencies, some East Asian countries began to liberalize capital flows under American and WTO pressure. In South

Korea the chaebol corporations were already borrowing too much when the government perversely opened up short-term while controlling long-term foreign borrowing. Thus much hot capital flowed in, and at the first sign of economic difficulties, flowed out again (Gemici, 2008). This vulnerability was encouraged by IMF- and World Bank–supported policies like the exchange rate peg, the sterilization of capital inflows to prevent currency appreciation and inflation, the liberalization of capital accounts, and domestic financial liberalization. Hedge funds were thus permitted to become very active in speculation against East Asian economies, leveraging positions of up to 100 to 1 (investments to reserves) to target a currency and make money out of its subsequent devaluation (Krugman, 2008). This package of policies and actions caused the Asian crisis of 1997. Despite this the U.S. Treasury, American financial firms, the IMF, and OECD continued to pressure the South Korean authorities to open up their financial sector further to foreigners, who in 1998 were allowed to establish bank subsidiaries and brokerage houses in Korea. "Lobbying by American financial services firms, which wanted to crack the Korean market, was the driving force behind the Treasury's pressure on Korea," says Blustein. IMF officials disliked these "ulterior motives." One said, "The US saw this as an opportunity, as they did in many countries, to crack open all these things that for years have bothered them." The United States also shot down a Japanese attempt to lead a rival East Asian financial consortium to solve the crisis (Blustein, 2001: 143–5, 164–70; Amsden, 2001).

Further financial crises recurred across Asia, and in Russia and Brazil between 1997 and 1999, too vulnerable to short-term capital flows and specifically to hedge fund manipulations. Finally, however, neoliberalism came under attack from within the international establishment. The 1997 World Development Report of the World Bank accepted the utility of what it called an effective state, not a minimal one, which should be armed with infrastructural and investment programs (World Bank, 1997: 27). The complementarity of state and markets turned into a "Post-Washington Consensus." Stiglitz argued that state policies to promote financial regulation, R&D funding, environmental sustainability, equality, and workplace democracy were all needed – but only temporarily: "The government should serve as a complement to markets, undertaking actions that make markets work better and correcting market failures. In some cases the government has proved to be an effective catalyst.... But once it has performed its catalytic role, the state needs to withdraw" (Stiglitz, 1998: 26). Yet since markets are always imperfect, the state is here to stay.

Developing countries learned from the Asian crisis. To comply with WTO rules, governments formally withdrew their subsidies to exports but actually renamed them as supports to science, technology, or poorer regions (Amsden, 2001). The South Korean government let fourteen chaebols go bankrupt and closed or restructured twelve of the biggest banks, while funneling $60 billion to write off bad loans and boost the remaining banks' cash reserves. As the chaebols were tamed, so the autonomy of the central bank was reduced, restoring financial regulation from private hands to state control (Lim, 2010). Countries with high growth rates realized they were attractive to foreign investors and so could impose conditions on them. Gemici (2008) says the goal is (1) to attract long-term productive cold money, not short-term speculative hot money by imposing taxes on short-term withdrawals of funds, and (2) to put the foreign capital into productive investment not into boosting consumption (which sucks in imports) or reducing government deficits. If a government seeks to use loans to win the next election by boosting consumption without increasing productivity, then inflation, rising imports, and balance of payments crises will result, followed by foreign capital's demanding further structural adjustments. Government skill matters and Gemici shows that in Chile, South Korea, and Turkey the policies adopted, some wise, others foolish, were mainly explained by domestic power configurations, not foreign pressures. These states remained sovereign enough to adjust the limits of investor confidence – and to make their own mistakes.

The lesson was that governments retain some sovereign autonomy unless their debts mount or they are vulnerable to volatile flows of hot money. Most middle-income countries soon resumed economic growth and so could increase their reserves to avoid debts to international banks (this had the downside of boosting the global imbalances that contributed to the Great Neoliberal Recession of 2008, discussed in Chapter 11). All the East Asian and ASEAN countries did this. Neoliberalism lingered on among officials trained in its models; no country seeks to go back simply to preneoliberal days, and it sometimes remains the default mode of policy. However, in most countries there were adaptations, creating variations some of which might be called centrist neoliberalism, with more active government planning, restrained regulation, and some welfare programs, while other adaptations were more corrupt forms of politicized capitalism. Neoliberalism in the Anglo-American mode did not overwhelm the world. Developing nation-states could resist or pervert it. It is ironic that whereas by the end of the twentieth century regulation of finance was revived by some developing countries, in the old North financial regulations were still being dismantled. There the lessons of the East Asian and Russian financial crises were being ignored. The West was sinking; the Rest were rising.

This unexpected contrast between the West and some of the Rest is also revealed in welfare policies. In East Asia the authoritarian regimes of the 1970s and early 1980s had not developed welfare programs, with the notable exception of education. But democratization coupled with economic growth in the late 1980s had led to increased welfare spending and the Asian crisis did not halt this. The coverage of health programs in Taiwan and South Korea steadily widened through the 1990s to the whole population, with South

Korea also moving toward the single-payer insurance model that Taiwan had already established. Since Koreans must still contribute about 40 percent of costs in copayments, and Taiwanese about half of that, these are not yet complete European-style health care systems, but they are moving in that direction. The 1997 crisis actually had a positive effect on welfare, exposing the gaps in welfare programs, which had formerly focused on employees of large corporations. In response programs were extended to cover those not working, including the poor, the elderly, and the unemployed, for whom retraining programs were also introduced. This also increased mass demand in the economy. Since economic growth soon returned, there was no enduring fiscal crisis to prevent such welfare state expansion, while democratic development rhetoric now promoted it (Wong, 2004; Haggard & Kaufman, 2008).

Latin America recovered more slowly from its debt crisis. But economic growth did eventually occur. Some of the groundwork had been laid by neoliberal programs that had achieved macroeconomic stability; reduced imbalances, inflation, and debt; privatized inefficient industries; streamlined government; and increased foreign capital flows. However, these achievements had been at severe cost. There were higher unemployment, lower wages, and more poverty, all of which reduced demand and led to lower growth – in Brazil the lowest growth rate in the entire century. Neoliberal reforms were not a success story, but they could be a platform. Brazil began to profit when the Lula government (from 2003), while maintaining market programs, introduced more proactive macroeconomic planning, including more government investment, social welfare programs (especially the Bolsa Familia), and minimum wages, all aimed at increasing mass demand. Primary education was also greatly expanded, large-scale cash and land transfer programs to the poor began, and the state poured investment into infrastructures including transport and energy and high-tech industries. Welfare programs shifted from being the privilege of highly paid workers toward being universal rights. By the 2000s this combination had produced more diversity in the Brazilian economy, able to exploit its abundance of natural resources with internationally competitive corporations. Other center-Left regimes across the region followed suit with active macroeconomic policies, aided in the Andean countries by pressure from newly organized indigenous peoples.

The results were higher growth rates coupled with declining poverty and inequality in most Latin American countries in the first decade of the twenty-first century (López-Calva & Lustig, 2010; Evans & Sewell, 2011). Brazil under Lula was the exemplary case of what might be called leftist neoliberalism. Between 2004 and 2010, the Brazilian economy grew at 4.2 percent per annum, more than twice the rate achieved between 1980 and 2004, despite the Great Neoliberal Recession of 2008, which produced zero growth in 2009. In Brazil a smaller but more proactive state embodying greater citizenship helped propel the country into membership of the BRIC group of countries

(Brazil, Russia, India, and China), which some believe will inherit the earth. So during the decades when social citizen rights in the West were under threat, they were being expanded in East Asia and Latin America.

In Africa until 2000 economic decline persisted regardless of development strategy (Nugent, 2004: 326–47). Some postcolonial states had followed the capitalist road; others pioneered African socialism. But all had floundered amid desperate rural and shantytown poverty caused by dependence on raw materials exports, often of a single product; by the 1970s global downturn; by volatile yet generally falling commodity prices; by population growth; by rising trade and budget deficits and debts; and by political corruption. In the 1980s the states went cap in hand to the international banks for loans and received structural adjustment programs in return for opening up markets and weakening their states. The program seemed appropriate in one sense, for many African states were corrupt and ineffective. They are essentially too small, typically raising revenue of only 10 percent of GDP, compared to the 30 percent–50 percent of advanced states. This means they lack the basic health, education, communications infrastructures, and court and police institutions necessary for a modern state. On top of that, many are also corrupt and some experience considerable violence. None of Fukuyama's (2011) three prerequisites for good government – the provision of order, the rule of law, and accountability of government – has been present in about one-half of African countries.

Whether neoliberal reforms worked in Africa is difficult to determine, given inadequate statistics and the dislocations brought about by contingent factors like civil wars (destructive) and mineral finds (bonanzas). Debt repayments always exceeded total foreign aid, and in the late 1990s the debt to GNP ratio in Africa stood at 123 percent, compared to 42 percent in Latin America and 28 percent in Asia (Sassen, 2010). Privatization of inefficient state industries produced benefit especially where union rights were entrenched in law. If they were not entrenched, then efficiency gains by the new owners, usually foreign, were largely due to lower wages while profits went abroad, with little benefit to Africans. Where privatization merely handed over nationalized industries to friends of the regime, not much benefit flowed at all. Overall, the annual rate of growth in sub-Saharan Africa declined from 1.6 percent during 1960–80 to −0.3 percent during 1980–2004, a terrible trend (Chang, 2009). Neoliberal programs increased inequality amid policies that deliberately cut back health and education programs – just as the AIDS human immunodeficiency virus (HIV) struck the continent. Without economic growth greater than population growth, they also increased indebtedness.

Then came a salutary shift in developmental economics. International programs for Africa in the 1990s began to encourage good governance and infrastructural development. Harrison (2005) says this was a rollout neoliberal phase, rolling out state powers to create efficient markets by building more physical infrastructures, developing schooling, and extending central and local government infrastructural powers in rural areas so that property rights could be guaranteed. The programs also involve poverty reduction, partly through extending welfare safety nets for the poor. NGOs were partners in the programs in order to strengthen civil society. But it seems a bit of a stretch to continue calling such policies neoliberal, since they were now encouraging good statism as well as freer markets. Neoliberalism was in reality faltering and compromising in Africa as elsewhere. This seems to have been a spur to the economic growth of around 5 percent that was occurring in the first decade of this century, driven by the oil economies of Angola, Nigeria, and the Sudan; by China's increasing demand for raw materials; by big inflows of profitable foreign direct investment especially from China; by foreign aid and debt relief; sometimes by relatively successful privatizations; and by governments able to plow back some of the profits into reducing debts and improving infrastructures. The average African growth rate during the 2000s was about the same as the Asian. Most African economies recovered quite quickly from the Great Neoliberal Recession discussed in Chapter 11, though unemployment, especially youth unemployment, remains high and in some countries population growth threatens to swallow up economic growth. Nonetheless, the continent is benefiting from global growth, and especially from the shift in economic power toward China.

Worker and peasant protest movements are also now increasing in the South of the world, especially in China (as we see in Chapter 8). The world's workforce has doubled in the last three decades, with almost all the expansion in the South. The feminization and informalization of work have increased, and labor unions have had to develop strategies to cope. Deindustrialization is northern, since manufacturing jobs are relocated to the South. Capitalism has tried to solve its profitability crisis with what Harvey (2005) and Silver (2003) call a spatial fix, not ending class conflict but relocating it. But tendencies toward democratization in the South give labor protest and indigenous peoples' movements more political power. There are limits to this, for a tendency toward enclave economies makes organized workers a privileged group in some southern countries, while greater international competition among manufacturers weakens the ability of labor to demand better and costlier employment conditions, as do the prevalence of subcontracting and automation (what Silver calls the organizational/technological fix). Nonetheless, structural adjustment programs were greeted with a great wave of popular protest movements around the world, and protest seems set to continue.

So global patterns and capitalist limits have been varied, as the inequality statistics also indicate. More countries saw some widening in inequality during the period 1990–2006 (ILO, 2008). In van Zanden et al.'s (2011) study the global average of national Gini coefficients rose from 0.35 in 1980 (lower than any previous point since their data began in 1820) to 0.45 in the year 2000, a substantial rise. But this was largely contributed by two regions. The biggest rises were in postcommunist countries (including China), under communism the most equal countries, now usually the most unequal. The next biggest rises were in the Anglo countries. But two regions deviated. East Asia apart from China remained relatively egalitarian, while after 2000 most Latin American countries became more equal (López-Calva & Lustig, 2010). The sustained economic development of Asia was also reducing inequality among the world population considered as a whole. Though inequality between the *countries* of the world is still increasing, as indicated previously, this is an artifact of the large number of small but poor countries. The single global Gini coefficient among the world's *people* actually fell from 0.56 in 1980 to 0.51 in 2000 (van Zanden et al., 2011: table 5A). Because India and China are still reducing poverty, and they account for 40 percent of the world's population, it is still falling. So that is good global news.

The South: II. Phony free trade

Growing economic globalization, greater international trade, and the mutual interests of states whose industries are strong enough to withstand foreign competition produce positive results for the world. This includes developing countries once they have developed competitiveness through initially protectionist and statist means. In Chapter 5 we saw this switch to more openness occurring in countries like Taiwan, South Korea, and India. We will see it in the case of China in Chapter 8. Thus recent globalization has increased world trade to the benefit of most of the world's population. Living standards have risen. Traditionally, there were relatively few middling-income people in the world. Now they are the majority.

Neoliberals press for trade liberalization, which is no bad thing. Liberalization resulted mainly from the General Agreement on Tariff and Trade (GATT), which in 1995 became the World Trade Organization (WTO). In the 1970s, like the two banks, GATT was turning toward a focus on the South, extending freer trade into a greater realm of manufacturing and into services, especially financial services. Its grasp was also deepening, as its rulings became backed by a body of international law constraining the North as well as the South. By the twenty-first century protectionism like Bush the Younger's steel tariffs received heavy fines. This reinforced the power shift occurring within northern capitalism, diminishing the power of sectors favoring protection and increasing those favoring liberalization, especially corporations in booming sectors, like finance and pharmaceuticals. There was increasing corporate lobbying at the GATT and WTO.

The interest of all countries is to free up the markets of others. Poor countries know that others got rich by protecting their infant industries, repressing finance, and subsidizing exports. But tariffs that redistribute from rich to poor countries are not geopolitically feasible, and so the second-best solution for the poor is genuine free trade for all, since their agricultural and low-end manufacturing exports would then be competitive – the downside would be being condemned to specialize in low-value, low-tech goods. But the poor got a worse option. The WTO pressured them to open up their markets while the rich countries subsidized their own agricultures. Such phony free trade is opposed by genuine neoliberals for they want the removal of all barriers to trade. But in the real world utopian ideologies are undermined by the self-interest of the classes and nations that proclaim them.

Despite an ostensibly democratic constitution, the WTO was dominated by the North, especially by an informal alliance known as the Quad – the United States, the EU, Japan, and Canada. Poorer countries complained about tariff negotiations that lacked transparency, with closed-door late night sessions, late release of meeting transcripts, and exclusion from the decisive meetings. Countries refusing to support Quad initiatives were placed on a blacklist of unfriendly states and some had their preferential trade agreements suspended (Jawara & Kwa, 2003). This especially characterized the 1994 Trade-Related Aspects of Intellectual Property Rights agreement, TRIPS. This protected the patent rights of inventors and the copyrights of writers, musicians, and artists, but its chief beneficiaries were big pharmaceutical companies. Big Pharma's patented drugs against AIDS were too pricey to be used widely in poor countries, and so hundreds of thousands died. "Generic" drugs costing a fraction of the price were produced by India and China, but TRIPS prevented their sale. TRIPS also kept a northern lock on creativity in cutting-edge technologies. It registers more than 90 percent of the world's patents. TRIPS had largely resulted from the Quad states and their big corporations' working together. This offensive reached even natural resources, as monopoly property rights over water, the soil, and plants were increasingly asserted. Natural herbal remedies from the South were being patented by northern corporations. This, unlike most nationalizations, really was privatization of the commons, a new enclosure movement (Drahos & Braithwaite, 2002: 72–3, 114–19; Roberts & Parks, 2007: 52–4). It was the perversion of a patents system that we saw in Volume 3, Chapter 2 had been an important part of the technological innovation of the second industrial revolution. Now it was preventing the global diffusion of technological knowledge.

Eventually there was a southern backlash. Resentment boiled over at the Seattle Ministerial Meetings in 1999, which broke up in disarray. After bitter negotiations, some breaches of TRIPS were allowed. In 2003 developing countries were allowed to import generic drugs to treat diseases that were epidemics, constituting public health threats. This struggle continues, since Indian and Chinese companies in 2011 were nearing the manufacture of much cheaper drugs to combat diabetes, cancer, and heart ailments. Since none of these can be defined as an epidemic, poorer countries are pressing for further relaxations of TRIPS. The United States also failed to commit the

OECD to grant corporations complete freedom to set up foreign branches and buy up local companies to the point where they could dominate local product markets. In 1998 France, followed by others, refused to sign. The Doha Development Round of WTO negotiations was blocked from 2001 onward and abandoned in 2008. The United States, Japan, and the EU had taken turns to block progress on agriculture, the item of greatest concern to poor countries. The entry of China added a large ally to India, Brazil, and other G-20 members who begun formal organization at the Cancun meeting in 2003. Four very big countries with middling levels of wealth were now experiencing sustained high growth rates: Brazil, Russia, India, and China – the BRIC countries. Their growth was now signaling a major shift in power in the global economy, away from northern domination led by the United States toward a more multipower-actor globe.

Collective organization by the BRIC-led South remains a direct challenge to American/northern neoliberal imperialism, and it has been aided in the streets by a motley alliance of protectionists and antiglobalists, environmentalists, feminists, indigenous peoples, and others, new social movements beginning to coordinate on a global scale. Their World Social Forum, rivaling the World Economic Forum of the world's dominant classes, is now an advocacy forum commanding global attention. Their power to disrupt and to command media attention at the beginning of the twenty-first century forced the WTO and the World Bank to make big rhetorical shifts and smaller shifts in actual policy (Aaronson, 2001; Rabinovitch, 2004). It was not good news that the WTO was stalled, since poor countries would have benefited from freer trade. But it was a sign of collective resistance to phony free trade. The United States and the EU tried to counter this by making bilateral agreements with poorer countries, as China also did with the ASEAN countries. Yet in Latin America it was not successful. The Free Trade Area of the Americas, proclaimed by President Clinton in 1994, proved dead in the water. The Latin Americans objected to U.S. protection of its agriculture through subsidies and noted that American proposals for the Free Trade Area would frustrate their comparative economic advantages. Instead the Mercosur countries of the Southern Cone made their own regional free trade deal and then extended it to Andean countries and to India. China has now displaced the United States as Brazil's main trading partner and has signed bilateral deals with some Latin American countries. The United States has been mainly left out in the cold, negotiating deals with minor and allied countries of the hemisphere.

Neoliberalism was faltering as the new millennium began. Previously it had risen almost everywhere, though only among the Anglophones and the post-Soviet countries did it become truly dominant. Privatization was a global trend, though for mixed motives and with rather varied results across the world. Finance capital also became more globally powerful. Yet in the Nordic countries and some countries of continental Europe, as well as in successfully developing countries of the South, neoliberalism met more resistance and was being blended with more proactive states at the beginning of the twenty-first century. This has had the effect of creating new economic regimes that fit less well into varieties of capitalism or welfare regime models. The key was not to become heavily indebted. If it did not, a country rich or poor could withstand quite well the icy winds of neoliberalism, which was not quite so global after all. Perhaps the most important conclusion to this chapter is just how varied and malleable the world is. Though we can detect neoliberal growth followed by faltering, the different nation-states and macroregions of the world reacted to this in varied ways. Capitalism does not impose strict limits on states. Once again both nation-states and transnational capitalism were expanding together. Then, however, occurred neoliberal disaster, the Great Recession of 2008, to be discussed in Chapter 11.

7 The fall of the Soviet alternative

In Volume 3 I sought to explain the Bolshevik Revolution. Here I examine the fall of the state socialism built by that revolution, and its replacement by versions of capitalism and democracy. The Fall was a world-changing event. Together with the economic reforms of the Chinese Communist Party (analyzed in the next chapter) it ensured the end of the cold war, the abandonment of state socialism, and the global triumph of capitalism over the last remaining alternative segment of the world economy. Explaining the Fall is of obvious sociological importance. For more than sixty years state socialism had been held together by Soviet power. Once it collapsed, so almost everywhere did the desire for world revolution. Marxist ideals for a wholly better society were largely finished, only Marxism as a pessimistic analysis of capitalism remained useful.

The Fall differed from the Bolshevik Revolution. It began from the top down as attempts at reform by the communist party failed and generated crisis. The usual term for this is a revolution from above, but was it a revolution at all? It contained relatively little turbulence coming from below, few mass demonstrations, with the big exception of Central Europe, and relatively little violence, except in Romania and between certain ethnic groups. So this chapter gives a more elite-centered explanation, the inverse of what I gave in earlier chapters. The Fall was threefold – the end of state socialism, the collapse of the Union of Soviet Socialist Republics, and the end of Soviet empire abroad. The subsequent transitions were twofold, toward capitalism and toward democracy. I discuss all these.

Faltering thaw 1945–1985

In Volume 3 I described the twin accomplishments of the Soviet Union under Stalin's leadership: good economic growth filtering down into modest improvements in social citizenship; and a formidable military power grinding Hitler down to defeat. This had come at considerable cost. There was almost no civil or political citizenship and a despotic party-state had caused millions of deaths. Victory in World War II then had conservative effects, increasing the legitimacy of institutions while crippling Soviet capacity to adapt to change. Yet by leaving Stalin's rule unchallenged, the war enabled him to lower the level of repression. Trusting no one, he still made sure his subordinates lived in fear. Though associates like Beria and Malenkov knew that reforms of the

Gulag prison system and of agriculture were essential, they dared not initiate them. Stalin did allow the Council of Ministers more autonomy in economic matters, while younger party people with technical qualifications could exercise their specialist competencies (Gorlizki & Khlevniuk, 2004). The regime made minimal housing and health concessions to the people for winning the war (Zubkova, 1998). Overall there was little change and the people dug in, hoping for a better life after Stalin died. Economic growth did resume. By 1950 the war-damaged economy had recovered to its 1940 level, and thereafter it grew rapidly.

Major changes came from 1953 after Stalin's death. Under Khrushchev (1954–63) coercion was lessened, terror wound down, camps closed, restrictions on labor mobility ended, and there was more investment in consumer goods and housing, plus a mild easing of censorship. The regime persisted with grand development projects, like the Virgin Lands agrarian program, an unsuccessful attempt to solve the agricultural crisis by more extensive cultivation of marginal steppe lands. More successful was the space program climaxing in the 1957 flight of *Sputnik I*, the first spacecraft to orbit the earth, followed by Yuri Gagarin's flight into space in 1961, remarkable technological achievements. In 1960, bursting with confidence, Khrushchev declared the Soviets would "bury" the West and promised his people socialism by 1984. But his erratic personal behavior alienated many, and his humiliation in the Cuban missile crisis led to his replacement by Leonid Brezhnev, who remained first secretary until his death in 1982.

Brezhnev expanded the nomenklatura system, whereby reliable party members were appointed to senior state offices. Party organs administered virtually all institutions – from Komsomol youth organizations, to trade unions, to the welfare state – but state socialism was no longer so centralized. The regime turned a blind eye to the informal networks, *blats*, by which people exchanged favors. Officials exploited their positions by rent seeking, while the people were bought off by a little consumerism. The Brezhnev era was one of stagnation. Elites had a nice quiet time, détente with the West grew, and urbanization continued. The Prague Spring was easily repressed while at home repression diminished. While open political dissent was not tolerated, higher education expanded and intellectuals could read much from the West and cautiously test the bounds of censorship. The economy chugged along, its innovation largely confined to a semiautonomous military-industrial complex, deadened by excessive central planning, for the prices of about sixty thousand commodities were set centrally. Hayek had identified the key weakness of command economies: information and coordination costs rise faster as the scale and complexity of an economy grow than in a market economy. But on the shop floor there was some relaxation. Lateness and absence were decriminalized, output norms were raised less often, and payment shifted from piece rates to fixed wages per hour (Ellman & Kontorovich, 1998: 10–11). The ironic results were more lateness, absenteeism, and turnover, and more open display of protest on the shop floor. The Soviet Union was thawing but losing its drive.

Workers had acquired an adequate deal of job security, a living wage, and some welfare benefits for which they did not have to work too hard. As long as they had believed in socialist ideals they had rioted to protest flawed socialist reality. But ideals became "squeezed out of mass consciousness by the conformism, consumerism and individualism of the Brezhnev era" and so riots stopped (says Kozlov, 2002: chaps. 12–13; quote from 313–14). The development of an urban, educated, and hereditary working class produced workers with a sense of collective identity and opposition – a we-they model of workers against management – but with any socialist alternative appropriated by the regime and discredited. There was ritualized and peaceful collective action at the shop-floor level, and these strikes did achieve some concessions (Connor, 1991).

Controls over white-collar and managerial strata weakened. The five-year plans and targets laid down for each enterprise were lowered. Administrators had less incentive to work hard or innovate and more opportunity to use blat networks to extract rent and exchange economic rewards for favors. Officials could also use their networks to achieve their targets by informal means. The party was no longer the transmission belt for major development plans. It conserved the privileges of the nomenklatura, who lived in segregated neighborhoods with weekend dachas in the country, purchasing luxury goods in their own shops. Suny (1998: 436) tells the story of when Brezhnev was visited by his mother. His life of luxury worried her. "What's the matter, Mother?" Brezhnev asked. "But Lyonya," she asked, "what will you do if the Bolsheviks return?"

Inequality remained much lower than in the West and corruption was not great yet both were less easy to legitimate in a supposedly socialist country. Everyone complained of corruption and a debate began about equality. Some sociologists argued efficiency would increase if more incentives and inequalities based on skills were introduced; others argued that reducing inequalities would lead to better collective morale, restoring commitment to socialist efficiency (Grant-Friedman, 2008). But economic growth continued. Between 1950 and 1975 real consumption per capita increased at a rate of 3.8 percent per year. By 1975 the Soviet Union had crept up to somewhere between 40 percent and 60 percent of the American level of GNP and the Soviets had more literacy, more doctors and hospital beds, full employment, and welfare benefits generous by the standards of comparable developing countries. Up to this point the masses could believe that the sacrifices might have been worth it, that controls could be eased and life get better, while the elites could believe that the regime might regain its popularity and its capacity to deliver something vaguely resembling socialism.

Unfortunately, the rate of economic growth then began to fall. GDP growth continued, but at a steadily declining rate, 5–6 percent during the period 1928 to 1970, 3 percent during 1970–5, 1.9 percent in 1975–80, and 1.8 percent in 1980–5 (Lane, 2009: 153–4, 162). Labor productivity and technological progress languished. It was an inefficient economy, producing many products that no one wanted and sacrificing 40 percent of its state budget and at least 20 percent of GDP to the military (compared to 5–7 percent in the United States). Gorbachev (1995: 215) confirms the accuracy of these figures, adding that they were double what the Politburo itself had believed, and what he himself had been told when he first entered office. The military-industrial complex had much more autonomy than in the United States and did great damage to the rest of the economy. In the Eastern bloc Western banks were increasingly providing investment; yet its own exports were never sufficient to pay this back and so indebtedness to the West was rising steadily (Kotkin, 2009). Yet not until 1990 did growth actually turn negative, the consequence of botched reforms. An unreformed Soviet bloc of low economic growth could have probably survived for a while, restraining the process of universal globalization.

The Soviets had already exploited extensive growth to the full. There was no more surplus agricultural labor and natural resources were dwindling except for oil and natural gas. The only technology-based growth was in the military-industrial complex. Unlike in the United States, security concerns meant that military innovations did not spin off into civilian products. The Soviets put 80 percent of R&D funds into military projects, says Gorbachev, while the U.S. rate had varied between 40 percent and 60 percent. The authorities then compounded the problem by pouring vast resources into massive Siberian cities and retooling obsolete factories (Allen, 2004: chap. 10). The model was still of catch-up industrialization to which central planning was appropriate, but capitalism was superior with "creative destruction" in the more complex and fluid high-tech post-Fordist era. Yet inflation was low, living standards were still just rising, the country's credit rating remained high, and falls in output were modest compared to capitalist recessions (Ellman & Kontorovich, 1998: 17; Kotz, 1997: 34–47, 75–7). It was not evident that crisis was looming until the mid-1980s.

Yet some of the nomenklatura began to fear disaster earlier. They had access not only to the downward-dipping economic statistics, but also to surging mortality statistics. From the late 1960s the death rates of men of working age began to rise, especially deaths due to accidents and other external causes, which typically result from alcohol, whose consumption was now the highest among all countries keeping statistics (White, 1996: 33–40). Infant mortality also began to rise in the early 1970s. The combination was enough to stop the publication of Soviet mortality statistics. It now seems likely that rising infant mortality rate was mainly due to better reporting in backward Central Asian republics, which also had higher birth rates. Infant mortality rates did not necessarily indicate decline – though at the time Soviet leaders did not know this.

But they attributed rising alcoholism among men to low workplace morale, probably correctly.

This was not a crisis in the ordinary sense of the word. They could have carried on for decades. But the steady slowing of growth and rising debt were clearly structural, and here Soviet ideology entered in. The leadership had substituted a material goal for socialist utopia. The socialist system was to be judged by its ability to overtake the West, specifically the United States, measured by comparative output and growth rates. This concrete goal survived doubts about utopian socialism and had seemed achievable while the gap from the United States was closing, until around 1975. But then the American lead had begun to widen again. Much of the leadership could not accept an economy of low growth since it made overtaking impossible. They thought the root of the problem lay in the economy. But state socialism had clearly failed in two ways, in the economy, but more fundamentally in politics, where, though despotism had lightened, there was no movement toward democracy. But failure was exacerbated by ideology – it was supposed to be much, much better. This was a failure of ideological power, and it was especially marked within the party-state elite.

What was to be done? Within the party arose a "new thinking" movement among a new generation of technocrats who under Khrushchev and Brezhnev had been allowed to study the West and appreciate its economic and technological strengths. They became the main reform influence on Gorbachev (English, 2000). They believed in reform to create a socialism with a human face (Kotkin, 2001). They realized that the USSR as presently constituted simply could not match a United States that was both a rich consumer society and a global superpower. In the 1970s Gorbachev (then a high apparatchik) was taken to a Canadian supermarket, a cathedral of consumption. He was impressed but suspected a fake Potemkin village stocked for his benefit. He asked his driver to stop unscheduled at a second supermarket. It was just as abundant.

Capitalism was a success and the cadres knew it. Their historic aspiration for world leadership sagged. "If socialism was not superior to capitalism, its existence could not be justified," says Kotkin (2001: 19). Ideology now played a lesser but destabilizing role, for it obstructed the possibility of continuing with a comfortable second-division existence. Fundamental overhaul seemed necessary. In Stalin's time the party had seen forced industrialization as a necessary step toward the development of socialism. Whatever the pain, when the Soviet Union became an industrial society like the West, it would then become more genuinely socialist. Suffering was necessary for a better future. After Stalin it did become a little more humane, the people became a little richer and a lot more educated. But Khrushchev's denunciation of Stalin at the 20th Party Congress had told the shocked party that its period of suffering had not been a necessary stage in the development of socialism but "criminal leadership." Subsequent liberalization had not produced socialism but crass consumerism and corruption. The nomenklatura were living lies, combining lip service to Marxism-Leninism with exploitation of office for material gain. Like others they were dissolving the contradiction in alcohol. Their children preferred Western jeans and pop music to the Party Program and Marxism-Leninism (Service, 1997: 370). No one believed the ideology anymore. Technocracy had replaced ideocracy (Hall, 1995: 82). The story was told of a man entering a health clinic, asking to see an ear-and-eye doctor. He was told there was no such specialism, but he persisted. An exasperated official asked why. "Because," the man replied, "I keep hearing one thing and seeing another." By mid-1917 almost no one in Russia had believed in monarchy; by 1980 almost no one believed in Marxism-Leninism. The regime could keep the populace compliant without much violence but it lacked heart and soul, morale and legitimation (Hollander, 1999). There was "moral depletion," said Soviet commentators, openly. Its ideological power had been shredded.

The regime was in decline but not at breaking point. This was not France in 1789 with its financial crisis nor Russia in 1917 nor China in the 1930s, both devastated by war. American pressure was not great. The collective leadership remained solid. The Soviet Union could have continued, with a repressive eye open in Eastern Europe, but maintaining an implicit contract elsewhere – the regime provided an adequate standard of living; the people acquiesced in its rule. It was not collapse that brought reforms. Reforms brought collapse.

The elite perceived that the root problem was lack of discipline. There was much debate about the two ways of providing it. Conservatives said tighten controls, make people work harder, go back to piecework. Liberals said introduce market discipline to generate productivity. Experiments with the latter occurred in the late 1970s and 1980s but seemed not to work well in an economy that was still overwhelmingly plan-, party-, and *blat*-dominated. Many party officials subverted the experiments. Conservative reforms followed under Yury Andropov, briefly first secretary, which yielded a minor economic revival (Ellman & Kontorovich, 1998: 14–15). If Andropov had not suddenly died, the Soviet Union might have survived longer.

Andropov had wanted Gorbachev as his successor, but the party old guard appointed the elderly Chernenko; he was sick and did not last long. After his death, Gorbachev's succession in 1985 was unchallenged. He initially resumed Andropov's conservative strategy with a more rationalized command structure through the creation of superministries, greater quality control, and a crackdown on absenteeism and alcoholism. He added more investment in machine building, computers, and robotics. Yet he also added market elements to trim the bureaucracy, increase enterprise autonomy, and allow private cooperatives. But the combination seemed not to work well. He then announced he would deepen market reforms, as the way to preserve socialism. He had no notion that this might be the road to capitalism.

Much of what followed depended on the power of Gorbachev and his office. Perhaps no other leader would have pursued such deep reforms. Gorbachev was respected for his abilities, but he had not been chosen as a great reformer and at this point he was not one. But using the immense powers of the general secretary of the Central Committee of the Communist Party, which neither the Politburo nor anyone had been accustomed to challenge, he pushed reform and promoted like-minded reformers to high positions. This had to be done gradually, except in the realm of foreign policy, where the general secretary's power was almost absolute (Brown, 2007: 201, 230, 256–7). After a year or so he had a pack of reformers around him. The main problem was to induce the party-state actually to implement reforms.

The reform period, 1987–1991

In foreign policy Gorbachev was prepared to make concessions to the West on arms control and regional disputes. This would defuse an arms race that diverted scarce resources to the military-industrial complex and erected barriers against economic cooperation with the West. In the economy he saw two problems: an absence of work discipline and motivation, and an over-rigid command structure. He made the radical switch of seeing market discipline and market competition as the twin solutions. To increase discipline, pay should be based on productivity. Gorbachev attacked "the tendency of levelling," which "negatively influenced the quality and quantity of work." Instead, he declared, "the incomes of working people should be linked to their performance on the job." People would thus work harder, while different levels of skill should get different rewards (Kotz, 1997: 57). But Gorbachev also saw productivity as requiring less hierarchy and more democracy in the workplace. Managers and workers together would make collective decisions about production goals and methods. Enterprises should compete with each other on the market rather than be cushioned by achieving a basic plan target. It all sounded fine in theory. He and his allies were borrowing from capitalism yet still saw reform as compatible with socialism. There would not be private ownership, just more decentralization of state property, a more efficient and democratic form of socialism. This was called *perestroika*, restructuring, initially understood as being economic.

Under Gorbachev's reforms of 1986–7, state enterprises were granted independence in production, though within overall nonbinding plan targets. They were able freely to allocate enterprise income and put more into incentive funds for workers. But they could not fire workers or set prices, most of which were still state-controlled. This was not a good combination. Enterprise autonomy meant they did not have to supply the state with their products at the fixed price. Instead they could sell them at greater profit to whomever they liked, or they could barter among themselves instead of selling them on the market for rubles. As bartering grew to about half of all trade, the central allocation mechanism broke down, as did trade among the republics. The newly empowered republican and municipal governments took advantage of devolution to reduce their deliveries to other areas. Decentralization and democratization at the workplace led to immediate pay increases since the workers were now paying themselves. Since most prices were fixed, the result was not rising prices and inflation, but since people had more money to spend, they bought all they could, hoarding and emptying the shops. Hence the enormous queues and inability to buy basic goods during 1990 and 1991 reflected policy errors more than general economic weakness. But this was now an economic crisis.

The crisis hit the state hard. It became unable to extract taxes from the more autonomous enterprises and republics just as oil prices and revenues began to fall. Then the government gave itself another a revenue headache. An unpopular crackdown on alcohol was undermined by Russians' thirst and massive illicit distilling and brewing – as in America's Prohibition period. Since a fifth of the state's revenue had come from legal alcohol, this compounded the revenue crisis. The budget deficit grew and the government took the easy way out of printing money and borrowing abroad. Inflation spiraled upward.

One joke has a man waiting in line to buy vodka. Because of restrictions imposed by Gorbachev, the line is long. The man loses his temper, shouting, "I can't take this waiting in line anymore. I hate Gorbachev! I am going to the Kremlin right now to kill him!" After half an hour he returns. The people in the line ask him whether he succeeded and he replies, "No, I got to the Kremlin, but the line to kill Gorbachev was far too long, so I decided to come back and queue for my vodka."

These reforms were not geared to the two crucial goals: to reduce state subsidies to industries and to allow prices to rise toward market levels. Gorbachev, like later neoliberals, underestimated the problem of authority involved in a transition from state to market controls. He destroyed the state socialist institutions, which had provided authority and stability, and put little in their place. He ignored evidence before him from the Chinese reforms. There carefully controlled, state-administered market reforms were already generating economic success. There was also the successful example of Hungarian goulash (mixed) socialism, in which agriculture but not industry had been turned over to the market (Hough, 1997: 16–22, 119, 269–73, 491). Chinese leaders, influenced by East Asian models of development, saw a strong state as necessary to implement reforms, preserve tariffs against imports, subsidize exports, and limit international capital flows. But the Soviets looked down on their younger brothers, expecting the Chinese to learn from them, not vice versa. Of course, all governments make errors, and those attempting wholesale transformations will make more of them. In Chapter 9 we see that the initial reforms of the Chinese communists were often counterproductive. But the CCP leadership learned by trial and error what seemed to work and what did not. The precondition, they recognized, was to keep control of the state, so that the top could judge the programs to be pushed. The Soviets, in contrast, went for a double revolution, in both economic and political power simultaneously, and failed (Pei, 1994).

Unlike the Chinese, Gorbachev was hindered by party disunity. Though factionalism had arisen in China as Mao was sidelined, party chiefs were disciplined by their unhappy experience during the Cultural Revolution. They argued over reforms but not in public, and they stood collectively behind decisions taken. In contrast, the Soviet leaders retained memories of the opposite: too much discipline under Stalin. Their arguments over reform turned into bitter factionalism.

I distinguish five emerging factions. On Gorbachev's Right were two types of conservative: reforming conservatives seeking to tighten controls, and temperamental conservatives who feared any change (which might threaten their own positions). Third was Gorbachev's own reform socialist faction. To his "Left" lay two types of liberals: genuine ideological liberals, believers in capitalist markets and liberal democracy, and opportunist liberals, who saw they could get rich quickly off markets – "elite self-emancipation" determined to turn reform to their own advantage (Tucker, 2010). Increasingly allied with these opportunists were nationalists, exploiting the decentralization of power involved in Gorbachev's reforms, enhancing the power of the republics and provinces. Their nomenklatura might grab more autonomy, waving nationalist flags but feathering their own nests. A liberal-nationalist alliance, led by Boris Yeltsin, eventually won out. But factionalism was unfortunately blossoming just as Gorbachev was weakening the party-state.

Gorbachev might still have pushed his reforms through the party, but he lacked a clear sense of economic priorities. Dobrynin, a fellow Politburo member, says he "never once heard Gorbachev present any broad and detailed plan for reforming the economy – whether one-year, or five-year, or some other kind of plan that had really been thought through." He left this to the chairman of the Council of Ministers, Ryzhkov, who had less power to push things through. Gorbachev focused on political reform where he could decree the necessary changes. Denouncing the conservatives as a "gigantic party-state apparatus that, like a dam, lay on the path of reform" (Hough, 1997: 105), he went outside the party and ministries, appealing to the people with *glasnost* (openness). This was popular but it also emboldened liberals who wanted more market reform than he did. Once freedom of expression and organization blossomed so did popular oppositional movements. Unlike the pragmatism of Gorbachev's reform faction and the gut reactions of the conservatives, some liberals did have an ideology, a view of an alternative society. Lawson (2010) says their ideas "of freedom, justice and equality may not have been new, but they were certainly utopian," and they applied to political, economic, and military power relations alike.

Glasnost started in March 1986 when Gorbachev encouraged the media to criticize the government. Being mostly staffed by liberals, they eagerly did so. It did not help Gorbachev that oil and natural gas prices were now falling. At the end of April the nuclear power station at Chernobyl exploded, its radiation eventually killing thousands. Gorbachev saw this as caused by the autonomy of the military-industrial complex, which ran the nuclear industry. Though military power was subordinated to party political control, the price for military acquiescence had always been autonomy and great resources in its own sphere. Even the Politburo had been left in the dark about nuclear safety. This strengthened his desire to trim military autonomy. The fractious debate that ensued about secrecy firmed up his commitment to *glasnost* (Chernyaev, 2000: 8; Service, 1997: 445–7). In 1986–7 political prisoners were freed and censorship of the press ended. In January 1987 he called for democratization throughout society, including freedom of assembly and organization. In response small movements began to organize lobbies and demonstrations. Liberals called for marketization, democratic clubs demanded democratization and honest investigation of the Soviet past, labor groups demanded economic reforms to benefit workers, and nationalists demanded regional autonomy.

Gorbachev was a democrat and rather optimistically expected that free elections within the party, including secret ballots and multiple candidates, would give him a mandate to continue reforms. But the party had long been more of an administrative agency than a party in the Western sense. When Gorbachev downsized its administrative role, its members could not easily shift to debating policy or election strategies. The party retained a conservative bias but had little collective political life and tended to fragment into its local parts (Gill, 1994: 184). There were now two unexpected outcomes. First, *glasnost* began to spawn off numerous social movements, generally small but active, debating a plethora of ideas, including distinctly Western ones. Second, party officials began to see they could seize the local state assets they controlled to become entrepreneurs. They were more experienced in self-promoting maneuvering than in party politics. The Central Committee was losing its grip. The way to reestablish Gorbachev's political control, suggested Yakovlev, one of his lieutenants, was to split the party and lead a Social Democratic reform party against a conservative Communist Party. Gorbachev rejected this. Brown (2007: 204–5) thinks this might have worked despite a risk that it would precipitate conservatives into launching a coup. It might have produced a more coherent reform strategy and an easier transition to democracy.

When democratizing the Communist Party did not work, Gorbachev turned to reducing its powers. Politburo and Party Central Committee powers were largely destroyed in 1989. The Central Committee Secretariat was reduced from twenty to nine departments, eliminating all the economic ones except for agriculture; Gosplan, the central planning authority, was abolished in 1991, as was Gosnab, which supervised supply chains among enterprises. The economy was cut adrift from the state. The 1989 election was the first one contested by candidates offering different policies, and those elected promptly rejected some of Premier Ryzhkov's ministers. Gorbachev drew back a little from democracy when he agreed in early 1990 to be nominated to the new post of executive state president by the legislature rather than risking fighting a national election for the post. This was a mistake, as he himself later recognized. At that point he would have beaten his main rival, Yeltsin, in an election, achieving more legitimacy to preserve the Soviet Union. If Yeltsin had won, he would then have had no incentive to destroy the Union. Key supporters also felt that the new presidential office needed more power than Gorbachev had given it, for some powers had gone to the leaderships of the individual republics. Then in 1990 Gorbachev forced the party to renounce its leading role in society. Though the Soviet Union did not fall until 1991, communism really ended then (Brown, 2007: 202, 209–10, 298–302; Kenez, 2006: 258–61).

Throughout these shocking political changes, many nomenklatura were recalculating how to retain their positions and perks. In the republics high officials were enjoying the greater autonomy that Gorbachev's destruction of the central party gave them. Lane (2009: 162–4) emphasizes the emergence of an acquisition class, essentially a middle class generated by the educational expansion of the Khrushchev and Brezhnev periods, composed of technical, managerial, and professional workers. It was attracted by Gorbachev's policies of gearing rewards to productivity and skills and increasing their representation in the party at the expense of workers and peasants. Hough sees parallels with the French Revolution, identifying the unfolding events as "a true middle-class revolution ... of the bureaucrats, of the bourgeois who managed the means of production," backed by masses of "urbanized, well-educated, skilled workers and white-collar personnel who had been created by the communist regime" (1997: 1, 24). At first these groups provided Gorbachev's main constituency, and he started off with considerable popular support. Not until May or June 1990 did he slip behind Yeltsin in the popularity polls.

Gorbachev found it easy to dismantle state powers, but botched reforms were difficult to undo. His own cautious economic reforms did not work well since conservatives within the bureaucracy obstructed them. Various plans of reform were aired. The Eastern European pattern of at first retaining fixed prices for essentials, free prices for luxuries, and maximum prices on other goods was advocated by some. Clearly, some prices had to be raised – and by the state rather than by a nonexistent market. Once reform got started across Eastern Europe and the Soviet Union, two schools of thought arose as to how this should be done. Neoliberals advocated rapid shock therapy, liberalizing everything quickly. Gradualists said things should be done more slowly, and selectively, in accordance with the particularities of each country, ensuring that institutions providing norms and rules for economic transactions were preserved. Market-price mechanisms might be introduced gradually, product by product, with a concomitant reduction in state orders. Gradualism was the less disruptive reform strategy. But neoliberals wanted to dismantle state controls and privatize industries to institute a market, supposing that the destruction of state control would allow markets to flourish. Many saw markets as natural. After all, this was the currently dominant view of Western economists.

Premier Ryzhkov, who favored gradual price increases, said Gorbachev made gradualism more difficult, for he "proposed to liquidate the existing mechanisms of economic administration without creating absolutely anything in their place." Gorbachev (1995: chap. 17) describes repeated delegation of plans to commissions that came up with different designs that were never reconciled. As economic deterioration and political disintegration at the center continued, republican leaders, especially Yeltsin in Russia, began obstructing too. Any plan would have caused pain for the Soviet people. Maybe Gorbachev was delaying administering pain until after the 1989 Soviet and 1990 Russian elections. If so, that was another miscalculation, for he lost them (Hough, 1997: 16–22, and chap. 4, quotes from 130 & 104; Kenez, 2006: 267–70).

Stalin, Khrushchev, Brezhnev, and Gorbachev were sitting in a train that had suddenly stopped. Nothing could get it to move. "Shoot the driver," shouted Stalin. It did not move. "Tell the driver's mate that socialism is just around the corner," shouted Khrushchev. Nothing happened. "Let's pull the blinds down and pretend the train is moving," suggested Brezhnev. Finally, Gorbachev threw the windows open and asked them to stick their heads out and shout, "There are no tracks! There are no tracks!"

The economy turned negative in 1990. Workers were restive, disillusioned first with communism, then with Gorbachev. Enormous miners' strikes in 1989 made broad demands amid a deteriorating economy, and Gorbachev had to yield costly wage and price concessions (Connor, 1991: chap. 7). The crisis was now felt by almost every household in the land. As the economy plummeted, so did Gorbachev's popularity. A poll of fall 1990 revealed that 57 percent thought life had become worse under him and only 8 percent thought it had become better (Levada, 1992: 66; Kotz & Weir, 1997; 77–83). His liberal and nationalist opponents triumphed in the elections of 1990–1. Many of the nomenklatura and the acquisition class now decided to ditch the faltering bureaucracy and take their chances in a market economy, without any socialism. The liberal intelligentsia was now prominent. The more educated a person, the more likely he or she was to support market reforms. In the parliament professionals and the liberal intelligentsia were small minorities among the conservatives but the majority among the reformers and they dominated Yeltsin's procapitalist group (Lane, 2009: 168–9). In late 1990 Gorbachev became alarmed at the liberal drift and turned back to seek support from the conservatives, but this was a mistake. He would not do what the conservatives really wanted and this only angered liberals. Liberals and opportunists were now seeking similar means to quite different ends – more decentralization of power to those who possessed resources in markets.

The end of the Soviet Empire

This political crisis quickly led to the collapse of the Soviet empire. The tsarist empire had been inherited, but the Bolsheviks had given most non-Russian nationalities their own republican or provincial governments and subsidized and granted given them linguistic and cultural privileges. Minorities had nonetheless learned the Russian language as the ticket to modernity. The Soviet Union was not an empire in the sense of the core exploiting the periphery – many Russians believed it was the reverse! But it was different in lands that had been conquered around World War II, for the European satellites and the Baltic republics had prior histories of national independence, and intermittent postwar revolts had revealed their restiveness under Soviet rule. They were ultimately held down by force, though they too were subsidized from Moscow.

As soon as they sensed Soviet weakening, the Polish and Hungarian oppositions began demonstrating for more autonomy, then for independence. Breaking with the past, Gorbachev encouraged them. In 1985 he had already told East European leaders to expect no more military interventions to help them. They had to become more popular. His foreign minister, Shevardnedze, gave a terse reply to a query from the Hungarian government when in 1989 there was an influx of East Germans into Hungary en route to fleeing into Austria and Germany: "This is an affair that concerns Hungary, the GDR and the FRG" – not us, he was implying (Brown, 2007: 242, 235). Gorbachev and his associates actually wanted the old-guard communist regimes of Eastern Europe to fall, expecting that they would be overthrown by reform communists like him. He did not realize there were not any in Eastern Europe (Kramer, 2003b; Kotkin, 2009: xvi–xvii).

Gorbachev was also unhappy with the satellite communist regimes since they supported his conservative opponents at home. But Ligachev, a leading conservative, has said that no one in the Politburo suggested sending in the Red Army to quell the 1989 disturbances in Berlin. Since the West no longer threatened, why keep such costly buffer states? These were now pressured to come to terms with their oppositions. Without this, they would have rejected reform and repressed the population. Whatever the outcome of such repression, velvet revolutions would have been unlikely. But now the end of the satellite empire was inevitable, held down by a military power, which the Soviets now refused to use.

The new thinking included a foreign policy that stressed political self-determination and saw the world as interdependent, embodying universal interests and values that trumped class interests and the cold war. Gorbachev became the man who ended the cold war. Instead of responding in kind to

Reagan's Strategic Defense Initiative and interference in Afghanistan, he rejected the zero-sum game of the cold war by offering negotiations on arms reductions and more. He then made most of the concessions, offering nuclear and conventional arms reductions, renunciation of force in satellite countries, and tolerance of internal dissent. It was fortunate that his adversary was Ronald Reagan, who, despite earlier hard-line rhetoric, converted to the same cause from late 1983. His turnaround was not due to electoral considerations or to a change of advisers. Three incidents changed Reagan: the shooting down by the Soviets of an off-course Korean Airlines plane and Soviet misinterpretation of the NATO Able Archer exercise in Europe as an attack on the Soviets made him realize that they really did fear American aggression, while a graphic television film *The Day After*, depicting the aftermath of nuclear war in Lawrence, Kansas, scared him. He believed in Armageddon but did not want it on his watch (Fischer, 1997: 112–38). When Gorbachev made overtures in 1985, Reagan met him halfway and would have gone further had his advisers let him. Reagan Mark II, the peacemaker, was good news for the world. But Gorbachev was even better news. He hated his military-industrial complex, lacked the power to confront it directly, but thought disarmament would do that indirectly. He had also realized that even if he got rid of all his country's nuclear weapons, no one would attack it (Chernyaev, 2000: 103–4; 192–8; Brown, 2007: 266–74; Leffler, 2007: 466ff.). It is doubtful that any other Soviet leader would have begun this peace process, though other possible American presidents might have responded if faced by Gorbachev and Soviet weakening. Gorbachev even convinced Margaret Thatcher of his sincerity.

Gorbachev almost always made the right moral choice. In Europe this again involved optimistic miscalculation. He assumed that through elections the satellite countries would endorse socialism with a human face, but they saw socialism as oppressive imperialism. Yet even as Solidarity took power in Poland, as the Berlin Wall was demolished by cheering mobs, and as the Ceausescus were shot in Romania, the Gorbachev reformers supported the noncommunist regimes that emerged. Not a single shot was fired by the Red Army as the Soviet bloc fell. By late 1989 Gorbachev had lost the option of military intervention. Since all the satellites were aflame, not even the Red Army could have suppressed them now.

Gorbachev now fell back on second-order benefits of nonintervention, saying it would improve East-West relations and allow defense spending to be reallocated to investment in consumer industries to save the economy. But there was not time enough for this to take effect since defense expenditure only began reducing in 1990, as the Soviet collapse began. The geopolitical cost was enormous: the collapse of the Warsaw Pact and the Soviet common market, the unification of Germany within NATO, and the advance of NATO to the borders of the Soviet Union. In fact, Gorbachev had been deceived by U.S. Secretary of State Baker and German Chancellor Kohl. He had agreed to the unification of Germany, which he had initially vehemently opposed, in return for Baker's and Kohl's promises that NATO would not be extended into Eastern Europe. But they had lied, and they did extend it. There would be no demilitarized zone in Central Europe. Instead the region was incorporated into the West, now reaching to the Russian border (Sarotte, 2009; Kramer, 2003). Conservatives and Russian nationalists were aghast at Gorbachev's striking geopolitical failures.

The loss of Central Europe then encouraged dissident nationalism within the Soviet Union itself. Only a few of the 127 officially recognized national groups of the Union were to cause trouble, and they were almost all in the western and southern rim of the Union. Beissinger (2002) shows that they were the most urbanized, educated nationalities in control of republics and autonomous districts. Some had also been only recently incorporated. Lithuanian, Latvian, and Estonian nationalists were the first to demonstrate, in July 1988, initially for more autonomy. The three Baltic republics had been incorporated by force into the USSR at the end of the war, and this was backed up by settling large numbers of Russians there, a policy that created colonial settler-native tensions. The events of 1989 in Eastern Europe then impacted heavily on the Baltic states, especially since Polish television, now visible there, had broken through Soviet control of information flows. Independence was now demanded, feeding discontent among the Russian settlers, whose cause was then taken up by nationalists within Russia.

The Baltic republics were soon joined by Georgia and Moldova, some of whose nationalists also wanted independence. Georgia had briefly been an independent state after the Bolshevik Revolution and Moldova had been part of Romania until 1944. Their conflicts were less between the local nationalities and Russians than between two local nationalities. This was also true in the South in the Armenian-Azeri conflict, where the Soviet authorities were conscious of the danger of interethnic blood baths. In these situations a nationalism versus imperialism interpretation is not appropriate (unlike in Eastern Europe and the Baltics). This was about rival ethnic conceptions of to whom each republic belonged. Demands for democracy thus fueled ethnic conflict and cleansing here, as they did across the twentieth century in many countries (Mann, 2005). But the Soviet authorities were drawn willy-nilly into these conflicts, which were a public test of their ability to preserve public order.

The regime had a different view of nationalists inside the Soviet Union. Secession here was considered unacceptable, a breach of the Soviet constitution. Though Gorbachev would negotiate appropriate forms of autonomy, he would not countenance independence. But the leadership underestimated the intensity of the Baltic nationalisms. Politburo members sent to investigate were horrified by it yet reluctant to sustain repression. When faced in 1988 with murderous cleansing between Azeris and Armenians over the disputed enclave of Nagorno-Karabakh, the head of the KGB urged military intervention, but

Gorbachev and the Politburo majority overruled him. Gorbachev sympathized with the Armenians but did not want to alienate the Azeris, so he dithered. In Baku, when faced with a pogrom of Armenians, he authorized military intervention, the only time he did so. But when he learned it had killed innocent people, he stopped it. In the other cases of repression in the Caucasus and Baltic republics local authorities had decided to repress and Gorbachev overruled them. This seemed to signal weakness and emboldened nationalists into ever-bigger demonstrations between 1988 and mid-1991 (Tuminez, 2003; Kramer, 2003a; Beissinger, 2002; Chernyaev, 2000: 181–91).

Beissinger (2002: chap. 7) identifies weakening "regimes of repression" in the Soviet Union. Stalinist-era repression had been wielded by NKVD security troops using overwhelming force, without much local party participation. Under Khrushchev this changed as local officials were charged with maintaining public order. They developed routines that relied on less violence. Under Brezhnev the focus was on rounding up ringleaders and dealing mildly with the rest. Thus violent repression had grown rare. As part of *glasnost* Gorbachev allowed free assemblies and demonstrations. As in the West organizers had to get permission from the local authorities and negotiate the size, location, route, and duration of the demonstration. Police and security forces were issued with riot control equipment rather than lethal weapons. Yet as the nationalist demonstrations grew, their organizers simply ignored the regulations, relying on popular support and sometimes supportive local officials. The Gorbachev public order reforms were failing, and by the 1980s the authorities had little experience of more severe repression. Beissinger sees a window of opportunity for repression opening in late 1988 and early 1989, but then closing as nationalist agitation spread, involving industrial strikes, especially by miners (cf. Connor, 1991: chap. 7). The army, says Beissinger, could not have intervened everywhere at once, while generals were restive at being used for domestic repression. He claims this was a tide of nationalism (2002: 160) without which the USSR would not have collapsed. Kramer (2003a: 24–9) disagrees, saying that the regime still had the option of force but rejected it. He emphasizes the conciliatory values of Gorbachev's faction. Beissinger also downplays the way republican leaders used nationalism as a cover for their own power grabs.

By 1990 common opposition to repression was drawing liberals and nationalists together. Gorbachev did not feel strong enough consistently to overrule either the liberals-nationalists or the conservative hard-liners and zigzagged. His own vision was of a socialist Soviet Union reformed by peaceful, political means. Eventually he let the Baltic republics and Central Europe go, and he recognized the limitations of any Soviet government dealing with Nagorno-Karabakh or Moldova. His final rationalization was that these difficult cases were around the periphery. The peripheral Empire might be let go. The core of the Soviet Union could be preserved, he believed.

But by 1990 he was forced to recognize a more serious nationalist threat. It came in Russia, the very core of the Union. Its opposition movements now claimed they had been exploited by the Soviet empire (Hough, 1997: 216, 238). Yeltsin and his liberal allies linked up with Russian nationalists and Yeltsin became the unofficial leader of a Russian nationalist-liberal alliance demanding more reforms than Gorbachev would countenance. In an election of January 1990 Yeltsin narrowly secured control of the government of the Russian Republic, which contained almost 60 percent of the entire Soviet population and 75 percent of the territory. Next month he got passed a resolution declaring the Russian government sovereign over its territories. Other republics then passed sovereignty resolutions, just in case Yeltsin succeeded in breaking away. So now the struggle also became one between Russian and Soviet elites, personalized by the mutual loathing between Gorbachev and Yeltsin. This caused a closing of the ranks between Gorbachev and the Soviet conservatives, usually perceived as his moving rightward.

Among Soviet economists there were now widespread disillusion with planning and admiration of Western economic performance. They knew all about the failings of planning, nothing about those of unregulated markets, and this was the high tide of neoliberalism. Assisted by Western advisers, with the promise of aid from the West, many Russians became neoliberals committed to shock therapy. They fastened on Yeltsin as the man most likely to do it. He had the same enemies as they did even if he lacked much commitment to economic principles. As the mixed economy planned by Gorbachev only seemed to worsen conditions, the terminology used for the desired economy shifted from a "socialist market economy," common in 1988–9, to a "regulated market economy" in 1990, and then to a "free market economy." Gorbachev was unwilling to go the whole way, unlike Yeltsin and the liberals of the Democratic Russia movement. For two years there were struggles over how far markets or privatization should go and how prices should be set. The Soviet elite were factionalized, advocating numerous rival plans.

These disputes were solved by two political power grabs, one successful, the other failed. In December 1990 Yeltsin used his narrow majority in the Russian parliament to slash the Russian contribution to Soviet taxes from one-half to one-tenth of total revenue, a body blow to Gorbachev. There was now dual power: Russian versus Soviet institutions. However, the leaders of the other major republics, the Ukraine, Belarus, and Kazakhstan, did not yet want to destroy the Union, and Yeltsin seemed not to believe it was possible. There had been few separatists in these republics. In the Ukrainian referendum in March 1991, almost three-quarters had supported "preserving the Union of Soviet Socialist Republics as a renewed federation."

The second power grab was by conservatives, and their botched coup inadvertently delivered the Soviet Union's deathblow. A putsch was launched in August 1991 by men Gorbachev himself had appointed as vice president, prime minister, and heads of the army and KGB. But the putschists lacked the guts to use the forces at their disposal fully in the absence of authorization from Gorbachev or other civilian leaders. In the USSR the military had never intervened in political power relations, and the generals could only half shake off habits of obedience. Gorbachev was resting at his holiday home in the Crimea. A group of plotters flew down to get his authorization for the coup, but he refused and the coup fizzled out. Those chosen to lead what would have been a bloody storming of the parliament building (the White House) lacked stomach for the fight. Kryuchkov, the head of the KGB, wrote a groveling letter to Gorbachev afterward, saying, "In general, I am very ashamed" (Brown, 2007: 366–71; Taylor, 2003; Knight, 2003; Dunlop, 2003; Beissinger, 2002: 366–71). Two of the key plotters were drunk during the coup. Valentin Pavlov, Gorbachev's prime minister, missed the plotters' main press conference, being drunk at the time, while Gennady Yanaev, Gorbachev's vice president, the coup's acting president, was too drunk to recognize the people who came to arrest him (White, 1996: 60, 163; Hough, 1997: 429–30). This presumably eased his pain at the time, though his hangover in prison must have been truly dreadful.

The failure of the putsch, launched by Gorbachev appointees, was definitive. The Communist Party had already faded, reformed out of existence by Gorbachev. But the Union now collapsed, and capitalism now began to replace communism. Yeltsin's brave and highly publicized denunciation of the coup in front of the White House, standing atop an armored personnel carrier, had contrasted with Gorbachev's absence in a southern sanatorium, amid false rumors of his complicity. The Ukrainian leader Kravchuk had announced on television his willingness to cooperate with the coup but now promptly reinvented himself as a nationalist and (even less plausibly) as a democrat. But he retained control of his republic's security police, which counted for a lot.

So a Ukrainian referendum in early December 1991 favored independence. Later that month Yeltsin made a joint agreement with the Ukrainian and Belorussian leaders to dissolve the Soviet Union and create a loose Commonwealth of Independent States. The bosses of the republics now forgot about communism and appropriated nationalist rhetoric in order to grab the material resources of their governments, supported by the rising acquisition class (Lane, 2009: 174–5). The nationalism that delivered the final deathblows to the Soviet Union was less sincere ideology than seizure of the spoils. The death of the Soviet Union resulted from Beissinger's nationalist tide in Eastern Europe and the Baltic republics, but elsewhere few conflicts were characterized by nationalism versus imperialism (Suny, 1993; Pearson, 1998; Bunce, 1999).

The direct role of the West in the collapse was not great. The cold war had certainly worsened Soviet economic difficulties by diverting a large proportion of Soviet resources to military needs. That and continued economic growth were easily the biggest Western contributions, long-term, indirect pressures. The American Reagan myth is that pressure from his administration was a major cause of collapse, but rising cold war tensions had tended to strengthen Soviet conservatives, justifying militarized socialism and the search for internal enemies. Most Russians believe Reagan-era pressure prolonged the Soviet Union and made reform initiatives more difficult. Some stress the impact of Reagan's SDI Star Wars program, yet meetings between Gorbachev and his military and space experts concluded that this could not work and that the existing Soviet ballistic missile arsenal equipped with multiple warheads provided a more effective and cheaper defense than trying to develop a Soviet SDI system (Brown, 2007: 246).

Nor do defense expenditure figures support the story of American military pressure. Though U.S. defense expenditure rose in the early eighties, it declined again from 1985. Soviet defense expenditure continued rising until the forced cuts of 1989–91, but these were too late to help the economy. In the early 1980s Gorbachev considered the U.S. deployment of intermediate-range nuclear forces (INFs) in Europe his major military headache and pulled out of Afghanistan partly to help him reach an agreement on INFs. The Afghan war was a defeat, but only on quite a small scale. Soviet troops there were only a fifth of U.S. forces in Vietnam, their casualties were only a quarter of U.S. ones, and the pro-Soviet regime in Kabul survived the Soviet pullout in 1989 and lasted until 1992 (Halliday, 2010). Bush the Elder did not pressure the Soviets. He did urge Gorbachev not to use force across Eastern Europe but Gorbachev was not intending this anyway. Indeed, the Bush administration feared that Soviet collapse might produce chaos in the region and preferred that Gorbachev succeed in his quest for a reformed communism. At the end of 1989, when Romania was engulfed by violence between the Ceausescu regime and dissidents, Secretary of State Baker told Gorbachev that the United States would not object to Soviet armed intervention there. Shevardnadze, the Soviet foreign minister, laughed at the idea, saying it was stupid (Pleshakov, 2009). But though Soviet diplomats never feared American direct aid to dissidents, the reformers did hope to get American aid to help them out of the economic mess.

On the other hand, Reagan Mark II did assist reform (and so the Fall). The negotiations between Gorbachev and Reagan, continued by Bush, strengthened the hands of the liberals and weakened the power of the military, the KGB, and the conservatives for it showed that the West was benign (Brown, 2009: 601–2). The liberals were also boosted by the tide of neoliberalism sweeping Western, especially American, economic and financial institutions. That was important in widening the fissures within Soviet elites and in boosting the certitude of the liberals that they really did possess the keys to the future. The pope's moral denunciations of communism had an influence on Polish dissidents, strengthening their morale. But in general the biggest influences from the West were indirect, mediated by Russian perceptions. To them the West appeared economically dynamic, and they could introduce reforms to get the same end result. The West and especially the United States were simply *there* and that alone exercised pressure on the Soviets, much more than any direct Western interventions – at least until the arrival of the neoliberals. But the main causes of the Fall were internal. Soviet bloc citizens destroyed their regime (Wallander, 2003; Kramer, 2003a: 31–9; Brown, 2007: chap. 9).

Explaining the fall: Was it a revolution?

The Fall had included mistakes, contingencies, and unintended consequences of action. After the fact, this downward slide through errors had a misleading air of inevitability, but a different outcome might have resulted from more decisive action and especially by following the Chinese path of economic before political reform. Gorbachev's fallibility was important. He was in power during the whole reform period, and he was skilled at political infighting. But he achieved almost the exact opposite of what he intended. The Soviet Union was admittedly difficult to reform. Its economy was antiquated, its Communist Party obstructive, its leaders divided. Yet I have indicated alternative directions of reform that would likely have done better. Gorbachev made a difference for it was his initiatives at home and abroad that made the Soviet Union fall faster and fuller than it otherwise would. The great man theory of history works here: this morally courageous but politically incompetent man, with just enough power to demolish institutions but not enough to rebuild them, changed the course of history.

The Fall had been unexpected. Almost no one had predicted it, least of all in the USSR. It resulted from a sequence of often unintended consequences of actions, in which moderate reformers who wanted to stay within the existing system found that their reforms set off further movements and demands that they could not control. In this respect it resembled the French Revolution. But there was a difference for the radical reformers who came out on top did not emerge from below but from the elite itself. The initial cause of Soviet weakness was prolonged economic slowdown, which, when contrasted to the economic performance of the West, contradicted the ideological basis of the regime. This led to strong desire for reform within the elite. But in a Communist Party that was more of an administrative agency than a producer of political programs there was no consensus over what reforms should be. Gorbachev's proposals then produced divisions among five main factions, which stymied not only his reforms but all other consistent reform lines.

This became a state resembling those depicted in earlier chapters as engendering revolution: factionalized, unable to repress severely or reform consistently. But this resulted from the reform process; it was not its original cause. Gorbachev then reacted to failure by weakening the party-state, without putting in place any alternative guarantee of law and order. This encouraged the Central European and Baltic nations to demand independence, almost the only time mass movements from below surged forward (alongside the miners' strikes of 1989). Then came the backing off from repressive militarism by the only two factions who could have wielded it – the Gorbachev reformers and the coalesced conservatives. The halfhearted conservative coup revealed the subordination in communist regimes of the military to the party-state. Even when that state was tottering, the generals could not move decisively – or soberly!

The coup triggered the final Fall, enabling former communists turned liberals, like Yeltsin, to combine with an opportunist acquisition class by now often spouting nationalism. The Soviet Union itself collapsed from the top down, with the decisive pushes in fluid situations from a fairly small group of leaders, many of whom made grave errors producing unanticipated consequences. In the later stages popular forces became more important, overlapping with dissenters in the party-state, and in Eastern Europe and the Baltics it was different. There the party-state elite was successfully challenged by mass movements. Nobody got what he or she had originally wanted, but many adapted along the way, positioning themselves to reap benefits from the Fall. No one should shed a tear for the fall of the Soviet Union. It had already lost its ideological attractions. It had successfully implemented catch-up industrialization but then stagnated into economic obsolescence. It was a great military power but it lost the cold war. It had risen above its worst political atrocities, but it remained repressive. It was no longer seen as a viable alternative to democratic capitalism. China remained that but for the peoples of the former Soviet bloc the issue in 1991 was, Could they do any better having overthrown it?

Political transitions: To democracy and dictatorship

The Soviet Union was replaced by fifteen states. The satellite empire was succeeded by six more states, plus East Germany absorbed into a united Germany. This is usually described as a transition to capitalism and democracy, though that is too simple a formula. Political power relations are easier to understand, since there was one big divide. On one side lay the successor states of the Soviet Union apart from the Baltic republics. These had never had parliamentary institutions of any depth, and communist rule had allowed almost no civil society organizations – independent business groups, labor unions, peasant associations, newspapers, universities, or religions. Emerging political parties therefore had little organizational basis in civil society. They were mostly networks of notables. Where existing republics or provinces declared independence, they formed single popular fronts, often one-party regimes. The dismantling of the communist state and economic decline also weakened political capacity (Strayer, 2001: 386–8). There was not much democracy here.

Further West democratization was a lot easier. The Central European and Baltic countries were neighbors of democratic Western Europe; they had earlier experience of parliamentary institutions; they had not been so long under Soviet domination; and their communist regimes quit rather than remaining in power in nationalist disguise. These countries also wanted to join the European Union, and the terms of accession required democracy. It is difficult to weight the relative importance of these democratizing pressures since they were highly intercorrelated. The timing of their democratic reforms was, however, related to their application for accession to the EU. Later so was the timing of reform by most former Yugoslav countries plus Albania (Cameron, 2007). Huntington (1991) classified this zone as part of his third wave of democratization, begun in Southern Europe and Latin America, and then continuing in East Asia. However, it was really a separate regional wave, not influenced by other regions, nor by shifts in U.S. or papal foreign policy as in other continents. Its democratization began as Gorbachev's policies entwined with Central European attempts to free themselves from the Soviet empire, then intensified by pressures from the European Union (Brown, 2007: 216–23).

These have been imperfect democracies. Four countries, Slovakia, Romania, Croatia, and Serbia, took a decade before government approximated roughly to democracies. A few remain marred by ethnic extremism directed against minorities (including Gypsies) as they had been more seriously in the interwar years. In some ways Central Europe returned to its interwar format. The locals said this was the return to Europe for the borders of Europe had been pushed eastward back to its interwar limits. Central European, Baltic, and some Yugoslav states gained from the Fall, for they are free and largely democratic. Habermas (1990) suggested that these were rectifying or recuperating revolutions, rejecting the fifty-year detour of communism and returning to earlier Western liberal models of modernity. Yet there had also been two major changes. First, in its economic structure Western Europe had changed fundamentally into the European Union. Second, in military power relations the extension of NATO eastward to the boundaries of Russia actually put much of Central and Eastern Europe into the American realm.

Politics are more complicated farther east in the CIS states. The transition was politically disastrous in countries where Soviet collapse meant the flaring up of rival ethnic and religious claims that each was the real soul of the new nation-state. Moldova, Armenia, Azerbaijan, Georgia, and Tajikistan were devastated by civil wars over who should possess the state and which lands it should control. Many in these countries would have preferred the iron hand of a Stalin or a Brezhnev, able to keep ethnic peace, to an attempt at democracy, which turned into ethnocracy. These dangerous national aspirations were accompanied by the desire of ruling communist elites to preserve their powers in nationalist guise. The combined result was a movement during the 1990s and early 2000s *away* from democratic institutions. This was true of Russia,

Moldova, Belarus, Armenia, Armenia, Azerbaijan, and Uzbekistan, while Georgia, Kyrgystan, and Tajikistan oscillated, closer to authoritarianism than democracy. In 2003–5 Georgia, the Ukraine, and Kyrgystan did have apparently progressive Rose, Orange, and Tulip Revolutions, though ethnic-regional rivalries were also involved, limiting subsequent democratization. The CIS countries have stronger presidencies and weaker parliaments than almost all the countries further west (Cameron, 2007).

Regimes have lasted or been overthrown by nonparliamentary means. Of the communist republican presidents who signed the original CIS Treaty in 1991, Nazarbaev in Kazakhstan and Karimov in Uzbekistan still rule repressively today. Niyazov in Uzbekistan ruled until his death in 2006 and was succeeded by another dictator. Several other presidents were deposed or forced to resign, their iron hands rusting and breaking amid crises. Of all those CIS state presidents only Snegur in Moldova left office as the result of a normal contested election. Russia has come closest to democratic elections yet Yeltsin was essentially able to appoint his own successor, Putin. Russia has never had an entirely fair national election, while Georgia has had a varied mix of elections and coups. Yet despite the lack of democracy in the CIS states, and except for civil war situations, this is an improvement on the Soviet era, for there are partially autonomous parliaments, parties, and media, even though their freedoms are curbed. Add the more radical democratic improvements found among the ex-satellite countries and the Baltic states, and the Fall of the Soviet Union was in general positive in terms of political power relations.

Economic transitions: Capitalism and neoliberalism

The economic transition was complicated by the fact that the Soviet bloc was turning capitalist just when neoliberalism was at high tide in the West. Early talk of a second Marshall Plan for the postcommunist states went nowhere. They got structural adjustment programs in shock therapy mode instead. Whereas 90 percent of Marshall aid had been in the form of grants, 90 percent of the funds now were in loans, with strings attached. Neoliberals believed that the state should be torn down so that the market could automatically take its place. That was the thinking of Russian neoliberals like Burbulis and Gaidar and their mainly American advisers.

The main American in Russia was Lawrence Summers, deputy secretary at the U.S. Treasury Department, then a man of influence in the IMF, later President Obama's leading economic adviser. He explained to Deputy Premier Victor Chernomyrdin the principles that the IMF was imposing on Russia in return for loans: "The rules that governed IMF lending weren't arbitrary or intrusive," he said; "they were a reflection of the immutable principles of economics, which operated in a way similar to the rules of physics" (Talbott,

2002: 82). This is the neoclassical version of the notion that capitalism imposes strict "limits" on what the state can (rationally) do. But this is false. Human rules are very different from the rules of nature. They are not objective, they represent particular power interests and so always favor some over others, and they require norms, laws, and institutions for enforcement. Had Summers read any sociology – and from the classics he could have picked any of Marx, Durkheim, or Weber – he would have known that for free markets to flourish, human institutions are required and their rules and norms must be widely accepted. Institutional economists like North and Stiglitz belatedly came to the same conclusion. A lawmaking legislature, an independent judiciary, an honest administration, institutionalized private property relations, the peaceful exchange of goods, genuinely competitive enterprises, and above all normative solidarity among the participants are required. Virtually none of these preconditions existed; indeed the reformers were trying to destroy some of them. Nor did they realize that markets always embody power relations, and that they are used by those with power in the market to increase their own resources and only second (and sometimes not at all) to increase the resources of society as a whole. Turning Russia over to its markets, which were in reality dominated by massive monopolies, would merely entrench monopoly power.

Summers's immutable principles submitted Russia to what he called "the three '-ations – privatization, stabilization, and liberalization," which "must be completed as soon as possible" in a single wave. Privatization of all state industries would create incentives to pursue efficiency and profit, stabilization would come through combating inflation by fiscal austerity, and liberalizing prices and trade would permit markets to reallocate resources. Jeffrey Sachs, another neoliberal who also alienated Russians with his arrogance, dismissed any criticism of shock therapy as "politically motivated rather than analytically sound" and argued that "enormous scope exists for increases in average living standards within a few years" (quoted by Pomer, 2001). This form of neoliberalism is a transcendental ideology applying the same principles to all times and places, though some of the neoliberals did advocate privatizations in stages – small-scale ones first, then big ones – and showed some sensitivity to unemployment.

The biggest defender of neoliberal shock therapy is the Swedish economist Anders Aslund (2002, 2007), adviser to the Russian, Ukrainian, and Kyrgyz governments. He says the most efficient economies are always free markets. States only add distortions and rent seeking, and the postcommunist transition was a struggle against rent seeking, profit seeking in noncompetitive, monopoly environments. If government officials remain in control of economic resources during a gradual process of liberalization, says Aslund, they will extract rent from every monopoly that they control, aborting overall economic performance. Only by comprehensive and rapid liberalization, that is, by shock therapy, can such transitional rent seeking be averted. He accepts that this will increase unemployment and widen inequality but they will provide incentives to entrepreneurs and workers alike and produces more growth than prolonged rent seeking.

His data on twenty-one former communist countries seemed to show that countries undergoing shock therapy in the 1990s did better than those experiencing a more gradual or a minimal transition. Shock therapists like Poland and the Czech Republic suffered drops in GDP of less than 20 percent over the first three or four years, while others, like Romania, had a drop of 25 percent. This was then followed by substantial growth in Poland and rather lesser growth in Hungary and Slovakia. By 1998 their GDPs (at purchasing power parities) were higher than they had been in 1989, while the Czech Republic's was about the same. In contrast Bulgaria and Estonia suffered initial drops in GDP of about a third, and by 1998 Estonia was almost back to its 1989 level, though Bulgaria's and Romania's recoveries were slower. The other two Baltic republics, Lithuania and Latvia, had bigger initial drops, close to 50 percent, and then recovered, though not to 1998 levels. In general the countries of Central Europe and the Baltic were to see steady growth rates in the range of 4–6 percent per annum in the late 1990s, while Romania and Bulgaria accompanied Russia into serious macroeconomic crisis in the period 1996–8. The CIS states mostly did worse than this in the 1990s. Georgian GDP dropped 76 percent. The Ukraine, Azerbaijan, Moldova, and Tajikistan dropped 50–65 percent; Kyrgystan and Armenia about 50 percent; Russia and Kazakhstan almost 40 percent; Belarus and Turkmenistan around 30 percent; and Uzbekistan only 20 percent. In the late 1990s there was some recovery in Armenia, Georgia, and Kyrgystan, while Belarus, Azerbaijan, and Uzbekistan held steady. Russia, the Ukraine, Moldova, and Kazakhstan continued to decline by about 4 percent per annum and Tajikistan and Turkmenistan declined by almost 10 percent per annum. The CIS states that initially appeared to do best were those that reformed least, while those that did worst were scarred by the ethnic civil wars that were also a legacy of the Fall (Aslund, 2002: 115–20).

Yet we should be wary of Aslund's conclusions. The better performing countries of the 1990s were Baltic and Central European countries, which were geographically and ideologically closer to the West. They could trade more with the West and receive more investment from it, most already had bigger private sectors and/or civil society institutions, and they had more past experience with capitalism. Soon thereafter most of them entered the European Union. These were all significant advantages, which may have been more decisive than shock therapy in aiding a speedier adjustment to capitalism, though they also permitted shock therapy programs with less political opposition. Among the states formed out of communist Yugoslavia, Slovenia and the Croatia are the closest to the West and again were the best economic performers.

Did gradualism lead to more rent seeking than shock therapy? The former Polish finance minister Kolodko (2000) and Nobel laureate Stiglitz (1999), backed by four other Nobel economic prizewinners, argue that mass neoliberal privatization of banks and industrial enterprises allowed nomenklatura capitalists to seize control of major assets and exact monopoly rents from them while the liberalization of finance enabled them to spirit their profits abroad. The bigger the shock, they said, the more the rent seeking. This was not market capitalism but what I have called politicized capitalism. The Nobel laureates stressed the need to maintain institutions and social capital to restrain this. Since the transition was from communism, the institutions and social capital mostly lay in the public sector. The laureates also believe that a sense of equity was essential to establish the legitimacy of a market economy, and so were wary of neoliberal reforms, which typically benefited the rich and widened inequality. This dispute among economists is ongoing.

In the first decade of the twenty-first century the ordering of GDP growth reversed. Gradualists and even minimally reforming states in the East now grew more than the westerly neoliberals. Over the whole period 1989–2008 these trends virtually cancelled each other out, giving the three main groups of countries – neoliberals, gradualists, and minimalists – similar growth rates. The ratio of real GDP in 2008 to that in 1989 in the CIS states was only slightly lower than that of the former satellite and Baltic countries. There was more variation among the CIS states, especially in Central Asia. The highest growth ratio of all was in natural gas–rich Turkmenistan (226) and the lowest of all was Tajikistan (61), while the Europeans and Baltics only varied between Latvia's 118 and Poland's 178. The high-performing Turkmenistan also scored the lowest on the European Bank for Reconstruction and Development's [EBRD] transition score – a measure of progress toward economic liberalization. As a group the Central Asians scored much lower on liberalization than did the Europeans, yet their growth rate was only slightly lower. Russia itself had almost no growth over the period (a ratio of 108) and a higher than average liberalization score. Belarus had a high growth ratio of 161 but a low score on liberalization, while the Ukraine had the reverse, with negative growth (61) but a quite high liberalization score (the same as Russia's). In all the postcommunist countries, there is *no* overall relationship either way between liberalization and economic growth (European Bank for Reconstruction and Development [EBRD], 2009: tables 1.1 & A1.1.1; Tridico, 2009).

Two groups of countries have done best over the whole period in terms of GDP growth. The first is composed of Slovenia, the Czech Republic, Slovakia, Poland, and Hungary, the most Westernized countries. They liberalized their economies, though only the Czech Republic and Poland underwent the full shock therapy treatment. The second high-performing group comprises Turkmenistan, Belarus, Uzbekistan, and Azerbaijan, who reformed very little. Oil and natural gas benefited three of them, while the fourth, Belarus, benefited from getting oil at a cheap price from Russia. These countries have seen laggard, partial privatization. Presence of natural resources like oil and gas is also more conducive to authoritarian regimes, as the Middle East also shows.

After twenty years of transition few countries had done markedly better than they might have done had they continued under communism. The average EBRD ratio of 2008 over 1989 for all former Soviet bloc countries (that is, excluding the Balkans, Mongolia, and Turkey, which the EBRD bizarrely includes among the transition countries) was 127. This is an average growth rate of 1 percent per annum. This is not much success, and as Lane (2009) has shown, the ex-communist countries in the European Union were hit harder by the Great Neoliberal Recession of 2008 than were CIS states precisely because they were more integrated into the Western economy, and especially into its financial sector, which caused the crisis.

Aslund (2007) responded to earlier EBRD figures, which were already casting doubt on his argument by blaming the lagging growth of Central Europe and the Baltic on a social welfare trap caused by excessive welfare payments. But it is hard to claim that shock therapy has been any better than gradual or even minimal reform in generating growth. This is not the main reason why some countries have done markedly better than others. No one model fits all: growth depended on policies attuned to conditions in each country.

Arguments rage over the quality of these GDP figures, especially late Soviet ones, but mortality and poverty statistics are simpler to construct, more reliable, and more revealing of impacts on the lives of ordinary people. In only a little more than half of the former Soviet bloc countries had life expectancy recovered in 2006 to 1990 levels, and this was true of less than half the CIS countries (World Bank, 2007). The United Nations Development Program [UNDP] (1999) says ten million died prematurely as a result of these transitions – about the same number as in all Stalin's atrocities (Mann, 2005a: 329–30). The atrocities of markets are not so visible as those of plans, but the suffering and the death rate may be similar.

Mass privatization programs led the way into disaster. Milanovic and Ersado (2008) say they were responsible for rising poverty and inequality, as were big cuts in subsidies to infrastructural programs. Stuckler, King, and Hamm (2009) in a study of twenty-one postcommunist countries show that programs that transferred at least 25 percent of large state-owned enterprises to the private sector within a two-year period were responsible for an average increase in male mortality rates of almost 13 percent. Where privatization was absent or gradual, mortality rates rose much less. These authors also found that mass privatization reduced economic growth, state capacity, and property rights protection. This conclusion was also supported by firm-level data from a sample of managers in 3,550 companies in twenty-four postcommunist countries. They found that in countries that implemented mass privatization, newly privatized firms were less likely to engage in industrial restructuring but much more likely to use barter and accumulate tax arrears than their state-owned counterparts. They say that their data support a neo-Weberian model of economic growth, which, as well as free markets, presupposes an autonomous, efficient, and bureaucratic state. Mass privatization did not produce autonomous private property or the separation of economic and political power, as its advocates intended. Instead it weakened the autonomy of both the state and private property and pushed countries toward crony or politicized capitalism. We will see some examples of this later. So a different type of political capitalism, emphasizing patron-client ties and a nonbureaucratic state, emerged in many of the post-Soviet countries, while countries that proceeded more gradually in creating a private sector, like Poland and Slovenia, are now much closer to the Western capitalist ideal, with a relative separation of political and economic power (Hamm, King, & Stuckler, 2012). A study by Davis (2001) also showed that mass privatization also increased unemployment and slashed health and welfare programs, mostly provided through state enterprises. The ending of state subsidies on basic foodstuffs, consumer goods, and utilities also bit hard, especially among the retired, older workers and ethnic minorities. Shock therapy was a disaster.

Neoliberals certainly knew privatization would cause unemployment to surge. State socialist countries had provided most welfare benefits at the workplace coupled with full employment, so there were hardly any systems of unemployment insurance in place. These were hastily devised with help from the World Bank and the OECD. In the mid-1990s, when leftist parties appeared to be making a comeback in Central Europe, there was a big increase in World Bank and Western European funding – a distinctly Bismarckian-type attempt to defuse class conflict through welfare, as had happened a century earlier. Unemployment pay in Central Europe rose to 30 percent of pay levels compared to only 10 percent or less in the CIS countries (Orenstein, 2008). Other welfare schemes were slower to come, but Central European countries began to introduce them in the late 1990s. Pension plans took the form of a unique regional combination of two of Esping-Andersen's welfare regimes, privatized liberal schemes pushed by the international agencies and more indigenous conservative corporatist welfare first developed in the region by the German and Austro-Hungarian Empires (Cerami & Vanhuysse, 2009). European Union pressure for better labor standards, health and safety regulations, public health, and treatment of national minorities then broadened welfare states. By 2007 Central Europe and the Baltic had welfare provisions more generous than most countries at their level of development, though the CIS countries were much less generous.

Past Austro-Hungarian and present German influences on this region were clear, says Tridico (2009; cf. Cerami & Vanhuysse, 2009). He distinguishes two measures of success. Whereas competitive capitalism, a liberalizing model (usually shock therapy), did best in GDP growth, a corporatist model did best on the United Nations Human Development Index, which combines life expectancy, infant mortality, education, and social welfare expenditure. The corporatist countries had formerly been Austro-Hungarian: the Czech Republic, Hungary, and Slovenia had the least poverty, the highest minimum wages, the lowest unemployment, and the greatest social investment – as well as pretty good economic growth. State capitalist countries (Turkmenistan, Uzbekistan, Belarus) also did better than competitive capitalist countries on the UN Index, and so also hybrid countries. Most people would prefer to live longer than have a high GDP, for they might not be alive to benefit! The word "liberalization," applied to the ex-satellite countries, needs refinement. The most successful transitions were social liberal, a mixture of the Euro and Anglo models of social citizenship.

A tale of happy neoliberal transition is not told by postcommunist citizens. In polls in the 1990s and 2000s conducted by Eurobarometer and the Pew Charitable Trust most people in most former Soviet Bloc countries said that economic conditions had deteriorated. There are big variations over whether they prefer capitalism or state socialism, with those now in the European Union preferring capitalism, and those farther east either evenly split or preferring state socialism. Generally, majorities want further reform, a very positive word, but their responses do not indicate the direction of desired reform. Gini coefficients for twenty postcommunist countries reveal widening inequality, and polls indicate that this is perceived and disliked by people in these countries. Aslund (2002: 311) comments as a true neoliberal that growing Gini coefficients of inequality are "expected and desired" – but not by the citizens themselves.

The most westerly countries of the Soviet bloc have had a fairly good transition, combining democracy with either high GDP growth or high Human Development performance. Farther east came democratic deficits and worse economic performance except for countries endowed with natural resources. In the East wars and civil wars generated by Soviet collapse brought disaster. Once again we see the continued variety of nation-states and macroregions. After two decades of fluctuating fortunes, the overall economic picture is that the varied countries of the former Soviet empire have converged on the economic performance of their non-Soviet neighbors. This is progress of a sort. In some senses, the midway point in this range is Russia itself, slightly below average in economic and human development, but with more democracy than most CIS states. Since it is also the biggest and most significant country, I now focus on it.

The Russian transition: Political capitalism, perverted democracy

Gorbachev's policies had dismantled the administrative powers of the state while allowing nomenklatura members to acquire control industries and banks.

They could now pursue rent seeking, whether under shock therapy or gradualism. To emphasize either their origins as statists or their destinations as capitalists seems relatively unimportant for this was political capitalism, a blend of the two. They were robber barons, mafia bosses, and since the public could see this, the process of liberalization, and especially of privatization, became deeply contested. It was in this context that U.S. vice president Gore replied to Summers by remarking that U.S. policy ought to be "a synthesis between the iron laws of economics and the hard realities of Russian politics" (Talbott, 2002: 85). There were no iron laws, but in Russia and several other countries political realities did stymie shock therapy by making it too unpopular to complete except by force.

The Russian government did at first try to implement the whole capitalist shock treatment (unlike most CIS countries). Days after the dissolution of the Union, at the beginning of January 1992, Russian President Boris Yeltsin appointed Gennady Burbulis as his deputy premier and Yegor Gaidar as the overseer of the economics ministries. These neoliberals, advised by Americans, promptly ordered the liberalization of foreign trade, prices, and currency. Soviet price controls were removed in an attempt to move goods back into understocked Russian stores, legal barriers to private trade and manufacture were removed, and subsidies to state farms and industries were slashed while allowing in foreign imports to break the power of state-owned local monopolies.

Inflation had started when the Central Bank printed money to ease the government's lack of revenue, but these reforms produced stratospheric inflation rising by double digits per month. This wiped out pensions and middle-class savings. Under the stabilization program, the government let most prices float, raised interest rates and taxes, and sharply cut government subsidies to industry, construction, and welfare. These policies caused widespread hardship. Many state enterprises now had no orders or means of financing. Many closed, bringing on a protracted depression. Both real per capita personal income and overall production declined by an astonishing 50 percent between 1991 and 1994 and investment declined by more than two-thirds, much worse than in the Great Depression discussed in chapter 7 of Volume 3 (Klein & Pomer, 2001: statistical appendix). Regions dependent on giant enterprises and industries were devastated.

The social impact was stunning. Whereas 1.5 percent of the Russian population was defined as living in poverty in the late Soviet era, by mid-1993 this had risen to somewhere between 39 percent and 49 percent (Milanovic, 1998: 186–90). Per capita Russian incomes fell by 15 percent by 1998, according to government figures. Life expectancy fell dramatically, for men from sixty-four years in 1990 to below fifty-eight in 1994, while women's dropped from seventy-four to seventy-one years. People were dying as a result of the transition! Even by 2004 life expectancy had not regained the levels of 1990. Alcohol-related deaths shot up 60 percent in the 1990s, overwhelmingly concentrated among men, indicating low morale. Deaths from infectious and parasitic diseases doubled. The poor could no longer afford medicines. There were now roughly one and half times as many deaths as births per year in Russia. Tikhomirov (2000: 8) shows that the scale of economic crisis in post-Soviet Russia up to 1996 was greater than the crises induced by World War I, the Civil War, and World War II. The economic collapse in the transition period far outweighed the extent of decline in the late Soviet era.

This is how Gorbachev (2001: xiii) later described shock therapy

"Shock therapy" did irreparable harm. Most dangerous are the social consequences – the sharp drop in standards of living, the enormous inequality of incomes, the decline in life expectancy – not to mention impoverishment of education, science and culture. All of this was bound up with deeply flawed privatization, a flare-up of crime, and moral degradation.

American economic advisers were accused of deliberately seeking to bring Russia to its knees in the interests of the United States! As Arbatov said, "Many of my countrymen now understand shock therapy as a conscious design to undermine Russia completely as a great power and transform her into a kind of Third World country. The actual results of shock therapy have not been far from this goal" (2001: 178). This is unfair. Most blame must be placed not on evil intent but on folly, in macroaffairs the normal partner of transcendental ideology, as it had been under Stalinism and was now again under neoliberalism. In both ideologies a limited set of simple principles was believed to give ultimate meaning to the workings of societies and economies, which are in reality varied, complicated, and delicate. If submitted to revolution or structural adjustment, they prove brittle. Neoliberalism, like Stalinism and fascism, wore blinkers that allowed clear but tunnel vision. Its proponents arrived in Russia not as scientists but as missionaries (says Cohen, 2001: 50).

To their credit Summers and Sachs also favored extensive aid programs and were disappointed by the meager $16 million loan given by the United States to Russia. They also tried to persuade the IMF to finance Russian social-safety-net programs (Talbott, 2002: 107, 286). They knew Russian markets needed boosting, they had asked for much more, and American politicians had initially promised it. But the notion of giving money to the recent evil enemy did not appeal widely within Congress and little aid was forthcoming. The postcommunist countries had to pay more to Western governmental organizations to service debts incurred in the communist period than they received in credits and grants now (Aslund, 2002: 411ff.). In any case, aid went overwhelmingly to the Central European and Baltic countries, not farther east. Private investment was greater, but it went to the same places. Western aid was trying to detach European countries from Russia more than it was seeking to build up Russia.

Russians were attempting to do something that had never been tried before: introduce capitalism into an already industrial society. It would have been a difficult task anyway, since there were many giant dinosaur plants with a slim chance of being globally competitive. Any regime would have had difficulty in turning this economy around. But China faced problems that were not dissimilar and let many state enterprises go to the wall without destroying the economy. I discuss the comparison with China more systematically at the end of the next chapter. Yet the neoliberalism adopted in Russia focused on destroying the twin guarantors of laws and rules in the society and the economy – the state and the Communist Party. It also destroyed the legitimating ideology for both. The command system was destroyed and nothing was put in its place. It was thought that free markets would follow automatically. They did not; nor have they ever.

Of course, no Soviet or Russian political leader seeking reelection could contemplate complete shock therapy. It might have shocked the people into another revolution. In 1992–3 the Communist Party was reviving because of the ongoing disaster and together with nationalists formed a majority of deputies in the Russian Supreme Soviet. Economic realities were also awkward for neoliberal remedies. Leaving it to the market would not produce much domestic competition, as intended. A single large enterprise, the state, made 77 percent of all products. It was an economy of monopolies, which if given freedom would charge what they liked. It was rational for them not to restructure but to raise prices, causing massive inflation. Shock therapy also involved opening up the Russian market to foreign competition, but imports were generally better made and cheaper and would wipe out most Russian firms. No politician could allow this, and so the government continued subsiding industries with credits. The Gaidar government, ostensibly neoliberal, restored subsidies in mid-1992. But this was not enough to stifle criticism, so Yeltsin fired Burbulis and then Gaidar in late 1992.

The communist/nationalist majority in parliament would not pass Yeltsin's shock therapy program. His response was military. He had already launched a military assault on Chechnya, in contrast to the conciliatory policies of Gorbachev. According to a Russian interior minister, the two wars in Chechnya launched by Yeltsin and Putin killed as many Russians as had the war in Afghanistan (Brown, 2007: 316). But in October 1993 Yeltsin sent forces in to storm the White House and arrest the deputies holed up inside. Hundreds were killed in this assault. The United States did not protest because it wanted Yeltsin to press ahead with shock therapy. Neoliberalism ranked higher for the United States than democracy at this moment. Yeltsin now devised a new constitution concentrating more powers in the presidency. This still endures, as does the absence of an independent judiciary. Presidential powers enabled Yeltsin to push ahead with mass privatization between 1994 and 1996, but further bad election results then forced him to compromise. Premier Chernomyrdin called for an end to market romanticism and muddled along between state and markets, mitigating the disaster.

But one neoliberal disaster could not be undone. Gaidar had removed restrictions on capital flows, and enterprise bosses could now export capital as part of shady foreign trade deals. Since they knew how uneconomic their enterprises were, their safest personal strategy was to spirit away all they had (mainly state credits) into foreign bank accounts. The capital flight was enormous, probably almost $100 billion in the period 1992–7. If privatization was considered the solution, it should have been coupled with more tariff protection and more regulation of capital flows. But by the time privatization was undertaken, most state firms were in such dire financial straits that the politicians could not refuse them continuing state subsidies (Tikhomirov, 2000: 16–22, 60–3, 141–58).

So the Russians got not the capitalism they had envisaged but crony, political capitalism. In the absence of good government, and in an economy originally configured for monopolies not competition, economic power was based on political connections, theft, monopoly, and exploiting the disjuncture between the old and the new system. Since it was hard to enforce contracts legally, KGB bosses used businessmen as their front men or mafia-style hit men helped out. In a November 1996 poll 52 percent of Russians said they believed that "the mafia" ran Russia. There were several routes to wealth. Those commanding state resources, like high officials of the Communist Party, the KGB, and the Komsomol (Soviet Youth League), could liquidate the assets of their organizations and spirit them into overseas accounts and investments. Others exploited the fixed prices of the Gorbachev period. By using their connections within the party-state elite to buy up scarce Soviet goods at low prices, they could sell them in Russia at a higher market price. Even bigger profits came from using connections quietly to buy up Soviet raw materials, especially oil, and export and sell and keep the profits abroad – doing no good for the Russian economy. Another route was through currency speculation, either in Soviet gold or dollars and yen, assuming that the deterioration of the economy would yield big profits when they later resold them. These opportunities meant Russia got profits without markets, "capitalists without capitalism" – in contrast to most of the former satellite countries dominated by markets, plenty of small owners, small shareholders, and networks of cross-ownership, "capitalism without capitalists" (in the words of Eyal et al., 1998).

Vladimir Gusinsky made his first money as the king of copper bracelets (a Russian fad). His connections in government got him into property development and banking. He speculated in currencies, selling rubles for dollars, waiting for the ruble to fall, then selling the dollars, paying back the ruble loan and pocketing the difference. As long as the ruble interest rate was below the pace of devaluation, this was a surefire way of making money. Betting on failure was a great idea. Then he moved into mass media. He was given the NTV television network for political favors done for Yeltsin, along with a state loan of more than $1 billion, which disappeared and was never repaid (most biographical details of the oligarchs are taken from Hoffman, 2003).

Then came Yeltsin's mass privatization programs, intended (like Thatcher's) to spread share ownership to create support for his reforms. Free share vouchers were distributed to the population, and then to the employees of the companies being privatized. Yet amid economic disaster most people were desperate for cash and sold their shares to rich intermediaries. Yeltsin, short of funds for the upcoming elections in which the Communist Party made a comeback, launched a loans for shares program in 1995, auctioning off packages of stock shares in desirable enterprises as collateral for loans to the government made by banks. In exchange for the loan, the state granted the bank assets worth many times the value of the loan. If the government did not repay the loans within a year (which it was in no position to do), the lender acquired title to the stock. The auctions were organized by a corrupt state, which allowed only a few banks to bid low. This kept the auction prices low and rewarded friends. Major share packages were transferred to a few banks, which appropriated prime economic assets at knockdown prices. The informal deal was that the oligarchs' media empires would endorse Yeltsin in the election. This was not neoliberalism but politicized capitalism, and indeed Summers, the neoliberal, tried to persuade Clinton to stop Yeltsin. Clinton rejected his advice, deciding that this was a small price to pay to finance Yeltsin against the communists (Kotkin, 2001: 130; Tikhomirov, 2000: 236–54; Cohen, 2001; Talbott, 2002: 206–9). Economic yet politicized power was invading and perverting a political democracy and the United States was still sacrificing ideals for anticommunism.

The oligarch Mikhail Khodorkovsky was by 2004 the richest man in Russia. From a middle-class background, he joined the Komsomol as a way to climb. His first business ventures used Komsomol properties, which he appropriated for himself and his Komsomol and KGB backers. People trusted him because they knew he had powerful backers. In 1987 he opened a center of science and technology, Menatep, originally importing and reselling computers, then "French" brandy and "Swiss" vodka (probably both counterfeit). With cash from these and using his connections, he obtained a banking licence for Menatep in 1989. He received big deposits from government agencies to finance import-export operations, and he may have stolen Soviet Treasury funds during the period of the collapse of the Union. Bank Menatep enabled him to fund a bid for the state-owned oil company Yukos in 1995. This was a loans-for-shares deal, using his connections inside the government. He paid only $350 million to acquire 78 percent of Yukos, which was worth many times that price. A higher bid was ruled out by his associates on the inside. After a few years in which Khodorkovsky outfoxed Western banks and oil companies by dubious methods, he had built up a substantial oil-based empire. He then saw that to get bigger he had to become respectable. His businesses became models of transparency. But he made the mistake of using his wealth to fund parties and media outlets opposed to President Putin. He met Vice President

Cheney to discuss a possible merger with an American oil giant, which would offer him powerful foreign support against Putin. Yet Putin was not intimidated and Khodorkovsky now languishes in jail after being found guilty in 2005 and 2010 of fraud and tax evasion. Currently, his sentence runs until 2017. Though he was probably guilty of some offenses, this is so common in Russian business as to indicate that he was singled out for political reasons. Political power had trumped economic power and most Russians approved.

Alexander Smolensky began trading on the black market in Soviet times. He was arrested in 1981 and sentenced to two years hard labor for economic crimes. He then went into construction and with the help of Moscow's mayor transformed his business into Bank Stolichny, which specialized in currency speculation. In the loans-for-shares deal he got the agroindustrial bank network Agroprombank, the second largest in Russia. The minister who oversaw the deals, Anatoly Chubais, received a $3 million interest-free loan from Stolichny at the same time. Smolensky merged his banks into SBS-Agro Bank, which grew into the largest Russian bank. It collapsed in the Russian financial crisis of 1998, but the Central Bank issued the bank $100 million in credits, which mysteriously vanished. Since then Smolensky has been regularly accused of embezzlement and currency fraud but with powerful political and security friends he has so far wriggled out of trouble. He now owns major newspapers.

Many successful capitalists over the world have begun by using dubious methods; many exploit political connections to secure government contracts and privileges, and many exploit monopolies rather than markets. The term "robber baron" capitalism was invented in early twentieth-century America. But I doubt that any country has ever been so dominated by robber baron or mafia capitalists as Russia in the 1990s. Yet, like their counterparts elsewhere, the Russians became respectable with time, entering into joint ventures abroad, sitting on the boards of Western corporations, converting their loot into private corporations operating on more-or-less private markets. Origins can be forgotten once the business is institutionalized.

Since political connections and insider access to productive resources mattered more than technical knowledge or manufacturing skills, most entrepreneurs were former party-state apparatchiks. Khodorkovsky exaggerated this, declaring, "90% of the prosperous people in business originated in the old nomenklatura structures and those close to them." But in one study 68 percent of Moscow businesses were headed by former managers of state enterprises; in another national study of the top hundred businessmen in Russia 62 percent were formerly state or party elite. The main pushers for a free market were party-state elite persons who longer believed in socialism but scented the opportunity to acquire wealth without having to curry favor with the party and socialism. They could also now display their wealth openly and pass it on to their children.

The political elite did not change much either. Around 75 percent of Yeltsin's top advisers and ministers were from the former Soviet apparatchik class. In 1995 former secretaries of local Communist Party committees headed eighty-three of the eighty-nine Russian regional and local administrations. About a fifth of the largest enterprises that were privatized became the private property of their former "red directors" and another 60 percent were controlled by them (Kotz & Weir, 1997: 117–18, 121, 126, chap. 7; Kotkin, 2001: 7; Tikhomirov, 2000: 289). Violent mafias aided the oligarchs from the shadows and curtailed the monopoly of the means of violence that political elites are supposed to wield. By the end of the 1990s, says Kenez (2006: 291), Russia "was ruled by a combination of crime syndicates, corrupt bureaucrats, and oligarchs." Better than Stalinism, yes, but better than late communism? It was not entirely clear.

Russia crawls out of the Abyss – the 2000s

The East Asian financial crisis spread to Russia in 1998, hitting an economy that had just begun to recover. Yet recovery soon recommenced and was sustained until the financial crisis of 2008. Russian governments were pragmatically managing an energy-rich economy generating fairly steady growth while maintaining high inequality amid power struggles between oligarchs, regional political bosses, and the central state. Under Vladmir Putin, Yeltsin's successor, neoliberalism was abandoned.

The state formally acquired more power, renationalizing industries, wielding reinvigorated security forces and more media control. About 35 percent of Russian GDP in 2006 was in state hands. Putin enjoyed a degree of performance legitimacy. He was popular because under him wages and pensions were paid regularly, living standards rose, a stronger state battled both the oligarchs and the regional governmental bosses and provided more public order, while Putin himself expressed a genuine Russian nationalism defiant against Western encroachments into its backyard. For a decade even if elections had not been rigged, Putin would have won them.

Under Putin a monetary economy was largely restored and informal bartering declined. Economic growth averaged around 7 percent through the first eight years of the new century. This was followed by a year of negative growth in 2009, due to the Great Neoliberal Recession, but since then growth has resumed at about 4 percent – better than Western countries. Because it was less tied to the global economy, except as an energy supplier, Russia weathered the financial crisis better than the countries of Eastern Europe, which embraced neoliberalism (Lane, 2009). There is abundant foreign investment and capitalists have become less preoccupied with asset stripping, more with rationalizing and investing in production. However, the Russian economy depends heavily on oil, natural gas, and metals and has not yet upgraded its technology to be able to compete in most semifinished or manufactured goods in Western markets.

Hanson (2003) emphasizes variety. In some sectors, despite the weak rule of law and insecure property rights, entrepreneurs recognize a viable framework of informal rules and are willing to invest and expand production. In others crude, illegal state intervention damps down capitalist rationality. This is a dynamic economy, he concludes, but it could do better if the rules of the game were more formal and predictable. Though Voigt and Hockmann (2008) perceive some growth in technical efficiency in industry (not agriculture), they attribute most recent growth to ruble devaluations after the 1998 financial crisis and to rising raw materials prices, especially energy, which Russia has in abundance. External shocks and not the success of transition, they conclude, have fueled Russia's growth.

Inequality remains high though it has stopped rising. Milanovic (1998) and Milanovic and Ersado (2008) estimated that the Gini coefficient almost doubled between 1988 and 1993 from 0.24 to 0.48, contributed by the richest 10 percent doing much better, the poorest 10 percent doing much worse, and the middle doing only a very little worse. More recent estimates see the Gini remaining relatively stable after 1995, at around 0.40, with each decile's share also remaining relatively stable. This is lesser inequality than in the United States. Milanovic and Ersado conclude that the large, corrupt privatization packages contributed most to inequality. The most visible inequality lies between Moscow and the rest of the country. Moscow, the link with the outside world, "the fiefdom of thieves," saw diffusion of wealth among a new middle class, in stark contrast to most of poverty-stricken Russia.

Putin did cut down some of the oligarchs. They had overestimated their power, believing that their capitalism was now more important than the state. Putin proved them wrong by arresting them and seizing their assets. In 2000 Gusinsky was briefly arrested, and that was enough to make him flee to Spain. Berezovky fled to London. Khodorkovsky, the richest man in Russia, unwisely stayed put and languishes in jail with several of his Yukos associates. On balance, most Russians seemed to think this acceptable, though there were murmurs that many of the industries confiscated from oligarchs were handed over to Putin's cronies. Tucker (2010) argues that this was a second wave of the self-liberation of the nomenklatura, and especially of the KGB. Those left behind in the first privatization wave now got their piece of the action. Virtually all the bureaucrats around Putin doubled as managers of large, informally state controlled corporations. In 2008 the leading business magazine estimated that Putin's personal and political allies headed the boards of companies controlling 40 percent of the Russian economy. This highly politicized capitalism implies a partial remerging of political and economic power after an interlude of fuller capitalist separation (Aron, 2009). The Wikileaks trove of U.S. State Department documents contained reports by U.S. diplomats that the Interior Ministry (the MVD) and the federal intelligence services (the FSB) now dominated. One cable reads, "Moscow business owners understand that it is best to get protection from the MVD and FSB (rather than organized crime groups), since they not only have more guns, resources and power than criminal groups, but they are also protected by the law. For this reason, protection from criminal gangs is no longer so high in demand."

However, the extent to which Putin or any central administrative agencies can control this sprawling crony state and capitalism is unclear. Putin's Russia has not returned to a Soviet-style despotic state. The party-state has gone, for the party was dissolved and state administrative agencies fragmented and have not been recomposed. Harding comments on the Wikileaks U.S. diplomatic cables from Moscow, "Privately, it seems, U.S. diplomats in Moscow take the same bleak view of the Kremlin that I do: that it isn't so much a state as a private-sector moneymaking business, in which stealing is a pathological habit." He quotes a Transparency International estimate that bribery costs Russia $300 billion a year, which is no less than 18 percent of Russia's GDP (2011: 230, 242). Putin's state has enough power to do simple things like rig elections and assassinate troublesome dissidents, but a kleptocracy is the opposite of a bureaucracy for it is not controllable from the top. Even cronies can become difficult to control if they have their own fiefdoms. A U.S. diplomat noted in 2006 that "at the height of Putin's control in a booming economy – it was rumored within the presidential administration that as many as 60% of his orders were not being followed" (*New York Times*, December 2, 2010). In 2011 many Russians turned against Putin's state for precisely this combination: the state cannot curb corruption but it can rig elections and shoot dissidents.

Nonetheless, Russia is much more democratic than was the Soviet Union, and military autonomy has been cut down since Soviet times. In negotiations with the United States over the nuclear arms limitation treaty of 2010 the Soviet military pressured the Kremlin to reject arms reductions unless the United States agreed to reciprocal limits on its missile shield in Eastern Europe. But the military was overruled for political reasons. That had not happened in Soviet times, as Gorbachev ruefully remarked. Perhaps Putin's Russia may be turned toward a more democratic and egalitarian distribution of power benefiting Russian citizens in general. But that has not yet happened.

The Fall of the Soviet empire was good news for Eastern and Central Europe and the Baltic states. It was good for nuclear disarmament, world peace, and globalization. This amounts to considerable good. The few progressives who still saw the Soviets as a beacon of socialism suffered a grave blow, though for most leftists the Fall was a relief for they thought this might end the tarnishing of their own cause with Soviet atrocities. The Fall soon led to improvement in most of the East European Soviet bloc countries. But so far Russia and most of the former republics of the Soviet Union have attained only the despotic, unequal, capitalist alternative to state socialism that might have been reached in the first third of the century in the absence of World War I. In the meantime millions of people died in both socialist and neoliberal experiments.

Revolutions are rarely a good idea, since they introduce immense dislocations into functioning power structures, and their outcomes are usually perverted versions of their original utopian goals. Russia was unfortunate enough in the twentieth century to have two of them. Russia can certainly stand as the exemplary case of both the limited role of reason in human affairs and the failure of humans to solve adequately the crises they bring on themselves. What Russian in 1914 would have wished for such a century!

8   The Maoist alternative reformed

Consolidation and crises: Maoism, 1950–1976

Chinese communism had a very different trajectory. It had shared Soviet utopian aspirations amid a similarly inhospitable environment and stabilized under
a highly repressive regime. Yet after one disastrous false start, Chinese communists found an economic solution, which has so far avoided the dislocations
of further revolution, they have generated enduring economic growth and they
have restored China's historic status as Asia's giant. Though this has not yet led
toward either democracy or equality, it has been much the better outcome for
the mass of the people. How did this remarkable trajectory happen?

There were major differences from the Soviet Union. Time was one, for
China became communist later, in a less threatening geopolitical environment, and it could learn from Soviet mistakes. China was far more ethnically
homogeneous, which provided more social cohesion and enabled less centralized government. Its greater provincial and county level political autonomy
proved an advantage. Yet at the time of its revolution China was much more
backward than Russia. Its revolution had been not urban-industrial but agrarian, based on core support among poor and middling peasants. Most leaders,
unlike the Bolsheviks, were of peasant origin. The ascent to power differed
too, following civil war, not preceding it. The Red armies took much of the
credit inside China for victory in the War against Japan, and they defeated
the Nationalist armies in the civil war that followed. By 1950 communist rule
and the personal leadership of Mao Tse-tung were unchallenged. Support was
widespread, especially in the countryside, where 85 percent of the population
lived. The communists had restored peace, national unity, and freedom from
foreign domination – and the peasants had the land.

The communist party-state embarked on a radical class-leveling project. Its
twin political principles remained unchallenged: the "leading role of the party"
(i.e., its monopoly of power) and a mythical "democratic centralism." They
made this a despotic party-state. Yet the country had been conquered piecemeal by various Red armies expanding out from their base areas, setting up
their own regional governments, as we saw in Volume 3, chapter 14. At the
center Mao's leadership was unquestioned, for his faction had seemingly made
all the right decisions in the long haul to power. But he now had to coordinate the party's regional mountaintop factions and in the new constitutional
arrangements regional parties and administrations had about the same strength

as the central party and ministries (Huang, 2000). Much depended on Mao to make it work.

The communists continued the forcible land redistribution they had already practiced in their base areas. Though the policy was ordered from above, it was embraced enthusiastically and violently by poorer peasants once they realized that the KMT and the local ruling classes were not returning. The land of rich peasants and landlords was seized and given to the poor and middle peasants to hold as private household property. By mid-1952 90 percent of rural China was a rather homogeneous mass of middle peasants freed from class exploitation, able to "develop household fortune" and maintain their customary cultures (Friedman et al., 1991). At this point in time the regime was enjoying popular support, peasant productivity was rising, and local communist elites focused on maintaining this happy state of affairs.

Not everyone was so fortunate. Between one and two million "counter-revolutionaries" – landlords, rich peasants, and supporters of the KMT and Japanese – were killed, and between four and six million were sent into penal labor and reeducation camps. The CCP was initially cautious in the cities, where it had less support. It needed cooperation from those with technical skills, including entrepreneurs. Yet within five years it had turned on any it deemed counterrevolutionaries or criminals. Perhaps a million more died and two million were dispersed to the camps. These are all very large numbers, though tiny in relation to the 580 million Chinese population at that time, and most skilled personnel remained in their former positions. From now on there was reverse class discrimination. Those from property-owning families had bad backgrounds and were disprivileged, while those from peasant and worker backgrounds were privileged.

China was geopolitically aggressive during the Korean War and persistently used all necessary force to keep Tibet compliant. Under Mao's successor, Deng Xiao Ping, it made a disastrous incursion into Vietnam in 1979 and occasionally saber rattled over Taiwan and the Soviet and Indian borders. The army was politically important in the Cultural Revolution and was used to repress it in a few areas. But despite large armed forces, Chinese communism has been mostly rather defensive. Its soldiers have been deployed more often as work brigades than warriors.

The communists confronted the same economic problem as the Bolsheviks. Above all, they wanted to industrialize their country, but to do this they would have to take resources from consumption and from agriculture. Yet (as in the Soviet Union) the peasants now controlled the land and were unlikely to welcome this. Chinese participation in the Korean War made the leadership doubly keen to industrialize since the poor equipment of the People's Liberation Army had made for terrible losses at the hands of the Americans. For a decade the CCP remained painfully dependent on Soviet military supplies.

Mao sought to maintain revolutionary momentum by class leveling and mass mobilizing "hero projects," while his charged foreign policy rhetoric whipped up Chinese nationalism (Chen, 2001). Class leveling was redistributive, though among those with "good" class backgrounds, a second criterion entered in determining privileges. The 10 percent–20 percent designated as "activists," politically reliable, did better than others. These two political and ideological principles of merit were in continuous tension throughout the period of communist rule (Andreas, 2009). But at the same time Mao did not want to emulate Stalin's forced industrialization, which he said was tantamount to fishing "by emptying the water of the pond." He found lesser ways of increasing control over the peasants. The severest was that peasants were banned from moving away from their homes. This was really a socialist version of serfdom, forcibly tying peasants to the land. Other controls were milder. From 1952 state purchasing agencies bought agricultural produce at fixed low prices, sometimes to subsidize industrial workers' consumption, sometimes to sell on to consumers at higher prices. Either way provided more investment capital for industry by keeping industrial wages low and using the surplus for investment. But though the state monopolized marketing, it initially left production to the peasants.

Mao then sought more control over peasants through agricultural collectives, which also provided them with some benefit, for it enabled them to share tools and draft animals. From 1949 groups of about five to fifteen households were joined together in mutual aid teams, which were enlarged in 1953 into elementary agricultural cooperatives of twenty to forty households. These changes did not seem to encounter much resistance. The regime also built up state-run heavy industries – coal, electricity, iron and steel, construction materials, chemicals, and engineering. Following the Soviet model, big capital-intensive plants were established, often with Soviet technical and financial assistance. In 1953 the first Soviet-style Five-Year Plan, shifted resources into heavy industry and major construction projects. Labor was controlled through state-run unions, party secretaries were placed in each factory, and workers were recruited into the party. Almost all those in the cities were incorporated into a work unit that was responsible for their welfare, and in the villages, all were members of the production brigade. Even housewives were gradually drawn into the work unit system. A basic level of welfare was obtained through what was called "the iron rice-bowl," organized by the work unit. In periodic major mobilizations of labor resembling the hero projects of the Soviet Union workers were exhorted to work harder for the good of the country. By the mid-1950s the party had destroyed such capitalism as had existed in republican China, and by 1960 it had absorbed the household economy into more collectivist forms.

Once again, as in the Soviet Union, state socialism was successfully applied to late development. GDP rose 9.2 percent per annum in the period 1952–7 and 6.8 percent when adjusted per capita to take account of rising population. This was as good as anywhere in the world at that time, though consumption

did not rise as much. Like the Soviet Union, communist China was successful at developing education, literacy, and health programs and at keeping the
level of inequality below that of most industrializing societies (Bramall, 2000:
table 2.2; Naughton, 2007: 80–2).[1] Overall, life expectancy rose rapidly from
thirty-five in 1949 to fifty in 1960 to sixty-five in 1980, and the mortality
rate halved between 1953 and 1970. These are more reliable measures than
GDP statistics, indicating substantial achievements, greater than most countries at a comparable level of economic development. The virtues of communism – relatively uncorrupt political elites committed to relatively egalitarian
development – could mobilize the advantages of planned development of the
known parameters of catch-up industrialization. It is important to note that
growth did not begin with the reforms of the post-1978 period. Communism
had its virtues. It also had its vices, for it was a rigid control structure, the party
penetrating most of social life, mobilizing intermittent but harsh persecution
campaigns against supposed class enemies. This was the familiar communist
combination of economic progress, political-ideological despotism, and military power subordinated to the party.

A major hiccup was in 1956, when taking too much labor from agriculture reduced agricultural output and generated famine and unemployment.
Mao now upped the controls. Higher cooperatives of more than one hundred
peasant families were introduced. These were unpopular since peasants were
controlled in them by party officials who kept prices low while demanding
more work output. But the increase in control had been gradual, effectively
trapping peasants within the communes without the terrible coercion to which
Stalin had resorted. On balance, therefore, the early years of communist rule
were an economic success story, unless you were one of the purged classes;
while the rigid one-party dictatorship provided order, which was valued after
decades of war and civil war. The regime's atrocities also declined after the
first wave. It was an improvement on the republican interwar period. The great
unknown is whether the Nationalists could have made similar achievements
had they won the civil war. They did so in Taiwan, though this was a much
easier proposition.

However, the geopolitical environment seemed threatening as tensions rose
with the Soviet Union as well as the United States. Mao grew impatient with
slow economic improvement. He turned to the hero projects, which perennially
lured communist regimes. The Second Five-Year Plan of 1958 included the
Great Leap Forward. Mao declared, "Three years of hard work and suffering
and a thousand years of prosperity." He whipped up tensions with the United
States over the Straits of Taiwan in order to mobilize Chinese nationalism

[1] There is much debate about the accuracy of Chinese economic statistics (see Naughton,
2007: chap. 6 for a review). The majority view is that they are inflated, though only
slightly.

behind the Leap (Chen, 2001). It was a seemingly attractive solution to China's two-sector problem, developing both the agricultural and the industrial sectors by exploiting China's one great natural advantage, cheap rural labor. China could industrialize by substituting plentiful labor for imported heavy machinery. Economies of scale would be gained by merging existing collectives into communes containing around five thousand households. The rural part of the Leap also contained some decentralization. Most enterprises controlled by ministers of the State Council were transferred to local governments, whose officials together with commune leaders were given some autonomy and resources to develop brigade industries and construction projects, able to disburse some of the profits of their enterprises. The proportion of output of industrial enterprises under central government control fell suddenly in one year, from 40 percent in 1957 to 14 percent in 1958 (Wu, 2004: 44–7). Backyard steel furnaces were the centerpiece of the Great Leap Forward. Led by local officials caught up in the enthusiasm of the Leap, in the furnaces they burned whatever wood could be found in order to smelt whatever iron, often scrap, could be found. Labor was removed from agriculture to operate such projects.

It was a disaster. The steel produced was low-quality pig iron, local stocks of wood and iron were often exhausted, and the diversion of agricultural labor meant appallingly that crops could not be harvested. The people were overworked amid food shortages, and this generated major famine in 1959 and 1960. Suffering was compounded by a quota system whereby local officials would report levels of production much higher than reality, and so top officials did not at first realize the extent of the disaster. Even when they did, Mao was reluctant to change what were mostly his own policies, and almost no one dared tell him the truth. Eventually, in January 1961 word came down to abandon the Great Leap Forward. Some provincial officials had already quietly jettisoned it (Macfarquhar, 1983; Yang, 1996).

In the meantime perhaps as many as 30 million Chinese had died of the famine, out of a total population that was then 650 million – an almost 5 percent casualty rate. The deaths were not deliberate, unlike the early killings of landlords and others. It had not been conceived of as an attack on the peasants, as Stalin's collectivization partly had been. It had resulted from appalling policy mistakes made by an unchallengeable dictator backed by enthusiastic local party radicals. It revealed a characteristic ideological vice of communist regimes: utopian ideology insisting on the total transformation of society could instead devastate it. Those provinces whose leaders had most fervently embraced the policy suffered most. The great famine ensured that overall growth was negative between 1957 and 1965, despite continuing industrialization (Bramall, 2000: table 2.2). As Naughton observes, "What good does it do to provide for your citizens basic needs for 27 years if you force on them policies of starvation in the other three years?" (2007: 82).

So the Great Leap Forward also had political consequences. It dented Mao's authority and he had to step back from public leadership. Party factionalism became more overt amid a radical/moderate split, which was sometimes cross-cut by regional conflicts. The state weakened. Shirk (1993) has analyzed the selectorate, the top five hundred or so party and state officials who participate in the selection of the top leaders. She found heavy representation among them of provincial party-state officials. Whenever there was a weak leader or a struggle over the succession, these provincial leaders were courted and concessions made to them. Now was such a time. The postrevolution phase of strong leadership had ended, and the provinces reacquired more autonomy.

But an unanticipated benefit was that the economic decentralization of the Great Leap continued. Popular pressure led to the communes being broken up and individual production team and brigade industries given more independence. A household responsibility system was for a time encouraged (Yang, 1996: 98), reflecting a view that peasants would produce more if they could benefit directly from the fruits of their labor. The state retained control of agricultural prices but peasants were allowed some price rises. Investment in rural infrastructures increased. Labor moved back from the cities to the countryside, since in the famine they could not be fed in the cities, and industrial investment was reduced to free resources for agriculture. So after a period in which ideology was supposed to triumph over reality, the CCP reversed itself, adjusting pragmatically to real peasant motivations. It had learned pragmatism decades previously, as we saw in Volume 3, chapter 14. Now it was repeated.

Between 1965 and 1978 GDP grew again, by a respectable 4.9 percent per annum (2.6 percent when adjusted per capita). The share of industry in GDP continued to rise, from 10 percent in 1952 to 35 percent in 1978, while the irrigated land area of China tripled. The later market reforms could take off from this base. The market alone could not have achieved this (says Bramall, 2000: table 2.2, 130, 300, 415; cf. Maddison, 1998). Though markets remained ideologically anathema, decentralization was further boosted in 1970 when Mao decided that geopolitical tensions might lead to another world war. If so, the best military defense for China would be in depth (as during the Japanese invasion). So the country was divided into ten cooperation regions, which were told to plan their own defense industries, under the dubious motto "Decentralization is a revolution and the more decentralization, the greater the revolution" (Wu, 2004: 53). Regional variations increased. In some provinces the peasant household reappeared as the primary productive unit; in others (especially formerly radical provinces) vestiges of the Great Leap Forward remained in the small but growing rural enterprises producing varied goods, sometimes with ownership vested in households or groups of households, sometimes in local public authorities. These had greater significance in the later reform period (Yang, 1996).

But the coherent ideological vision of socialist development had weakened amid political splits. In 1966 Mao launched the radical student Red Guards into a Cultural Revolution challenging the entrenched privileges of the party-state. Andreas (2009) says this was bringing about a convergence of the ex-peasant political elite and the highly educated intelligentsia into a single ruling class. Mao was concerned that both groups were now in effect able to transfer their privileges to their children, since political reliability and meritocracy were the two main criteria of admission to both the party and higher education. Mao wanted to reduce their power, renew the class-leveling project, and reestablish his own power. He encouraged student demands for a revolutionary renewal, but the Cultural Revolution span out of control by fall 1966 as it spread among workers and peasants. The students split into moderate and radical factions and infighting spread from the universities to the cities and countryside. Even a few army commanders supported the radicals. There was chaos, with a severe impact on economy and party.

Mao did acquire more power, though without a revolutionary renewal. Party unity was rhetorically reestablished. Chastened, all sides expressed their goals in terms of Mao's slogans. In 1968 he retook control, purging opponents and promoting loyalists, and then turning on the radicals. When a show of force did not intimidate them, he sent in the army. Perhaps a million and a half people died in the Cultural Revolution, including more than 100,000 party cadres (Chen, 2001: 846). It took many months for effective party and administrative institutions to be reestablished. The universities were closed, and about 17 million urban high school and university students, a whole generation, were exiled to the countryside for reeducation in manual tasks. It had been a bad experience for the leadership. But though everyone now genuflected to Mao, factionalism between the radical Gang of Four arraigned against moderates endured. Mao always divided and ruled, promoting and then purging leaders if they threatened to become his rivals.

Mao died in 1976. His anointed successor, Hua Guofeng, managed to have the Gang of Four arrested, though real power was accruing to Deng Xiaoping, who effectively attained power by late 1978. He reinstated others like him who had been purged by the Gang and reopened the schools in 1978 and the universities from 1980. The authority and unity of the party were restored with Deng as unchallenged leader. The ultimate effect of the Cultural Revolution had been to reestablish the unity of the party elite and educated technocrats. Their political and educational credentialing systems were restored and universities returned to meritocratic ways. The elderly leaders holding political authority since 1949 were retired, opening up positions for a younger generation of technocratic communists, Red Engineers, who were to rule China during the reform period (says Andreas, 2009). It also firmed up their commitment to order, if necessary through military power, and so the influence of the PLA in higher party circles increased.

The one-child policy was introduced in 1978–9, reinforcing the effect of the demographic transition normal to industrialization. Combined, they stabilized the population, helping growth. In 1979 Deng's reformism was stiffened by a military debacle, an invasion of Vietnam in which the PLA was worsted by the more battle-hardened Vietnamese. The armed forces clearly needed modernization, and that depended on more economic growth. Again geopolitics pressured change and Deng now headed a long period of economic reform lasting into the twenty-first century. Unlike the late Soviet reforms, economic reform was not accompanied by much political reform, though ideological reform came with the dominance of a market ideology coupled with meritocratic rather than political criteria for advancement.

Economic reform: The Deng era, 1979–1992

Economic reforms started similarly to Soviet reforms. Though there was not the spur in China of dipping growth rates, the leadership had become concerned about lagging behind capitalist Japan and the East Asian Tigers – including annoyingly Taiwan, ruled by the KMT. It is not true, as Harvey (2005: 211) says, that Chinese reform "was in part an unintended consequence of the neoliberal turn in the advanced capitalist world." China had to catch up and, as we shall see, its marketization was limited and not very capitalistic. Reform came from the top. In the immediate aftermath of the Cultural Revolution were reforms (like those of Andropov and the early Gorbachev) that attempted to recentralize and tighten discipline. When these also stuttered, a rather bland notion of Four Modernizations of agriculture, industry, technology, and defense originally proposed by the moderate Zhou En Lai in 1975 took over. This did not initially contain a vision of the release of market forces. This proved to be more the unintended consequence of piecemeal reforms. Deng and his faction referred constantly to Mao's criterion of practice as the only guide to truth, which meant if something worked, continue with it; if not then discard it – pragmatism once again.

By the mid-1980s it became evident that outside heavy industry the leadership was taking a different path to the Soviet Union, involving some market reforms while keeping intact the leading role of the party. The party had a dual role. It still acted as a developmental state, appointing enterprise directors, setting criteria for success, and having direct control of financial levers – unlike the Russian postcommunist trajectory. But second, state coercion was a safety mechanism: if economic reforms produced undesirable political effects, the party could crack down. The security police were active, the courts were subordinate to the party, and prisons and labor camps remained. Order must come first. Whereas Russia had experienced sustained Stalinist order and then reacted against it, the Chinese had been rescued from disorder by communism and then went through more disorder resulting from party disunity. So there was popular support for the party's "leading role," if that meant order. In 1979 Deng was as explicit about democracy as Gorbachev, but in the opposite direction: "Talk about democracy in the abstract will inevitably lead to the unchecked spread of ultra-democracy and anarchism, to the complete disruption of political stability, and to the total failure of our modernization program. … China will once again be plunged into chaos, division, retrogression, and darkness" (Deng Xiaoping, 1984: 171). But the economic reforms involved little coercion. Macroeconomic manipulation was the main thrust of policy. Economic was somewhat separated from political power.

There were also other differences from the Soviet Union. In terms of political power, Deng's faction had far more control over the party-state than did Gorbachev's faction and so they never felt the need to turn against it. Nor was Chinese economic planning ever as centralized as Soviet. Industry was only half-nationalized and independent town and village enterprises (TVEs) and collective farms were already expanding. In the 1970s TVEs were termed "commune and brigade enterprises" and almost all agriculture was collective. In the 1980s, TVEs were largely run by village and township officials, but collective farming had gone. Fewer than six hundred commodity prices were now allocated nationally (Strayer, 2001: 394). The leadership retained control of aggregate demand, balancing the needs of agriculture, trade, industry, and defense and pursuing a growth- and technology-promoting agenda. Benefiting from the easing of relations with the United States, which had begun with Nixon's 1972 visit, Deng opened up China to foreign direct investment (FDI). China was slowly joining the world economy, but by initially focusing it on state owned enterprises (SOEs) Deng limited its autonomy.

However, the main boosts to growth were domestic. China could build on the achievements of Maoism as well as on China's own comparative advantages. There was no foreign debt, a large pool of rural labor, fairly good infrastructures, education and health standards that provided a skilled, disciplined labor force, and a very high domestic savings rate, which made for lots of investment capital. This was responsible for more than half the increased labor productivity over the reform period (Hofman & Wu, 2009: 11). The first year in which growth reached 11 percent was 1981, before reform had really got going. Not all China's economic resurgence can be attributed to the market reforms. And all leaders from Mao onward, regardless of their varying attachments to plan versus market, made sure that these earlier preconditions for growth were maintained. Living standards rose, though not by as much, since more resources were poured into industrial investment than consumption, and the service sector remained comparatively undeveloped. Rapprochement with the United States meant that the military was not a drain on resources, unlike in the USSR. Thus the share of investment in GDP rose as planning lessened, thus accelerating overall growth and productivity growth. Between 1978 and 1988 GDP rose at about 8.4 percent per annum, while GDP per capita rose almost 7 percent, rates matched over a ten-year period in history only by three other countries, Japan, South Korea, and Taiwan, the only countries that could also match China's investment rate (Bramall, 2000: table 2.3; Naughton, 2007: 142–8). Poverty rates were slashed in the 1980s. Only the Chinese then managed to continue such a rate of growth over a much longer period. Over the first thirty years of the reform period the average annual growth was more than 9.5 percent (8.1 percent per capita), absolutely unparalleled in the world. The inevitable periodic slowdowns (in 1981, 1989, and 1990) were followed by more accelerated growth (Hoffman & Wu, 2009: 10–12).

The initial phase of the economic reform period reflected the virtues of a relatively pragmatic and technocratic state socialism, which had abandoned collectivization, hero projects, and military force in its economy. This was possible because Deng's leadership was firmly established, the radicals were eliminated, and the bureaucracy was rendered subservient. The reforms were pragmatically controlled from above. Pressure for a certain reform might come from below, but typically the leadership would agree to its being tried out in a particular locality. If it worked, it was applied elsewhere too. But the leadership decided whether it had worked. No power group, such as landowners, industrialists, or local party oligarchies, could thwart policy. Nor could officials yet mount sizable rent-seeking coalitions from the state. However, Deng had made a deal with provincial leaders to secure his leadership by increasing their representation in the party's Central Committee. In 1987 they constituted 43 percent of the committee, the largest single bloc. This made any reforms likely to maintain decentralization (Shirk, 1993: 149–52).

Policies through most of the 1980s varied between the urban and rural sectors. In the cities the state sector remained dominant, with market forces restricted to small providers of services. Here the traditional socialist goal was to rationalize production and prices within the plan. As usual this proved unattainable. The planners repeatedly tried but failed to specify optimal prices, which could work on the ground, given that the Stalinist option of force had been abandoned. Thus in practice state-owned enterprises (SOEs) began to exercise more autonomy in order to achieve a healthy balance sheet. The planners allowed some relaxation of price controls. Once an enterprise met its quota set by the planners, it could sell additional produce and buy in further resources at market prices. This gave an incentive for enterprise managers and workers to seek profits, and this revealed a growing divide between profitable and unprofitable SOEs, the former living substantially off the market, the latter state-subsidized. The latter still dominated, but the planners did not prefer them, for they were costly. During the 1980s power to appropriate profits devolved from ministries to the local SOE managers. The state now taxed the enterprises rather than directly appropriating revenue from them. SOE managers still had to go to state banks for funds, but this was not a major budgetary constraint since banks operated under old assumptions that they should bail out weak enterprises rather than refuse them loans (Lardy, 2002). The government was still indirectly protecting the big SOEs, at an economic cost, for most were inefficient and they incurred costly welfare programs for workers. But the regime seems to have feared more the potential cost of more radical reform might have caused mass worker discontent These were big, concentrated workforces quite capable of collective action.

Gorbachev had tried to rescue the Soviet economy by radically reforming the state-owned enterprises dominating the economy. When that seemed not to work, they were privatized. But it proved impossible to introduce such radical changes while also expecting this sector to provide the overall health of the economy. In contrast, there was no serious attempt in China to privatize the big SOEs until after 1992, well after reforms in nonstate sectors in the countryside had made them profitable enough to support more of the overall economy. The most fundamental Chinese reforms were "growing out of the plan" (as Naughton, 1995: 129–30 & 2007: 92, put it), leaving alone the planned state sector in the cities but expanding autonomy and markets in nonstate agriculture and local-government-run rural and small-town enterprises. There was no attempt at a big bang. The reforms were gradual but cumulative. Deng expressed it as "crossing the river by groping for stones."

So for almost two decades two different modes of production cohabited: state socialism in the urban sector and household-centered and small business enterprises in the rural sector, which were nonetheless state-subsidized and closely entwined with local government officials (Wu, 2004: 64, 434–5; Pei, 2006: 22–6; Naughton, 2007: 91–8; Andreas, 2008: 127–9). The Maoist system of household registration, plus food rationing and tight police control on mobility reinforced the creation of two different worlds. The cities contained permanent employment, government supplied housing, pensions, education, and the lion's share of investment. The rural economy had poorer living standards, less welfare, but could grow, left more to its own devices.

The peasants became freer. Work team size reduced and between 1980 and 1984, after experiments in some provinces, peasant households were given complete autonomy over production. China was back to a household peasant economy, this time without landlords. The state retained formal ownership of the land (it still does) and controls over pricing. By 1983 household had replaced team contracts for almost all peasants, and they could buy their own means of production. Agriculture boomed for a time in consequence. In the Soviet transition agriculture played a much lesser role (absorbing 14 percent of the labor force, compared with 71 percent in China), and peasants seemed conservative, content to remain in collective farms, rejecting Gorbachev's inducements to privatize (Strayer, 2001: 397–8). In China the Peoples' Communes lost their administrative powers to township governments, whose officials could now devise their own policies to increase local prosperity and their own tax revenues. The concessions made to peasants and local officials during and after the Great Leap Forward and the Cultural Revolution had increased their autonomy while also raising the state's fixed agricultural prices. A succession of good harvests then furthered a flowering of rural light industries, the TVEs, still collectively owned and run by village and township officials until the late 1980s. Huang (2008) claims that the great growth of the 1980s was due to the dominance of private enterprise in rural areas, but that is because he conflates together enterprises and the still very large numbers of the traditional self-employed – artisans, peddlers, and others. In fact growth in the 1980s was mainly from smallish manufacturing collective enterprises, helped by government policies of easy credit and the right to negotiate their tax rates with ministries. In 1985 they were given the power to buy and sell off-plan products at prices they chose. They could even enter into joint venture agreements with foreign firms. A dynamic market economy was growing out of the plan (Huang, 2008: chap. 2; Andreas, 2010: 68; Wu, 2004: 64–5; Gittings, 2005: 123–5; Pei, 1994: 43–4, 74–6: Naughton, 2007: chaps. 10 & 11).

Contracts and property rights in rural enterprises were guaranteed less by law than by power structures in which officials and local family lineages had reached an accommodation. In coastal Fujian Province entrepreneurs employing migrant laborers developed tiny textile businesses in their living rooms. A few grew into large family lineage businesses – a distinctive version of classic bottom-up capitalism. But in neighboring Jiangsu Province some large manufacturing plants employing local village labor were mostly run by local officials. Chen (2003) says that village party secretaries had become profit-driven capitalist bosses, influencing China's economic development, a version of post-Soviet rent-seeking bureaucrat-entrepreneurs. Private cooperatives flourished, given preferential government credit. Some used remittances from overseas Chinese. The military set up its own enterprises, which grew into a military-industrial empire. In the mid-1980s even the terrible conditions in prison camps improved as prison directors realized that prisons could also become manufacturing enterprises so their workers must be healthy and well fed (Lau, 2001).

Variety was furthered by the regime's decision to subsidize the coastal provinces, which could most easily import raw materials, semifinished products, capital, and technology and export finished goods. Four special economic zones were set up in 1980, and fourteen port cities were opened up to foreign trade and investment in 1985. The interior would specialize in import-substitution industrialization, capitalizing on China's net trade surplus. From the special enterprise zones models of private ownership based initially on investments made by overseas Chinese diffused widely across the country. In these zones Chinese segmentalism was ending. Yet property rights remained ill defined and lightly protected since the private was so entwined with the public (Oi & Walder, 1999: Wu, 2004: 66–9; Wedeman, 2003: 35–6).

Local officials were involved in all these projects. They could use industry profits to increase their revenues at a time when central planners were reducing their revenue flows. "Rural enterprise – that's our second treasury!" said one. In return officials could assist local enterprises by steering them state bank loans at preferential interest rates on insufficient credit, renaming an enterprise so that it qualified for start-up funds, reporting that an enterprise was managed by a school (which gave them a tax break), or inflating the size of a workforce to maximize claimed outgoings. Tax evasion was the norm, and corruption increased as relations tightened between local officials and enterprises. After experiencing revenue shortfall, the central state tightened up the tax system, but local officials became ingenious in developing their own local taxes.

TVEs could take advantage of abundant rural labor. Where the state had set high prices for products, they could undersell the SOEs selling at the fixed prices. As they expanded, the competitive environment increased and prices fell. This put more pressure on inefficient SOEs, while central officials, seeking greater efficiency, began to prefer market processes. Even conservatives like Premier Li Peng appreciated the contribution rural enterprises made to stability, while conservatives also wanted to prevent provincial officials from siding with their reforming rivals. Markets were often the unintended consequences of decentralization (Shirk, 1993: 154, 177, 195). The reforms were working, generating growth and public satisfaction, while keeping party elites mollified. Even the SOEs benefited in a more round-about way. They could subcontract work to TVEs and since there were no welfare benefits in the TVE sector, and under the one-child policy retirees could not get much support from children in old age, workers and peasants saved in state banks, which then invested the proceeds in the SOEs.

In the mid-1980s regional officials even introduced export embargoes to prevent local produce from leaving their region and restricted imports to protect local producers. Commodity wars threatened the integration of national markets and contributed along with a credit squeeze aimed at curbing inflation to a period of lesser growth between 1988 and 1991 of 5.5 percent in GDP and 4 percent in GDP per capita (Braman, 2000: table 2.3). Yet rural industry remained buoyant, helping offset faltering agricultural growth, while the regions were sufficiently large, and start-up incentives sufficiently strong, that competitive pressures were strong. Some regional governments then stopped protecting uncompetitive industries and made interregional trade agreements with each other (Naughton, 1995: 153–8, 186; Shirk, 1993).

The capitalist party-state: 1992 onward

Jiang Zemin became president in 1989. The support of the urban population for the students demonstrating in Tiananmen Square in that year alarmed the leadership, which responded with repression. Yet this conservative political reaction did not reverse the economic reforms. In 1992 Deng made his southern tour, giving speeches praising the reforms, declaring, "To get rich is glorious" and "Let a few people get rich first." The distinctive role of little homily-slogans always remained a feature of Chinese communist ideology. The 14th Party Congress declared for the first time that the goal of reform was a socialist market economy. Whereas earlier leaders had feared the growth of big private business and so had subsidized both SOEs and TVEs, Deng was impressed in his tour by the efficiency of export-oriented foreign-invested firms in the special economic zones. He concluded that large-scale private business operating on capitalist principles was necessary to compete with foreign businesses. From 1992 the government opened up more channels to FDI and China became more dependent upon the international economy, with foreign trade constituting no less than 60 percent of GDP. The privatization of SOEs and TVEs began in the same year, private enterprises became much bigger and more independent of government, the government stopped giving easy credit and other benefits to small collective enterprises, and the downsizing of the industrial ministries began. The proportion of the urban workforce in the public sector fell dramatically (Pei, 1994: 43–4, 81; Naughton, 1995: 273–4; Wu, 2004: 82–3; Yang, 2004: 25–6, 37; Andreas, 2008: 130; 2010: 69–74).

These were dramatic changes. From this point on it is difficult to find a term that sums up the Chinese economy. "Socialism with Chinese characteristics" is the regime's own designation but this is vague and exaggerates the socialism. Some Westerners see it as a variant form of a capitalist mode of production (e.g., Andreas, 2008). China is now bound into the single global economy, the last autarchic holdout against universal globalization collapsing. Yet domestically China remains quite different from Western capitalism. It remains under heavy state tutelage, and since there is not private property as understood in the West, it is not quite capitalism, not even politicized capitalism, since the state still dominates private corporations. Fan et al. (2011: 1) rather nicely call it "a successful stir-fry of markets, socialism, and traditional China that is fully none of the three, ... all tossed together over very high heat."

Oi and Walder (1999) introduce the notion of a bundle of property rights, separating out rights to control, rights to derive income from property, and rights to transfer property. They perceive a gradual and uneven pattern of change in China involving a transition from traditional state and collective firms to reformed firms, to contracted and leased firms, and to fully private firms, though complicated by regional variations, and variations between corporatist property relations with much state involvement in the interior and private entrepreneurship more important in coastal areas. Diversity and competition among these different forms help to explain how economic expansion has been possible despite highly imperfect property-rights. The Chinese seem to have demonstrated, contrary to the conventional wisdom of economists, that absolute, secure property rights are not a precondition of economic success – for they have been more successful than capitalist economies. As Fukuyama (2011: 248–50) observes, Western economists exaggerate the importance of absolute property rights: just "good enough" rights will work, he says. In China the party can abrogate any right to property, but out of desire for economic growth it rarely does so. Economic actors seem to regard this as good enough to risk sinking their resources into enterprises. What also mattered in the absence of fully guaranteed property rights was that ownership forms aligned together the interests of local government with local enterprises.

The 1990s saw much privatization, though it also turned many state-owned enterprises into shareholder-owned companies yet with the government holding a controlling or majority stake. Many shares were sold to foreign investors eager to grab a piece of China's economic growth, but it seems that the biggest companies remain in government hands though apparently the internal managerial hierarchy and not the ministries makes the management decisions.

But the CCP's Organization Department, not the company's board of directors, controls personnel decisions. It is secretive, has no public phone number, and posts no sign on the huge building it occupies near Tiananmen Square. The department handles high-level personnel decisions, secretly. If such a body existed in the United States, says McGregor (2010: 72), it

would oversee the appointment of the entire US cabinet, state governors and their deputies, the mayors of major cities, the heads of all federal regulatory agencies, the chief executives of GE, Exxon-Mobil, Wal-Mart and about fifty of the remaining largest US companies, the justices of the Supreme Court, the editors of the *New York Times*, the *Wall Street Journal* and the *Washington Post*, the bosses of the TV networks and cable stations, the presidents of Yale and Harvard and other big universities, and the heads of think-tanks like the Brookings Institution and the Heritage Foundation.

That is true of those that were still state-run, for many more have been privatized. But the party was in its own way highly meritocratic. The main criteria for promotion were a proven ability to foster growth, to create employment, to attract FDI, to control social unrest, and to achieve both control targets. As Hoffman and Wu (2009: 20) note, four of these five were closely aligned with growth. To some this recalls the examination-based civil service Confucian meritocracy of China's imperial past – including the stress placed on the maintenance of order. But now incentives were also maintained. Local officials who promoted growth were allowed to keep much of their surplus for reinvestment, while success at the local level was rewarded with promotion into the central government hierarchy.

In 2004 property rights were supposedly constitutionally guaranteed, and they were strengthened in 2007, but as is also the case with labor rights, implementation lagged. State and economy remain entwined and the central state sets the macroeconomic parameters, partly through the stability of the state sector, partly through its robust saving and investment. Party leaders are members of "leading small groups," which bring together ministers, experts, company managers, and officials in key policy areas. The economics body, the Communist Party Leading Group on Economics and Finance, is headed by Premier Wen Jiabao himself. The leading groups then give the relevant ministry its orders. There is special concern to keep control over the financial sector. The leading group on economics and finance tells the People's Bank of China to adjust interest rates. These leading groups are powerful but as in other party bodies, their membership is secret (McGregor, 2010; Naughton, 1995: 13). At the top there is much more state regulation than in any capitalist country, and the principal regulator remains the party, not ministerial bureaucracies, again unlike relatively statist capitalist countries like Japan or South Korea. The central state retains ownership of land while local governments are active in dispossessing peasants for purposes of development. The Chinese stock market is not like others. It is a funny money casino (say Walter & Howie, 2003). Of its shares 70 percent are owned by the state and a controlling interest in every listed Chinese enterprise is reserved for the state. Chinese bonds are mainly held by Chinese banks, which are mostly owned by the Chinese state. Foreigners put up much of the money, but the state controls. The purpose of the stock market is not to make profit either for individuals or the state but to direct savings to their highest use values. And though most formal investment by banks is in SOEs, an informal financial sector has arisen to provide credit to the other hybrid enterprises. The private savings rate is high in China, as is the case in most of East Asia. But the Chinese have more incentive to save since health insurance and pensions remain stunted. Their savings finance growth (Fan et al., 2011: 6–8, 13) This does not seem like capitalism, though future movement toward capitalism remains possible.

Lower down and at the local level, party cadres and entrepreneurs or their family members merge into a unique Red capitalist class of cadre-tycoons. Ever since the failures of the Great Leap Forward and the Cultural Revolution local officials had distrusted the central state and managed to wrest some autonomy for themselves. Now they could profit from economic decentralization. Officials sit on enterprise boards, charge matchmaker fees to arrange joint ventures, and feed taxes to themselves and their superiors. This is a more statist version of the political capitalism that is widespread in the world, and its two components, officials and entrepreneurs, have generally had quite harmonious relations. Dickson found that officials and entrepreneurs had similar conservative views. The entrepreneurs were embedded in the state even before they were formally admitted into the party. Since the state had created institutions within which entrepreneurs could flourish, they did not favor democracy (Dickson, 2003: 84–5; Tucker, 2010). In 1993 Jiang Zemin changed the constitution to allow capitalists into the party, where they are now over-represented. Gone is affirmative action for workers and peasants. Including entrepreneurs in the party was intended to discipline them but also to use their control over their workers to increase state power. In Fujian Province the local party recruited entrepreneurial lineage heads in order to preserve united local control. Capitalists became merged into the local party-state, exploiting the villagers in part-capitalist, part-statist forms (Chen, 2003). This is not state capitalism in the Trotsky/Djilas sense, indicating a unified state elite, a nomenklatura, controlling all the sources of social power, exploiting all beneath them. Nor is it the politicized capitalism now beginning to dominate much of the world. Access to the state does confer economic resources, but the result is not fully private corporations. The balance of power remains more tilted toward the state than is found in other versions of political capitalism, so I prefer the term "capitalist party-state," retaining a sense of duality between economic and political power and between central state direction and local party autonomy – with the party-state ultimately decisive.

There are entwined economic and political markets. Neither is self-reproducing; each needs the assets of the other. Sato (2003) says that rural families with the most political capital were the most entrepreneurial. He also found regional variations. In Wujiang Province the party and state cadres took over the economy, whereas in Wenzhou private entrepreneurs took over the local state. The economic market exchanges goods and factors, while the political market creates, trades, and diverts state assets to private interests, in corrupt rent seeking. Private owners are often the kin of officials. In the Maoist period local officials could act in an arbitrary way, but the diversion of public funds to private gain was not easy to conceal since it ran against the ideology of most officials. Rampant corruption followed from the introduction of market processes into the local state (Yang, 2004: 12–13; Wu, 2004: 74; Wedeman, 2003: 27, 242; Lin, 2001: 3–6, 18, 98, 144–5). Yang analyzed thirteen hundred corruption cases to conclude that corruption grew in frequency and scale and penetrated further up the hierarchy after 1992 – after the main erosions of the command economy. Huang (2008) is wrong to see corruption as being purely bureaucratic, located within the state. It characterizes economic enterprises as well, and their partial liberation has increased corruption. Opening up to international trade, investment and cultural exchanges also endowed trade, customs, and educational officials with a gatekeeper role from which they could extract rent. The more diverse the markets and their regulation, the more the opportunities for rent (Zweig, 2002: 44, 162).They were often seized gratefully in this extreme form of political capitalism.

During the reform period Chinese officials had more autonomy within the official administrative system than their Soviet/Russian counterparts (Solnick, 1996). They could profit from playing a double role as a shareholder in the state and a tax gatherer for the state. Some officials seized state assets in a privatization bid, not as often as did the Soviet/Russian officials at the moment when they sensed that the state was weakening, but more continuously so. Through all these practices of political capitalism, the Chinese hierarchy remains nonetheless intact, providing a surprisingly orderly framework for development.

As provincial inequalities grew, and as local officials increased their rent seeking and became quasi-capitalists, the central government sought to reregulate. Jiang and Premier Zhu Rongji were spurred on by crises like the Tiananmen Square insurgency of 1989, the collapse of the Soviet Union, and the Asian financial crises of the 1997–8, which toppled other governments across Asia. The leadership fired thousands of corrupt officials, executing the most egregious. It increased its authority over tax collection, bank lending, investment, the stock and bond markets, environmental standards, the customs, and various other policy realms. It sought a leaner but more disciplined bureaucracy, more transparent, with more horizontal accountability of officials, though it is unclear how successful this was. There seem to be cycles, in which a phase of larger, more autonomous markets and enterprises is then countered by a burst of reregulation by the state, which nonetheless continues to reform, generating another phase of corruption – and so on (Whiting, 2001; Bramall, 2000: 459; Yang, 2004: 20–1; Oi & Walder, 1999).

This is not just two steps forward, one step back. The efficiency of this capitalist party-state derived from a dialectic between the entrepreneurial dynamism of local officials and businesspersons and the ability of party leaders to restrain their rent seeking, to maintain some shreds of its former incorruptibility, of its former ideology of egalitarian development, and of its own despotism. Whereas the Soviet state was paralyzed at the time of transition, the Chinese state remained intact, manipulating its political machinery and continuously revamping the economic levers it still possessed (Yang, 2004: 297–8). This is not lost on the Chinese people. While often expressing contempt for the party, many see it as needed to prevent the chaos and rampant corruption they see in the Russian transition to capitalism and democracy (Gittings, 2005: 12–13).

The capitalist party-state has continued to deliver the goods. Between 1991 and 1996 GDP growth was a remarkable 12 percent and per capita it was 11 percent. This despite a period of deflation! Growth of 8 percent–10 percent per annum was maintained until the world financial crisis of late 2008, in a country of more than a billion people. China also recovered quicker than any other country back to that level of growth in 2009–10. No other country has ever maintained such growth over such a long period. East Asian competitors maintained it for ten to twelve years, and Japan followed its high-growth period with stagnation. Chinese growth continues to owe most to a high level of investment, in the new millennium outstripping that of any other country. Since growth is concentrated in industry, China has become the world's factory. India, currently with the second-highest level of growth, has much less industry, more services and agriculture. It remains about fifteen years behind China. But note that India also moved from being a relatively planned economy with high educational levels to a more market economy – like China it grew out of the plan. China and India are also moving up the international technology ladder, while China is now among the leaders in green technology

(Naughton, 2007: 143, 153–6; Maddison, 2007: 169). Infant and child mortality rates virtually halved between 1990 and 2006, and average life expectancy rose to seventy-three, only five years lower than in the United States.

During this time China also emerged as a major player in the world economy. It applied for membership of GATT in 1986, when its tariffs averaged 43 percent. Negotiations with GATT and the WTO lasted until the new millennium, with China steadily reducing its tariffs to 15 percent in 2001 and less than 10 percent by 2005. With the establishment of the China-ASEAN countries free trade area in 2010, all tariffs were abolished. There was full current account convertibility by 1996. Helped by overvaluation of the Renminbi in the new millennium China emerged as the world's largest exporter and the second largest recipient of foreign direct investment, behind the United States. It takes in very little short-term hot money and so avoids the volatility of finance plaguing the neoliberal era of capitalism. By 2000 almost a third of Chinese manufacturing was in factories affiliated with foreign companies (Lardy, 2002: 4, 8, 32–3, 61; Naughton, 2007: 401–23; Andreas, 2008: 130). When the financial crisis hit the world in 2008, Chinese manufacturing exports were immediately hit. However, by immediately undertaking the world's biggest domestic stimulus program, China recovered quickly and embarked on a healthier path of political economy to increase domestic consumption and perhaps even to reduce regional inequalities. This seemed to prove the virtues of the party-state part of the capitalist party-state.

This has amounted to a Chinese miracle, a sustained rate of development unique in the world during the twentieth and twenty-first centuries, and likely to continue for a while yet. The number and proportion of people in poverty between 1981 and 2004 were also slashed, though two-thirds of this occurred during the 1980s and was probably due to TVEs and agricultural growth following decollectivization, egalitarian land reform, and increased state prices for farm produce. As Perry Anderson (2010: 95) notes, this has been the most dynamic form of either capitalism or communism. Never have modern industries and urban infrastructures grown so fast, never have people moved out of poverty so fast, but never have both inequality and corruption grown so fast, and never have workers or peasants, formerly theoretical masters of the state, been treated so ruthlessly. The balance for most Chinese seems positive. They do not much like the regime, but it satisfies both material and ideal desires. China eats and China is great.

Skeptics see the economy as containing problems, with poorly functioning financial and accountancy sectors, inefficient SOEs, a large trade surplus stimulating an urban industrial sector creating relatively few jobs, and great urban-rural inequality, which combines with low workers' wages to damp down domestic consumption. Lin and Liu (2003) show that when more investment was put into the interior provinces, it went disproportionately into nonprofitable capital-intensive heavy industry SOEs. Better, they say, if investment went into sectors in which interior provinces have comparative advantages, above all in labor-intensive industries. The Chinese entry into the WTO in 2001 on not very favorable terms was probably an attempt to correct these problems with more foreign investment and trade (Lardy, 2002). The bottom line, however, is that growth continues and that China quickly bounced back after the Great Neoliberal Recession, unlike the United States, Japan, or most of Europe.

Inequality and resistance

The major problem concerns equity rather than growth. Decentralized markets have grossly widened inequality, and the emergence of the capitalist party-state has greatly increased corruption. Poverty rates have been slashed and all provinces' incomes have risen, but the cities and the coastal provinces have been privileged over the countryside and the interior provinces, especially during Deng's time. Per capita GDP in metropolitan Shanghai and in Zhejiang, a coastal province, are, respectively, thirteen times and five times that of Guizhou, a western province (Lin & Liu, 2008: 56). Markets created Weberian-type class divisions, enabling those taking economic or political resources to the market to benefit at the expense of those who have only their labor to sell. Thus inequality between persons and households has rocketed. Estimates of Gini coefficients of inequality between individuals in 1979–81 were in the range of 0.29–0.31, among the lowest in the world. They rose to around 0.38 in 1995–8, to 0.43 in 1994, and to almost 0.50 in 2006, slightly higher than that of the United States. According to the World Bank half the increase was due to urban-rural differences, a third to interregional disparities, and the remainder to differences within the rural or urban sectors. In the Deng era this was worsened by the privileging of large private enterprises and the special enterprise zones. The latest figures are exceeded only by Russia and a few Latin American countries. The trend through the whole reform period has been increasing inequality and a form of class exploitation distinctive to this dual system. The regime now worries that this could lead to serious conflict (Lee & Selden, 2007; Chai & Roy, 2006: 191–2; Naughton, 2007: 217–25; Huang, 2008; Andreas, 2008: 134–8). But the dismantling of rural health and education programs had begun earlier, though intensified during the demise of the TVEs and the decline of the SOEs. The iron rice bowl is gone. These trends do not fit easily with the regime's claim to be giving a more genuine form of human rights to its people – not individual civil or political liberties, but social citizen rights in the form of material security, freedom from absolute poverty. Compared to other developing countries, especially the rival success story, India, Chinese communism did mean freedom from absolute poverty, but not freedom from relative poverty.

This is not just a problem for China but for the world. The relative poverty of the masses amid the enormous productivity of the economy means that there

is insufficient domestic demand for Chinese goods. They must be disproportionately exported. China exports vastly more than it imports and so earns
enormous sums of foreign currency, especially dollars, which because of insufficient demand back home it has to invest in the advanced countries. This fuels
the "global imbalances" that we will see in Chapter 11 were one of the major
causes of the Great Recession of 2008. So the world has an interest in raising
the standard of living of the Chinese masses.

Perhaps the Chinese can remedy this through class struggle. China has a
long history of worker and peasant resistance, and there has been much recent
discontent. In the 1980s students led the way, with a series of demonstrations
culminating in 1989 with the Tiananmen Square protest. Students wanted more
political liberalization, but they were galvanized into action by rising prices and
official corruption, and these grievances attracted support from urban workers
and many party officials. This seemed very dangerous to the conservatives and
their arguments persuaded the Central Committee into repression. Then workers became more important. For SOE workers, the reforms whittled away the
former welfare advantages of their "iron rice bowl" welfare system. The eighty
million migrant workers in the private coastal industries have never enjoyed
such benefits. Until 2008 this sector of the economy was buoyant, unemployment was much less of a problem, and female migrant labor was more docile.
Yet exploitation in both sectors is severe. Now protests in the export sector are
more frequent, often involving strikes, which are less common in the SOEs.
The "second generation" of migrant workers (most of whom will not return
to the village) are becoming more self-confident and more inclined to protest.
Thus labor protests have multiplied, as has the volume of labor dispute arbitration – part of the big increase in popular litigation in the courts against employers and officials that developed from the late 1990s. As Lee (2002) says, the
transition from state socialism to what she calls market socialism has produced
a radicalization of workers quite unlike in the Soviet Union.

Lee (2007a) has compared worker protest movements in the late 1990s in
two regions. In the northern rust belt city of Liaoning the collapse of the SOEs,
generated by the government's own reform program, produced substantial
unemployment, while many workers had not been paid for months or were
not paid their pensions or other benefits to which they were entitled by law.
About half the SOEs had collapsed or were terminally declining, unable to
continue paying benefits. The workers believed it was the responsibility of
local and regional governments to step in and pay them but this was not done.
So workers complained volubly and repeatedly to officials, organizing peti-
tions and noisy demonstrations in the streets and outside local and regional
government offices. There was much community support as well as some sympathy from officials. Even the police surrounding their demonstrations showed
sympathy. Though the workers welcomed outside support, they were careful to
confine their mobilization within single work units, the *danwei*, which in the

state socialist system had also been residential and social welfare units. This resulted in cellular protest movements, with translocal organization rare – an obvious weakness.

Lee adduces two main reasons for this. First, though gross exploitation was widespread, it took varying forms in different factories and among different categories of worker (according to age, skill, and prior class status). Thus most grievances varied locally. Second, the workers knew the authorities would be quick to repress broader movements. Unit-level protests were OK, but as one worker put it, "There is no need to associate with other units. The state will consider us rioting if we coordinate with others." The workers appealed to the norms and laws to which the regime formally adhered. This was not a challenge to the state, but a request that the state do what it was supposed to do, couched within the class, comradely, and citizen norms of Chinese socialism. The workers asked that the regime adhere to the norms of Mao's socialism during which they perceived they had been treated quite well and fairly. The odds against this tactic's working are quite high. They would have to continue making trouble to get concessions, but the tragedy of that route, as usual in state socialism, is that those who lead demonstrations and riots risk very harsh treatment by the state. The best outcome here would be that if more democratic rights were acquired by Chinese workers, their demands might develop into a social democratic workers movement. As yet, however, there is little sign of this.

In the booming coastal sun-belt industries, Lee emphasizes the low wages and poor treatment of the mainly migrant workers. Often working twelve hours a day, six or even seven days a week, sometimes physically abused, often not even knowing their own pay rate, this was exploitation at a level comparable to that depicted by Friedrich Engels in his classic *The Condition of the Working Class in England in 1844*. Laws that supposedly protected workers' rights were ignored often with government connivance since it wanted to attract foreign capital and making big profits depended on flouting the law. The courts backed up employers, arguing that if labor laws were observed, there would be no foreign investment. Lee notes that Chinese wages in the booming sectors are low not only because of oversupply of labor but also because not the employers but the rural communities pay the costs of reproduction of the labor force. Thus they too are being exploited indirectly. These workers protested only sporadically, generally lacking the work-unit structure of older industries. Migrant workers are more difficult to organize and there were fewer protests, generally by small groups of workers united by native-place ties. They focused on wage issues and again appealed to the regime's values and norms, especially its recent emphasis on the rule of law. In China workers and peasants appeal to the law, and the bourgeoisie – employers and officials – flout it (Lee, 2002). Here workers also tread a fine line between demonstrations appealing to the rule of law and forms of action that might seem more threatening to employers and officials, who are usually closely connected.

So most protests are ineffective. Workers can no longer rely on protection from party secretaries who used to be located within the enterprise. Party officials often share in enterprise profits, and so are unsympathetic to higher wages or benefits. Unions are underresourced and ineffective. Managerial prerogatives are almost absolute. Reforms have not brought freedom for workers. Conditions are often better for workers in European, American, and Japanese companies in China, provided these do not subcontract their production. They are worse in private Chinese, Hong Kong, overseas Chinese, and Korean enterprises. But the regime believes exploitation is necessary for China's comparative advantage of a well-educated but cheap labor force (Taylor et al., 2003; Chan, 2001; Lee, 2007b, is less sanguine about the influence of Western firms).

Successive regimes have declared that they wish to reverse rising income inequality, yet the reforms have undermined their capacity to do so. Autonomous local officials do not want to change a system that benefits them. As the state devolved activities onto private or local actors, its own resources fell. Revenue fell from being 35 percent of GDP in 1979 to only 10 percent in 1996. Decentralizing reforms also displaced basic health and education costs onto local government. Since poor villages had few resources, health care weakened across the countryside and the interior, as did pensions, especially once SOEs began to be downsized, causing wider regional disparities in mortality rates. However, the government began to regain powers in the late 1990s, and by 2005 its revenue had risen to 20 percent of GDP. More could now be possible.

But there are political problems. Jiang had advocated "GDP First and Welfare Second," supported by the party in the big cities and coastal provinces. Hu Jintao succeeded him as party general secretary in 2002 and together with his premier, Wen Jiabao, proclaimed an interest in lessening inequality and upgrading welfare. With great fanfare they toured China's poorer regions and promised better welfare provision and more jobs. Rural taxes were lowered, subsidies increased, and slight improvements made in rural education and health. The declared intent was to steer the economy away from investment and exports toward domestic consumption and public services. But the pace of reform was slow and the richer regions resisted reform. This is a policy dispute where we can perceive a Left versus Right division (Naughton, 2007).

Though the regime took steps to rein in corruption, opinions differ as to how effective they were. This is potentially a serious matter for the regime. If the party-state loses control of its own officials and economic growth is undermined by massive rent seeking, then the state becomes vulnerable to discontent from below. Lee (2007b) has seen grounds for optimism in this since worker movements have recently produced gains for the workers involved and the government has made progressive reforms in pensions, unemployment, bankruptcy proceedings, anticorruption drives, and emergency funds for disasters. The regime fears social unrest, though it remains hostile to broader-based movement. Thus she sees Chinese labor as more of a force for social policy reform than for political change, which would be more gradualism.

In contrast, Pei (1994, 2006) sees disaster lurking. At first he saw China pursuing a fairly successful evolutionary authoritarian transition toward market coordination and private ownership. Though he noted some "spill-over" effects, transferring powers from the state to civil society, possibly encouraging some democratization, these were very limited. More recently he has perceived a contradiction in the Chinese path. As the authoritarian state marketizes, officials up the state hierarchy extract more and more rent from their positions and corruption expands to such a point that the state becomes predatory and threatens market efficiency. China, he argues, is caught in a trap that will bring it down. The party is very conscious of this possibility but handles it in its characteristically secretive way. In the anticorruption struggle if a high functionary is involved in corruption, the Central Commission for Discipline Inspection, a high party organ, investigates the charges. It is not restrained by legality and suspects may be kidnapped, harshly interrogated, and held for months. The verdict will depend not only on the facts but also on secret negotiations between party cliques. If the functionary is found guilty, he or she is handed over to the courts. This trial is a formality, though the sentence is sometimes negotiable. But the source of most corruption is the party itself. Its higher levels of top party, state, and business officials communicate through their own unlisted phone network, the Red Machine. A vice minister confided that "more than half of the calls he received on his 'red machine' were requests for favours from senior Party officials, along the lines of: 'Can you give my son, daughter, niece, nephew, cousin or good friend and so on, a job?'" (McGregor, 2010).

China certainly remains despotic. Economic power has been partially separated from the state but is in itself also despotic. During the entire reform period there has been no glasnost. The masses are becoming more restive yet they fear chaos or retribution if the boat is rocked. A clause of the constitution bans subversion of state power and punishment remains certain and harsh. The media are government controlled. Since 2001 the *hukou* pass laws preventing people defined as rural from migrating to the towns have been lightened. But if they do migrate, they are still treated in the towns as second-class citizens. Labor laws have been intensified, but it is not clear they are actually implemented. Since 1988 elections for local village governments have spread to cover most of the Chinese people, but they are not really free and there are no political rights at the national or regional level. Rule in Xinjiang, parts of Inner Mongolia, and Tibet still depends on military power, though other minorities are treated well if they do not seek autonomy.

Comparing the Chinese and Russian reform paths

China has not completely abandoned communism. Some of Brown's six key features of communist regimes (presented in Chapter 6) remain, as he has noted (2009: 604–6). In economic power, the plan has been replaced by the market in matters of detail but not in overall macroeconomic control, which the party-state elite holds. Ideologically, the twin principles of communism are abandoned: the long-term achievement of an actual communist society (of which no one speaks anymore) and any sense of belonging to a world communist movement. Chinese nationalism, growth, and order provide the new legitimating principle. Its ideological power is gone, and that decline is the central cause of greatly increased corruption. But the monopoly of political power by a party remains unchanged, though it is not democratic nor especially centralized. One would not call this ensemble communism. But it is not capitalism either. I have called it a capitalist party-state. This label would broadly fit Vietnam and Laos too. Cuba has less capitalism but a softer party-state. Only North Korea seems to endure grimly as a block of Stalinist granite amid the soft putty of the formerly communist regimes.

In terms of collective economic power the contrast with the Soviet Union is extreme. In 1978 Chinese per capita income was still only 15 percent of the Soviet Union's, but by 2006 it had outstripped it and each year since continues to do so (Maddison, 2007: 170–4). Whereas the Russian economy depends on the price of oil and natural gas – the vast bulk of its exports – China's economy is based on diverse manufacturing and cheap but disciplined and skilled labor. In response to the Great Neoliberal Recession it invested more in its domestic economy in order to broaden that base. We saw in the last chapter the disaster that befell the Soviet Union's transition out of highly centralized communist economic planning. This chapter, in contrast, has revealed a Chinese success story. Against this, we can balance the greater respect for individual civil and political rights in postcommunist Russia. Though Russian democracy is imperfect, it is much less authoritarian than China. Indeed, the most commonly adduced reason for China's economic success is that it kept firm political control over the economic transition while Soviet controls collapsed because economic perestroika and political/ideological glasnost were pursued simultaneously (e.g., Pei, 1994). This also meant that the Chinese transition has been more leisurely over a thirty-year period, compared to the Soviet six years. China could grow out of the plan, while Gorbachev and then Yeltsin destroyed the plan and failed to put anything in its place. This was the key. This was how they did it.

But why did they do it this way? It is often said that China had the advantage of possessing a lower initial level of economic development, with far fewer unreformable industrial behemoths. Yet backwardness is not generally beneficial and it initially gave the Chinese far fewer highly trained technocrats – scientists, engineers, factory directors, economists, agronomists, and so forth. As Strayer (2001: 402) notes, the higher-performing economies of Eastern Europe, including Hungary, Poland, and the Czech Republic, were more successful because they were more advanced and closer to the West than Russia or China. The sudden loss of Eastern Europe and the Baltic republics dislocated Soviet/Russian trade relations. Alcoholism and its fiscal ramifications were also distinctively Russian. Nothing comparable affected the Chinese.

The Chinese did benefit from other Asian economic networks – from Japanese and Korean development and from the overseas Chinese diaspora, which had revived in the 1950s and 1960s (Arrighi, 2007). But since they also benefited from American and European networks, adaptations were made from global as well as macroregional models.

Yet political power relations probably mattered more. The Chinese party-state elite was less centralized yet more united than the Soviet party-state. Decentralizing measures in the economy had begun much earlier, in the 1960s, starting with measures encouraging rural industry in the Great Leap Forward, continuing with the return to peasant household production in 1963 after its disastrous failure, both boosted further in 1970 – all under Mao. It is from 1979 that we generally date the reform period, but its base had been laid earlier and it included both decentralization and pragmatism. After the Cultural Revolution and its echoes of civil war disunity the backlash led to political conciliation between the educated and political elites, while the post-1976 purge of the radicals restored party unity. The new collective leadership was based on a new, younger generation of Red Engineers, technocrats but also communists, committed to development through technocratic reforms and less to feathering their own nests (Andreas, 2009).

Thus China could sponsor decentralization, letting loose the market dynamism of local industries and farms, under the umbrella of rules and macro-economic plans set by a cohesive party-state elite. There was in China a more enduring and higher ideological valuation placed on order, and this restrained, though it could not eliminate, the tendencies to corruption and rent seeking inherent in political capitalism. In contrast, Soviet party-state elites had lost their ideological bearings; they were already more corrupt under communism and were more attuned to the personal opportunities provided them by the privatization of state and republican assets. The Soviet and Russian reformers who kept an ideological faith shifted it to faith in free markets, and this was encouraged by their much greater ideological links to the West, then at the high tide of neoliberalism.

The Chinese were right; the Russians and their neoliberal advisers were wrong. Economies need order and markets do not automatically provide it. As we saw in Chapter 2, a measure of statism has generally aided recent economic development, especially in catch-up – provided the state elite is genuinely committed to development and not to feathering its own nest. The problem in most developing countries is that their elites are not thus committed. The Chinese combined the two ideologies, which have so far been most conducive to low corruption development: communism and the East Asian combination (shared with Japan and the Tigers) of normative solidarity, hard work, and a frugality generating high rates of savings and investment.

Neoliberals viewing their failures in Russia argued either that markets had not been pushed far enough or that Russia was inherently not reformable, too corrupt, carrying too many industrial behemoths (Aslund, 2002: 13–15). Yet an alternative had been possible. Had the Soviet leadership delayed glasnost until after perestroika was firmly institutionalized, supervised by a state and law, then Russia too would have benefited economically, though civil and political liberties would have waited a while. Gorbachev probably could not have done this, since he became more committed to glasnost than perestroika. Since he was the party secretary no one else could do it. It was achievable in principle, but principles do not rule the world. Yet just as most Chinese welcomed the growth-order combination that their leaders provided, most Russians applaud Putin because he half-embodies this ideal.

Archie Brown (2009: 616) concludes flatly, "As an alternative way of organizing human society, Communism turned out to be a ghastly failure." McGregor (2010) is also unsympathetic but more ambivalent. He concludes that the Chinese communist system was "rotten, costly, corrupt and often dysfunctional. But the system has also proved to be flexible and protean enough to absorb everything that has been thrown at it, to the surprise and horror of many in the West. For the foreseeable future, it looks as though their wish, to bestride the world as a colossus on their own implacable terms, will come true." But though communism had more than its share of ghastliness, capitalist markets have had their problems too, while communism also had some successes. In developmental catch-up, first the Soviet Union and then China and Vietnam did as well as any other comparable developing society. In economic adaptability and creativity in reaching beyond communism – and in both long-term growth and the raising of basic living standards – the Chinese achievement is unparalleled. The Soviet Union provided a military might, which saved most of the West from fascism, while China since 1950 has used its armed forces more for domestic development than for imperial aggrandizement. China has been careful to make peace with the United States and not to claim leadership over its region. Its relations with the ASEAN countries remain quite good, though hegemonic strategies may be now emerging. Relations with Japan are bad for historical reasons; the Taiwan issue remains potentially dangerous, as do China's claims to various islands in the China Sea – and almost all mainlanders believe Taiwan is part of China. Chinese nationalism has stirred all these pots, countered by Japanese and Taiwanese nationalisms. But at present China is more pacific than the United States and in terms of economic growth is more successful. Within an overall growth of a more universal globalization, in which communist regimes no longer present a distinctive segment of human society, a sea change in global power is under way.

What of the future? Optimistic observers of China see a gradual movement toward more civil and political rights. Yang (2004) believes that the corruption and arbitrary powers of local bosses are being cut back, adherence to the constitution is increasing, the courts are becoming more independent and effective, and the local legislatures are providing genuine oversight of the executive.

This might be the way to more democracy and equality. Others disagree. If the response to corruption and regional inequality is serious protest, it is difficult to envisage the regime's lessening its controls. The regime does provide order, which is a valued and scarce resource among developing countries. It seems especially valued in China. A more realistic optimism is that the party elite, alarmed by the rising tide of protest, might make more determined efforts to reduce inequality and corruption – though this might increase despotism, not democracy. Genuine democracy might be out of reach for quite a while yet, while further decentralization without democracy would not be likely to reduce either inequality or corruption. After all, market decentralization was what caused them to intensify in the first place.

9   A theory of revolution

I have defined a revolution as a popular insurgent movement that overthrows a ruling regime and then transforms substantially at least three of the four sources of social power – ideological, economic, military, and political. A political revolution is one that only changes political power relations, as happened in 1911 in China, and as the 2011 Arab Spring attempted to do. I gave fuller explanations of the main twentieth-century revolutions – successful and unsuccessful – in Volume 3 and added a little more about post–World War II Latin American and Asian cases here in Chapter 5. Chapter 7 presented what was initially a revolution from above in the fall of the Soviet Union, and I will spend some time discussing the special case of the Iranian revolution of 1979 later in this chapter. Other chapters have discussed the development of the main reformist alternatives to revolution through the century. From all of this some broad comparative and historical generalizations, amounting to an approximate theory of revolution, are possible, though history always presents new challenges to revolutionaries and counterrevolutionaries alike. These generalizations involve all four sources of social power.

First, in the twentieth century revolutions up to the Iranian revolution of 1979 successful insurgent leaders embraced Marxist theories of class exploitation, struggle, and revolutionary transformation, though they did not always do this at the beginning of their struggle while Marxism proved a supple ideological instrument in their hands. A substantial component of ideological power was necessary for modern revolutions, for this gave a vision of the march of history, which solidified an insurgent ideological power elite and drove them on to take highly risky actions during insurgency and wholesale social transformations after they seized power. This meant that the insurgents kept sight of their ultimate transformative goals even while engaging in pragmatic, reformist actions in the present, as was notably so among the Chinese communists. It also ensured that seizing political power was not the end of the revolution. These revolutionaries did not settle down into comfortable enjoyment of power but driven on by their ideology sought to transform the other sources of power.

Second, the plausibility of notions of class exploitation to very large numbers of workers and peasants indicated that class struggle was a key cause of modern revolutions – as Marxists claim. But I found little support for the Marxian notion that distinct relations of production in the rural sector – peasant proprietorship, wage-labor, and others – were especially helpful or harmful for the

246

revolutionary cause. It was much broader conceptions of class, often focused on the state as much as upper classes, that fueled revolution. The revolutionary elite then had to add on an explanation of their own role in revolution hastily, for they were mostly not workers but bourgeois intellectuals. More importantly, since revolutions occurred in relatively backward countries, they found they had to extend Marx's theory of industrial class conflict into the realm of peasants, but they were quick to do this – since their own survival depended on it! Class struggle was the main contribution of economic power relations to revolution. It meant that parties led by ideological elites had mass backing, either persistently, as in China, or at the vital moment, as in Russia. Without this, all revolutions would have failed against even weak and faction-ridden states and armies.

Third, as Lenin himself remarked, and as many have since repeated, political weakness or division within the ruling regime was also a necessary feature of revolution. Here I bend slightly the conventional view to say that the state that is repressive, exclusive, and *either* infrastructurally weak or factionalized is most vulnerable to revolution. This is the main role of political power relations in causing revolution. As we see later, the revolutionaries had also to extend their own theory of exploitation and revolution out of the economic realm and more into the political realm than they had previously done. Note therefore that democracies are only very rarely vulnerable to revolution. They can normally process discontent through institutionalized electoral processes. It needed a series of crises and over a decade in which such institutions became very strained before the Weimar Republic fell.

Fourth, in revolutions in this period, except for most Latin American cases (most of which were not successful), defeat in major war precipitated revolutions, as in Skocpol's model of revolution. Yet war also continued to determine the form of the revolution itself. Revolution, and in response counterrevolution, became militarized, accompanied by civil war. This was true in Russia, China, Korea, Vietnam, Laos, Cuba, Nicaragua – and it is true in Nepal today. This was the principal role of military power relations.

Thus all four sources of social power provided necessary preconditions for revolution, and since they were all required, it is not really possible to claim that any one of them was primary. Indeed, it was possible for a larger component of one to substitute for a lesser component of another. Thus the Chinese Nationalist state was not particularly weak. It was much stronger than the communist soviets opposing it, but it was crucially weaker than the Japanese state whose military proceeded to shred its powers, eventually allowing the communists to seize victory. The few revolutions and attempted revolutions in Latin America did it without war, because their regimes had become highly personalized and exclusive. Similarly, as we shall see, in the Iranian case the absence of war was compensated for by the extreme personalism and weak infrastructures of the shah's regime.

These are the broadly common elements. However, not all revolutions were the same. We can perceive the development of two (which might become three) distinct historical waves of revolution. The first wave occurred in the years 1917 to 1923, spearheaded by the Bolshevik Revolution in Russia, then spreading unsuccessfully through the center and east of Europe. As I noted in Volume 3, chapter 6, the Bolshevik Revolution remains the sole case of a successful revolution in a somewhat industrialized society. The leading actor, as Marx had predicted, was the organized proletariat, the industrial working class. The Bolsheviks had begun 1917 as only marginal actors. Then they grew rapidly in influence, but partly through playing catch-up with workers whose actions were already revolutionary. The workers needed armed support from peasant soldiers, while peasant occupations of the land immobilized the regime in the countryside, and the workers eventually also needed leadership from the Bolsheviks. Yet workers remained the core of the insurgent forces through both the revolution and the ensuing civil war. Yet in the rest of the industrial world – and in the currently industrializing world – the destiny of the industrial working class was not to make revolution but to reform capitalism. Workers were the leading (though again not the sole) actors in reforming capitalism and deepening democracy, generating not revolution but what T. H. Marshall called social citizenship. So why were the Bolsheviks and the Russian working class uniquely successful in achieving revolution?

The initial answer is simple: war. World War I caused the collapse of the Russian state's infrastructural power, with consequent loss of popular legitimacy. But Russia was the only case of a country with a major industrial sector (especially important in its two capital cities) in which a major war generated a series of massive military defeats for an infantry army used as cannon fodder to make up for deficiencies in logistics and weaponry, which led to a major soldiers' revolt *during the war itself*. The soldiers were mostly former peasants though former workers were prominent in the navy. In their revolt they used their arms to aid striking workers, demonstrators demanding bread, and peasants seizing land. For all of these groups a more political and military version of the Marxist notion of exploitation made sense. Only the workers were likely to identify capitalists as the main enemy, but all dissidents identified the state as exploitative, especially when the regime was sacrificing millions of their lives in a pointless, fruitless war. The Bolsheviks were by now the only party talking about exploitation in the broadest sense. They offered a program of land, bread, and peace, which might plausibly end all the major sources of exploitation and so people listened to them. It was the failure of all monarchist or liberal alternatives that Trotsky was referring to when he declared, "A revolution takes place only when there is no other way out." Note that the soldiers did more than simply refuse to repress the revolution: they were its shock troops and they specifically bridged the gap between workers and peasants, which elsewhere in Europe helped defeat revolution.

Trotsky later gave an economic analysis of the revolution in terms of "combined and uneven development," whereby he argued that in Russia the contradictions of feudalism (principally impacting peasants) and capitalism (impacting workers) exploded at the same time. This was acute, but on its own this would have generated separate risings, which would have been separately and successfully repressed, as in Spain at the time. The Bolsheviks also relied on war for their success. In Russia two major causal sequences stand out: first, a causal sequence involving class struggle spearheaded by the industrial proletariat, Marxist ideology, and Bolshevik political organization; then a second sequence involving repeated defeats in a major war that weakened the ruling regime, armed the revolution, and allowed soldiers to paper over major gaps between workers and peasants. Combined, these two sequences yielded success.

This conclusion was reinforced in Volume 3, chapter 6, by analysis of the failed revolutionary wave in Germany, Austria, Hungary, and Italy during the period 1918–23. Again war defeat weakened existing regimes (the battered Italian forces were only victorious in a formal sense). In these countries the difference in war experience from that in Russia was that the defeated armies revolted only at the very end of the war. Soldiers' councils did immediately form alongside workers' councils, and some of both types of council demanded revolution. But the new postwar centrist regimes had a solution: they demobilized the troops and let them go home, without their weapons. The soldiers melted away, leaving only a hard core of revolutionary soldiers facing more effectively organized counterrevolutionary paramilitaries, led by army officers. This also meant that soldiers could not bridge the gap between workers and peasants, an important weakness in these countries, since most peasants remained passive in the postwar disturbances. There were also other differences between these countries and Russia. In Germany and Austria reformist workers could make gains in the postwar republics, undercutting leftist revolutionaries. In Hungary a Romanian counterrevolutionary army invaded to help put down a revolutionary regime that had captured the state in the capital, the one case where foreign counterrevolutionaries played a major role after World War I.

The Bolsheviks seized power rather easily, and there was no immediate attempt at a counterrevolution in the capitals. However, conservatives regrouped and formed White paramilitaries in various provinces, forcing the Bolsheviks to raise a Red Army to repel them. The ensuing civil war lasted several years and was very destructive – especially of the Bolsheviks' resources. Yet once the Western allies stopped substantially aiding the Whites, their atrocities against civilians and their internal factionalism resulted in a Red victory. From there on there was no serious internal counterrevolution movement, except in Stalin's mind. The Bolshevik leaders used supposed counterrevolutionary threats to legitimize their growing despotic powers, but the main cause of these was their own utopian transformational goals imposed on a reluctant population. True, there was a counterrevolutionary threat to the Soviet Union posed by foreign powers, especially after Hitler seized power in Germany. Building up Soviet defense forces meant prioritizing rapid industrialization, which in turn meant diverting agricultural surplus into industrial investment – which required coercing an unwilling peasantry. Thus the Russian Revolution increased the despotic power of the state beyond the rather inefficient level attained by tsarism. This was a combination of the power and transformational goals of the Bolshevik and especially of the Stalinist state encountering both geopolitical pressure and an unwilling peasant population.

Skocpol (1979) noted that revolutions increased government bureaucracies. This had not been correct of the French Revolution (as I noted in Volume 2). It was true of the Russian Revolution though in a way distinctive to the new invention of a party-state. The state's infrastructural power depended not only on increased government administrative agencies but also on a party, wielding its own security services, surveilling both state officials and the general population. The party was not a bureaucracy in Weber's rather dispassionate sense of the most rational means of attaining known goals, but an ideologically suffused instrument devoted to ultimate values. Moreover, its tendency to launch mass mobilization hero projects was not at all bureaucratic. But the limits of state power were exposed by the psychological withdrawal of the citizens (and finally of the party itself) from the regime. Nonetheless, this revolution had increased both the despotic and infrastructural powers of the state – overall, probably not a good thing.

The second revolutionary wave was inspired by the Chinese communists. Their revolution was also led by Marxists but like almost all subsequent revolutions it was perpetrated not in the name of workers but of peasants. The Chinese Communist Party (the CCP) led by Mao transformed Marxism into a theory of rural exploitation and rural class struggle: poor and middle peasants against rich peasants and landlords, exploited by labor, rent, taxes, and other dues. This version of exploitation made sense to the mass of peasants, and it became crucial to communist success since most peasants grew to recognize that they would get more material help from the communists than from the Nationalists or the Japanese. Like the Bolshevik one, this was a class revolution, proclaimed in Marxist terms, led by a cohesive communist party. Yet since peasants feared the power of the propertied classes and the state (and then the Japanese), they had rarely attempted more than local, rather ritualized demonstrations-insurrections with limited goals, and they did not usually welcome the entry of the communists into their villages, since they believed that it would bring down regime repression on their heads later.

So the second essential requirement for revolution was that the communists could militarily protect the peasants of the soviet base areas they entered and ruled. The CCP *was* an army from the period of the first soviet in Kiangsi in 1931 to its final victory in 1949, and its policy always included building up self-defense militias for the base areas so that initially reformist land, rent, and tax redistribution could be introduced inside them. The further military precondition was the Japanese invasion of 1931, which, merging into the Pacific War, lasted until 1945. Chiang Kai-shek's Nationalist forces were distracted by this war from the probable final elimination of the communists, and his regime was weakened by its inability to defeat the Japanese. The communists could thus protect and gradually extend their base areas, ready to finally confront the Nationalists after the Japanese surrender.

Again, we find similar overall causes: class struggle, given a Maoist rural ideological twist; second, a succession of war defeats on China's own territory, enabling a cohesive and ideological communist party elite to build up defensive military strength necessary to build local soviets and win peasant converts and then to achieve final military victory.

Almost all subsequent revolutions in the second wave that now ensued after 1949 were in the name of the peasants, and most were influenced by the Chinese communists, though also aided materially by the Soviet Union. Yet there was a difference from China and Russia. Outside Latin America revolutions were also anticolonial, and this blended together peasant class struggle and nationalist anticolonialism. Especially in Asia peasants perceived two linked enemies: the colonial state and its principal collaborators, who had been local landowners and merchants. All these were greatly weakened by World War II, first, when the Japanese overthrew British, French, and Dutch colonies in Asia, and, second, when the United States, the British Empire, and China defeated the empire of Japan. In Africa, the Caribbean, and elsewhere, the war had weakened even the British imperial victors in the eyes of the locals. The French, Belgians, and Dutch who were defeated but then restored were weakened even more. Nationalist movements now achieved independence across the world's colonies, mostly through purely political revolutions, but occasionally through social revolution where class struggle entwined with anticolonial nationalism. In Asia revolutionary insurgent movements in Korea, Vietnam, Laos, and Cambodia all combined Marxist and nationalist ideologies. So did the more social insurrections in Africa, in Algeria and Angola. Yet in Angola as in the many anticolonial political revolutions in Africa, a nation was only a gleam in the eye of the revolutionary elites. In reality there was almost no sense of national identity, unlike in most of the East and Southeast Asian countries with long political histories. In Africa the appeal was more to race – throw out the whites – in Muslim Africa mixed with throw out the Christians. Though I rejected Chalmers Johnson's explanation of the Chinese revolution in terms of peasant nationalism, his theory was much closer to the truth in all these cases since they thrived on antiimperial nationalism.

So this second revolutionary wave had three main causes: rural class struggle, nationalist/racial anticolonialism, and defeat of the ruling regimes in major war. Note that the British, who were victorious in the world war, suffered only political revolutions and successfully repressed armed insurrections in Malaya and Kenya. Macroeconomic conditions and the precise relations of production mattered somewhat, but not usually much. The peasants embracing communism were sometimes tenant farmers, sometimes small proprietors, sometimes landless laborers. The movements had different social bases, as Goodwin (2001: 82–4) shows against the more economistic arguments of Paige and Wolf. What mattered most was an indigenous, rural, and military struggle between peasants and landlords complicit in alien colonial rule and weakened by its defeat.

Thus the successful revolutions did not usually have to contend with powerful internal counterrevolutionaries after their seizure of power. This was true of China, North Korea, and Vietnam, where to begin with the regimes had much more popularity among the masses than their domestic opponents did. However, these revolutionaries had to contend with more powerful counterrevolutionary forces posed by a new geopolitical context. This centered on the determination of the United States not to lose more Chinas but to defeat communist revolutions by all necessary force. The United States gave threatened regimes billions of dollars in aid and was also prepared if required to go as far as a scorched earth strategy of exemplary repression, killing so many people or destroying so much of an economy that any communist regime there would be greatly weakened and would remain unattractive to nationalists in neighboring countries. At first the Soviet Union and China matched this effort by giving support to revolutionaries in Korea and Vietnam, but they tired of their uncontrollable local allies before the United States did. In contrast, the Russian revolutionaries had been largely left alone at the end of World War I, despite brief, half-baked Western interventions in its civil war. Unlike revolutionaries in the second wave they had no outside support; nor did the revolutionaries of Central and Eastern Europe. One might say that the feebleness of intervention by the Western powers after 1918 was due to war-weariness, but the United States, the Soviet Union, and China were also war-weary after World War II, yet they all intervened more. The United States had been involved in supporting Chinese Nationalists during the Pacific War, but when the civil war began, they largely stood aside. But as a result of this defeat American counterrevolutionary strategy strengthened along with American global power to reduce the overall prospects for revolution.

American strategy might not seem very successful, a draw in Korea and a failure in Vietnam, while outcomes in Laos and Cambodia were not good either. Yet this can be seen differently. In Korea devastating bombing of the North helped defend the southern regime and produce a compliant capitalist and eventually democratic government in the South of the country. But the devastation and militarization of the North in the civil war also helped make its communist regime unattractive in the South and abroad. In Vietnam bombing also helped cripple its communist regime, though it eventually recovered – to make a move toward capitalism. In Cambodia American bombing campaigns helped produce so terrible a communist government, the Khmer Rouge, that a neighboring communist regime, Vietnam, invaded Cambodia to overthrow it. In Laos American (and also Vietnamese) interventions resulted in civil wars and very weak regimes, mostly communist, which could not effectively govern the country. So there were in effect two levels of success for American counter-revolutionaries. The higher level would be to produce a democratic capitalist regime, which was rarely achieved. The lower level was scorched earth, so to devastate a country that it would constitute a powerful incentive for people across all classes to desert the revolutionaries, and for people in nearby countries not to follow this example. U.S. policy proved successful in the latter strategy, constituting a major blockage to revolution, especially in small countries, which could be devastated more easily.

My explanation is recognizably Marxian in emphasizing class struggle, but it is not Marxian in any other way. Neither the macroeconomic fortunes of capitalism nor the microrelations of production mattered greatly to revolutionary outcomes. Revolutions did not occur at particular points in economic cycles or through the expansion of the capitalist world system. They did often occur at periods of unusual economic suffering, usually when this was caused by war. The workers embracing revolution were sometimes skilled, sometimes unskilled; the peasants were sometimes tenant farmers, sometimes small proprietors, sometimes landless laborers. The movements had different social bases, though activists were much more often men than women, and the risk takers were mostly young, single adults. But the popular classes in these cases shared in common a profound sense of exploitation, emanating from more than just the capital-labor relationship, for it involved a sense of political, military, and ideological (in the colonial cases, racial) exploitation as well. The combination allowed flexible Marxist ideologists plausibly and often correctly to identify the causes and remedies of exploitation.

After the revolution they were soon not so flexible. After a honeymoon period, they cracked down hard on supposed counterrevolutionary classes as well as on any political dissent. The despotic power of the state elite increased in the same way and basically for the same reasons as in the Soviet Union. Utopian transformational goals, geopolitical pressure, and peasant unwillingness to sacrifice for the sake of industry and armaments combined to increase despotic powers. Infrastructural powers wielded by a party-state intermittently launching hero projects also increased, with seemingly less psychological withdrawal than in the Soviet Union. But then in China extraordinary economic flexibility was introduced by the regime, then imitated in Vietnam, which gave the regime a combination of market and statist economic tools, which has enabled the country to achieve massive and still continuing economic growth. This is by far the happiest line of development of twentieth-century revolutionaries, even though the reforms have not yet spread significantly to the political realm.

However, not all modern revolutions can be interpreted along either Soviet or Chinese lines. Africa differed somewhat, though its anticolonial revolts were encouraged by the two world wars in which Africans were encouraged to kill Europeans, a big dent in supposed European superiority. Latin America differed more, for the continent saw no major wars. Instead it had extreme inequality reinforced by ethnic-racial disprivilege and a long tradition of peasant insurgency. Above all perhaps, it had vulnerable ruling regimes, highly personalist and exclusionary. These factors led to many attempted revolutions but only two successful ones, in Cuba and Nicaragua, alongside a host of repressed revolutionary guerrilla movements in both the mid-1960s and the mid-1970s. There were faint echoes here of anticolonialism, for ruling elites were generally supported by the American empire, and university-educated intellectuals spread utopian Marxist ideas of antiimperialist revolution as reinterpreted by Fidel Castro and Che Guevara, rechanneling insurgent Latino traditions that stretched back to Zapata and Sandino. In general, however, local regimes were up to the task of combating such insurgents, if given a little outside help from the United States. The two successful revolutions were launched against extreme examples of that repressive, exclusionary, infrastructurally weak, and personalist state generally identified by sociologists as being especially vulnerable to insurgents. They even alienated many elite groups; they refused to conciliate popular grievances, which might have detached reformists from revolutionaries; and they lacked the military professionalism that might have repressed insurgency. These were personal praetorian guards not real armies (Wickham-Crowley, 2001). But both these revolutions then encountered American led counterrevolution and its scorched earth policies destroyed the credibility of the Nicaraguan Sandinistas and Castro's Cuba.

So most of the individual relevant causes, as identified by previous theorists or by me, were not strictly necessary for revolution. A major, devastating, and continuing war in China or an unusually ineffective state in Cuba and Nicaragua might compensate for the relevant absence of some other causes. Compensation was even clearer in the deviant case of Iran in 1979, which was not significantly Marxian, which did not occur in response to war, and which had a different outcome. It also raises the possibility that, like the Russian and Chinese Revolutions, it might inaugurate another wave of revolutions. I turn to it in more detail.

Third wave precursor? The Iranian Revolution of 1979

Before 1979 Iran was ruled by the Pahlavi monarchy.[1] This was of recent origin, founded in 1925 by an army officer, Reza Shah, the son of an army major with a humble peasant background. In 1941 during World War II the British

---

[1] I am indebted in this section to the work of Hazem Kandil (2012).

began to doubt his loyalty to the allied war effort, and Iranian territory was crucial for supplying the Soviet Union with Western aid. So the British invaded, easily destroyed his army, and replaced him with his son, Mohammad Reza Pahlavi, who ruled until 1979. Since his dynasty was not hallowed by time, he would stand or fall by his personal success or failure. The shah increased the pressure on himself by creating a personalist absolute monarchy initially resting on a feudal landowning aristocracy, a type of regime that had become obsolete everywhere else in the world. In the 1960s, however, he sought land reforms to destroy the power of the landowning class and to build up a class of loyal peasants. Unfortunately, most of these did not get enough land to survive, and they were forced to migrate to a marginal urban existence (Kian-Thiébaut, 1998: 127; Kandil, 2012). The shah's basis of support thus narrowed.

The economy was narrowly based on oil, by 1978 accounting for 98 percent of exports. This led to imports of foreign goods undercutting Iranian business, especially the merchants and artisans of the bazaars, the bazaaris, whom the shah regarded as backward. Oil money financed the state, including all its state capitalist projects. This led to substantial economic growth in the early 1970s, but the benefits did not trickle down much beyond the shah's client networks, and for ordinary people inflation wiped out the benefits of growth. The shah was a true reactionary, avoiding terms like "modernization" or "development," declaring rather that he would rebuild the Great Civilization, which meant retaining the court, the trappings, the divine right rhetoric, and the clientelism of bygone monarchism. The rights of women and education and health did improve, and the regime was quite secular. The shah imagined that he might rule absolutely through a new technocratic class, yet court clientelism and corruption undermined this. His nouveau riche clients conspicuously appropriated most of the wealth, causing a widespread sense of relative deprivation among the population. The shah's relentless and grandiose monarchist propaganda merely created the kind of mass cynicism also found in the Soviet Union (Azimi, 2008: chap. 8). Arjomand (1988) adds that petrodollar wealth created moral confusion. A few Iranians were enriched, most were not, and their material aspirations became dislocated, enhancing relative deprivation and perceptions that the regime was unjust and immoral, so fueling Islamic ideas of social justice.

Geopolitically, the shah initially adopted the pose of America's policeman of the Gulf, though it was mainly his oil that gained him masses of the latest American (and other) military equipment. This drew persistent charges that he was a tool of foreign imperialism, which was not really true of the 1970s, during which he tried to play off the United States against the Soviets. But he was spending enormous sums on a defense that was not needed, and on the latest military equipment, which his troops could not operate. As the regime became more corrupt and authoritarian, losing popular support, holding phony elections, imprisoning thousands of dissidents, this generated a fundamental problem. Statist development based almost entirely on oil was creating larger middle and working classes, more educated people, and more lawyers, in short a larger constituency for more constitutional rule. Yet he refused absolutely to go down this route and all would-be reformers could see this. As Tocqueville long ago observed, liberalization of despotic rule is dangerous for the monarch. Given the absence of reformers within the Iranian regime, reform from outside – that is, a revolution – became more likely (Azimi, 2008: 348–53).

Most theories of revolution see personalistic dictators as the most vulnerable to revolution. This regime was highly personal for the shah divided and ruled among all his acolytes, who all reported individually to him. This was also true of his army commanders and there was no collective high command. He would brook no dissent from his policies and there was no security of office in either the civil or military administration. As Kandil (2012) observes, this was a monarchical absolutism in the sense that its political core was the royal court, which dominated the military and security organs of the state. For the shah to weaken his military power was obviously dangerous, and his whole system of rule severely weakened the infrastructural power of the state. Like the Americans, the shah was most focused on the danger posed by the Left opposition, but he was also careful to divide and rule among the Islamic hierocracy, the ulama. While he severely repressed and exiled the few dissident clerics like Khomeini, he tolerated the bulk of the ulama leaders, who were politically conservative and fiercely anticommunist. There was little threat to his regime from Islam until its final days.

Classes played a part in this revolution, but not in a narrowly Marxian sense. In the mid-1970s global stagflation hit both the middle class and the urban poor. Foran (2005: 75–80; cf. Moshiri, 1991: 124) says this economic downturn precipitated revolution, confirming J-curve theories of revolution, since the downturn followed a period of growth. However, Kurzman (2004: 91–104) notes that the recession was no worse than in comparable developing countries, which did not have revolutions, and in Iran those who suffered most were not more likely to join the dissidents. Nonetheless, the major problem for the shah was that he had politicized and even personalized the economy. His own family plus ten other allied families owned all the five hundred largest industrial and financial corporations in the country (Kandil, 2012). This was a fairly extreme version of political capitalism, but it had a potential downside for those who benefited from it. The regime – that is, the shah – might be praised in good times but reviled in hard times in an economy dependent on oil and so on an international capitalist economy not controlled by the shah. Neoliberalism was the response in some other countries; discontent leading to revolution was the outcome in Iran. Some were more hurt than others, of course. Parsa (1989: chap. 5) says the movement centered on bazaaris, hurt by the shah's antiinflationary policies (he imprisoned merchants who raised their prices), aided by the relatively privileged workers of the oil and construction industries, plus white-collar workers and leftist students – a broad but pre-dominantly middle-class opposition. Insofar as class played a causal role in the revolution it pitted a narrow court and capitalist elite against most of the middle class – though the urban poor were also eventually mobilized.

There were also ideological grievances – disgust against the corruption and supposed libertinism of the Westernized Pahlavi court. Its combination of cul-tural liberalism – including tolerance for religious minorities and women's rights – and political despotism was anathema to lower levels of the ulama and to young seminarians. The clergy wielded considerable ideological power in a pious country, and this was grounded in their simple life-style and notable lack of corruption. The hierarchy had effected a compromise with the shah: the regime would leave them alone and they would not criticize it. Yet there were stirrings amid younger, more radical clerics (Arjomand, 1988: 201; Moshiri, 1991: 126; Azimi, 2008: chap. 9). This revolution obviously did depend on broad economic discontent but it brandished more ideological and political than economic banners (Kian-Thiébaut, 1998: 202–9). The organized oppo-sition was small and varied, stretching from the Tudeh communist party and small guerrilla movements on the Left, through liberal and nationalists, to the Islamist populists on the Right. Common experience of repression pushed them toward minimal cooperation under nationalist, populist slogans. Discontent was growing, as foreign diplomats, but not the shah, could perceive. He was trapped inside his delusions of grandeur institutionalized into an Orientalist court. Surrounded by obsequious acolytes and foreign arms dealers, he could not believe the danger he was in.

U.S. policy was in its usual dilemma, supporting a son-of-a-bitch because of his anticommunism, while hoping against hope that he might move toward liberal constitutional rule. Kennedy had tried pressure, with few results. Jimmy Carter's policy was ambiguous. He declared that foreign aid would only be given to regimes recognizing human rights, but in practice he made an excep-tion for the shah, whom he also praised lavishly as a bulwark against commu-nism – and whose oil he needed. Although the Americans were now unhappy about the shah's attempts to play off the superpowers against each other, his role in OPEC and Arab oil embargos, and his nationalization of Iranian oil, nonetheless the shah still had the Americans over an oil barrel.

The opposition movements survived since repression on the ground was somewhat sporadic, as a result of the shah's own policies. SAVAK, the secret police, was kept understaffed and underfinanced, since the shah feared it as a potential rival (Kandil, 2012). It was not as all-powerful as many have argued. The army was equipped with the most modern weapons of war but lacked low-lethality weapons suitable for crowd control, as did the police. There was no paramilitary police force. Strikes and demonstrations grew through 1978. Islamic movements could mobilize networks of people based on the mosques, and they learned to exploit the tradition of public mourning on the fortieth day after someone's death, turning funeral marches into protest demonstrations against the victims of repression. Some mosque networks were then taken over by more radical lower clergy articulating Ayatollah Khomeini's slogans. Khomeini had adapted some leftist slogans while adding that only Islam could combat American imperialism and its stooges. From exile he was the most forceful and articulate critic of the regime, and the other opposition groups found it difficult to disagree with what he said. His followers accepted his every word and identified him as another charismatic religious leader (Azimi, 2008: 342–7). By the autumn of 1978 the Islamists were collaborating quite closely with striking blue- and white-collar workers and the Left more generally.

In mid-November 1978 the Shah showed some resolve when he dissolved the civilian government and installed a military regime. For a few days a show of military power in the streets seemed to cow the demonstrators, but he was reluctant to up the repression when demonstrations resumed, and he refused to appoint hard-line generals to the top government positions. A favorable view of him (offered by Kurzman) is that he was using both the carrot and the stick, repression of mass demonstrations alongside conciliation of liberals. But the opposition – and most later scholars – saw him as vacillating. A severe cancer had weakened his capacity to take decisions, already found wanting in earlier crises. Aware of his impending mortality, he was reluctant to bequeath to his eighteen-year-old son a regime of terror. He refused army requests for more repression, while the army, weakened by years of divide and rule, could not mount its own coup.

The demonstrators grew in confidence and numbers. December 10 and 11, 1978, saw enormous demonstrations demanding that the monarchy be replaced by a constitutional republic. Foreign observers estimated their number in Teheran at up to a million, with hundreds of thousands marching in several other cities. At most, 10 percent of the population was mobilized, which would be a higher proportion than in most revolutions. It was predominantly middle class. The peasantry was never much involved; the urban poor were to be involved later, after the shah was deposed. Faced with very large demonstrations, the army and the shah were caught in a dilemma. They lacked riot control weapons like tear gas, rubber bullets, and body armor. The army could only repress with weapons of high lethality, causing many deaths and further alienating the population. Some generals nonetheless urged the shah to authorize more shootings but he was unresponsive. There were some deserters although the army basically remained intact yet inactive (Kurzman, 2004: chap. 6; Parsa, 1989: 241–7; Arjomand, 1988: 120–8).

The Carter administration dithered. The National Security Council urged an "iron fist," but the State Department preferred conciliation and a more constitutional monarchy. U.S. General Huyser was sent to work with Iranian generals on preparing a coup but was frustrated by their total inability to move collectively. They remained loyal to the shah but were unable to mount collective pressure on him. Military officers lacked corporate solidarity as a result of the extreme personalism of the shah's regime (Kandil, 2012). Carter was in any case reluctant to endorse force and was focused on problems in other parts of the world until too late. The State Department desk officer for Iran at the time has penned a narrative depicting confusion and inaction in Washington (Precht, 2004; cf. Moshiri, 1991: 129). Iranians were not sure what to make of the American signals they detected, but by mid-December most thought the United States was abandoning the shah, and he himself believed so (Arjomand, 1988: 128–33). U.S. officials were already in touch with Khomeini's aides and seemed to have believed their assurances that they would work with both liberals and the army to form a new constitutional government. This was the kiss of death.

In January 1979 the demoralized and very sick shah, now aware that the United States might not defend him, fled the country (he had also done so when challenged in 1953 by the republican premier Mossadeq). Army loyalty was ended by his flight. The demonstrations turned in February into insurrection led by armed bands of Islamists and leftists. The army stood aside and there was a peaceful transition to a republican regime seemingly headed by liberal politicians. But the liberal, nationalist, and leftist parties had been weakened by years of repression, and the inheritor of revolution was Khomeini, an acute political operator able to mobilize after the shah departed through the mosques, the more numerous bazaaris, and urban marginal people against the modern parts of the middle and working classes (Arjomand, 1988; Keddie, 2003: 222–39; Moshiri, 1991; Foran, 2005: 80–7). A referendum in April 1979 voted in favor of an Islamic republic and in December Ayatollah Khomeini was installed as supreme leader.

Was this a revolution? It certainly involved a popular insurgency, though its size has been often exaggerated. Estimates of the numbers killed vary wildly, but the likeliest ones total around one thousand over fifteen months in 1978–9, which is not particularly high. This was only as many as died in less than three weeks in the Egyptian demonstrations of 2011. These figures "do not match the image of vast masses standing up to machine-gun fire" (says Kurzman, 2004: 71; cf. Kandil, 2012). It was a political revolution, replacing an authoritarian monarchy with a republican constitution supervised by a theocracy. It also turned into an ideological revolution, from Western secularism to Islamism, while more than two-thirds of the members of the first parliament of 1980 were lay or clerical intellectuals (Arjomand, 1988: 202), resembling the French revolutionaries whose intellectual activities I documented in Volume 2, and rather like the communist elites discussed earlier in this volume.

The unraveling of the new regime after the coup also resembled France. For most participants "the revolution of 1978–9 was in crucial respects an attempt to fulfill the objectives of the Constitutional Revolution" (says Azimi, 2008: 440). Yet that was not how events played out. The liberals and civic nationalists who formed the first postrevolutionary government possessed only small organizations. They lacked mass mobilization. Their timorousness also alienated both the Left and the Islamists, and cooperation between any of the three main revolutionary groups was at an end. Khomeini won the ensuing power struggle because he had promised to form a constitutional government, taking the wind out of its rivals' sails; because he did a deal with the military, which the Left could not do (promising them immunity from reprisals if they would stand aside); and because after the shah was overthrown Khomeini had mobilized mass support with promises of economic benefits for all. Especially drawn were the bazaaris and the poor urban classes. In the end he was the leader with most mass support. He did not keep his promises, of course, and his reprisals were savage.

The economy remained capitalist, though the Khomeini regime national-ized many industries, pursued infrastructural economic projects, and in conse-quence doubled the size of the state administration. But the Iranian version of a party-state was unique, for the state was supervised not by a party but by the powerful clerical elite – a theocracy. This power structure was reinforced by a military transformation with the establishment of the Islamist version of the party militia, the Revolutionary Guards, who have so far lasted longer than any Red Guards. Their power was greatly enhanced by the Iran-Iraq War. Though that war had been provoked by Khomeini's appeals to Iraq's Shi'a majority to rise up against Saddam Hussein's Sunni regime, the actual war started with an Iraqi invasion of Iran. So the religious elite could proclaim the war as being "sacred defense." It was also seen as "a providential gift," the "blessing of the war," as Khomeini described it, for it produced both a patriotic rally around the flag and the regime and a strengthening of the Revolutionary Guards (Azimi, 2008: 336). The regime did not maintain its popularity for long, of course. The last few years have indicated that the majority of Iranians would wish to be free of the ayatollahs.

Overall, the changes in Iran were important enough to be considered revolu-tionary. The revolution had mainly domestic causes. Unlike most other modern revolutions, the regime was not weakened by geopolitical instability. Iran was not involved in war before its 1979 revolution, nor was its state weakened by external events. The main external influence was that the shah was weakened by his dependence on the United States, although by the time of the revolution their alliance was very shaky and the United States did not in fact help him in the crisis. But their relationship was perceived in Iran as American imperialism. This may have been a necessary cause, for it was a factor in generating such a broad inclusionary alliance against his regime, comprising liberal centrists, left-ists, and Islamists – hardly natural allies. Yet it was not the only factor involved. Geopolitical factors contributed but not fundamentally to this revolution.

Since there was no war, no financial crisis, and no peasant uprising, Iran does not fit Skocpol's model of revolution. She has acknowledged this, calling

Iran an exceptional case (Skocpol, 1994; Arjomand, 1988: 191, 202–3). This was also an exclusively urban revolution, without peasant involvement, the only case in the twentieth century when this was so. It was also exceptional in ranging religious revolutionaries against a secular state, the reverse of the usual modern revolution, which tends to be leftist secularism launched against state and religion alike. Finally, it was unusual in having a ruler who would neither reform nor wholeheartedly repress. Had the shah authorized the army to repress the demonstrations with all guns blazing, he could have survived, as many despots have. But he lacked the stomach for this, given his self-delusions, his illness, and his concern for his young son and heir. These qualities do make the Iranian case different.

Yet in one other very important respect Iran fits very well into standard models of revolution. This was a personalist, repressive, and exclusionary regime – the type of regime considered to be most vulnerable to revolution. Since it was exceptionally personalist, it was also exceptionally vulnerable. The shah and his family and close friends had also commandeered the economy so that any economic recession would also be blamed on him. Outside this narrow circle he had deliberately divided and ruled among all the elite groups who might otherwise have offered him concerted support. This did not result in a factionalized regime with serious disagreements about policy such as hindered the response of some other regimes faced by serious insurgency. The problem was rather that the regime produced passivity among its potential allies and a failure to act collectively. The key self-inflicted wound was from the military. This military seemed powerful, for it was very large and magnificently equipped for war. But it had never fought a war and it lacked the skills to operate most of its modern weapons. That cannot be good for officer morale. But its crucial weakness was the absence of a high command. All generals reported individually to the shah. Most of them were loyal to the shah. But they were incapable of collective action or collective advice. If the shah was unwilling to repress, they could not, and nor could they mount a coup. In a sense therefore the unusually intense degree of regime personalism compensated for the lack of geopolitical instability and peasant support, and turned what might have been grumbles during an economic recession into virulent attacks on the ruling regime. The political and military weaknesses of the regime were here the most important cause, with ideological and economic grievances contributing but structured by them into revolution.

Might Iran become the inspirer of a third wave of revolution, in this case confined to Muslim countries, and unlike the other waves in being led by religious groups? By now Marxism and socialism were very weak across the region, unlikely to generate many revolutionaries. The experience with Arab socialism had not been happy, as supposedly socialist Ba'athist parties had degenerated into despotic, repressive clientelism failing to produce much economic development. Alone, the Syrian Ba'athist Party continued to rule, to no great popular acclaim and encountering massive resistance first in 1982, which it managed to repress, and then again in 2011 and 2012. Its Ba'athist brethren in other countries are gone. From the 1990s most of the popularly acclaimed movements of the Middle East have been Islamist and they are revolutionary in the sense that they seek to overthrow political regimes and install Shariah law. Except for the Muslim Brotherhood, they endorse violence and form their own paramilitaries. But we must not exaggerate their powers. The schism between the two branches of Islam, Shi'a and Sunni, limits collaboration across the region. Hezbollah, like the Iranian regime, is Shi'a, while Hamas, the Muslim Brotherhood, the Taliban, and al Qaeda are Sunni. Cooperation across the schismatic divide can occur, since they have common foreign enemies, but is infrequent. Indeed, Hezbollah and Hamas resemble national liberation movements more than schismatic Islamist revolutionaries. The Muslim Brotherhood, though seeking Shariah law, has been forced by repression into reformism at the local community level. The more radical Sunni terrorist movements who were the antecedents of al Qaeda split off from the Brotherhood in disgust at its endorsement of nonviolence. Al Qaeda today is a polarizing force across the Muslim world. Osama bin Laden achieved popularity in the Arab street principally because of his courage in oppositing American imperialism. It is American imperialism that keeps Al Qaeda, the Iranian ayatollas, and other forms of Islamic extremism quite vigorous. Without that, their lack of real social and economic programs, their killing of civilians, and their fundamentalist ideology would leave them with very little support. This would amount at most to an artificially, externally induced third wave of revolution, with little indigenous staying power.

Attempts have been made to emulate the Iranian revolution, though without much success. The Taliban seized power when Afghans were resisting the Soviet invasion of their country but they did not succeed in ruling the whole of the country. In the Sudan, Yemen, and Somalia, Islamist movements have struggled hard, without attaining or retaining power. So far Islamic fundamentalism has revealed itself capable of profiting from and reinforcing a degree of chaos (especially when helped by foreign imperialism), but its only revolution remains Iran. Most of its strength (apart from the reformist Muslim Brotherhood) derives from backlash against American imperialism and Israeli colonialism. Settlement of the Palestine conflict would seriously weaken Islamist revolutionary forces, and so would American withdrawal from Iraq and Afghanistan. The first seems unlikely in the near future; the latter is underway. But the radicals like Al Qaeda have been largely defeated in their attempts to mount revolution in the Middle East, though they only need a few terrorists to maintain a certain amount of mayhem. These revolutionaries are better at creating (a little) chaos than revolution. It seems unlikely that this will be a third wave of any kind, at least in the immediate future.

However, it is possible that the desire right across the Middle East for more political representation and more economic justice, as revealed in the Arab revolts of 2011, might interact with some of these movements and their off-shoots to generate broader-based dissident movements and even revolutions that were not merely political. Most Middle Eastern countries are ruled by despotic regimes whose dynasties and elites are not hallowed by time and who appropriate most of the wealth of the country through a coercive and corrupt state-capitalist nexus – resembling the shah's Iran. The state's repressive agencies remain its main form of infrastructural power, and no other ruler has pursued the shah's suicidal path of emasculating the army. Yet in other cases the unity of the army and security agencies cannot be taken for granted. Since these despots do not fully trust the army, they build up their own praetorian guards in the form of paramilitary security agencies who do most of the repression. However, this can alienate the army, especially if the military feels it is losing out on the struggle for the resources of the new state capitalism. This happened in Egypt and was the key factor in the refusal of the army to join in the repression of the mass 2011 demonstrations involving somewhere between ten and fifteen million people. The military's disloyalty to Mubarak made their success possible (Kandil, 2011, 2012).

In Tunisia, Egypt, and Libya in 2011 dissidents protested vociferously the economic corruption and exploitation embodied in entwined state and capitalist agencies. In Egypt the combination of U.S. aid and neoliberal privatizations enabled friends and relatives of Mubarak to seize much of country's economic resources. This newly enriched capitalist class was tied closely into the apparatus of the regime. There was considerable economic growth, but it did not reach down to improve the life of the people. While corporate taxes were reduced, taxes on the people were increased. Food subsidies were reduced and labor conditions worsened, while a debt cycles ensured that foreign investors also did well out of neoliberalism. This new level of exploitation by the regime and foreign banks was the economic grievance fueling the revolt in Egypt (Kandil, 2011). We saw in Tunisia and Egypt two persistent conditions for revolution: the discontent and sense of injustice of the masses and a split within the ruling regime, which especially weakened its repressive capacity. As in Iran temporary alliances formed among leftist, liberal, and Islamist dissidents, creating the broad base that might potentially overturn more than just the form of state – and then perhaps generate a postpolitical revolutionary struggle among the victors. Where the rulers are of a different sect or ethnicity from the mass of the population, such populism becomes inflected by religious or ethnic sentiments too, as in Bahrein and Syria, though here the ruling ethnic/sectarian group is also more determined to resist and repress, fearing the worst from any political revolution.

There remains therefore the possibility that Iran may have inaugurated a third revolutionary phase, though that depends, first, on whether the current nonviolent dissident movements can achieve political stability and engage in substantial economic and political reforms. If the West wants order, reforms, and modernity across the Middle East it might help these dissidents – though not by military interventions. But if the reformists fail and are repressed, that will boost the appeal of revolutionaries, probably of an Islamist type. But most revolutions in the first two phases were not successful. Revolutionaries fail more often than they succeed.

Soviet fall: Revolution from above?

The collapse of the Soviet Union was substantially revolutionary, though it differed from all others considered here. The Soviet Union from 1990 meets all but one of my criteria for a revolution. Politically, fifteen states replaced a single state, and a colonial empire gave way to six more states; a single one-party-state was transformed into democracy in half these cases and into personalistic dictatorship in the other half. This was clearly a political revolution. The economy was transformed from perverted socialism to a sometimes perverted capitalism, also revolutionary. The ideology of Marxism-Leninism was discarded in favor of Western liberal ideologies, again revolutionary. Even military power was partially transformed, as a superpower collapsed and the cold war ended. There were further resemblances to other revolutions. It proceeded through a sequence of unintended escalations, as did other revolutions discussed in this book, though most of these "revolutionaries" lacked much ideology, except for liberals and neoliberals, who did not in the end win out. Also different from other cases except the Iranian revolution was the absence of geopolitical crisis or an opening of the world system. There were no major outside causes of the Fall, save the existence of a more successful model of development in the West, which corroded the ideological power of the party-state elite. Outside influences were to become more important after the Fall, for it ensured the dominance of Western ideas and practices over the former Soviet bloc. Though these were adapted and often perverted to suit local power holders, the ex-Soviet countries no longer offered an alternative to Western capitalist democracy led by the United States. Universal globalization was nearing reality. The effects of the Fall were indeed revolutionary in a geopolitical sense too.

Yet was this an insurgent revolution? Can one really call it a revolution when much of the communist ruling class remained a ruling but capitalist class afterward, and were motivated less by ideology than by crass materialism? It was usually the same people who were transforming the sources of social power and benefiting personally from the shift! Popular insurgency was also much less than in 1917. In 1991 large crowds with mass support were involved in Central Europe and in the Baltic republics, and here there was less continuity of elite rule. These places did indeed see revolutions – and luckily revolutions with not much violence. Among these cases the Polish Solidarity movement stands as the only major working-class insurgent movement, though it was not violent. Only Romanian crowds were very violent in overthrowing their communist regime, with several hundred dead. The others were velvet revolutions, nonviolent. I stressed military power struggles in most twentieth-century revolutions, but not here. The regimes barely resisted their overthrow and mighty armed forces could not bring themselves to act effectively. Farther east part of the existing elites made the necessary ideological adjustments to hold on to power, and so to avoid a real revolution. The difference in all the Soviet bloc had been rule by a profoundly ideological regime, which had now been ideologically corroded from within. Its elite no longer believed it had the moral right to intervene, and many of its members preferred to enrich themselves from the Fall.

The Fall presupposed a populace alienated from state socialism. Yet it was mainly elites who decided what would happen. The famous demonstration supporting Yeltsin's stance in front of the White House was estimated at the time to constitute twenty thousand to forty thousand people, below the size of earlier demonstrations favoring a variety of causes. Lane's acquisition class and Hough's bourgeoisie offered a larger social base but did not represent the masses as a whole and they were moved by more calculative sentiments than is normal in revolutions. Most citizens wanted some kind of reform that would bring them higher living standards and political freedoms. That was the important mass base from which reformers could act. But there is no indication that the masses wanted to move to capitalism or to dissolve the Soviet Union, and they did not act to do so. There was, however, popular support for politicians who were leaning in such directions. Yeltsin was prodemocracy and had the common touch. He was also an opportunist who could mobilize antielitism and Russian nationalism and he promised markets yielding abundance for all. The public even tolerated his bouts of inebriation in public. He rose to power through largely free elections. But during campaigns he never publicly favored a free market economy and never mentioned the word "capitalism." This was wise. In a poll in European Russia in May 1991, 54 percent said they wanted to continue with a version of socialism. Most of these wanted a more democratic form of existing socialism, while another 23 percent chose the Swedish model of social democracy. Eighty-one (81) percent wanted the state to guarantee food and shelter to all. In a referendum conducted across almost all the Soviet Union in March 1991, 76 percent of the voters approved of the Union, just as it was being dismantled. They wanted the end of communism, but not the breakup of the Soviet Union, rather its reform, and not the embrace of capitalism.

We should not take these polls too seriously, however. As the pollster, Levada (1992), reported, opinion was volatile, changing as the situation deteriorated and as new panaceas descended from above. The masses were mostly reactive, responding in elections and polls to the latest initiatives, but without making sacrifices to attain any goal. This began as a revolution from above and remained so outside of the European part of the Soviet bloc. This makes it different from other major revolutions discussed in this book. It also fortunately made it virtually bloodless – apart from the few republics engulfed in ethnic civil wars.

Conclusion

Like human societies in general, revolution mixes together the universal, the particular and the developmental. I have discerned some general characteristics of modern revolutions, but set amidst the peculiarities of each country and amid both a broad process of world-historical development and short-term processes of interaction between regimes, insurgents and outsiders. This has inserted mistakes, unintended consequences, and uncertainties into revolutionary outcomes. Right through the twentieth century we see a learning process among insurgents, who drew lessons from previous attempts at revolution and adapted their own strategies accordingly. On the other side came counterrevolutionary learning strategies, with American military power central in its ability to make revolution a highly undesirable goal. And always the participants argued over strategy and tactics, responding to their perceptions of the threat and tactics of the other side, and pondering how they could obtain further support (or weapons) from other classes, from moderates, and from outsiders. An overall theory of all this cannot be too precise. In the social sciences laws are not possible, but some broad generalizations work quite well for most twentieth-century revolutions.

Three generalizations seem particularly apposite. First, most revolutions have resulted from class struggle linked to a sequence of authoritarian regime defeats in wars. Second, most revolutions involve rather unhappy sequences of events. The revolutionaries seize their chance due to unexpected power contingencies and they have utopian transformative goals at odds with the preferences of either the mass of the people or those of particularly powerful actors, domestic or foreign. In the ensuing violent struggle with counterrevolutionaries the revolutionaries either lose (as happens most of the time) or succeed by imposing such a level of coercion on the people as both to induce much suffering and to prevent them from achieving most of their goals. The exception is in the sphere of economic power, where communist revolutionaries have achieved some success in sponsoring growth. I do not mean this as a blanket condemnation of revolutionaries. I emphasize that disasters ensue as the result of the combined but conflicting actions of revolutionaries and counterrevolutionaries. Where dissidents feel with Trotsky that there is no other way out, meaning that the suffering is already great and the regime will only repress, then they must seize hold of revolutionary means. But they should be looking for forms of structural reform that do not require heavy coercion on the mass of the population to achieve.

Third, however, revolutions do not happen in democracies, where compromise reform is instead institutionally privileged, and where the infrastructures of more routinized and accountable administrative agencies can actually diffuse the reforms throughout the land. As democracies have spread gingerly across the world, so has revolution receded. Unless some major crisis erupts across the world – and, as we shall see, that might be brought about by climate change – we might see revolutions gradually diminishing in frequency and scale. The high point of revolutions was probably the twentieth century.

10 American empire at the turn of the twenty-first century

In February 1941 Henry Luce proclaimed the beginning of the American Century. America, he declared, must now: "accept wholeheartedly our duty and our opportunity as the most powerful and vital nation in the world ... to exert upon the world the full impact of our influence, for such purposes as we see fit and by such means as we see fit .... We must now undertake to be the Good Samaritan to the entire world ...." This was global imperialism for a good cause. As we saw in Chapter 5, American imperialism after World War II had been quite varied. Over Europe it was hegemonic, even legitimate. Over East Asia it was a mixture of indirect empire and informal empire through military intervention, yet domination then became more benign and now legitimate hegemony predominates there too. Latin America and the Middle East were at the receiving end of informal empire through military intervention or proxies, though this has recently declined in Latin America while increasing in the Middle East. The United States had no colonies in this entire period and tended to move toward milder forms of domination. Yet, as Chalmers Johnson (2000, 2005) says, the size and sprawl of its military base network constitutes a new type of global empire, intended to militarily coerce without formal occupation.

This chapter deals with two recent crystallizations of American imperialism: economic imperialism, centered on dollar seigniorage occurring from the early 1970s; and military imperialism intensifying in the 1990s and 2000s. I try to explain them and I ask whether the two were in fact distinct or whether they became merged into a single global imperial strategy, as world systems theorists and others argue. I will ask how successful the two were and whether they reversed the drift toward lighter forms of American empire. Since Chapter 6 already discussed some of the economic intensification, I focus here more on military power relations, and especially on the two main wars of the twenty-first century so far, in Iraq and Afghanistan. I begin with the economy.

The new economic imperialism, 1970–1995: Dollar seigniorage

The postwar global economy had benefited from the American hegemony, which set its rules. It boomed in the 1950s and 1960s, boosted first by American growth, then European, then Japanese. The dollar was the reserve currency, backed by gold, and a lower tariff regime boosted trade. All continents shared

268

to some extent in growth. Though the Bretton Woods system gave the United States privileges, it was administered by multilateral agreements between nation-states, allowing them to implement their own development plans and repress international flows of capital. This was more American hegemony than empire. But then came crisis, as we saw in Chapter 6. A slowdown at the end of the 1960s became stagflation, which Keynesian countercyclical policies seemed only to worsen. The prices of export commodities on which poorer countries depended were falling, creating balance of payments difficulties, which their Import Substitution Programs could not resolve. The sharp hike in oil prices in 1973 worsened their problems.

The Bretton Woods financial system collapsed between 1968 and 1971. The slowdown, plus U.S. deficits compounded by spending in Vietnam, and increasing financial volatility, all meant a faltering of its financial repression. The United States was importing and spending abroad much more than it was exporting, resulting in big American deficits. Since the dollar was at first still on the gold standard, this resulted at the end of the 1960s in a run on its gold. Fort Knox was being emptied. This seemed a threat to American power. The United States might soon have been forced to sell off its investments abroad to pay for its military activity abroad. Foreigners might have also used their surplus dollars to buy up American industries, as Americans had earlier done in Britain. But after some arm-twisting by U.S. diplomats, the major central banks agreed as a stop-gap measure to stop converting their dollars into gold, thereby sacrificing their immediate economic interest to the common good produced by American global responsibilities. At this point neither they nor the U.S. administration realized how costly this would become. This informal mutual restraint held the line until August 1971 when President Nixon took the dollar off the gold standard – to save his war, his expansionary economic policies, and his reelection chances (Kunz, 1997: 192–222). The reasons were domestic plus Vietnam, not a premeditated drive for economic imperialism. That was an unintended consequence – though some disagree (e.g., Gowan, 1999).

The dollar remained the reserve currency. The only use for surplus U.S. dollars held abroad was now to invest them in the United States. Since most were held by central banks, they bought U.S. Treasury notes in bulk, which lowered their interest rate. U.S. adventures abroad could now be financed by foreigners, despite American current account deficits, and at a very low interest rate. The alternative, the foreigners felt, was worse: disruption of the world's monetary system, weakening U.S. resolve to defend them, while a fall in the value of the dollar would make U.S. exports cheaper than their own. U.S. governments were now free of the balance of payments constraints faced by other states. If necessary, the Federal Reserve Bank could just print more dollars, now politely called quantitative easing. Americans could spend more on social services, fight in Vietnam, and consume more, all at the same time. This held off the European challenge in the real economy, as it was to hold off the challenge of Japanese capitalism, which so taxed American politicians in the 1970s. Power was not yet passing to Asia. Whether premeditated or just seen through hindsight, for the United States it was not a crisis at all, but an opportunity to enhance its seigniorage over the world economy. No military force was involved, only the exploitation of an already existing dollar seigniorage. The end of financial repression made for more volatility in the world economy, but other states were forced to hold even larger reserves in dollars, so reinforcing their dependence on the United States. The alternative of moving away from having the dollar as the reserve currency still seems riskier to the players. So this regime is seen as partially legitimate, a hybrid form of economic imperialism/hegemony.

World systems theory (and some others) regards this shift toward domination by finance as a sign of American decline. Yet there was no further decline in the aggregate strength of the American economy vis-a-vis others. Because of World War II, the U.S. economy had been unusually dominant in the 1940s. The U.S. share of world GDP (measured in terms of purchasing power parity) had been an extraordinary 35 percent during the war, due to peculiar wartime conditions. It was still recovered to 27 percent in 1950. Then, as the European and East Asian economies recovered from the war, it fell to 21 percent in 1973. But since 1973 two alternative measures put it as either stabilized at around 21 percent for the whole period up to 2005, or as slightly rising to 24 percent by 2010 and then levelling off (IMF, 2010; Maddison, 2001: Table 1–3; Chase-Dunn et al., 2003). Some (e.g., Boswell, 2004: 518–20) say that American decline is evidenced by the fact that its GDP is now no higher than that of the EU, but that is because the EU has admitted more and more countries. Though the EU has a single market, it is not backed by a single state or treasury and it moves at the pace of the slowest country. The problem of the EU as a would-be economic hegemon is that it can be rarely pointed in a single direction, let alone set rules for anyone else.

Moreover, during the 1990s and early 2000s, U.S. production levels and productivity outstripped those of Europe and Japan by a considerable margin, helped by escalating investment by foreigners in the United States (Schwartz, 2009: chap. 5; Dooley, 2003). World systems theorists say that the United States is now going the same way as Britain did in the late nineteenth century: a shift from manufacturing to finance and services ensures its decline. But whereas late nineteenth century British manufacturing corporations had fallen behind their American and German rivals in technology, managerial practices and productivity, this is not true of American corporations today. The share of foreign exchange reserves of the dollar increased greatly in the 1990s, enabling U.S. corporations to borrow and invest at low rates of interest. Helped also by the world's best educational system for the upper middle classes, and by U.S. technology and managerial practices its productivity improved in the 1990s to remain around 2 percent per annum superior to its rivals. Schwartz suggests that the clear separation made by world systems theorists between manufacturing and finance mis-perceives the nature of contemporary capitalism. Control of global productivity chains, the circulation of capital among productive units, is what matters for economic strength, and the depth and range of financial institutions are crucial in this. The bulk of foreign investment in the United States is in the form of passive holdings of low-yielding Treasury and mortgage bonds, which generates additional housing-based aggregate demand in the United States. This increases U.S. profits and enables American arbitrage so that most American investment abroad is in active, higher-yielding equities and FDI. This arbitrage borrows at low and lends at high interest, as had the British around 1900. Now it ensures U.S. domination of the global economy. Of course, as I noted in Chapter 6, most ordinary Americans benefited very little from this, while the Great Recession of 2008 did serve notice on U.S. hegemony in the long-run.

As we saw in Chapter 6, world systems theory was correct in seeing that this economic imperial intensification also involved a shift of power from states other than the United States to transnational finance capital, manifest after 1970 in structural adjustment programs. These interventions in southern countries were so forceful as to constitute imperialism. It was also global as country after country was forced to yield control of capital flows to international finance capital. So though this *was* American economic dominance, it was not that alone. It also shifted some power from the interstate level to the transnational-market level, a disembedding trend. A state's credit now depended less on agreements between central banks and the IMF than on private financial markets run on neoliberal principles. World systems theory sees this growing transnational capital as escaping from the control of the declining U.S. hegemon (Arrighi & Silver, 1999: chap. 2). Yet there was actually close coordination between the U.S. government and private finance. Gowan (1999: chap. 3, 2004; cf. Soederberg, 2004) calls this "the Dollar-Wall Street Regime," since it gave both the U.S. government and financiers far more power over the world's monetary and financial relations than had the Bretton Woods regime. This included European and Japanese finance capital. So it was a dual kind of imperialism, of the United States and transnational finance capital, at the expense of other nation-states, though we saw in chapter 6 that resistance to this was rising in the new millennium.

Through the postwar period the United States sought to open world markets. In most IMF negotiations over countries' economic crises, the United States pursued the most neoliberal line. In the Asian crisis of 1997 it also shot down a Japanese attempt to lead a rival East Asian financial consortium to solve the crisis (Blustein, 2001: 143–5; 164–70). Imperial powers do not like collective organization around the periphery. Yet this offensive ground to a halt as the East Asian economies found new ways to repress capital and cut foreign borrowing and as resurgent Latin American leftists stalled the U.S. plan for the Free Trade Area of the Americas. The Great Neoliberal Recession further shifted the balance of power against American and northern capitalism.

Yet the new economic imperialism did halt American relative economic decline for three decades. The continued rise of China, India and others will eventually end this phase, but the dollar continues to operate as the hub of the world's financial markets. In 2009 just less than 90 percent of the $3 trillion daily foreign exchange dealing involved the U.S. dollar, while Wall Street and Nasdaq traded 60 percent of all the world's stock exchange trades, and U.S. government bonds comprised about 40 percent of all world bonds. The U.S. needs this to continue financing its ever-increasing trade and budget deficits. In 2009 Americans' total debts to foreigners totalled about $3.8 trillion, more than a quarter of its GDP, while U.S. government debt is 85 percent of its GDP, lower only than Japan (whose debt is 90 percent owed to Japanese citizens), Ireland and Greece. The United States depends on a massive inflow of foreign capital. It must therefore keep capital markets open and prevent any return to policies of national development involving capital controls. It continues to push financial neoliberalism (Soederberg, 2004: 125; *New York Times*, February 7, 2010).

Foreigners must continue to invest in the United States rather than elsewhere. Despite many voices saying this cannot continue, it does. Some export surplus economies, like Germany or the oil states or Japan, have little choice since their own economies cannot generate much more domestic demand and the United States remains the safest haven for their surplus capital. The Chinese wish to maintain their levels of exports, which they believe increase employment and social stability in China. Chinese economists have believed that if the U.S. economy suffers a 1 percent decline, so does the Chinese. There are signs that as Chinese industries proceed upstream into higher-tech products, they create less employment. But all countries with dollar surpluses would take a substantial capital loss if they noticeably withdrew from holding dollars. There is no immediate exit strategy for them. The American and Chinese dominant classes both do very nicely out of the arrangement, at the expense of their peoples – and they are the ones who take the decisions (Schwartz, 2009: chap. 6). Sovereign Wealth Funds – direct activity by states on financial markets – now emerging may lead to more buying of American equities than bonds. That would undo U.S. global arbitrage. It would not lessen these countries' interdependence with the American economy, but within that relationship some power would shift toward the foreign states. That could begin a graceful American hegemonic decline.

Eventually Chinese GDP will overtake that of the United States. Estimating when is not an exact science, but current estimates date GDP overtaking in dollar terms converted at market exchange rates at 2019 (Economist.com/chinavusa), while the IMF has recently estimated that the dollar's reign will end by 2025, being replaced by a basket of three currencies, the dollar, the euro and the renminbi. Yet that could be upset by political upheavals, environmental disasters, or water or fuel shortages, all of which could affect China more than the United States. If China chose to become a military rival this might also lessen its economic growth. India's economy would also grow, perhaps as fast as China's. But it is fifteen years behind China in its level of development. Brazil and Russia would be somewhat further back. Europe will probably not advance much in relation to the United States. It is a positive force on its periphery, especially encouraging democracy among its neighbors, who want to join the EU. Democratization is formally a requirement for membership, though in practice this is sometimes breached (for example, Cyprus was admitted but not Macedonia). True, there are conditions, one of which is democratization, but the economic incentives are assumed to be large and worth it. Yet the EU has no unity in the financial, military or geopolitical realms, while the majority of referenda over the last two decades have clearly shown that its citizens do not want further deepening of the Union. All this makes it more likely that the United States will survive as the leading power of an evolving multilateral world economic order during the first half of the twenty-first century.

Informal Empire through military intervention, 1990–2011

U.S. military power is now hyper-active. Military spending (in constant 2008 dollars) is higher than at any time since 1945. Between 2001 and 2009, spending on defense rose from $412 billion to $699 billion, a 70 percent increase, larger than in any nine year period since the Korean War. Including the supplementary spending on Iraq and Afghanistan, we spent $250 billion more than average U.S. defense expenditures during the cold war – when the United States faced Soviet, Chinese and Eastern European potential adversaries. In the 2000s the United States had no serious adversaries yet its defense spending went up from about a third to half of total worldwide defense spending. Nor is the upward trend solely due to spending on the Iraq and Afghan wars, for normal spending has also risen significantly. The United States currently spends about half of the entire military expenditures of the planet! No other power has ever had what the Pentagon calls full spectrum dominance, that is dominance over land, air, sea, and space, able to defeat any adversary in the field and control any situation across the range of military operations (Bacevich, 2002). Britain's nineteenth century Navy was kept at a two-power standard, equal to the next two navies combined and its army was weaker than those of some of its rivals. There is no comparison between American military dominance and any other known to history. The lack of real military threat to the United States when compared to other empires is also striking. What's the military for?

In fact America's wars are now entirely wars of choice, since no state threatens the United States. War has become the default mode of American diplomacy, like European diplomacy of previous centuries. Between 1989 and 2001 the United States averaged one large-scale military intervention every eighteen months, higher than all prior periods except 1899 to 1914 (discussed in Volume 3, Chapter 3). Since 2001 war has been continuous. 2012 is the twelfth year in which the United States has been at war in Afghanistan and the tenth in Iraq – the longest period of continuous warfare in American history. 2011 saw a lesser and more multilateral intervention in Libya led a little covertly by the United States. In 2001 the Bush administration had intended more wars. Military threats were openly made by U.S. officials against Syria, North Korea and Iran. Bush's projected antiballistic missile sites in Eastern Europe was a threat aimed at Russia as well as Iran. To the Russians, if the American missiles really could intercept theirs, Russia would lack deterrence against an American first-strike nuclear attack for the first time since the 1940s. No wonder they were alarmed. Israel received far more economic and military aid than anyone else and was given a free hand militarily, feeling free to invade Lebanon in 2006 and the Gaza Strip in 2008. Only the United States and its allies now make war. So far there have been no other international wars in the twenty-first century. President Obama did slow the tempo a little, offering more conciliatory diplomatic language and saying he wanted to negotiate with Iran over its nuclear program. He withdrew most of the troops from Iraq. Yet he balanced this with troop increases in Afghanistan and Predator drone strikes in Pakistan and the Yemen. Despite administration unease at Israel's encouragement of Jewish settler land grabs, the United States does nothing to restrain Israel and this fuels conflict across the Middle East. The United States also quietly increased its military presence in Latin America, especially in Colombia, where in tandem with a reinvigorated Colombian government it had some success against the FARC rebels. How did we arrive at this – a highly militaristic power in a peaceful international system?

Creeping imperial expansion in the 1990s

The collapse of the Soviet Union left an enormous American military preponderance in the world. Military expenditures in the former Soviet bloc were slashed, while Europe, Japan and China continued to focus on economic growth. The United States already possessed almost 40 percent of the world's military budget during the 1990s. The 1990s saw what was hyped as the Revolution in Military Affairs (RMA), precision-guided missiles and advanced communications systems. America was so superior militarily to its enemies that it did not really need RMA weapons, but they enabled more fighting at a distance, and this saved American lives. Martin Shaw (2006) calls this "risk-transfer war," transferring the casualty burden from American forces to the enemy, including enemy civilians. Wars need no longer involve mass mobilization for which the consent of the masses would have to be bought. It seemed easier. The temptations toward military aggression were obviously strong amid the climate of naïve triumphalism that swept America in the 1990s.

Since there seemed no threat to the United States, such military preponderance brought forth Secretary of State Madeleine Albright's famous question posed to Joint Chiefs of Staff Chairman Colin Powell in 1995: "What are you saving this superb military for, Colin, if we can't use it?" (Albright, 2003: 182). There might be two responses: downsize the military or use it. Increasingly, the United States used it. At one level we do not need to find elaborate explanations for this. It is what all imperial powers do until they feel they have reached a satiation point. The United States does not yet feel satiated. I have emphasized throughout this volume, together with classical realist theorists, that Great powers will expand if they think they *can* do so. Weaker states are there for the taking if one has the military capacity to do so, accompanying it of course with fine-sounding rhetoric about improving the world. That is what Assyria, Rome, Spain, Britain, France and others had done in the past. Eventually, they became satiated. Rome turned to defensive wall-building, Britain and France began to feel overstretched. But the United States had just seen its main rival collapse, leaving it dominant and armed with risk-transfer militarism lowering American casualties. It was far from feeling satiated, indeed some thought its greatest imperial period was just beginning. The one difference from most previous empires was that the United States was not seeking a direct empire of colonies, but an informal empire of client states.

Thus Bush the Elder and Clinton expanded NATO to the borders of Russia, profiting from East European fears of Russia and desire for American aid. The Americans argued that the purpose of NATO extension was to stabilize democracy and market reform in Eastern Europe (Ikenberry, 2001: 234–9, buys this), yet the peaceful European Union was sufficient for this purpose. The main purpose of NATO expansion was to extend American influence and intimidate Russia. These two administrations also extended U.S. military interventions against so-called rogue states. Tiny Panama was invaded at the order of Bush the Elder in 1989. Its dictator, Manuel Noriega, formerly an employee of the CIA, was behaving egregiously, alienating most Panamanians as well as the United States. There was plenty of local opposition from which the United States could assemble a more popular regime. A swift U.S. invasion quickly established such a regime. The military lesson drawn was that success would result from launching the overwhelming force which the United States possessed. Not the mission creep of Vietnam, better intervene with maximum force immediately. This became the Powell Doctrine, though Powell himself was careful to pair it with a clear exit strategy. The political strategy of having an alternative regime ready was not heeded later on.

The military lesson was visible in the United States-led First Gulf War of 1990–1 launched by Bush the Elder after Saddam Hussein had invaded Kuwait. Unlike the invasion of Panama, denounced by the UN, this one came with both

UN and Arab support since Saddam had flouted international law by invading Kuwait and since the other Gulf states now felt he threatened them too. United States-led forces, almost 400,000 strong, quickly rescued Kuwait and moved into southern Iraq to devastate Iraqi forces exposed in desert terrain. Only 293 U.S. losses were recorded. Then U.S. forces withdrew, leaving Saddam bruised, battered and (it was thought) vulnerable to a military coup. When Saddam nonetheless survived, the United States and Britain began intermittent bombing, enforcing a northern no-fly zone so that Kurds could establish their own regional government.

There were also air-strikes in Yugoslavia, launched by President Clinton, allowing Bosnian Muslims and Croats and Kosovo Albanians to recover their lands from Serb domination. There were no American losses in these ventures, which could be seen as defensive operations rescuing peoples who had suffered aggression. They were not in any obvious sense imperial. U.S. bombing forced Serb President Milosevic to back down, and this precipitated his fall when Russia abandoned him, reluctantly, for it had thought that Serbia lay in its sphere of interest. In reality, Russia no longer had one.

But U.S. success in Yugoslavia had been in tandem with local forces operating on the ground. Croat, Bosniak and Kosovo Albanian forces could take advantage of Serb disarray and recover their lost territories. The United States helped produce what might seem a lamentable solution, a series of ethnically cleansed states in the former Yugoslavia, a project still being completed in Kosovo. Yet this was probably the best solution available when most people had been coerced into seeing their ethnic identity as primary and other ethnicities as enemies (see Mann, 2005: chap. 13). The United States may have found the least bad solution through its limited use of military force. In 1994 Clinton also threatened a Haitian military junta, which in 1991 had overthrown the elected government of Jean-Bertrand Aristide and then refused to step aside. Clinton's motives were mixed, for he also wanted to stem the flow of Haitian refugees streaming into the United States. He sent off a naval invasion force, which was en route to the island when the Haiti military backed down and let Aristide resume office. This did not end Haitian woes, of course. Yet these interventions seemed successful, feeding the confidence that America had military solutions to the world's problems. They were also conducted within defined limits, with local allies, and mostly in response to the aggression of others. These successes were contrasted to the Clinton administration's disastrous little intervention in Somalia in which eighteen U.S. Rangers were killed. But this was intervention by few American troops with no clear goals in a very confused local environment.

These cases were accompanied by rhetoric implying America's right to decide alone when intervention was justified, even though Iraq was invaded under the cloak of UN legitimacy, and the former Yugoslavia under the NATO umbrella. Clinton declared America to be "the indispensable nation" in his election campaign of 1996, while his staffers coined the phrase "multilateralism if we can, unilateralism if we must." Secretary of State Albright declared absurdly "If we have to use force, it is because we are America. We are the indispensable nation. We stand tall. We see further into the future." (cf. Gelb, 2009). She and other Democrats were staking a claim to humanitarian interventionism, military intervention for humanitarian purposes. This included liberal intellectuals like the security expert and Clinton adviser Kenneth Pollack, Paul Berman, a leading liberal hawk, Michael Ignatieff (later leader of the Canadian Liberal Party), and Philip Bobbitt, constitutional law scholar and adviser to both Bush the Elder and Clinton.

Bobbitt's massive book (2001) concluded that if a state is not democratic and does not protect human rights, its "cloak of sovereignty" should no longer protect it from military intervention. Who is to decide whether a state has infringed democracy and human rights? Bobbitt says the UN is not capable of this, since the interest of its members is to protect state sovereignty. The only possible contender is the United States. Immensely powerful, but also democratic and committed to human rights, the United States is the *only* power that combines both the might and the right to attack deviant states. The United States should have immunity in such attacks from international law. The United States is Hobbes' Sovereign, the only power capable of restraining global anarchy. Since more than half the states in the world are neither genuinely democratic nor very respectful of human rights, Bobbitt's theory would place much of the world at risk of American invasion – especially if they have defied the United States, have something the United States wants, or merely occupy a piece of highly strategic turf. The liberal becomes indistinguishable from the neo-conservative.

Democrats argued that in Somalia and Haiti "restoring the democratically elected governments, with military force if necessary, was the morally correct thing to do." Democratic enlargement became the ideal. Clinton's 1996 National Security Strategy used the words democracy or democratic more than 130 times (Chollet & Goldgeier, 2008: 98, 318–9). Republicans were a little more Realist and more likely to justify interventions in terms of the national interest, but they did not oppose the policies. Nobody saw this as aggressive nationalism. The nationalism was more implicit than explicit and the aggression was directed only against despots and their acolytes – or so it was said. It was justified, so argued all American leaders, by America's responsibilities to the world. Nor did the world seem to object. The UN accepted American leadership in these ventures. Russia and China barely demurred, showing no interest in balancing U.S. power – for they could not. Nor could the Europeans. There had never been a single global empire before.

Clinton himself had to be pushed into these interventions. He lacked much interest in foreign policy, except for global trade. Put more positively, he hated war and sought to reduce its casualties. Bombing selected targets from a safe distance became his forte in Yugoslavia and Iraq, while lobbing Tomahawk cruise missiles in the general direction of Bin Laden or Saddam Hussein completed his harder foreign policy (Chollet & Goldgeier, 2008; Hyland, 1999; Cohen, 2005). This was better than war, even if it sometimes hit inoffensive civilians and pharmaceutical factories. Faced with a 9–11 Clinton would probably have invaded Afghanistan and he might have eventually gone to war with Saddam Hussein though not until the Afghan war was over (says Indyk, 2008). As the threat of proliferation of weapons of mass destruction (WMDs) and state support for terrorism loomed larger, Clinton alternated carrots (aid) and sticks (sanctions and threats of war) for Iran and North Korea. With the election of the moderate President Khatami in Iran in 1997, Clinton moved toward the more carrot-oriented policy of the Europeans and Russia. There seemed a possibility of a deal. North Korea and Iraq were more problematic because of enormous mutual suspicions. Republican pressure forced Clinton into harsher measures. Thus when escalation came under Bush the Younger, Democrats were ill-equipped to oppose interventions clothed in the moral mission of bringing democracy to the world.

The rise of the Neo-Cons in the court of Bush the Younger

Once Republicans took control of Congress in 1994 they demanded tougher foreign policy. Through the 1990s conservative Republicans merged with hawkish Scoop Jackson Democrats to become self-styled neo-conservatives urging bigger military budgets and more military interventions, set amid a global mission of bringing democracy to the world. They did not call this imperialism, except allusively, as in the Cheney family Christmas card sent out in 2003 containing some words of Benjamin Franklin: "And if a sparrow cannot fall to the ground without His notice, is it probable that an empire can rise without His aid?" Neo-con pressure, when coupled with the failure of sanctions and bombings to precipitate an Iraqi revolt against Saddam, resulted in 1998 in a Congressional commitment to overthrow him by funding an emigre Iraqi opposition. The Democrats were now trapped. They had escalated the pressure on Saddam, committed themselves to overthrowing him, but had no way of effecting this. They had actually contained Saddam more than they knew, for he had abandoned weapons of mass destruction (WMDs). But realist arguments about containment and offshore-balancing were for foreign policy wonks not the mass media or the public who increasingly accepted the Republican view of Clinton as weak (Cohen, 2005: chap. 5).

Neo-cons could also operate within a broader myth cultivated electorally by the Republicans, that President Reagan had destroyed the evil empire. In Chapter 7 I argued that Soviet bloc citizens, not Americans, had destroyed the Soviet Union, while Reagan himself had contributed more to that destruction after he converted to detente. But the Reagan myth of naïve triumphalism came to dwarf older memories of military hubris in Vietnam. When Bush the Younger took office, among the leading policy-makers only the moderate Secretary of State Colin Powell and his moderate deputy Richard Armitage had fought in Vietnam. The leading administration hawks had evaded the draft to Vietnam, including the president and vice president. It was impossible to get a straight answer from Bush on his own evasion, but the blunter Cheney declared "I had other priorities in the sixties than military service." John Bolton, Bush's ambassador to the UN was even blunter: "I confess I had no desire to die in a Southeast Asian paddy field" (quoted by Packer, 2005: 26). These were chicken-hawks.

Though neo-cons had domestic policies, they focused on foreign policy. They sought a revival of patriotism, a powerful military, and an expansionist foreign policy, which would preempt foreign threats with American aggression. This was imperialism, though few used the I-word. Nor did they even see it as aggression. Kristol, Paul Wolfowitz, Douglas Feith and others proclaimed a mission to spread freedom by military expansion: power with a moral purpose. This mission was espoused especially by intellectuals who did not have administration posts, like the staff of *The Weekly Standard* and the American Enterprise Institute. But they focused on one under-populated, third-rate Middle Eastern power whose tin-pot dictator had long defied the United States, Iraq.

There was no necessary reason why these people should come to dominate American foreign policy. Yet the hawks had three great strokes of luck – more than the fair share of any politician. First, though Al Gore probably won the presidential vote in 2000, the Supreme Court voted along partisan lines to give the presidency to Bush the Younger. I think Gore would not have invaded Iraq. Second, recognizing his own ignorance of foreign policy, Bush asked his experienced running-mate Richard Cheney, former Defense Secretary, to pick his foreign and defense team. By now Cheney was a hawk, regretting his support for the 1991 decision not to carry the U.S. attack in Iraq on to Baghdad. He mostly chose the like-minded. Neither Cheney himself, nor Defense Secretary Donald Rumsfeld, nor National Security Adviser Condoleeza Rice, were really neo-cons. They were less ideological, more hard-nosed. They saw their main mission as increasing American power across the world, though (like all imperialists) they thought this would be a force for good. They had four main beliefs, shared by Bush himself, say Daalder and Lindsay (2003): (1) America should not be constrained by alliances, traditions or friendships; (2) American power should be used for America's benefit – but this would also bring benefit to the world; (3) No strategic equal or competitor should be allowed; (4) America is best protected against threats by preemptive strikes.

It is not easy to categorize President Bush himself, an incurious man who rarely read official reports, ignoring advice based on serious knowledge of facts, preferring to listen to simple advice from a coterie of White House and Pentagon hawks. He repeatedly said of his own actions "I went on instinct."

His Treasury Secretary, Paul O'Neill, thought these qualities indicated an ideologist, since "ideology is a lot easier, because you don't have to know anything or search for anything. You already know the answer to everything. It's not penetrable by facts. It's absolutism." (Suskind, 2004: 165, 292). The White House was taken over by ideologues.

They could count on support from the conservative religious side in America's culture wars. A few Americans believed Jews must occupy the Temple Mount to prepare for the Second Coming of Christ. Far more preferred Judhaism to Islam. I doubt that Bush himself bought into a scenario taken straight from the Book of Revelations, but he did need the votes of the Bible Belt and he himself had been born-again while campaigning across small-town Texas for his father. It is unlikely the religious right was influential in formulating foreign policy. It does not figure in insider accounts of the administration. Yet the president's language added chiliasm to imperialism: good must triumph over evil, God over the devil. In turn this resonated among Republican voters, many of whom were prioritizing moral over material issues, which I try to explain in Chapter 11. Though not many rated foreign policy as a top priority, they did support an American nationalism imposing morality on the world – the Old rather than the New Testament, vengeful Jehovah over Christ the peace-maker, the mirror image of jihadi Islam. Through the 1980s and the 1990s the Republican Party was captured by the religious right in moral matters, by big business conservatives in economic matters, and by hawks in foreign policy. These were distinct political crystallizations, but since Bush the Younger endorsed all their views – perhaps he was the only one who did so – each was given a rather free hand in its own sphere. There was overall unity in this polymorphism. Given the different factions and the confusion of labels here, I prefer to use the term hawks when writing collectively of them rather than neo-cons, Vulcans (James Mann, 2004), or assertive nationalists. They were only implicit nationalists, while this was an imperialism that dared not speak its name.

The Middle East had become the most troubling region and the hawks could build on traditional U.S. policy. As we saw in Chapter 5, earlier administrations from Eisenhower onward had threatened military action against anyone interfering with the free flow of oil to the West. Saddam Hussein had for so long blocked American interests that establishment opposition to the war was muted. Men like Brent Scowcroft and Zbigniew Brzezinsky only objected to the way intervention was conducted. The fact that under Bush the Elder and Clinton Iraq had been contained at rather low cost to the United States cut no ice amid the near-universal desire to have Saddam overthrown and amid confidence in American military-cum-moral power.

Few Americans realized that Middle Eastern states now posed less of a threat than nonstate terrorists. Sunni radicalism had bred jihadi terrorists, ironically nurtured for years by the United States as anticommunist allies. They seemed to pose a significant threat to secular Middle East regimes like Egypt and Algeria in the early 1990s but these regimes had successfully repressed them. The militants fled to more peripheral Muslim countries like Afghanistan, Sudan and the Yemen, and also to Western Europe. There they moved from national terrorism fighting their own country's regime to international terrorism aimed as well at the United States and its Western allies who supported Israel and secular apostate Muslim regimes. Bin Laden had been forced out of the Sudan into Afghanistan. Its Taliban government did not expel him but tried to restrict his activities when Clinton lobbed Cruise missiles into Afghanistan (Ensalaco, 2008: 265).

Yet the imperialists were focused on states not stateless terrorists. The incoming Bush administration immediately began planning an invasion of Iraq. While Clinton had been aware of the dangers of nonstate terrorism, and had taken some steps against Al Qaeda, he had not developed a comprehensive policy. But the incoming Bush team derisively called terrorism a Clinton issue. Cheney, Rice, Rumsfeld and especially Wolfowitz were focused on Iraq, says Richard Clarke (2004), the then White House counterterrorism coordinator. His warnings of terrorist threats were brushed aside and whereas he had enjoyed direct access to Clinton, he never got to see Bush. He did see National Security Adviser Condoleeza Rice but says she ignored his warnings. Treasury Secretary O'Neill remarked of his first National Security Council meeting, ten days into the new administration, that the discussion was all about Iraq and possible invasion (Tenet, 2007: 225–38; Suskind, 2004: 75, 129; cf. Ensalaco, 2008: 242–60; Chollet & Goldgeier, 2008: 310; Gordon & Trainor, 2006: 14–16; Packer, 2005: 39–40; Suskind, 2006: 1–2). Yet all this was in private and until 9–11 the Bush team doubted that overthrowing distant states would be popular among Americans. Foreign policy had not figured much in the election campaigns of 1992, 1996 and 2000. In 2000 Bush had argued against nation-building abroad. Foreign adventures would have to be provoked by evil foreigners.

9–11 was the third great stroke of luck for the hawks. Bush confided to his diary "The Pearl Harbor of the 21st century took place today" (Woodward, 2004: 24). Like Pearl Harbor it could unleash American Empire. It was the chickens coming home to roost, for it had been American foreign policy not American or Western values that had provoked the turning of existing Islamic terrorists focused on local issues against the United States. Osama bin Laden (2005), the figurehead of the al Qaeda terrorist network, made three demands of the United States: removal of American troops from the holy places (in Saudi Arabia); ending mass killing of Iraqi children (through sanctions and bombing raids); and ending support for Zionist expansion, Jewish settlements in Palestine. At other times, he added American support for apostate Muslim regimes and its greed for Arab oil. Other terrorists went through the same repertoire (Ensalaco, 2008, chap. 9; Bergen, 2011).

Islamic terrorism had started with local grievances. The failure of secular Arab Socialist and military regimes had given Islamists their chance to attack these secular, corrupt and authoritarian rulers – what they call the near enemy. Arguing that adherence to Sharia law would bring a Middle Eastern revival, they launched local attacks during the 1990s. But Saddam, Mubarak, and the Algerian military had been too strong for them and their ranks had been decimated by repression. The survivors fled abroad. Some now advocated attacking the "far enemy," the United States and the West, whose commitment to the Middle East they saw as weak. If the United States was forced out, that would undermine the near enemy and Islamist states could be founded. That was the view of the Egyptian Zawahiri, and his influence on bin Laden generated Al Qaeda. Terrorism went global, though jihadis focused on the near enemy always opposed the global strategy (Gerges, 2005). But the far enemy jihadis could now capitalize on widespread hostility to the United States, enough to generate much Muslim support for the 9–11 terrorists. Bin Laden grossly misjudged the American reaction. In an interview with CNN's Peter Bergen in 1997 he had derided U.S. withdrawals from the Lebanon and Somalia when, respectively, only two hundred and twenty of its soldiers were killed. He expected the strike of 9–11 to precipitate U.S. withdrawal from the Middle East (Bergen, 2011). There were major misjudgments all around.

9–11 was an incident without precedent in American history. 3,000 people were killed in an extremely lucky suicide attack on New York and Washington using civilian airliners to demolish buildings symbolizing American power. There was understandable outrage among Americans, as there was abroad. The desire for revenge was the dominant popular emotion. Bush said "My first reaction was outrage. Someone had dared attack America, They were going to pay"(2010: 127). 9–11 made it almost impossible for Democrats to publicly dissent from an aggressive Middle Eastern policy. The Afghan and Iraq wars received overwhelming support in the House and Senate, and so did increasing military budgets. The joint resolution passed by both Houses on 9–14 not only authorized the president "to use all necessary and appropriate force against those nations, organizations or persons" who had perpetrated 9–11 but also authorized him "to prevent any future acts of international terrorism against the United States." This was a blank check indeed. The Kerry and Obama Democratic presidential campaigns of 2004 and 2008 were noticeably light on foreign or military challenges to Republican policy. Democrats had long preferred to focus on what they believed were their strengths – the economy, health care, education, and the environment – while hard geopolitics were left to a Republican agenda.

There was enormous support within America for retaliation against the Taliban, which was harboring Osama Bin Laden, universally assumed to be behind 9–11. I wrote in *Incoherent Empire* (2003: 124) that it would have been better if in the first place the United States had supported a proposal whereby the Taliban would hand Bin Laden over to Pakistan for trial there on terrorism charges. That proposal would have brought more Muslim support for the

United States whether or not the Taliban accepted it. Yet it was not surprising that an enraged American political establishment rejected this and went to war. I doubt a President Gore would have done differently. We humans have emotions, we are not just calculating machines.

Yet more was brewing inside the White House. Paul Wolfowitz, minutes after fleeing his office in the Pentagon on September 11, told aides he suspected Iraqi involvement in the attack. George Tenet, then Director of the CIA, recounts that the day after 9/11, he ran into Richard Perle, the neo-con head of the Defense Policy Board, outside the White House. Perle said: "Iraq has to pay a price for what happened yesterday. They bear responsibility." This, says Tenet, despite the fact, that "the intelligence then and now" showed "no evidence of Iraqi complicity" in the 9/11 attacks (Tenet, 2007: xix). Richard Clark recalled that Bush ordered him to "find a link" to Iraq. Six days after the attack Bush told his War Council "I believe Iraq was involved"; while Wolfowitz urged that this was the opportunity to hit Iraq. According to Bob Woodward the vice president was "hell-bent," a "powerful, steamrolling force" for military intervention in Iraq. But Cheney said little in these meetings (Packer, 2005: 40–4) since he did see that revenge required hitting Afghanistan first. Most of the world's governments supported the invasion of Afghanistan, as they did not support one of Iraq, and Powell also argued strongly against any Iraq adventure. Wolfowitz was overruled. "We won't do Iraq now" concluded the president "we're putting Iraq off. But eventually we'll have to return to that question." It was in less than three months, on November 21, 2001, that Bush ordered Rumsfeld to begin planning for war with Iraq. "Let's get started on this," Bush recalled saying. "And get Tommy Franks looking at what it would take to protect America by removing Saddam Hussein if we have to." Rumsfeld reported every month to Bush on progress (Woodward, 2004: 26)

9–11 and the War on Terror were godsends for the hawks. They could now cultivate a permanent war mentality, which would support their ambitious projects. Rumsfeld compared the war on terror to the "50-years, plus or minus" of the cold war. Secretary of State Powell warned that the war "may never be finished, not in our lifetime." Homeland Security Director Tom Ridge warned that the threat of terrorism "is a permanent condition to which this country must permanently adapt." This climate made it possible for the imperialists to frame military interventions as defense against terror. Better to engage them over there than here, said the president. Some drew analogies with 1898 and 1945: temporary colonies were necessary to create client, democratic regimes and end dictatorship and terrorism (Boot, 2002).

The goals of the invasions

In Afghanistan the objective was simple and as stated: to get Bin Laden and overturn the regime that harbored him. The latter goal was quickly achieved, seemingly reinforcing the case for also hitting Iraq. So in February 2002 Bush ordered General Franks to begin shifting forces from Afghanistan to the Gulf. Next month he interrupted a meeting between Condoleeza Rice, his national security adviser, and three senators with the words "Fuck Saddam. We're taking him out." (Packer, 2005: 45). The then head of Britain's special forces says that in February 2002 the British military were told to begin planning for Iraq (Gilligan, 2009). Blair and Bush discussed the plan on April 6–7 at Bush's Texas ranch and Blair promised British support, though he wanted UN backing too. It was all decided much earlier than either the American or British governments were to claim. But deception is normal in foreign policy.

Opposition within the administration evaporated as Colin Powell dramatically ended his opposition to the Iraq war. Realizing it was inevitable anyway, on February 5, 2003, in the United National General Assembly he gave a transparently false case for the existence of Saddam's WMDs. He asked us to believe that trucks, which in his slides clearly had canvas sides, were carrying chemical weapons across Iraq. The trucks would have whipped up contaminating dust as they trundled across the desert, making chemical weapons unusable! As the Iraqis claimed, the trucks were carrying weather balloons. Nonetheless, despite the derision with which the Assembly greeted Powell's presentation, it was uncritically fed to and received by the American public. Despite sizeable antiwar demonstrations in U.S. cities, 70 percent of Americans agreed that "going to war in Iraq was the right thing to do." Similar numbers believed Saddam Hussein had close ties to Al Qaeda, that he had WMDs, which could hit the United States, and that he had been involved in the planning of the attack of 9–11.

We should not expect mass opposition in such a context. The public generally remains indifferent as international crises germinate and foreign policy tends to be dominated by political elites plus interested pressure groups (Mann, 1988b). American Jews and oil companies played major roles in U.S. policy in the Middle East. I discuss oil later. Jews were influential in urging support for Israel against the Palestinians and contributing negative views of Arabs in general and of Saddam in particular, who donated funds to suicide bombers' families. Some around the administration – Richard Perle, Douglas Feith and Elliot Abrams especially – seem to have favored overthrowing Saddam because it would be good for Israel (Packer, 2005: 32). But once a government declares that a crisis has erupted, popular nationalist emotions tend to explode. The political leadership wraps itself in the flag, stresses the danger to the country, and manipulates information flows to an ignorant electorate. Administrations perceive electoral utility in a good war – one they can easily win. They normally exaggerate the real threat by trading on stereotypes of menacing foreigners, exploiting their monopoly of the means of domestic communication regarding far-off lands. In 1939 Hitler invented Polish attacks on Germans along the border; in 1964 the United States invented the second Gulf of Tonkin incident to justify war in Vietnam. The Japanese government justified Pearl Harbor as a response to the strangulation of Japan by U.S. trade and oil embargoes. Bush the Younger invented links between Al Qaeda, Saddam Hussein and Iran and greatly inflated the WMDs that Saddam might posses.

Saddam Hussein was indeed a cruel dictator, and he might have had a few WMDs. Saddam did not have links to terrorists, yet few Americans knew that he espoused secular Arab nationalism, and so was hated by Al Qaeda and others. The Shi'a ayatollahs in Iran also despised the Sunni al Qaeda and the Taliban. It was wildly unlikely that Khomeini Shi'as, Ba'athist Arab nationalists, and Sunni al Qaeda would collaborate and share deadly technology. The administration especially exaggerated Saddam's threat to the world, and skeptics (like me) were denounced as unpatriotic or antisemitic.[1] Saddam contributed greatly to his own downfall by bluffing that he did have WMDs – a very big mistake. On neither side did reason prevail.

Underlying the administration's, and indeed most Americans' responses was overconfidence. American patriots in Congress and in bars routinely proclaim the United States to be the greatest country in the world and by greatness they mean it has both might and right on its side. The memory of Vietnam had been obliterated by triumphs against the Soviet Union and lesser enemies in the 1990s, followed by seeming Afghan success (in reality it was far from that). Few expected Iraq to be a difficult war. They did not think it would last long and they did not think they themselves would be asked to make significant sacrifices. They were imbued with what I have described as spectator-sport militarism, cheering on their team from the side-lines without having to make sacrifices themselves (Mann, 1988b).

If the enemy backs down or the war is quickly won, the legitimacy of the regime is enhanced and elections can be won – as Mrs. Thatcher had proved in the Falklands/Malvinas War. If war endures longer, emotional commitment gradually diminishes. If war seems to be going badly, the response will vary according to whether the war is perceived as in genuine defense of the homeland or as a war of choice, where one can choose to desist without dire consequences. Thus, even when things seemed very bad, the commitment of the British, Russian, German and Japanese populations in World War II remained strong, whereas the British over several centuries and Americans in the period 1898–1902 could choose to engage and then disengage from colonial wars, and the United States could also turn against engagement in Vietnam – and Iraq.

The Bush administration purged the military, State, and the CIA, dismissing or side-lining critics and even those who wrote balanced reports on looming difficulties. These were labeled defeatists. Enemies were seen everywhere, inside the administration, among liberals, and across the Muslim world. In the

---

[1] My own views at the beginning of 2003 on the likely disaster that would ensue in Iraq and Afghanistan were expressed in *Incoherent Empire*.

neo-con book of Richard Perle and David Frum (who coined the phrase axis of evil), Muslim states are seen as hostile, but so too are the Pentagon, he CIA and the State Department. They recommend purges for all (2003: 194–228). The hawks succeeded in finding compliant replacements (Gordon & Trainor, 2006; Tenet, 2007). With so much skepticism coming from the State Department, the hawks ignored it. Disgusted with the CIA, they set up their own intelligence agency, the Office of Special Plans, operating out of Cheney's office under the direction of Douglas Feith. He provided intelligence reports confirming their ideological predilections. Feith's Gestapo Office, Powell called it (Woodward, 2004: 292; Packer, 2005: chap. 4). This was a conspiracy, a few key players acting secretively, doctoring intelligence, concealing motives, and feeding Americans false information.

It is difficult to know whether the reasons given for the invasion of Iraq were ideology-driven mistakes, wish fulfillment, or lies rationalized as the ends justify the means. That their allegations about Saddam's WMDs were grossly exaggerated was known to the CIA and its Director Tenet (Tenet, 2007: 321). Wolfowitz admitted that "for reasons that have a lot to do with the U.S. government bureaucracy, we settled on the one issue that everyone could agree on, which was weapons of mass destruction" (Packer, 2005: 60). When I read widely in 2002 in preparation for my book *Incoherent Empire* (2003), I found that most experts suspected Saddam might have a few short-range rockets and some barrels of chemical weapons, which by then were probably degraded and unusable. Defenders of the invasion (e.g., Bush himself, 2010: 262, 268–9; James, 2006: 108–9) claim that most knowledgeable Americans believed there was a significant risk of Saddam unleashing WMDs. This was not true. The UN weapons inspectors had found hardly anything over several years' diligent searching. Postinvasion U.S. searches turned up nothing at all. The claimed links between Saddam and al Qaeda and 9–11 were simply absurd. They may have been lies though it may be more likely that the imperialists wanted the invasion so badly they jumped at every straw – the wish fulfillment alternative.

That was probably true of Bush himself, who only read what the hawks wanted him to read. In his memoirs (2010) he says "One intelligence report summarized the problem: 'Since the end of inspections in 1998, Saddam has maintained the chemical weapons effort, energized the missile program, made a bigger investment in biological weapons, and has begun to try to move forward in the nuclear area' " (2010: 229). This probably reveals he saw only doctored reports. The only evidence Bush ever offered at the time for the relations between Iraqi WMDs and Al Qaeda was based on the interrogation of a Libyan militant, yet the Defense Intelligence Agency and the C.I.A. had both concluded his evidence was fabricated – well before the president used it publicly (Bergen, 2011). Afterward, when nothing was found, Bush blamed false intelligence. Had he bothered to read even documents in the public realm, he would not have been so misled. He comments pathetically "no one was more shocked or angry than I was when we didn't find the weapons. I had a sickening feeling every time I thought about it. I still do." (Bush, 2010: 262).

Tenet is loyal to his president and polite about the vice president, saying only that his bellicose speeches about Saddam "exceeded available intelligence." He is ruder on Wolfowitz, Feith and their staffs, who he says circulated pseudointelligence reports, "Feith-based analysis," at odds with those of the professionals (2007: 348). The intelligence agencies wrote reports dismissing allegations of meetings between the 9–11 hijacker leader Mohammed Atta and an Iraqi agent in Prague, and allegations of Saddam's supposed attempts to buy uranium and tubes for nuclear centrifuges from Niger. But the president, the vice president and others just ignored the agencies and continued making the allegations. The vice president said, rather remarkably, "It's not about our analysis, or finding a preponderance of evidence. It's about our response." (Suskind, 2006: 308). Condoleeza Rice lied at least twice. She testified that the White House was on high alert against terrorism even before 9/11, and she assured us that "the United States has not transported anyone, and will not transport anyone, to a country when we believe he will be tortured" – both "demonstrably false" (says Bergen, 2011).

Abu Zubaydah, a deranged low-level Al Qaeda helper was labeled by the president as Al Qaeda's chief of operations. He was repeatedly tortured and so revealed many imaginary plots. He wrote a diary in prison in which he adopted three different schizophrenic voices. This induced the top CIA official dealing with Al Qaeda to say to a colleague "this man is insane, certifiable, split personality." Word got out of this and the president turned on the CIA Director, saying "I said he was important. You're not going to let me lose face on this, are you?" "No sir, Mr. President," responded Tenet obediently, since the president had let him keep his job even after 9–11 (Suskind, 2006: 99–100). Fear of losing face is of perennial importance in geopolitics, as we have seen.

After the war, when no weapons and no links to al Qaeda were found, the public justification shifted to bringing democracy to Iraq – though for some neo-cons this had always been an important motive. Yet the chances of bringing democracy to Iraq were slim. Quantitative studies of attempts to export democracy by force do not offer much cheer. In all U.S. interventions in the twentieth and twenty-first centuries, the failure-rate in bringing even a modest level of democracy (the level of Polity Score +4 used by political scientists, of which Iran until 2011 was an example) was 60 percent–70 percent, worse than even odds. Most of the successes came just after 1945 in countries with existing democratic traditions, like Germany and Italy, or in Central American cases in the 1990s when the regional tide of democratization was strong anyway. With countries like Iraq or Afghanistan, lacking democratic traditions, the prospects were near-zero – with recent examples like Somalia or Haiti in mind (Coyne, 2007). Peceny (1999) offers a glimmer of hope from his analysis of cases of intervention. Where the United States intervenes with the intention of introducing liberal reforms, some liberalization tends on balance to occur but only where other conditions are favorable. Favorable conditions do not include the prevalence of ethnic/religious conflict as found in these two countries. If the goal was democratization across the Middle East, it would be much better to start with Egypt or Jordan or some of the small Gulf states, in which middle-class opposition movements and some limited elections existed. In any case in Iraq rhetoric about democracy was not backed up by a plan for actually installing it.

Ultimately none of these given reasons were really what mattered. Saddam was chosen as the first victim for three other reasons.

(1)   Because he was already available as a man who had defied and supposedly humiliated the United States and so been vilified to the American people for a decade. Revenge was desired both by the Bush administration and by many Americans, to reassert their imperial status.

(2)   Not because he was strong and dangerous, but because he was weak, debilitated by the 1991 Gulf War and then by sanctions and bombings. He was a hated yet easy target, a good example to all enemies of what would happen if you defied the United States. Wolfowitz said this openly – this was why he considered Iraq more doable than Afghanistan (Woodward, 2004: 21; Suskind, 2004: 187–8). That Saddam had also defied the United States so openly was felt as a humiliation. In order to maintain U.S. credibility as a super-power, the hawks felt they had to destroy him. Yet again, status mattered in geopolitics. There was only one way left to destroy him, the others had failed.

(3)   In the climate of enhanced support for Israel and the war against terror, the hawks had become unhappy with the Saudi alliance. They detested the Saudi Wahhabi brand of Islam, which was financing madrassah schools devoted to teaching the Koran. They were considered to be a breeding-ground for terrorists. This was an exaggerated fear and the Saudis hated both Shi'ite Iran and radical Sunni movements like al Qaeda, who threatened them as much as the United States. But it was a very high-risk strategy to think of replacing Saudi with Iraqi oil. There was less of it, it would take over a decade to develop, and the Iraqis would not have the price flexibility that the Saudis had manipulated to the interests of the United States.

Yet the neo-cons were supremely confident that the tide of history and American military power made them invincible, and by claiming that the Democrats were weak, the Republicans had virtually forced themselves into an invasion to maintain U.S. imperial credibility. This war was mostly about maintaining imperial status, backed by confidence in military power. Material goals concerning oil came only through their prism.

How did our oil get under their sand?

However, there was oil. In 1991 a war in Iraq had resulted when Saddam invaded Kuwait, a sovereign country, so acquiring much greater oil resources.

That war was at bottom about oil. In 2003 one of the main reasons for invading Iraq was obviously oil. It has the second-biggest oil reserves in the world, after Saudi Arabia. In 1991 Saddam had invaded Kuwait angered by Kuwait exceeding its agreed oil export quota, which reduced the price he could get for his oil. Then Bush the Elder had publicly declared "We cannot permit a resource so vital to be dominated by one so ruthless" (Ensalaco, 2008: 188). Vice President Cheney's Energy Task Force Report of 2001 also identified Saddam Hussein as "a destabilizing influence to U.S. allies in the Middle East, as well as to regional and global order, and to the flow of oil to international markets." Its recommended policies included a potential "need for military intervention. "By now the U.S. Fifth Fleet, based in Bahrain, was spending most of its time patrolling the Straits of Hormuz, guaranteeing this vital shipping lane for the free flow of oil. Bush had also added military advisers in Georgia and a rapid-reaction force in Kazakhstan to protect oil and natural gas reserves in the Caucasus and Caspian Sea (Klare, 2004: chaps. 3 & 4).

The Bush team did discuss oil in Iraq in private. If Iraq had not had oil, it would probably have escaped invasion, even though Afghanistan was also invaded and it did not have oil, or indeed anything of value – unless the United States followed the example of the British Empire and start mass production of opium. The United States invaded Afghanistan because it contained Bin Laden and the Taliban and U.S. leaders wanted revenge on them to reassert imperial status. Iraq was invaded because it had both oil and Saddam Hussein – evil, defiant, a source of supposed status humiliation for American leaders, yet easy to knock over and replace with a client state.

Yet oil is an economic resource with a price. This would seem to invite rational calculation. The most rational way to get oil might be to either befriend Saddam or, at least, not to let ideological conflict interfere with market terms. The contrast with Venezuela is striking. The United States is the biggest importer of Venezuelan oil despite hostile rhetoric thrown between the two countries. Saddam, like President Hugo Chavez in Venezuela, had every incentive to sell his oil, and Americans to buy it. But Saddam had invaded Kuwait and the United States then spent ten years sanctioning and bombing him. It was difficult for any American politician to ignore his bad points for the sake of buying his oil. Admitting that real politik should triumph over morality is especially difficult for empires that trumpet their noble mission to the world. But that would mean that these motives are thicker than oil.

The United States only gets 10 percent of its oil from the Middle East. It depends much less on it than do the Europeans, Chinese or Japanese, who have managed their access to Middle Eastern oil by peaceful bi-lateral agreements with the producer countries. Of course, they don't have the military power to do otherwise. Some think that the oil motive was to deprive America's economic rivals of oil. Harvey says "whoever controls the Middle East controls the global oil spigot, and whoever controls the global oil spigot controls the global economy." Faced with greater global competition, he says, "what better way for the U.S. to ward off that competition and secure its own hegemonic condition than to control the price, conditions and distribution for they key economic resource upon which its competitors rely?" (Harvey, 2003: 19, 25). This is not plausible. Remember what happened in 1940 when the United States cut off Japan from the global spigot. The immediate consequence was that Japan went for broke, for war. For the United States to do it now would be virtually an act of war. It would break up NATO and cause China to be much more aggressive in seeking oil. It would break with America's traditional pursuit of open markets. But if, nevertheless, this was the American motive, it would not need an invasion of Iraq. It could turn off the spigot merely by air and sea military power, without an invasion (Brenner, 2006b).

It is true that in the Middle East U.S. oil politics had never gone strictly along market lines. The securitization of oil, its conversion into a matter of national security, was by now traditional, and national security for the United States meant military intervention as the default mode of diplomacy. The United States had for a long time done deals with the oil producers against the Soviets. Then it allied with Saddam, lining him up as an ally to balance against Iran, another major oil producer. Now the United States was allied only to a Saudi Arabia disliked by the neo-cons plus the small Gulf States perhaps vulnerable to insurrection, against both Iraq and Iran. This offshore balancing might have seemed a little imbalanced. Throughout this volume, as in Volume 2 (1993: 33) I have distinguished between market and territorial conceptions of profit. One might seek profit through market advantage or through authoritative control of territory, in extremis by war and empire. We have seen the latter pursued by the British, the Japanese and even the Americans in earlier periods. Were they doing it again here? The plan might be to invade Iraq to make it a strategic ally for its oil. But if national security and geopolitics were important we should add other motives: to better protect Israel, to intimidate Russia and China, to make America's allies grateful for guaranteeing their oil, and to transfer America's Middle East military bases from Saudi Arabia, whose future seemed uncertain, to the new client state of Iraq. Many of the hawks exaggerated the Saudis' support for terrorism (by way of financing madrassa schools)and wanted to be free of Saudi Arabia. In this scenario material desire for oil plays a role but entwined with strategic and imperial motives. This is more likely.

However, Vice President Cheney did think a lot about Iraqi oil. His energy task force drew up maps of the Iraqi oil-fields indicating which companies controlled them all. There were several meetings between the task force and American and British oil industry chiefs. The Americans denied this but leaked secret service documents confirm the meetings, while the former head of Conoco did admit attending. Some critics conclude that they involved a conspiracy between the administration and the oil industry to invade Iraq (Juhazs,

2006). But the evidence indicates a more complex picture, for two rival plans were competing, imperialist hawks and neoliberals supporting one plan, the oil magnates the other.

The first policy originated in the document "Moving the Iraqi Economy from Recovery to Sustainable Growth," produced by the Treasury Department with help on Iraq from USAID. This document was then reworked in 2003 by an American consultancy firm to become a neoliberal structural adjustment program similar to those discussed in Chapter 6. Paul Bremer wrote much of it into his draft Orders, which became Iraq's laws during his reign as proconsul. The draft included the privatization of all state industries except oil. Foreigners could own 100 percent of any other enterprise and repatriate all the profits abroad. Taxes on business and labor union rights were both lowered, markets strengthened, and foreigners were given immunity from prosecutions for infractions within Iraq. Bremer himself regarded political and market freedoms as identical, typical of neoliberals (Juhazs, 2006: chap. 6; Bremer, 2006). Some of his Orders were written into the Iraqi Constitution, but hostile Iraqi lawmakers blocked implementation. At the end of 2009 Iraq still had 240 state owned factories employing between 100 and 4,000 workers each and the minister of industry and minerals said there would be no privatizations until after 2012, while utilities such as water and electricity, and industries such as cigarette manufacturing would not be privatized at all. He preferred joint ventures between Iraqi state industries and foreign private business, and most of these deals have been with non-American firms (Reuters, July 28, 2009). Like most aspects of the occupation the neoliberal bonanza proved disappointing.

Nonetheless, before the invasion, the hawks expected that after victory foreign oil companies would begin pumping enough oil to pay for the occupation. This would also cause the global price of oil to fall, weakening OPEC, Iran and Saudi Arabia alike. Regimes might fall, replaced by a blend of American domination and democracy (Perle & Frum, 2003). But the major oil companies were in any case horrified by this plan. Any collapse in prices would slash their profits, and they were appalled by the notion that the United States might undermine OPEC. Their whole business strategy was to divide the spoils with the oil producing states, not undermine them. They didn't even mind Iraqi oil being kept under the ground for future use. As the occupation failed and violence dragged on, oil supplies remained disrupted while demand increased, increasing profits. Obviously the oil companies had not planned this. But they had stalled Bremer's privatization program by placing a former CEO of Shell Oil USA, Philip Carroll, as head of Iraqi oil resources. As he later told the BBC "There was to be no privatization of Iraqi oil resources or facilities while I was involved." He saw privatization as pure ideology. The oil industry's rival plan, spearheaded by Carroll, was to form a single nationalized Iraqi Oil Company, which would then act as a responsible member of OPEC. This was pitting

neoliberals and imperialists seeking radical change against industry conservatives who wanted to keep things as they were (Greg Palast, *BBC Newsnight
Report*, March 17, 2005).

Stalemate between Big Oil and the neoliberals/imperialists helped empower
the new Iraqi government to insist upon state ownership of the oil fields. This
was the first policy area in which the new government showed it was not just
a U.S. stooge. An Iraqi state oil company owns the oil but the oil companies
produce the oil and develop new fields, in return for a royalty of $2 paid to
the government for every barrel sold. Auctioning off the rights to the oil-fields
started in December 2009. The first buyers were mainly European, Chinese
and Russian, not American oil companies. Not yet settled are the conflicting
claims to ownership of the oil by the Shia, Sunni and Kurdish communities in
Iraq. That remains deeply controversial.

It was not immediate oil profit that helped initiate the invasion but regional
strategic visions. These involved oil, but set within an imperial strategy advocated by the hawks, not the oil industry, which favored continuity and stability.
The hawks believed that shown the might of the super-power in Iraq, other
rogue states would cave in; if not, they could be confronted too. Rumsfeld
stressed the demonstration effect of Iraq (Gordon & Trainor, 2006: 4, 19, 131;
Suskind, 2004: 85–6, 187). The president labeled Iraq, Iran and North Korea
as the other axis of evil countries, but Syria, Libya and Cuba were also given
warnings. General Wesley Clark (2007) says that a senior general told him less
than two weeks after 9–11 that the administration had decided to attack Iraq.
Six weeks later, he met the same general and asked if the Iraq plan remained
active. The reply came: "Oh, it's worse than that ... Here's the paper from the
Office of the Secretary of Defense outlining the strategy. We're going to take
out seven countries in five years.' He named them, starting with Iraq and Syria
and ending with Iran." General Clark later responded to my question by adding that the other four were Lebanon, Libya, Somalia and Sudan. There would
be punitive restructuring of the Middle East, followed by its rebirth as Muslim
states became peaceful, democratic and Israel-tolerant, under American tutelage. In 2011 Defense Secretary Gates seemed to give some discrete support to
this claim by hinting that he had restrained Bush from more aggressive policy
toward Iran.

This was imperialism on an unprecedented scale. The Afghan and Iraq invasions marked a reversal of the historic drift of the United States toward milder
forms of domination. Now the United States was escalating back up the hierarchy of domination, from informal imperialism, through proxies, into massive
military intervention. 300, 000 troops were assembled to support the invasion
of Iraq and 150,000 occupied the country for six years. The troops stayed for
so long that Iraq and Afghanistan were in effect temporary colonies. O'Reilly
(2008) and Porter (2006) claim this was direct empire, but the intention was
always to leave soon, leaving a friendly client regime in place.

The invasion and occupation of Iraq

The way the Iraq invasion was conducted was also unprecedented. Quite different was the unilateralism. First, there were virtually no foreign allies. Though various countries participated nominally, only the British had rules of engagement permitting the use of their troops in all combat situations. And though most Middle Eastern states were privately pleased Saddam Hussein was being taken out, they offered no visible support. The Americans and British were on their own. Bush appreciated Blair, telling Blair's principal adviser, "Your man has got *cojones*" – still little boys in the playground. Some normal allies, like France and Germany and later Spain, opposed the intervention. Whenever Americans turned nasty – at Fallujah, at Guantanamo Bay, at Abu Ghraib and in torture and extraordinary rendition across the world, it lost further legitimacy, especially since all these excepting Abu Ghraib were defended by the highest levels of the administration. It can be retorted that an empire has only to be feared, not liked. But as we have seen, America has often enjoyed legitimate hegemony. This was being ideologically undermined by actions that made any moral claims difficult to sustain. Can an administration that tortures and defies Geneva Conventions be trusted to spread democracy? Since the advanced countries cannot contest U.S. leadership, their disgust may not matter much. But the destruction of American prestige across the Muslim world was more damaging, encouraging many terrorists into thinking *they* occupied the moral high ground. America lacked real ideological power.

The second aspect of unilateralism was more immediately damaging: the absence of significant local allies on the ground, apart from Kurdish forces in the North. Some American generals hoped that entire Iraqi army units might come over to their side and then fight for them, but they had not secured the cooperation of a single Iraqi officer in advance, and this did not happen. Hopes of an army of thousands of Iraqi exile freedom fighters also faded before the actual invasion. Only seventy-three Iraqi exiles went through the training that made them ready for action (Gordon & Trainor, 2006: 105–6). In all previous interventions since World War II (apart from the fiascos at the Bay of Pigs and Somalia) the United States had counted on significant local allies. As we saw in previous chapters, these were usually the military plus either the upper classes or particular ethnic groups. In the former Yugoslavia the allies were Croatian, Bosnian and Kosovo Albanian forces and they were the ones who captured territory on the ground. Even in Afghanistan there were allies in the shape of the Northern Alliance plus various discontented tribal leaders. There were very few exiled Iraqi leaders with the Americans and the reliance on one rather dubious character, Ahmed Chalabi, seemed pathetic. CIA Director Tenet remarked "You had the impression that some office of the vice president and DOD. reps. were writing Chalabi's name over and over again in their notes, like schoolgirls with their first crush" (2007: 440). Chalabi exploited this with fake intelligence supplied directly to his friends in the Pentagon and White House, bypassing the intelligence professionals (Bergen, 2011).

This was not incompetence in the securing of allies, since there were none available, except for the Kurds. Local allies had been getting more difficult to find through the twentieth century as nationalism became the legitimating principle of political power. Being a traitor to the nation – or alternatively in this case, to Islam – an uncommon sentiment in the nineteenth century, was now a significant deterrent to disaffected local elites against joining in on the imperial side. Empire was getting more difficult. Class allies had been dominant in Asia and Latin America, as we saw in Volume 3, Chapter 3 and this volume, Chapter 5, but were not appropriate to Iraq, where there was neither a military nor a capitalist class independent of Saddam, and nor was there a popular insurgent movement. Only ethnic/religious conflicts could potentially bring forth allies, though allying with one group to attack another was hardly conducive to social peace after the intervention. Iraq was a good example of this. Kurdish nationalists were keen to ally with the United States, for they rightly saw this as an opportunity to create their own state. The Shi'a/Sunni religious divide might also enable the Shi'a to seize control of the Iraqi state from Saddam's Sunni-based regime. However, at the time of the invasion neither the Shi'a nor the Americans thought in these terms, the Shi'a because negotiations if leaked would incur reprisals from Saddam, the Americans because they would have had to negotiate through Shi'a Iran, an enemy. After the invasion the two did gradually become allies, which then fueled the Sunni insurgency. Adding to the quagmire, several strands of antiimperialism surfaced – a rather secular Iraqi nationalism, a pan-Arab solidarity and an even broader sense of Islamic solidarity. As with earlier anticolonialism, nationalism was not actually the main driver. But it was clear that the United States lacked ideological and political power for the imperial venture on which it had embarked.

Shadid (2005: 280–8) interviewed Iraqi combatants, both insurgents fighting against the United States and Iraqis fighting with the United States. By now most opposed the United States out of a sense of national pride and honor, coupled with distrust of Western colonialism and America's unswerving support for Israel. These diverse sentiments could be rolled up together in Islam: "We" were Muslims, "They" were infidel imperialists. But whereas the insurgents voiced ideological reasons for fighting, those helping the Americans said they did so for the wages. "Should I sleep without dinner and not work with the Americans? No. I should work with the Americans and have dinner." Denounced as infidels by the local clergy, they wryly responded "They pay us and we'll stop working with the Americans." They were fearful of retribution from their communities. Only the Kurds were committed allies. In realist power terms that was the main reason why the Americans should not have invaded.

This was also the main reason why the size of the American occupying force was too small. Cheney, Rumsfeld, Wolfowitz and Feith believed a light force of

120,000 American soldiers would suffice. They were proved right for defeating the Iraqi Army. But for subsequent occupation, pacification and rebuilding, the absence of allies required an enormous number of Americans. In his memoir, Ambassador Bremer, the proconsul of Iraq from May 2003 to May 2004 says he asked for many more troops, but to no avail. An occupying force of 250,000 (suggested by dissident generals) might have been sustainable for a time. Yet a RAND Corporation report thought 500,000 might be necessary, and that would have required reintroducing conscription, which would be deeply unpopular and might even destroy the whole operation. But it was putting an inappropriate political burden on its armed forces.

In any case the administration barely planned for the aftermath. British officers complained of the lack of American planning (Gilligan, 2009). American officials in Iraq interviewed by Ferguson (2008) say that there was no plan at all and their own attempts to devise plans were thwarted by ideologues in Washington (we see later that there was an oil plan). Actually, plans had been hatched very late in the day within the Pentagon. Invasion preparations had taken eighteen months, postwar planning began only two months before the invasion. The State Department, with the only officials experienced in the Middle East, was side-lined, but the Pentagon starved its own planning officers of resources and influence in the White House. Rumsfeld had his own policy team, derisively termed "the black hole" by one Joint Staff officer. " We'll know what we're going to do when we get there," said Jay Garner, the ex-general designated at the last minute to head the occupation administration (Gordon & Trainor, 2006: chap. 8, quotes from pp 142, 152, 157). The army assumed government would be turned immediately over to Iraqis (Wright & Reese, 2008: 25–8). The military was told to make plans for a draw-down of U.S. troops within a few months of Saddam's fall.

The Bush administration thought the Iraqis would welcome them with sweets and flowers, security would be turned over to friendly Iraqi police and army units, government institutions would remain intact, and a friendly government would promptly form. The model was perhaps from Eastern Europe in 1989: "topple the leader, pull down his statue, and let civil society take over" (Kopstein, 2006: 88). Assistant Defense Secretary Paul Wolfowitz testified to Congress that the costs of the invasion would be paid with oil money. Barbara Bodine, Garner's deputy, said she was told "we were going to be out of there in a couple of months." This was then prolonged to the end of August, four and a half months after the fall of Baghdad. Rumsfeld's spokesman said "we will be out of there in three to four months" (Ferguson, 2008: 88; Packer, 2005: 132–3; Gordon & Trainor, 2006: 162, 463–4). The "plan" was get out quick.

The political scientist Larry Diamond served in the civilian administration. He observed that to build a democracy in Iraq, "the first lesson is that we cannot get to Jefferson and Maddison without going through Thomas Hobbes. You can't build a democratic state unless you first have a state, and the essential condition for a state is that it must have an effective monopoly over the means of violence." (2005: 305). Saddam had been a rather dark Hobbesian sovereign but the United States tore him down without putting much in his place. Communications, electricity, and water supplies were devastated, ministries and police stations were deserted. Garner could not even communicate with his officials across town, let alone keep public order.

An orgy of looting swept the cities with U.S. troops gazing on from the side-lines, seemingly preoccupied with guarding the Oil Ministry and Garner's officials. Thousands joined in a highly professional looting of Baghdad, which began April 9, 2003, the day Saddam's regime ceased to function. At least sixteen of the twenty-three ministries were gutted, as were police stations, hospitals, schools and food distribution centers. Equipment was stripped from power plants, delaying the restoration of electricity to Baghdad. American occupation officials estimated the cost of the looting at $12 billion, equaling projected Iraq oil revenues for the year after the war (Packer, 2005: 139). The idea of paying the costs of invasion out of oil revenue would have to wait awhile. In fact, postinvasion oil profits were never sufficient for this.

Most officials and many army officers in Iraq felt the army should have stopped the looting. It remains unclear why they did not try. Their hi-tech weaponry was ill-suited to policing, but Barbara Bodine adds that "the needs of the average Iraqi simply were not that high on our priority list. That was the day that their... caution turned to skepticism about our commitment to them (Ferguson, 2008: 138). Rumsfeld's response made it worse: "Freedom's untidy," he declared, "free people are free to make mistakes and commit crimes and do bad things. They're also free to live their lives and do wonderful things. And that's what's going to happen here." "Stuff happens," he added by way of consolation. Packer (2005: 136–7) comments: "The defense secretary looked upon anarchy and saw the early stages of democracy. In his view and that of others in the administration freedom was the absence of constraint. Freedom existed in divinely endowed human nature, not in man-made institutions and laws. Remove a thirty-five-year-old tyranny and democracy will grow in its place." This is the neoliberal theory of politics – simply remove despotism and they will flower again. No sociologist would agree.

In May 2003, Bremer compounded the problem by two decisions, one political, one military. There was radical de-Ba'athification as those in the top four levels of the ruling Ba'ath Party were banned from holding public office. They amounted to between 30,000 and 50,000 people. All lower level Ba'athists had to pass stringent vetting procedures, which took a long time, harming administrative efficiency. So many sacked officials joined the insurgency, accompanied by other Sunnis who perceived that this policy ensured Shi'a and Kurdish dominance. General Garner told Ferguson his policy had been to selectively purge only in the top two levels (about six thousand people) and Bodine said they were more worried about corrupt and incompetent officials than Ba'athists. Douglas Feith in Washington wrote the de-Ba'athification Order and Rumsfeld, Wolfowitz, and Cheney backed him up. The president also did after Bremer notified him (when Bush later tried to deny this, an infuriated Bremer released the relevant letters). But Powell, Rice, the National Security Council principals and the generals had not been consulted. In Iraq Garner, CIA officials, and most generals were furious, some calling it madness. Chalabi was the man implementing the policy in Iraq and he had a vested interest in wholesale purging (Gordon & Trainor, 2006: 475–85; Tenet, 2007: 426–30; Ferguson, 2008: chap. 5; Bremer, 2006: 39–42, 53–9). The U.S. lack of political power worsened.

The second woeful decision was to disband the Iraqi army. More than half a million men, more than 7 percent of the national labor force, lost their jobs – but not their guns. Many joined the insurgency. Most U.S. officials and most Iraqis wanted the disbandment of the dreaded Security Police and the Republican Guards, but not the regular army. They knew that soldiers had obeyed Saddam's orders or were shot. Here the disbandment decision seems to have been taken by three people, Bremer, his main security adviser, Walter Slocombe, and Rumsfeld, though Bush immediately approved it, if in vague terms. Others were surprised and mostly appalled. They had expected to recall much of the Iraqi army, and a list of more than 100,000 acceptable soldiers had been prepared (Ferguson, 2008: chap. 6). Since it would take years to train a new force, it would be impossible to leave in three to four months. Developing local military power would take a lot longer. Bush later conceded these were mistakes (2010: 259).

Most have been struck by the incompetence of the Bush administration in making these two political and military decisions, to do the job without the Iraqi army, and without Ba'athist administrators. But they were not just mistakes. Together with the failure to bother about local allies they were all of a piece. They revealed great imperial arrogance. First came the assumption that U.S. armed forces could conquer, pacify, and create a *tabula rasa*, a blank slate, from which benign institutions would rise up in a country with a vastly different culture. Second came the assumption that the American values of freedom and democracy would somehow outweigh in Iraqi minds all the horrors of foreign invasion and occupation. This revealed both an ignorance of the necessary conditions for democracy (including the secure provision of public order) and an inability to empathize with a defeated people. Most occupation staff had no local knowledge. They were ex- Washington lobbyists, Congressional staffers, and public- relations specialists – enthusiastic Republicans but without any knowledge of Iraq or Islam. They were carpet-baggers, not settlers. Once again the United States lacked Americans who wanted to settle down in such a place. An empire without settlers needs friendship from much of the local population, but this could not be achieved. Once in Iraq they rarely dared stray out of the Green Zone, the U.S. fortress in Baghdad. The Americans visible to most Iraqis were heavily armored soldiers and military contractors. They could not win Iraqi hearts and minds (Shadid, 2005: 260–1). Since the United States lacked the ideological as well as the political power necessary for the intended light imperial policy, the American imprint had to be much heavier. But though military power can destroy, it can rarely construct.

Costs and benefits of the invasion

And so the death-toll was enormous. The increasing technological disjunction between the United States and its enemies generated "risk-transfer militarism" whereby the United States could transfer the risks of war from its own soldiers to enemy forces and civilians. U.S. bombing in Afghanistan had probably killed about three thousand civilians – though as in earlier colonial wars, native deaths were not counted. In Iraq the wave of shock-and-awe bombing was followed by intermittent repressed rebellions, suicide bombings and fire-fights involving indiscriminate firing by edgy, frightened American and British soldiers.

No one knows how many died. The United States has never released data on Iraqi casualties while the Muslim requirement that the dead be buried within twenty-four hours means that many deaths are unrecorded. The Iraqi Health Ministry came up with an estimate of 150,000 but this counted only those taken to hospitals and morgues. The NGO Iraq Body Count has carefully counted deaths reported in English-language journalistic sources, and that total comes to about a hundred thousand, but since English is not the language of Iraq this must be a gross undercount. In 2010 Wikileaks released 400,000 classified U.S. military logs from Iraq covering the period January 2004 to January 2010. These detail 109, 000 deaths witnessed by U.S. troops, 65 percent of them civilians. This too must be an undercount, since U.S. forces could not see everything. This convergence of estimates around 100,000 has persuaded most journalists to settle on this as the total. Yet it must be far too low.

A survey of deaths in Iraqi households as a result of the war conducted by a team of epidemiologists published in the *Lancet* also included deaths resulting from increased lawlessness, degraded infrastructures and poorer healthcare. It allowed the family to decide whether each death was war-related. It came up with a massive total of 650,000 up to June 2006 (Burnham et al., 2006). Of the households asked to produce a death certificate 92 percent did so. An even higher figure of a million up to January 2008 was reported by the Opinion Research Business Survey (2008), but its methods were more dubious. Given the explosive nature of the *Lancet* article's findings, there have been attempts to discredit it. Yet epidemiologists and survey researchers confirmed that it conformed to best current practices, though adding that it is difficult to conduct surveys in countries with poor infrastructures. This could only be a ball-park estimate. It may nonetheless be the best one available but I think we should reduce it a little because of the discretion allowed to the families in defining war-related deaths. That would produce a ball-park estimate of around 500,000. I should add that most were not killed by U.S. soldiers. The Wikileaks documents reveal many killings by Iraqi military, police and paramilitary forces. This would be the total deaths caused by the invasion and occupation.

The UN additionally estimates that at least 2.5 million Iraqis fled to become refugees abroad, and another 2.5 million were displaced within the country – out of a total population of only about thirty million. This is an enormous amount of suffering. Every death leaves a devastated family; and most refugee flights do the same. Coalition casualties seem trivial in comparison: 4,500 U.S. soldiers, 2,000 soldiers of other countries, and 1,300 military contractors. About thirty thousand U.S. soldiers have been wounded. The dead and wounded leave a smaller trail of suffering across American families too. The cost of the war now exceeds $2 trillion (some say it is even $3 trillion). Violence is still ongoing. It was on a downward path during 2009 and 2010 but ticked up again in 2011. In Afghanistan and Iraq, the ratio of American soldier to native civilian casualties was probably in the order of 1: 50, risk-transfer militarism with a vengeance. Insufficiently discriminate fire-power at a distance predictably resulted in mass civilian deaths. It is incapable in an age dominated by antiimperialism of achieving the desired results, for it enrages the affected population and brings more terrorist recruits and more killing by both sides. No one has been prosecuted for disproportionate bombing or fire-power.

But was all this justified by securing a better future for Iraq? On the positive side a terrible dictator was overthrown and executed, and elections were held. Saddam was indeed terrible. The death-toll he inflicted was high, though it was strategic rather than mindless, for it spiked upward in response to two revolts. The first came in 1988 during the war with Iran when more than 100,000 Shi'a Kurds were probably massacred. Some Kurds were alleged to have helped the Iranians. This atrocity occurred when the United States was supporting Saddam and when Donald Rumsfeld was ferrying him arms. Then in 1991 Saddam's defeat at the hands of the Americans unleashed revolts in the Kurdish North and in the Shi'a South. Saddam again retaliated fiercely, killing perhaps 100,000 Kurds and Shi'a. Other smaller waves of repression including the persecution of the Marsh Arabs, may have caused another 50–100,000 dead. Any suspicion of opposition to Saddam could result in torture and perhaps death. This would yield a grand total of 300,000 to 400,000, though some have claimed more, up to 800,000 without providing supporting evidence. Again, these are only ball-park estimates.

Perhaps we can say no more than that the American invasion and Saddam's regime may have caused deaths of a similar order of magnitude. Whereas Saddam's casualties were intentionally inflicted, this was much less true of the Americans. We can only guess what Saddam might have inflicted had there been no invasion. That would have depended on whether he was threatened by revolt and whether he survived. The best outcome might have been if a successful coup against him had been mounted. Both regimes also brought a culture of violence to the country. Saddam's is evident in the anguished testimony of survivors from his prisons, while the postinvasion regime's is evident in the anguished testimony of American soldiers in the Wikileaks war logs, witnessing terrible atrocities by insurgents, comrades and Iraqi allies. Saddam's killings were generally more predictable. If you opposed him you were in danger. Today's regime also tortures and kills its enemies, though today's terrorist violence also threatens mere bystanders. Under Saddam street and social life remained more-or-less normal. Today they are not (Rosen, 2010: 9).

The United States did encourage democracy but also (unintentionally) sectarianism, wrongly identifying Saddam's regime as exclusively Sunni and handing Iraq over to organized groups who were almost exclusively Shi'a or Kurdish. The result was that in 2005 the first election produced satisfyingly large turnouts, but 95 percent voted for the parties of their own ethnic/religious group – more ethnocracy than democracy, with majority groups tyrannizing minorities. An uneasy coalition between Shi'a and Kurdish parties then ruled, dominating the Sunni community. Kurdish parties remain entirely Kurd-based, though some Shi'a and Sunni parties have recently projected a more secular, nationalist image and there are signs that people are tiring of sectarianism. Yet they are more physically segregated today, since multiethnic neighborhoods disappeared as their minorities were terrorized into flight (Rosen, 2010: 17–18, 45–9, 64–5, 549–50). This is like other cases of sectarian cleansing, like Northern Ireland and the former Yugoslav republics. The Ba'athist regimes of the Middle East, including Saddam's, had been more secular, more tolerant of ethnic and religious minorities (except for Jews), and favoring more rights for women than do America's Arab allies. In today's Iraq major constitutional issues are ethnically defined, for they specify which ethnicity will dominate each province and the nation. In practice that means determining which notables will head local administrations, distributing government jobs and revenues to their friends and relations. According to U.S. diplomats whose cables were leaked by Wikileaks and published by the Lebanese newspaper *Al Akhbar*, in 2010 under the guise of de-Ba'athification Prime Minister Maliki fired experienced and competent security and intelligence personnel and replaced them with his party loyalists.

If the three rival ethnic/religious communities could compromise through more representative procedures it would be a political improvement over Saddam, though an internal coup against Saddam might have produced the same result. General Ray Odierno, the American commander in Iraq, replied fairly candidly to a journalist when asked whether the United States had worsened the ethnic conflict "I don't know. There's all these issues that we didn't understand and that we had to work our way through. And did maybe that cause it to get worse? Maybe." (*New York Times*, February 6, 2011). This was a decidedly pessimistic evaluation coming from a man in his position.

The United States had finally learned how to acquire local allies. It added Shi'a support to its Kurdish allies and in 2006 armed Sunni tribal chiefs against the Sunni insurgents. Their success was important to the "surge," the infusion in early 2007 of an additional 21,000 American troops. In his memoirs Bush (2010) claims that his military commanders on the ground, plus Rumsfeld, opposed the surge but that he acted on the advice of four neo-cons. "Fred Kagan, a military scholar at the American Enterprise Institute, questioned whether we had enough troops to control the violence. Robert Kaplan, a distinguished journalist, recommended adopting a more aggressive counterinsurgency strategy. Michael Vickers, a former CIA operative who helped arm the Afghan Mujahideen in the 1980s, suggested a greater role for Special Operations. Eliot Cohen ... told me I needed to hold my commanders accountable for results." Rumsfeld was fired and the surge began. It also involved Iraqis, putting almost 100,000 Sunni militiamen on the U.S. payroll, at a cost of $30 million a month, and this emboldened Premier Maliki to launch a surprise attack on the Shi'a Sadrist militias, many of which had degenerated into criminal gangs.

The combination of Iraqi and U.S. forces eventually brought success and the disarming of the Sadrist militias in 2008 ended the sectarian civil war (Rosen, 2010: 363–75). U.S. troops were then gradually reduced, down to about 15,000 by September 2012. The surge did work. The Status of Forces Agreement of November 2008 set a withdrawal date for all U.S. troops of October 2011. The Agreement ratified the full sovereignty of Iraq, Iraqi ownership of all industries, including oil, and all former U.S. military bases and establishments, plus the subjection of all subcontractors to Iraqi law. There are now more military subcontractors in Iraq than U.S. troops, two-thirds of whom being foreign nationals, more than a third of them armed and carrying out security duties – another attempt to displace the risk away from American citizen-soldiers. Iraq is still in difficulties and killings continue. The number of those killed as given by Iraqi ministries rose slightly from 3,481 in 2009 to 3,605 in 2010. In 2011 the level of killing remained about the same. Nor is the new regime in Iraq a reliable ally of the United States. It is Shi'a, supporting Iran and Hezbollah while refusing to recognize Israel. The invasion has boosted Iranian power. The United States still relies on Saudi Arabia and Israel, just as it did before the invasion.

Other than the killing of Saddam Hussein, none of the original U.S. goals was attained. Saddam Hussein may have been a son-of-a-bitch, but his was an Iraqi regime. He was *their* son-of-a-bitch. He could provide more order than the Americans. This had been a fairly pointless and extremely costly military intervention.

Afghan quagmire

There was a more obvious reason for invading Afghanistan, since the probable perpetrator of 9–11 was lurking in his training-camps there. There were no major ulterior motives since Afghanistan had nothing that served U.S. national interests. At first all went well. The Taliban government was toppled by American fire-power and local Afghan allies. With local allies on the ground, it required less than 300 Americans on the ground to capture Kabul. Half of them were target-spotters with GPS phones, and half were CIA operatives with suitcases stuffed full of dollars for the allied warlords. But then came difficulties. It remains unclear why in November 2001 the White House and the Pentagon refused military requests to insert another 6000 Army Rangers into the Tora Bora mountains when the CIA had intelligence Osama was there. Most assume, as Ensalaco (2008: 227; cf. Bergen, 2011) says, that "The Bush administration's planning for the coming war in Iraq suffocated the efforts to kill Bin Laden." General Tommy Franks the man who made the final decision on Tora Bora was abruptly removed to prepare the Iraq battle-plan. Now the United States is stuck in an Afghanistan from which most of al-Qaeda has departed.

By 2011 it was unclear what the United States and its NATO allies are doing there, apart from taking sides in a civil war, which had been raging for thirty-five years, pitting the urban, educated, more secular peoples of the North against the more rural and traditional Pashtun peoples. The Taliban regrouped, found allies within Pakistan and assumed the leadership of many Pashtun clans. Though Karzai himself is a Pashtun, the Pashtun are substantially under-represented in his regime. Since they form more than 40 percent of the population, they cannot be suppressed, especially in terrain that favors guerillas, and given assistance from Pakistan, and probably Iran too. The Afghan army has been built up to 134,000 men, but it remains of doubtful utility, has an attrition rate of 24 percent per year, and cannot operate independently of NATO forces. The best outcome would be a deal between the Taliban and the Karzai regime lasting long enough for NATO to get out quickly, saving face. Karzai seems to want this but the Uzbek and Tajik parts of his regime oppose any deal and their independent drug revenues give them much autonomy from Karzai. Some Taliban leaders are believed to favor talks but recent loss-rates have brought younger, more radical Taliban into leadership positions. They may not have much incentive to negotiate, since they believe they can outlast the United States. The Taliban are "seamlessly embedded into communities" and are more ideologically committed than the Karzai regime with its corruption and brutal warlords. Since the dominant ideology is Islamist nationalism, those who side with the infidel Americans are automatically hated (Rosen, 2010: chap. 11, quote from p. 491).

It has proved a hard struggle against guerillas able to swim like fish in a tribal sea. Up to mid-2011 almost 2500 NATO troops had been killed. 100,000

U.S. troops plus 40,000 NATO allies can flush the Taliban out of the cities but control of villages and hills proves fleeting. Allied troops drive out the Taliban fighters but then leave, and then the Taliban come back. If we repeat the calculations made for Iraq by U.S. generals and the Rand Corporation, Afghanistan would require an overall troop strength of between 250,000 and 500,000. Nobody has proposed a surge of such size. Casualties increased up to 2011 and then fell slightly. The UN estimates that more than 3 million Afghan refugees have fled abroad. Attempts to eliminate the Taliban kill civilians as well. The UN estimates that almost 10,000 civilians were killed between 2006 and 2010, more than two-thirds by Taliban-allied forces, less than one-third by coalition and government forces. Thus it is doubtful that either side can capture enough hearts and minds to win over the whole country, still less can the many other local warlord militias across the country. Afghanistan earned its title of the graveyard of empires by defeating both the British and the Soviets. Now it may be adding the American Empire. It is unlikely that any victory will result before the deadlines set by Obama for a series of troop withdrawals initiated in July 2011 and ending in 2014. Obama's own commitment to this war was neither wholehearted nor sincere since it resulted from electoral opportunism, to balance his withdrawal from Iraq. He is seeking an exit strategy, egged on by Vice President Biden and other Democrats, while the generals pressure him for the opposite policy, a further troop surge, which would stay longer. He is well aware that this might be his Vietnam.

The United States again wrongly assumed that military power could deliver democracy. But this remains a tribal society, with each village, each province being controlled by local big men and small paramilitaries – though some doubt these even do control their neighborhoods. Elections consist of stuffed ballots and voters marshaled by tribal warlords controlling the country's only lucrative trade, the opium poppy. The defect of majoritarian democracy in ethnically or religiously divided countries is revealed here, as it was in Iraq: people vote for the parties representing their own ethnic or religious group, so heightening ethnic tensions. Karzai's regime is corrupt, as stolen elections in 2009 and 2010 revealed to the world. Wikileaks' release of State Department documents, reported in the *New York Times* (December 3, 2010), reveal U.S. frustrations over corruption. In October 2009 U.S. Ambassador Eikenberry after a meeting with President Karzai's brother cabled his despair at "how to fight corruption and connect the people to their government when the key government officials are corrupt." The documents provided the evidence. The first vice president was caught smuggling $52 million in cash into the United Arab Emirates; the Transportation Ministry collected $200 million a year in trucking fees but registered only $30 million with the government; the Minister of Health told U.S. diplomats that parliamentary deputies had offered to confirm his appointment for $1,000 per vote. There were many more instances. Most international diplomats and NGO workers interviewed by Rosen (2010: chap. 11: esp. pp 462–3) remained pessimistic about the outcome, and thought the new "counterinsurgency strategy" (COIN) would change little. Most of the interviewed Afghans believed that after the Americans leave, Karzai would flee abroad and the Taliban would form a coalition government with other opposition groups. I find this a little pessimistic. The Karzai government can probably hold most cities and major roads since Afghan security forces have improved and since the Taliban does not appeal to most urban Afghans. Yet the Taliban and their allies will probably control rural areas, especially in the East. The elections promised for 2014 might further divide Afghans along ethnic and tribal lines. Afghanistan remains a mess.

Worse, however, is that Pakistan has also been destabilized by the Afghan mess, and it has nuclear weapons, which may not be securely protected from theft or sale. The Conflict Monitoring Center says that in 2011 the CIA carried out 132 drone attacks in tribal areas of Pakistan, claiming the lives of 938 people, overwhelmingly Pakistani civilians. This dwarfed the total number of strikes during the whole of the Bush administration. The United States is shifting policy away from new invasions to drones, not only in Pakistan but also in the Yemen and Somalia. Drones can accurately bomb designated targets, and they kill far fewer innocent civilians than do invasions – and zero Americans. But they depend on intelligence reports of more variable accuracy. When added to numerous covert raids on the ground by U.S. forces into Pakistan, this creates blowback, especially among northeastern tribal Pakistanis. U.S. policy has done the opposite of what was intended: it has strengthened jihadi Islamism across Pakistan and weakened the Pakistani government. The assassins of Pakistani moderates are cheered by large crowds.

Success of a sort came on May 2, 2011, when U.S. forces found and killed Osama bin Laden in a raid on a compound just outside Islamabad, the capital of Pakistan. He had been already marginalized by being forced to live in extreme clandestinity. Documents taken from his compound and released by the U.S. military in May 2012 reveal a man unhappy at what he thought was al Qaeda's takeover by advocates of the "near enemy" strategy, and he railed against terrorists who attacked fellow-Muslims. His death probably made little difference to the international terrorist movement, which is much more dependent on the current Arab uprisings against despotic regimes. If the uprisings succeed, terrorism will be discredited, but if they fail terrorism may grow in response. But the death of bin Laden does offer a quick and dirty way out of Afghanistan for the United States. The killing of the main target of the invasion by U.S. forces could be an excuse for leaving, leaving Karzai to his own resources. This will happen soon, since support for the war in the United States has drained away. It would be a superficially face-saving withdrawal, as in Vietnam, though few American politicians, sensing humiliation, support this. Americans should heed the words of British army chaplain the Reverend G.

H. Gleig, one of the handful of survivors of the disastrous First Anglo-Afghan War. He wrote in his memoir of 1843 that it was

a war begun for no wise purpose, carried on with a strange mixture of rashness and timidity, brought to a close after suffering and disaster, without much glory attached either to the government which directed, or the great body of troops which waged it. Not one benefit, political or military, was acquired with this war. Our eventual evacuation of the country resembled the retreat of an army defeated.

Blowback

The main negatives of these two invasions and occupations do not concern the two countries themselves but the international blowback. Before the invasion, Afghanistan contained a few international terrorists and Iraq almost none. The invasions created far more across many Muslim lands. Even Bush (2010) acknowledges this: "When al Qaeda lost its safe haven in Afghanistan, the terrorists went searching for a new one. After we removed Saddam in 2003, bin Laden exhorted his fighters to support the jihad in Iraq. In many ways, Iraq was more desirable for them than Afghanistan. It had oil riches and Arab roots. Over time, the number of extremists affiliated with al Qaeda in Afghanistan declined to the low hundreds, while the estimated number in Iraq topped ten thousand." Al Qaeda became more active in Iraq, Jordan, the Lebanon, the Yemen, Somalia, Western Europe and elsewhere as a consequence of the invasions. The U.S. National Security Estimate for 2006 admitted "The Iraq conflict has become the "cause célèbre" for jihadists, breeding a deep resentment of U.S. involvement in the Muslim world and cultivating supporters for the global jihadist movement" (Ensalaco, 2008: 273). The improvements to Iraq that might eventually flow are outweighed by international escalation of terror and the war on terror. Jihadis have stayed global, and as Rosen (2010) observes, "The United States adopted Al Qaeda's view of the world, and it too treated the entire world stage as a battlefield." This, says Gerges (2005), is a big mistake for both sides. There is much opposition among the jihadis to attacking the far enemy, but the aggression of the far enemy undermines the power of the near faction. Neither the United States nor the terrorists can win this engagement. All they can do is bring mayhem to a few places and major inconvenience to many.

The United States is protected by great oceans from terrorist blowback and its Muslim communities are small, diverse and conservative. Britain has proportionately a much bigger Muslim population, mostly drawn from a Pakistan now being destabilized by U.S. and British government policy. Of the 119 persons 69 percent convicted in Britain of Islamic terrorism offenses between 1999 and 2009 were of Pakistani descent born in the UK with British passports. Those caught attempting or plotting bombings *all* gave their main reason as British foreign policy (Centre for Social Cohesion report of July 5,

2010). The overwhelming majority of Pakistanis in Britain are law-abiding citizens. But many are enraged by Britain killing large numbers of Muslims in Afghanistan and Iraq, and by the failure to deal with the Israel-Palestine conflict. In a poll of British Pakistanis in the *Guardian* newspaper, 13 percent defended suicide bombings. When asked if they had to live in the same situation as a Palestinian, they might consider becoming a suicide bomber themselves, an amazing 47 percent said yes (*Guardian*, March 15, 2004; cf. UK Foreign and Commonwealth Office/Home Office "Draft Report on Young Muslims and Extremism," April 2004). The former Director General of MI5, the main British intelligence agency, revealed to an official enquiry that a big surge of warnings of home-grown terrorist threats after the invasion of Iraq got MI5 a 100 percent increase in its budget. She continued, "Our involvement in Iraq radicalised ... a whole generation of young people – a few among a generation – who saw our involvement in Iraq and Afghanistan as being an attack on Islam. Arguably we gave Osama bin Laden his Iraqi jihad so that he was able to move into Iraq in a way that he was not before." (*The Independent*, July 21, 2010). A U.S. diplomatic cable released by Wikileaks reveals that prominent British Muslims, including two Members of Parliament, warned the British government in 2007 about blowback in the British Muslim community from "the debacle in Iraq" and the Israeli invasion of the Lebanon. The U.S. diplomat did not like what he called this "knee-jerk reaction." He wrote "the Muslim community is not the only element in Britain blaming ... foreign policy for inciting radical elements ... even the mainstream press has expressed the belief, reportedly widespread, that homegrown terrorism is an 'inevitable' response to the UK's involvement in Iraq and reluctance to call for an 'immediate ceasefire' in the Middle East." (*The Guardian*, December 13, 2010). He did not add that they were right.

Spain had its only major terrorist attack on March 11, 2004, followed by a failed attempt the following month, during the period when its conservative government allied itself with U.S. policy in Iraq. 191 people died in this terrible incident. After the successor socialist government withdrew from Iraq there were no more jihadi attacks in Spain.

Robert Pape analyzed every reported case of suicide terrorism occurring anywhere between 1980 and 2005 (315 cases). He concluded there was "little connection between suicide terrorism and Islamic fundamentalism, or any one of the world's religions .... Rather, what nearly all suicide terrorist attacks have in common is a specific secular and strategic goal: to compel modern democracies to withdraw military forces from territory that the terrorists consider to be their homeland." "The taproot of suicide terrorism is nationalism ...." It is "an extreme strategy for national liberation" (2005: 4, 79–80). Pape (2010) recently extended his analysis to the 2,200 attacks between 1980 and 2010. In each single month from 2002 there were more suicide terrorists trying to kill Americans and their allies in Muslim countries than in all the years before

2001 combined. From 1980 to 2003, there were 343 suicide attacks across the world. At most 10 percent were directed against Americans. But once the United States occupied Afghanistan and Iraq total suicide attacks worldwide rose dramatically – from about 300 in 1980–2003, to 1,800 in 2004–9. However, terrorist attacks have peaked and have been recently declining and are now overwhelmingly perpetrated by locals against locals in the war zones of Afghanistan, Iraq, Pakistan and Somalia. In 2010 only 15 of the 13,000 people killed in terrorist attacks were Americans.

But the danger to us has diminished. Muslim terrorism directed against Americans is now negligible, more as a consequence of the dominance of near enemy factions among the terrorists plus homeland security provisions than of American foreign policy. At its peak it was a response to our long-standing but recently escalated aggressive foreign policy in the Muslim world, plus the increasing aggression of our ally Israel. This is what suicide bombers themselves have emphasized, that is what Al Qaeda itself has said. If we respond to terrorist atrocities with aggression in the Muslim world and atrocities against Muslims, we simply create more terrorists aiming at us. But the consequences are even worse than this might suggest. In their attempts to deny that their own policies had created the terrorist threat against us, the British and American governments fall back on arguments about civilization, culture and values. President Bush described terrorists as "a threat to civilization and our way of life," deploying "the demented logic of the fanatic," requiring us to mount a "crusade" against them; Prime Minister Blair perceived "an attack on our values." For others the struggle is between Western civilization and an Islamic terrorism rooted in a more primitive, backward and even savage Muslim civilization. Policies can be quickly changed, unfortunately "culture" is much slower-changing. Culturalist views condemn the United States to long-term war (Jacoby, 2010).

They also encouraged atrocities. Most CIA professionals doubt the efficacy of torture. Khalid Shaikh Mohammed, the apparent mastermind of 9/11, was waterboarded 183 times, yet revealed nothing more about 9/11 than he had already freely told a journalist from Al Jazeera two years earlier (Bergen, 2011). Guantanamo Bay and extraordinary rendition lost the United States the moral high ground. These atrocities plus attacks on mosques and Muslims in the West, further encouraged extreme reactions on the Muslim side. As always in severe conflict situations, the rival sets of extremists dance the tango together, each boosting the importance of the other. Islamic fundamentalism is not intrinsically popular in the Middle East. Neither in its Sunni nor its Shi'a forms (e.g., the Iranian ayatollahs) has it done any better in social development than did previous more secular movements. Al Qaeda in particular offers no positive vision for building a better society. It has nothing to say about education, health care and jobs. It kills indiscriminately, including many Muslim civilians, and few share its fundamentalist values. Those who bomb civilians contravene both Enlightenment and Muslim values. But so do state terrorism and aerial bombing. Since the terrorists are brutal and unpopular, we ought to be able to occupy the high ground in the eyes of most of the world. But we do not. We have lost our ideological power.

The second blowback is nuclear proliferation. U.S. policy has been admirable on one front, the attempt by American diplomats and politicians to secure under lock and key (with the cooperation of Russia) the materials of the former Soviet nuclear program. This effort was begun in the 1990s and President Obama promised to finish it, securing all remaining material within four years. Though this goal was hindered by Congressional refusal to vote funds to the project, Wikileaks documents (*The Guardian*, December 19, 2010) reveal American diplomats tirelessly monitoring the suspected smuggling of nuclear materials across the world. We must thank them for that.

A different success was claimed by Bush administrations: that Libya's development of nuclear weapons was deterred by the Iraq invasion. Indeed Muhammed Qaddafi had announced that he was abandoning his weapons program just three days after the Fall of Baghdad – in return for increased economic, military and security cooperation with the United States and other Western countries. Had the American invasion persuaded him? Maybe this had helped, though Qaddafi had been negotiating with the British and Americans for years, the talks had been making progress, and his main motives seemed to be to end his international isolation and economic sanctions so that his sons would not inherit a pariah regime – which looks ironic today! Nonetheless, Libya might offer a little support to the Bush case.

However, the Iranian, Korean and Pakistani cases are not success stories. Even before it became obvious that the Iraqi occupation had been botched, the supposed "demonstration" effect boomeranged. Iran's reformist President Khatami had wanted to negotiate with the United States in what he called a Dialogue Between Civilizations. Under his leadership Iran condemned the 9–11 attacks, rounded up Al Qaeda operatives and assisted the United States in Afghanistan. But Bush's bellicosity undermined Khatami, strengthened clerical conservatives, and led Iran to intensify efforts to get a nuclear deterrent. Khatami was succeeded as president in 2005 by the Holocaust-denying Ahmadinejad. The North Koreans also moved faster toward nuclear weapons. The demonstration effect understandably scared these regimes, since Saddam and colleagues were killed. But it also increased their desire to get nuclear weapons in self-defense. When the Iraq occupation bogged down, nothing could be done to stop the Korean and Iranian governments, and the Bush team had stopped focusing on them, leaving policy to the Europeans, Russians and Chinese (Cohen, 2005: 135–9, 184–6). That did help prevent the United States heeding Saudi King Abdullah's advice to "cut off the head of the snake," that is to bomb Iranian nuclear sites (Wikileaks State Department documents, *New York Times*, November 28, 2010)! The blowback of U.S. and Israeli interventions in Iraq, Afghanistan and the Lebanon also strengthened Iran's regional power, a bizarre outcome, since earlier the United States had successfully used Iraq under Saddam Hussein to balance Iran. If Iran does acquire nuclear weapons (though intelligence services began to cast some doubt on this in mid-2011) it may be difficult to dissuade Israel from preemptive strikes, including nuclear strikes, and it also lead to Iran's regional rivals like Iraq, Saudi Arabia and Turkey acquiring them too. In the Middle Eastern and Pakistani contexts, if the requisite technology for a suitcase nuclear weapon appeared, it is possible to imagine suicide bombers exploding them. After all, highly ideological suicide bombers have become commonplace. They are unlikely to heed the dangers of MAD since they go willingly to their deaths seeking glory in the afterlife.

Elsewhere in the Muslim world United States policy remained more traditional, without major interventions or threats, favoring despotic but friendly regimes against riskier progressives. Having earlier helped destabilize Arab socialist regimes, the United States now acquired Islamists as its main populist enemies. Together they wreaked havoc. Lebanon, the Yemen and Somalia lack effective government, Pakistan is on the brink. Egyptians and Tunisians overthrew U.S.-supported dictators in early 2011, with no help from the United States. Wikileaks cables from Tunisia (*New York Times*, January 16, 2011) reveal that over several years U.S. diplomats had been describing the regime as corrupt and authoritarian, run by a mafia-like ruling family, yet they still praised our ally, dictator Ben Ali, for providing stability and repressing Islamists When the mass demonstrations of the Arab Awakening of 2011 spread to Bahrein, home port of the U.S. Fifth Fleet, the Obama administration urged moderation on the king, but he ignored it and with the aid of troops sent from our neighboring ally, Saudi Arabia, he repressed the demonstrators. The United States will do nothing to hinder repression even though it is uncomfortable with it. This is described in the American media as walking a tightrope between stability and democracy, yet the metaphor is not apt since the United States consistently falls off the rope on the despotic side. In Algeria in December 1991 the Islamic Salvation Front won an election, but the results were immediately overturned by a military coup with the support of the United States. The United States refused to accept the Hamas electoral triumph in Palestine in 2006 and Hezbollah electoral successes in Lebanon in 2009. Democracy is a goal of U.S. policy only if it can bring its friends to power. Ironically, the one Muslim country in this region with a genuine democracy, Turkey, is at present ruled by the mildly Islamist AK party.

Only in Libya in 2011 did the United States intervene to help overthrow a dictator, but Qaddafi was never a U.S. ally. Libya also has oil, obviously a necessary reason for the intervention of the American and European governments, though the desire to rescue rebels from a murderous regime was also a genuine motivation, and this time the powers secured the approval of the UN and even of the Arab League, most of whose members had been alienated by

Qaddafi's erratic behavior. The intervention was not unilateral, but a combined NATO operation, with a substantial British and French presence yet depending heavily on U.S. air power, which Obama sought in public to minimize. Air power degraded Qaddafi's military infrastructure so completely that the rebels were able to achieve victory on the ground. Whether they can also wield stable and reasonably representative political power afterward remains doubtful. Democracy is not that easy and political chaos would certainly lead back to despotism. The casualty rate of the intervention – estimated by the new government of Libya to be 30,000 – may have equaled that which might have been consequent on Qaddafi repressing the uprising. It is impossible to say as yet whether intervention was a worthwhile venture. Perhaps it was a risk worth taking. However, on balance I would expect a better future for Arab countries to come from indigenous political struggle, as in the Arab Awakening.

In general American policies added instability to the region and international terrorists to the world, the opposite of what empire is supposed to do. The most obvious policy implication of blowback is to stop invading foreign countries. Try offshore balancing instead, says Pape. I would add put more pressure on Israel and offer more economic and less military aid to Muslim countries – which would also be much cheaper than invasion. Islam has always been resilient when faced with foreign imperialism – British, French, Soviet or American. Terrorists can find ideological power in mobilizing the language of Islam to rally support. That is why it sometimes seems that Islamic fundamentalism is our enemy. The conclusion from this appearance is that the solution is to invade and reconstruct hostile Muslim countries, imposing Western values on their culture. But these conclusions are false. The reverse is true. The major political parties in the United States and Britain say terrorism is the main reason for keeping our militaries in Muslim countries. On the contrary, it is the main reason for pulling them out. As long as Western powers threaten or invade Muslim countries, the more terrorists are created. Not only do our policies fail in the invaded countries, but the blowback they bring is exactly what we were trying to combat in the first place. Yet the lesson has still not been learned. Earlier offshore balancing had not seemed good enough. But in retrospect it looks fine.

Two imperialisms or one?

Were the two imperial crystallizations, economic and military, closely linked? In three senses they were. First, oil was important when linked to an overambitious geopolitical strategy. Second, economic domination allows the United States to afford its enormous military without overtaxing Americans. Foreigners have paid for it through dollar seigniorage. Third, the two imperialisms share a home within the American tradition of equating political freedom with the economic freedom of the entrepreneur. The Project for the New

American Century had been the key conservative lobby in the late 1990s and its founding statement had called for "a Reaganite policy of military strength and moral clarity ...[to] ... promote the cause of political and economic freedom abroad." All three of these links were part of the intensification of economic imperialism, and, to a lesser extent, of military imperialism. But have the two ventures been part of the same imperial strategy?

World-systems theorists say "yes." They claim that the United States chose military aggression to reverse relative economic decline, as they claim previous failing hegemons also did (Harvey, 2003; Wallerstein, 2003). Harvey distinguishes between two logics of power, territorial and capitalist (as I have also done) but he tends to reduce the first to the second. He argues that with a failing economy, revealed by de-industrialization and the turn to finance capital, trade deficits and ever greater consumer debts, the Bush administration sought to reverse economic decline by a military aggression, which would secure control of all Middle Eastern oil. World systems theorists add an analogy with the British Empire: as each hegemonic power weakened, it became more aggressive, attempting to hold onto empire by military force. The analogy is false, since we have seen that the British became less aggressive as they declined, declaring they were a satiated power interested only in defending what they had. But is it true of the Americans?

Each of the wars since 1991 (the Gulf War, Bosnia/Kosovo, Afghanistan and Iraq 2003) has resulted in more U.S. bases ringing the oil and natural gas fields of the Middle East and the Caucasus. Is this the consistent element in the new imperialism? If the United States can no longer rely on its coercive powers within economic markets, perhaps it is turning to military power to ensure its energy needs. Some in Washington do think this way. Yet the ring of bases does not bring more oil or gas, for the bases do not create client states. When the United States tried to influence President Karimov of Uzbekistan to lessen his repression, he refused. Indeed he asked American troops to leave his country and began to negotiate an alternative deal with Russia, though this was only to secure a better deal from the Americans. The Saudis asked the Americans to close their local bases, believing the U.S. presence weakened their hold over their country. The United States complied. Bases do not confer much local coercive power.

As I showed previously, American economic power did not decline between 1970 and 2000. Indeed, the intensification of structural adjustment and dollar seigniorage, plus technological dynamism in the 1990s, *increased* American economic imperialism. Harvey accepts Arrighi's theory that hegemons decline as they shift from production to finance. In Chapter 6 I doubted whether this is true of the United States. Yet there is no indication that the hawks even knew of the existence of such a theory, let alone believe in it. They seemed supremely confident in all America's powers, economic, ideological, military and political. Overconfidence was their undoing. American strategy was not to stem economic decline by military means, as in world systems theory, but to *increase* global dominance by both economic and military means. This was the intention of Vice President Cheney, Defense Secretary Rumsfeld, and Assistant Secretary Wolfowitz. They sought to extend American power across the world, out of a mistaken sense of strength, not a sense of weakness.

However, the economic and military strategies were often pushed by different actors. Economic intensification was pushed by the states of the global North and by finance and corporate capital more generally, while military imperialism was pushed unilaterally from Washington (except for Tony Blair). The Clinton administration had focused on international trade and finance, supported by major capitalists. Clinton had great faith in globalization as free trade. He believed this produced common benefits for all nations, which was quite unlike the neo-con zero-sum conception of foreign policy, us against them. He opposed the protectionism, which was important in his own party, and was supported by business Republicans, not by neo-cons. He achieved most of his goals: NAFTA, the rescue of the Mexican peso, the conversion of a voluntaristic GATT into a WTO with enforcement powers, and getting China into the WTO (Chollet & Goldgeier, 2008: 148–69, 326). In contrast, militarism had come to dominate the writings of the neo-con intellectuals, while international economic issues interested them little. The book of essays edited by Weekly Standard stalwarts Kagan & Kristol (2000) contains only one economic recommendation: double the military budget. The book edited by Republican Party Chairman Haley Barbour (1996) has a chapter endorsing free trade. But its twenty-four pages are greatly outweighed by the ninety-two pages devoted to "hard" foreign policy and the military. Richard Perle paid little attention to issues of trade or economics (according to Weisman's, 2007 biography). Kristol gave only two cheers for capitalism, saying that while it promoted freedom and wealth for most people, it lacked morality. He, like other neo-cons, favors a much stronger state than do neoliberals. The hawkish policy-makers, Cheney, Rumsfeld and others showed little interest in economic imperialism in general – with the major exception of oil.

There was not total separation, for there was common interest in undermining Saddam Hussein and in opposing American isolationism, and there was a brief attempt to foist neoliberalism on Iraq. But there was also a shift of departmental powers as Clinton was replaced by Bush. The Pentagon rose above both State and Treasury in influence and the office of the vice president under Cheney grew stronger. The fights between Defense and State became legendary, but as the wars were prepared the Pentagon dominated. Treasury and Commerce continued Clinton trade policies, quietly continuing the shift toward bilateral free trade agreements, but this was separate from "harder" foreign policy. The civilians running the Pentagon dominated foreign policy, but secretively. So different parts of the state were involved in the two intensifications, using different methods. This was not two imperialisms, but they were not intimately connected and they did not comprise a single grand scheme.

Those favoring a more conspiratorial capitalist interpretation of the invasion cite the interlocks between the administration and maintenance and construction corporations like Haliburton, Bechtel and Parsons. Juhazs (2006) notes that 150 U.S. corporations made $50 billion profit out of three years of rebuilding Iraq, with Haliburton easily the biggest beneficiary at $12 billion. But the major oil corporations made much bigger profits than they did. Perhaps Cheney's connections with Haliburton, or George's Schultz's with Bechtel got the contract for their firm rather than another, though it does not seem that Condoleeza Rice's ties with Chevron brought a payoff. It would be hoped that the administration had indeed at some point consulted construction companies about the costs of rebuilding, especially given the likely extent of American bombing. But has a war ever been instigated by construction firms hoping to profit from its devastation? This would be an amazingly irrational subordination of American national interests to a small fraction of politically connected capital. No, the war was led from within the administration, and not at the behest of powerful outside pressure groups – always excepting the Israel lobby.

Of course, American economic strength provides the resources for its military, while its military position since World War II had guaranteed economic strength. There was current linkage between the two in the brief attempt to subject Iraq to structural adjustment programs, though this did not include oil and it derived less from economic principles than from what I called a slash/burn/rebirth sense of mission anathema to most economists. The connection while the Republicans were in power (up to 2008) was weaker: two conservative interest-groups agreed to a trade-off – you can have your policy, if we can have ours. But they showed little interest in the other's policies, and economic imperialists had done better under Clinton.

Overall the economic and military imperialisms were rather distinct crystallizations of power. Economic imperialism was successful at maintaining American power over three decades, while its military imperialism was a failure. The former intensified gradually, step-by-step, as it dawned on Americans what new powers they possessed to secure the interests of the United States as seen through the lens of American finance and corporate capitalists. In contrast military intensification was ideologically germinated and enacted through overconfidence in military power. It involved a sweeping simplification of modern history and a roughshod ride over global and regional realities. Its failure diminishes somewhat the extent of universal globalization. Huntington's 1996 claim of a fundamental clash of civilizations was not true at the time he wrote, but its core – a clash between Christian and Muslim civilization – became truer since he wrote, thanks to the joint efforts of American administrations and terrorists. They converted a religious into also being a political and geo-political divide, though they probably also widened divides within Christian and especially within Muslim civilization.

Conclusion

Under Bush the Younger faith in America's ideological mission and military power had overwhelmed a sense of realism. The imperialists proposed slashing-and-burning their way across the Muslim world in order to see it reborn in the American image. They believed the United States possessed the power to achieve this. National Security Adviser Condoleeza Rice declared "American values are universal" and the United States is "on the right side of history." Yet values are more diverse, history more complex – and the United States lacked the political and ideological power to accomplish the mission. This was an example of Weber's value rationality in which commitment to ideological goals overwhelms instrumentally rational calculations about the relation of available means to ends. The answer to Madeleine Albright's famous question is that having almost half the world's military expenditure is of little use in securing either American interests or the betterment of the world. A military of this size has come to serve no discernible purpose.

The American and British publics also came to realize this. The U.S. government had striven to control the information flow and create an atmosphere of fear, just as it had done in previous wars. Dissident reporters were fired and war correspondents were embedded within U.S. military units, and publicity for returning coffins and funerals was banned. The United States refused to publish Afghan or Iraqi casualty figures. It rejected conscription knowing that Americans would not sacrifice in this far-off cause, and it relied on risk-transfer militarism to avoid bargaining with ordinary Americans for their support. Despite these precautions, public opinion soured. Support for the Iraq war halved, to around 30 percent in both the United States and Britain by late 2006, and Obama's announced intention to quit was popular. By late 2010 a majority of Britons and Americans saw the Afghan war as a lost cause. These had been wars of choice, and most now chose to end them. Public opinion, like the Bush administration, had not endorsed military intensification out of a sense of weakness or decline, as world systems theory has it, but out of a sense of pride in strength. But the public accepted its mistake quicker. So did Defense Secretary Robert Gates who had been in charge of these two occupations since December 2006, and who served for twenty-six years before this in the CIA and the National Security Council. In a speech to West Point cadets reported in *the New York Times*, February 26, 2011 he declared: "In my opinion, any future defense secretary who advises the president to again send a big American land army into Asia or into the Middle East or Africa should 'have his head examined,' as General MacArthur so delicately put it." Gates suggested that future interventions should be by the navy and air force – informal empire with gunboats. Americans, including Republicans like Gates, seem to be developing combat fatigue.

The policy of preemptive military interventions had conspicuously failed. I and others predicted that beforehand. When it began to fail, the imperialists demanded more surges, more militarism. That is characteristic of ideologists whose policies begin to fail. Turning back would be an admission of failure and end their political influence. That had also been the view of Japanese militarists in the late 1930s. When most army strategists were advising an end to Japanese expansion, since no matter how many colonies Japan conquered, she would still depend crucially on American- and British-controlled markets, the Tokyo leadership ignored or sacked them. American imperialists did likewise but luckily America is a democracy and they were cast from office.

Yet we cannot comfort ourselves, as Ikenberry (2006: chap. 10) does, by proclaiming "the end of the neo-conservative moment," for that moment became a self-fulfilling prophecy. The Obama administration has continued what are essentially neo-conservative and militaristic policies. Despite his gentler rhetoric and his bizarre Nobel Peace Prize, Obama has upped the military offensive in Afghanistan and expanded it over the Pakistani border with his own drone offensive. He is still engaged in conflicts in five Muslim countries: Afghanistan, Pakistan, Iraq, Somalia, and the Yemen. He has not closed Guantanamo Bay nor stopped extraordinary rendition and he became the first American president to authorize the assassination of an American citizen. Bush the Younger must be proud of him.

Thanks to such imperialist policies, terrorists have proliferated. They are mobile, difficult to target, dedicated to killing Westerners, especially Americans and Britons, and they are willing to die in the process. They are another example of "interstitial emergence," power dynamics throwing up unexpected problems for society. A handful of militants, though with a larger body of sympathizers, unexpectedly emerged to create threats out of all proportion to their numbers. Encouraged by hawks in Washington and London they created a war on terror affecting all our lives. 3,000 U.S. citizens were killed on 9/11, a terrible single atrocity. The U.S. response has cost $3 trillion, an enormous sum, yet doing very little good. There are now almost no terrorists attacking targets outside of their own homeland. International police action, not militaries, have been responsible for this decline. The few remaining terrorists attacking us remain real and we must obviously get them before they get us, though not through aerial bombing. Let us declare ended this war on terror and the national hysteria and restrictions on civil liberties this has generated. I forgive Bush his emotionally understandable "get them dead or alive" outburst, though not his role in causing the eruption of terrorists in the first place, nor his cultivation of subsequent terror hysteria in order to restrict our civil rights. I do not forgive Obama for continuing this.

Enlightenment values of democracy, freedom and tolerance must be defended, against jihadi and other terrorists but also against our own national security states. Guantanamo Bay, extraordinary rendition and bombing raids undermine these values. The USA Patriot Act passed in 2001, renewed in 2006, gave the state new powers to tap telephones, e-mails, and medical, financial, and even library records; it eased restrictions on foreign intelligence gathering within the United States; expanded state authority to vet financial transactions, especially of foreigners; and broadened state discretion in detaining (if necessary indefinitely) or deporting immigrants it suspects of terrorism-related acts or intentions. Stone (2004: 528) says "the United States has a long and unfortunate history of overreacting to the dangers of wartime. Again and again, Americans have allowed fear to get the better of them." He observes that it was now doing so again. The other invader of Iraq, the UK, introduced comparable powers in its Terrorism Act of 2006. Other states have introduced less draconian tightening security measures. Habeas corpus, long fought for by our ancestors, becomes endangered. Agamben (2005: 2–4,14, 22) detects "a continuing tendency in all of the Western democracies, the declaration of the state of exception has gradually been replaced by an unprecedented generalization of the paradigm of security as the normal technique of government." He claimed Bush the Younger was "attempting to produce a situation in which the emergency becomes the rule, and the very distinction between peace and war … becomes impossible." The State of Exception becomes the rule. Universal Enlightenment values are being eroded by establishment forces.

We can curse the fools who got us into this, but they succeeded in thoroughly immersing us in their folly. The Obama administration is immersed in the neo-con legacy, partially trapped by Congress. It fails to pressure Israel to stop stealing Palestinian land and strangling the Palestinian state. Israel told U.S. diplomats that they deliberately kept the economy of the Gaza strip "on the brink of collapse" without "pushing it over the edge," a U.S. diplomatic cable of 2008 revealed (WikiLeaks cable, posted online by Norwegian daily *Aftenposten*, January 5, 2011). The Israeli human rights group B'Tselem says that by July 2010, Jewish settler councils had fenced off 42 percent of the Palestinian West Bank, an incredible proportion, illegal under international law. It included 21 percent of land that the state of Israel itself recognized was privately owned by Palestinians, which was against Israeli law. The Israeli state still aids land-grabs and the United States complains verbally but does nothing. Its idea of pressure in November 2010 was to offer Israel twenty jet fighters, worth $3 billion, in return for a mere ninety-day moratorium on settlement-building! Israel did not accept even this. Israel has absorbed 20 percent of the U.S. foreign aid budget plus military aid to the tune of $27 billion since 2000. Its survival depends on American aid, which *should* give the U.S. leverage, but it never exercises this. The poverty-stricken Palestinian state is even more dependent on its much lesser U.S. aid. In 2011 the United States went to the wall to defend Israel, vetoing the Palestinian application for membership as a state of the United Nations, with great damage to its international status and its pretensions to be the peacemaker in the Middle East.

President Clinton set out his parameters of peace after the failure of the Camp David summit in 2000. Israel and a new Palestine state would recognize each other; their border would follow the pre-1967 line except for adjustments for new border-adjacent Jewish settler communities for which the Palestinians would be compensated with land elsewhere; Jerusalem would become a shared capital; and refugees would be resettled and/or compensated, but without an automatic right of return. These were the terms Israeli premier Olmert and Palestinian premier Abbas almost agreed to in September 2008 and remain the obvious basis of a peace agreement. The United States, and only the United States, has the power to drag the parties toward signing one. It is the single step most likely to win the United States friends across the Middle East and stem the terrorist flow. But the pro-Israeli government lobby in the United States prevents it, convincing both parties that a pro-Israel policy might tip the balance in half-a-dozen House seats and perhaps even in two Senate seats (Florida and New York).

Much of the foreign policy establishment – Republican and Democrat alike – still believes military action remains necessary to defeat the terrorists, and all of it believes in an American responsibility to bring order to the world (e.g., Gelb, 2009; Kagan, 2012; Brzezinsky, 2012). It is now difficult for prominent American politicians to publicly urge withdrawal from such ventures. They do not want a repeat in Iraq or Afghanistan of those last desperate scenes from the U.S. embassy in Saigon on April 30, 1975, as U.S. helicopters whirred above, picking up the last Americans, as crowds of their Vietnamese friends jostled and pleaded desperately and unavailingly to be airlifted out. How can the greatest power in the world admit defeat at the hands of such puny Iraqi and Afghan foes? How do we get out gracefully, without losing face? We cannot, but then face is not the worst thing to lose.

The United States does not now bring order to the world. The evidence of the last decade points to the opposite conclusion: the United States tilts the balance toward disorder – at least this is the case in the Middle East, and also in a different way in Mexico and Colombia, riven by bloody drug wars caused by Americans' demand for drugs. But it is difficult for Americans to accept this. Kagan and Brzezinski have been reduced to arguing that the world under American domination is better than a world under the domination of Moscow or Beijing. Ernest Gellner always argued the same. But today and tomorrow that is no longer the realistic alternative. Kagan and Brzezinski themselves argue that China's power is far less than that of the United States and that China is unlikely to become hegemonic, surrounded as it is by distrustful neighbors. Sooner or later, a multipolar world will return, not domination by one or two powers. And that will offer no threat to democracy (where it exists) or to open trade (such as it is), which are the twin defenses supposedly mounted by the United States. Indeed, a multilateral order probably offers a better chance of combating climate change, the biggest threat to the world, than does American domination (as we will see in Chapter 12).

Yet I have little confidence that this view will prevail, since imperialism is deeply embedded in contemporary American ideology and politics and many American politicians believe they can only be reelected if they do not antagonize the pro-Israeli government lobby. This war on terror will last a while yet. The United States has the military power to destroy but it does not have the political or ideological power to reconstruct. But almost no American politician and few Washington think-tank intellectuals accept that. A sense of responsibility for world order combined with the loss of face consequent upon a withdrawal prevent it. Status concerns remain important in geopolitics, making leaders prefer war to backing down. Afghanistan in this respect may do for Obama what Vietnam did for Lyndon Johnson and Iraq did for Bush the Younger.

These are not major wars. In time they may be of no great global significance. For an imperial power this quantity of military killed and wounded is expendable – and the United States is constantly devising new risk-transfer schemes for protecting the lives of its soldiers. Iraqis, Afghans, Pakistanis, and foreign mercenary contractors take the brunt. The financial costs of somewhere around $3.5 trillion are enormous but supportable in an economy worth $14 trillion. The inconvenience of high security when we travel by air is annoying, while the seemingly permanent state of emergency should cause alarm, since it is a regression in civil citizenship rights. Yet these wars are not very intrusive in our privileged Western way of life. For the few critics and suspects wire-tapping, searches and arrests without warrants, indefinite detention without trial, extreme rendition and torture are occasionally horrific intrusions, undermining the universal values the United States claims to embody. Not only is American military power unsuited to the task at hand, the United States has also lost some of its moral authority, its ideological power.

These American failures do not indicate American decline, yet. The United States has not failed to win victories that in the past were within its capabilities. When it fought in Vietnam against guerilla foes as determined as those in Afghanistan, it was defeated. And it has *never* tried to invade a country since World War II in which it had no significant local allies on the ground, as it did in Iraq. The United States could never in the postwar period have been victorious without such allies in a country the size of Iraq, and American administrations had been too sensible to try. America was not overstretched but overstretching, for the collapse of the Soviet Union had given the United States delusions of grandeur. In military terms the United States can retain a degree of global dominance while not seeking absurdly ambitious global goals.

At least the Iraq experience seems to have taught America lessons. In the Libyan intervention in 2011 there were allies both local and international. There were planes in the air, but no American boots on the ground. Let us hope the lesson lasts. The United States must only intervene with the support of neighbors and locals who can lead the military campaign on the ground and who could form a credible, popular government afterward. These conditions are not often found in this age of nationalism. They were found in Grenada and Panama (tiny countries, of course), they were found in a more complex way in the former Yugoslavia, perhaps they are there in Libya, and they were present but not acted upon in Rwanda. But they were not found in Somalia, Iraq or Afghanistan, and they are not likely to be present in many other countries. Failing these conditions, nonintervention is the better policy. Unpleasant as it is to watch dictators launching repression against their peoples, we should have learned by now that military intervention is often likelier to make things worse. Disturbing as are some of the beliefs of some Islamists, they are no business of ours unless they are aimed at us. Rather than claiming the right to intervene inside foreign countries anywhere, the United States should live up to its security promises to countries like South Korea, Taiwan, and Israel, while pressuring them toward good behavior. It should preserve military power not to overwhelm but to deter potential enemies. This could reduce U.S. military expenditure by somewhere between 25 percent and 50 percent and the world would be a safer place. The United States must especially learn a lesson learned earlier by other empires: Muslims do not easily accept foreign empire. That is difficult to swallow since almost all the countries presently identified by American administrations as hostile are Muslim.

Folly not weakness has been the problem and U.S. strengths remain. The dollar still rules. More than 60 percent of the world's foreign reserves are held in dollars (only 27 percent are held in euros) and the dollar is the base-line for about half the world's currencies. An unrivaled higher education system still produces Nobel prizes and technological innovation. Combined with a flexible immigration policy, this pours out scientists, social scientists and engineers. In 2006 37 percent of PhDs in science were foreign-born and 20 percent of engineering and computer science PhDs were Asian-Americans (*Statistical Abstract of the United States*, 2009: 761).

Nonetheless a sense of American decay is in the air. A failed imperialism has plunged a region further into political difficulty and a failed neoliberalism has led much of the world into economic difficulty. America seems unable to address government debt, climate change, a dysfunctional health system, declining secondary education, potholes in the roads, and levels of class inequality which undermine the universal social citizenship laboriously constructed over half a century. One major political party rejects science and social science, including evolution, climate change, and the ability of governments to create jobs. The other party is timorous and disunited, in principle willing to confront problems but in practice unable. Their combination inside a separation of powers yawning wider is a stalemated polity corrupted by big business, perversely legitimated by the judiciary. Around 40 BC Cicero listed a series of woes of a Roman Republic sliding into Empire. He finished by declaring "one realizes that finally everything is for sale." The possibility suggests itself that the combination of capitalist corruption, fantasy ideology, and political incompetence indicates the terminal end of this empire/hegemony sooner than we might think.

Relative American economic decline will come. The U.S. contribution to world GDP (measured by purchasing power parity) is level with the European Union, just below that of the four BRIC countries combined. But this level is falling. The United States still has a lead over any single nation-state and this matters for a reserve currency. Eichengreen (2009) suggests the dollar will remain "the principal form of international reserves well into the future." He predicts the euro will gain market share, and in the longer run, the Chinese renminbi will join it. "But for as far as one can see clearly into the future, the dollar will remain first among equals." The IMF is less sanguine, seeing the reign of the dollar over by 2025.

Yet though the Recession has harmed American economic prestige, the Euro is troubled and does not have a single coherent state behind it. The EU spends less than 1 percent of European GDP, an indication of its tiny size and power. Its Constitution was designed so that politics would move at the pace of the slowest country. For its part, the renminbi is a state-controlled currency, not freely convertible. Neither it nor the euro could yet serve as a reserve currency. But a basket of currencies has been the more normal international reserve currency in the past and will probably reappear in the future. The BRIC countries recovered from recession more swiftly than did the United States, and this enhanced the gradual swing in economic power away from the West. Creditors in China, Japan and the oil-producing states will slowly diversify their foreign investments, which will dent U.S. hegemony. At some point down this trajectory of slow decline, current levels of U.S. military spending will become politically unsustainable, for without the dollar as reserve currency they would require higher taxes from Americans. Indeed, the U.S. budget deficit brought in 2011 acceptance in Washington that the growth in military expenses must be slowed, and eventually slightly reduced from 2017 onward. But bigger cuts are desirable and likely. In their origins American economic and military imperialism were closely linked, and they will decline together. This may amount to somewhat less than the "American century" which Henry Luce predicted in 1941. But it is not quite over yet.

American IR theorists divide on whether China's rise might raise the threat of war. Postcommunist China has emphasized economic growth and cooperative geopolitics. It has joined international bodies and settled most territorial disputes amicably. No military officer has served on the standing committee of the Politburo since 1992. But Deng Xiaoping's famous advice had an unspecified ending: "Coolly observe, calmly deal with things, hold your position, hide your capacities, bide your time, accomplish things where possible" – and then? Some worry over China's economic assertiveness in Africa, geopolitical assertiveness toward Japan, missiles positioned against U.S. domination of the South China Sea, and claims to islands therein. China will not brook interference in Tibet and Xinjiang and Taiwan remains a potential flash-point. Chinese popular nationalism has surged and military spending increasing, though SIPRI figures give it only a sixth of U.S. spending in 2009. Chinese leaders seem to have decided to seek a geopolitical status commensurate with their economic power. However, Japan apart, China has good relations with the countries of Southeast Asia, and China also depends on the Chinese capitalist diaspora. If China did become more aggressive, the other countries of East and South Asia, including the powerhouses of Japan and India, would ally together to balance Chinese power, and this is a disincentive for China. Moreover, China is deeply integrated into the American economy – and vice-versa. Such interdependence makes war between them unlikely. Some observe that World War I broke out despite increasing interdependence between the rival powers, but the level of mutual enmeshing of the American and Chinese economies is much deeper than in the earlier period. Both economies would collapse if war brought the banning of trade with the enemy. Arrighi (2007) additionally suggests that a Chinese-led Asian resurgence is likely to be pacific because of its generally peaceful historical record (which I evidenced in Volume 3, Chapter 2, when contrasted with historical Europe) and because of the "archipelago" nature of the East Asian economy with strong transnational linkages spearheaded by the overseas Chinese. The other economic powerhouse, the European Union, is very peaceful and currently fragile. In the famous words of a former Belgian foreign minister, Europe is "an economic giant, a political dwarf, and a military worm." On matters of war and peace there is much room for optimism.

In this volume I have traced the decline of imperialism across the world, with only one empire left standing, if floundering. American Empire has in the post–World War II decades been the third pillar of polymorphous globalizations, but it has recently been asked to support too much weight and is now teetering. Global peace would seem to depend most on American ability to decline gracefully. Though the long-term future may be brighter, the new American militarism charted here has been anything but graceful.

11 Global crisis: The great neoliberal recession

Chapter 6 narrated the rise of neoliberalism and its faltering at the beginning of the twenty first century. But deregulation and financial growth had continued to steam ahead, especially in the North of the world. As many have noted, periodic surges in financialization have occurred since at least the fifteenth century and they have tended to lead to major financial crises, like the South Sea Bubble or the Great Depression. The problem is generated by an overaccumulation of capital, which becomes too great to be invested in productive activity. Thus investors switch to investing in financial instruments, which are less bound by real material resources. Keynes had worried about this tendency in his *General Theory* (1973 edition: 159–61), noting "So long as it is open to the individual to employ his wealth in hoarding or lending money, the alternative of purchasing actual capital assets cannot be rendered sufficiently attractive ... except by organising markets wherein these assets can be easily realised for money." Such financialization might deepen and become more leveraged and Keynes feared lest the "enterprise becomes the bubble on a whirlpool of speculation ... When the capital development of a country becomes a by-product of the activities of a casino, the job is likely to be ill-done."

Hyman Minsky (1982) then built on Keynes to advance his financial instability hypothesis, according to which advanced capitalist economies shifted toward more fragile financial structures not supported by the underlying accumulation process, thereby generating crises. These came in three phases, he believed. The first one, "hedge finance," remained healthy since expected future revenue from investments exceeded running costs, while payments of debt and interest charges conformed to normal accounting standards. The second phase involved riskier "speculative finance," in which debt and interest charges must be met either by selling assets or by further borrowing. Then in the third disastrous phase, "Ponzi finance," debt and interest charges can only be met by selling on the assets, which sales then continue upward until finance so outruns the real economy that the system collapses.[1] Minsky did not offer an explanation of this sequence, but as a description it is what actually happened over the last three decades, and on a global scale. I seek now to explain its causes and initial consequences. Obviously this chapter will deal mainly with economic power relations, though ideological and political power will also figure.

---

[1] Named after Charles Ponzi, a notorious American fraudster of the early 1920s.

In Chapter 6 I charted the continuing stagnation from around 1970 of the economy of the global North. There had been several attempts made to stem it. Neo-Keynesian efforts ground to a halt in the 1970s when growth-stimulating policies that accepted a mild level of inflation now failed to work. Productivity was stagnant, and unemployment and inflation unexpectedly rose together. For a period, governments tolerated higher levels of inflation. When these reached unacceptable levels, they began to deflate but without reducing government expenditures. This produced unacceptable levels of budget deficit. Since politicians wanted to be reelected, they did not respond with higher taxes. Instead they attempted to cut government expenditure. They succeeded but at the cost of stagnant wage levels, greater inequality, and more poverty. The root cause of this was a faltering of capitalism in the global North. Manufacturing industry was increasingly moving south, where costs (especially wage-costs) were lower. Capitalism needed another dose of creative destruction. It certainly got the destruction (of manufacturing) and it also got the creation of new microelectronic, dot-com, and bio-technology industries, but these were not big enough to restore profit levels or full employment. There were then two main reactions. At the level of capital, entrepreneurs began to invest less in industries creating physical goods and more in financial instruments, which became more and more abstruse and more and more outstripping the real productive base of the economy. And at the level of labor, decisions were taken to keep up demand and contain unrest by making credit much easier for the mass of the population. Combined, these forces were to produce a credit crisis, not of government but of both the top and the bottom of the private economy. That is the story I will narrate in this chapter.

As we also saw in Chapter 6, the United States, which was to be the epicenter of the coming storm, had effected a major redistribution from labor to capital, from ordinary Americans to the rich. Capital's share of pretax profit and interest in national income had risen from around 12 percent in the 1930s and 1940s to 17 percent in the 2000s. Effective corporate tax rate had fallen, from 55 percent in the 1940s to less than 30 percent in the 2000s, and posttax corporate earnings had increased dramatically. All this pushed up stock market valuations. Investors believed net profits would continue rising and so stock market capitalization rose four times faster than gross national income. It would have needed great economic growth to support such expectations. Yet U.S. GDP growth actually fell from 3.6 percent p.a. between 1950 and 1975 to 3.1 percent afterward and world GDP growth dropped from 4.7 percent to 3.5 percent.

Before the 1980s American financial services had been highly regulated by the state. Reagan had then begun a process of deregulation (Prasad, 2006). Yet the 1933 Glass-Steagall Act was still in place and it had erected a firewall between commercial and investment banks. Commercial banks are regular High/Main Street banks, which take customers' deposits in cash, offer low rates of interest, make loans at slightly higher interest rates, and pocket small but regular profits on the difference. They take in real money and they create real money whenever they extend a loan. In contrast, investment banks accept money for investment into stocks and commodities. When they take in deposits or make loans, they have to clear these through deposits held at commercial banks. Unlike the latter, they cannot create money. Theirs is a higher-risk enterprise, but their investments were limited by the rules of the commercial banks. But if the two types of bank are merged, then the investment wing of the new bank has access to real cash as well as the power to create money, and so the constraints might be lessened. But most countries had no such firewall and their banks continued to act conservatively.

In the 1980s American commercial banks began to exploit loopholes in Glass-Steagall to enter the securities markets. They pressed for complete abolition and achieved it in 1999. It was a Republican initiative, though with bi-partisan support and it was signed into law by President Clinton. Since only the United States had such an Act, its repeal might not seem too dangerous. But two things differed in the United States. First, Americans – governments and people – ran on credit much more than any other country, and so their debt needed more supervision. Second, in countries like Germany, Japan, or Sweden the major role of big banks remained investment in manufacturing industry. Close relations between finance and manufacturing made for less speculative banking.

Glass-Steagall repeal was not the only deregulation. Interest rate ceilings had been abolished, capital requirements for savings-and-loans institutions had been slashed, variable rate mortgages and money market funds spread widely, and altogether regulation was now considered as bad. The Fed under Greenspan gradually abandoned any attempt to steer the economy and any attempt to set maximum interest rates that banks could offer savers. Instead in a series of steps it began simply to follow the market (Krippner, 2011: chaps. 3 & 5). Fed chairman Greenspan, Treasury Secretary Robert Rubin, and Securities and Exchange Commission Chairman Arthur Levitt opposed any regulation of derivatives, backed by heavy lobbying from Wall Street and by the presence of bankers within the administration. One leading investment bank, Goldman Sachs, provided numerous Treasury and White House officers. The top ten U.S. banks control more than 60 percent of all financial assets, and their top personnel staff most key government advisory positions. Johnson (2009) comments that this resembles the crony capitalism of banana republics. This level of corporate concentration threatens democracy, especially since it is heavily biased toward the interests of the rich.

The causes of the Great Recession

Numerous forces had contributed to financial expansion: the role and the floating of the dollar reserve currency, OPEC, removing capital controls, merging commercial and investment banks, an internet enabling financial transactions to be globally instantaneous, and more volatile interest rates all contributed. But underlying all this was a relative stagnation in the real economy, and especially in manufacturing. Between 1973 and 2000 the average annual growth of American labor productivity – that is, GDP per hour – has been less than 1 percent per annum, which is almost a third of its average for the previous century. Over this period real wage growth was lower than at any other point in U.S. history. In 1997, the hourly real wage for production workers was about the same as it had been in 1965. Despite this, the rate of return on capital investment declined. This squeeze on manufacturing profits resulted from overcapacity and overproduction, which was in turn the consequence of increased international competition, and this problem gradually spread from the United States to the North in general. America was hit first in the late 1960s by later-developing, lower-cost producers in Germany and Japan. Then in the 1970s Germany and Japan were hit by the rising value of their currencies against as a consequence of an international monetary crisis and the collapse of Bretton Woods. Then the other East Asian countries joined in, able to produce at lower cost than America, Europe, and Japan. Overcapacity, overproduction, falling profits became general, and capitalist corporations were not able to find major new industries that were able to compensate for that. So capital shunned manufacturing and went instead into finance. The subsequent financial crisis therefore ultimately depended on the weakness of manufacturing, especially in the United States and Britain, but in other countries too (Brenner, 2002).

In the burgeoning financial sector, there were then three direct causes of the crisis of 2008: unregulated shadow banks, global imbalances, and debt. Investment bank profits shot up in the 1990s and 2000s, which made commercial banks envious for they had been losing traditional savings and deposits business to pension funds and insurance companies. Corporate financing was also providing less profit than formerly. So some commercial banks abandoned conservatism and went for the profits – averaging 12 percent – of the derivative markets. They were using the savings of their many millions of customers in risky ventures, without their knowledge. They invented a host of derivatives like securitization, interest-rate swaps and credit-default swaps, which they believed insured them against risks except those with extremely low probability of occurrence. For example mortgage-holders may default on their loans but default is usually a fairly random and rare result. Securitization, making the loan more secure, might result if one bundles loans together. The few bad loans will then be outweighed by the many reliably paying back.

A derivative can provide a hedge against risk. If Bank A worries about a loan it has made, it strikes a derivative deal, paying a fee to Bank B in exchange for Bank B's promise to compensate Bank A if the loan sours. Bank A sheds some of the uncertainty related to its loan and is now happy to make further loans. Bank B assumes some of the risk but gets fee income now. It's win-win, they told each other. They then mixed derivatives with securitization: lenders sold their loans to an investment bank, which bundled the loans together and sold pieces of the bundle to pension funds and other investors. The original lenders, having offloaded their loans, could make new ones. The investors acquired a slice of the loan bundle and its interest income without going to the trouble of assessing the borrowers. Then they securitized not just loans but credit derivatives, selling securitized debt. One can buy and sell the price movement of an asset rather than the asset itself; or the risk of default on a loan, even by a country, as Greece discovered in 2010. What is happening through this process, as Crouch (2011: chap. 5) notes, is that the value of any derivative becomes more and more divorced from the reality of the original asset. The buyers and sellers know nothing of this, only what the market valuation is. It is an extreme version of shareholder value. Assets are not assessed, only stock market valuation. In this game of pass the parcel, value is created by the act of passing, and so the velocity of passing also increases. Financial services were moving up Minsky's scale of risk.

Leveraging is borrowing against one's capital stake. The instruments noted previously helped banks increase their leveraging. Nineteenth century banks had leverages of about two, that is they borrowed twice the level of their capital stake. This meant that half your assets must go bad before you go bust. But in the 2000s leveraging had reached the range of 20–30 in many banks. With a leverage of 20 you go bust if you lose only 5 percent of your assets. The risks were increasing exponentially (Haldane, 2012).

Yet the bankers were delighted. Not only were they using other people's money without their knowledge to make profit, but this increased the number of transactions on which banks could charge up-front fees and commissions for trades. Most CEOs and market traders were not taking personal risks. They could book profits on their trades and build up their end-of-year bonuses, which mattered more to them than the long-term health of the firm. The faster they could buy and sell, the bigger their bonuses. Risk-taking, which generated big returns now but possible bankruptcy later, was not risky for them, for they had sold on the debt. So finance sector profits kept on increasing. In the United States between 1973 and 1985 the financial sector had never made more than 16 percent of domestic corporate profits. By the 2000s this had reached 41 percent. Financial sector pay also rose. Before 1982 it had never averaged more than 108 percent of pay in private industries. By 2007 it had reached 181 percent (Johnson, 2009). Bankers were coining it, seemingly without much risk. The more politically savvy ones had even figured out that by now they were too big to fail. In the last resort the government would bail them out. Gains were privatized, losses socialized.

It made some criminal behavior inevitable. Greed is necessary to capitalism. To quote Streeck (2009) profit-seeking is "constitutionally devious." The typical capitalist, he says, is a rule-bender, a rational- utilitarian exploiter of gaps in the rules, a quality that is even admired in our culture. Quantitative research reveals that the neoliberal deregulation implemented between 1986 and 2000 created greater opportunities for managers to engage in financial malfeasance (Prechel & Morris, 2010). The multilayer-subsidiary corporate form, legally permitted since 1986, enabled them to make capital transfers among legally independent corporate entities in ways hidden to regulators and to the investing public, enabling fraud and its concealment. The increased use of stock options gave managers incentives to misrepresent and inflate corporate financial statements. The legal creation of off-balance-sheet entities meant that financing and assets could be placed in companies that did not appear in the parent companies' financial statements. These and over-the-counter derivative markets enabled managers to make hidden and unregulated capital transfers, which also gave them information advantages over the investing public. There is no clear divide between such information asymmetries and insider trading. The 2000 Commodities Futures Modernization Act also enabled managers to transfer risk to unsuspecting investors through the use of extremely complex financial instruments. Information asymmetries also meant that no one knew just how much fraud was being perpetrated. Yet it is unlikely given the strength of the capitalist profit motive and the incentives to bend bankers' fiduciary trust norms, that malfeasance was the work of a few bad apples. It had become normal behavior. Former Goldman Sachs executive Greg Smith is bitter about his former colleagues: "I attend derivative sales meetings where not one single minute is spent asking questions about how we can help our clients. It's purely about how we can make the most money off of them.... It makes me ill how callously people talk about ripping their clients off" (*New York Times*, March 14, 2012). Stricter regulation and more criminal prosecution is the way to deal with this, but both were lacking.

Expansion was helped by the second cause of crisis, global imbalances. These reveal that nation-states and macroregions both remain important in the global economy. During the postwar period the United States initially ran large trade surpluses and capital exports, but this had reversed itself to trade deficits and inflows of capital, become large by the mid-1980s and increasing again after 2000. The United States was running especially large current account deficits, while exporters like Japan, China and the oil states had large surpluses. Chinese high savings rates fed a global liquidity boom, which increased asset prices and lowered interest rates. Money was so cheap, anyone could borrow. Imbalances seemed manageable as long as foreign creditors continued to hold assets denominated in debtor currencies. After the bursting of the dot.com bubble, private foreign investors had been largely replaced by central bank purchasers, sovereign wealth funds (SWFs), especially by Japan and China. These state-run enterprises were willing since this facilitated their massive exports to the West and in the case of China it made for rapid economic growth and social stability at home. It would have been better for China and the world had the regime boosted domestic demand by higher wages and lower inequality. Then China would have exported less and the United States and Europe could have exported more to China, lessening global imbalances. Creditor countries feared more the global contraction that would result if the United States went in for austerity in order to reduce its debt levels. But the United States benefited more, being able to borrow at low interest rates and then use the cash to invest in ventures with a higher rate of return. Thus the United States got an economic boom in the 1990s, with faster rates of economic growth than either Europe or Japan.

This imbalanced global economy seems to some to indicate the strength, not the weakness of the American economy (Schwartz, 2009). An analysis of the economic history of 14 developed countries over the last 140 years showed that credit growth was the single best predictor of financial instability, with imbalances playing a smaller role. But the collapse of Bretton Woods made a big difference. While it lasted, there were no financial crises, afterward there were many, plus a correlation between lending booms and current account imbalances (Jorda et al., 2010).

Moreover, the whole edifice also depended on what might be a fragile base: rocketing Western household debt. These debts rather than global imbalances directly caused the Great Neoliberal Recession. Debt is normal in capitalism, being merely investment seen from a different angle. Schumpeter defined capitalism as "that form of private property in which innovations are carried out by means of borrowed money," though he regarded the entrepreneur as the agent of creative destruction, whereas the banker was merely a facilitator (1982, orig. 1939: pp 92–4, 179; 1961, orig, 1911, pp 107, 117, 405–6). But bankers now saw themselves as the real creators of value and the debts which they were handling had become the key to the global economy. By 2008 world debt was $160 trillion, three times the world's GDP, while the value of all derivatives was $680 trillion, an astounding sixteen times world GDP. In the 1920s world debt had been around 150 percent of GDP. In the Great Depression it had briefly risen to 250 percent but from 1940 to 1980 it hovered again around 150 percent. Then it kept rising to 350 percent by 2007. Debt was consuming millions of people, especially in America where household debt had been about 64 percent of disposable income in 1980, up to 77 percent by 1990 and zooming up to 121 percent by 2008. Over the same period savings declined from 9.8 percent to 2.7 percent. Debt was proportionately greatest among the poorest households. Underlying this was a weakness of aggregate demand. Ever since the downturn of the 1970s government policies had tried to cope with the problem of insufficient demand by borrowing. But because profitability had not recovered, interest rates were lowered to make everyone's borrowing easier. Since the neoliberal offensive had kept wages low and reduced welfare and other public spending, demand and investment were reduced, and so private debt became the supposed way to restore profitability (Brenner, 2002).

But debt was not being regulated. By 2005 75 percent of lending in the United States was done by nonregulated shadow banks. Hedge funds were the dominant form, but there were also asset-backed commercial paper conduits, structured investment vehicles, auction-rate preferred securities, tender option bonds and variable rate demand notes – more and more arcane financial products. Hedge funds and their shadow comrades typically escape regulation, managing to organize their legal shell in tiny offshore countries like Bermuda or the Cayman Isles where no one wants to regulate them because they added significantly to the local economy. The Securities and Exchange Commission could have restricted the quantity and quality of investment banks' debts but it failed to do so. In 2004 it even permitted them to increase their leverage and by 2008 they were borrowing up to thirty times their reserve capital. The commercial banks were also developing new structured investment vehicles and other off-balance-sheet transactions. These over-the-counter, in-house derivatives were not being regulated either. They had created a whole new meaning for Schumpeter's creative destruction, destroying an economy by ingenious means!

Debt was much higher in the Anglo countries, especially the United States. Their minimal welfare states pushed people into borrowing to finance their children's education, health care, and retirement, which in other countries were financed by general taxation. Thus the proportion of private health care in a country and the proportion of credit in its GDP are correlated (Prasad, 2006). The ideal of a property-owning democracy was also more developed among Anglo politicians, and governments of both right and left were drawn into subsidizing home mortgages, which became consumers' biggest debts. Renting was more common in most other countries (Schwartz, 2009), and rents were subsidized in the more generous welfare states.

As we saw in Chapters 2 and 3, American postwar economic growth had depended on a combination of market forces and government macroeconomic planning. Together they had generated mass consumerism centered on house purchase, automobiles and other consumer durables. Over more than two decades GDP and family incomes had risen together. But from the 1970s family incomes began to stagnate and inequality widened, with depressing effect on mass consumption, which was now only financed by taking on debt. As we saw in Volume 3, Chapter 7, this had been also one of the causes of the Great Depression.

Ordinary American households had already gone through two attempted solutions to their difficulties. The first solution was that more women in the household took up paid employment – for other reasons too, including declining fertility, improving education and feminism. The participation rate of women increased from 44 percent to 60 percent between 1973 and 2003, while women's median personal income almost doubled. But their wages were lower than men's, and the increased labor supply also had the effect of lowering men's wages. Though women's wages relative to men's were rising throughout the period, the absolute gains of women in employment were rather small, except near the top of the income scale. Thus average overall household income barely changed (Massey, 2007: 42–4) while inequality between households was rocketing.

The second attempted solution was to work longer hours to keep up wages. But hours and wages increased much more for better-educated, higher-skilled women (Hout & Fischer, 2006: 122–4). Working women guaranteed the American Dream for the upper middle class. But they barely enabled working class households to keep their heads above water. Yet they wanted to maintain their consumption levels.

So a third solution was adopted by governments and households: let the people take on more debt. This proved possible in two interrelated ways. First, increasing national debt and global imbalances enabled the mass import of cheap Chinese and other Asian goods, which big retail outlets in the United States like Walmart and Target recycled to ordinary households. Since many consumption goods got cheaper, a potential American debt bubble did not yet burst. But second, household debt, gradually increasing through the postwar period, saw a major surge after 1995 due to home mortgages (Massey, 2007: 178). Foreign capital inflows resulted in lower interest rates and higher house prices, both of which made it possible to remortgage cheaply. This seemed an ideal way to minimize the social discontent that might arise from rising inequality. People could maintain their consumption and their standard of living by taking on more debt, secured against the rising value of their home. This was the single largest factor enabling the United States to keep up consumer demand and experience a national economic boom and faster growth than any other country from the late 1990s into the mid 2000s. Crouch (2009) calls it privatized Keynesianism, not like the real thing of course (cf. Schwartz, 2009: chap. 4).

There were now two short booms in mortgage markets. The first, in the late 1990s, mostly involved refinancing homes especially in nonwhite communities. Since housing prices were steadily rising, consumers thought they could borrow using their housing equity as security. They were using their homes as ATMs to finance the American Way of Life. The second boom came from 2002 as interest rates fell, more capital was looking for outlets, and more poor people were suckered into new variable-rate mortgages (made legal by the Reagan administration) starting at very low interest rates. The specialized occupation of mortgage originator broker had arisen, taking over from the loan officers of banks and savings-and-loans institutions. The brokers were paid commission on the value of each mortgage sold and so had an incentive to clinch deals regardless of the client's resources (which they sometimes falsified). The client also often ended up with a costlier mortgage rate in order for the broker to increase his/her cut. The banks acquiring the mortgages then protected themselves by selling on riskier pooled mortgages in securitized packages to investors. Markets were structured so that brokers and the issuers of securitization were actually increasing the risk of default yet passing that risk onto others (Immergluck, 2009: chaps. 3 & 4). This combination of perverse incentives and dishonesty did keep working class families afloat while interest rates remained low. But note that behind this combination, and ultimately the major cause of the Great Recession itself, was the increasing level of inequality and poverty in the United States. The country would have been better off if more of the national income had been in the hands of middle- and working-class families, for they would have spent it on real necessities, which would have generated real jobs. But why had this not happened? Let me first document the extent of inequality.

Economic inequality: The arrival of American exceptionalism

I resisted the notion of American exceptionalism in chapters dealing with previous periods. Between the mid-1890s and 1929 the United States had lagged in union power and social citizenship, though not in education or women's rights. Its racism was distinctive, but only because it was felt mainly at home. Britain practiced it abroad in its Empire – and whereas 90 percent of its imperial subjects were excluded from meaningful citizenship, that was only true of 10 percent of America's. Then in the Great Depression, the New Deal and World War II, the United States pioneered together with the other Anglophone countries progressive taxation, and it also developed its own welfare programs. It was also catching up in union power. From then to the late 1970s, the United States had mixed experiences, again lagging somewhat in social citizenship and woefully in union power, but maintaining progressive taxation, enfranchising its black population, and fully sharing in the growth of rights for women and other identities. Since the 1970s, however, more regressive taxation, lagging social citizenship and income inequality has steadily gathered momentum.

At the beginning of the twenty first century the United States became exceptional among advanced countries in the extent of its inequality, especially at the top of the income scale. Among twenty-four OECD countries only Mexico and Turkey – the least developed countries – had higher inequality and more poverty in 2005 (OECD, 2008; Piketty & Saez, 2003; Saez, 2009; Massey, 2007: 35–6, 166–8; Hacker & Pierson, 2010: 155–9; Brandolini, 2010: 213–6). The share of all incomes going to the top 10 percent of Americans rose steadily from 33 percent in 1980 to almost 50 percent in 2007, the highest share ever recorded. Between 1974 and 2007 the higher the income, the bigger the increase. This was true for every income decile. At the very top the super-rich saw the biggest gains. The top 1 percent almost tripled its share of national income, the share of the top 0.1 percent (about 150,000 families) more than quadrupled, and the top

0.001 percent (15,000 families) share increased six-fold. These small groups comprise the core of the capitalist class. experiencing very large increases in its absolute levels of income.

In contrast, middling income deciles – mainly managerial, technical and professional occupations – saw a very slight gain in household income, but the lowest deciles – the working and lower middle classes – were stagnant. At the bottom, adjustments to the federal minimum wage became rarer and meaner, so that by 2006 its real value had declined by 45 percent from its 1968 peak. There is little sign of any change in these trends. Census returns reveal that in 2010 the median household income had declined back to the level reached in 1996, while 15 percent of Americans were below the poverty level, the highest figure since 1993. The median annual income for a full-time male worker in 2010 was $47,715 – slightly lower than its level in 1973. Indeed, the United States continues to invest less and less in the programs that can create more skilled and relatively high wage jobs. In 2010 48 million Americans aged between eighteen and sixty-four failed to work a single week, while 50 million lacked medical insurance – both figures being higher than any annual figures over the last decades. Ethnic minorities and young people have been the hardest hit. No relief is in sight since spending on job training, infrastructures, and research and development has declined and in the new millennium has formed less than 10 percent of all federal spending.

Among the twenty countries with the best data the United States had seen the biggest rise in inequality, though the UK and Canada followed its steep upward trend from the mid-1980s. The Gini coefficients of fourteen of these countries also rose, though by lesser amounts, in the 1980s and 1990s. In the 2000s, however, trends were more variable. Half the Ginis remained fairly static, a quarter fell – including the UK – and a quarter continued rising, especially the United States. Russia and China (see Chapters 7 and 8) also rose substantially, along with India's, though these cases lack comparable data on deciles and the super-rich. In contrast, the share of the top groups in the main Euro countries and in Japan had remained virtually static throughout the last few decades. By 2005 the American Gini coefficient was distinctly higher than any other Western country and was double the Ginis of several Nordic countries, a remarkable disparity! (OECD, 2008; Atkinson et al., 2009; Mann & Riley, 2007).

This remarkable increase in American inequality, sustained over more than three decades, affecting all strata but benefiting the superrich most, has occasioned much debate. Most declare it an example of American exceptionalism and attribute it to purely domestic causes. Yet this is a mistake, for other Anglophone countries were exhibiting similar tendencies. Some downplay this or attribute it to American domination of English-language business (Hacker & Pierson, 2010: 160–1); others leave it for further research (Brandolini, 2010: 216). But we can distinguish three main causes of rising inequality. First came pressures felt across the world, though better resisted in some countries than others, and which rarely affected the very top of the income distribution. Second came pressures common to the Anglo countries, some of which did affect the super-rich. Third came those American peculiarities, which made the trend greatest in the United States, though they might have been only exaggerations of causes shared with Anglos or others.

I briefly recapitulate my comparative conclusions reached in Volume 3, Chapter 9, and Chapter 6 here. The common pressures felt in all advanced countries were economic, though entwined with demography. This was a period of relative stagnation or low growth and the export of manufacturing industry, punctuated by recessions in which employers sought to lower their wage-bills and in which unemployment (especially in Europe) and/or casual employment (especially in America) increased. De-industrialization and the export of jobs to poorer countries added a decline in the proportion of skilled and supposedly secure blue-collar workers. The expansion of higher education, and the maturation of welfare programs plus the ageing of the population placed a scissors of need from young and old on government finances. Changing marriage and divorce patterns especially widened female inequality and created the need for more income support at the bottom, especially among single mothers. Rising burdens and lower tax yields were bound to produce some cuts in every country. However, as we have seen, the Nordic and some Euro countries coped without increasing inequality as much. This was because their welfare states were popular among the middle as well as the working class, plus the combination of corporatism, high labor union density (or militancy in the case of France) protecting them from the cold winds of market forces, and ample free child-care facilities allowing mothers, especially single mothers, to work full-time.

But the other Anglo countries tended to shadow the United States because of their shared voluntarism rather than corporatism, their plummeting union membership, the emergence of a divide in the working class, with secure and skilled workers turning against a welfare seen as subsidizing scroungers at their expense, and the success of women of high occupational attainment compared to poor women, who suffered more single motherhood, the need to pay for child-care, and low, casual wages. In 2005 of the Anglo countries only Australia fell (slightly) below the average level of inequality in all the OECD countries, and only the UK fell below the average extent of poverty (OECD, 2008). In the United States resistance to market forces was especially low while the resentments of workers were exacerbated by more racism. These are the main reasons why general inequality increased only slightly in most advanced countries, and why it increased more in the United States than in the other Anglo countries.

Yet none of these pressures could explain the extraordinary widening of inequality at the top of the income scale. Many economists argue that top incomes have become more unequal as a result of technological changes. They often compare CEOs to basketball or football stars whose extraordinary incomes reflect their extraordinary skills (and whose wealth is therefore regarded by most fans as legitimate). In this model CEOs should get paid much more than anyone else because their skills are rare. Dew-Becker and Gordon (2005) tested this by examining productivity and income growth over the years 1966–2001. They first noted that only the top 10 percent of the population enjoyed income growth commensurate with U.S. productivity gains, while the top 1 percent and especially the top 0.1 percent reaped the biggest gains. Yet these gainers formed "much too narrow a group to be consistent with a widespread benefit from SBTC" [Skill-biased technical change]. The earnings of hi-tech occupations either increased only slightly or they declined, while those of CEOs more than doubled. But CEOs and top managers make decisions that can make or lose millions of dollars. Maybe only a very few people have a gift for this, and so really are worth million-dollar salaries.

Yet this argument took a knock in the Great Neoliberal Recession when it became evident that CEOs were receiving enormous salaries whether or not the corporation made money under their stewardship. There is also a vital difference between CEOs and sports stars: the CEOs are paying themselves. In Chapter 7 we saw what happened when ordinary workers at the end of the Soviet Union were given the power to decide their own wages. Wages shot up without any increase in productivity. Dew-Becker and Gordon also note another uncomfortable fact for the SBTC argument: Europe saw the same technical and corporate changes but no significant rise in inequality and only modest CEO pay rises. European enterprises are no less efficient or productive than American ones. Britain and Ireland within Europe did shadow U.S. salary patterns, but there was no correlation between rocketing inequality at the top and economic efficiency.

Over half the pay increases of top executives came from stock options, which they could claim if the stock market price of the firm went up (Fligstein, 2010: 237–8). Since the entire stock market went up in the 1980s and 1990s the earnings of most company executives surged upward, regardless of how well their firm compared to its competitors. Maximizing shareholder value had become the dominant business strategy. The recession of the 1970s had left many corporations undervalued, holding more cash and assets than they were apparently worth, and aided by the Reagan administration's deregulating program a wave of mergers and takeovers followed. To protect their own positions from takeover, top managers took on debt, sold off undervalued assets, downsized and fired workers and low-level managers, and raised short-term share prices and profits. The argument followed that managers own performance could and should be measured by the short-term share price of their corporation. This would align the interests of shareholders and executives so that massive salary increases were not at the (short-term) expense of the shareholders. Since one way to boost share prices was simply to close or export a branch or fire workers – the markets believed this signaled a drive toward efficiency – it resulted not only in rocketing top salaries and share values but also some redistribution from labor to capital. These greatly increased inequality at the top.

Stock options were rarer elsewhere. Nordic and Euro corporations were less oriented to the stock market. More concentrated ownership, block share-holding, and more financing by the banks reduced the salience of short-term share prices and stock options. In 2001 50 percent of nonfinancial listed companies in Austria, Belgium, Germany, and Italy had a single block-holder controlling over half the voting rights, mostly wealthy families or banks protecting their corporations from the short-term vagaries of the stock market. The traditional upper class has its virtues! Anglos differed because of dispersed shareholding. In the UK the median block-holder controlled only 10 percent of votes, and in the United States only 5 percent. There was some movement across Europe in the 1990s toward stock options, but the difference from the Anglos remained (Ferrarini et al., 2003; Schwartz, 2009: 156). Macroregions matter. In the United States gains from stock options as well as all the profits of hedge fund managers are liable to capital gains not income taxes, and these are paid at lower rates. This is true of some British hedge funds too. Tax policy increased top incomes in both the UK and the United States.

So the disproportionate rise of top incomes in the two biggest Anglos was substantially due to CEOs paying themselves more, with the consent of shareholders, and this was due to the distinctive nature of Anglo share-holding. This involved distributive not collective economic power and it did long-term harm to capitalism as well as short-term harm to other classes, since it threatened the basis of the high growth – high consumer demand economy, which capitalism, assisted by states, had managed to devise. It was aided by the neoliberal ideology more prevalent in Anglo countries. If business wanted to pay its leaders more, it was not government's role to interfere. Politicians trumpeted the economic virtues of incentives for the rich, and geared tax policies to this. [2]

The conundrum of inequality in the United States

From the 1980s onward Republican administrations, especially those of Reagan and Bush the Younger, cut welfare programs, failed to increase minimum wages, and ended the progressive bias of the tax system. In Bush the Younger's tax cuts the top 1 percent received a remarkable 25 percent tax cut compared to the 5 percent enjoyed by most people (Massey, 2007: 5). Democratic administrations held the line, but not much more. Clinton slightly increased the average tax rate on rich households, while leaving others unchanged, and the working

[2] I have presented almost no data on Australia and New Zealand, and few on Canada and do not know whether this is also the case there.

poor were slightly helped by his Earned Income Tax Credit. But his welfare reform hurt the poor. We saw previously that the British, Australian and New Zealand Labour Parties joined in such regressive policies. Studies of posttax and postwelfare transfer incomes shows that U.S. politicians have regressed most since the early 1980s. But Canada and the UK were not far behind from the 1990s (Kenworthy, 2010: 218–9). So we also need to explain why the center-left parties in Anglo countries did not seem to fight harder against fiscal and welfare regression.

What has especially puzzled analysts is how few Americans seemed to mind grossly widening inequality. Since America is a democracy, why no backlash at the polls? Polls show that most Americans are aware that inequality has greatly widened and they believe the rich should pay more taxes. They espouse some abstract conservative principles, believing in individual responsibility, free enterprise and the American Dream, but they also embrace government programs of greater equality, particularly those that provide social security and educational opportunities for all. Most Americans, whether they vote Democrat or Republican, favor government intervention in health care, education, and provision of jobs, and say they are even willing to pay higher taxes for them. In these respects they do not differ much from the citizens of other advanced countries (Osberg & Smeeding, 2006; Page & Jacobs, 2009). Americans also say that if cuts are made in expenditures, they should come first in defense, not in social programs. Yet none of this translates into political action. Why not?

Since America is a liberal democracy, parties and elections are supposed to reflect citizen preferences. Over the last decades the Republican Party has become decidedly neoliberal in its rhetoric, favoring letting markets rule. If that means more inequality, so be it. Indeed, it has gone further, actually encouraging more inequality because then, it says, entrepreneurs will invest more and create more jobs. The Party is also close to the rich and to big business. So one part of our explanation must address the issue of why masses of ordinary people vote for such a Republican Party. But we must also address the issue of the Democratic Party's timidity, even pusillanimity, in seeking to reverse the trend toward greater inequality.

It might be that class-based voting has declined. But this is not true, since the correlation between class and voting actually increased since the 1970s. Republicans got more of the votes of the rich, Democrats more of the poor. However, there is a difference in who gets to vote. Lower turnouts among the poor and immigrants hurt the Democrats and any redistribution to the poor. Immigration to the United States almost doubled between 1970 and 2000 and shifted toward being mostly people from poor countries with lower skills. Since most are not citizens, they cannot vote. The presumption is that if they could, more would vote Democrat. The effect is that the median voter's income has not fallen much, and so the average *voter* is not too bothered about inequality

(McCarty et al., 2006). This combination of nonvoting and immigration is greater than in Europe, including the UK. It is part of the explanation.

Structural, especially class shifts in voting might provide a second part of the answer. Yet shifts among voters have tended to cancel each other out, giving no overall advantage to either party. Professionals and nonmanagerial white-collars became more Democrat. However, this was more out of identity politics than economic liberalism and was counterbalanced by the self-employed and managers voting more Republican, mainly for economic reasons. Women did shift to becoming mostly Democrat, with feminist issues becoming important from the 1990s. African-Americans became overwhelmingly Democrat, while more Latinos voted in the 2000s, disproportionately Democrat. Religion benefited the Republicans more from the 1990s as Evangelicals became solidly Republican and those regularly attending religious services became twice as likely to vote Republican. So overall, neither party gained much from these shifts (Hout et al., 1995, Manza & Brooks, 1997, 1998; Brooks & Manza, 1997; Olson, 2006).

Perhaps economic issues matter less than they used to. Houtman et al. (2008) say that they remain important in America and working class voters continue to express views favoring redistribution, yet this has increasingly played second fiddle among many workers (and others) to moral issues like abortion, the Christian family, law and order, and a supposed breakdown of traditional values in the face of morally lax liberalism. This may be an indirect reaction against the success of capitalist consumerism, which is pervasively felt to be corrosive of moral and family values. Or it may be a broader sense of malaise in a nation that senses injustice and/or decline but has no clear economic sense of who to blame.

There are parallels to this in Europe but in America the reaction became bigger and more politically organized, amounting to another Great Awakening sweeping across the old southern Bible Belt and then broadening out to rural, small-town and parts of suburban America where churches are the principal social institutions. The resurgence of religion fueled conservatism and hostility to "materialistic" issues, and it bent economic radicalism toward a conservative populism. More white workers listened to politicians putting the blame for their economic stagnation on high taxes, big government, and a welfare state supposedly favoring immoral scroungers, welfare queens, feckless blacks and immigrants. Since racism had gone covert, polls cannot tap it accurately, but the Republicans were deploying Atwater-type covert racism, which helped them in the South among white workers and contributed to the tarnishing of welfare programs in the eyes of whites. Racism may have outweighed all the other moral issues in swinging workers' votes rightward, against their class interests. On the other side, more higher managers and professionals were also voting against their own economic class interests, choosing moral liberalism over wealth. Recently, European racism has also been increasing and generating far-right parties, pushing traditional conservative parties rightward, but the potential damage to the universal welfare state has not yet become actual.

In his study of Kansas Frank (2004) found moral issues dominant. Kansas Republicans used cultural wedge issues like abortion, gun control and moral decline to persuade working class people to vote against their economic interests. Control of local Republican parties shifted from business worthies to religious middle class whites passionate about repealing *Roe* v. *Wade*, blending economic and moral interests in a cultivation of the backlash of the people against big government and liberal elites. This was a genuine ideology, involving passionate attachment and hatred. Bartels (2008) disagreed with this, however, claiming that cultural issues only affected relatively affluent white voters, not working-class whites, who still rated economic issues higher and still favored economic redistribution. These two studies had different samples. Frank researched rural and small-town Kansas, but this part of America was under-represented (for practical reasons) in the national polls relied on by Bartels. Frank's study was thus of the Republican heartland. Rural and small-town America votes much more Republican than the rest of the nation. After two hundred years of electoral democracy, the United States finally has national, not regional politics, but they are urban-rural ones. 2004 election data "indicate a 20-point gap...between inhabitants of counties with more than a million people and those in...counties of less than 25,000." This gap has widened to become bigger than the class or gender gap (Gimpel and Karnes, 2006). Its size is unique to the United States.

In 2004, as well as being more Republican, rural voters were more white, more Evangelical, more church-going, and more elderly, and they were less educated and poorer than those in the cities and suburbs. They owned more guns, more often strongly opposed abortion, and lived in more traditional families. They were more likely to be homeowners and self-employed. Numerous surveys also show that they are more satisfied with their lives and jobs. Incomes are also more equal in rural and small-town America. The upshot, say Gimpel and Karnes, is that "many rural voters are comfortable voting Republican because they see themselves as independent business persons rather than on-the-clock wage slaves. Actual monetary income plays a smaller role in their economic evaluations than self-perceived economic status."

So country folk in the United States can connect ideological and economic reasons for voting more conservative than can suburban folk (who provide most swing voters) and much more conservative than city folk (which are Democrat). They are rather insulated from matters of inequality and their insularity has a pronounced moral tone. They see the coasts and the cities as alien dens of iniquity (and the cities do contain "new age" lifestyles and more multiethnic crime) or as the home of hated big government and big corporations. Rural and small-town communities believe themselves to be more communitarian and more virtuous than the materialistic suburbs and cities. In contrast the cities flaunt diversity and recognize conflict. This might also explain why Republicans have become more ideologically cohesive and so more effective in Congress, while Democrats remain more factionalized, like traditional American parties. Ideological power in America is asymmetric: it is more powerful on the Right than the Left. Finally, rural folk are also grossly overrepresented in Senate elections. Wyoming (population 500,000) has two Senators, the same as California (population 34 million). Politics on the Hill are thus more conservative than in the nation. This is an imperfect democracy.

One traditional aspect of American ideology is often said to lessen the importance of economic redistribution. Surveys find that Americans believe it is easier for the ordinary person to get ahead in the United States, regardless of background, than do people in other advanced countries (www.economic mobility.org). Greater social mobility is assumed to soften the blow of greater inequality. Yet that faith is deluded. The OECD (2010: chap. 5) collected studies of the relationship between sons' and fathers' earnings in twelve countries. The relationship is much stronger in the United States than in Denmark, Australia, Norway, Finland, Canada, Sweden, Germany and Spain, and a little stronger than in France. Only in Italy and the UK is social mobility (slightly) less than in the United States. No less than 47 percent of the economic advantage of high-earning fathers in the United States is transmitted to their sons, compared to only 17 percent in Australia and 19 percent in Canada. These countries do what Americans believe the United States does: they compensate for inequality with greater social mobility. But the United States does not – it actually reinforces inequality, making it half-hereditary. Of course, these data refer to men. Given the relative importance of labor market gender equality in the United States (noted in Chapter 5), women may well have better mobility chances – yet women vote more Democrat than do men. Yet in politics ideology can matter more than reality. In this case, not believing in the ideology might lead working class men to consider themselves as failures, which is difficult to do.

Bartels also argues, as I did some time ago (Mann, 1970), that popular attitudes are often contradictory and confused. In polls most Americans believed inequality had gone too far, yet most also supported Bush the Younger's tax cuts, despite their transfers to the rich. The main reason was that Bush's tax cuts were carefully designed to give ordinary tax-payers a 10 percent cut, which obscured their vision of the 25 percent cuts given to the rich. Republicans emphasized the 10 percent and the elimination of the lowest tax bracket (as Bush does in his memoir, 2010: 442–3). In the United States there is also a problem of terminology. Welfare is an unpopular term and even those on welfare often deny it. Almost half those receiving Social Security, unemployment benefits, or Medicare say they have not used a government program (Mettler, 2010: 829). That also reveals a lack of solidarity among Americans. Welfare is associated with unworthy others, not with oneself.

People also have limited knowledge of the extent of inequality. Runciman's (1966) classic study of relative deprivation showed that English workers compared their lot not to the rich, of whom they knew little, but to those near them in the class structure. They felt deprived only if they were doing less well than them. Page and Jacobs (2009: 37–42) show that most American make quite accurate estimates of the incomes of those they know personally. But their knowledge of the top end is hazy. A 2007 sample estimated the average income of a CEO of a large national corporation as $500,000 p.a., 12 times that of a skilled factory (whose income they estimated fairly accurately).They thought a CEO should only get 5 times as much, $200,000. In reality the average CEO got $14 million p.a., 350 times the skilled worker's income! Ignorance may be heightened by the fact that this continental country produces greater geographical distance between rich and poor (Massey, 2007: 192–5). Inequality at the national level may not have much political resonance. Even in the Great Depression Americans did not march in the streets protesting against inequality but against unemployment and poverty.

The voters also have short memories. Though Democratic administrations tended to improve the living standards of ordinary Americans, while the Republicans did the reverse, the Republicans were electorally shrewder, for they produced mini-booms just before elections, while the Democrats produced them earlier. The electorate then forgot this and voted more Republican than their economic interests would warrant. In a CBS/New York Times poll of January 2010 only 12 percent of respondents said President Obama had reduced their taxes since coming into office, though one year previously he had done just that for 95 percent of Americans. Now it was forgotten. Knowledge is also class biased: the poor know less about economic issues than the rich who have greater access to the media

Bartels found that senators didn't do what ordinary voters wanted anyway. Their roll call votes were much more in line with their own views than with those of their constituents. They sometimes deferred to the opinions of the affluent but did not care at all what the lowest third of the income distribution thought. This was especially true of Republican senators. Brooks and Manza (2006) say that responsiveness by politicians to public opinion on welfare programs was also lower in other Anglophone countries than in Nordic or Euro countries. Again, this was democracy imperfect.

Redistributive politics requires popular mobilization. The main traditional pressure group for more equality has been the labor union, yet by 2008 American labor union membership was down to 12.4 percent across all nonagricultural sectors, and a tiny 7.6 percent in the private sector. We saw in Chapter 6 that this was due to several causes: structural changes in the economy, a series of employer offensives, the emergence of identity rather than class politics, and timidity by the unions themselves. I think the decline of labor unions in the United States explains quite a lot, for without them a class explanation of inequality has few advocates. Moreover, mobilization through unions has decreased while through churches it has increased, which steers many Americans away from economic toward moral issues. Among Democrats, the decline of unions and the rise of "identity politics" of race, gender and sexual orientation also reduced the salience of class issues while saddling the Democrats with support of rights for minorities, sometimes unpopular ones. New postmaterialist movements also wield plenty of emotion but they have been led by educated professionals with less concern for the economic conditions of workers. Thus the Democratic Party emphasizes economic equality less than do most center-left parties. From the 1960s relatively affluent members began to take over the Democratic Party and liberal money went mostly into civil rights, feminism, environmentalism, and gay rights (Hacker and Pierson, 2010: 180). Except for feminism, these are not big vote-winners.

Elections have also got more expensive, favoring business funding of parties. Spending by the two parties' presidential candidates had gone steadily upward for most of the century until 1972, but then it leveled off, fluctuating between $50 million and $100 million until 1988. This was the period of relatively effective campaign finance laws. Then spending moved upward again and continued to do so, reaching $450 million in 1996, $1 billion in 2004, and $2.4 billion in 2008. The cost of winning a House seat doubled between 1988 and 2010 and that of a Senate seat went up 30 percent (all figures in constant dollars).[3] But these figures may exaggerate the upward trend. If we adjust them by the increasing size of the electorate, this wipes out most of the increase until the first decade of the twenty first century. The average cost per voter fluctuated but within the same overall range – until this last decade. Moreover election expenditures as a proportion of American GDP actually fell in the period from 1972 to 2000. They then rose sharply but only to the level of spending through most of the twentieth century. As a proportion of GDP election spending was actually at its highest in the Nixon victory of 1968. It seems that elections have quite suddenly got more expensive. Most spending is by business. In elections since 2000 business provided more than 70 percent of all donations, with labor unions providing less than 7 percent. The trend here is less a rise in business contributions than a decline in labor contributions. Republicans have received most of the funding in all elections except for Obama's 2008 campaign, when business perceived Obama would win. Getting reelected is the prime motive of most politicians and it requires them to go cap in hand to business, pushing them rightward on economic issues. Corporations buying votes is an American tradition. It has always been so and it is doubtful therefore whether the rise of inequality, at least between 1970 and 2000, can be attributed to it. The main

---

[3] Historic data from Alexander (1980); recent data from Federal Election Commission Data and the online contributions of Dave Gilson (*Mother Jones* online, February 20, 2012) and Erik Rising (blogspot February 23, 2012).

change is the continuous decline of labor, which has been clearly responsible for part of the rise.

Hacker and Pierson (2010) suggest that financing elections is less important than prior agenda-setting. Here changes have occurred. In the past most lobbying at the federal level came from the peak business associations, now it comes from individual corporations and industries. Thus the number of Washington corporate lobby offices had increased from just U.S. Steel in 1920 to 175 in 1968 to more than 600 in 2005 and their spending rocketed between 1998 and 2008 from $1.4 billion to $3.4 billion (far more than the increase in GDP in that period). Three-quarters of all lobbying costs were incurred by business (figures in constant dollars, from www.opensecrets.org). Much of this lobbying is to secure federal subsidies or exemptions from taxation or regulation, increasing inequality through the back door, hidden from voters. It is impossible to know how much policy lobbying and donations buy, since there is little accountability (Repetto, 2007). But to suggest that lobbying and money have little effect would be to imply that businessmen are fools, spending big dollars for no return. One egregious case involved the Obama healthcare reform bill of 2009. Health insurance, pharmaceutical, and for-profit hospital corporations deployed six lobbyists for each member of Congress and spent $380 million dollars to help defeat the proposed national insurance fund. The biggest contribution, of $1.5 million, went to the Democratic Senator chairing the committee drafting the bill (*The Guardian*, October 1, 2009). This proved a good investment, since the scheme as amended involved state-subsidized profits for health corporations. Lobbying may be partly responsible for the rise in inequality.

Lobbying and corruption are not merely an American phenomenon. The phone-hacking scandal erupting in Britain in 2011 revealed what may be the norm in many countries. Rupert Murdoch and his family control the world's largest media empire, one that is extremely important in Britain. It was revealed during the scandal involving a Murdoch newspaper that Prime Minister Cameron had met privately with the Murdochs or their senior executives on twenty-six occasions in the first fifteen months of his administration, and that senior cabinet ministers had met with them privately on no fewer than sixty occasions. The Conservatives responded to public criticism of this by saying that the previous Labour administration had done just the same. But European electoral laws are clearer. Europeans have stringent limits on campaign spending and give free air-time on broadcast media to political parties so that expensive media campaign advertisements need not absorb most party finances. Europe has intermittent scandals about election and party financing but these are small change when viewed from America.

Distinctive to the United States is that the bias toward business-dominated policies is supported by the Supreme Court. In a series of decisions culminating in January 2010, the Court struck down part of a 2002 campaign-finance reform law limiting the amount of campaign contributions. It declared that this law violated the free-speech rights of corporations to engage in public debate of political issues. "Government may not suppress political speech on the basis of the speaker's corporate identity," said Chief Justice Roberts in writing the court's majority opinion, explicitly equating the rights of a large corporation with those of any individual person. This is hard to reconcile with democratic theory, which emphasizes the need for equality of political citizenship. The United States today is less one person one vote than one dollar one vote. Economic power inequalities have invaded political and judicial power relations, generating a highly imperfect democracy. With the exception of the civil rights period the Supreme Court has been distinctively conservative and procapitalist. I am not sure why this is so.

I have presented a multistranded explanation of why Americans do not much challenge rising inequality. Voters are better-off than nonvoters; racism tarnishes views of the poor; and ordinary white people, especially white men, in country districts and the South have become more Republican and more concerned with conservative moral values than economic issues. Americans are politically myopic and ignorant and have false views about social mobility. Republicans are more skilled at exploiting all that rhetorically while Democrats, being more divided, have more difficulty in finding simple resonant rhetoric. Ideological power is wielded by the Right, social science by the Left – poor compensation! American unions have faded, and with them class struggle, partially replaced by identity and moral politics. The politicians are more conservative than the voters, and this is due in part to having been corrupted by big business, a corruption legitimized by the Supreme Court.

One must finally admire the skill of Republican leaders. Effective politicians try to frame complex issues with simple but resonant rhetoric. Republicans do exactly this in opposing "taxes taken from out of your pockets," "big government," "socialized medicine," while Democrats insist on talking about detailed policies. Though it is tempting to think that poor Republican voters are stupid, perhaps Democratic politicians are even stupider. Why can't they also focus on slogans and leave the economic inducements to just before elections? High-mindedness and democracy don't mix. In contrast Republican politicians manage to comfortably straddle two core constituencies with almost nothing in common: big business demanding more power and more profits, and small-town America distrusting both Washington and Wall Street, worrying about declining moral standards, and fearing the plague of big cities and other races. The party's ability to keep the loyalty of the latter even against their own material interests is rather remarkable, a tribute to their political skills.

Some of this long list of causes is found to a lesser extent in other advanced countries, especially in Anglophone countries. But their full extent is distinctively American. Thus at the very end of the twentieth century the United States became *for the first time* exceptional. It became more unequal but less bothered by this. This was achieved, not as a result of foundational American culture or institutions – not a liberal tradition, or no socialism, or democracy before bureaucracy, or weak government with multiple veto-points or other variants of standard tropes of exceptionalism. Though America had long supported relatively unfettered property rights, this was at times overcome and at other times reinforced by influences from both national and global forces. Viewed close-up, the long-term was a combination of several short-term conservative surges, sometimes allied with a rhetorical neoliberalism, as already documented in Chapters 3 and 6. Of course, it was not genuine market fundamentalism. Throughout this period the government was subsidizing agriculture, retaining a gigantic military, expanding prisons, and pouring subsidies into hi-tech projects from which the private sector would profit. Neoliberalism was administered to the poor, not the propertied. Inequality continued to widen – and then its chickens came home to roost.

The 2008 recession

As the Fed lowered interest rates in the 1990s, there followed easier money and a stock market boom. Two bubbles seemed to initially indicate vitality. The bursting of the first one, the dot-com bubble, in 1998–2000 resulted from the massive imbalance between the expectations held by finance capital of dot.com companies and their actual economic performance. Fear that the bubble might lead to a recession led to further reductions in U.S. interest rates. Greenspan's Fed between December 2000 and June 2004 successively lowered the federal funds rate target from 6.5 percent to 1 percent. This combined with an even greater influx of foreign, especially Chinese, money into U.S. Treasury bonds to produce a speculative boom centered on real-estate, much bigger in value than the previous bubble in technology stocks. Again, this seemed to indicate economic health, though it depended on increasing personal and corporate debt (Brenner, 2006). In The Black Death of 1346–9 those who were about to die developed rosy cheeks. So too did American consumers.

The bubble burst in the U.S. subprime mortgage market, which aided house purchase by quite poor people, especially blacks, Latinos and the elderly. The virus spread quickly to the other countries, which Schwartz (2009) calls the "Americanized rich" – the other Anglos, the Netherlands and some Scandinavian countries. The seven countries with the highest residential mortgage debt as a ratio of national GDP are Switzerland, the Netherlands and Denmark, which do not have subprime mortgages, plus the United States, the UK, Australia and Ireland, which all do (Sassen, 2010). The combination of both is distinctively Anglo. At a time of unusually low interest rates subprime clients had been offered variable rate mortgages. But sooner or later interest rates would rise, threatening their ability to pay, which would lose them their savings and their homes. If this happened, risk would no longer be a matter of random individuals but of a collective class. Its default might overwhelm some of the derivatives. Neoliberals criticized subsidies for subprime mortgages as introducing market distortions. Prudent lenders would not give mortgages to such people, they said. They were right. Yet brokers and mortgage managers were booking profits on the transactions and politicians were trumpeting property-owning democracy to win elections. Neoliberals cannot control the economic and political power actors who implement policies. Yet politicians' strategies owed much to the ideological climate of neoliberalism.

In 1998 subprime loans had been 5 percent of all U.S. mortgage lending, but by 2008 they were almost 30 percent. Risky loans had been hidden and sold on in derivatives like Collateralized Mortgage Obligations (CMOs) and Credit Default Swaps (CDS). Many of these were then repackaged and sold as Collateralized Debt Obligations (CDOs) whose value rose from $52 billion in 1999 to $388 billion in 2006. Bad debts were being sold on, though mixed in with better ones, so the original lender had no interest in ensuring that the debt could be honored. My own house mortgage was sold on three times in the period from 2007 to early 2010. Complex mathematical models manipulated by whizz-kids reassured the banks, but they were faith-based since bank directors did not understand them. Mathematical economists had developed models so abstruse as to be beyond ordinary human understanding, a form of ideological power like that of priests or sorcerers who alone know how to communicate with the spirits. In reality, it all depended what you put into the equations. Models supposed to predict losses on mortgage-backed securities were estimated on data only since 1998, a period during which housing prices only rose! The banks did not know the real value of the assets they were trading. These were like Iraq's weapons of mass destruction – toxic but impossible to find (though toxic mortgages really did exist).

The first-line regulators were the commercial ratings agencies like Moody's and Standard and Poor's. The financial services industry depends heavily on their seal of approval. Yet they had given many toxic subprime mortgage-dominated CDOs their highest AAA rating. The main reason for their failure to assess accurately was probably that they are not in fact independent. They are paid their commission for rating products by the investment banks and shadow banks producing and selling the CDOs, not by those buying them. Thus their paying customers benefit from high ratings and the agencies therefore have an incentive to please them. Unfortunately, the paying customers want to simply make loans, not good loans. But the deals were also growing in number and complexity, putting the agencies under too much strain, especially since their best assessors were being lured by higher wages into the banks (Immergluck, 2009: 118). The regulating ratings agencies themselves need regulation.

As Davis (2009: 106) emphasizes, notions of market efficiency and shareholder value had downsized corporations and increased the complexity of actors involved in the financial services industries. While Wall Street had become more powerful and the biggest banks were now bigger, they were not in control of financial markets. A former SEC Chairman observed in 1996 that while most countries' investment decisions were made by only a few dozen "gatekeepers," the United States had "literally hundreds of gatekeepers in our increasingly decentralized capital markets" – and they were also more shadowy, making informed decision-making more difficult and criminal greed more tempting.

Meanwhile the regulators-in-chief remained blissfully unconcerned. In 2004 Fed Chairman Greenspan said the rise in home prices was "not enough in our judgment to raise major concerns." In 2005 his successor Ben Bernanke said a housing bubble was "a pretty unlikely possibility." In 2007 he said "do not expect significant spillovers from the subprime market to the rest of the economy," for the economy had reached a new era of stability that he called "the great moderation" (Leonhardt, 2010). They had not understood that financialization produced volatility, which, though unrelated to the fundamentals of the economy, could nonetheless bring it down. Even most of President Obama's economic advisers believed in the new era of stability. The top three, Timothy Geithner (Treasury Secretary), Peter Orszay (Office of Management and Budget) and Lawrence Summers (White House economic adviser), were all protégés of Robert Rubin, former Chairman of Goldman Sachs and a major derivatives trader. Summers is a neoliberal (as we saw in Chapter 7). In his academic publications he argues that corporation and capital gains taxes stifle growth, while unemployment insurance and welfare payments fuel unemployment – the hallmarks of class-biased neoliberalism. Would such advisers move radically against the bankers? Prominent economists proposing more reform – like Paul Krugman, Joseph Stiglitz, or Simon Johnson – were kept away from positions of authority.

The addition of variable rate subprime mortgages brought on Minsky's third phase of Ponzi finance, a scheme that promises high returns to investors on the basis of money paid in by subsequent investors, rather than from net revenues generated by any real ongoing business. The scheme requires the underlying asset values (here housing) to keep on increasing. But when only mild economic trouble came, between June 2004 and September 2007, the U.S. federal funds rate was successively hiked back up again from 1 percent to 5.25 percent. Fewer could afford to buy houses, and many variable-rate mortgage-holders could not repay their loans, especially, it seems, those arranged by brokers (Immergluck, 2009: 103). Housing prices fell and the derivatives and securities tied to variable rate subprime mortgages abruptly lost value. Since nobody knew exactly where they were, it affected the whole derivatives market. This triggered in 2008 the collapse of the whole Ponzi scheme. The low probability risk had happened, and no one was insured against its losses.

Wall Street's models hadn't anticipated a housing crash. The supposedly benign dispersal of risk turned into a virus spreading to most major financial institutions. Actually, risk is the wrong term. It refers to situations in which the probabilities of different random outcomes can be determined, as in poker or roulette. But Keynes (1936: chap. 12; 1937) distinguished between risk and uncertainty, situations in which probabilities cannot be calculated. Ultimately, he observed, outcomes in capitalist economies are uncertain – like the prospects of war – and both expectations and confidence were extremely precarious. No mathematical formulas can predict them and yet whizz-kid economists had been blinding their bosses with arcane mathematical formulae. In 2008 since lenders did not know how many toxic assets they held, nobody would now lend. Bankers were playing pass the [toxic] parcel, some of them passing into zones of criminality. In the end the bankers did ultimately know exactly what game they were playing, for when just one part of the derivatives market collapsed, no one would take the parcel. Investors panicked and stock markets crashed. The United States and Britain led the way into disaster, but Ireland and Spain also had mortgage and housing development crises, and most European banks were left holding toxic assets. Theirs were estimated by the IMF as being about 75 percent the level of American toxicity.

The result was the Great Recession of 2008, the biggest since the Great Depression. Since it was a financial crisis fueled by inequality and deregulation, I call it the Great Neoliberal Recession. Banking failures dried up the credit on which manufacturing and service enterprises depended on a week-to-week basis. World trade promptly fell relative to GDP by 30 percent in 2008 and 2009. The impact on ordinary people was immediate. Survey data reveal that almost 40 percent of U.S. household had at one point or more between November 2008 and April 2010 either experienced either marriage partner been unemployed, or had negative equity in their house, or been in arrears for over two months in their house payments. Reductions in spending were normal following unemployment (Hurd & Rohwedder, 2010). Since people were trying to reduce their level of debt, they were not spending, and consumer spending is the main driver of aggregate demand. U.S. unemployment officially rose to almost 10 percent in late 2009, though the real rate would be about 16 percent if we include those working part-time who wanted full-time work or who had given up looking for work. The comparable UK rate was probably about 14 percent–15 percent, while the European Union real rate would be about 12 percent–13 percent. Long-term unemployment was increasing and into 2012 overall unemployment only fell a little. Japan escaped more lightly, with only 5 percent unemployment. Major exporting nations like China and Germany were hit, though they had not been responsible for the financial collapse, and they recovered quicker. When the crisis hit China, its banks reacted instinctively just like Western banks, radically cutting back on lending to companies wishing to expand. But the Communist Party still rules China and its fiscal leading group (explained in Chapter 8) ordered the banks to release the credit in a massive stimulus program, thus reviving Chinese growth (McGregor, 2010). It was not an example liberal democracies could follow.

One might assume after this debacle that neoliberalism would be finished. This seemed so for a short while, since most countries plumped for Keynesian stimulus programs. Yet the political power of the banks remained intact and much of the Republican Party and Wall Street bizarrely saw the causes of crisis not as lack of regulation but as political interference with markets. They particularly blamed the two government-sponsored mortgage companies Freddie Mac and Fanny Mae for the crisis. This is implausible since these were latecomers to the subprime market, they provided only about a sixth of subprime mortgages, and they held a much lower percentage of nonperforming loans than did the banks (Schwartz, 2009: 183–5). Republicans saw the solution not as government pump-priming but as tax cuts and rolling back the state at all levels to balance the budget. But doing this in a recession worsens it by reducing demand and increasing unemployment. Business is not investing because it lacks customers and big spending cuts will produce even fewer. Since Republicans believe they benefit electorally from espousing lower taxes and a slimmer state, ideological politics trumps economics In this case business confidence becomes contested – manufacturing wanting stimulus programs, finance wanting only bail-out. The resulting pump-priming was not Keynesian, since it focused on bailing out the banks. They were supplied with cheap money and bad assets were taken off their hands – Keynes for the bankers. They did eventually repay the loans but no other regulatory conditions were attached – no structural adjustment for the rich! As soon as the banks recovered with the aid of government welfare they were spouting the efficient market and shareholder value once again, and they were paying themselves as much as before the crisis.

The ultimate irony was that neoliberals were receiving massive state subsidies from taxpayers to survive. Banks recovered because of direct transfers of wealth from taxpayers. They were defined as too big to fail, not too big to exist, and they became even bigger. Bank of America and J. P. Morgan Chase, the two biggest, were helped by the government to acquire Merrill Lynch and Bear Stearns. Some neoliberals did object to this, believing that banks should be allowed to fail whatever their size. The markets, they said, will step in to correct and to provide the needed investment funds. Not quite sharing their optimism, Keynesians back away from going this far. They say it is right to bail banks out, but not at the long-term expense of the taxpayers and only if there is further regulation (Krugman, 2008). Restoring a Glass-Steagall-type act is essential to separate the utility functions of banks from their riskier activities. Paychecks must be deposited, small business must get normal seasonal loans, truckers must be able to buy gas on credit, debit and credit cards must work etc. These bank activities should not be allowed to fail. But risky CDOs, credit default swaps, multimillion currency transactions etc. should not be subsidized. Indeed, they should be more tightly regulated.

Yet these requirements have not been met. An opportunity to escape from sacrificing all to investor confidence was lost. Yes, restore their confidence with immediate subsidies, but in return for more regulation and higher liquidity requirements and higher taxes. Confidence does not have to prevent states from ever challenging capitalism. But without pressure from below and in a period of the decline of leftist parties, upper class interests and ideology have once again ruled political economy, imposing limits on states.

A second phase of the Great Recession came when debts were shuffled off from the private to the public sector. In most of the Mediterranean countries plus Ireland the initial problem was not that the lending boom had gone to profligate states. It had gone to the private sector, especially financing unsustainable housing booms, as in the Anglo countries. But when the crisis hit and lending ceased, there was some initial pump-priming to bail out the banks plus an attempt to maintain public spending amid falling tax revenues in order to compensate for the collapse of household consumption and private-sector investment. So public sector deficits rose up to 10 percent or more of GDP in the United States, the UK, and Mediterranean countries. This shuffling of debts merely postponed the day of reckoning, since no institution can indefinitely spend much more than it receives in revenue. So, as the financial sector recovered its confidence, investors began to attack government pump-priming, generating currency runs where they considered budget deficits too high. What had originally been a combination of mortgage debt crisis, global imbalances and an unregulated and near-criminal financial sector became a sovereign debt crisis affecting above all the Southern European states (especially Greece, but also Italy, Spain and Portugal), plus Ireland. Their high levels of debt made them vulnerable to speculation against their currencies, forcing them to pay very high interest rates to investors and to deflate their economies and slash government spending in order to restore investor confidence. Again, ordinary taxpayers and especially poor welfare recipients paid the price of the Great Neoliberal Recession. The only alternative would have been to raise the level of taxation, especially for the rich, but rich investors would not like that. Esping-Andersen's Euro welfare regime was dividing in two, while Ireland and Britain were moving even closer to the United States to form a coherent Anglo bloc. Once again, neoliberalism had widened inequality, this time internationally and this time because of its failure.

Though the first phase of the crisis bottomed-out in 2010, it was mostly a jobless recovery. Inequality continued widening. Bankers' profits grew again. Manufacturing recovered more slowly, mainly by cutting back its permanent labor force and rehiring casual workers at lower wages. Governments focused policy not on job creation but fiscal soundness. Krugman (2008) calls this "the return of Depression economics." Ordinary people did not get back their jobs, their houses or the value of their pensions. The share of wealth held by the top 10 percent of American households increased yet again, from 49 percent in 2005 to 56 percent in 2009, while the poor, especially minorities, got poorer.

Quite against neoliberal explanations, countries with more controlled labor markets like Germany and the Nordic countries did better than those with more flexible markets, like the United States and Britain. Though as usual debt-laden states (except the United States) had to bow to the power of financial confidence, most OECD states remained in better shape. All the major OECD governments could borrow long-term at an interest rate of less than 3 percent, indicating that the bond markets were not worried that their current budget deficits would undermine their long-term fiscal viability. Moreover, states with surpluses saw their sovereign wealth funds strengthened. They had previously mostly bought U.S. Treasury bonds, but in the new century they were diversifying into more portfolio investment. They bought big chunks of the U.S. banking groups in trouble, like Morgan Stanley, Merill Lynch and Citigroup. The growth of sovereign wealth funds is another harbinger of power shifting away from the United States toward Asia (Davis, 2009: 182–3). It also demonstrates the resilience of economically stronger and more cohesive nation-states against the supposedly stronger limits imposed by transnational capitalism.

The recession spread through the world through both trade and financial channels. Most developing countries had few toxic bank assets but they felt the effects of lower foreign direct investment and lower remittances from citizens working abroad. Those with reserves fought back by setting up wealth funds to boost investment and to finance more effective stimulus programs. But in the years 2008 and 2009 trade fell 30 percent relative to global GDP. The most open economies, especially those trading a narrow range of products and trading manufactured rather than raw material commodities were most harmed, as were those exporting to the most affected developed countries – like Mexico, highly dependent on its trade with the United States. Prices of most commodities fell while their increasing volatility also increased revenue uncertainty, making capital investment and government planning more difficult. But food prices rose, increasing food poverty in the poorest countries. The number of those living in poverty had fallen steadily between 1980 and 2008, partly as a result of lower rates in China. Indeed, a quick Chinese recovery from the Recession will reinforce this. Overall, GDP fell most in the richer countries and least in poorer countries, though there was much variation among the poor (Nabli et al., 2010). The Great Neoliberal Recession widened the gap between successfully and unsuccessfully developing countries – China, India, Vietnam, Poland, Turkey, Brazil versus most of Africa and central Asia – furthering the obsolescence of the North-South divide.

In the richer countries, especially the Anglophones, neoliberals responded to failure by claiming their policies had not been pressed far enough – the traditional response of ideologists. In the United States and the UK in which neoliberal ideology is stronger, they had their way. Britain had easily the biggest financial sector in proportionate terms, contributing 40 percent of Britain's foreign earnings, with a high debt level (11 percent of GDP), just above the U.S. rate, twice as high as Germany's. Britain had good credit, however, for most of its debt was long-term and at low rates of interest. Britain was not very vulnerable. Yet in 2010 the new Conservative government announced a 19 percent cut in public expenditures, the firing of 490,000 public sector workers and effectively privatizing higher education. Such slashing of expenditures and employment in the teeth of a Great Recession completely disregarded the experience of the Great Depression. Indeed, it threatened to repeat it. In reality Conservatives were taking advantage of the recession to realize their long-held ideological desire to downsize the state. The need for some cuts in public spending, smaller and more gradual, was widely recognized, and was proposed by the prior Labour government, but this sudden butchery worsened the crisis.

The United States followed suit in August 2011 when President Obama and the Democratic Party leadership concocted a last-minute deal with Republicans, pressured by Tea Party extremists, to avoid the United States defaulting on its debts. Obama abandoned his stimulus program and agreed to slash government expenditure in a recession, just like the British. With interest rates at historic lows, governments should be borrowing money to spend on stimulating the economy. But they were actually cutting such programs. In the United States big cuts in state and local government spending were especially damaging to employment and consumption levels. The Anglos were sliding together into disaster. The outcome is less clear elsewhere, where most politicians hesitate to press neoliberalism further. France and Germany have been more cautious and are recovering better. Yet collectively the European governments imposed on Greece austerity programs so severe as to make likely a Greek default on its loans, with knock-on effects on other Mediterranean countries; while the European Central Bank continued to advocate austerity in order to raise business confidence. Yet short-term fiscal austerity programs create more unemployment and increase the tax burdens on firms and consumers. This will not restore growth, pay off debts, or restore international investor confidence. Indeed, the IMF has changed its tune, now urging stimulus programs for troubled countries.

The consequence of the Recession was that especially in the Anglophone and Mediterranean countries the poor got screwed, the working class movement seemed finished, the middle class had to be thankful for small mercies, and transfers from them all helped the rich get richer – though they had been responsible for the crisis in the first place! It is difficult to see economic growth coming from the cuts implemented in 2011 by Greece, Britain and the United States. In Britain and the United States they were driven not so much by economic theory as by a class ideology privileging the rich and especially the banks, but not manufacturing industry, at the expense of the people.

Reform

More regulation of finance and transnational corporations is needed to reembed the economy in the social structures of citizenship, which they are supposed to serve. This should involve not just more activism by individual states but also more global, multilateral cooperation between states. In turn this requires multilateral institutions like the IMF and World Bank to reform their own voting structures so that they become more representative of nation-states across the globe, not just those of the North (Abdelal & Ruggie, 2009). The same need will appear in the next chapter, which deals with climate change.

But very little has been done as yet. Governments did seek to make banks hold bigger deposits and to regulate some types of trading. Under the Basel III agreement made in 2010 between many countries banks' minimum equity to capital ratios are required to rise from 2 percent to almost 10 percent in the case of the biggest banks. But even that is not enough, for it means that losses in a bank's assets of only 4 percent would make it insolvent. The Obama administration favored stronger regulatory agencies, wanted over-the-counter derivatives traded on exchanges or through clearinghouses, with restrictions on commercial banks and institutions that own banks operating and investing in hedge funds and private equity firms. It also wanted a cap on trading activity done for in-house accounts. But its legislation of July 2010 was much weaker, merely giving power to new regulatory bodies, which will decide which derivatives would be regulated and which trades must be disclosed. Will they be tough enough? Regulators have not been effective so far, and there is little progress as yet on implementation of the new laws. Most financial institutions oppose any new regulation. If they can be bailed out by tax-payers each time a bonanza pay-out period ends, they already have the ideal solution! This is not moral hazard but immoral certainty.

Nor is there international consensus on solutions like firewalls or Tobin taxes on short-term financial transactions, while each country wants to protect its own banks. Bankers lobby against regulation by claiming it will stifle them unless they flee abroad to a more hospitable country – and unlike manufacturers they have few fixed assets tying them to their homeland. Most Europeans blamed the Anglos for bringing about the crisis but their own desire for radical reform was weakened by the fact that their generous welfare states did not depress consumer demand down to Anglo levels. Canada is unconcerned since it had retained strict financial regulation and so did not suffer much recession. The BRIC countries, especially India with a more insulated economy and China with its massive domestic savings, recovered quickly and are even less concerned. Chinese imports of Japanese and Australian goods also pulled these countries into growth. That is a sign of hope for the global economy, and also a sign of shifting power toward non-Western economies and to economies, which are more state regulated.

The European Union had its own problems. The introduction of the Euro had yoked together economies of very different strengths and led to massive investment in its less developed national economies, since investors believed that the euro made Greek or Spanish debt just as secure as German or French. The crisis revealed this to be false. These economies cannot compete with the more dynamic countries within the Union, especially Germany. Yet saddled with the euro, they cannot devalue their currency to improve the competitiveness of their exports. The fundamental weakness is not economic but political, for the Union lacks a coherent political mechanism for implementing effective economic policy. There is a European Central Bank but there is no single Treasury to apply fiscal as well as monetary discipline and to make fiscal transfers to depressed areas, as nation-states can do. To develop a true Treasury would improve the ability of Europe to weather future crises, but this implies more federalism and the last two decades have revealed fierce popular opposition to deepening the Union. Any government proposing deeper fiscal integration faces the risk of being thrust out of power, a major deterrent for politicians. This is the macroregion of the world in which multilateral institutions have developed furthest, but behind the backs of the people. This has come back to haunt the Union.

There is a global consensus that more regulation of banks is necessary, but there is a plethora of regulators and standards in the global economy. In the United States the Dodd-Frank Act, in the UK the Vickers Commission, in the European Union the Capital Requirements Directive IV, and in the European insurance sector the Solvency II rules – all provide different rules for minimum liquidity. At the global level the Basel III agreement pledged governments to gradually increase the liquidity coverage ratio, requiring banks to hold enough easily saleable assets to withstand a 30-day run on them. But this will remain a voluntary scheme until 2015 and it remains politically contentious. Banks argue that it will not only reduce their profits but also their lending capacity, and they add that it may even increase the profits of less-regulated shadow banks. Because of their pressure, the Basel rules may be softened. This looks like rather marginal regulation though it is a start and it reveals more international cooperation than happened in the Great Depression, when states' competitive devaluations and tariffs worsened the crisis. Through institutions like the EU, the G20, the Basel institutions, the IMF and the World Bank, none of which existed in the 1930s, there is potentiality for multilateral global regulation, which could be intensified by tougher bank rules, breaking up the biggest banks, and introducing Tobin taxes on short-term capital flows. Indeed in 2011 the European Union proposed a Tobin tax of 0.1 percent on transactions but the UK, home to 80 percent of European capital transactions, vetoed it.

A genuine solution requires more than just regulation. As we have seen, there were two underlying crises, of global imbalances and American-led inequality, both increasing debts. Global imbalances meant that by the end of 2010

American consumption was nearly 70 percent of its GDP, almost exactly double that of China's. Both figures are unsustainable in the long-run, one too big, the other too small. They reveal the same underlying problem: lack of demand by the two peoples, which depresses the economy. This could be remedied by redistribution in both countries. Additionally, the United States should provide additional stimulus funds for investments on sectors like infrastructure and education while the Chinese solution would be to expand the domestic market and allow the appreciation of the renminbi. But would China and Japan allow their currencies to appreciate, making their exports more expensive? For their part, American politicians have abandoned the remedies of a further stimulus program and higher taxes. At the G-20 meeting in November 2010 there was no agreement on steps to curb imbalances.

A stable U.S. housing market requires more than a prudent supply of houses and mortgages. It needs more people able to buy or indeed rent houses without risk of default (Coates, 2010; Immergluck, 2009). That would require major redistribution from rich to ordinary Americans. As we have seen, a conservative-neoliberal alliance had skewed the distribution of national growth to the rich, depressing mass consumption levels except through debt. That needs reversing, but at present the distribution of political power does not permit this. Gamble (2010) advocates a radical New Deal type program, involving reregulating financial services, redistributing income and assets, investing in infrastructure projects, new technologies, education and skills and, to pay for it, austerity and lower consumption to reduce debt and free up resources for investment. It might work, but it is pie in the sky. There is not pressure for this from the streets, unlike the 1930s. Today class struggle and ideological polarization are largely absent. There have been major strikes and demonstrations in the weaker countries, like Greece, Ireland, and Spain, but they align their citizens not only against their own governments but also against Germans who are angry at having to bail them out. There have been riots in Britain against a background of racism, high youth unemployment, and major government cuts, but they have been rather apolitical. There have been smallish demonstrations across U.S. cities against Wall Street. But there is little sign of an alternative ideology comparable to the social democracy-cum-Keynesianism of the 1930s and 1940s. No big social movement is demanding radical changes, though we should not discount the possibility that this might appear, for the crisis is likely to last awhile. But so far the clamor is much less than during the Great Depression. The working class and the Left have declined, but the capitalist class and the Right are flourishing. Against this balance of forces, "experts" are powerless. It seems reasonably clear what policies *should* be pursued to rescue the economies of the North of the world, but the prospects of this happening are currently poor. In this case it is less capitalism and business confidence in general that is imposing strict limits on states, but a specific fraction of capital expressed in investor confidence.

In the United States there is much "Main Street" versus "Wall Street" rhetoric, but it generates two rival populisms, of the Democratic left and of the Republican right, at its most extreme in the Tea Party, railing against Wall Street, Washington and the eastern Establishment alike. In reality this rightist populism is more opposed to big government than big capitalism. Given the importance of big business to the Republican Party, the party will not support much regulation of finance capital, whatever the populist rhetoric in its heartlands.

There has been an astonishing degradation of the Republican Party, seeking ever more redistribution to the rich, increasingly little-American and so ignorant of the world, antiscience, imperialist, espousing a market fundamentalism at odds with American reality, crying "socialism" at every reform that might help ordinary people from the strengthening of collective bargaining to health care, to regulation of the banks, to climate change. But the pusillanimity and divisions of the Democratic Party are worrying too, making the party unwilling to stand up for the necessary reforms. Financial services corporations were the leading campaign contributors to both parties in 2008. Both parties are constrained by the invasion of political space by economic power actors. Republicans and blue-dog Democrats drag their heels on reform. The separation of powers became the stalemating of powers, as the polarization of constituencies yielding safe seats, plus a highly cohesive and ideological Republican Party encountered changes in congressional procedures involving party control of committees, plus changes in campaign funds, plus the spread of filibusters and the 60-seat Senate majority from major bills to almost all bills (Zelizer, 2009). All of this stymied reform proposals, including necessary financial regulation and economic stimulus programs.

The Great Neoliberal Recession resulted from the growing power of deregulated finance capital. Consumption amid rising inequality and global imbalances, endorsed by neoliberals, held up only through unsustainable levels of debt. Finance capitalists and attendant top managers wanted the freedom promised by neoliberalism, and they got it because neoliberalism dominated the finance sector in most countries. But liberating bankers' greed proved harmful to the economy and the population as a whole. More than any other sector, finance needs regulation, for it is the most volatile, dangerous sector of capitalism. But economic and political power distributions prevented this, and will likely do so for a while longer yet. There will be more financial crises, probably affecting the North more than the South, assisting the passing of global power.

Yet in its Anglophone heartland the crisis of 2008 ironically revived neoliberalism. In crises the power of speculators is at its greatest – as it was also in the 1920s. Those who caused the crisis saw their powers increased! Unless there is a powerful upsurge of popular revolt against this, we must conclude once again in this volume that collective interests and rationality do not govern human societies. Fed. Chairman Greenspan famously chided the stock market for irrational exuberance, but this crisis demonstrated irrational malignance. If this Recession follows the pattern of the Great Depression, almost all governments in power at its beginning will fall. This happened in the United States in both 2006 and 2008, and in the UK in 2010. In these countries the first momentum was rightward, though since their new regimes will likely also fail economically, they may also fall. Some conservative governments in power in Europe may fall, replaced by center-leftists. The 2012 elections in France provided the first case of this, though it remains to be seen how far the new President Francois Hollande can go while retaining investor confidence.

Conclusion

As we saw in Chapter 6, neoliberalism did not dominate the world, nor did it roll back many states. State size as a proportion of GDP stopped growing, but usually remained at about the same level as it had reached before the neoliberal onslaught. Moreover, neoliberal influence was faltering at the end of the twentieth century. It had not brought much growth in either the South or the North and it had grossly widened inequality in the countries that most embraced it. Legitimated in the United States by the Supreme Court, it had allowed economic power to corrupt democratic politics and weaken social citizenship, both of which had been the crowning glories of the twentieth century. Neoliberalism greatly increased the power of the financial sector, especially in the Anglophone countries, and its power also increased greatly in countries that became indebted to foreigners. In the leading Anglo country, the United States, inequality widened and citizenship weakened most, though it did not at first lower mass consumption because a society of debt had emerged. This precipitated the Great Neoliberal Recession, and is likely to soon precipitate another one. When Chicago School rational expectations models so grossly mis-price risk and put pathological values on assets that should be very familiar to everyone, how can we believe in the magic of the market? In Chapter 7 we saw that neoliberalism's impact on the post-Soviet economies was also negative. Overall, on efficiency, collective power grounds, neoliberalism should be abandoned.

Yet neoliberalism still thrives in the financial sector because of its distributive power, for it benefits the most powerful classes and nations that are still able to impose their interests on much of humanity. The cutting edge of its power lies with speculators who can attack the currency of countries resisting its policies. Politically, it resonates amid fiscal pressures on welfare states coming largely from noneconomic causes, like ageing and the growth of higher education. In some countries it became entrenched politically through an alliance with conservatives like Thatcher and Reagan. The liberal Anglophone countries have been the most hospitable to neoliberal ideology. Northern corporatist and southern developmental countries have been able to bend and blend it with their more proactive states. There the potential losers from neoliberalism are more politically entrenched, abler to resist. In the South neoliberalism was strongest where international debt was highest. But stronger southern states learned to resist neoliberal pressures by building up their financial reserves, while in very poor countries the international banks began to abandon rolling back the state. Good governance was in. Neoliberals do not think they have won the political battle since northern states still distribute 30 percent–50 percent of national GDPs, about the same proportion as in 1980. Their need to form alliances with conservatives contributed to this, for statism has been resilient on the Right as well as on the Left. There has been little state-downsizing. The minimal state has not arrived and probably will not do so unless we envisage disaster scenarios.

There remains much global variation. Though the global triumph of capitalism is near-complete, it remains volatile through time and varied through space. It adapts to crises mediated through nationally and regionally varied ideologies and institutions. The nation-state is still the entrenched regulator, and nation-states turn to their regional neighbors and their cultural kin to find best practices. Institutionalized centrist ideologies reduce the power of capitalism and specifically of business confidence from sweeping transnationally through the world. The citizenship institutions that solved the turmoil of the first half of the century remain and no capitalist expansion, no ideology and no crisis of sufficient depth has yet erupted to undermine them across much of the world. Yet retaining citizenship remains a struggle. The United States, Britain, Ireland, and much of Mediterranean Europe are seeing social citizenship rights diminished. Elsewhere in the North social citizenship hangs on. But the momentum has switched to the bigger countries of the former South, and there the economic prognosis is healthier. Whether the distribution of the rewards from growth will benefit most citizens remains to be fought over. Capitalism does not impose such strong limits as either neoliberals or pessimistic Marxists believe. Human beings can choose – though they may not choose well.

Is this a further phase of Polanyi's double movement within capitalism: between the self-regulating market on the one hand, and social demands for "self-protection" against this on the other? Streeck (2009) endorses such a Polanyian cyclical model, arguing that market capitalism perennially seeks to break free from the noncontractual institutions containing it, yet in turn inducing pressures for the restoration of noncontractual obligations. Certainly, neo-Keynesian success had built up the power of finance capital, and then neo-Keynesian failures led to neoliberal demands for market self-regulation. It did not have success across all spheres of the economy (states remained the same size), but in finance its excesses then led again to demands for the protection of social life through reregulation and the setting up of institutions able to protect us from the destructive potential of market expansion. Yet the demands were initially ignored and it may be that would-be reformers like Hollande lack the power to enforce them. It seems overambitious to develop a model of economic development on two-and-a-half episodes: first the growth of classical liberalism, second the growth of Keynesian social democracy – with the half being the success of neoliberalism in dominating the financial sector of capitalism. Polanyi's model also seems a little too functionalist and too rationalistic. It is functionalist because it assumes that development is a process internal to the capitalist mode of production. Yet we have seen ideologies, wars and states greatly influencing the development of capitalism. It is rationalistic because it seems to believe that human beings can rationally solve the excesses of an existing order. Yet these were all closely contested power struggles yielding different outcomes in different countries, and though I have argued that capitalism and capitalists need more regulation, I am not at all confident that this will happen. These cycles are neither regular, uniform nor inevitable, so they are not actually cycles.

What are we to make now of Schumpeter's creative destruction? In his later work, he argued that a bureaucratized capitalism of giant corporations would stifle the creativity of the entrepreneur and lead the way toward socialism (1942: 134). Today's giant corporations are not very bureaucratic, for they have learned how to subcontract and asset strip, how to move globally and become leaner and meaner. But in becoming subordinate to the bankers they have encouraged a whole new meaning of creative destruction, of derivatives, securitization and the rest destabilizing capitalism and risking the sacrifice of the high-consumption, high-employment capitalism, which made them rich in the first place.

Once again is revealed the fundamental contradiction of capitalism. Capitalists' drive for immediate profits can destroy the economy from which their profits derive. In search of profit they have screwed down wages and union organization, they have captured states and slashed welfare, and they have financialized – all crass, short-term self-interest given the ideological veneer of neo-classical economics and neoliberalism. But all these successes have undermined the high demand economy on which their wealth ultimately depends. This is also largely true for China's party-state capitalists. They have repressed wages and unions, captured the state, and exported and invested the profits abroad, thereby lowering the potentiality of their own domestic economy. The combination of Western entrepreneurs and Chinese party-state capitalists creates the global imbalances that harm the globe. It seems the world has not learned the lesson that a market capitalism coordinated and regulated by nation-states in the interests of the people is the pragmatically best solution to the contradictions of capitalism and socialism. This bodes ill for the greater and more global regulation that climate change should thrust upon us.

Are the Great Depression and the Great Neoliberal Recession sufficiently similar to indicate a cyclical process? Both were precipitated by financial crises generated by transnational finance capital outflanking regulation within the nation-state in the absence of effective international regulation. They had been preceded by credit-fueled bubbles and they were then worsened by a debt crisis. The financial sector will likely continue to be the bringer of periodic harm far greater than that of the ordinary business cycle. Both disasters also came after a period of rising inequality and sagging mass incomes, and both came after a period of technological ingenuity, which had failed to generate much growth. In both the United States led the way into global recession – though recovery from the Depression also involved a world war.

But this current recession is lesser, so far. There was no recent equivalent of the 1929 stock market crash, though Greece may have a similar role to that of the Austrian Credit-Anstalt bank in 1931, the harbinger of a Depression. There has been no equivalent either of the severe monetary contraction inflicted by the financial authorities – though the Anglo governments seem embarked on a comparable contraction. But the fiscal mistakes of government were then driven by the desire to preserve the value of currencies against gold. There is no Gold Standard today, nor mass banking collapses induced by clinging tenaciously onto the Standard. Little regulation had existed before the Great Depression, whereas this Recession followed a long period of regulation, some of which still remained in place, especially in corporate and developmental states. In what is supposed to be an increasingly transnational age, variations between nation-states and macroregions have grown so that the Great Recession has struck much less evenly across the world. Now there is 10 percent unemployment, not 25 percent, and unemployment insurance, especially generous in Europe, meant consumption did not fall so precipitously. The international response in the 1930s was beggar-thy-neighbor devaluation and protectionism. Today there is more of a balance between international and domestic regulation – though global imbalances today are much bigger.

History does not repeat itself. Capitalism does not have regular cycles for its nature changes through time. I charted the rise of a technologically innovative high productivity/low demand phase around the beginning of the twentieth century, followed by a high productivity/high demand phase (often called Fordism) from World War II to the 1960s, followed by the lower productivity/ lower demand neoliberal phase. Each phase of capitalism has had a different logic of development, different institutions, and different contradictions, as French Regulationist theorists argue (Boyer, 1990). Nation-states also have their own rhythms of development, which in phase three have been much more variable, adding to the distinctiveness of each period. Political power relations have played significant roles in the present crisis, which were not present earlier on. The political crises of both the European Union and the United States were new, and so was the ideological commitment to a property-owning democracy.

So I am skeptical of cycles. Capitalism perennially generates new instruments, new institutions, and new problems – for example, joint-stock companies (in phase 1), national accounts (phase 2), Eurodollars, CDOs, sovereign wealth funds (phase 3), with a CO_2 emissions crisis perhaps leading to a phase four of modern capitalism. Such novelties emerge unexpectedly through the cracks of existing institutions, interstitial emergence versus institutionalization. At first each escapes much regulation, adapting to and bending and straining existing institutions. Then come demands for more regulation, though these are politically and ideologically contested and variably implemented. This may force regulation on the innovators, though this is not necessarily so. In phase three neoliberals have not yet been restrained. In some countries they have gained ground, in others lost. Unlike Polanyi and Streeck, I see no inherent cyclical logic necessarily moving capitalism forward. Bankers think they have solved their own problem without any cyclical change. If they get into market trouble, the state steps in, but not to regulate them, to give them welfare. This is not good for capitalism, but their distributive power may prevail. The pessimistic scenario for the Anglophone countries above all is that neoliberalism-plus-handouts to bankers may hasten on their economic decline. But the world remains uneven and the Great Recession did further the impression that economic power might be shifting from the North to some countries of the South. Current optimism fastens on Asia, and especially on the enormous nation, which combines plan with market in only a semicapitalist way. But what if China or India, accumulating financial reserves so rapidly, wanted to actually use them domestically? That would pull the rug out from the United States. Growth on such scale is likely to lead at some point to an abrupt reversal of capital movements, especially if countries liberalize their capital accounts. There would be speculative domestic bubbles, overinvestment and a collapse of confidence on a far greater scale than the Asian Crisis of the 1990s. In this globalized economy few countries would be able to isolate themselves from such volatility. More rules are needed, but will they come? Economic globalization does not necessarily integrate the world in harmonious fashion. It can tear it apart. Another potentially more serious global threat also loomed on the horizon, as we see in the next chapter.

12   Global crisis: Climate change

Introduction: Three villains: Capitalism, states, citizens

Volumes 3 and 4 have charted the growth of globalization processes. In Volume 3 I dealt with the "segmented globalization" of rival empires and with the Second Industrial Revolution, which diffused new industrial technologies through larger swathes of the world. I analyzed the crises posed for most of the world by two World Wars and a Great Depression and noted the diffusion of liberal, socialist and fascist ideologies. In this volume I have charted the further global diffusion of capitalism and nation-states, and the coupling of a decline in international wars and a growth of civil wars across the globe. Yet in truth the global dimension of all this was not particularly interesting from a sociological point of view. For the most part I was merely describing the global expansion of social structures long familiar to us on more local scales. Does capitalism change because it is global rather than regional? Do geopolitics change because they concern 190 nation-states rather than 30? Yes, but not greatly.

However, a major exception was noted in Chapter 2. The emergence of international peace across most of the world was a world-historical change come quite suddenly upon us. This happened for several reasons, but the major one was the threat of nuclear weapons to the globe. This made warfare between the greatest powers completely and utterly irrational. The use of nuclear weapons could be the most extreme form of globalization. They could cause many millions of casualties, ending civilization as we know it, making the world uninhabitable for humans. Insects might inherit the earth. Military power relations had become fully globalized, for they had hit up against the limits of the earth and then ricocheted back on us. Perhaps the most appropriate metaphor is a lethal boomerang, our own inventions coming back to kill us. But humans took evasive action against nuclear war and this transformed societies. There has never been an entity like the European Union, an economic giant but a military dwarf. On a lesser scale many other states show the same novel imbalance, their civilian far outweighing their military functions. The military backbone of most states has turned to jelly, and for them soft have largely replaced hard geopolitics.

But a second, slower-paced boomerang of equal global lethality has been launched, and is just beginning to fly back on us. This is climate change, generated by our own supposed mastery over nature, humanity's peak of

361

collective power. More specifically, the problem has been created by capital-ism ably assisted by both nation-states and individual consuming citizens. These, unfortunately, are the three most fundamental social actors of our time. Their powers must now all be curbed to avoid planetary disaster – a formidable task. And this, like nuclear weapons, is a global threat since car-bon emissions anywhere affects everywhere. The climate knows no national boundaries. It is global.

Throughout this book, as is conventional, I have used GDP statistics to measure economic health. GDP growth has measured the success of national economies. Volume 3 charted the success of the white settler colonies, the Japanese Empire, early Nazi Germany, and the Soviet Union. This volume has focused on the "golden age" of capitalism in the West after 1945, and on recent Chinese and BRIC growth. GDP growth is why capitalism is seen as a great success story. Conversely, we deduce failure where growth has been absent or minimal – as in most colonies, most countries during the 1920s and 1930s, the Soviet Union from the 1960s onward, and most OECD countries very recently. Yet an insistent ironic theme of my volumes has been that almost nothing comes as unalloyed success or failure. Out of wars has come good, while the regimes securing economic growth were sometimes monstrous. The white colonies got economic growth out of genocide; Hitler and the Japanese got growth out of militarism, and Stalin got it with mass murder. But modern economic growth also has a universal dark-side: environmental degradation threatening the destruction of humanity. That would be hubris indeed: our greatest success might become the slayer of our world.

The environmental disaster looming ahead of us has many facets – climate change, ozone, particulates and acid rain, the depletion of the seas, soil and forest erosion, water shortages etc. Here I focus on climate change, popularly known as global warming, caused by the release into the atmosphere of "green-house gases" (GHGs). Carbon dioxide, CO_2, comprises more than two-thirds of all GHGs. Once released, most GHGs cannot escape the earth's atmosphere. Trapping the sun's rays, they gradually heat up the planet, its atmosphere, seas, and lands. Over the last twenty years the scientific community has come to accept that global warming is happening at an accelerating rate and as an overwhelmingly "anthropogenic" process, that is, caused by human activity. In 2005 the heads of eleven national academies of science wrote a letter to the G8 heads of government warning that global climate change was "a clear and increasing threat" requiring immediate political action. The academies were those of Brazil, Canada, China, France, Germany, India, Italy, Japan, Russia, the UK and the United States – the major developed countries and all four BRIC countries. There is no longer significant room for scientific denial (Oreskes, 2004). As the chief scientific adviser to the Australian government, Professor Ross Chubb, recently declared "There are probably people now who think I am partisan because I'm saying the science is in on climate change.

Well, I don't think that's partisan, I think that I can read English" (*The Sydney Morning Herald*, June 22, 2011).

Such scientists advise government agencies dealing with the environment and provide an inner channel of concern to politicians. This is the one case where my refusal to make science a distinct source of social power wavers. In general I have regarded scientists and technologists as subordinate to other power holders. Ralph Schroeder has argued that in the modern period the enormous growth of the institutions of science technology have converted them into another source of social power. Up until now I have disagreed. In Volume 3, chapter 3, for example, I argued that though inventions powered the Second Industrial Revolution, the inventors were largely subordinated to business corporations. Some became entrepreneurs themselves, if they could find investors; others worked for corporations or sold their patents to them. In the mid-twentieth century atomic scientists produced the most devastating weapons ever, but their employers were the major military powers. They were mostly patriots supporting their own nation's war effort. But now the autonomy and collective solidarity of environmental scientists is much greater, for they have taken the lead in bringing the issues to global consciousness. They do not produce an ideology in the sense of an ultimate meaning system, for their knowledge is "cold," based on observation of facts, and they accept that their theories are refutable – unlike religious or socialist ideologists. Scientists have coped with uncertainty not through faith but probability theory, alternative scenarios and ranges of possibilities. Few are committed to a faith, though James Lovelock's attachment to "Gaia," the Earth as a super-organism, is perhaps one such, while many other environmentalists espouse "ecocentrism," viewing the environment as a moral entity in its own right, of which we humans (like other species) are only a small part. There is in fact tension between science and morality among environmentalists, though scientists tend to stick to the former. As a social scientists I will do likewise. But scientists and social scientists cannot carry the day unaided by mass movements and governments, though as a caste the scientists do have some clout. I hope their views carry the day and that they will prove an exception to my model of power, but I doubt it.

There are two main aspects to climate change, global warming and greater variability. The reports of international scientific agencies are the main way climate scientists explain their research. The "Intergovernmental Panel on Climate Change" (IPCC), set up in 1988 by the UN, produced its 4th Report in 2007. The UN Environment Programme GEO-4 Report (UNEP, 2007), the UN Human Development Report of 2007/2008, the OECD Environmental Outlook to 2030 (2008), and the UK government's Stern Review (2007) all concur that global warming is gathering pace and has a more than 90 percent chance of being anthropogenic. The human activity responsible is industrialization, principally its burning of fossil fuels, above all coal, then oil. Fossil fuels combined produce about two-thirds of GHGs, deforestation another 20 percent,

[margin note, handwritten, right side: Climate change as global science]

[handwritten note at bottom: Burning of oil and coal / deforestation.]

and agriculture and other land use practices produce the rest. James Hansen (2009), with an impressive track record of accurately predicting global warming trends, says any mitigation policy must have as a central strategy the rapid phasing-out of coal emissions so that they are ended by 2020 in the developed world, and by 2030 in the whole world, except if CO_2 can be captured in safe storage units. Agricultural and forestry practices that sequester carbon must also be adopted. Much of the world's remaining supply of fossil fuels – coal, oil, gas, tar sands and shale oil – must be kept securely in the ground if our grandchildren are to have a livable planet. So I focus on fossil fuels.

Contemporary anthropogenic shocks are new only in scale. Radkau (2008) discerns five historic eras of human-nature interaction: subsistence hunter-gathering, ancient civilizations dependent on water and wood, modern colonialism, the Industrial Revolution, and the most recent, which he calls globalization. Throughout, human groups impacted nature in ways which often had dire consequences for the local environment and sometimes for their own existence. Diamond (2005) gives examples of social collapse through destruction of natural habitats, reduction of wild foods, loss of biodiversity, soil erosion, freshwater pollution, exhaustion of natural photosynthetic resources, human introduction of toxins and alien species, artificially induced climate change, and overpopulation. A fairly recent example came from China. After its seventeenth century crisis the Qing dynasty restored an imperial system based on large granaries, intensive marketing of foodstuffs, and more efficient use of natural resources. Yet its very success brought a massive population surge, which again overtaxed available natural resources. Nature was being overworked by the dawn of the twentieth century. Radkau's industrialization phase first posed only local environmental threats. But with the onset of the global era in the 1950s, the "deepest rupture in the history of the environment" began (2008: 250).

The main culprit has been industrial capitalism, with its relentless short-term search for private profit with no responsibility for the public good or for payment for public harm. A "treadmill of profit" has generated technological change, population growth, and consumer affluence, its exponential economic growth based on fossil fuels – the power of capitalism's creative destruction taken to a ghastly end that Schumpeter never envisaged. Yet capitalism is not acting alone. It is buttressed by political power relations, that is states and politicians whose principal goal is economic growth. They have economic and political interests of their own, for to expand industrial capitalism brings more state revenues and more political popularity. Political success is actually measured by economic growth, driven in democracies by electoral cycles – or in despotic regimes in other ways in which popularity is judged (secret police reports, riots etc.). Yet the political treadmill is not imposed by states on unwilling subjects, for these measure their own success by material consumption, and they will support politicians who they think will deliver this

treadmill of profit
political treadmill
treadmill of military destruction

right now. Politics are also overwhelmingly caged by the nation-state, making the raising of a genuinely global issue like climate change especially difficult. Rational, national and very short-term calculation is essential to capitalist profit, politicians and citizens alike. We want it now, they all cry: this is how we define success! The task of climate mitigation is therefore a very big one – to take human beings off the three main treadmills and the villains of climate change, the arch-villain, capitalist profit, ably assisted by political elites and ever-increasing citizen consumption.

Military power is also involved in a more minor capacity, since industrialization boosted war-fighting ability, which remained the main function of states into the twentieth century. Coal and then oil became critical in war. Since oil is located in relatively few places across the world, and since navies, air forces, tanks and trucks cannot operate without oil, it became the greatest strategic resource, helping precipitate wars. Wars produce the most destructive human impact on the environment, and they consume the most fossil fuels. Thankfully this threat has eased across much of the world. Yet the U.S. Department of Defense is the world's largest consumer of petroleum and the world's biggest polluter. Jorgensen and his colleagues (2010) in a comparative study in the period 1970 to 2000 found that the scale and intensity of carbon dioxide emissions as well as the per capita ecological footprint of nations was directly related to the military participation ratio (the number of military personnel per 1000 population) and military expenditures per soldier (controlling for other variables, like GDP and urbanization). The more militarized a country is, the more it damages the environment. Hooks and Smith (2005) aptly call this "the treadmill of military destruction." They also note a particularly horrific aspect of modern war. Nuclear, biological and chemical weapons brought a new goal to warfare: not merely to crush human bodies but also to render the whole environment uninhabitable, as in the use of napalm in Vietnam and Cambodia. Biological and chemical weapons potentially pose a distinct nightmare ecological scenario of how the human world might end. But this scenario apart, the worst military scenario for climate change is to have large militaries and not use them, for using them in war inflicts great damage on economies and produces decline in GDPs!

Finally, all these practices resonate inside a powerful ideology of modernization in which nature is explicitly subordinated to culture. Humanity's destiny in common-sense proud parlance is to conquer and exploit nature. This ideology outgrew capitalism, for state socialism was equally endowed with it. Though Engels had doubts about the conquest of nature, and though the early Bolsheviks had green ideals, Stalinism brought industrial gigantism and devotion to Five-Year Plans of growth. Progress toward socialism was now measured by gross indicators of production (Goldman, 1972: 18–19, 64–70). McNeill (2000: 336) says the "growth fetish" became a "state religion" everywhere: "The overarching priority of economic growth was easily the most important idea of the twentieth century." All four sources of social power are together destroying the planet. The task of combating this is formidable.

It is unclear whether capitalism or state socialism has been worse at despoiling. The "hero projects" of state socialism produced the most terrible episodes of destruction. Capitalism cannot compete with the destruction of the Aral Sea. This has led some to argue that state socialism – sometimes all authoritarian regimes – have done more damage than capitalism or liberal democracy (e.g., Shapiro, 2001; Josephson, 2005). Yet they produce no comparative statistical data. Goldman (1972: 2–5) says the Soviet record was only about as dismal as the West's, while studies of China say environmental destruction became worse as the economy marketized since local actors became freer to pursue profit at all costs and better at evading government pollution controls (Muldavin, 2000; Ma & Ortolano, 2000). A comparison of post-Mao China with capitalist Taiwan says their levels of destruction were similar (Weller, 2006). Nazi Germany was Nature-conscious, taking especial care with swamp drainage, highway construction and deforestation – forests were a key part of Nazi Teutonic myths. Yet in air pollution the Nazis were no better than the democracies, for they sacrificed the environment to industrialization, especially of military goods (Uekoetter, 2006; Brüggemeier et al., 2005). All modern states have sacrificed the environment to GDP, regardless of regime type. The economic problem is now capitalism only because it became the world's dominant mode of production. If we all had state socialism, the problem would be just the same.

Global warming trends: Past, present, future

Scientists acknowledge limitations in their ability to measure and predict and they qualify their statements in terms of both statistical probability and the degree of scientific agreement. All figures given later are merely mid-points of possible ranges. Scientists are also just a normal bunch of academics, of varying abilities and research diligence, sometimes too attached to particular paradigms, too keen to grab the headlines, or too beholden to those who finance their research. For all these reasons, exactitude is impossible and controversies and minor scandals intermittently erupt. However, none of the scandals have been serious enough to cast doubt on what is now consensus wisdom.

Scientists use two main alternative measures of GHGs. One focuses only on carbon dioxide, CO_2, while the other converts all six groups of greenhouse gases to CO_2 equivalents, which is labeled CO_2e The preindustrial concentration of CO_2. in the atmosphere was about 280 parts per million (ppm) while CO_2e was about 290 ppm. By 1990 these had risen to 353 CO_2 and 395 CO_2e. These were the levels at which the Kyoto Protocol agreement hoped to stabilize emissions, and 1990 is often taken as the "baseline" for subsequent rates of increase. By December 2011 the CO_2 level had reached 393 ppm, and was still rising.

Points out that capitalism is by default problem here. (wrestling for consensus)

This produces global warming. For at least one thousand years up to the twentieth century there were small temperature swings in the oceans and the near-surface air, due to natural forces like solar radiation and volcanic activity. Yet the first five decades of the twentieth century saw a much bigger rise in temperature of about .07° C per decade, and since 1980 it has been rising at. 2° C per decade. The World Meteorological Association produces global average annual temperatures. It says that the hottest ten years have all been since 1998. In the 2000s the rise has slowed slightly but this seems to have been due to the explosive industrial growth in China, which was powered by coal-fired power stations. As well as carbon, these emit vast quantities of sulphur, which reflect the sun's rays and so tend to temporarily cool the atmosphere. Whereas CO_2 emissions impact on the atmosphere for a hundred years, SO_2 emissions fall out in weeks or months. When the Chinese start fitting sulphur dioxide scrubbers to their power station chimneys, as they will, atmospheric temperatures will surge again.

Global warming is also confirmed by rising sea levels due to thermal expansion and losses of glaciers, ice caps and polar ice sheets; by the decline in global biodiversity; by the shifts of bird, insect and plant ranges; by earlier insect emergence, bird egg-laying, and tree flowering each year; by deforestation; by lengthier crop growing seasons in mid- to high-latitude ranges; and by changes in rainfall and ocean currents (United Nations Environmental Program [UNEP], 2007: 59; Speth, 2008: xxi-xxii). Warming has also a more than 50 percent chance of causing greater extremes of temperatures and winds. In fact the greater variability of weather has now become visible to us, whereas warming is less perceptible. Exceptionally cold weather on the eastern seaboard of the United States in 2010 was assumed by many climate skeptics to discredit the notion of global warming. But it was outweighed by a warmer winter elsewhere in the planet. The IPCC Report (2007: 38) says industrial era growth has a more than 90 percent probability of producing a warming effect unprecedented in more than ten thousand years.

The problem is exacerbated by population growth combined with successful industrialization in developing countries. The OECD countries had contributed about 85 percent of GHG emissions through almost all the twentieth century, but by 2004 their relative share had declined to 46 percent. The enormous population size of China means that it has now overtaken the United States as the biggest polluter, though Australia and the United States remain the biggest per capita. Though GHG emissions per unit of GDP have begun to decline because of increasing efficiency in reduction techniques, the absolute growth in global GDP has outweighed that, especially in China (OECD, 2008).

The IPCC Report projected alternative scenarios of warming ranging between 1.8° C and 4.0° C during the twenty-first century, with the median being about 3° C. This level is almost certainly higher than human beings have ever experienced. More recent studies suggest even higher future temperatures. The Stern

Review (2007: chap. 1) says an increase of 5° C is more than 50 percent likely (so does the MIT Joint Program on the Science and Policy of Global Change, 2008), while the Global Carbon Project of the University of East Anglia (2009) suggests 5°–6° C. Since our temperatures today are only 5° C above those of the last ice-age, these warming projections might make a very big difference to life on earth.

How much difference no one can say precisely. The reports indicate likely horrific consequences, including hundreds of millions of people lacking water or exposed to flooding, numerous species extinctions, reductions in cereals, and increased exposure to malnutrition, diarrhoeal, cardio-respiratory and infectious diseases. These would be more likely if warming was reinforced by variability. The IPCC Report gives a range of temperature rises, which might bring on each disaster, meaning that we cannot correlate a specific temperature with definite consequences. Impacts are also variable across the globe. Temperature rises are greater in northern than southern latitudes and less damaging in temperate zones. For flooding, the numbers affected will be largest in the densely populated mega-deltas of Asia and Africa while small islands are especially vulnerable (Intergovernmental Panel on Climate Change [IPCC Report], 2007; Stern Review, 2007: chap. 3). On top of these projections, "feedback loops" or "tipping-points" might suddenly worsen consequences (UNEP, 2007: 62–5). The ability of the planet to hold increased emissions within natural carbon sinks is declining. If the sinks fill up, the atmosphere will start warming at a much faster rate. A melting Greenland glacier might change sea currents weakening the Gulf Stream on which Western Europe depends for its warmth. Without this, its climate might resemble Labrador's, for it is on the same latitude. The melting of frozen peat bogs in Siberia and Canada might release enormous amounts of methane into the atmosphere. Increased methane already results from a global shift toward meat-eating. Cows fart a lot more than we do, and the planet does not like it.

These official reports may be overoptimistic, since they assume economic growth will bring much greater energy efficiency. The IPCC "business as usual" strategy (BAU), the do-nothing strategy, assumes that at least 60 percent of carbon emission reduction will occur through greater efficiency, without any mitigation policies. They expect substantial contributions from such innovations as carbon capture, hydrogen fusion fuel, solar panels, or cellulosic biofuels, and from more nuclear power. But it is likely that global population and GDP will continue to grow, wiping out whatever savings are made through greater energy efficiency. Throughout the history of capitalist industrialization increases in energy-efficiency have been outweighed by the growth in population and production that this generates. Growth outpaces efficiency (Raskin et al., 2002: 22). Why should that change now? True, there is now new, single-minded focus on research on alternative energy technologies. Perhaps the ITER international hydrogen fusion fuel project located near Aix en Provence in France could produce a working plant like a mini-sun, which would put ten times as much electricity into the grid as it consumes. ITER projects an "Age of Fusion" commencing in the last quarter of the twenty-first century. The physics of creating a mini-sun are known, the problem is essential an engineering one: how to construct a building, which could safely contain the energy released by a mini-sun. According to its own engineers, there is no sign of any such breakthrough.[1]

Even stabilizing emissions at present levels would not stop warming, since changes already "baked in" will take decades to work their way through. Thermal expansion of the seas would continue for centuries, due to the length of time required for heat to penetrate deep oceans. Stabilization at today's emissions levels would bring greenhouse gas levels close to 550 ppm COe by 2050 and a rise in temperature of anywhere between 2 percent and 5 percent – extremely dangerous levels. Radical mitigation measures are almost certainly necessary. The Stern Review (2007: 13) suggests that we must reduce annual global emissions by 80 percent from the 1990 level by 2050 to avoid disaster. Hansen and colleagues (2009) say we have to get back to 350 ppm carbon emissions. So mitigation measures must be global, involving cooperation at the very least between the major OECD polluters and the major new polluters, the BRIC s. Though they are egged on to action by the transnational community of scientists and environmental movements, the core of mitigation must come through an unprecedented global extension of soft geopolitics.

The future is not certain. Revolutionary new technologies, driven by the profit motive, might emerge to solve the emissions problem. There are some who believe so. If so, we should go down on our knees before the public and private laboratories that make the breakthroughs and the businesses and governments financing them and bringing them to the market. It would be a third great achievement of capitalism in the present period, a third great burst of creative destruction, after the second industrial revolution and the great postwar boost of consumer demand. If the breakthroughs came in China, it would be a second great achievement of that capitalist party-state. Conversely, without breakthroughs, a disastrous war or pandemic disease killing much of the global population might also send global emissions downward. But the climate modelers have been proved right for over two decades. The threat is highly probable and would be disastrous if it did come to pass. It would seem prudent and rational to take serious mitigating action now.

First steps toward mitigation, 1970–2010

Some actions have been taken already. Legislation against visible pollution became widespread from the 1970s. Then came the CFC crisis. Scientists

---

[1] Personal communication, Les Michels, France, July 10, 2010.

noted a thinning of the ozone layer protecting the Earth's atmosphere from solar radiation and traced it to chlorofluorocarbon gas propellants (CFCs), then used in air conditioners, refrigerators, aerosols and other industrial processes. Luckily, the aerosol industry began finding technological alternatives just as a number of countries banned CFCs. In 1987 the Montreal Protocol agreement between 191 countries began phasing CFC production out. Less harmful gases now power aerosols and it is believed that natural processes will heal the ozone layer in about fifty years. This was a success of soft geopolitics, though made easier by technological innovation.

Popular consciousness of global warming made rapid progress after the publication of Rachel Carson's best-seller of 1962, *Silent Spring,* a bitter attack on chemical industry pollution. By the 1970s polls were showing that protecting the environment enjoyed majority support, though it was not usually a very deep sentiment. Popularization of environmental science grew after the Club of Rome's pioneering book of 1972, *Limits to Growth,* and was sealed by the statement of the eleven major national academies of science in 2005. Once achieved, scientific consensus diffused inside government administrations as scientific advisers made their presence felt. Here experts did make a difference. As Frank notes, environmentalism took a leap forward with the rise of conceptions of nature as an ecosystem. This enabled a global conception of danger, which was not really possible while environmentalism centered merely on aesthetic celebrations of the beauty of nature. The two combined began to seem like a genuine ideology.

Beck (1992) suggests that the traditional class cleavages of industrial society have given way to a new "risk society" in which he says there is consensus about common environmental and other concerns. States, corporations, social movements and ordinary citizens are all motivated to combat such danger. He is right about the decline of class but where is this consensus? True, scientific pressure has been paralleled by the rise of green movements. Their expansion also dates from the 1970s, as environmental problems were publicized more and as traditional left parties ran out of steam. The movements originated in the New Left, in feminism and in 1960s countercultures among a generation disillusioned with established politics. They fought not only for better ecology but for more local democracy, parading strong ethical sensibilities toward the human and the nonhuman world (Doherty, 2002; Taylor, 1995). Again, the combination tends to make a social movement, which is truly ideological, going beyond mere science. But it is a very diffuse movement. Green NGOs are many and varied. Some are large and global, like Greenpeace with its membership of more than five million, offices in twenty countries, and an annual budget more than $300 million. Others are small, local, and quickly come and go. Many have a direct radical action fringe. There is little overall leadership or coordination.

Green NGOs began much bigger in the North than the South though they now do have a genuinely global presence. In the North they attract highly educated groups, more from the arts and social sciences than hard sciences or engineering (except for environmentally related sciences). They are predominantly middle class, dominated by professions in the media, arts and crafts, public sector and social welfare professions like teachers, health professionals, and social workers. These people have more autonomy from hierarchy in their work-lives (and so more freedom of expression), their jobs are more concerned with values or politics, and they are less connected than others to corporate capitalism. They are in a figurative sense the herbivores, not the carnivores, of capitalist democracies. Some of these professions are also highly transnational. Such groups provide the core activists of new social movements more generally, especially those concerned with postmaterialist identity politics, world peace, and human rights, all of which also generate large quasi-transnational INGOs – though like the bigger environmental groups they are in practice international federations whose individual branches are nationally organized. Women are as numerous as men, but youth predominates, especially in direct action groups. Even elementary schools are hot-beds of green sentiments, and this has enabled continual replenishment of the base (Doherty, 2002: 57–66, 217). Public opinion polls generally reinforce this picture, with more concern for the environment among the better educated, those with postmaterialist and leftist values, though they also find that religious people, especially non-Christians, are more concerned than the irreligious, and they sometimes find that the middle-aged, not the young, worry most (Kvaloy et al., 2012).

World polity theory places this little world of highly educated, herbivorous, young people and NGOs amid a much broader "world polity." It argues that since the mid-nineteenth century a "rationalized world institutional and cultural order" has emerged embodying universally shared and applicable models that shape states, organizations, and individuals' identities alike (Boli & Thomas, 1997; Meyer et al., 1997; Meyer, 1999). Its adherents argue that common conceptions of the individual, of progress, of sovereignty, and of human rights have arisen and are driven onward, structuring the actions of states, groups and individuals, and providing a common framework for solving global problems. Though they accept that nation-states remain the principal policy-makers, this is essentially a transnational model in which a common ideology diffuses right across national boundaries, persuading all states that certain policies are simply the right thing to do. This vision is one of an emerging common ideology, but it has a strongly pragmatic content too. It is a blend of useful policies and institutions for the world as a whole to adopt set amid a broader moral liberalism, which is said to derive from the Enlightenment – though perhaps that is too eurocentric. Its highly pragmatic and rational streak makes it only half-ideological, and it is not very transcendent or immanent. It is also a highly optimistic scenario. We will eventually do the right thing about climate change, as we will do about most policy issues.

I have so far failed to perceive much of this optimism through much of the twentieth century. Liberalism, socialism and fascism were probably the most important ideologies, and they all derived to one degree or another from a common Enlightenment tradition but they went to great lengths to exterminate each other. From the 1950s world polity theory became a little more plausible, as interstate wars declined, as class conflicts were compromised, and as many states across the world did adopt some common institutions amidst a host of emerging international organizations, from scientific associations to United Nations agencies, from global standard-setting agencies to feminist and environmental NGOs. By the twenty-first century, so say world polity theorists, a single world culture had crystallized as the constitutive element of an emerging world society, a set of "scripts" to be followed anywhere across the globe. No longer confined to the West, world polity, culture and society are now supposedly the common heritage of humanity, institutionalized across the globe. But we have seen that neoliberalism has become one of these scripts, and that is hardly conducive to social harmony or intervention to secure climate change.

Of course, such agencies and movements do exist, exerting some influence. Gender politics have made global progress, and shrewd INGOs have also found lowest common denominators to press their causes. Feminist INGOs shifted their rhetorical framing from discrimination against women (which is interpreted differently in different cultures) to violence against women's bodies (which is deplored in virtually all cultures), and this has been internationally quite successful. Yet theirs is a constant struggle not a mere enactment of global scripts. They also rely on a "boomerang effect" whereby INGO pressure on international agencies like the UN result in pressure on recalcitrant states, weakening their caging (Keck & Sikkink, 1998). In the field of sex offenses there are stronger indications of a global script. Legal codes have moved in concert across most of the world to tighten laws on rape and child sexual abuse (especially between 1980 and 2000) while loosening laws on adultery and sodomy (especially in the 1960s and 1990s) – though it is the deviant cases like Iran, which tend to grab the media headlines. The authors of this study (Frank et al., 2010) says this is evidence of the growth of a world culture constituted by individualized personal identities, free-standing personhood, at the expense of the protection of the traditional family and nation. But John Meyer's assertion that there is a single national welfare script is not true, as we saw in Chapters 6 and 11.

Environmental activism has also been viewed from a world polity perspective. Bromley et al. (2010) analyzed about five hundred history, civics, and social studies textbooks used for children of between eleven and eighteen years in sixty-nine countries for the period from 1970 to 2008. They say that the environmental content of textbooks increased substantially over the period, and the issues discussed were increasingly global rather than national, and contained more discussion of universal human rights. The most developed countries' textbooks showed most concern, while Soviet and then post-Soviet countries showed least. The authors choose to emphasize a common global postnational trend. However, their data indicate that the changes in textbooks resulted from pressure from teachers, administrators and scientists involved in educational institutions. This sector and these professionals are at the heart of the environmental movement, as we saw earlier. Though the authors insist that the textbooks reflect an emerging global culture rather than activist pressure, their results seem to indicate the reverse – scientific and ethical pressure applied by committed environmentalists. Seeing environmentalism as merely part of a blander world culture or world polity is a mistake. Environmentalism is growing, it has a strongly moral quality, and it may blossom into becoming one of the most significant ideologies of modern times. It would be only the second really significant novel ideology created in the twentieth century, after fascism, but it has not yet had much success (and look what happened to fascism).

There are important weaknesses in environmental movements. There is little presence of either capitalist carnivores or the working class. Environmental activism tends not to be a class struggle issue in the North of the world. Labor unions are still more oriented to jobs and fear that green policies will reduce them. For the foreseeable future this movement will have to develop quite differently from previous radicalisms and socialisms. The movement in the South sometimes differs, for peasant movements in the hinterlands are often prominent, angered by dam-building and deforestation of their habitats by governments and big corporations threatening their cultivation practices and their livelihood. The World Social Forum gives them a little global organization. However, their political clout is limited, except in Andean countries where indigenous peoples have recently surged into power. Yet the bottom line of pessimism is that every government in the world is committed to economic growth.

In most countries environmentalist activists come more from the Left than from the Right, though East Asia is an exception. There environmentalism resonates in the region's traditional religions, Confucianism, Buddhism and Taoism, which are much more ecocentric than either Christianity, Judaism or Islam. This results not only in more environmental protest there than in the West, but it comes at least as much from the Right as from the Left (Kern, 2010). Nonetheless, in the West astute framing by NGOs has led them to blend popularized scientific findings with vivid depictions of habitat damage, endangered cuddly species (the polar bear above all) and idealized Nature, and this makes converts right across the political spectrum. Astute framing is also revealed by their linguistic shift from the goal of "limits to growth" – who wants to limit their standard of living? – to "sustainable development" – two positive words!

The global master frame is that humanity needs a new relationship with nature to achieve a sustainable future. The UNDP Report (2007: 61) declares a moral imperative rooted in universal ideas about stewardship of the earth, social justice and ethical responsibility. In a world where people are often divided by their beliefs, these ideas cross religious and cultural divides. The Report quotes a famous American Indian proverb "We do not inherit the Earth from our ancestors, we borrow it from our children" and quotes comparable homilies in all the major world religions. To the chagrin of the do-nothings, the greens have seized the moral high ground. They respond by trying to shift the argument away from greening toward the cost of mitigation programs and against "big government." Ideological battle has been joined, if indirectly.

Greens have sought to bring rather abstract and scientific issues into everyday moral behavior through tree-hugging, recycling, individual carbon-offsetting, and other forms of personal mitigation. Thus individual action might be seen as making a difference. If I bicycle instead of driving, or if I drive a hybrid vehicle, there is both a morally uplifting effect and a miniscule impact on the climate. Ordinary consumers have a lower impact on GHG emissions than do the fossil fuel industry and major industrial consumers, but they are important in bringing pressure and votes. In international polls support for green solutions averages 75 percent, though the intensity of commitment is not high (Scruggs, 2003: chap. 4). In democratic response, the main political parties in Europe and Japan (but not alas the United States) have begun to compete rhetorically for the title of the environmental party, though their actions lag behind their words, especially in a recession. Against the tide of public opinion, the Gillard Labour administration in Australia has passed the world's first national carbon tax on the 500 biggest corporations, combined with an emissions trading scheme second in size only to the European Union's. But will it knock them out of power at the next election?

Some countries have mitigated more than others. In Esty's 2010 Environmental Performance Index Iceland, Switzerland, Costa Rica and Sweden were the best performers, followed by most Western European countries, Japan and New Zealand, plus a few poorer countries like Mauritius, Colombia and Cuba. The United States lags in 61st place, alongside Paraguay and Brazil, but ahead of China and India. On Esty's ranking of 2007 CO_2 emissions data the top-ranked countries were poor countries without much polluting industry plus Switzerland, the Nordic countries, and (nuclear-powered) France. Then come diverse countries, including Brazil, the remaining West Europeans and Japan. The United States is the lowest-ranked advanced country except for Australia, but ahead of India and China (data available at http://epi.yale.edu). The contrast between the two biggest Western economies, Germany and the United States, is enormous. The movement in Germany has conquered some regional governments and achieved notable victories over the utility companies; the movement in the United States has done neither – and its influence there is currently declining. As we shall see later, national and regional divergencies are currently increasing. There is no common global script in sight.

Among this great variety, however, there is one pattern. Scruggs (2003: esp. chap. 5) found among OECD countries during the period 1970–2000 that corporatist countries did better. They have brought labor and business organizations together inside government offices to hammer out compromises on class issues, and on environmental issues scientists and environmentalists have been added. But having peak business and labor organizations present means that lobbying is not confined to industries who have most to lose from environmental policy, which is a major obstacle in the United States. Under corporatism compromises between less and more polluting industries are made before their common program is presented to government and labor. Germany, Sweden, the Netherlands, Denmark, Austria and Finland were the high performing corporatists, while the three liberal countries in the study, the UK, the United States, and Canada, performed worst along with Italy and Spain. Ozler and Ohbach (2009) similarly found that countries high on the Freedom House Index of economic freedoms (a measure of neoliberalism) had a worse ecological footprint, even after controlling for urbanization, per capita GDP, exports and climate. They conclude that the more the market freedom the more relentless the treadmill of profit. Growth and constant reinvestment, driven by market competition, led to greater resource exploitation and higher emissions. The greater the government regulation, the less the footprint. The more states embrace the free market ideal, the more difficult it is achieve sustainability.

This is a worrying finding since this is a neoliberal era in which government regulation is often viewed as bad, especially in the United States, which has the heaviest global footprint per capita but now lags greatly in environmental negotiations (Speth, 2008: 73). The United States has forgotten its environmental tradition surrounding the preservation of wilderness, a popular theme in American culture. New Deal Democrats had favored resource conservation and wilderness preservation, and administrations up to President Nixon continued the tradition. Clean Air and Clean Water Acts were passed under Nixon in 1970–2. But that proved to be the high point. Much of this legislation remains on the books, but subsequent administrations weakened implementation.

Some business sectors remain the main opponent of emissions control proposals, especially in America. The electric utilities, mining, petroleum and natural gas industries have led, aided by big corporate consumers like the auto industry and agricultural crop and livestock producers. Since their bottom lines would be hurt by effective emissions policies, they are willing to spend heavily to avert them. The market fundamentalism of conservative think tanks, which would bring death to the planet, also began to conquer the Republican Party. Conservatives tended to be also progrowth in population policy, being against sex education, contraception and abortion. For their part, many American liberals favoring individual human rights were dubious about state intervention and population control. For the global environment all this was ominous (Hulme, 2009: 274–5; Kamieniecki, 2006: chaps. 4 & 6). Indeed, by 2012 the near-collapse of moderate Republicanism left a field of presidential contenders vying to outdo each other in ridiculing the whole notion of climate change. They had also found a new energy goal: resource independence, the exploitation of national reserves of newly discovered shale gas deposits so that the United States would no longer need to import oil. They see this as enhancing national security, currently the most sacred goal of American politicians. It actually entails the death of the planet.

Business and political opponents of the environmental movement do not contest the goal of a cleaner environment. Instead they dismiss global warming as a hoax. Business prefers not to discuss green issues but instead finances candidates who can be counted on to oppose emissions bills as a part of a broader rightist agenda. Business has also set up industry environmental groups, whose green titles belie their mission. These emphasize scientific dissensus, aided by their own tame scientists, and the large costs and job-losses of emissions proposals (on costs they are right). Until 2007 the conservative think-tank the American Enterprise Institute was offering grants of $10,000 to any scientist who would write a skeptical report about climate change (Newell & Paterson, 2010). Faux-green groups denounce big government and call for more domestic energy extraction to increase national security. This is backed up by billions of dollars to finance the election of conservatives, to defeat green candidates, and to finance litigation against government environmental agencies. This helps them set congressional agendas and intimidate the agencies into not implementing legislation. Thus the Environmental Protection Agency, the EPA became "a more flexible, pro-business, cost-conscious, power-sharing facilitator" (Miller, 2009: 57). Subsequent Republican presidents and congresses did nothing to change this trend, and Clinton and Gore, who wanted to change it, were prevented from acting by a Republican-dominated Congress.

Environmental concerns grew nonetheless, energized by pollution scandals like Times Beach, the Love Canal neighborhood, Three Mile Island and the Exxon Valdez oil tanker spillage. The greens shifted focus to the state and local level and regulation followed. Mandatory emissions reductions policies appeared in the 1990s and 2000s in a third of U.S. states. Some U.S. corporations now realized that to comply with standards that varied by state and city was not cost-effective. Seeing that federal legislation was bound to come, they began to put forward their own proposals, usually weaker and more attuned to their bottom lines in order to win a seat at the table where legislative proposals would be discussed. Low-emitting business was ready to accept emissions standards at the Kyoto standard, business as a whole was prepared to support mild cap-and-trade proposals, and investors and some businesses geared themselves up to make profits out of carbon trading and other climate reform proposals (Miller, 2009: chaps. 3–6; Kamieniecki, 2006; Kraft & Kamieniecki, 2007). There is less reason why low-emitting corporations – retailers like Walmart, banks, and many others – should fear greener policies, since their costs would barely rise. Indeed for several years in the new millennium major business interests did seem to be shifting toward a carbon compromise (Newell & Paterson, 2010: chap. 4). The World Economic Forum organized one hundred CEOs of major global corporations to submit a brief report to the G8 meeting of 2008, urging it to do better than Kyoto in reducing emissions. The report endorsed public-private initiatives, mainly to pioneer new technologies. An unexpected silver lining from the 2008 Recession was the conversion of U.S. auto companies. Having received enormous government subsidies to avoid bankruptcy, they accepted in July 2011 tougher government standards of fuel efficiency that they had earlier fought tooth-and-nail.

But Bush the Younger and a Republican Party becoming more conservative were not helpful. Bush abandoned his earlier promises to regulate CO^2 emissions and withdrew the United States from Kyoto under pressure from conservative Republicans and industry groups (Suskind, 2004: 127). Vice President Cheney's Task Force on Energy recommended an increase in fossil fuel extraction and billion-dollar subsidies to its producers. This was legislated by Congress in 2005. The administration's political appointees to head the EPA, the Forest Service, the Interior Department, and the Department of Agriculture undermined existing environmental oversight, paying back the contributions that the logging, farming and energy industries had made to Bush's election campaign. Nonetheless, by 2006 Congress was beginning to respond to the scientific consensus. Senate leaders began to craft a proposal that might satisfy business and a congressional majority. In 2007 Bush was also pressured by a Supreme Court decision forcing the EPA to accept responsibilities for climate change. He was forced to release more federal climate data and in 2008 he declared he would support federal limits on GHG emissions, though adding enough qualifications to undermine that commitment. Since most Democrats were already convinced, and since most polls (as in most countries) revealed consistent, if skin-deep support for green reforms, President Obama's initial intentions were greener. However, the Great Neoliberal Recession and Republican gains in Congress in 2010 made further progress impossible in the short-term. Indeed, in 2010 some prominent corporations like BP, ConocoPhillips, and Caterpillar withdrew from the U.S. Climate Action Partnership, the leading business NGO pressing for cap-and-trade schemes.

There was more progress in other OECD countries. Increased regulation, taxes on emissions and cap and trade schemes appeared from the late 1990s. The Kyoto Protocol was signed in 1997, though it only came into force in 2005 when enough countries had ratified it. The European Union has consistently been the global leader in environmental matters because it is fully aware since the Chernobyl nuclear disaster in the Ukraine had spread radiation clouds over its borders that emissions are transnational. The EU proposed an average reduction of emissions of 15 percent from their 1990 level by the year 2012, but the final agreement at Kyoto was only for 5.2 percent. The withdrawal of the United States from the Kyoto process in 2002 was also a major blow. It now required Russian participation to get the necessary number of countries to put the Protocol into effect, and so the Russians could leverage minimal targets for themselves. Kyoto's coverage came down from 66 percent to 32 percent of 1990 world emission levels. During the compliance period of 2008–2012 countries emitting less than their quota can sell emissions credits to those that exceed their quota. Developing countries were not given targets but urged to propose Clean Development Mechanisms (CDMs), administered by the UN, which would qualify them for carbon credits that they could then sell to OECD countries. Compliance mechanisms are weak and most of the signatories are not on course to achieve the reductions, though these were ironically helped by the collapse of former Soviet bloc economies. Economic recession is good for the climate.

The EU has introduced a mandatory cap and trade scheme. A mandatory carbon tax was considered but rejected after pressure from the UK. The European Trading Scheme (ETS) began in 2005. Its first phase was too soft on business and states for they were given the freedom to negotiate their own terms. There was a race to the bottom as each state favored its own business by issuing too many emissions credits. But the scheme was tightened up in a phase two beginning in 2007 (Skjærseth & Wettestad, 2009). European emissions fell 3 percent in 2008, and 40 percent of this is attributed to the scheme (the recession contributed 30 percent). The EU now said that it could meet its Kyoto commitments (European Environment Agency, 2009). Further tightenings are underway, including the inclusion of an aviation fuel scheme imposed on all airlines flying into Europe for the whole length of their journey, more policing power granted to the European Commission, and reductions in the cap. The EU Commission is a quasi-international state, currently supervising twenty-seven states, an advantage in climate change policy, which no other part of the world enjoys. "The aim is that the European Union leads the world in accelerating the shift to a low-carbon economy," boldly declared José Manuel Barroso, president of the European Commission in 2007.

But the EU was brought back to earth by the Copenhagen UN Climate Change Conference in December 2009. This was commandeered by the United States and China who produced only a nonbinding Accord. This recommended but did not mandate a reduction of emissions to 2° C above preindustrial levels. Most countries noted the Accord without signing it, and it set neither binding commitments nor deadlines. It pledged $30 billion to the developing world over 2010–12, rising to U.S.$ 100 billion per year by 2020, to help them adapt to climate change. Tougher proposals to limit emissions were dropped. Individual countries had published their own pledges for reducing emissions provided general agreement was reached, but since there was no agreement, it was unclear whether they would implement them. Copenhagen was somewhere between a disappointment and a disaster. Predictably, the 2010 Conference in

Cancun achieved little, not even publicity since the world's media ignored it. A fund to provide $1 billion aid per annum to poor countries was approved, without indicating where the money would come from.

Few environmentalists are impressed by this recent history. As of 2010 we have had many nonbinding statements of principles, a climate treaty that fails to protect climate, a convention on desertification that merely documents its extent, and a Law of the Sea that has prevented neither pollution nor fish-stock depletion. Copenhagen was a defeat for the more ambitious goals of the EU which had hoped to get agreement to share out carbon budgets to 2020 and beyond. But neither the United States nor China, nor the other BRIC countries, nor the oil producing countries would go this far. The United States and the Arab oil producers had twice before stymied attempts to set time-bound targets (Jaggard, 2007: chap. 6). In 2011 came signs that the larger developing countries, now become major emitters themselves, were pragmatically allying with the major polluting advanced economies to slow the pace of international conventions. Overall, the most that can be said of existing commitments and programs is that they are a start. Yet they are nowhere near enough.

Every year that commitments are not made, global GDP and emissions grow further, requiring evermore radical reform. It is now doubtful whether emissions could be stabilized at their present level of around 450 ppm CO_2. The Stern Review (2007: 475) said that to reach 450 ppm, emissions in developed countries should peak in the next ten years and then fall by more than 5 percent per year, reaching 70 percent–90 percent below 1990 levels by 2050. It added that this goal "is already almost out of reach." The UNDP Report (2007: 43–51) thought stabilization at 450 ppm CO_2e would cost about 1.6 percent of global GDP up to 2030 (less than two-thirds of global military expenditures). It would aim at 50 percent reductions of GHGs by 2050 from 1990 levels. Stern believed stabilizing at 550 ppm CO_2e was possible, provided emissions peak in the next 10–20 years and then reduce by up to 3 percent per year so that by 2050 emissions would be only 60 percent of 1990 levels. The question is how? Gilding (2011) believes a more radical plan is necessary. Its Phase One would seek a global reduction of 50 percent in emissions over five years. Phase Two would follow, a fifteen year push to net zero emissions. Phase Three would be an eighty year program of removing enough emission from the atmosphere to return the world to preindustrial emissions levels. All these estimates would involve radical, global policies involving restraints on production and consumption, and probably also the end of economic growth and the arrival of a steady-state economy.

Alternative policy responses: Statist and market solutions

In presenting his environmental Review to the U.S. Senate in 2007, the economist Nicholas Stern declared "Climate change is the greatest market failure the world has ever seen," since pollution is an "externality" for market actors. If a factory pollutes the surrounding environment, its pollution and the costs of clean-up are external to the firm, costing it nothing. Since external social costs do not figure in company balance-sheets, companies will continue to pollute with abandon. Furthermore, wherever a scarce resource comes free of charge, as with the air we breathe, it is likely to be used to excess. Coal is the worst offender. Its external costs have been estimated as being equivalent to 70 percent of its market price. So if the coal industry was forced to pay for the costs it inflicts upon us, the price of coal would almost double, which would be a substantial incentive for consumers to switch to less polluting energy sources – and for the coal industry to diversify its activities into such sources. The only agency that could organize this is the state.

States have regulated capitalism since its beginnings, as Polanyi emphasized – regulating factory safety, setting protectionist tariffs, legitimizing and regulating labor unions, permitting corporations an individual legal entity etc. The environmental challenge requires further national regulation but this time combined with international coordination of regulation since emissions in all countries affects everyone's climate. Emissions are transnational, INGOs are half-transnational, and legislation must be international. This is why a major change of direction for human societies is required. Whereas the civilizing of capitalism so far has consisted of individual state regulation, raising the bars of national cages, this next stage of the civilizing process must lower those bars. For climate change is also an externality for states.

The bedrock of policy, however ineffective it has been so far, must be the global setting and monitoring of emission reduction targets for a minimum of the major polluting countries by binding international agreements, a great extension of the role of soft geopolitics among states. Without this there would be such leakage of GHGs elsewhere that a country imposing, say, a carbon tax on its own would harm its international competitiveness. The free rider problem looms large, for a state might think it rational to do nothing, for if other states reduce emissions such a state benefits too. Let the others bear the costs, we can share the benefits (Nordhaus, 2008). This is why existing protocols do not enter into force until a given number of countries have ratified them. This involves trimming the autonomy of the individual nation-state, while increasing the power of the collectivity of nation-states. State caging needs to be reduced, international caging increased.

But just think how difficult that is. Domestic policy disagreements are usually decided by a simple majority vote in parliament or a ruling elite, but international agreements would require near-unanimity, at least among the main polluters – the United States, the EU, Japan, China, India, Brazil and Russia – and a truly effective regime would require many more states. The diversity of the interests represented across countries is much greater than in any individual nation-state. Many must get international agreements ratified by their own parliaments, which are often very inward-looking. In the United States international treaties must be ratified by two-thirds of the Senate, nowadays a formidable hurdle. UN and other agencies dealing with environmental issues are among the weakest and worst-financed international agencies. Regulatory slippage results. A regulation might cover 80 percent of the problem, and 80 percent of those being regulated might try to implement it, resulting in an 80 percent success-rate. Not bad, one might think, except that the mathematical outcome is that only 50 percent of the problem would be regulated (Speth, 2004: 103–5; 2008: 84).

It is conventional to distinguish between statist and market-oriented policies (though I will tend to downplay the difference). Statist policies regulate directly by setting national and international quotas for energy consumption and emissions, backed by mandatory energy standards for businesses, buildings, appliances, automobiles, airplanes etc. They also pour public money into investment in cleaner technologies. Regulations have the advantage that they can be targeted so as to directly penalize the most damaging types of emission, with no market signals needed as intermediaries. Regulations can also encourage high-emitting business, like the fossil fuel, power generating and auto industries to diversify into cleaner fossil technology or renewable energy technology, like wind, water or biomass. Deadlines and penalties also signal clearly to investors the potential rewards and time-frames involved in technological innovation; and governments can target their own R & D efforts at the most damaging emissions. The OECD and BRIC countries could provide credible implementation and so could some other developing countries – enough to cover most emissions.

A radical proposal has come from Myles Allen, an Oxford climatologist. He suggests oil, gas and coal companies take responsibility for burying all the carbon dioxide emitted by the fossil fuel products they sell. As he says, "Carbon comes into Europe through a couple of dozen pipes, ports and holes in the ground. It goes out through hundreds of millions of flues and exhaust pipes. Yet European climate policy is all about controlling the flow at the point of emission. It's like blowing air into a sponge and trying to slow it down by blocking up the holes." (*The Independent*, October 7, 2010). He slyly adds that this would involve less government, not more. But given the political power of such industries, this is pie-in-the-sky.

Regulation is often easier for the public to appreciate. It already pervades our life and millions of people have been involved in local struggles for mandated recycling, clean-ups and protection of species and lands in the South as well as the North of the world. Environmental regulations are probably more palatable than new environmental taxes, and the public finds them easier to understand than complex cap-and-trade schemes. There are already fines for exceeding vehicle emission standards in the United States, which give a financial incentive to auto companies to comply, while the EU mandatory labeling of the energy efficiency of refrigerators produced an immediate consumer response, with consumers preferring more efficient appliances. Households produce 35–40 percent of all CO_2 emissions, and in certain respects mitigation can come at lowest cost here (UNDP, 2007: 136–70).

I have argued in Volume 3 and here that state direction of economic activity is relatively efficient when the goal is known and simple and when the means are clear. This was true during the world wars, when the goal was to produce goods that would simply kill people. It is also true in late development programs when the agreed goal is to adapt methods already used by earlier developing nations – whether the late developers were capitalist, like Japan and the East Asian Tigers, or state socialist, like the Soviet Union and China. The weakness of state planning is in shifting gears toward a new type of economy. In climate change policies, however, the core goal is known and simple – to reduce the consumption of fossil fuels and to develop alternative energy technologies. Government regulation can achieve this first goal more directly than can markets, while it can at least assist private firms to develop new technologies with investment of its own.

But regulations also have drawbacks, especially internationally, since regulatory structures differ enormously between countries. The European Union can regulate across its large zone, but no effective global sovereignty exists. The UN is too feeble, other agencies too specialized. States must negotiate elaborately with each other to achieve global agreements, and this is more difficult for regulation than for the main alternatives, taxes or cap-and-trade. International monitoring of compliance is especially difficult. Not all national emission levels are known, while some countries refuse to submit to international inspections, like China. Scandals have also undermined private agencies verifying emissions.

In any case, since the currently dominant ideology is neoliberalism, market friendly solutions commodifying the environment are now all the rage among official bodies and among economists, especially in the Anglophone world (Hulme, 2009: 298–304). Market-friendly policies involve ways of setting a global price on carbon that is higher than the present market price, so that emitters themselves are charged the social costs of their products and given a market incentive to invest in new lower-carbon technologies. Nordhaus (2008) believes this is more efficient than regulations since a carbon price would efficiently transmit knowledge of the costs of GHG emissions to billions of people and thousands of organizations creating the problem. Estimates of the carbon price required today are around $25–$30 per tonne of CO_2, but it would have to steadily rise in the future. Different economists envisage different gradients but almost all estimates involve radical pricing changes (Nordhaus, 2008: 15–20; Stern, 2007: 370).

The idea is that this would shift capitalist calculations of profit and loss in green directions. After the initial coercion of setting prices, the treadmill of profit might be manipulated into reducing rather than increasing emissions. Finance capitalism in the persons of venture capitalists would then also shift its investments into greener industries and products. The advocates of such policies say that capitalism has shown enormous adaptability in the past. It can do so again in the future. Since capitalism is the only economic game in town, they say, we have to use it. Newell and Paterson (2010) note that some venture capitalists are already devising ways of making profit from decarbonization. I place more hope when climate crises really strike hard on a split among capitalists, with low-emitters turning against high ones. This need not be a class issue.

There are two main ways of effecting carbon price change, carbon taxes and "cap–and-trade" schemes, both backed by reductions in tariff and non-tariff barriers for low-carbon products to assist global uniformity. Since taxes and tariffs are the province of states these policies are not actually neoliberal but extensions of a mixed economy. Consider first carbon taxes. These do not guarantee a specific level of emissions reductions, for that depends on market reactions to the tax. But high carbon-emitting business would have a market incentive to shift in the direction of lower emissions – unless it can pass on the increase as price increases to consumers. A carbon tax is also relatively simple to enforce. But it is likely to be fiscally regressive, hurting the poor most. The upside is that since the tax base is so large, a quite low level of taxation would yield massive revenue that could be earmarked for directly environmental purposes or for subsidizing those populations hardest hit by the consequent rising energy prices. Carbon taxes also exercise pressure internationally. A country can impose a tariff on imports whose production involves high carbon emissions, putting market pressure on foreign business and governments. The WTO has said that this would be a legitimate use of tariffs, while it would also appeal to protectionists who rail against free trade. Unfortunately, however, current politicians' mantra in most countries is no new taxes.

In cap-and-trade schemes an overall authority – a national or regional government or an international body like the EU – distributes carbon permits to companies allowing them to emit GHGs. The cap is the total amount of GHG emissions allowed to all the permits in the system, while trade refers to companies buying and selling permits to each other. A company can either reduce its GHG emissions if its permits do not cover its needs, or it can buy more permits from companies who have surplus permits. In theory, firms that can reduce carbon emissions at a low cost will do so, and sell their excess permits, while firms finding it harder to reduce emissions will only buy enough permits to cover their continuing levels. The total amount of emissions allowed is then gradually reduced as the cap is lowered year by year. This is an incentive for businesses supplying or using fossil fuels to switch toward renewables. The existence of a free-market in emission certificates is supposed to ensure that incentives are administered efficiently, with little cost or corruption. Unlike taxes, a cap should produce a known quantity of GHG reduction. The key parts of cap-and-trade are the level at which the initial cap is set and the gradient of its annual reductions, for without a pain-causing level of caps, emissions would not be reduced sufficiently.

A third set of policies derive from the concept of ecosystem services. Ecosystems like wetlands and forests provide major environmental benefits like water-filtration and the absorption of carbon in the atmosphere. The idea is that those who own these lands should be paid to conserve them, meaning they do not have to make money by draining swamps for development or cutting down the forest for lumber. This redistributes resources to property-owners, though most of them might be poor peasants. But such schemes would be radical interventions in markets. Though these and cap-and-trade schemes do set up markets, the initial terms of those markets are set politically. This is not a neoliberal scheme.

The main disadvantage of neoliberalism lies elsewhere, in its unrelenting probusiness stance and in the increasing business influence on government. This influence results in the watering down of all emissions schemes. American high-emissions corporations and trade associations finance lobby organizations and politicians denouncing environmental science and urging that big government be rolled back. They pretend to be environmentally conscious. Oil company commercials depict green nature, not black oil, and business rarely fights environmental bills in public, preferring to operate on Congressional committees and subcommittees with the help of subsidized politicians and scientists, quietly stripping green bills of their teeth, slipping deregulation provisions into bills on different subjects (Repetto, 2007; Miller, 2009: chaps. 2 & 6). Business is now the main obstacle to mitigation in the United States, and that potential split between high- and low-emitting businesses has not yet emerged. James Hansen (2009) says that since "special interests have been able to subvert our democratic system," we get only legislation that "coal companies and utilities are willing to allow."

The fossil fuel industries are in reality a part of the big government they denounce. High-emitting industries get big tax concessions bringing their corporate taxes below the national average. The nominal U.S. corporate tax rate is 35 percent but almost all businesses receive exemptions and allowances, which put the real national average at half that. The lowest rate, less than 2 percent, is paid by the defense and aerospace industry, a major emitter with its gas-guzzling planes, ships and tanks. The transportation, petroleum and pipeline, and gas and electric utility industries also pay less than the average rate (Institute on Taxation and Economic Policy, 2004). U.S. mining companies also receive depletion allowances ranging from 5 percent to 22 percent of their gross income from extraction and processing. Fossil fuels got about $72 billion in subsidies between 2002 and 2008, while subsidies for renewable fuels were only $29 billion, half of which goes to corn-based ethanol whose climate effect is minimal. Of the fossil fuel subsidies, $70.2 billion went to traditional sources like coal and oil. Only $2.3 billion went to "carbon capture and storage," a technique designed to reduce GHGs from coal-fired power plants through massive underground storage silos (Environmental Law Institute, 2009). Whether carbon capture can work at an economic price is dubious. No working plant yet exists anywhere. "Clean coal," trumpeted by the mining corporations, does not exist.

This is not just an American problem, for subsidies are common across the world. One study estimated in 2000 that worldwide subsidies of pollution totaled $850 billion annually, 2.5 percent of global GDP (Speth, 2008: 100). Reform would lead to job losses and rising prices in this sector, and this has deterred governments from action. The leaders of the G-20 countries agreed in principle in September 2009 to phase-out inefficient fossil-fuel subsidies, saying that to eliminate them by 2020 would reduce overall GHG emissions by 10 percent by 2050. Principle has not yet led to practice, though it might. But since the status quo yields the energy industry high profits, it has little incentive to invest in new technologies. It is difficult to share the optimism of Newell and Paterson (2010) when R & D private investment in alternative energy sources has actually fallen in recent years. Most of the spending is public. One study found that of fourteen key innovations in energy sources in the past thirty years whose finances could be traced, only one was funded entirely by the private sector, while nine were totally public. The cost of educating scientists and engineers also falls on the government (Stern Review, 2007: 353–5, 362–3). For significant emissions reductions, states must become much tougher on fossil fuel industries. This is not anticapitalist, for it merely seeks to penalize those industries that are the worst carbon emitters.

Business says it prefers a cap-and-trade model because this interferes least with markets. Its real belief is that it can sway government policy toward a low cap to which it can easily adjust. Thus existing schemes have been ineffective. One problem is that states often see the high-emitting industries as their energy champions in international competition. They want them to remain profitable and so are responsive to their lobbying. Cap-and-trade is also vulnerable to corruption in credit allocation, though this could be solved by replacing free permits with auctions so that governments do not decide who gets them. The highest bidder gets the permit and this also yields revenue that, in theory, governments use for investment in renewable technology. The EU is scheduled to shift to an auction in 2012, though California is back-tracking on a similar commitment. The northeastern states of the United States already operate an auction but it is performing badly. The utility companies are simply passing on the cost to consumers in higher prices and states use the revenue to ease budget deficits rather than invest in renewables.

Since tough regulation, carbon taxes, and cap-and-trade schemes might all produce some effect, it matters little what blend of statist and market-oriented solutions are chosen. To work, all would involve government imposing radical restrictions on business and consumers. Only the mechanism is different. What is much more important is that business, especially energy business, be coerced into making concessions. However, this would require changed politicians, and they could only be changed by mass popular pressure, which requires mass consumers changing too.

I have presented these various schemes as if they were in themselves solutions. Yet they are not. All of them – carbon taxes, cap-and-trade, and state-imposed quotas – require a major shift to renewable forms of energy. But using existing greener technologies to solve the problem would require enormous expenditures. The global economy currently uses about sixteen terawatts of electric power generation. To get that total without the aid of fossil fuel from a mixture of current alternative technologies would involve massive industrial complexes spread over very large land-masses. Solar cells in the required quantity might spread over about thirty thousand miles of land. Solar thermal sources might require about a hundred and fifty thousand square miles, biofuels might occupy over a million square miles. Then there are wind turbines, geothermal sources, and nuclear power plants. One can play with the relative weights of each of these but, overall, the currently available alternative energy sources would require a space about equal to that of the United States. That would be a theoretical possibility but not a practicable one (Barnes and Gilman, 2011: 48–9). We can assume some improvements to these technologies over the years it would take to implement this, but absent completely new technologies, the savings would not be large enough to be politically feasible.

Of course, such emission-reduction costs can be set against the potential reductions in GDP and living standards that a do-nothing policy will eventually bring. The Stern Review (2007: 211; cf. OECD, 2007) calculated the cost of policies keeping emissions down to a CO^2e level of 500–50 ppm at 1 percent per annum of global GDP, though adding that the range of possible costs runs from –1 percent (net gains) to +3.5 percent per annum. In 2008, because of worsening climate change, Stern doubled the costs of his proposed policies to 2 percent of GDP (*Guardian*, June 26, 2008). Other economists envisage much higher cost figures of 5 percent reduction in GDP if emissions were kept down to such a level. The Stern Review claimed that all costs would be swallowed up amid large growth of the global economy through the century. It also warned that to do nothing might risk a recession lopping 20 percent off global GDP.

Unfortunately, politicians and electorates prefer to avoid smaller costs right now than much bigger ones some way down the track – when those politicians do not expect to be in office and those electorates are mostly dead. The discount rate is the tool economists use to compare economic impacts occurring today with those in the future. Most economists set a high discount rate for the future since people value the known present much more than an uncertain future. Using a high discount rate reduces the benefit of taking mitigating actions now, since future benefits are seen as lower. Nordhaus (2008: 10) sets his discount rate at 4 percent, which makes emission-reduction policies much more expensive. The Stern Review set its discount rate at only 1.4 percent, which make such policies profitable. The Review defended this low rate in terms of the increasingly severe future risks that science identifies – but sensing skepticism over its calculations it added an ethical argument as well, our responsibility toward succeeding generations. Objective risk plus ethics are crucial, they say (Stern Team, 2008; cf. UNDP Report, 2007: 62–3).

Unfortunately, the calculations in themselves do not make sense. The cost of building a United States-sized alternative energy complex would be immensely expensive, involving GDP losses of far greater than any of these calculations. It is simply impossible to avoid a major loss of GDP all over the world, given present technologies, if we are serious about climate change. Indeed, the main goal of effective climate change policy has to be a move to a permanently lower level of GDP. That is the only way to preserve the earth – unless some new and cheap miracle technology appears. It might happen, but giving people tax incentives to develop such a technology seems pathetic, the triumph of faith over probability – and faith in exactly the same kind of technological fix that got us into this mess in the first place (as Barnes & Gilman, 2011, note).

The coming political struggle

The main challenge to business domination has come from the small world of environmental NGOs. During the Kyoto negotiations, NGOs were officially accredited to the conference. Though not allowed to attend the core meetings between state delegates, they lobbied them in the corridors, participated in panel sessions, briefed delegates, and produced a useful daily newspaper about conference developments. Betsill (2008a) says that while NGO positions "are not reflected in the Protocol's text, the environmental community did shape the negotiating process in a number of ways and thus had moderate influence." However, Humphreys (2008: 169) says that in the case of forestry policy NGOs most influenced the outcome of negotiations if they framed recommendations in probusiness neoliberal discourse. Betsill (2008b), reviewing various studies, says "NGO influence was highest when the political stakes were lowest … [and when]… negotiations involve limited commitments for behavioral change" (p. 203). NGOs also wield more influence during early negotiations. During later discussions requiring actual commitments, business lobbyists overwhelm them. Business spokespersons are often appointed to states' negotiating teams and they take items off the agenda or otherwise pare down agreements (pp. 193–4). There is unequal power: business predominates over environmentalists, which helps account for the inadequate treaty outcomes. Green influence is felt more diffusely, over public and party opinion, but with lesser impact on policy crystallization. A world polity has not arrived.

Radical environmentalists completely reject the technical debate over discount rates. They add that any level of discounting ignores the irreversible damage inflicted in the meantime on biodiversity (the killing of plant and animal species) and low-lying countries. Climate change violates principles of sustainable development, earth stewardship, and the inalienable rights of future generations (Hulme, 2009: 124–32; Hansen, 2009). Yet unfortunately the peoples of the world do not endorse such moral absolutism while the unborn do not vote. At a time of recession, the jobs now demand – which conservative politicians say requires a reduction in environmental regulation – is hard to counter. Media reports of environmental problems declined once the Great Recession started, as did politicians' interest and environmental concerns revealed in opinion polls. In polls people often say they would take an x amount of reduction in living standards to save the planet, but when their living standards are actually threatened, they behave differently. Citizen consumption becomes even more desirable when we are deprived of it. Of course, if we were entirely short-term and selfish, we would take no mitigation steps at all, for the climate will probably not significantly worsen in our own lifetimes. But since we do try to make provision for our descendants, there is in principle some hope that we will begin mitigating. Yet the problem is too abstract. It does not hit us hard in our everyday lives – except for some of the poor in poor countries, who lack the power to resist much or to elicit more than a passing glance from us.

There will now unfold a long political struggle, with states hopefully pressured from below and from outside by green NGOs, scientists, and low-emitting business, to constrain business and consumers a little more, year by year. Yet interests vary according to where people are situated in the world. There is pronounced inequality in global emissions by consumers.

The world's poor are virtuous for they barely consume or emit, while the rich pollute greatly because they consume greatly. Those who earn more than $7000 per annum on average exceed what would be a fair personal emitting limit of 2 tons of CO_2 p.a. These overconsumers include almost all the citizens of advanced countries, though because of the size of the middle class in countries like India and China, overconsumers are now as numerous in developing as developed countries. They purportedly include almost twice as many men as women (Ulvila & Pasanen, 2009: 22–6, 37–8). It isn't just a question of overcoming business opposition. It is also necessary to overcome the short-term interests of the mass of northern citizens and of richer citizens everywhere. In developed countries emissions reductions would paradoxically fall heaviest on the poor since most policies would raise the price of fossil fuel energy and the poor pay a higher proportion of their income to heat their homes and power their cars. If President Obama's now abandoned cap-and-trade legislation were to cut emissions by 15 percent, households in the bottom fifth of the income scale would pay 3.3 percent more of their after-tax income, almost double the 1.7 percent more paid by the richest fifth (*Wall Street Journal*, March 9, 2009).

Equity suggests that redress for emissions programs be made through compensatory progressive taxes. Left parties might be expected to support this, though conservative parties would not.

Climate change impacts the global South more than the North. Poor countries already suffer most from climatic conditions. Roberts and Parks (2007: 71–96) assembled a dataset of more than 4000 extreme weather disasters between 1980 and 2002. This showed that rural people in poor countries suffered the worst and first effects – death, homelessness, and displacement from climate-related disasters on a scale between ten and a hundred times worse than people in the United States (even including Hurricane Katrina). As they say, "rich nations pay for climate change with dollars, and poor nations pay with their lives" (p. 37). The UNDP Report says global warming threatens most the poor and the unborn, the "two constituencies with little or no voice" (UNDP 2007: 2).

Poor countries already tend to be warmer, with more variable rainfall. They depend more on vulnerable agriculture, and have poorer health and infrastructural provision to deal with crises. Some richer countries, like Canada, the Scandinavian countries, Germany, Poland and Russia might actually benefit from global warming, since they could grow more crops and graze animals further north, burn less fossil fuel, and welcome more tourists. Latin America, the Middle East apart from Egypt, and especially Africa and South Asia would be the biggest sufferers. The richer countries also have more resources to adapt to threats. The Netherlands has long spent enormous sums on its flood defenses. Britain, coastal Florida and California could do the same – at least I hope so, since my Los Angeles home is less than a meter above the high-tide mark of the Pacific. In contrast more than a fifth of Bangla Desh would be under water if the sea rose a meter, and the country lacks the resources to do much about it. Yet the voters of the Southwestern states of the United States should be told they may inhabit a giant dust-bowl after the next decades.

The narrowness of a country's export base indicates the extent of its dependence in the world economy and this is correlated with environmental degradation. Poorer countries understand that structural inequality contributes to their climate vulnerability and constrains their national development, and so in negotiations over climate change they try to inject a broader sense of global injustice. Citing Durkheim, Roberts and Parks (2007: 48–66) argue that norms, trust and diffuse reciprocity are just as important in negotiations as are material interests. If wealthy countries wish to lower this hostility and improve cooperation on climate change, they must acknowledge the broader injustices of the international division of labor, and target them for reform. That, however, is a very ambitious goal, difficult to convey to northern electorates worrying about their own jobs and taxes.

Some developed countries might withdraw from all global negotiations on the grounds that they could weather the coming storm. The UNEP Report lists several alternative future scenarios. In Security First or Me First, government and business seek to improve or maintain only the well-being of the rich and powerful (2007: 401ff; cf. the Fortress World strategy identified by Raskin et al., 2002: 25–7). The rich could not entirely insulate themselves, for the catastrophes that might befall poorer countries would have knock-on effects, producing a decline in their own GDPs, while the clamor of massed refugees might make the borders unenforceable without enormous security costs. There might be wars between states competing for declining water, food resources etc. There is present-day evidence from Africa that greater variations in rainfall produces more violent conflict (e.g., Hendrix & Salehyan, 2012). If poorer countries cut down their rainforests in a desperate bid to expand their agriculture to feed their populations, that would intensify global warming for all. It seems more likely that countries would continue global negotiations, though some more enthusiastically than others.

But the North shares responsibility for growing pollution in developing countries, for it has exported many of its polluting industries to them. Poorer countries now produce more manufactured goods for export and so must endure more of the pollution involved in their manufacture, while wealthier countries, where those goods are consumed, shift to cleaner industries and claim moral purity (Jorgenson & Burns, 2007, Roberts & Parks, 2007). It is an illusion that the North is reducing its dependence on carbon, for our lifestyle relies heavily on carbon-intensive imports. When the North suggests using carbon intensity per unit of each country's GDP as a metric in negotiations, this is carbon colonialism for measuring domestic production leaves out the carbon values embedded in trade flows. Who is responsible for China becoming the biggest polluter, the Chinese or foreign capitalists, goes the rhetorical question? These ecosocialist arguments are morally valid. But morality does not rule the world.

The countries of the South naturally want economic growth. They want living-standards like those of Europe and the United States, and they want them now. Yet if the whole world enjoyed current Western life-styles, humanity's ecological footprint would require an astounding five planet Earths (Hulme, 2009: 260)! The tragedy is most evident for the poor of the world who walk the Earth with an exceedingly light carbon footprint. Whatever the morality of past versus future polluters – OECD versus BRICs – why should the people of sub-Saharan Africa or Bangla Desh or Pacific islands have to pay for the sins of others? Developing and poor countries will continue fighting for better terms. They should certainly do so, and we in the developed world should yield much more than we have yet. But morality does not rule the world.

There is some room for hope, for this is not a zero-sum game. Reductions in emissions anywhere benefit everybody. Where there is a common global interest, poor countries also have more leverage than usual. It particularly makes sense to target industries that are inefficient and relatively cheap to improve, wherever they are – and they are increasingly in poorer countries. Many power generating plants in the developing world and the countries of the former Soviet Union use obsolete, highly polluting technology. For the OECD countries to bring them more advanced technology would be relatively easy and cheap, and the consequent emission reductions would benefit them too. But it would not be enough.

To subsidize just two countries, Brazil and Indonesia, to better preserve their rain forests would bring major benefits. Combating deforestation probably offers the cheapest way to lower overall emissions. Deforestation contributes about a fifth of global GHG emissions. It is an especially perverse market failure. Indonesian farmers fell trees for palm oil, generating short-term profit but large carbon emissions. Their rate of profit is only about 2 percent of what they might get from the carbon market value of the timber if a carbon tax was set at \$25 per tonne, which would therefore be a very effective way of helping the global climate. Even the large-scale hardwood logging enterprises of Indonesia make profits of less than 10 percent of that carbon market value. Clearly, the world's interest is to subsidize Indonesians to reforest more than they deforest. Subsidies would also benefit Indonesians, especially the poor peasants and indigenous peoples who are being expropriated by big landlords, corporations and governments who are leading deforestation (UNDP, 2007: 157–9). At Copenhagen and then next year at Dubai the developed countries accepted the principle that they must subsidize developing countries' programs, though the amounts offered were small and were without enforcement mechanisms. This is not enough.

The two indispensable nations

To counter global warming, two nations are indispensable, the two on whom I have focused most in this volume, the two biggest polluters, the United States and China.

The United States has become a major obstacle to emissions reduction. It lags well behind the European Union and East Asia in climate sensitivity. Here it is definitely not the leader. Though its neoliberalism is highly selective, as earlier chapters emphasized, it is mobilized strongly over climate matters. Big government in this policy arena is supposedly bad. The diversity of this continent-sized country is reproduced by its federal political system. GHG emissions vary enormously between regions. In 2005 the average person in Wyoming emitted 154 tons of CO_2e, more than 10 times the emissions of a New Yorker's 12 tons or a Californian's 13 tons. The lowest 10 emitters were all East or West Coast states, while the highest 10 were all western, midwestern or southern. This is mainly due to the location of coal and oil reserves, though people in rural states also consume more gasoline. This regional distribution roughly corresponds to the division between Republican and Democratic states.

This is a major reason why Republican politicians tend to oppose climate legislation, while most Democrats support it. Many Republican politicians are also antiscience, more provincial, and more insulated from global issues. Congress itself tends to privilege local against national and global issues. A Democrat minority, the so-called blue dogs and black dogs (representing coal and oil districts) also believe they can better hang onto their seats by espousing environmental conservatism. They may be right since emission-reduction policies would require voters in their states to pay more for their fuel needs now. Senators and especially Congressmen often add riders to environmental bills, protecting local emitters (Miller, 2009: chap. 2). The interests blocking progress are strong, popular and can muster arguments with ideological and electoral resonance.

Regional inequality is difficult to redress, since tax systems are not as well-geared to counteract it. Federal grants to hard-hit states from the proceeds of carbon taxes or cap-and-trade might help offset the cost. At present, however, these states' voters and their politicians currently oppose carbon pricing and cap-and-trade. This is not primarily a class issue since labor's desire to reduce unemployment is stronger than their intermittently green rhetoric. Though Democrats are greener than Republicans, this is truer of middle-class than working-class Democrats. There is no mass movement from below pressing for much mitigation. Add on the recent changes in political power relations on the Hill and it becomes extremely difficult to get filibuster-proof majorities for emissions bills in the House and Senate, unless their bite is stripped out of them.

The passage of the American Clean Energy and Security Act through Congress during 2009 and 2010 presents a dispiriting case-study (Goodell, 2010). It set a goal of reducing carbon emissions by 20 percent by 2020, while permitting 2 billion tons of carbon offsets per year. It included a rather weak cap-and-trade scheme but quite strong measures to improve energy efficiency. It was stronger than the original business-friendly blueprint bill drawn up by the U.S. Climate Action Partnership, a coalition of moderate environmental groups and major corporations like GE and ConocoPhillips, which had set a goal of only 14 percent carbon reduction by 2020. The bill nonetheless alarmed the Republican Party, the blue and black dogs, and the coal and oil companies. They fought back by arguing that the climate bill was nothing more than a national energy tax that would cause energy prices to rocket and destroy jobs. Its cap-and-trade should really be called cap-and-tax, they said. Rep. Joe Barton (Republican, Texas) had just been replaced by Rep. Waxman (Democrat) as chair of the House energy committee. He promised to launch "crafty guerrilla warfare" on the bill. Waxman says "I talked to Joe Barton as this process began, expressing a desire to work together with him on this. He told me he didn't believe in the science of global warming, didn't think it was a problem and didn't want to try to solve it."

Big Coal spent $10 million on lobbying against the bill, and more than $15 million paying for the federal campaigns of politicians who opposed it. Between 2003 and 2009 the number of lobbyists devoted to climate change soared over fivefold to 2,810 – five lobbyists for every lawmaker. Only 138 of them were pushing for alternative energy. The lobbyists focused on Democrat blue-dogs. Rep. Rick Boucher, a Democrat from the coal fields of southern Virginia, got the biggest single coal cash handout, more than $144,000 in 2009. Boucher was a former chair of the House energy subcommittee and spoke for the blue-dog votes Waxman needed. Boucher spent six weeks in backroom negotiations between his coal friends and members of the House energy committee.

So the climate bill was amended to include more free permits for polluters, plus $1 billion a year to support clean coal research – on top of the $3.4 billion in research funds in the president's stimulus plan. The bill now contained $60 billion in support for coal – far more than the aid given to all forms of renewable energy combined. Boucher also got the forty or so coal-powered plants currently under construction exempted from the new regulations. The all-important target for reducing carbon emissions by 2020 was cut from 20 percent to 17 percent. The goals for boosting renewable energy were cut nearly in half. EPA authority to regulate carbon emissions was gutted. Instead of an auction for all emissions permits, as Obama had promised, the bill gave 83 percent of them free. All told, major polluters received $134 billion in allowances. The nation's dirtiest corporations got another government handout.

The climate bill squeaked through the House by a vote of 219 to 212. Almost all the Republicans plus 44 Democrats voted against the measure. Its passage in the Senate was halted when the administration realized it lacked the votes. This is likely to endure if future elections do not shift the balance of power leftward. Political power relations operating through the electoral cycle block progress toward emissions reductions. Yet the participation of the United States in any global program is essential, for the United States emits a quarter of the world's emissions and still has unrivaled geopolitical clout. It is difficult to escape a feeling of gloom when pondering likely American responses to the looming crisis, at least in the medium-term.

China, the other essential nation, is also problematic, though its authoritarian party-state has an advantage. It does not have to defer to business but can almost arbitrarily impose radical programs, including environmental programs. It also has an unusually long attention-span, planning decades ahead, as is also evident in its military and security policies. The extraordinary One Child Policy was forcibly imposed and it ensured that an estimated three hundred million extra births were avoided, the equivalent of a 5 percent reduction in carbon emissions, greater than the entire Kyoto process (Hulme, 2009: 270). Yet the regime's main everyday goal remains economic growth, believing this is what sustains order and its own power, and indeed this is what the people want. As we saw in Chapter 8, it is now facing serious disaffection among both peasants and industrial workers. In the short-term, therefore, it is unwilling to sacrifice GDP and employment growth in return for greater benefits in the future – like other countries.

Maoist hero projects aiming to conquer nature, like the Great Leap Forward, led to terrible environmental excesses. Contemporary projects like the Three Gorges Dams and the West-East Pipeline maintain this tradition. But rapid economic growth, privatization and power devolution – the arrival of the capitalist party-state – have made things worse, as protective infrastructures have weakened amid the primacy of profit-driven growth (Muldavin, 2000). The township and village enterprises (TVAs), the key to rural economic development, were causing 50 percent of national pollution by the late 1990s. The government recognizes its environmental problems and has enacted much antipollution legislation. But local officials entrusted with enforcing the laws rarely do so, since this might threaten local profits, revenue, jobs, and their own corrupt profits (Ma & Ortolano, 2000). Coal supplies two-thirds of China's energy needs and oil adds another 20 percent. Unsustainable logging, loss of grasslands, water scarcity, vehicle pollution, and serious loss of topsoil all lead to biodiversity losses, climate warming, desertification, and urban pollution. Six of the ten most polluted cities in the world are in China; five of China's biggest rivers are "not suitable for human contact." Yet China's performance may be no worse than other Asian states like South Korea, Malaysia, Indonesia and the Philippines where the problem is too-cosy a relationship between business and officials responsible for environmental protection, both linked to corrupt networks of political patronage (*Economy*, 2004).

The Chinese government is trying to move toward cleaner energy sources. In 2009 China announced it would spend $440 billion in clean energy R&D over the next decade and it has now overtaken Germany as the leading investor in clean fuels. An HSBC bank report (2009) estimated that 38 percent of China's stimulus package was green, with only South Korea and the EU having a higher green proportion, and its green programs were easily the world's biggest in dollar terms. By 2010 China gave the biggest subsidies to renewable energy users, and had created a National Energy Commission composed of cabinet ministers led by Prime Minister Wen Jiabao himself. China is already producing more than half the world's solar panels, and is the largest producer of wind turbines. The Chinese government, unlike the United States, sees the next generation of technology as centering on new alternative energies and is investing heavily to secure leadership in this field. China might prove to be the first case in which a state-dominated economy leap-frogged over capitalist market economies in the technological race, instead of merely playing catch-up. The main obstacle is China's economic success, its growth rate. Though improvements in energy efficiency have been considerable, out-performing those of the United States, they are more than swallowed up by economic growth. The emissions plan for

2006–10 aimed to reduce energy consumption by 20 percent per unit of GDP. Yet this was less than half the growth in GDP over the period. The Chinese Communist Party's legitimacy depends on it delivering economic growth. It is highly unlikely to go for lesser growth.

Nonetheless, China has been active in global climate change negotiations as de facto leader of the developing countries, the G-77. Most developing countries cannot assemble expert delegations themselves and rely on the BRIC countries, especially China. China has insisted that the developed countries must move first and must provide additional funding and technology transfer to the developing countries. It contrasts the "survival emissions" of developing countries with the "luxury emissions" of developed ones. The latter can be dispensed with, the former means food on the table. These are popular positions in the G-77, but they are not accepted by the United States.

At Copenhagen China refused to allow international inspectors into China. Its sensitivity is matched by the United States. Congress has refused to ratify foreign treaties that might infringe on its authority. National sovereignty as well as capitalism block solutions. American politicians have repeatedly said they will not move until developing countries present reduction proposals. The U.S. Senate said this when rejecting Kyoto by a resounding 95 votes to 0. President Bush the Younger commented "the American life-style is not open to negotiation." But it must be. China kept repeating that the United States must move first. At Copenhagen the United States and China finally agreed on something, but it was to block more definite treaty proposals. Global climate control without the two biggest polluters is impossible but they present major obstacles, the United States because of its neoliberal capitalism amplified by federalism, China because of its extraordinary statist success in achieving economic growth, and both of them because they are not fertile ground for transnational NGOs and they jealously guard national sovereignty. The two indispensible nations are hastening on disaster.

Conclusion

Our collective mastery over Nature was supposedly total but instead proved self-destructive. Greenhouse gas emissions are saturating the atmosphere, the sea and the land of planet Earth. At some point in the twenty-first century if the world does not adopt major mitigating policies, global warming will severely menace human society. It will hit unevenly, poorer countries hardest, but it will also reduce living standards everywhere. It is now virtually impossible that the scientific community has got it all wrong, but it is just possible that human technological ingenuity driven by the desire for capitalist profit will pioneer some alternative emission-free and cheap fuel. That would be a burst of creative destruction by capitalism greater than either the second industrial revolution or the great postwar boom in consumer demand. It seems unlikely. Necessity is not the mother of invention. A far gloomier possibility might actually have a silver lining: a nuclear war or a global pandemic or even a passing meteorite might wipe out half the human population and so substantially reduce emissions. But none of these look as likely as continuing climate change, bringing gradual disaster.

This will not be an unexpected crisis, like the others discussed in Volume 3. We know many years in advance what the future will likely bring if we do nothing. If human reason dominated societies we could avoid disaster by action now. But it does not. The reason of most actors is limited to short-term alternatives. This drives nationally caged politicians trapped by the electoral cycle and pressured by consumption-mad voters to steer us away from serious mitigation.

There are three major obstacles to any happy outcome. First, northern citizen rights have grown to include a high-emissions consumer culture, soaking up an enjoyable material present in preference to thinking about apparently more ascetic and still abstract futures. Southern citizens are also beginning to savor the immediate pleasures brought by economic growth and understandably want to consume still more. None of these peoples would accept severe rationing or taxing of fossil fuels. Global warming is an abstract threat not yet biting into everyday lives. By the time it does, decades down the line, it may be too late. People are especially unlikely to support major mitigation during a recession.

Second, successful policy would require cutting back the autonomous power of capitalism, driven on the treadmill of short-term profit to destroy the environment. Though there are potential splits between low and high emitting industries, these have not yet happened. The capitalist hurdle is raised higher by the fact that labor is not convinced that environmentalism is in its interest, as well as by the recent surge of neoliberalism denouncing government regulation. Class struggle is asymmetric here – most of the capitalist class opposes emissions regulation, but most of labor does not support it. Third, successful policy would require cutting back the autonomous power and the caging power of the individual nation-state and its politicians, who are driven on two treadmills, one of GDP growth, the other of the electoral cycle (or the authoritarian regime's equivalent). What politician would advocate severe rationing or taxing of fossil fuels?

On the positive side, soft geopolitics among states were boosted in the settlement of World War II, and these plus a burgeoning NGO sector do generate some international and transnational action. Yet far more is needed for effective mitigation. Action requires binding agreements between all the major states, and this is rendered more difficult by North-South hostility and by jealous protection of national sovereignty by the principal polluters. So tackling climate change requires attacking the autonomy of this period's three great success stories – capitalism, the nation-state, and individual citizen rights. This is a formidable, probably an impossible task.

It seems unlikely therefore that we can reduce emissions fast enough to avoid serious consequences. Humanity may have to go through a few disasters, like the wholesale flooding of some countries, before it begins to react. As such crises loom, the gravity of the threat might galvanize low-emissions businesses, electorates, and politicians into drastic global mitigation policies, a Great Awakening says Gilding (2011), accepting and imposing major sacrifices for at least one or two generations. Populations would live in reduced circumstances, but they would live. Alternatively, as crisis worsened, a Fortress World scenario might be adopted by those states and regions suffering less but possessing more power. That might be popular among their citizens who would turn their national cage into a fortress. This could generate new ideologies, not cuddly green ones but nastier ones generating ecofascist regimes or populist charismatic leaders in countries beset by massive refugee flows, enraged terrorists, local wars and mass deaths, producing not global integration but disintegration, with possible escalation into nuclear war. So far I have treated the ideological response to climate change as that of nice, gentle scientific-cum-ethical herbivores. But environmental ideologies might in the future be as varied as other ideologies were earlier in the twentieth century when humans confronted the rise of corporate capitalism and the working class. Ideologies comparable to revolutionary socialism, aggressive nationalism, and even fascism might emerge. We can see the first stirrings of this, perhaps, in the emergence in the United States of a nationalist drive for energy self-sufficiency, attempting to cut the country off from the rest of the world.

These two extremes are not the only possible paths. Some limited progress might be made in mitigation policies but not enough to outweigh the emissions generated by economic growth. This may be the likeliest path. We don't know how long-delayed would be its really bad consequences, but from general recognition of an undesirable trajectory toward disaster might gradually come stiffer mitigation policies. These would inevitably reduce living standards, but the two world wars did see willingness to sacrifice, provided sacrifices were seen as universal and therefore just. The onset of climate disaster might be comparable – indeed to my mind the likeliest possibility for saving human life on earth. The best possible path would be stiffer mitigation policies now or soon, along the lines laid down in recent official reports, but with tighter regulation and stiffer carbon taxes and cap-and-trade schemes – what Newell and Paterson (2010) call Climate Keynesianism. Yet they would have to be backed up by new greener technologies. This combination could still significantly reduce global warming by the mid-twenty-first century. Common to all of these alternative policies of mitigation would be more interstate coercion in regulating, imposing carbon taxes, and setting caps on emissions at both the national and especially the international level. Salvation can come only from a more international human society, pressured by scientific findings and quasi-transnational NGOs. But I don't quite see it happening.

Capitalism must also be reined in. It has been the main polluter yet remains unwilling to pay the social cost of its pollution. At a time when Marxism is almost dead and social democracy is on the defensive, eminent establishment environmentalists like James Gustav Speth (2008: chaps. 8 & 9) float schemes for "changing the fundamental dynamics" of capitalism. He asks governments to revoke charters of corporations that violate the public interest, exclude unwanted corporations, roll back limited liability, eliminate corporate personhood (which gives them the same rights as any person), get corporations out of politics, weaken corporate lobbying, and democratize corporations. He believes capitalism "profoundly threatens the planet" and must be replaced. He accompanies this with wider calls to the citizenry to end its growth fetish and its consumerism, and he asks for a new politics and a new ideology, including the cultivation of postmaterialist values appropriate for a postgrowth society, and an ethic of global equity and sustainability. He admits that all this – which amounts to restructuring all four sources of social power – might seem rather utopian in the United States. Actually, it would be in any country. Yet he is hopeful that it would be practicable if the coming environmental crisis creates citizen demand for radical action.

More moderate scenarios see mitigating policies coming more gradually but cumulatively over two or three decades, through a relatively democratic, integrative, soft geopolitical and peaceful process – assisted perhaps by some great capitalist or government laboratory technological breakthroughs. More malign scenarios foresee intensifying social strife, raising higher the border fortifications of the more prosperous world, while simultaneously making them harder to defend, amid authoritarianism, hard geopolitics and wars. In a future crisis GDP per capita would plummet, even in the richest countries, affected by collapse elsewhere, and likely to turn to costly forms of armed self-defense. Eventually such a decline might reduce emissions, though perhaps after a few climate wars along the way.

No one can predict which path might be chosen, for we are dealing with human beings, capable in the twentieth century of collectively launching two terrible wars for no good reason, while later capable of banishing interstate wars from much of the earth. Who knows what we will do? The choice, said Rosa Luxemburg in 1918, is between socialism and barbarism, though climate socialism would be very different to the socialism she envisioned, closer to the reformism she denounced. Free markets and business-corrupted governments got us into this mess, though the delusions of state socialism contributed mightily in some places too. Consumers' preferences and votes keep us there. But confronted by a common global problem, the survival of humanity requires devising effective collective decision-making, together with a more socially responsible way of life for its citizens. The twentieth century saw the drifting away from and then back toward market-dominance. Now it must needs to drift away again, but this time away from national caging too – an unprecedented move, Polanyi's double movement rolled into one. Yet the crisis and the threat remain abstract. Just like the neoliberal threat discussed in Chapter 11, it is not rooted in peoples' everyday experience. Until a very imaginative social movement can bridge the gap between climate change and everyday experience, I fear this chapter is blowing in the wind.

13 Conclusion

Overall patterns of globalization and development

In this volume I have depicted a narrowing followed by a widening of the ideological spectrum, capitalist triumph and tribulations, the decline of interstate wars and their replacement by either peace or civil wars, the intensification of national citizenship, and the replacement of all empires save one by nation-states. All this was happening on an increasingly global scale – a series of globalizations, which sometimes reinforced, sometimes undercut, and always differed from each other. As a result, the world is more interconnected, though it is not harmonious, and it is nowhere near being a single global system. It is a process of universal but polymorphous globalization.

My second volume identified capitalism and nation-states as the two main power organizations of the long nineteenth century in the advanced countries. In Volume 3 and here I have expanded my horizons to the globe and added empires. The entwined dynamics of capitalism, nation-states, and empires brought disastrous world wars and revolutions in the first half of the twentieth century. This was followed by a fairly sharp break after 1945 as power relations subsided into a short "golden age" of democratic capitalism, in which occurred the collapse of all but two empires, a degree of class compromise within capitalism, the institutionalization of both capitalism and state socialism, the emergence of mass social citizenship, and global economic and population growth. The principal military confrontation eased into a merely cold war, which eased further as the Soviet Union stagnated. This plus the advent of nuclear weapons brought a decline in usable military power and a rapid decline in interstate wars across the world. Reformed capitalism and American-led geopolitics between nation-states now jointly bestrode most of the world. In the North of the world a higher level of civilization, more prosperous, with more public caring, more literacy and greater human longevity was being developed, though the route to it had been circuitous and dangerous. But there was concern in this period that the South of the world was not sharing in much of this and indeed might be condemned to a limited and dependent development.

Then came a second break in the 1970s. This one affected the North and the South of the world quite differently. In the North what I called the Anglophone, Nordic and Euro varieties of social citizenship began to falter. Faltering was greatest among the Anglos but in general the power of center-left reformist parties began to fade. Their main goals were no longer to advance but merely to defend what had already been achieved. Social democracy and liberalism had become overinstitutionalized, overbureaucratized ideologies having difficulty coping with novel structural changes. Their subsequent defense has been more successful in the Nordic, northerly Euro countries and Japan than in the Anglophone and Mediterranean countries. There democracy and citizenship were becoming subordinated to those who had power within markets, especially finance capital. At the same time Soviet-style communism collapsed, deservedly so since it had never been remotely democratic. An alliance of neoliberals, finance capital, and conservatives emerged. This was strongest in former Soviet-bloc and Anglophone countries, and strongest of all in the United States. A long postwar drift to the right had finally made the United States exceptional, a trope I had resisted in earlier periods – though Britain also moved less far in the same direction. Capitalism, especially American capitalism, now contains an asymmetric class structure in which the capitalist class faces little challenge from below.

Yet neoliberalism failed to deliver on its promises. It delivered not growth but stagnation, inequality and poverty, plus corporate encroachments on political democracy. It then brought on the Great Neoliberal Recession of 2008. But the lack of challenge from below brought no effective solution to this crisis. Neoliberalism survives because it commands distributive power, the power of some over others, mostly expressed transnationally, but it does not bring more collective power for all. Prospects for the Anglophone countries do not currently look very good, even for their capitalist classes since they are now rejecting the policies that boosted the aggregate consumer demand on which their prosperity had rested during the golden age. It is doubtful in the long-run that capitalism can do as well if it consigns the lowest fifth or fourth of the population to the scrap-heap.

But this is not the whole global story. The world is big and it remains varied. The Middle East was distinctively turbulent, its regional problems worsened by a burst of aggressive American imperialism, which also brought terrorist blowback and encroachments on civil rights in the North. But during these recent decades of northern stagnation, large parts of the South have experienced substantial economic growth occurring amid relative peace. Neither dependency theory nor its offshoot, world systems theory, had expected this. Orthodox world systems theory had assigned countries rather fixed statuses in the world system, as core, semiperiphery or periphery, with the dynamism of the system being largely confined to struggles among countries of the core. It could not explain national or macroregional mobility, whereby countries rise from the periphery into the core. Thus some world systems theorists began to stress that capitalism was coping with a declining rate of profit in the North of the world by what they call a spatial fix, relocating to the cheaper supplies of the South, a shift that will eventually also produce a shift in global hegemony toward a more multicentric form.

Upward mobility is not confined to China. It has been spearheaded by all four of the so-called BRIC countries (Brazil, Russia, India, and China) but is now spreading to almost the whole of Southeast Asia, to much of Latin America, to Turkey, and even to scattered African countries like Algeria, Uganda, Ghana, Botswana, and South Africa. The BRIC countries and not the United States, Japan, or the European Union led the way out of the Great Neoliberal Recession of 2008 partly because they were less neoliberal. Instead their economies were export-subsidizing, somewhat protectionist, and state-coordinated. The most effective economies around the world contain more statism than neoliberal models allow, especially of course China. Whether they can continue their growth if the northern recession continues, thus reducing global demand, remains unclear. They also differ substantially from each other, none more so than the four BRIC countries. Thus the world retains great variety even while being globalized. Nation-states and macroregions retain their differences even when faced with intensification of transnational power processes.

So any crude distinction between North and South needs qualifying. First, some northern countries embraced much less neoliberalism and so emerged quicker out of the Great Recession – as did Switzerland, Sweden, and Germany. Second, many Southern countries, especially in Africa and Central Asia, remain desperately poor and under-developed. Third, many northern corporations had moved their manufacturing operations southward, creating an ambiguous national/transnational identity for themselves and their bosses. They make more of their profit from manufacturing within expanding southern markets and so are becoming less dependent on their home base in the North; yet they tend to repatriate their profits back home and they still tend to think of themselves as being American or German or Japanese. Their ambiguity is typified by that apparently quintessential American manufacturing corporation, General Electric, which now does more of its business in finance than in manufacturing and generates more of its profits abroad, yet whose CEO was appointed in January 2011 to head President Obama's American Economic Recovery Advisory Board. The capitalist class has a dual identity – it is not simply a global capitalist class, as some argue – while most other classes remain predominantly nationally segregated. All three qualifications blur any simple-North distinction. But they do not disguise the fact that the worm is turning: the balance of economic power is shifting away from the old West toward a more multilateral order that includes powerful southern countries, especially in East and South Asia. This shift is reinforced by a flailing American military imperialism, which after 2000 lost a realistic sense of its own limits, as well as by increasingly dysfunctional American and EU polities.

Though it remains unclear what the twenty-first century might have to offer as comparable sea-changes in power relations to those charted in this volume, we already know that the triumph of capitalism, the nation-state, and mass consumption citizenship will continue to incubate toxic levels of climate change, unless nonpolluting, cheap alternative energy technologies are miraculously invented and diffused. Global warming and greater weather variability might result in either of two extremes: geopolitically negotiated reforms on a global scale to reduce emissions, or the collapse of much of modern civilization. Perhaps more likely is a muddling through sundry disasters toward an intermediate solution, favoring some classes, macroregions and nations more than others – the normal outcome of human social development. However, for survival's sake, there *should* be another swing away from market domination and neoliberalism back toward a more socially regulated democracy, though this time on a global geopolitical scale. There is, of course, no guarantee that this will happen. It will have to be struggled for. These alternatives might bring either a more integrated or a more disintegrated form of globalization. That choice could make it a more dramatic century even than the last one.

The role of the four power sources

I now move to conclusions at a more theoretical level, beginning with the development of each of the four power sources.

Ideological power

This played a highly variable role in the struggles of the twentieth century, being especially prominent in its first half, then declining after mid-century before recovering somewhat at the advent of the twenty-first century. Racist ideology dominated the last century of imperial rule across the world, and contributed to its collapse, patriarchy maintained most of its power in both homelands and empires, while liberalism and social democracy came to dominate in the West, and Marxism empowered revolutionary transformations in Russia, China and elsewhere. Fascism did likewise in Germany and Italy and impacted considerably on Japan. The combination of these rival ideological struggles brought on World War II and the massive postwar transformations, which were due to that war. I emphasized that nationalist ideology had varied forms. Aggressive nationalism was a consequence more than a cause of World War I, but was generally short-lived, transmuting into a more populist and progressive longing for peace afterward. Pacific forms of national citizenship then dominated. However, one great exception, fascism, emerged to cause World War II. It is striking how similar problems of modernization – industrialization, mass mobilization warfare, and the political incorporation of the masses – brought such diverse ideological responses. Ideological diversity may also be the consequence of environmental crises in the twenty-first century. In my chapters dealing with the first half of the twentieth century I explained variability in terms of existing institutional differences between countries interacting with their varied experience of the major unintended dislocations of the period, which were two world wars and the Great Depression, all three of them global phenomena. Here globalization was expanding more disintegration than integration.

World War II saw off fascism while state socialism lost the cold war, resulting in an ideological discourse narrowing into a centrist spectrum ranging from social democracy through Christian Democracy and liberalism (in the American sense) to moderate conservatism. Racism also lost much of its power with the fall of colonialism and American segregation, though both rabid anticommunism and patriarchy began to weaken slightly later. "The end of ideology" was proclaimed by many. Daniel Bell (1960) argued that a great transformation had occurred from the late seventeenth century onward as dominant ideologies shifted from being religious to secular, which then had become exhausted by the 1950s, discredited both by the atrocities they had brought to the world, and by the success of reformed capitalism and welfare states. The Soviet Union and the West, he said, were gradually converging onto a single model of modernization – a victory for less ideological, more pragmatic conceptions of reform. His argument was later revived by Francis Fukuyama just as the Soviet Union was collapsing. He took the collapse of fascism and state socialism as proof of "the triumph of the West," and went on to boldly declare that "What we may be witnessing is not just the end of the cold war, or the passing of a particular period of postwar history, but the end of history as such: ... that is, the end point of mankind's ideological evolution and the universalization of Western liberal democracy as the final form of human government." (1989: 4). While Fukuyama was correct to stress Western victory, for him to declare "the end of history" seemed ludicrous, explicable only in terms of the naïve triumphalism then sweeping the U.S. History institutionalizes old ideologies but perennially throws up new ones through the interstices of social development.

And so the decline of ideology was interrupted toward the end of the twentieth century by new ideological contenders emerging from both inside and outside of the West – and especially from within America, the very heartland of the supposed new consensus. Here neo-imperial, neoliberal, and Christian fundamentalist ideologies all became more prominent, being responses to problems of American empire, capitalism, and the nation as a moral entity. While none claimed to oppose liberal democracy, one revived militarism, another stripped social protections for the masses, and the third showed intolerance toward alternative moralities and life-styles. All this threatened the liberal ideals that Bell and Fukuyama said were triumphant. In all prosperous countries globalization also brought more immigrants from other cultures, regenerating racial and religious divisions within them. Finally, environmentalists emerged with green, transcendent, and largely pacific ideologies.

Bell, Fukuyama and others were wrong in their assumption that liberalism/social democracy was the unassailable bedrock of Western civilization. Marxists and fascists had also thought that they could end history and look what happened to them! In reality liberal and social democracy had been fought for every step of the way and had never fully achieved victory. If liberals and social democrats weakened and stopped fighting so vigorously, they would become vulnerable to rightist counterattack – and this is what happened. They grew tired, their core constituencies declined or shifted toward different identity politics, and the mass media came under increasingly corporate, conservative control. Feminist, gay and other identities made considerable gains, but conservative ideologies resurfaced to take command of the political center and reverse some citizenship gains, especially in the Anglophone countries. There can be no end of ideology, only new ideological swings. The next swing might be in the opposite direction, toward the new forms of collectivism I saw as necessary to combat climate change. But what is certain is that history does not end, and nor does the human need for ideology.

Contemporary ideological threats have also come from outside the West, from new Islamic, Hindu, and Zionist fundamentalists, adding yet greater ideological variability to the world. They are ideological responses to the issue of who is to constitute the nation, and in the Islamic case also to Western and Soviet imperialism. Within the West, whereas Europe is now largely pacific, America remains imperialist – Europe is suddenly become Venus and America Mars, the reverse having been true in previous periods. Native-born Europeans have continued secularizing, unlike Americans, and religion in Europe depends increasingly on immigrants for its congregations and ministers. Secularism also dominates most (though not all) formerly communist states. Yet purportedly purer and more aggressive versions of Islam, Judaism and Hinduism have intensified over the last decades, while African and Latin American Christianity are seeing mass conversions from main-line churches to Protestant sects. American Protestantism, American and Israeli Judaism, Islam, and the world-wide Anglican Church are all experiencing internal religious wars between conservatives and liberals. It seems we have reached not the end of ideology but a surfeit of ideologies, many of them intolerant, leading to a revival of ideological conflicts in the world. This is not surprising, since new ideologies are responses to new social problems, and social development will perennially bring new crises which existing ideologies and institutions seem incapable of solving. However, most of these new ideologies are not as violent and not as mobilizing as those prevalent in the early part of the century. Nonetheless, some of them are what I called "immanent," strongly reinforcing an in-group identity and others are "transcendent," committed to the wholesale transformation of social life by the mobilization of new, interstitial social forces.

These ideologies are seductive but potentially dangerous. They mobilize intense emotions, commitment to ultimate values, and a sense of mission that often display extreme intolerance of others. We can never abolish these strivings from human existence but they tend toward what Max Weber called value-rationality – commitment to ultimate values to the exclusion of careful calculation of means-ends relationships (which he called instrumental rationality). Many people would prefer to call this irrationality, a quality, which has been very visible in this book. It was evident in the run-up to most of the major crises of the century, especially the two world wars and two Great Depressions/Recessions. Human beings were at their least impressive when sliding down slippery slopes into these crises, though the eventual settlement of crises brought some hope, indicating learning ability. Our ability to keep at bay the threat of nuclear war stands as the main hope that potentially disastrous crises might be avoidable altogether. On a lesser scale of irrationality, recent U.S. policies in the Middle East, powered by a resurgence of imperial ideology, were counterproductive, generating blowback in the form of increased international terrorism, nuclear proliferation, and clashes both within and between major world religions.

There is a second danger of transcendent ideology. It assumes one perfect way of organizing human society and so ignores the real diversity of human beings, their interests and their values. Revolutionary situations come the closest to revealing a near-consensus about desirable change among the people as a whole, but it is mainly a negative consensus, wishing to sweep away an existing regime now seen as deeply exploitative and incompetent rather than a consensus about what might succeed it. Successful positive revolutionary slogans tend to be simple and concrete: "Bread, Land and Peace" demanded the Bolsheviks, "Land to the Tiller" demanded peasant revolutionaries. But then what? How should postrevolutionary society be organized? On this, there was no consensus but conflict, and violence was the normal response by revolutionaries who nonetheless tried to impose their utopian blueprints on a recalcitrant population. Such was the life-course of Bolsheviks, Chinese communists, fascists, and Islamists, though neoliberals seek to control by less violent means.

It is therefore important for human societies to keep transcendent ideological power in its place, in a distinct sacred realm. We should separate Church from state, keep U.S. foreign policy focused on global pragmatism not global mission, and keep Chicago economists inside the University of Chicago. We should forever compromise our differences and gladly accept the kind of morally dubious political stratagems, which necessarily accompany backstairs compromise between politicians. We should allow other civilizations their own ideologies, however deviant and repugnant they might seem to us – and so should they allow us our choices. All this would largely prevent ideology from overwhelming the pragmatism and compromise, which more appropriately govern the economic, military and political realms of human societies.

Economic power

Capitalism proved its power and efficacy during this period. It triumphed partly because it could mobilize the bigger battalions in war, partly because the power of capitalists proved superior to the power of the working class and other oppositional movements. Yet capitalism also out-performed state social-ist and fascist alternatives while its own inherent tendencies to exploitation, volatility, and crisis were lessened by reformist pressure from below. State socialism was good at late economic development, when the future was known. It was especially good at late industrialization in which its despotic ability to redirect the agricultural surplus into industry was an advantage – though rarely for peasants. But state socialism also committed terrible atrocities, less-ening its attraction across the globe. Capitalism in contrast exemplified what Schumpeter called creative destruction, the ability to destroy old industries while jumping up onto more advanced levels of technology and organization. Of course, my comparisons in this volume between the efficiency of capital-ism and state socialism are in a sense too sophisticated. Most of the world understands something much simpler: capitalism works, communism didn't – though China's half-communist economic miracle is causing reconsideration across parts of the South of the world.

In Volumes 3 and 4 I have identified three phases of capitalist development in the North of the world. The first jump to a new phase occurred around the beginning of the twentieth century when the second industrial revolution gen-erated a corporate economy of high productivity but low mass demand. This combination came to grief in the Great Depression, though it may have laid the base for a Phase 2, boosted by World War II, which came to fruition with the release of massive consumer demand after 1945. Now a corporate economy coordinated by multiple states managed to combine high productivity with high consumer demand during the thirty-year golden age. Both phases had at their core nationally caged economies, even though globalization was contin-uing. Phase two was plunged into crisis in the 1970s leading to a third, neo-liberal, and more transnational phase. The neoliberal part of this was new but not creative in the sense that it was a return to old orthodoxies, and it resulted in slower growth and mass consumption fuelled increasingly by debt. More successful economies in the South of the world had a slower, more lagged development and are now beginning to move beyond phase one into mass consumerism, somewhat nationally caged (though export-oriented) and rather more statist than in the comparable northern phase, since that is a comparative advantage of late economic development. What is striking in all of this is the coexistence around the world of policies of national economic development combined with the global expansion of capitalism. These processes are closely entwined. For example, while we laud the economic performance of China, and that is substantially due to the policies of the Chinese Communist Party, it also received a considerable boost from the very large investments made in the country by American, European, Japanese, and overseas Chinese corporations, who actually provide much of the hi-tech parts of the economy. National and transnational networks of interaction have not been in a zero-sum relationship with each other – they have intensified together.

The economic success of capitalism was not due to capitalists alone. Luckily for the mass of the population, Marx's analysis of class struggle within capitalism proved half-right. He was wrong to expect revolution from the working class, except in unusual conditions determined principally by political and military power relations, especially war. But he was half-right in that the popular classes could usually mount enough collective action to force reforms on capitalism. Revolutionaries failed, reformists partially succeeded. This led to mass consumption prosperity and it deepened democracy through different varieties of the civil-political-social citizenship chain pioneered by T. H. Marshall in the 1940s. In the 1950s consumption citizenship enmeshed everyday citizen pleasures within capitalism. Freedom of speech, of organization and assembly, free elections and progressive taxes, full employment policies, welfare programs, and more and more consumption goods spread through the North of the world, and then to some countries of the South too. That process will doubtless continue across the South, though the North has seen some recent regression along this chain of citizenship as working class movements declined while capital developed more transnational organization beyond the reach of individual nation-states.

Economic progress had not come merely from market forces. Especially in the postwar period it has been boosted by coordination and regulation by nation-states. They are the main agencies of macroeconomic planning, and about 80 percent of trade in goods and services still lies within countries. Citizenship has been achieved within national cages. Big corporations have become more transnational (especially in financial services) and their supply chains span many countries, yet they remain dependent on states for assistance and regulation. Global capitalism remains a mixture of national, international and transnational networks, and its transnational organization has increased and has in some ways curtailed the economic powers of nation-states, but we are not yet near the transnational ruling class proclaimed by some (Sklair, 2001; Robinson & Harris, 2000). The organization of finance capital, armed with its speculative weapon, is the closest thing to that.

It is possible within the West to identify varieties of capitalism, with some considerable differences between relatively market-oriented Liberal Market economies and more corporatist Social Markets. Then we must add the distinctively corporatist economy of Japan. But the greatest deviations from these models can be found in the more statist economies of most of the South. In most times and places of late development across the last two centuries state-coordinated market economies have best provided economic growth, though policies vary according to local portfolios of resources and comparative advantages (Chang, 2003; Kohli, 2004). This was conditional upon economic and political elites being relatively cohesive and relatively uncorrupt, but the numerous success stories, especially in East and Southeast Asia, have provided a heartening rebuttal to dependency theory, which had suggested that the advanced countries might be able to keep developing countries in a state of stagnant dependence on them.

Yet the most widespread type of economy in the world today is even more statist. Decolonization generally resulted in moderately effective states but almost no entrepreneurial class. Development was therefore undertaken under considerable state patronage. The period during which socialism was an attractive ideal in the South of the world saw much nationalization of industry. This often became corrupted and in the reaction against socialism that began in the 1970s or 1980s privatization began. It too often became corrupt. Former Soviet bloc countries had a distinctive version of this. As we saw in Chapter 8, their transition to capitalism began with the seizure of state economic resources by former apparatchiks, joined by entrepreneurs who managed to secure privileged access to licenses granted by the state. Initially this produced a Mafia-like capitalist class of some autonomy, headed by the Oligarchs, but Putin's gradual consolidation of power forced them to deal with him. They lost some of their Mafia tendencies but became closely enmeshed with the state. The question of who wears the pants in this marriage of convenience is much disputed, but this is a much more politicized form of capitalism than is found in the West. China offers a variant form of this transition. Politicized capitalism is also found in many countries of the South. Privatized state assets have been allocated to the friends and relatives of the political elite, with militaries and security police forces sharing in the spoils in some countries. This is intended by the regime to buy loyal supporters. The Shah's regime in Iran and Mubarak's in Egypt were notable examples of this, while the issue of who was to control the state-dependent enterprises of Rwanda was an important issue at stake in the run-up to the genocide there. Such politicized capitalism is of course somewhat politically vulnerable, for it focuses much of the economic discontent that is expressed onto the regime, adding to whatever political discontents are voiced. Yet the overthrowal of a regime may not eliminate politicized capitalism, for the new regime may pursue the same clientelist policies – as happened in Iran after the 1979 revolution. So although capitalism dominates the world, it comes in varied forms and Western-style capitalism does not dominate the world.

The success of varied forms of capitalism and states is revealed by mortality trends. I gave some figures on improving mortality rates up to 1970 in the conclusion of Volume 3. The improvement has continued since then. Global average life expectancy in 1970 was fifty-nine years; in 2010 it was sixty-nine. Children have done even better. In 1970 the global child mortality rate (of children less than 5 per 1,000 children) was 141; by 2010 it had fallen by more than half, to 57. Though India and especially China contribute disproportionately to these improvements, and though most of sub-Saharan Africa and some post-Soviet countries have not seen improvement, the movement toward better human health has been near-global. Greater equality in life expectancy across the world is already here, the product both of capitalism bringing more abundant and healthier diets and governments creating infrastructures of water, sewerage, and public health. These two processes, bringing riches to the North and adequate living standards to much of the South have been the great economic achievements of the period. We must regard this recent period of human history in a positive light – though the shadows of climate change and nuclear war hang over it.

Nonetheless, the difference between the richest and poorest individuals in the world remains large. Despite China's growth the absolute gap in welfare between the average American and the average Chinese is still widening (though this will probably not continue long). International inequality still dwarfs intranational. One global estimate is that 60 percent of a person's income is determined by national place of birth, compared to 20 percent by inherited class position within a nation (Milanovic, 2010). The luck of where you were born determines most of your fate. This is why so many from the global South risk their lives trying to sneak into Northern countries. Nonetheless, we are beginning to see at last the groundwork being laid for a shift toward a truly global economy embodying a more equal distribution of power across the world.

This economic contribution to a civilizing process in the North and the South is currently threatened in some countries and macroregions by a neoliberal surge embodying growing debt, inequality, greed, and financial criminality threatening the living standards of ordinary people and the social cohesion of nations. Once again, unfettered capitalism leads to exploitation. There is no necessary self-correcting, self-protecting mechanism as Polanyi seems to have believed. Instead, the lesson for each generation is that civilizing capitalism and saving it from itself is a never-ending struggle.

What are the future prospects of capitalism? Accurate prediction of long-term trends is not possible, for three main reasons. First, the earth is a big and very varied place. It is impossible to make generalizations about macrosocial structures today that apply to the whole world. Still less can we hazard them for the future. Second, my model of the sources of social power is nonsystemic – that is, the four sources do not add up to a single social system and nor are there determinate relations between them. As I will argue a little later, they are orthogonal to each other, somewhat autonomous but interacting, which makes the outcome of their interactions unpredictable – and which produces globalizations, not a single process of globalization. Third, macrostructures emerge from human action and humans themselves are volatile, emotional, and capable of both rationality and irrationality. Humans are unpredictable. In view of these problems I will eschew hard-and-fast predictions and instead try to specify alternative scenarios for the future of capitalism, hazarding some rough guess as to their relative probabilities.

In Chapter 11 I discussed the Great Neoliberal Recession of 2008. I noted that most of the Northern countries were worse affected than were the successfully developing countries of the South. I also doubted whether current northern economic policies could cure the weaknesses and prevent the return of a recession some years down the road. This is a part of the shift in economic power away from the North toward the South, resulting most probably in a return to a more multicentric structure of capitalism, which I have just indicated might also be a capitalism of multiple forms. But I now want to go beyond this to ask what is the long-term future of global capitalism.

Marxists have confidently predicted the eventual doom of capitalism, although after the collapse of socialism some began to gloomily think that capitalism was eternal. Yet world systems theorists have recovered their nerve. Focusing on the sight of capitalists prolonging the life of capitalism by a "spatial fix," moving northern manufacturing abroad to cheaper labor and other costs, Marxists have predicted that capitalism will eventually exhaust its markets. When China becomes too expensive, manufacturing plants are moved to cheaper countries, like Vietnam. When Vietnam becomes too expensive they will go elsewhere, perhaps to Africa – and so it will continue. The move out of China is already beginning to happen. Wallerstein (2012) estimates that it takes about thirty years for labor movements in developing countries to form unions and raise wages and conditions so that their country is no longer one of cheap labor. But once the last receiving region, probably Africa, upgrades its labor conditions, there will be no cheap labor markets left. Further spatial fixes are not possible, the rate of profit falls, workers are globally organized to resist attempts to cut labor costs, and capitalism meets its final crisis. He does not give any dates for this, but his model might lead us to assume that it might occur in about sixty years time.

This is highly speculative and of course (as Wallerstein accepts) no one can confidently predict outcomes over such a long time-frame. Yet I am skeptical of some aspects of this model. First, I do not doubt the sequence of spatial fixes but its end-result might be different. If there were no cheap labor left, capitalists could no longer reap super-profits from this source, but the higher productivity of labor and the increased consumer demand in newly developed countries might compensate for this and generate a prosperous and reformed global capitalism, with full citizenship rights for all human beings. This would not mean the end of capitalism but a much better capitalism. The main objection to this rather happy scenario is that increased labor productivity tends to lead to fewer jobs, in which case this scenario would also require shorter working hours and job-sharing so that all could participate in this form of capitalism.

My second main doubt over the spatial fix model is that markets need not be restricted by geography. New markets can also be created by cultivating new needs. Capitalism has grown adept at persuading us that we need two cars per household, bigger and better houses, and innumerable electronic devices that become obsolete and need to be upgraded every year. We cannot begin to envisage the consumer fads of our great-grandchildren, but we can be fairly sure there will be some. Markets are not fixed by territory. Planet Earth can be filled and yet new markets can be created.

However, whether this can be the permanent solution for capitalism's ills remains to be seen. It depends on a second fix, what is called the "technological fix," the ability to continuously develop new products and industries. This is the heart of Schumpeter's notion of "creative destruction": entrepreneurs invest in technological innovation, which results in the creation of new industries and the destruction of old ones – and the maintenance of profits and further investment. Creative destruction can be a bumpy ride. The Great Depression in the United States was partially caused by the stagnation of the major traditional industries, while the new emerging industries, though vibrant, were not yet big enough to absorb the surplus capital and labor of the period (I discussed this in Volume 3). That was only achieved in the aftermath of World War II when enormous consumer demand held back by wartime sacrifices was released.

Today there are again new dynamic industries, like microelectronics and bio-technology. Creation is still flourishing but unfortunately these industries have not provided a satisfactory fix since they have not generated sufficient employment to offset the unemployment resulting from the transfer of manufacturing industry abroad. Innovations like computers, the Internet and mobile communication devices do not compare with railroads, electrification, and automobiles in their ability to generate employment growth, especially in low skilled occupations. Nor have they generated enough profit to boost the economy sufficiently. Overaccumulation of capital has resulted, with excess capital being invested in finance services, which has actually added to the recent woes of capitalism. More important perhaps is the expansion of the health and educational sectors, which are more labor intensive, especially for more intellectual and more middle class occupations. Their expansion is likely to continue, as the length of life, and especially the length of old age, plus educational credentialism both continue to increase. Randall Collins (2012) is skeptical of this and is already worried by recent tendencies for middle class intellectual labor jobs to be also transferred abroad. He sees no way for northern capitalism to generate sufficient employment to maintain the whole society. Yet another possible candidate for job creation in the future is the alternative fuels sector. At present this is not a significant job creator, but the future of this sector is as yet unknowable. As Collins notes, there is no necessary reason why the process of creative destruction should always save capitalism. Maybe capitalism was just exceptionally lucky in the postwar golden age.

There is a brighter side of current trends, however, for the expansion of capitalism in the South of the world has produced a big growth in global employment, greater even than the substantial rise in world population. Without this, the doubling and trebling of world population would have produced a major economic crisis of its own. Between 1950 and 2007 job growth was about 40 percent higher than population growth. In the OECD countries more people are working than ever before, although the absolute number of unemployed has also risen because the population is larger and a higher proportion of the population seeks jobs, including far more women. The growth in the numbers of women entering the formal labor market has been the biggest problem for the level of employment in the North of the world. But the globe has not shared in the travails of the North. The global unemployment rate remained fairly stable between the 1970s and 2007, at around 6 percent. Even through the Great Recession ILO statistics reveal that global employment has continued to grow, though at only half the rate before the crisis. But it is unevenly distributed. It fell in 2009 in the developed economies, including the European Union (by −2.2 percent) and its neighbors, and in the ex-soviet Commonwealth of Independent States (by −0.9 percent), but it grew in all the other regions of the world. The employment-to-population ratio also fell back in the advanced countries, and in East Asia, but elsewhere by 2010 this ratio was back to the 2007 level. Growing unemployment is as yet a northern not a global problem. Yet it is possible that the future of labor markets in the North may be labor shortages not high unemployment, since the length of life is growing and the birth-rate has fallen below the level necessary to reproduce the population. Europe, Japan and North America will probably need substantial immigration to make up the gap. Since these demographic tendencies will then also appear in developing countries as they get richer, overall world population will probably begin falling in the second half of the twenty-first century. These are reasons why global unemployment may not increase substantially and why we might feel more optimistic about the future of capitalism.

But supposing we did accept Wallerstein's negative conclusion on capitalism's future. This might produce one of two alternative futures quite apart from capitalist collapse. In the first and the more pessimistic one of the two structural employment is envisaged as remaining high and a "2/3–1/3" society emerges (though any exact figures are arbitrary ones). In this society most workers are well-educated, high-skilled, and in regular employment, but 1/3rd of the population are excluded from such positions and are forced to live on the margins of society in casual, part-time or no employment. They might receive enough welfare and charity to keep them from revolting, or they might be repressed (which might generate an expanded version of the "workfare to prisonfare" model sketched out in Chapter 6). The excluded would be a minority, so their chances of successful revolt would be small. It might be that the included 2/3rd would not sympathize much with them, viewing them negatively as worthless drop-outs, scroungers, welfare queens etc. In some countries ethnic or religious minorities would be overrepresented among the poor, and negative ethnic/religious slurs would be added to these stereotypes. The excluded might become a hereditary lower class. Most of the included might vote to maintain this gulf, while many of the excluded would not vote. The extent of welfare might continue to differ among the various welfare regimes of the world, with countries like Sweden and Germany being willing to keep the poor within the mainstream society, while countries like the United States might not be. We can recognize this pessimistic scenario, for it is already present in the United States, and sociologists have perceived its rise in Europe too. It would be the final demise of the working class – but not of capitalism. Economies have been moving unsteadily toward the first part of the model proposed by Marx and Engels, the triumph of capitalism, though the two great radicals would lament the lack of the second part, the prospect of a revolution overturning it. For capitalism has developed into an asymmetric mode of production, in which there is an organized and self-conscious capitalist class – if generally with a dual global-national identity – but little collective organization or consciousness and much greater national divides among the middle and lower classes. The class challenge to capitalism diminished in the second half of this present period. On its own that asymmetry would prolong the life of capitalism, though perhaps a sequence of spatial fixes will gradually strengthen the global working and middle classes. Moreover, nation-states, wars and ideologies remain perennially capable of disrupting and rechanneling capitalism.

Social institutions survive even when they do not perform very well, unless counterorganization emerges among the oppressed. In the North of the world this is at present hindered by the fact that never has the Left been so weak as today, though there has been a leftist upsurge in some countries of the global South.

The second alternative scenario is more optimistic. It agrees that capitalist markets will fill up the planet and that profit and growth rates will fall. But it suggests that this will stabilize into an enduringly low-growth capitalism. That would not be new, of course. Capitalism's great breakthrough came in eighteenth and nineteenth century Britain. Yet the British growth rate never exceeded 2 percent in any one year. The British success story was rather that an average growth of just above 1 percent per annum continued for a very long time. In the twentieth century, however, the pace quickened. Between the wars, the most successful developing countries (Japan, its colonies, and the Soviet Union) achieved historically unprecedented growth rates of around 4 percent. Then in the late twentieth century China and India (and now others) achieved growth rates of around 8 percent. Though those rates have endured for at least two decades, they will inevitably decline. Then Africa and Central Asia might do even better. But when capitalism fills the earth they might have all been reduced down to the 1 percent level of the historic British success story. Why should a growth rate of 1 percent produce a capitalist crisis? Japan has experienced that for over a decade yet remained remarkably stable. Capitalism might continue as a low growth global system, as it was for much of its history. The period 1945–1970 in the West and the end of the twentieth and beginning of the twenty-first century in the East would then be both viewed as having been utterly exceptional. This low-growth scenario would also reduce the role of speculation and downgrade the power of finance capital, with repeats of our present Great Recession (which are at present quite likely) becoming in the long-run less likely. Indeed, as labor conditions improve throughout the world, that is very good news. Then all of humanity might live in an almost steady-state economy. The future of capitalism might not be exciting, but boring.

If forced to choose one scenario as the most likely to occur sometime around or after 2050 (provided nothing very major in the meantime interfered), I would plump for a global capitalism spreading lower levels of growth but more equality of condition across the world, except that it would carry a casually employed or unemployed lower class of somewhere between 10 percent and 20 percent of national populations – a mixture of the two scenarios depicted above – very much like the nineteenth century industrializing countries.

I would not predict crisis and revolution. The future of the Left is likely to be at most reformist social democracy or liberalism in the American sense. In the North of the world the pessimistic scenario presented previously might even finish them off too, but this is unlikely to be so under my optimistic scenario. This assumes that employers and workers would continue to struggle over the mundane injustices of capitalist employment (factory safety, wages, benefits, job security etc.), and their likely outcome would be compromise and reform. Developing countries will likely struggle for a reformed and more egalitarian capitalism just as Westerners did in the first half of the twentieth century. Some will be more successful than others, as was the case in the West. China faces severe problems. The benefits of its phenomenal growth are very unequally distributed, generating major protest movements. Revolutionary turbulence is certainly possible there, but if it succeeds, it would probably bring in more capitalism and perhaps an imperfect democracy, as happened in Russia. The United States also faces severe challenges since its economy is overloaded with military and health spending, its polity is corrupted and dysfunctional, and the ideology of its conservatives has turned against science and social science – all amid the inevitability of relative decline and some realization that American claims to a moral superiority over the rest of the world are hollow. This seems a recipe for further American decline.

Of course, all these scenarios are voided if climate change brings the disaster many predict. Then the human condition would be much worse than in a mere crisis of capitalism. The challenge in the twenty-first century is for electorates and political elites to devise policies to counter the tendency toward an included/excluded divide, to restrain mass consumerism, and to accept more global international coordination. The challenge for capitalism is to jump creatively again, especially onto a phase of a higher level of alternative energy-efficient technology. Yet these economic goals need to be struggled for and we cannot predict the outcome of such immense struggles.

Military power

Global empires and two world wars proved the culmination and ruination of a millennial European tradition of militarism, older than capitalism. Military power has its own logic of development, different from the economic logic of capitalism and from the political logic of states. But in this period military development has drawn substantially on the growing economic powers of capitalism as appropriated by states. Military technology and tactics developed enormously throughout this period. I do not identify distinct phases here, just a continuous escalation in the ability to kill people. With the eventual advent of nuclear weapons war at the highest level became completely irrational, and indeed interstate wars diminished almost to vanishing point. Unfortunately, the United States then pioneered a new generation of smart conventional weapons in the so-called Revolution in Military Affairs of the 1990s. This intensified risk-transfer war, whereby the risks of war are transferred from one's own troops to enemy soldiers and civilians. The United States could go on killing people extremely efficiently without suffering much in consequence. Not all killing inventions have been hi-tech, however. Soviet Tank Sergeant Mikhail Kalashnikov achieved immortality by devising a semiautomatic weapon based on a few interchangeable parts, easy to manufacture at low cost, and suited to guerilla and paramilitary forces. Together with shoulder-held surface-to-air and antitank missiles plus improvised explosive devices (IEDs) these weapons of the weak have leveled the playing-field of low-intensity warfare across the world. Mighty states can be humbled by guerilla and terrorist bands.

Social development was buffeted and rechanneled during the twentieth century by mass mobilization warfare. Without the two world wars, then probably no fascist or communist regimes (only failed revolutions); Tsarist Russia and Nationalist China would have survived, along with other semiauthoritarian capitalisms; there would have been no global American Empire, nor the dollar as the single reserve currency but rather a basket of currencies. Phase two of capitalism – high productivity/high demand might not have emerged, or would not have emerged so quickly. The United States would still have been the leading power, endowed with abundant natural resources, attracting and educating skilled workers, but it would be followed at only a moderate distance by Germany, and then by Britain and France – both keeping their empires for longer, which might have been better for the development of their colonies afterward. There would be no European Union, and we might have had a Japan-China standoff in Asia, with the balance of power eventually shifting away from Japan (as it has anyway). Perhaps there would have been different patterns of development of social citizenship in the liberal countries, perhaps lesser Social Democratic/Christian Democratic compromise in continental Europe; the American New Deal might have persisted longer and the United States might never have become exceptional. Perhaps there would have been no nuclear weapons or nuclear power, and who knows what other technologies might or might not have developed. These are all only possibilities, though the probability is that some of them would have transpired. The world would have been different.

Wars like the two world wars are unlikely to be repeated. Either another major war would cause the destruction of the planet, or there will be no more major wars. I assume human beings will have enough rationality to choose the latter option, unless zero-sum issues concerning basic natural resources intervened. Yet the emergence of smaller "risk-transfer wars" mean that great powers can wage limited wars without having to buy mass popular consent, and so it becomes less likely that major legitimacy challenges coming from war will threaten regimes. That probably makes revolutions less likely since it would be harder to dislodge existing power elites. The Chinese Communist Party may be able to hold onto power for a long while, while rather corrupted forms of democracy found across the world, including the United States, may also be very durable. Democrats and Republicans can keep up their stalemating almost indefinitely, reinforcing gradual American decline but no catastrophe.

After the two great wars the two "marcher lord" empires on the edges of the old civilizational core of Europe, the United States and the Soviet Union (previously hesitant imperialists), dominated the world and managed to avoid a third war. Soviet rule was despotic but defensive, while the American Empire was more varied, in places very aggressive although its overall trajectory was toward lighter hegemony – an empire whose own self-interest was often bound up with a more general good. A zone of peace spread across most of the North of the world and across swathes of the South too. Apart from civil wars, peace was spreading.

Most social scientists have preferred a much simpler evolutionary story over this period of the growth of capitalism and democracy, with the nation-state succeeded by globalization. Yet they perform such theoretical feats by imposing pacific blinkers on the world. Of course, if we have succeeded in outlawing interstate wars (a big if), then for the first time in human history such pacific models of social development might explain more in the future. We can only hope so.

At the beginning of the new millennium this pacific drift was interrupted by a burst of American imperialism in the Middle East whose blow-back helped further spread what had been local Islamic terrorism. This mutually murderous escalation between the United States and *jihadi* Islamism is not currently lessening. Over poorer parts of the world a rising military threat came from civil wars, about half of which centered on ethnic or religious conflicts. The democratic ideal of rule by the people or nation was being perverted into murderous cleansing of other peoples, as I explained in my book, *The Dark Side of Democracy* (2005). Yet civil wars peaked in the 1990s and then declined slightly in the new century. Existing civil wars tended to drag on, but fewer new ones were starting – a sign of hope, which recent events in countries like Libya, Syria, and the Yemen might dash.

Some argue that the worst case of ethnic cleansing, the Holocaust of the Jews, was the transforming moment of the twentieth century, indeed sometimes of modernity itself. I do not share this view, though global recognition of the Holocaust has been good, since it led toward better appreciation of the more general problem of genocide. This was not the first modern genocide – that unhappy honor rests with colonized natives in the Americas, followed by colonized Australians, and in the early twentieth century by Armenians. Nor was it the last. Like other genocides the Holocaust occurred amid interstate war, some of which also involved mass bombing of civilians, though this is not generally recognized as also being an atrocity. The Holocaust was part of the broader dark side of modern militarism. The political struggle against militarism continues. It was won after enormous cost and eventual war-weariness in Europe and after much lesser cost in Latin America. It remains to be won in countries like the United States and North Korea, and across swathes of the Middle East and Africa. American militarism may now be restrained over a period of time because of the failure of its recent adventures – as happened for thirty years after the Vietnam defeat. The global balance of probabilities is that war and military power will decline over the coming decades, though future climate crises might well terminate this relatively pacific era. But so far in the period covered by this volume, military power has greatly declined across most of the world.

Political power

Nation-states are now the hegemonic political form across the world. Only one empire is left, and its decline has just begun and will continue. Nation-states continue to structure capitalism. Liberal and social democratic versions of democracy have proved their durability, though their diffusion across the world has been slow and halting. They have not shown universal superiority over despotic regimes in terms of economic performance, while attempts to export democracy by force have failed, except in a few countries that had already experienced democracy in the past. Democracy is instead validated by its intrinsic political merits, for it creates more freedom, considerably more than state socialism or fascism, whose failure was also less economic than political. They degenerated into repressive despotisms because their all-conquering revolutionary elites did not devise any mechanism whereby they might either permit open intraparty debate or cede power to others. We saw that the major communist and fascist revolutions of the twentieth century were born in wars and they always bore the marks of violence. In contrast liberal and social democracies have extended citizen rights, at first down the class structure, then to ethnic minorities and the female majority, then to people with disabilities and unconventional sexual identities. This process is still ongoing and it has been a great political achievement of the period.

Liberal and social democracy require continuing pluralism in civil society. This involves the ability to mobilize countervailing interest-groups against dominant ones as well as the autonomy of politics from encroachments by dominant military and economic power actors. This is often not so in countries calling themselves democracies – including the United States where democracy is now faltering due to the corruption of its politicians and mass media by capitalist corporations and the erosion of civil liberties by its national security state. Nonetheless, liberal and social democracy remain the least bad political systems we know. Since they are always imperfect, struggles to defend and improve them are also never-ending.

Though many believed that globalization would undermine the nation-state, in fact the nation-state has been globalized. The world is now filled with supposed nation-states. State functions have shifted but not declined overall. Curiously, since social scientists have long neglected military power relations, they have not much noticed the most important decline in state power – making war. Many nation-states no longer retain their traditional military backbone. Globalization enthusiasts have instead focused on the lesser decline whereby national economies have been somewhat undercut by a transnational capitalism given a dash of American economic imperialism. However, most states – especially the corporatist and developmental varieties discussed in earlier chapters – still remain in substantial control of their economies, while many other states never possessed such control. In all my chapters I have been at pains to differentiate between states, since they are all different. Even cousins, like Britain and the United States, or Japan and Korea, differ from each other. What transnational enthusiasts abuse as a nationalist methodology still has a significant place in social science, though of course nationalist blinkers should not prevent recognition of the continued importance of local, macroregional, transnational and international networks of interaction. And as if to offset major military and minor economic declines in state activities, northern states have acquired new legislative roles in areas of social life formerly considered private or taboo, like wife- or child-battering, life-style choices like smoking or junk food, consumer environmental pollution, sexual preference, and welfare rights. Thus the regulatory density of states has continued to increase, and new roles for states are still emerging while old ones like war making and protectionism are declining. New social movements continue to pressure politicians to create yet more spheres of government regulation.

The countries of the European Union are unique in having developed a two-level state, though the move of some political functions to Brussels and Strasbourg has not greatly weakened the governments of the member countries, the exception being in the expanding realm of competence of the European Court of Justice in Luxemburg. Though overall political roles have expanded in the EU, the expansion is divided between the individual nation-states and the EU. In terms of spending, most power lies with the individual states. Whereas the EU spends less than 1 percent of Europe's GDP, member governments spend between 30 percent and 50 percent of their GDPs. The EU remains more of a regulating than a redistributing state (though there is some redistribution toward agriculture and poorer regions). Nationally caged identities also remain more important than any common Euro identity, except for a few elites (including social scientists whose main paymaster for research has become the EU).

Social scientists are among the few groups who want to see more deepening of the Union. But the current momentum of the EU is not toward deepening. That was rejected in recent national referenda in which younger voters were especially opposed to further integration. Given this, the Union often moves at the speed of the slowest member, as it was fashioned to do. In particular, Euro currency troubles threaten to undermine the Union. It is unlikely that this two-level European model will inspire much imitation across the world. It is a unique case, the product of the continent's two great wars. It is to be hoped there will not be a third war, for it would be unlikely to generate comparable unexpected benefits afterward.

Yet many of the poorer countries of the world are nation-states only in terms of their elites' aspirations, not of realities on the ground. Real sovereignty and real national identity remain elusive. The creation of infrastructures genuinely integrating states' territories and the creation of the social cohesion necessary to form national identities remain projects for the future, requiring continuing struggle. Overall, power inequality among states is the most significant feature of political power relations in the world today, paralleling great global economic inequality. Whereas northern and a few southern states really can implement their policies across the whole of their territories, most southern states cannot.

The last of the empires survives. I have emphasized the great variety of the American Empire in the postwar period. In the West it was hegemonic, even legitimate. It was highly militaristic at first in East Asia, but then developed into hegemony also. While the United States has generally regarded Africa as of little strategic or economic interest, in Latin America and the Middle East it has intermittently deployed military force, overt and covert. In the Middle East American interventions escalated disastrously in the new millennium. Many take this as a result of American decline, but over the last few decades the American Empire seems to have been on a path of self-induced decline. In foreign policy it has been embroiled in pointless, unwinnable wars and obsessive backing of Israel, both of which only multiply its enemies. In domestic policy it has pursued a destructive neoliberal policy, weakening the state, failing to renew its basic infrastructures, and threatening the mass consumption economy that has brought Americans great prosperity. Many American political leaders ridicule the coming climate crisis as simply a hoax that stymies any constructive policy response. The development of major ideological divisions reinforce the traditional division of powers in the constitution to inhibit responses to most changes. All of this also reduces American political power in the world as foreigners gawp with appalled amazement at American politics.

But are these all separate follies, any of which could easily have gone otherwise and might still do so, or have they been conjoined even inevitable aspects of an Empire in decline? They might be viewed as the continued exercise of the traditional practices, which made America great in the first place, but in a changed environment to which they are unsuited – a fairly common feature of empires in decline (I once analyzed the decline of the British Empire in such terms (Mann, 1988c). This is true of America's enduring practice of profligate energy-extraction, which makes it now unwilling to embrace emissions reductions. And in the eyes of neo-conservatives and neo-liberals, military interventions and free markets made America great and must be embraced again. But, as I have shown, these two beliefs are false, since in earlier periods administrations had been much more cautious in launching military interventions, specifically only attempting them where they had considerable local support; while America's emergence as the greatest economy in the world owed much to state activism concerning macroeconomics, infrastructures and regulation. In fact, it was through forgetting these American traditions that decline partially came. So decline was not a general process conjoining all the sources of social power. It centered in the realms of ideological and political power, yielding false and damaging beliefs, globally unpopular but mobilized by political actors able to block policies more suited to the realities of the twenty-first century. In contrast American economic and military power remain formidable: global hegemony focused on the dollar as the world's reserve currency, and military dominance over the world's states (though not over the world's guerillas). These ideological and political failures are reversible, but as present constituted they inflict damage, hastening on an American relative decline, which would occur anyway in the medium-term.

We can already glimpse the likely successor as the guarantor of world order. It is not another empire, for it is unlikely in the foreseeable future that any single power could replace America. Instead it is likely to be a consortium of powers, perhaps the United States, the European Union, China, Japan and India. The dollar would be replaced as the reserve currency by a basket of currencies, but the United States might retain its military lead longer. However, this peaceful scenario might be shattered by more problematic Chinese-American relations or by severe environmental conflicts.

The modern dynamic

Through all of this we see an inventive dynamism, originally European, then Western, then more global as it involved ripostes by other world civilizations. A second industrial revolution followed by a postindustrial revolution, in tandem with rising nation-states, lengthened the life span, brought mass prosperity, deepened citizenship, perfected the arts of killing people and destroying the planet, and expanded international collaborative institutions. I have deliberately mixed the benign and the malign in the previous sentence in order to emphasize the duality of human dynamism. Each success brings its dark side, each calamity its silver lining. Globalizations bring both on an ever-enlarging scale. Wealth, health and leisure in most of the North and parts of the South have continued to improve but the risk it might end in mushroom clouds or melting glaciers has also grown. It is within human powers to choose to move down one of several paths.

On what does the dynamic ultimately rest? Max Weber argued that a spirit of rational restlessness underlay Western civilization, especially its religion, combining human reason with dissatisfaction with the present world, the combination generating a drive to improve the world by rational this-worldly action rather than merely accepting or retreating from the world (as he saw Confucianism, Hinduism and Buddhism doing). He traced this back to Calvinist sects of the sixteenth to eighteenth centuries. Today, his view seems distinctly Eurocentric, but on a more global scale rational restlessness might be a succinct characterization of modern civilization. It cannot simply result from human nature since some civilizations have been notably more dynamic than others, and ours is perhaps the most persistently dynamic of all. On what social structure does this rest?

When analyzing the origins of dynamism in medieval Europe in Volume 1, I emphasized that it was a multipower-actor civilization. That meant two main things. First medieval Europe comprised many power actors – multiple states, cities, bishoprics, monastic communities, guilds and local village-manor complexes – all enjoying some autonomy in competition with each other. Second, however, this competition lay within the common norms of a single Christian civilization. Its rivalries did not reach the depths of a war of all against all, for at a minimum level these actors were normatively regulated within a shared Christian ecumene. Fukuyama (2011) has recently argued that the core of medieval Christianity was the diffusion through society of notions of Natural or Common Law independent of any single state. But it also meant that the worst wars before the twentieth century came with religious schism. Perhaps Volume 1 overemphasized a little the religious element and under-estimated the class solidarity of armed lords backed by the Church. But the end-result was regulated competition, which as we also see in modern capitalism is probably the main recipe for productive dynamism.

Something comparable endured through later centuries, though much changed in forms. Dynamism has recently rested on capitalist competition entwined with competition between nation-states. Neither dominated the other's sphere, but both have been embedded in broader civilizational ideologies coming from distinct macroregions of the world and also from a broader ideological orientation conventionally termed Enlightenment values. The combination generated minimal but multiple institutions of regulation. We have seen the contributions of diplomacy, alliances and military deterrence, of cooperation over reserve currencies, the Gold Standard and Bretton Woods, of rapidly diffused scientific discoveries and technological applications, and of macroregional varieties of citizenship. They have been joined in the post–World War II period by international and transnational agencies like those of the UN, the EU and innumerable NGOs, often backed by internet-based organization, applying a little pressure on states and capitalism alike. None of this has been enough to prevent intermittent disasters, but out of most disasters came some further attempt at improvement, in the Keynesian aftermath of the Great Depression, in the establishment of international institutions after World War II, including peace in Europe through the European Union, in arms reduction programs after the ending of the cold war, and in the beginning of moves during the Great Recession toward a more multicentric regulation of global capitalism, most specifically in the growing stature of the G-20 group of countries, which includes all four BRIC countries. Peace dividends after wars have always been less than hoped for, but have been real. We are nowhere near the world polity or world culture trumpeted by some sociologists, but we have a sketch of what might eventually become a global multistate civilization capable of achieving a little more overall regulation, riven though it still is by ideologies and conflict. Any future world polity would be a combination of transnational and international networks of interaction. We need much more of both if humanity is to solve the problems now arising from the boomerang environmental effects of our supposed mastery of Nature.

The question of primacy

What ultimately determines this rational restlessness? Indeed, what determines social change more generally? I have selected out and focused on four sources of social power that I consider more decisive than everything else. This has necessarily involved relegating other important features of human life to the back-burners. In this volume I have sought to explain the social development of the last hundred years in terms of the complex combinations of these four sources of social power. But can we go further and select one among them as being preeminent? Karl Marx and Friedrich Engels said yes, Max Weber said no. It is worth quoting them.

Engels in a letter of 1890 written after Marx's death tried to define historical materialism:

According to the materialist conception of history, the ultimately determining element in history is the production and reproduction of real life..... The economic situation is the basis, but the various elements of the superstructure: political forms of the class struggle and its results ... constitutions established by the victorious class after a successful battle, etc., juridical forms, and then even the reflexes of all these actual struggles in the brains of the participants, political, juristic, philosophical theories, religious views and their further development into systems of dogma, also exercise their influence upon the course of the historical struggles, and, in many cases, preponderate in determining their form. There is an interaction of all these elements in which ... the economic movement finally asserts itself as necessary ... the economic [conditions] are ultimately decisive. But the political ones, etc., and indeed even the traditions which haunt human minds also play a part, although not the decisive one. (Letter from Engels to Bloch, in Marx & Engels, 1978 edition: 761).

In this famous statement Engels allows political and ideological power (he does not mention military power) a significant role in human history but then he returns twice to economic factors, claiming both times that they were "ultimately decisive." This is the kernel of his historical materialism. But how are they decisive? Marx was clearer:

The specific economic form, in which unpaid surplus-labour is pumped out of direct producers, determines the relationship of rulers and ruled ... It is always the direct relationship of the owners of the conditions of production to the direct producers ... which reveals the innermost secret, the hidden basis of the entire social structure and with it the political form of the relation of sovereignty and dependence, in short, the corresponding specific form of the state. (*Capital,* Vol III, p. 791)

Here Marx is saying that the *forms* of economic power, specifically the form of the relations between owners/controllers of the means of production and workers, determines the forms of other major power structures. He goes on to qualify this by saying that we must add in "innumerable different empirical circumstances, natural environment, racial relations, external historical influences etc." Translated into my terms, Marx would assert that the form of the mode of economic production ultimately determines the forms of the other three power sources. He would allow for empirical and extraneous complications, but he does not allow for equivalent causality from ideological, military or political power relations onto economic power relations.

Max Weber flatly rejected this, for he believed it was impossible to prioritize any one of what he called "the structures of social action." Indeed, he added,

Even the assertion that social structures and the economy are "functionally" related is a biased view ... For the forms of social action follow "laws of their own" ... and ... in a given case they may always be codetermined by other than economic causes. However, at some point economic conditions tend to become important, and often causally decisive for almost all social groups ... conversely, the economy is also usually influenced by the autonomous structure of social action within which it exists. No significant generalizations can be made as to when and how this will occur.(Weber, 1978 edition: II, 341).

At one point here Weber appears to be stressing economic causes, but then he backtracks and says we cannot even have "significant generalizations" about the relations between what he calls "the forms of social action." He appears to be condemning ventures like my own, which clearly does involve significant generalizations about the structures of social action. He is also clear that there cannot be an ultimately decisive cause.

I have generally tried to steer between the Marxian and Weberian positions, attempting significant generalizations while backing away from ultimate primacy. Let me first recall some of my generalizations in Volume 1. I found in ancient history two persistent though not invariant dialectical power processes. First, there was an internal dialectic between state and society, between the centralized and the decentralized, and between state elites and social classes in civil society, so that techniques and organizations developed by the one were then seized by the other and used to increase its power. The second dialectic was one expressed geopolitically over a broader macroregional scale between domination by centralized empires versus multipower actor civilizations – in the ancient Mediterranean world, for example, between the Assyrian or Roman empires and Greek or Phoenician city-states. Multiple city-states appeared in river valleys and along coast-lines, though with agrarian hinterlands, all set amid broader production-trade networks and culture. On the other hand, marcher lords adjacent to those civilizations, combining agriculture and pastoralism, intermittently conquered these city-state complexes, establishing empires in the process. These involved what early twentieth century theorists called superstratification: the imposition of the conquerors as a ruling class over the conquered. But when empires faded, multipower actor civilizations tended to reemerge. This might be about to happen again, with the fading of the American Empire. Yet there were also stabler periods in which modes of economic production seemed to develop more autonomously, and then came what Eisenstadt (1982) called the Axial Age in which the world religions and the power of clerical ideologists expanded over areas much greater than any single economic, political, or military network.

Thus no single power source was persistently more important than the others, and no clear, repeated principle of succession seemed to characterize the transitions between such different regimes. Ibn Khaldun, the great fourteenth century north African sociologist, developed a cyclical theory of Islam, which Ernest Gellner more recently expanded to include modern times. It is one of alternation between the city and the desert whereby warrior desert nomads sweep in on the decadent cities, conquering and ruling on the basis of a more austere, purer religious faith. But then they in turn become lax and decadent, and a new conquest sweeps in from the desert. Osama bin Laden obviously liked this theory, seeing himself as a new desert caliph. He is now dead and there is unlikely to be a replacement. Nor does the model apply very well to any other of the world's religions or civilizations – though the marcher lords might be seen as a variant form. Each civilization tends to have its own logics of development.

A further difficulty is that when we seek to explain any of these major civilizations, we must generally bring in all the sources of power. Take, for example, marcher lord conquests. They conquered because their military formations were usually more mobile and their morale was more solidaristic than that of their more sedentary opponents. This was an immediate military causality. But in turn there were economic and political causes of their military forms. Horse archers (their most effective troops) emerged among herding and hunting nomads and so were in a sense a product of their mode of production. Their particular tribal formations also seemed to have generated greater solidarism – which was mainly a political cause. Economic and political forces helped generate military superiority in a particular context. Yet nomadism or tribalism were not superior forms of economic or political power to those of the agriculturalists. They were in fact economically and politically backward. Their superiority only lay in the impact of their economies and polities on military power. In fact most of the nomads gladly embraced the superior mode of production and civilization of the sedentary elites after they conquered them. It was only through warfare that this particular transition occurred yet it presupposed all the sources of social power. Conversely, when the great religions swept in, there may well have been economic or political crises that made the converts embrace the new religion but it was through Christianity or Islam that the transition to a new form of society actually occurred. The result of all this was that I could not embrace statements of ultimate primacy in earlier times – though I felt I could make generalizations like those given previously concerning quite broad reaches of time and space and power source interactions.

In Volumes 2 and 3 and in this volume I have detected partially comparable dialectics in the modern period. Early modern and modern Europe was an example of a multipower actor civilization, successfully resisting attempts by any single empire to seize control of the continent. Yet as European states diminished in numbers and increased in power and scope, Europe became a rather unique synthesis of the two. Though a single empire never dominated Europe itself, its states established rival segmental empires across the world. Polanyi discerned a version of the centralization-decentralization cycle occurring over the nineteenth and twentieth centuries in the form of what he called a double movement in the advanced countries between capitalist markets and state regulation. I first used and then criticized this model (at the end of Chapter 11) as being too functionalist and too rationalistic. In the twentieth century we can contrast empires versus nation-states and state socialism/fascism versus democratic capitalism – all relatively centralized versus relatively decentralized societies. But the solution to their conflict was quite complex. Fascism was overthrown by a greater and more centralized military power wielded by an alliance between communism and democratic capitalism. Communism then faced an uphill battle not only against capitalism's superior decentralized ability to innovate, but also against the superior centralized power of its core, the American Empire. Here the model breaks down, as all models eventually do when confronted by the complexity of human societies. Democratic capitalism also triumphed because limited state regulation and de-commodification made it more acceptable to citizens in general. This in effect provided a synthesis to the dialectic, though in some parts of the world it is now under threat from a neoliberalism claiming to be entirely decentralized.

In the modern period I detected some continuity from the period discussed in my second volume: on the one hand, the unfolding of capitalism and its social classes; and on the other hand, the development of nation-states from an initially imperial world. The twentieth century has seen the victory of a reformed, socialized, and often politicized capitalism as the solvent of class struggle, and of major wars solved by an international order imposed by an imperial United States, though in tension with geopolitical relations between states, the combination avoiding further interimperial wars. Through the vicissitudes and disruptions of military and ideological power in the twentieth century, we can perceive continuity, increasingly global, of the economic predominance of capitalism, and a dual political predominance of the nation-state and (American) Empire. These have been responsible for all the major wars and most of the ideologies of the period. Contra Weber, I have therefore attempted significant generalizations but, contra Marx, without any assertion of ultimate primacy.

This also involves a view of globalization different to that of most commentators. They have seen it as a singular process whereby essentially *transnational* relations are undermining nation-states. I agree that transnational processes are underway, especially in the capitalist economy, above all in finance capital, but the main political principle of globalization has been *international*, regulation by and competition between states – geopolitical more than transnational relations. When capitalists and their opponents seek subsidies or regulation, they still turn to states, while most global issues are negotiated between states, especially the more powerful ones, and above all (though just beginning to decline) the American Empire. Ideological conflict and diversity have also revived again. But because of the increasing devastation and irrationality of war, soft geopolitics are chosen more often than hard geopolitics. It is hopefully through soft geopolitics that climate change, probably the major crisis of the twenty-first century, will be confronted. This is a polymorphous process of globalization, driven by several different logics of development, more complex than just a dual dialectical process.

What will follow? Since the process of globalization has now virtually filled the world, this introduces changes. After the American Empire there is no longer the space available at the margins for the marcher lords to develop independently. In certain respects globalizations have filled up the world. So though Chinese power is growing, it is already enmeshed amidst global capitalism, geopolitics and ideologies – and American debt! The normal historical dialectic though which the successor appears first on the periphery of the previously dominant one wielding quite distinctive powers, may be at an end. The likeliest successors to American Empire are actually old civilizations reasserting themselves, but within an emerging global framework. It also seems, as I argued in the last chapter, that the next bout of regulation and centralization might not be at the level of the individual state but at the level of global geopolitics, though egged on by transnational actors. History does not repeat itself. This is to bow toward Weber's agnosticism and to back away from a Marxian level of theoretical ambition. Determinism, even only ultimate determinism, is not a defensible position in sociological theory because societies are too complex and human beings too creative, emotional and irrational to permit it.

A further characteristic of my power sources complicates causal arguments. The four sources generate nonequivalent powers – their relations are, as it were, orthogonal to each other. As I noted at the beginning of this volume, each has unique qualities. Ideological power is not in its origins autonomous, for ideologies are overwhelmingly a response to crises presented by the other power sources. Ideologies emerge as plausible solutions to the unexpected outcomes of the others' interactions but they then exercise emergent powers of their own. Ideologies are also unique in having no necessary geographical boundaries. They can penetrate human consciousness wherever people communicate. In this century ideologies have been repeatedly communicated across much of the globe. Ideologies may also explode quite suddenly, changing mass behavior relatively quickly before settling down into more institutionalized forms. Ideological leaders are also more likely to be seen as charismatic by their followers than are other power-holders. Founders of new religions are striking examples of this, but I also noted in Volume 3, chapter 8 that three of the main six fascist leaders in Europe were viewed by their followers as being highly charismatic (Hitler, Mussolini and Codreanu). Religious leaders claim a close relationship to the divine and this is believed by their followers, and fascists believe that leadership is the essential precondition of social development. In both cases the followers have a need to believe the leader is charismatic, given the content of their own ideology.

Economic power is very different from ideological power for it is distinctively stable yet cumulative, enduringly embedded in everyday life, generating mass behavior of a relatively steady, cumulative form. It does know boundaries, but only those of the logistics of production and trade, which are often very extensive, especially today. Economic power relations today, and probably in most societies, form the deepest- and broadest-rooted power structures, inducing gradual but major change, in modern times adding economic growth over long periods of time.

Military power is different again. It is easily the most suddenly destructive force, killing people, ruining their habitat, bringing political realms crashing down, even capable of destroying the higher levels of whole civilizations. But it can only do this according to the logistics of military striking-ranges, which in historical societies were often quite limited – though not today. It is also the most contingent power source, for many battlefield outcomes could have gone otherwise, as I have emphasized. Military power also has a close relationship with and dependence on economies and states. The better-organized states and the bigger, more materially resourced battalions usually triumph on the battle-field, though overall war outcomes may differ, since guerilla tactics and morale may wear down great powers, while weapons of mass destruction today also threaten to level the playing-field. Military power is also the only one of the four that could, in principle, be abolished. All human groups need economic production, ideologies and political and judicial regulation. They do not need war, nor even defense if no one else mounts offense. For many states (though not all) that outcome is at present nearing, though a failure to respond to climate change may bring crises that might revive militarism.

Political power is also distinctive in being the institutionalization of other power relations over given territories, very clearly bounded, capable of more extensive organization only through geopolitical relations with other states. It offers a national cage, trapping its subjects or citizens. Its character depends heavily on the natural and social configuration of its territories, and so states are extraordinarily varied.

Given such noncongruence of powers, it becomes difficult, if not impossible, to claim that one is ultimately decisive, though in specific periods we may rank the power of one or more sources above the others. The power sources are different rather than contradictory and all have been (so far) necessary to civilized human societies. In any case there are plausible competing views on ultimate primacy. If nuclear war broke out and destroyed most of the earth as a human habitat, military power would have been decisive, though few would be around to do the necessary rewriting of Marx and Weber. Conversely, if weapons of mass destruction continue to act as a powerful deterrent against war, military power might continue to decline across the world. Given the very varied degrees of rationality shown in this volume by social actors confronted by the possibility of major war, I would not bet on one of these eventualities over the other. Similarly, the economy would have been ultimately decisive if capitalism destroyed the environment of the earth, though again who would be around to debate it? On the other hand, religious and other fanatics privilege the ultimate power in the sense of the ultimate truth of their own ideology, and will never be convinced otherwise. If there is a God, religious ideology might loom larger than if there is not. Note that these alternative scenarios all concern extreme ends, the death of societies or of ourselves. It is difficult to imagine ultimacy in any other context, since human interaction chains are otherwise never-ending. All this offers more support to Weber than Marx on the question of ultimate primacy. It probably does not exist over the whole of human history and it is certainly beyond our ken. But Marx was right to try to explore it, and Weber was wrong to so flatly deny the possibility of major historical generalizations.

In the specific period discussed in this volume, two of the sources of social power have been more significant than the others: economic and political. Although capitalism is not quite singular across the globe, it tends in that direction. There is one capitalism. In contrast, there are many ideologies, claiming fundamentally different truths, all endorsed by only a minority of humanity. There is great military variability: one superpower, a handful of other nuclear powers, a few highly armed militaries in flashpoint regions, states beset by civil wars and nonstate paramilitaries, and the now-ubiquitous terrorists. While there is a hierarchy in principle in military power among states, in reality nuclear states cannot bring their full powers into action, and none of them can easily squash guerillas or terrorists. There are also many states, embodying enormous differences of size, power, constitutions and policies. Some cannot implement decisions beyond their capital cities, others are in control of all their territories. Some are quite advanced representative democracies, some are phony democracies, others are brutally or benignly despotic. These power networks coexist within a more limited range of varieties of capitalism, which may seem to confer greater global power on capitalism.

Yet it is not that simple. Two types of political power continue to constrain capitalism. First, the main variation within capitalism is between relatively market and relatively statist versions, that is in terms of the relative importance of economic vis-à-vis political power relations. In ascending order of statism, the main types distinguished in this book are liberal market, social market, developmental, and politicized economies, with China the most extreme statist case remaining – although state socialism was in its time the most extreme case of statism. Whereas the first three types enshrine the overall dominance of capitalism over states, it is difficult to say this in the case of politicized capitalism, which we have seen to be very common across the world. Here property rights are essentially acquired through access to the state. With time, this may develop into relative secure and autonomous property rights, or it may remain vulnerable to reappropriation by the state if the nature of the regime changes, as it did in Iran, and might do so in Egypt today. In state socialism the state obviously controlled the mode of economic production. This degree of statism was not capitalism at all. Amid this range only in some cases does the state severely constrain capitalism. Of course, it is possible to envisage a future in which politicized capitalism disappears and the range of variation diminishes considerably, but that is not the reality that confronts us.

There are also lesser and more idiosyncratic varieties of capitalism like the Islamic type, which bans the taking of interest. Islamic banks provide finance without interest through a contract in which both parties share both profit and risk, amid a distinctive rhetoric of justice. But since the giant Hong Kong and Shanghai Bank (better known as HSBC) has launched an Islamic Amanah Bank, and Citibank and Merrill Lynch have followed with Sharia-compliant products also, Islamic finance is evidently compatible with Western banking practices and it lacks significantly different rights of ownership. The same can be said for the difference between Japanese and American capitalism, the latter more dependent upon lawyers to enforce contracts, the former relying more on normative trust between the parties. These varieties do not significantly shift the balance of power between markets and states.

The decline of state socialism and of social democracy did tilt the balance of global power toward market-oriented capitalism. Yet I have emphasized that the supposed limits, which neo-classical economists and pessimistic Marxists say constrain states, most concretely through forcing them to defer to business confidence, are not fixed. Pressure from various interest-groups can force business to bend. As both Keynes and FDR realized, and the recent Great Recession also exemplifies, capitalists sometimes need rescuing from themselves. In these contexts the rescuers, political actors, have the potential power to exact a price from capitalism and bend its supposed limits. Whether this power will now be exercised again in the aftermath of the Great Recession remains to be seen.

Political power relations exercise a second and more universal constraint on capitalism, for they continue to fracture it into national capitalisms. In my volumes I have referred to this as the caging of the population into nation-state cages. Here conceptions of national interest dominate the global economy alongside private capitalist interest, and in modern times there has always been some tension between them. Although the varieties of capitalism are limited, the number of nationally caged capitalisms is large. Although capitalism's trans-national organization is now stronger than in the recent past, most economic activity remains within nation-state boundaries and most economic regulation and macroeconomic planning, and virtually all economic statistics gathering, is by the state. As I have noted, many powerful corporations now have a dual identity, national and transnational. Moreover, economic activity beyond state boundaries is international as well as transnational, being partially negotiated between nation-states. This may increase significantly if climate change continues, cutting back the autonomy of both capitalism and the individual state. The more pessimistic scenario would be that international cooperation did not increase, which would raise the bars of the national cages once again.

In these two ways political power relations significantly structure economic power relations, just as the reverse is also true. That capitalism is the economy of the world confers on it a degree of routine, institutionalized, global power – and it gives capitalists a degree of collective consciousness – which is only rivaled by nation-states and national identities. When concluding in Volume 2 that capitalism and nation-states dominated the world, I neglected empires. Now with only one empire left and its decline in sight, my generalization is even truer. Marx was only half-right. As early as 1848 (when he and Engels issued *The Communist Manifesto*) he had realized that capitalism would grow to become truly global, but he did not realize that nation-states would also grow to fill the globe.

Capitalism has seen two high-points in the North of the world. The first was the Second Industrial Revolution (discussed in Volume 3, chapter 3) when new corporations pioneered a plethora of new technologies generating much higher productivity. The second was the period after World War II (discussed in Chapters 2 and 6), when reformed capitalism generated mass demand and prosperity for its citizenry. Neither of these golden ages was a purely capitalist development. The first one owed much to the development of science and technology, the second one might not have even occurred without World War II.

Much of the South of the world caught up with the first phase from the 1950s, and some of it is now entering the second phase. But in the North, and especially in the Anglophone countries, a crisis-point has been reached, in which the short-sighted greed of the capitalist class, the crassness of contemporary conservatism and neoliberalism, and the decline of the labor movement combine to put in question the ability of capitalism to continue maintaining a mass demand-based economy benefiting all its citizens, or to create the regulatory reform needed to solve its current finance-centered crises. The high-point of capitalism may have passed in the North. It seems healthier at the moment across large swathes of the South, though in more statist guises. So while it may seem plausible to choose the development of capitalism as the key structural process of the long twentieth century, this has not been a process autonomous from the other sources of social power, especially political power, and it might not reproduce itself forever.

Looking back on the period covered by this book should induce some contentment. By and large it has been a good period for the human race. Though I have often criticized American foreign policy, lamented the rise of neoliberalism, worried about the future of democracy, and commiserated with Russian sorrows, these difficulties are far outweighed by the really good news of the decline of war and the diffusion of better health and wealth to most of the people of the world. Westerners and Americans may lament the beginnings of their relative decline, but they continue to live well, while the rise of the Rest and the emergence of a more multicentric global capitalism and geopolitics are also surely good news.

No one can accurately predict the future of large-scale power structures. The most one can do is to give alternative scenarios of what might happen given different conditions, and in some cases to arrange them in order of probability, as I did in the cases of climate change and the future of capitalism. There are possible dark clouds on the horizon. All good cheer might be overwhelmed by the two great looming threats to contemporary society: nuclear war and climate change. It remains unknowable how humans will react to these planet-threatening crises. Assuming some rationality by political leaders, which they have indeed shown so far, nuclear war might be avoided. Climate change is more problematic. On the one hand pressure from new social movements might lead to an international collectivism restraining states, capitalists, and consumers from destroying the planet. If not, and climate change became insupportable, civilization might be overwhelmed by wars, massive refugee flows, chaos, and new extremist ideologies. There is no end of history, no ultimate primacy, no necessary continued progress, for the unintended consequences of human action constantly create new interstitial problems, plural outcomes are always possible, and human beings have the capacity to choose well or badly, for good or ill, as we have seen repeatedly in this volume.

Bibliography

Aaronson, Susan 2001 *Taking Trade to the Streets: The Lost History of Public Efforts to Shape Globalization*. Ann Arbor: University of Michigan Press.

1996 *Trade and the American Dream: A Social History of Postwar Trade Policy*. Lexington: University Press of Kentucky.

Abdelal, Rawi 2007 *Capital Rules: The Construction of Global Finance*. Cambridge, MA: Harvard University Press.

Abdelal, Rawi & John G. Ruggie 2009 "The Principles of Embedded Liberalism: Social Legitimacy and Global Capitalism." In David Moss & John Cisternino (eds.), *New Perspectives on Regulation*, pp. 151–62. Cambridge, MA: The Tobin Project.

Abramowitz, Alan 2010 *The Disappearing Center: Engaged Citizens, Polarization, and American Democracy*. New Haven, CT: Yale University Press.

Abramowitz, Moses 1979 "Rapid Growth Potential and Its Realization: The Experience of Capitalist Economies," in Edmund Malinvaid (ed.), *Economic Growth and Resources*, Vol. I, pp. 1–30. New York: St. Martin's Press.

Acemoglu, Daron, Johnson, Simon, & Robinson, James 2001 "The Colonial Origins of Comparative Development." *American Economic Review*, 91, 1369–401.

Ahn, Jong-chul 2003 "Siming'gun: The Citizens' Army during the Kwangju Uprising." In Gi-Wook Shin and Kyung Moon Hwang (eds.), *Contentious Kwangju: The May 18 Uprising in Korea's Past and Present*. Lanham, Md.: Rowman & Littlefield.

Alam, Shahid 2000 *Poverty from the Wealth of Nations: Integration and Polarization in the Global Economy since 1760*. Basingstoke: Palgrave.

Albright, Madeleine (with Bill Woodward) 2003 *Madam Secretary*. New York: Miramax Books.

Albrow, Martin 1996 *The Global Age: State and Society Beyond Modernity*. Stanford, CA: Stanford University Press.

Aldcroft, David 2001 *The European Economy 1914–2000*. 4th ed. London: Routledge.

2002 "Currency Stabilisation in the 1920s: Success or Failure?" *Economic Issues*, 7, Part 2.

Alesina, Alberto & Drazen A. 1991 "Why Are Stabilisations Delayed?" *American Economic Review*, 81, 1170–88.

Alexander, Herbert 1980 Financing Politics: Money, Elections and Political Reform. 2nd ed. Washington, DC: Congressional Quarterly.

Alic, John 2007 *Trillions For Military Technology: How The Pentagon Innovates* And Why It Costs So Much. New York: Palgrave Macmillan.

Allen, James & Lyle Scruggs 2004 "Political Partisanship and Welfare State Reform in Advanced Industrial Societies," *American Journal of Political Science*, 48, 496–512.

Allen, Robert 2004 *Farm to Factory. A Reinterpretation of the Soviet Industrial Revolution*. Princeton, NJ: Princeton University Press.

Amenta, Edwin 1998 *Bold Relief: Institutional Politics and the Origins of Modern American Social Policy*. Princeton, NJ: Princeton University Press.

Amenta, Edwin & Theda Skocpol 1988. "Redefining the New Deal: World War II and the Development of Social Provision in the US." In Margaret Weir, Ann Shola Orloff, & Theda Skocpol (eds.), *The Politics of Social Policy in the United States*. Princeton, NJ: Princeton University Press.

Amsden, Alice 2001 *The Rise of "the Rest": Challenges to the West from Late-industrializing Economies*. New York: Oxford University Press.

Anderson, Perry 2010 "Two Revolutions," *New Left Review*, January–February, 59–96.

Andreas, Joel 2008 "Colours of the PRC," *New Left Review*, No. 54.

    2009 *Rise of the Red Engineers: The Cultural Revolution and the Origins of China's New Class*. Stanford, CA: Stanford University Press.

    2010 "A Shanghai Model? One Capitalism with Chinese Characteristics," *New Left Review*, No. 65.

Andrew, Christopher & Vasili Mitrokhin 1999 *The Sword and the Shield: The Mitrokhin Archive and the Secret History of the KGB*. New York: Basic Books.

Andrew, John III 1998 *Lyndon Johnson and the Great Society*. Chicago: Ivan R. Dee. Los Angeles: University of California Press.

Angresano, James 2011 *French Welfare State Reforms: Idealism versus Swedish, New Zealand and Dutch Pragmatism*. London: Anthem.

Appadurai, Arjun 1990 "Disjuncture and Difference in the Global Culture Economy." *Theory, Culture, and Society*. 7, 295–310

Arbatov, Georgi 2001 "Origin and Consequences of 'Shock Therapy.'" In Lawrence Klein & Marshall Pomer (eds.), *The New Russia: Transition Gone Awry*. Stanford, CA: Stanford University.

Arjomand, Said Amir 1988 *The Turban for the Crown: The Islamic Revolution in Iran*. Oxford: Oxford University Press.

Armony, Ariel 1997 *Argentina, the United States and the Anti-Communist Crusade in Central America, 1977–1984*. Athens: Ohio University Center for International Studies.

Armstrong, Charles. 2003 *The North Korean Revolution, 1945–1950*. Ithaca, NY; Cornell University Press.

Arnson, Cynthia & William Zartman (eds.) 2005 *Rethinking the Economics of War: The Intersection of Need, Creed, and Greed*. Baltimore: Johns Hopkins Press.

Aron, Leon 2009 "The Merging of Power and Property," *Journal of Democracy*, 20, 66–8.

Arrighi, Giovanni & Beverly Silver 1999 *Chaos and Governance in the Modern World System*. Minneapolis: University of Minnesota Press.

Arrighi, Giovanni 1994 *The Long Twentieth Century*. London: Verso.

    2007 *Adam Smith in Beijing: Lineages of the 21st Century*. London: Verso.

Aslund 2002 *Building Capitalism. The Transformation of the Former Soviet Bloc*. Cambridge: Cambridge University Press.

    2007 *How Capitalism Was Built: The Transformation of Central and Eastern Europe, Russia, and Central Asia*. Cambridge: Cambridge University Press.

Asselin, Pierre 2002 *A Bitter Peace: Washington, Hanoi, and the Making of the Paris Agreement*. Chapel Hill: University of North Carolina Press.

Atkins, Pope & Larman Wilson. 1998 *The Dominican Republic and the United States: From Imperialism to Transnationalism*. Athens: University of Georgia Press.

Atkinson, Anthony & Thomas Piketty, 2007 *Top Incomes over the Twentieth Century*. Oxford: Oxford University Press

Atkinson, Anthony et al. 2009 "Top Incomes in the Long Run of History," NBER Working Paper No. 15408.

Austin, Gareth 2004 "Markets with, without, and in Spite of States: West Africa in the Pre-Colonial Nineteenth Century, *LSE Working Papers of the Global Economic History Network*, No. 03/04.

Azimi, Fakhreddin 2008 *The Quest for Democracy in Iran: A Century of Struggle against Authoritarian Rule*. Cambridge, MA: Harvard University Press.

Bacevich, Andrew 2002 *American Empire: The Realities and Consequences of U.S. Diplomacy*. Cambridge, MA: Harvard University Press

Bairoch, Paul 1982 "International Industrialization Levels from 1750 to 1980," *Journal of European Economic History*, Vol 11.

Baldwin, Peter 1990 *The Politics of Social Solidarity: Class Bases of the European Welfare State, 1875–1975*. Cambridge: Cambridge University Press.

Barber, William 1985 *From New Era to New Deal: Herbert Hoover, the Economists, and American Economic Policy, 1921–1933*. New York: Cambridge University Press.

Barnes, William & Nils Gilman 2011 "Green Social Democracy or Barbarism: Climate Change and the End of High Modernism." In Craig Calhoun and Georgi Derluguian (eds.), *The Deepening Crisis: Governance Challenges after Neoliberalism*. New York: Social Science Research Council.

Bartels, Larry 2008 *Unequal Democracy: The Political Economy of the New Gilded Age*. Princeton, NJ: Princeton University Press.

Bass, Warren 2003 *Support Any Friend: Kennedy's Middle East and the Making of the U.S.-Israel Alliance*. New York: Oxford University Press.

Baumann, Zygmunt 1998 *Globalization: The Human Consequences*. New York: Columbia University Press
2000 *Liquid Modernity*. Cambridge: Polity.

Bayly, Christopher & Tim Harper 2004 *Forgotten Armies: The Fall of British Asia, 1941–1945*. Cambridge, MA: Bellknap Press.
2007 *Forgotten Wars: Freedom and Revolution in Southeast Asia*. Cambridge, MA: Harvard University Press.

Beck, Ulrich 1992 *Risk Society, Towards a New Modernity*. London: Sage.
2001 *What Is Globalization?* Cambridge: Polity Press.

Beissinger, Mark 2002 *Nationalist Mobilization and the Collapse of the Soviet Union*. Cambridge: Cambridge University Press.

Belknap, Michael 1995 *Federal Law and Southern Order: Racial Violence and Constitutional Conflict in the Post-Brown South*. Athens: University of Georgia Press, 2nd edition.

Bell, Daniel 1960 *The End of Ideology: On the Exhaustion of Political Ideas in the Fifties*. Glencoe, IL: Free Press.

Bell, Jonathan 2004 *The Liberal State on Trial: The Cold War and American Politics in the Truman Years*. New York: Columbia University Press.

Ben-Zvi, Abraham 1998 *Decade of Transition: Eisenhower, Kennedy, and the Origins of the American-Israeli Alliance*. New York: Columbia University Press.

Benford, Robert & David Snow 2000 "Framing Processes and Social Movements: An Overview and Assessment." *Annual Review of Sociology* 26, 611–39.

Bergen, Peter 2011 *The Longest War: The Enduring Conflict between America and Al-Qaeda*. New York: Free Press.

Berman, Larry 2001 *No Peace, No Honor: Nixon, Kissinger, and Betrayal in Vietnam*. New York: Free Press.

Berman, William 1998 *America's Right Turn: From Nixon to Bush*. 2nd ed. Baltimore: Johns Hopkins University Press.

Bernhard, Michael et al. 2004 "The Legacy of Western Overseas Colonialism on Democratic Survival," *International Studies Quarterly*, 48, 225–50.

Beschloss, Michael 2002 *The Conqueror: Roosevelt, Truman and the Destruction of Hitler's Germany, 1941–1945*. New York: Simon & Schuster.

Bethell, Leslie 1991 "From the Second World War to the Cold War: 1944–1954." In Lowenthal, Abraham F. (ed.), *Exporting Democracy: The United States and Latin America: Themes and Issues*, pp. 41–70. Baltimore: Johns Hopkins University Press.

Bethell, Leslie & Ian Roxborough 1988 "Latin America between the Second World War and the Cold War," *Journal of Latin American Studies*, 20, 167–89.

Betsill, Michele 2008a "Environmental NGOs and the Kyoto Protocol Negotiations: 1995 to 1997." In Betsill & Elisabeth Corell (eds.), *NGO Diplomacy*. Cambridge, MA: The MIT Press.

Bewley-Taylor, Dave et al. 2009 "The Incarceration of Drug Offenders: an Overview," *The Beckley Foundation*, Report 16. Kings College, University of London.

Biersteker, T. 1992 "The 'Triumph' of Neoclassical Economics in the Developing World: Policy Convergence and the Bases of Government in the International Economic Order." In James Rosenau & E.-O. Czempiel, *Governance without Government: Order and Change in World Politics*. Cambridge: Cambridge University Press.

Bill, James 1988 *The Eagle and the Lion: The Tragedy of American-Iranian Relations*. New Haven, CT: Yale University Press.

Block, Fred & Matthew Keller (eds.) 2011 *State of Innovation: The U.S. Government's Role in Technology Development*. Boulder, CO: Paradigm.

Block, Fred 1977 *The Origins of International Economic Disorder*. Berkeley & Los Angeles: University of California Press.

1987 *Revising State Theory: Essays in Politics and Postindustrialism*. Philadelphia: Temple University Press.

2008 "Swimming against the Current: The Rise of a Hidden Developmental State in the United States," *Politics & Society*, 36, 169–206.

Bloom, Jack 1987 *Class, Race and the Civil Rights Movement*. Bloomington: Indiana University Press.

Blustein, Paul 2001 *The Chastening: Inside the Crisis That Rocked the Global Financial System and Humbled the IMF*. New York: Public Affairs.

Bobbitt, Philip 2001 *The Shield of Achilles: War, Peace and the Course of History*. New York: Knopf.

Boli, John & George Thomas 1997 "World Culture in the World Polity," *American Sociological Review* 62(2): 171–90.

Bombach, G. 1985 *Postwar Economic Growth Revisited*. Amsterdam: North-Holland.

Bonds, John Bledsoe 2002 *Bipartisan Strategy: Selling the Marshall Plan*. Westport, CT: Praeger.

Boot, Max 2002 *The Savage Wars of Peace: Small Wars and the Rise of American Power*. New York: Basic Books.

Boswell, Terry 2004 "American World Empire or Declining Hegemony," *Journal of World Systems Research*, Vol.10

Boyer, Robert 1990 *The Regulation School: A Critical Introduction*. New York: Columbia University Press.

Brady, David 2009 *Rich Democracies, Poor People: How Politics Explain Poverty*. Oxford: Oxford University Press.

Bradley, David & John Stephens 2007 "Employment Performance in OECD Countries: A Test of Neo-Liberal and Institutionalist Hypotheses," *Comparative Political Studies*, Vol. 40.

Bradley, David et al. 2003 "Distribution and Redistribution in Postindustrial Democracies," *World Politics*, 55, 193–228.

Bradley, Mark 2000 *Imagining Vietnam and America: The Making of Postcolonial Vietnam, 1919–1950*. Chapel Hill: University of North Carolina Press.

Bramall, Chris 2000 *Sources of Chinese Economic Growth, 1978–1996*. Oxford: Oxford University Press.

Brandolini, Andrea 2010 "Political Economy and the Mechanics of Politics," *Politics and Society*, 38, 212–26.

Brands, Hal 2010 *Latin America's Cold War*. Cambridge, MA: Harvard University Press.

Brauer, Carl 1982 "Kennedy, Johnson, and the War on Poverty," *The Journal of American History*, 69, 98–119.

Bremer, Ambassador L. Paul III 2006 *My Year in Iraq: The Struggle to Build a Future of Hope*. New York: Simon & Schuster.

Brenner, Robert 1998 "The Economics of Global Turbulence," New Left Review, No. 229.

2002 *The Boom and the Bubble: The U.S. in the World Economy*. London: Verso.

2006 "What Is, and What Is Not, Imperialism," *Historical Materialism*, 14, 79–105.

Brinkley, Alan 1996 *New Deal Liberalism in Recession and War*. New York, Vintage.

Bromley, Patricia et al. 2010 "The Worldwide Spread of Environmental Discourse in Social Science Textbooks, 1970–2008: Cross-National Patterns and Hierarchical Linear Models," unpublished paper School of Education/ Department of Sociology, Stanford University.

Bromley, Simon 1997 "Middle East Exceptionalism – Myth or Reality." In David Potter et al. (eds.), *Democratization*. Cambridge: Polity Press.

Brooks, Clem & Jeff Manza 1997 "The Sociological and Ideological Bases of Middle-Class Political Realignment in the United States, 1972–1992," *American Sociological Review*, 62, 191–208.

2006 "Social Policy Responsiveness in Developed Democracies," *American Sociological Review*, 71, 474–94.

Brown, Archibald 2007 *Seven Years That Changed the World: Perestroika in Perspective*. Oxford: Oxford University Press.

2009 *The Rise and Fall of Communism*, 2009. New York: HarperCollins.

Brown, Michael 1999 *Race, Money and the American Welfare State*. Ithaca, NY: Cornell University Press.

Brüggemeier, Franz-Josef, Mark Cioc, & Thomas Zeller (eds.) 2005 *How Green Were the Nazis? Nature, Environment and Nation in the Third Reich*. Athens: Ohio University Press.

Brzezinski, Zbigniew 2012 *Strategic Vision: America and the Crisis of Global Power*. New York: Basic Books.

Bucheli, Marcelo 2005 *Bananas and Business: The United Fruit Company in Colombia, 1899–2000*. New York: New York University Press.

Bulmer-Thomas, Victor 1994 *The Economic History of Latin America Since Independence*. Cambridge: Cambridge University Press.

Bunce, Valerie 1999 *Subversive Institutions: The Design and the Destruction of Socialism and the State*. Cambridge: Cambridge University Press.

Burn, Gary 2006 *The Re-Emergence of Global Finance*. London: Palgrave Macmillan.

Burnham, Gilbert et al. 2006 "Mortality after the 2003 Invasion of Iraq: a Cross-Sectional Cluster Sample Survey" *The Lancet*, October 11.

Burnham, Peter 2001 "New Labour and the Politics of Depoliticisation," *British Journal of Politics and International Relations*, 3, 127–49.

Burns, James M. 2009 *Packing the Court: The Rise of Judicial Power and the Coming Crisis of the Supreme Court*. New York: Penguin Press.

Busch, Andrew 2005 *Reagan's Victory: The Presidential Election of 1980 and the Rise of the Right*. Lawrence: University Press of Kansas.

Bush, George W. 2010 *Decision Points*. New York: Crown.

Calder, Lendol 1999 *Financing the American Dream: A Cultural History of Consumer Credit*. Princeton, NJ: Princeton University Press.

Cameron, David R. 2007 "Post-Communist Democracy: The Impact of the European Union," *Post-Soviet Affairs*, 23, 185–217

Campbell, Ballard 1995 *The Growth of American Government: Governance from the Cleveland Era to the Present*. Bloomington: Indiana University Press.

Cardenas, Enrique et al. (eds.) 2000 *An Economic History of Twentieth-Century Latin America*. Vol. III, *Industrialization and the State in Latin America: The Postwar Years*. New York: Palgrave.

Carrothers, Thomas 1991 "The Reagan Years: The 1980s." In Abraham Lowenthal (ed.), *Exporting Democracy: The United States and Latin America*. Baltimore: Johns Hopkins University Press.

Castells, Manuel 1997 *The Power of Identity*. Vol. 2, *The Information Age: Economy, Society and Culture*. Oxford: Blackwell.

Castles, F. G. & I. F. Shirley 1996 "Labour and Social Policy: Gravediggers or Refurbishers of the Welfare State." In F. G. Castles et al. (eds), *The Great Experiment*, Allen and Unwin, Sydney, pp. 88–106.

Castles, Francis 1985 *The Working Class and Welfare in Australia and New Zealand*. Sydney: Allen & Unwin.

  1998 *Comparative Public Policy: Patterns of Post-War Transformation*. Cheltenham, UK: Edward Elgar.

Castles, Francis & Deborah Mitchell 1993 "Worlds of Welfare and Families of Nations." In Castles, (ed.), *Families of Nations: Patterns of Public Policy in Western Democracies*. Hanover, NH: Dartmouth University Press.

Castles, Frank & Herbert Obinger 2008 "Worlds, Families, Regimes: Country Clusters in European and OECD Area Public Policy," *West European Politics*, 31, 321–44.

Centeno, Miguel 2002 *Blood and Debt: War and the Nation-State in Latin America*. College Park: Pennsylvania State University Press.

Cerami, Alfio & Pieter Vanhuysse 2009 *Post-Communist Welfare Pathways*. New York: Palgrave Macmillan.

Cesarano, Filippo 2006 *Monetary Theory and Bretton Woods: The Construction of an International Monetary Order*. Cambridge: Cambridge University Press.

Chai, Joseph & Kartik Roy 2006 *Economic Reform in China and India*. Northampton, MA: Edward Elgar.

Chan, Anita 2001 *China's Workers under Assault: The Exploitation of Labor in a Globalizing Economy*. Armonk, NJ: M. E. Sharpe.

Chang, Ha-Joon 2003 *Globalisation, Economic Development and the Role of the State*. London: Zed Books.

  2009 *23 Things They Don't Tell You about Capitalism*. London: Allen Lane.

Chase-Dunn, Christopher et al. 2000 "Trade Globalization since 1795: Waves of Integration in the World System," *American Sociological Review*, Vol. 65.

Chase-Dunn, Christopher & Andrew Jorgenson, 2003 "Interaction Networks and Structural Globalization: A Comparative World-Systems Perspective," *Society in Transition* 34, 206–20.

Chen Jian 2001 *Mao's China and the Cold War*. Chapel Hill: University of North Carolina Press.

Chen, Chih-jou 2003 *Transforming Rural China: How Local Institutions Shape Property Rights in China*. London: Routledge.

Chen, Jian & Yang Kuisong 1998 "Chinese politics and the collapse of the Sino-Soviet alliance." In Odd Westad (ed.), *Brothers in Arms: The Rise and Fall of the Sino-Soviet Alliance, 1945–1963*. Washington, DC: Woodrow Wilson Center Press.

Chernyaev, Anatoly 2000 *My Six Years with Gorbachev*. University Park: Pennsylvania State University Press.

Chirot, Daniel 1986 *Social Change in the Modern Era*. San Diego, CA: Harcourt Brace Jovanovich.

Chollet, Derek & James Goldgeier 2008 *America between the Wars: From 11/9 to 9/11: The Misunderstood Years between the Fall of the Berlin Wall and the Start of the War on Terror*. New York: Public Affairs.

Clark, Daniel 1997 *Like Night and Day: Unionization in a Southern Mill Town*. Chapel Hill: University of North Carolina Press.

Clark, General Wesley 2007 *A Time to Lead: For Duty, Honor and Country*. New York: Palgrave MacMillan.

Clarke, Peter 2008 *The Last Thousand Days of the British Empire: Churchill, Roosevelt, and the Birth of the Pax Americana*. London: Bloomsbury Press.

Clarke, Richard 2004 *Against All Enemies*. New York: Simon & Schuster.

Cline, William 2004 *Trade Policy and Global Poverty*. Washington, DC: Institute for International Economics.

Coates, David 2010 "Separating Sense from Nonsense in the U.S. Debate on the Financial Meltdown," *Political Studies Review*, 8, 15–26.

Coatsworth, John 1994 *Central America and the United States: The Clients and the Colossus*. New York: Twayne.

Cohen, Lizabeth 1990 *Making a New Deal: Industrial Workers in Chicago 1919–1939*. Cambridge: Cambridge University Press.

2003 *A Consumers' Republic: The Politics of Mass Consumption in Postwar America*. New York: Alfred A. Knopf.

Cohen, Stephen 2001 *Failed Crusade: America and the Tragedy of Post-Communist Russia*. New York: Norton.

Cohen, Warren 2005 *America's Failing Empire: U.S. Foreign Relations since the Cold War*. Oxford: Blackwell.

Collier, Paul 2000 "Doing Well out of War." In M. Berdahl & D. Malone (eds.), *Greed and Grievance: Economic Agendas in Civil Wars*. Boulder, CO: Lynne Rienner.

2003 "Breaking the Conflict Trap: Civil War and Developmental Policy," World Bank Policy Research Report, Washington, DC: World Bank.

Collins, Randall 2012 "Technological Displacement of Middle-Class Work and the Long-Term Crisis of Capitalism: No More Escapes." In Georgi Derleugian (ed.) *Does Capitalism Have a Future? A Sociological Polemic*. New Haven, CT.: Yale university Press.

Connor, Walter 1991 *The Accidental Proletariat: Workers, Politics, and Crisis in Gorbachev's Russia*. Princeton, NJ: Princeton University Press.

Cooper, Frederick 1996 "*Decolonization and African Society: The Labor Question in French and British Africa*," African Studies Series. Cambridge: Cambridge University Press.

2002 *Africa since 1940: The Past of the Present*. Cambridge: Cambridge University Press.

Cowie, Jefferson 2010 *Stayin' Alive: The 1970s and the Last Days of the Working Class*. New York: New Press,

Cox, Ronald 1994 *Power and Profits: U.S. Policy in Central America*. Lexington: University of Kentucky Press.

Coyne, Christopher 2007 *After War: The Political Economy of Exporting Democracy*. Stanford, CA: Stanford University Press.

Creveld, Martin van 2008 *The Changing Face of War*. New York: Ballantine Books.

Cronin, James 1996 *The World the Cold War Made*. New York: Routledge.

2001 "The Marshall Plan and Cold War Political Discourse." In Martin Schain (ed.), *The Marshall Plan: Fifty Years After*. New York: Palgrave.

Crouch, Colin 2005 *Capitalist Diversity and Change: Recombinant Governance and Institutional Entrepreneurs*. Oxford, Oxford University Press.

2009 "Privatised Keynesianism: An Unacknowledged Policy Regime," *British Journal of Politics and International Relations*, 11, 382–99.

2011 *The Strange Non-Death of Neoliberalism*. Cambridge, UK: Polity.

Cullather, Nick 1999 *Secret History: The CIA's Classified Account of Its Operations in Guatemala, 1952–1954*. Stanford, CA: Stanford University Press.

Cumings, Bruce 1981 & 1990 *The Origins of the Korean War*. Vol. 1, *Liberation and the Emergence of Separate Regimes, 1945–1947*. Vol. 2, *The Roaring of the Cataract, 1947–1950*. Princeton, N.J.: Princeton University Press.

2004 *North Korea: Another Country*. New Press.

Cusack, Thomas & Susanne Fuchs 2002 "Ideology, Institutions and Public Spending," *Discussion Paper of the Research Area Markets and Political Economy*, Wissenschaftszentrum Berlin.

Daalder, Ivo & James Lindsay 2003 *America Unbound: The Bush Revolution in Foreign Policy*. Washington, DC: Brookings Institution Press.

Dallek, Robert 1998 *Flawed Giant: Lyndon Johnson and His Times, 1961–1963*, New York: Oxford University Press.

2003 *John F. Kennedy. An Unfinished Life, 1917–1963*. London: Penguin.

Davis, Christopher 2001 "The Health Sector: Illness, Medical Care, and Mortality." In Brigitte Granville & Peter Oppenheimer (eds.), *Russia's Post-Communist Economy*. Oxford: Oxford University Press.

Davis, Gerald 2009 *Managed by the Markets: How Finance Re-Shaped America*. Oxford: Oxford University Press.

Deng Xiaoping 1984 *Selected Works (1975–1982)*. Beijing: Foreign Language Press.

Development. Oxford: Blackwell.

Dew-Becker & Robert Gordon 2005 "Where Did the Productivity Growth Go? Inflation Dynamics and the Distribution of Income," *National Bureau of Economic Research*, Working Paper No. 11842.

Diamond, Larry 2005 *Squandered Victory: The American Occupation and the Bungled Effort to Bring Democracy to Iraq*. New York: Times Books/ Henry Holt.

Dickson, Bruce 2003 *Red Capitalists in China: The Party, Private Entrepreneurs, and Prospects for Political Change*. Cambridge: Cambridge University Press.

Dittmer, John 1994 *Local People: The Struggle for Civil Rights in Mississippi*. Urbana: University of Illinois Press.

Dodge, Toby 2003. *Inventing Iraq: The Failure of Nation-Building and a History Denied*. New York: Columbia University Press.

Doherty, Brian 2002 *Ideas and Action in the Green Movement*. London: Routledge.

Domhoff, William 1996 *State Autonomy or Class Dominance? Case Studies in Policy Making in America*. New York: Aldine de Gruyter.

1990. *The Power Elite and the State. How Policy Is Made in America.* New York: A. de Gruyter.

Forthcoming. *The Committee for Economic Development.* unpublished ms.

Dominguez, Jorge 1999 "U.S.-Latin American Relations during the Cold War and Its Aftermath." In Victor Bulmer-Thomas & James Dunkerley (eds.), *The United States and Latin America: The New Agenda.* Cambridge, MA: Harvard University Press.

Dooley, Michael et al. 2003 "An Essay on the Revived Bretton Woods System," NBER Working Paper No. 9971.

Doreenspleet, Renske 2000 "Reassessing the Three Waves of Democratization," *World Politics* 52, 384–406.

Douglas, Roy 2002 *Liquidation of Empire: The Decline of the British Empire.* Basingstoke, UK: Palgrave Macmillan.

Dower, John 1999 *Embracing Defeat: Japan in the Wake of World War II.* New York: Norton.

Drahos, Peter & John Braithwaite 2002 *Information Feudalism: Who Owns the Knowledge Economy?* New York: New Press.

Dreyfus, Michel et al. 2006 *Se protéger, être protégé. Une histoire des Assurances sociales en France.* Rennes: Presses universitaires de Rennes.

Drukker, J. W. 2006 *The Revolution that Bit Its Own Tail: How Economic History Changed our Ideas on Economic Growth.* Amsterdam: Aksant.

Dudziak, Mary 2000 *Cold War Civil Rights: Race and the Image of American Democracy.* Princeton, NJ: Princeton University Press.

Dunlop John 2003 "The August Coup and Its Impact on Soviet Politics," *Journal of Cold War Studies*, Vol 5.

Ebbinghaus, Bernhard & Jelle Visser 1999 "When Institutions Matter. Union Growth and Decline in Western Europe, 1950–1995," *European Sociological Review*, 15, 135–58.

Ebbinghaus, Bernhard & Mareike Gronwald 2009 "The Changing Public-Private Pension Mix in Europe: from Path-Dependence to Path Departure," draft paper, MZED, University of Mannheim.

Eckes, Alfred 1995 *Opening America's Market: U.S. Foreign Trade Policy since 1776.* Chapel Hill: University of North Carolina Press.

Edsall, Thomas 1984 *The New Politics of Inequality.* New York: Norton.

Eichengreen, Barry (ed.) 1995 *Europe's Postwar Recovery.* Cambridge: Cambridge University Press.

1996 *Globalizing Capital: A History of the International Monetary System.* Princeton, NJ: Princeton University Press.

2009 "The Dollar Dilemma: The World's Top Currency Faces Competition," *Foreign Affairs*, September/October.

Eisenstadt, Shmuel 1982 "The Axial Age: The Emergence of Transcendental Visions and the Rise of Clerics," *European Journal of Sociology*, 23, 294–314.

Elliott, David 2003 The Vietnamese War: Revolution and Social Change in the Mekong Delta, 1930–1975, 2 vols. Armonk, NY: M. E. Sharpe.

Ellman, Michael & Kontorovich, Vladimir 1998 *The Destruction of the Soviet Economic System: An Insiders' History.* London: M. E. Sharpe.

Ensalaco, Mark 2008 *Middle Eastern Terrorism: From Black September to September 11.* Philadelphia: University of Pennsylvania Press.

Environmental Law Institute 2009 "Estimating U.S. Government Subsidies to Energy Sources: 2002–2008."

Epstein, Philip et al. 2000 "Distribution Dynamics: Stratification, Polarization and Convergence Among OECD Economies, 1870–1992," *London School of Economics, Department of Economic History Working Papers*, No. 58/00.

Eriksson et al. 2003 "Armed Conflict 1989–2002," *Journal of Peace Research*, 40, 593–607.

Eskew, Glenn T. 1997 *But for Birmingham: The Local and National Movements in the Civil Rights Struggle*. Chapel Hill: University of North Carolina Press.

Esping-Andersen, Gosta 1990 *The Three Worlds of Welfare Capitalism*. Cambridge: Cambridge University Press.

1999 *Social Foundations of Postindustrial Economies*. Oxford: Oxford University Press.

2011 "Families and the Revolution in Women's Role," three unpublished lectures available at the author's web-site.

Estévez-Abe, Margarita, Torben Iversen, & David Soskice 2001 "Social Protection and the Formation of Skills: A Reinterpretation of the Welfare State." In Peter Hall & David Soskice (eds.), *Varieties of Capitalism: The Institutional Foundations of Comparative Advantage*, pp. 145–83. New York: Oxford University Press.

European Bank for Reconstruction and Development 2009 Transition Report.

European Environment Agency 2009 Greenhouse Gas Emission Trends and Projections in Europe: Tracking Progress Towards Kyoto Targets, EEA Report No. 9/2009.

Evans, Peter & William Sewell, Jr. 2011 "The Neoliberal Era: Ideology, Policy, and Social Effects," unpublished paper.

Ewell Judith 1996 *Venezuela and the United States: From Monroe's Hemisphere to Petroleum's Empire*. Athens and London: University of Georgia Press.

Eyal, Gil, Ivan Szelenyi, & Eleanor Townsley 1998 *Making Capitalism without Capitalists*. London: Verso.

Fairclough, Adam 1995 *Race and Democracy: The Civil Rights Struggle in Louisiana, 1915–1972*. Athens: University of Georgia Press.

Fan, Joseph et al. 2011 "Capitalizing China," *NBER Working Paper* no. 17687, December.

Federico, Giovanni 2005 *Feeding the World: An Economic History of Agriculture, 1800–2000*. Princeton, NJ: Princeton University Press.

Ferguson, Charles 2008 *No End in Sight: Iraq's Descent into Chaos*. New York: Public Affairs.

Ferrarini, Guido et al. 2003 "Executive Remuneration in the EU: Comparative Law and Practice," EGGI Working Paper Series in Law, No. 32, *European Corporate Governance Institute*.

Filene, Peter 2001 "Cold War Culture Doesn't Say It All." In Peter J. Kuznick and James Gilbert (eds.), *Rethinking Cold War Culture*. Washington, DC: Smithsonian Institution Press.

Fineman, Daniel 1997 *A Special Relationship: The United States and Military Government in Thailand 1947–1958*. Honolulu: University of Hawai'i Press.

Fiorina, Morris & Samuel Abrams 2009 *Disconnect: The Breakdown of Representation in American Politics*. Norman: Oklahoma University Press.

Fischer, Beth 1997 *The Reagan Reversal: Foreign Policy and the End of the Cold War*. Columbia: University of Missouri Press.

Fischer, Claude & Michael Hout 2006 *Century of Difference: How America Changed in the Last One Hundred Years*. New York: Russell Sage Foundation.

Fischer, Fritz 1998 *Making Them like U.S.: Peace Corps Volunteers in the 1960s*. Washington, DC: Smithsonian Institute Press.

Fitch, Robert 2006 *Solidarity for Sale: How Corruption Destroyed the Labor Movement and Undermined America's Promise*. New York: Public Affairs.

Fligstein, Neil & Taekjin Shin 2007 "Shareholder Value and the Transformation of the U.S. Economy, 1984–2000," *Sociological Forum*, 22, 399–424.

2010 "Politics, the Reorganization of the Economy and Income Inequality, 1980–2009," *Politics and Society*, 38, 233–42.

Flora, Peter 1983 *State, Economy, and Society in Western Europe 1815–1975: A Data Handbook.* Vol. I, *The Growth of Mass Democracies and Welfare States.* London: Macmillan.

Flora, Peter & Heidenheimer, Arnold 1981 *The Development of Welfare States in Europe and America.* New Brunswick, NJ: Transaction Books.

Foran, John 2005 *Taking Power: On the Origins of Third World Revolutions.* Cambridge: Cambridge University Press.

Forsberg, Aaron 2000 *America and the Japanese Miracle: The Cold War Context of Japan's Postwar Economic Revival, 1950–1960.* Chapel Hill: University of North Carolina Press.

Fourcade-Gourinchas, Marion & Babb, Sarah "The Rebirth of the Liberal Creed: Paths to Neoliberalism in Four Countries," *American Journal of Sociology*, 108, 533–79.

Fousek, John 2000 *American Nationalism and the Cultural Roots of the Cold War.* Chapel Hill: University of North Carolina Press.

Frank, David John. 1999 "The Social Bases of Environmental Treaty Ratification, 1900–1990." *Sociological Inquiry*, 69, 523–50.

Frank, David John, Bayliss J. Camp, & Steven A. Boutcher 2010 "Worldwide Trends in the Criminal Regulation of Sex, 1945 to 2005." *American Sociological Review* 75, 867–93.

Frank, Thomas 2004 *What's the Matter with Kansas? How Conservatives Won the Heart of America.* New York: Metropolitan Books.

Fraser, Steve 1989. "The 'Labor Question.'" In Fraser & Gary Gerstle (eds.), *The Rise and Fall of the New Deal Order*, pp. 55–84. Princeton, NJ: Princeton University Press.

Friedman, Edward et al. *1991 Chinese Village, Socialist State.* New Haven, CT: Yale University Press.

Friedman, Milton 1962 *Capitalism and Freedom.* Chicago: University of Chicago Press.

Frum, David & Perle, Richard 2003 *An End to Evil: How To Win the War on Terror.* New York: Random House.

Fukuyama, Francis 1992 *The End of History and the Last Man.* New York: Free Press.

2011 *The Origins of Political Order.* New York: Farrar, Straus & Giroux.

Gaddis, John 1972 *United States and the Origins of the Cold War, 1941–1947.* New York: Columbia University Press.

1982 *Strategies of Containment: A Critical Appraisal of Postwar American National Security Policy.* New York: Oxford University Press.

1997 *We Now Know: Rethinking the Cold War.* New York: Oxford University Press.

Gaiduk, Ilya 1996 *The Soviet Union and the Vietnam War.* Chicago: Ivan Dee.

Gamble, Andrew 2010 "The Political Consequences of the Crash," *Political Studies Review*, 8, 3–14

Gambone, Michael 1997 *Eisenhower, Somoza, and the Cold War in Nicaragua, 1953–1961.* Westport, CT: Praeger Publishers.

2001 *Capturing the Revolution: The United States, Central America, and Nicaragua, 1961–1972.* Westport, CT: Praeger.

Garrett, Geoffrey 1998 *Partisan Politics in the Global Economy*. New York: Cambridge University Press.

Gasiorowski, Mark & Malcolm Byrne (eds.) 2004 *Mohammad Mosaddeq and the 1953 Coup in Iran*. Syracuse, NY: Syracuse University Press.

Gelb, Leslie 2009 *Power Rules: How Common Sense Can Rescue American Foreign Policy*. New York: Harper.

Gemici, Kurtulus 2008 "Hot Money. Cold Money: Managing Global Capital in Emerging Economies." Ph.D. Dissertation, UCLA.

Gerges, Fawaz 2005 *The Far Enemy: Why Jihad Went Global*. New York: Cambridge University Press.

Giddens, Anthony 1990 *The Consequences of Modernity*. Cambridge: Polity.

Gilding, Paul 2011 *The Great Disruption: How the Climate Crisis Will Transform the Global Economy*. London: Bloomsbury.

Gilens, Martin 1999 *Why Americans Hate Welfare*. Chicago: University of Chicago Press.

Gill, Graeme 1994 *The Collapse of a Single-Party System: The Disintegration of the CPSU*. Cambridge: Cambridge University Press.

Gill, Lesley 2004 *The School of the Americas: Military Training and Political Violence in the Americas*. Durham, NC: Duke University Press.

Gilligan, Andrew 2009 "Iraq Report: Secret Papers Reveal Blunders and Concealment," *The Telegraph*, London, November 21.

Gimpel James & Kimberly Karnes 2006 "The Rural Side of the Urban-Rural Gap," *Political Science & Politics*, 9(3), 467–72.

Gittings, John 2005 *The Changing Face of China: From Mao to the Market*. New York: Oxford University Press.

Gleditsch, Kristian 2004 "A Revised List of Wars between and within Independent States, 1816–2002," *International Interactions*, 30, 231–62.

Gleijeses, Piero 1991 *Shattered Hope: The Guatemalan Revolution and the United States, 1944–1954*. Princeton, NJ: Princeton University Press.

Glenn, Evelyn Nakano 2002 *Unequal Freedom: How Race and Gender Shaped American Citizenship and Labor*. Cambridge, MA: Harvard University Press.

Goldfield, Michael 1987 *The Decline of Organized Labor in the United States*. Chicago: University of Chicago Press.

1997 *The Color of Politics: Race and the Mainsprings of American Politics*. New York: New Press.

Goldin, Claudia & Robert Margo. 1992 "The Great Compression: Wage Structure in the United States at Mid-Century," *Quarterly Journal of Economics* 107, 1–34.

Goldman, Marshall 1972 *The Spoils of Progress: Environmental Pollution in the Soviet Union*. Cambridge, MA: MIT Press.

Goldstone, Jack 2001 "Toward a Fourth Generation of Revolutionary Theory," *Annual Review of Political Science* 4, 139–87.

2004 "Its All about State Structure: New Findings on Revolutionary Origins from Global Data," *Homo Oeconomicus*, 21, 429–55.

2009 "Revolutions." In Todd Landman & Neil Robinson (eds.), *The Sage Handbook of Comparative Politics*, pp. 319–47. Los Angeles: Sage.

Goodell, Jeff 2010 "As the World Burns. How Big Oil and Big Coal Mounted One of the Most Aggressive Lobbying Campaigns in History to Block Progress on Global Warming," *Rolling Stone Online*, posted January 6.

Goodwin, Jeff 2001 *No Other Way Out: States and Revolutionary Movements, 1945–1991*. New York: Cambridge University Press.

Gorbachev, Mikhail 1995 *Memoirs*. New York: Doubleday.

Gordon, Colin 2003 *Dead on Arrival: The Politics of Health Care in Twentieth-Century America*. Princeton, NJ: Princeton University Press.

Gordon, Michael & Trainor, General Bernard 2006 *Cobra II: The Inside Story of the Invasion and Occupation of Iraq*. New York: Random House.

Gorlizki, Yoram & Oleg Khlevniuk 2004 *Cold Peace: Stalin and the Soviet Ruling Circle, 1945–1953*. Oxford: Oxford University Press.

Goto, Ken'ichi 2003 *Tensions of Empire: Japan and Southeast Asia in the Colonial and Postcolonial World*. Athens: Ohio University Press.

Gourinchas, Pierre Olivier, & Olivier Jeanne, 2007 "Capital Flows to Developing Countries: The Allocation Puzzle," *NBER Working Papers* No. 13602, National Bureau of Economic Research.

Gowan, Peter 1999 *The Global Gamble: Washington's Faustian Bid for World Domination*. London: Verso.

2004 "Contemporary Intra-Core Relations and World Systems Theory," *Journal of World-Systems Research*, Vol. 10.

Grandin, Greg 2004 *The Last Colonial Massacre: Latin America in the Cold War*. Chicago: University of Chicago Press.

Grant-Friedman, Andrea 2008 "Soviet Sociology, Perestroika, and the Politics of Social Inequality," Ph.D. Dissertation, UCLA.

Griffin, Keith 1991 "Foreign Aid after the Cold War," *Development and Change*, 22, 645–85.

Griffith, Barbara 1988 *The Crisis of American Labor: Operation Dixie and the Defeat of the CIO*. Philadelphia: Temple University Press.

Gross, James A. 1995 *Broken Promise: The Subversion of U.S. Labor Relations Policy, 1947–1994*. Philadelphia: Temple University Press.

Habermas, Juergen 1990 "What Does Socialism Mean Today? The Rectifying Revolution and the Need for New Thinking on the Left," *New Left Review*, 183: 3–21.

Hacker, Jacob & Paul Pierson *Winner-Take-All Politics*. New York: Simon & Schuster.

Haggard, Stephan & Robert Kaufman 2008 *Development, Democracy, and Welfare States: Latin America,. East Asia, and Eastern Europe*. Princeton, NJ: Princeton University Press.

Hahn, Peter 2004 *Caught in the Middle East: U.S. Policy towards the Arab-Israeli Conflict, 1945–1961*. Chapel Hill: University of North Carolina Press.

Haldane, Andrew 2012 "The Doom Loop," *London Review of Books*, 34, 21–2.

Hall, John A. 1995 "After the Vacuum: Post-Communism in the Light of Tocqueville." In Beverly Crawford (ed.), *Markets, States and Democracy: The Political Economy of Post-Communist Transformation*. Boulder, CO: Westview Press.

Hall, Michael 2000 *Sugar and Power in the Dominican Republic: Eisenhower, Kennedy, and the Trujillos*. Westport CT: Greenwood.

Hall, Peter & D. W. Gingerich 2003 Discussion Paper 04/5, Cologne, Germany, Max Planck Institute for the Study of Societies. Available at www.mpi-fg-koeln.mpg.de

Hall, Peter & David Soskice 2001 *Varieties of Capitalism: The Institutional Foundations of Comparative Advantage*. Oxford: Oxford University Press.

Halliday, Fred 1999 *Revolution and World Politics: The Rise and Fall of the Sixth Great Power*. London: MacMillan.

2010 "Third World Socialism: 1989 and After." In Lawson et al. (eds.), *The Global 1989: Continuity and Change in World Politics*. Cambridge: Cambridge University Press.

Hamm, Patrick, Lawrence King, & David Stucker 2012 "Mass Privatization, State Capacity, and Economic Growth in Post-Communist Countries, *American Sociological Review*, 77, 295–324.

Handler, Joel 2004 *Social Citizenship and Workfare in the United States and Western Europe: The Paradox of Inclusion*. New York: Cambridge University Press.

Hansen, James 2009 *Storms of My Grandchildren: The Truth about the Coming Climate Catastrophe and Our Last Chance to Save Humanity*. New York: Bloomsbury.

Hanson, Philip 2003a *The Rise and Fall of the Soviet Economy: An Economic History of the U.S.S.R. From 1945*. London: Pearson.

    2003b "The Russian Economic Recovery: Do Four Years of Growth Tell Us That the Fundamentals Have Changed?" *Europe-Asia Studies*, 55, 365–82.

Harding, Luke 2011 *Mafia State: How One Reporter Became An Enemy of the Brutal New Russia*. London: Guardian Books.

Hardt, Michael & Antonio Negri 2000 *Empire*. Cambridge, MA: Harvard University Press

Harrington, Michael 1962 *The Other America: Poverty in the United States*. New York: Macmillan.

Harrison, Graham 2005 "Economic Faith, Social Project and a Misreading of African Society: The Travails of Neoliberalism," *Third World Quarterly*, 26, 1303–20.

Harrison, Robert 1997 *State and Society in Twentieth Century America*. London: Longman.

Harvey, David 1989 *The Condition of Postmodernity*. London: Basil Blackwell
    2003 *The New Imperialism*. Oxford: Oxford University Press.
    2005 *A Brief History of Neoliberalism*. New York: Oxford University Press.

Hearden, Patrick 2002 *Architects of Globalism: Building a New World Order during World War II*. Fayetteville: University of Arkansas Press.

Heinlein, Frank 2002 *British Government Policy and Decolonisation 1945–1963*. London: Frank Cass.

Hendrix, Cullen & Idean Salehyan 2012 "Climate Change, Rainfall, and Social Conflict in Africa," *Journal of Peace Research*, 49, 35–50.

Hicks, Alexander et al. 1995 "The Programmatic Emergence of the Social Security State," *American Sociological Review*, 60, 329–49.

    1999 *Social Democracy and Welfare Capitalism: A Century of Income Security Politics*. Ithaca, NY: Cornell University Press.

Higgs, Robert 1989 *Crisis and Leviathan: Critical Episodes in the Growth of American Government*. Oxford: Oxford University Press.

Hinrichs, Karl 2010 "A Social Insurance State Withers Away." In Bruno Palier (ed.), *A Long Goodbye to Bismarck? The Politics of Welfare Reform in Continental Europe*. Amsterdam: Amsterdam University Press.

Hirsch, Susan 2003 *After the Strike: A Century of Labor Struggle at Pullman*. Urbana: University of Illinois Press.

Hirst, Paul & Grahame Thompson 1999 *Globalisation in Question*. 2nd ed. Cambridge: Polity Press.

Hobsbawm, Eric 1994 *The Age of Extremes: The Short Twentieth Century, 1914–1991* London: Michael Joseph.

Hoffman, David 2003 *The Oligarchs: Wealth and Power in the New Russia*. New York: Public Affairs.

Hofman, Bert & Jinglian Wu 2009 "Explaining China's Development and Reforms." *Commission on Growth and Development*, Working Paper No. 50.

Hogan, Michael 1987 *The Marshall Plan, Britain, and the Reconstruction of Western Europe, 1947–1952*. Cambridge: Cambridge University Press.

1999 *The Ambiguous Legacy: U.S. Foreign Relations in the "American Century."* New York: Cambridge University Press.

Holden, Robert 2004 *Armies Without Nations: Public Violence and State Formation in Central America 1821–1960*. Oxford: Oxford University Press.

Hollander, Paul 1999 *Political Will and Personal Belief: The Decline and Fall of Soviet Communism*. New Haven, CT: Yale University Press.

Holloway, David 1994 *Stalin and the Bomb: The Soviet Union and Atomic Energy, 1939–1956*. New Haven, CT: Yale University Press.

Holton, Robert. 1998 *Globalization and the Nation-State*. New York: St. Martin's Press.

Honey, Michael 1993 *Southern Labor and Black Civil Rights' Organizing Memphis Workers*. Urbana: University of Illinois Press.

Hooks, Gregory 1991 *Forging the Military-Industrial Complex: World War II's Battle of the Potomac*. Urbana: University of Illinois Press.

Hooks, Gregory, and Chad Smith 2005 "Treadmills of Production and Destruction: Threats to the Environment Posed by Militarism." *Organization & Environment* 18(1): 19–37.

Hoopes, Townsend & Brinkley, Douglas 1997 *FDR and the Creation of the U.N.* New Haven, CT: Yale University Press.

Horne, John & Alan Kramer, 2001 *The German Atrocities of 1914: A History of Denial*. New Haven, CT: Yale University Press.

Hough, Jerry 1997 *Democratization and Revolution in the USSR, 1985–1991*. Washington, DC: Brookings Institute.

Hout, Michael et al. 1995 "The Democratic Class Struggle in the United States, 1948–1992," *American Sociological Review*, 60, 805–28.

Houtman, Dick et al. 2008 *Farewell to the Leftist Working Class*. New Brunswick, NJ: Transaction.

Howard, Christopher 1997 *The Hidden Welfare State: Tax Expenditures and Social Policy in the United States*. Princeton, NJ: Princeton University Press.

HSBC Global 2009 *A Climate for Recovery: the Colour of Stimulus Goes Green*. London: HSBC Bank.

Huang, Jing 2000 *Factionalism in Chinese Communist Politics*. Cambridge: Cambridge University Press.

Huang, Yasheng 2008 *Capitalism with Chinese Characteristics: Entrepreneurship and the State*. Cambridge: Cambridge University Press.

Huber, Evi & Stephens, Johns 2001 *Development and Crisis of the Welfare State*. Chicago: University of Chicago Press.

Huggins, Martha 1998 *Political Policing: The United States and Latin America*. Durham, NC: Duke University Press.

Hulme, Mike 2009 *Why We Disagree about Climate Change*. Cambridge: Cambridge University Press.

Humphreys, David 2008 "NGO Influence on International Policy on Forest Conservation and the Trade in Forest Products." In Betsill & Corell (eds.), *NGO Diplomacy*. Cambridge, MA: The MIT Press.

Hunt, Michael 1987 *Ideology and U.S Foreign Policy*. New Haven, CT: Yale University Press.

1996 *Lyndon Johnson's War: America's Cold War Crusade in Vietnam, 1945–1968*. New York: Hill & Wang.

Huntington, Samuel 1991 *The Third Wave: Democratization in the Late Twentieth Century*. Norman: University of Oklahoma Press.

1996. *The Clash of Civilizations*. New York: Simon & Schuster.

Hurd, Michael & Susann Rohwedder 2010 "Effects of the Financial Crisis and Great Recession on American Households," *NBER Working Paper* No. 16407.

Hutchinson, M. 2001 "A Cure Worse than the Disease? Currency Crises and the Output Costs of Supported Stabilization Programs." In M. Dooley & J. Frankel (eds.), *Managing Currency Crises in Emerging Markets*. Chicago: University of Chicago Press.

Hyam, Ronald 2006 *Britain's Declining Empire: The Road to Decolonisation, 1918–1968*. New York: Cambridge University Press.

Hyland, William 1999 *Clinton's World: Remaking American Foreign Policy*. Westport, CT, Praeger Publishers.

Ikenberry, John 2001 *After Victory: Institutions, Strategic Restraint, and the Rebuilding of Order after Major Wars*. Princeon, NJ: Princeton University Press.

2006 *Liberal Order and Imperial Ambition*. Cambridge: Polity.

Immergluck, Dan 2009 *Foreclosed: High-Risk Lending, Deregulation, and the Undermining of America's Mortgage Market*. Ithaca, NY: Cornell University Press.

Indyk, Martin 2008 *Innocent Abroad*. New York: Simon & Schuster.

Ingham, Geoffrey 1984 *Capitalism Divided?* London: Macmillan.

2009 *Capitalism*. Cambridge: Polity Press.

Institute on Taxation and Economic Policy 2004 "Corporate Income Taxes in the Bush Years," Report No. 9/2004.

Intergovernmental Panel on Climate Change 2007 *Climate Change 2007, the IPCC Fourth Assessment Report. Synthesis Report*. Geneva: IPCC.

International Government Office 2008 *World of Work Report 2008: Income Inequalities in the Age of Financial Globalization*. Geneva: ILO.

International Monetary Fund 2010 "World Economic Outlook."

Iversen, Torben & David Soskice 2009 "Distribution and Redistribution: The Shadow of the Nineteenth Century," *World Politics*, 61, 438–86.

Iverson, Torben & John Stephens 2008 "Partisan politics, the welfare state, and three worlds of human capital formation." *Comparative Political Studies*, Vol. 41.

2005 *Capitalism, Democracy, and Welfare*. New York: Cambridge University Press.

Jacoby, Sanford 2004 "Economic Ideas and the Labor Market: Origins of the Anglo-American Model and Prospects for Global Diffusion," Unpublished paper, UCLA, November.

Jacoby, Tim 2010 "The 'Muslim Menace,' Violence and the De-Politicising Elements of the New Culturalism." *Journal of Muslim Minority Affairs*, 30, 167–81.

Jacoway, Elizabeth 1982 "Introduction," and "Little Rock Business Leaders and Desegregation." In Jacoway & David Colburn (eds.), *Southern Businessmen and Desegregation*, pp. 1–14, 15–41. Baton Rouge: Louisiana University Press.

Jaggard, Lyn, 2007 *Climate Change Politics in Europe: Germany and the International Relations of the Environment*. London: I. B. Tauris.

James, Harold 2001 *The End of Globalization: Lessons from the Great Depression*. Cambridge, MA: Harvard University Press.

2006 *The Roman Predicament: How the Rules of International Order Create the Politics of Empire*. Princeton, NJ: Princeton University Press.

Jian, Chen 1994 *China's Road to the Korean War*. New York: Columbia University Press.

Johnson, Chalmers 2000 *Blowback: The Costs and Consequences of American Empire*. New York: Henry Holt.

2005 *The Sorrows of Empire. Militarism, Secrecy, and the End of the Republic*. New York: Henry Holt.

Johnson, Simon 2009 "The Quiet Coup," *Atlantic Online*, May.

Jorda, Oscar et al. 2010 " Financial Crises, Credit Booms, and External Imbalances: 140 Years of Lessons," *NBER Working Paper* No. 16567.

Jorgenson, Andrew K., Brett Clark, & Jeffrey Kentor 2010. "Militarization and the Environment: A Panel Study of Carbon Dioxide Emissions and the Ecological Footprints of Nations, 1970–2000." *Global Environmental Politics* 10, 7–29.

Jorgenson, Andrew & Thomas Burn 2007 "The Political-Economic Causes of Change and the Ecological Footprints of Nations, 1991–2001: A Quantitative Investigation." *Social Science Research*, 36, 834–53.

Josephson, Paul 2005 *Resources under Regimes: Technology, Environment, and the State*. Cambridge, MA: Harvard University Press.

Juhazs, Antonia 2006 *The Bush Agenda: Invading the World, One Economy at a Time*. New Haven, CT: Yale University Press.

Kagan, Robert 2012 *The World America Made*. New York: Knopf

Kagan, Robert & William Kristol 2000 *Present Dangers: Crisis and Opportunity in American Foreign and Defense Policy*. San Franciso: Encounter Books.

Kamieniecki, Sheldon 2006 *Corporate America and Environmental Policy*. Stanford, CA: Stanford University Press.

Kandil, Hazem 2011 "Revolt in Egypt," *New Left Review*, No. 68, March–April.

2012 "Power Triangle: Military, Security and Politics in the Shaping of the Regime in Egypt, Turkey and Iran," Ph.D. Dissertation, UCLA.

Kangas Olli 2010 "One Hundred Years of Money, Welfare and Death: Mortality, Economic Growth and the Development of the Welfare State in 17 OECD Countries 1900–2000," *International Journal of Social Welfare*, 19, S42–S59.

Karabell, Zachary. 1999 *Architects of Intervention: The United States, the Third World, and the Cold War 1946–1962*. Baton Rouge: Louisiana State University Press.

Kato, Junko 2003 *Regressive Taxation and the Welfare State*. Cambridge: Cambridge University Press.

Katz, Michael B. 2001 *The Price of Citizenship: Redefining the American Welfare State*. New York: Metropolitan Books.

et al. 2005 "The New African American Inequality." *The Journal of American History* 92, 75–108.

Katzenstein, Peter 1985 *Small States in World Markets: Industrial Policy in Europe*, Ithaca, NY: Cornell University Press.

2005 *A World of Regions: Asia and Europe in the American Imperium*. Ithaca, NY: Cornell University Press.

2010 *Civilizations in World Politics: Plural and Pluralist Perspectives*. New York: Routledge.

Katznelson, Ira 2005 *When Affirmative Action Was White: An Untold History of Racial Inequality in Twentieth-Century America*. New York: Norton.

Katznelson, Ira, Kim Geiger, & Daniel Kryder 1993 "Limiting Liberalism: The Southern Veto in Congress, 1933–1950," *Political Science Quarterly*, 108, 283–306.

Keck, Margaret & Kathryn Sikkink 1998 *Activists beyond Borders*. Ithaca, NY: Cornell University Press.

Keddie, Nikki 2003 *Modern Iran: Roots and Results of Revolution*. New Haven, CT: Yale University Press.

Keene, Jennifer D. 2001 *Doughboys, the Great War and the Remaking of America*. Baltimore: Johns Hopkins University Press.

Keesbergen, Kees van 1995 *Social Capitalism: A Study of Christian Democracy and the Welfare State*. London: Routledge.

Kelly, Matthew forthcoming "U.S. imperialism in the Middle East: an abbreviated survey," unpublished paper, UCLA Department of History.

Kenez, Peter 2006 *The History of the Soviet Union from the Beginning to the End*. New York: Cambridge University Press.

Kenworthy, Lane 2004 *Egalitarian Capitalism: Jobs, Income and Growth in Affluent Countries* New York: Russell Sage Foundation.

2010 "Business Political Capacity and the Top-Heavy Rise of Income Inequality: How Large an Impact?" *Politics and Society*, 38, 255–65.

Kern, Thomas 2010 "Translating Global Values into National Contexts: The Rise of Environmentalism in South Korea," *International Sociology*, 25, 869–96.

Keynes, John Maynard 1937 "The General Theory of Employment," *Quarterly Journal of Economics*, 51, 209–23.

Khalidi, Rashid 2009 *Sowing Crisis: The Cold War and American Dominance in the Middle East*. Boston: Beacon.

Kian-Thiébaut, Azadeh 1998 *Secularization of Iran. A Doomed Failure?* Paris: Diffusion Peeters.

King, Desmond & Wood, Stewart 1999 "The Political Economy of Neoliberalism: Britain and the United States in the 1980s." In H. Kitschelt et al. (eds), *Continuity and Change in Contemporary Capitalism*. New York: Cambridge University Press.

Kinzer, Stephen 2004 *All the Shah's Men: An American Coup and the Roots of Middle East Terror*. New York: Wiley.

Kirk, John 2002 *Redefining the Color Line: Black Activism in Little Rock, Arkansas, 1940–1970*. Gainesville: University Press of Florida.

Kirk-Greene, Anthony 2000 *Britain's Imperial Administrators, 1858–1966*. Basingstoke, UK: Macmillan and New York: St. Martin's Press.

Kissinger, Henry 2003 *Ending the Vietnam War: A History of America's Involvement in and Extrication from the Vietnam War*. New York: Simon & Schuster.

Klare, Michael 2004 *Blood and Oil: The Dangers and Consequences of America's Growing Dependency on Imported Petroleum*. New York: Henry Holt.

Klarman, Michael 2004 *From Jim Crow to Civil Rights: The Supreme Court and the Struggle for Racial Equality*. New York: Oxford University Press.

Klausen, Jytte 1999 *War and Welfare: Europe and the United States, 1945 to the Present*. London: Palgrave Macmillan.

Klein, Jennifer 2003 *For All These Rights*. Princeton, NJ: Princeton University Press.

2001 "Foreword." In Lawrence Klein & Marshall Pomer (eds.), *The New Russia: Transition Gone Awry*. Stanford, CA: Stanford University Press.

Knight, Alan 2008 "U.S. Imperialism/Hegemony and Latin American Resistance." In Fred Rosen (ed), *Empire and Dissent: The United States and Latin America*. Durham, NC: Duke University Press.

Knight, Amy 2003 "The KGB, Perestroika, and the Collapse of the Soviet Union," *Journal of Cold War Studies*, Vol 5.

Kohl, Juergen 1981 "Trends and Problems in Postwar Public Expenditures." In Flora and Heidenheimer, *The Development of Welfare States in Europe and America*. New Brunswick, NJ: Transaction Books.

Kohli, Atul 2004 *State-Directed Development: Political Power and Industrialization in the Global Periphery*. Cambridge: Cambridge University Press.

Koistinen, Paul 2004 *Arsenal of World War II: The Political Economy of American Warfare, 1940–1945*. Lawrence: University Press of Kansas.

Kolodko, Grzegorz 2000 *From Shock to Therapy: The Political Economy of Postsocialist Transformation*. New York: Oxford University Press.

Kopstein, Jeffrey 2006 "The Transatlantic Divide over Democracy Promotion," *The Washington Quarterly*, 29, 85–98.

Kornhauser, Arthur, 1952 *Detroit As the People See It: A Survey of Attitudes in An Industrial City*. Detroit: Wayne University Press.

Korpi, Walter 1978 *The Working Class and Welfare Capitalism: Work, Unions and Politics in Sweden*. London: Routledge.

Korstad, Robert 2003 *Civil Rights Unionism: Tobacco Workers and the Struggle for Democracy in the Mid-Twentieth-Century South*. Chapel Hill: University of North Carolina Press.

Kose, M. Ayhan, Eswar Prasad, Kenneth Rogoff, & Shang-Jin Wei, 2006 "Financial Globalization: A Reappraisal," unpublished paper, Harvard University.

Kotkin, Steven 2001 *Armageddon Averted: The Soviet Collapse 1970–2000*. Oxford: Oxford University Press.

2009 *Uncivil Societies: 1989 and the Implosion of the Communist Establishment*. New York: Random House

Kotz, David, with Fred Weir 1997 *Revolution from Above: The Demise of the Soviet System*. London: Routledge.

Kozlov, Vladimir 2002 *Mass Uprisings in the U.S.S.R.: Protest and Rebellion in the Post-Stalin Years*. Armonk, NY: M. E. Sharpe.

Kraft, Michael & Sheldon Kamienicki (eds.) 2007 *Business and Environmental Policy*. Cambridge, MA: The MIT Press.

Kramer, Mark 2003a "The Collapse of the Soviet Union (Part 2): Introduction," *Journal of Cold War Studies*, 5, 3–42.

2003b "The Collapse of Eastern European Communism and the Repercussions within the Soviet Union (Part 1)," *Journal of Cold War Studies*, 5, 178–256.

Krieckhaus, Jonathan 2006 *Dictating Development: How Europe Shaped the Global Periphery*. Pittsburgh: University of Pittsburgh Press.

Krippner, Greta 2005 "The Financialization of the American Economy," *Socio-Economic Review*, 3, 173–208.

2007 "The Making of U.S. Monetary Policy: Central Bank Transparency and the Neoliberal Dilemma," *Theory and Society*, 36, 477–513.

2011 *Capitalizing on Crisis: The Political Origins of the Rise of Finance*. Cambridge, MA: Harvard University Press.

Krugman, Paul 2008 *The Return of Depression Economics and the Crisis of 2008*. New York: Norton.

Kruse, Kevin M. 2005 *White Flight: Atlanta and the Making of Modern Conservatism*. Princeton, NJ: Princeton University Press.

Kunz, Diane 1997 *Butter and Guns: America's Cold War Economic Diplomacy*. New York: Free Press.

Kurzman, Charles 2004 *The Unthinkable Revolution in Iran*. Cambridge, MA: Harvard University Press.

Kvaloy, Berit et al. 2012 "The Publics' Concern for Global Warming: a Cross-National Study of 47 Countries," *Journal of Peace Research*, 49, 11–22.

Lacy, Nicola 2010 "Differentiating among Penal Rates," *British Journal of Sociology*, 61, 778–94.

LaFeber, Walter 1984 *Inevitable Revolutions: The United States in Central America.* 2nd ed. New York: Norton.

1994a *The American Age: United States Foreign Policy at Home and Abroad since 1750.* 2nd ed. New York: Norton.

Lane, David 2009 "Post-Socialist States and the World Economy: The Impact of Global Economic Crisis," unpublished paper, University of Cambridge.

Laothamatas, Anek (ed.) 1997 *Democratization in Southeast and East Asia.* New York: St. Martin's Press, Institute of Southeast Asian Studies.

Lardy, Nicholas 2002 *Integrating China into the Global Economy.* Washington, DC: Brookings Institute.

Lash, Scott & John Urry 1994 *Economies of Signs and Space.* London: Sage.

Latham, Michael 2000 *Modernization as Ideology: American Social Science and "Nation Building" in the Kennedy Era.* Chapel Hill: University of North Carolina Press.

Lau, Sanching, 2001 *Dix ans dans les camps chinois 1981–1991.* Paris, Dagorno.

Lawson, George et al. 2010 *The Global 1989: Continuity and Change in World Politics.* Cambridge: Cambridge University Press.

Ledeneva, Alena 1998 *Russia's Economy of Favours: Blat, Networking and Informal Exchange.* Cambridge: Cambridge University Press.

Lee, Ching Kwan 2002 "From the Specter of Mao to the Spirit of the Law: Labor Insurgency in China," *Theory and Society*, 31, 189–228.

2007 *Against the Law: Labor Protests in China's Rustbelt and Sunbelt.* Berkeley & Los Angeles: University of California Press.

Lee, Ching Kwan & Mark Selden 2007 "China's Durable Inequality: Legacies of Revolution and Pitfalls of Reform," *The Asia-Pacific Journal*, January 21, 2007.

Leffler, Melvyn 1999 "The Cold War: What Do 'We Now Know?'" *American Historical Review*, Vol. CIV.

2007 *For the Soul of Mankind: The United States, the Soviet Union, and the Cold War.* New York: Hill & Wang.

Lemke, Douglas 2002 *Regions of War and Peace.* Cambridge: Cambridge University Press.

Leonard, Thomas 1991 *Central America and the United States: The Search for Stability.* Athens: University of Georgia Press.

Leonhardt, David 2010 "The Fed Missed This Bubble. Will It See a New One?" *New York Times*, January 6.

Levada, Iurii 1992 "Social and Moral Aspects of the Crisis." In Ellman & Kontorovich (eds.), *The Destruction of the Soviet Economic System: An Insiders' History.* London: M. E. Sharpe.

Levinson, Jerome & Juan de Onis 1970 *The Alliance That Lost Its Way.* Chicago: Quadrangle Books.

Levy, Jonah 2005 "Redeploying the State: Liberalization and Social Policy in France." In Streeck and Thelen, eds., *Beyond Continuity: Institutional Change in Advanced Political Economies.* New York: Oxford University Press.

Lewis, George 2006 *Massive Resistance: The White Response to the Civil Rights Movement.* New York and London: Oxford University Press.

Lewis, Jane 1992 "Gender and the Development of Welfare Regimes," *Journal of European Social Policy*, 2, 159–73.

Lewis, Joanna 2000 *Empire State-Building. War and Welfare in Kenya, 1925–52.* Athens: Ohio University Press.

Lichtenstein, Nelson 2002 *State of the Union: A Century of American Labor.* Princeton, NJ: Princeton University Press.

2003 *Labor's War at Home: The CIO in World War II*. Philadelphia: Temple University Press, 2nd edition.

Lieberman, Robert C. 1998 *Shifting the Color Line: Race and the American Welfare State*. Cambridge, MA: Harvard University Press.

Lieuwen, Edwin 1961 *Arms and Politics in Latin America*. New York: Praeger.

Lim, Taekyoon 2010 "The Neoliberalisation of the Korean State: Double-Faced Neoliberal Reforms in the Post-1997 Economic Crisis Era," unpublished paper, UCLA Dept. of Sociology.

Lin, Justin Yifu & Peilin Liu 2008 "Development Strategies and Regional Income Disparities in China." In Guanghua Wan (ed.), *Inequality and Growth in Modern China*. Oxford: Oxford University Press.

Lin, Yifu & Liu Peilin 2003 "Chinese Development Strategy and Economic Convergence," *Economic Research Journal*, 2003–03.

Lin, Yi-Min 2001 *Between Politics and Market Firms, Competition and Institutional Change in Post-Mao China*. New York: Cambridge University Press.

Lindbom, Anders 2008 "The Swedish Conservative Party and the Welfare State: Institutional Change and Adapting Preferences," *Government and Opposition*, 43, 539–60.

Lindert, Peter 1998 "Three Centuries of Inequality in Britain and America," Department of Economics, University of California at Davis, Working Paper Series No. 97–09, revised version.

2004 *Growing Public: Social Spending and Economic Growth since the Eighteenth Century*. Cambridge: Cambridge University Press.

Lipset, Seymour & Stein Rokkan. 1967 "Cleavage Structures, Party Systems, and Voter Alignments: An Introduction." In Seymour Lipset & Stein Rokkan (eds.), *Party Systems and Voter Alignments: Cross-National Perspectives*. Glencoe, IL: Free Press.

Lipset, Seymour Martin 1960 *Political Man*. New York: Doubleday.

Little, Douglas 2002 *American Orientalism: The United States and the Middle East since 1945*. Chapel Hill: University of North Carolina Press.

Logevall. Frederik 1999 *Choosing War: The Lost Chance for Peace and the Escalation of War in Vietnam*. Berkeley: University of California Press.

Long, Ngo Vinh 1998 "South Vietnam." In P. Lowe (ed.), *The Korean War*. Basingstoke, UK: Macmillan.

López-Calva, Luis & Nora Lustig, eds. 2010 *Declining Inequality in Latin America: A Decade of Progress?* Washington, DC: Brookings Institution Press and United Nations Development Programme.

López de Silanes, Florencio & Alberto Chong 2004 "Privatization in Latin America: What Does the Evidence Say?" *Economia*, 4, 37–111

Lowe, Peter 2000 *The Korean War*. Basingstoke, UK: Macmillan.

Lowenthal, Abraham 1995 *The Dominican Intervention*. 2nd ed. Baltimore: Johns Hopkins University Press.

Lundestad, Geir. 1998 *"Empire" by Invitation: The United States and European Integration, 1945–1997*. New York: Oxford University Press.

Lynd, Michael 1999 *Vietnam: The Necessary War: A Reinterpretation of America's Most Disastrous Military Conflict*. New York: Free Press.

Ma, Xiaoying & Leonard Ortolano 2000 *Environmental Regulation in China: Institutions, Enforcement, and Compliance*. Lanham, MD: Rowman & Littlefield.

MacFarquhar, Roderick 1983 *The Origins of the Cultural Revolution. Vol. II, The Great Leap, Forward, 1958–60*. New York: Columbia University Press.

Maddison, Angus 1982 *Phases of Capitalist Development*. Oxford: Oxford University Press.
    1998 *Chinese Economic Performance in the Long Run*. Paris: OECD Development Centre.
    2004 *The World Economy: A Millennial Perspective*. Paris: OECD.
    2007 *Contours of the World Economy, 1–2030AD*. Oxford: Oxford University Press.
Mahler, Vincent & David Jesuit 2006 "Fiscal Redistribution in the Developed Countries: New Insights from the Luxembourg Income Study," *Socio-Economic Review*, 4, 483–511.
    1987a "The Politics of Productivity: Foundations of American Economic Policy after World War II." In *In Search of Stability: Explorations in Historical Political Economy*. New York: Cambridge University Press.
Mahoney, James 2001 *The Legacies of Liberalism: Path Dependence and Political Regimes in Central America*. Baltimore: John Hopkins University Press.
Maier, Charles 1987a "The Two Postwar Eras and the Conditions for Stability in Twentieth-Century Western Europe." In *In Search of Stability*. Cambridge: Cambridge University Press.
    1987b *In Search of Stability: Explorations in Historical Political Economy*. New York: Cambridge University Press.
Mamdani, Mahmood 1996 *Citizen and Subject: Contemporary Africa and the Legacy of Late Colonialism*. Princeton, NJ: Princeton University Press.
Mann, James 2004 *The Rise of the Vulcans: The History of Bush's War Cabinet*. New York: Viking Press.
Mann, Michael 1970 "The Social Cohesion of Liberal Democracy," *American Sociological Review*, Vol. 35.
    1986 & 1993 *The Sources of Social Power*. Vols. I & II. Cambridge: Cambridge University Press,
    1988a "The Autonomous Power of the State: Its Origins, Mechanisms and Results." In M. Mann (ed.), *States, War and Capitalism*. Oxford: Basil Blackwell.
    1988b "The Roots and Contradictions of Contemporary Militarism." In M. Mann (ed.), *States, War and Capitalism*. Oxford: Basil Blackwell.
    1988c "The Decline of Great Britain." In M. Mann (ed.), *States, War and Capitalism*. Oxford: Basil Blackwell.
    1997 "Has Globalization Ended the Rise and Rise of the Nation-State?" *Review of International Political Economy*, 4, 472–96.
    2003 *Incoherent Empire*. London: Verso.
    2005 *The Darkside of Democracy: Explaining Ethnic Cleansing*. Cambridge: Cambridge University Press.
    2006 "The Sources of Social Power Revisited: a Response to Criticism." In John Hall & Ralph Schroeder (eds.), *An Anatomy of Power: The Social Theory of Michael Mann*. Cambridge: Cambridge University Press.
Mann, Michael & Riley, Dylan 2007 "Explaining Macro-Regional Trends in Global Income Inequalities, 1950–2000," *Socio-Economic Review*, 5, 81–115.
Mann, Robert 2001 *A Grand Delusion: America's Descent into Vietnam*. New York: Basic Books.
Manza, Jeff et al. 1995 "Class Voting in Capitalist Democracies since World War II: Dealignment, Realignment, or Trendless Fluctuation?" *Annual Review of Sociology*, 21, 137–62.
    1998 "The Gender Gap in U.S. Presidential Elections. When? Why? Implications?" *American Journal of Sociology*, 103, 1235–66.

Manza, Jeff & Brooks, Clem 1997 "The Religious Factor in U.S. Presidential Elections, 1960–1992," *American Journal of Sociology*, 103, 38–81.

Mares, David 2001 *Violent Peace: Militarized Interstate Bargaining in Latin America*. New York: Columbia University Press.

2003 *The Politics of Social Risk: Business and Welfare State Development*. Cambridge: Cambridge University Press.

Marsh, Steve 2005 "Continuity and Change: Reinterpreting the Policies of the Truman and Eisenhower Administrations toward Iran, 1950–1954," *Journal of Cold War Studies*, 7, 79–123.

Marshall T. H. 1963 (1949) "Citizenship and Social Class." In *Sociology at the Crossroads*. London: Heinemann.

Mart, Michelle 2006 *Eye on Israel: How Americans Came to See Israel as an Ally*. Albany: State University of New York Press.

Martin, Nathan & David Brady 2007 "Workers of the Less Developed World Unite? A Multilevel Analysis of Unionization in Less Developed Countries," *American Sociological Review*, 72, 562–84.

Marx, Karl 1959 (1894) *Capital*. Vol. III. New York: International Publishers.

Massey, Douglas & Nancy Denton 1993 *American Apartheid: Segregation and the Making of the Underclass*. Cambridge, MA: Harvard University Press.

2007 *Categorically Unequal: The American Stratification System*. New York: Russell Sage Foundation.

Mastny, Vojtech 1996 *The Cold War and Soviet Insecurity: The Stalin Years*. New York: Oxford.

Matray, James 1998 "Korea's Partition: Soviet-American Pursuit of Reunification, 1945–1948" *Parameters, U.S. War College Quarterly*, 28, 50–62.

Mayhew, David 1986 *Placing Parties in American Politics*. Princeton, NJ: Princeton University.

McAdam, Doug. 1982 *Political Process and the Development of Black Insurgency, 1930–1970*. Chicago: University of Chicago Press.

McAdam, Doug et al. 2001 *Dynamics of Contention*. Cambridge: Cambridge University Press.

McAdam Doug et al. 1996 *Comparative Perspectives on Social Movements*. Cambridge: Cambridge University Press.

McCarthy, John & Zald, Meyer 1977 "Resource Mobilization and Social Movements: A Partial Theory," *American Journal of Sociology*, 82, 1212–41.

McCarty, Nolan et al. 2006 *America: The Dance of Ideology and Unequal Polarized Riches*. Boston, MA: MIT Press.

McCauley, Martin 1998 *Russia, America and the Cold War, 1949–1991*. London: Longman.

McGirr, Lisa 2002 *Suburban Warriors*. Princeton, NJ: Princeton University Press.

McGregor, Richard 2010 *The Party: The Secret World of China's Communist Rulers*. New York: Harper.

McIntyre, David 1998 *British Decolonisation 1946–97*. Basingstoke: McMillan.

McKibbin, Ross 1998 *Classes and Cultures: England, 1918–1951*. New York: Oxford University Press.

McMahon, Robert 1999 *The Limits of Empire: The United States and Southeast Asia since World War II*. New York: Columbia University Press.

McNeill, John 2000 *Something New under the Sun: An Environmental History of the 20th Century*. New York: W. W. Norton.

Mead, Walter Russell 2001 *Special Providence: American Foreign Policy and How It Changed the World*. New York: Century Foundation/Knopf.

Mettler, Suzanne 1999 *Dividing Citizens: Gender and Federalism in New Deal Public Policy*. Ithaca, NY: Cornell University Press.

2010 "Reconstituting the Submerged State: The Challenge of Social Policy Reform in the Obama Era," *Perspectives on Politics*, 8, 861–76.

Meyer, David 2004 "Protest and Political Opportunities." *Annual Review of Sociology* 30, 125–45.

Meyer, John et al. 1997 "World Society and the Nation-State," *American Journal of Sociology*, 103, 144–81.

1999 "The Changing Cultural Content of the Nation-State: A World Society Perspective." In G. Steinmetz (ed.), *State/Culture*. Cornell, NY: Cornell University Press.

Migdal, Joel 1974 *Peasants Politics, and Revolution*. Princeton, NJ: Princeton University Press.

Milanovic, Branko 1998 *Income, Inequality, and Poverty during the Transformation from Planned to Market Economy*. Washington DC: The World Bank.

2010 *The Haves and the Have-Nots: A Brief and Idiosyncratic History of Global Inequality*. New York: Basic Books.

Milanovic, Branko and Ersado, Lire 2008 "Reform and Inequality during the Transition: An Analysis Using Panel Household Survey Data, 1990–2005." *World Bank Policy Research Working Paper*.

Miller, Nicola 1989 *Soviet Relations with Latin America, 1959–1987*. Cambridge: Cambridge University Press.

Miller, Norman 2009 *Environmental Politics: Stakeholders, Interests, and Policymaking*. 2nd ed. London: Routledge.

Mills, C. Wright 1956 *The Power Elite*. New York: Oxford University Press.

Minchin, Timothy 1999 *Hiring the Black Worker: The Racial Integration of the Southern Textile Industry 1960–1980*. Chapel Hill: University of North Carolina Press.

2001 *The Color of Work: The Struggle for Civil Rights in the Southern Paper Industry, 1945–1980*. Chapel Hill: University of North Carolina Press.

Minsky, Hyman 1982 *Can "It" Happen Again?: Essays on Instability and Finance*, Armonk, NY: M. E. Sharpe.

Mittelstadt, Jennifer 2005 *From Welfare to Workfare: The Unintended Consequences of Liberal Reform, 1945–1965*. Chapel Hill: University of North Carolina Press.

Moore, Barrington 1967 *Origins of Dictatorship and Democracy*. Boston: Beacon Press.

Morgan Kimberley & Monica Prasad 2009 "The Origins of Tax Systems: A French-American Comparison," *American Journal of Sociology*, Vol 115.

Morgan, Kenneth. 2000 *Slavery, Atlantic Trade and the British Economy, 1660–1800*. Cambridge: Cambridge University Press.

Morley, Samuel 2001 *The Income Distribution Problem in Latin America and the Caribbean*. Santiago, Chile: CEPAL/ECLAC.

Morris, Aldon 1986 *The Origins of the Civil Rights Movement: Black Communities Organizing for Change*. New York: Free Press.

Moshiri, Farrokh 1991 "Iran: Islamic Revolution Against Westernization." In Jack Goldstone et al. (eds.), *Revolutions of the Late Twentieth Century*. Boulder, CO: Westview Press.

Moye, Todd 2004 *Let the People Decide: Black Freedom and White Resistance Movements in Sunflower County, Mississippi, 1945–1986*. Chapel Hill: University of North Carolina Press.

Moynihan, Daniel 1969 *Maximum Feasible Misunderstanding: Community Action in the War on Poverty*. New York: Free Press.

Mudge, Stephanie 2008 "What Is Neo-Liberalism?" *Socio-Economic Review*, 6, 703–31.

2011 "What's Left of Leftism? Neoliberal Politics in Western Political Systems, 1945–2004," *Social Science History*, 35, 338–68.

Muldavin, Joshua 2000 "The Paradoxes of Environmental Policy and Resource Management in Reform-Era China," *Economic Geography*, 76, 244–71.

Muravchik, Joshua 1986 *The Uncertain Crusade: Jimmy Carter and the Dilemmas of Human Rights Policy*. New York: Hamilton Press.

Nabli, Mustapha (ed.) 2010 *The Great Recession and Developing Countries: Economic Impact and Growth Prospects*. Washington, DC: World Bank.

Nagl, John 2002 *Counterinsurgency Lessons from Malaya and Vietnam*. Westport, CT: Praeger.

National Security Council 1950 "United States Objectives and Programs for National Security," NSC-68. Declassified in 1975 and published in *Naval War College Review*, 27, 51–108.

Naughton, Barry 1995 *Growing Out of the Plan: Chinese Economic Reform 1978– 1993*. New York: Cambridge University Press.

2007 *The Chinese Economy: Transitions and Growth*. Boston: MIT Press.

Nelson, Bruce 2003 *Divided We Stand: American Workers and the Struggle for Black Equity*. Princeton, NJ: Princeton University Press.

Nelson, Moira & John Stephens 2009 "Human Capital Policies and the Social Investment Perspective: Explaining the Past and Anticipating the Future." In Nathalie Morel et al. (eds.), *What Future for Social Investment?* Institute for Futures Studies Research Report, 2009/2.

Newell, Peter & Matthew Paterson 2010 *Climate Capitalism: Global Warming and the Transformation of the Global Economy*. Cambridge: Cambridge University Press.

Nicolaides, Becky 2002 *My Blue Heaven: Life and Politics in the Working Class Suburbs of Los Angeles, 1920–1965*. Chicago: University of Chicago Press.

Nordhaus, William 2008 *A Question of Balance: Weighing the Options on Global Warming Policies*. New Haven, CT: Yale University Press.

Nugent, Paul 2004 *Africa since Independence*. Basingstoke, UK: Palgrave Macmillan.

Nye, Joseph 2004 *Soft Power: The Means to Success in World Politics*. New York: Public Affairs.

O'Connor, Alice 2001 *Poverty Knowledge: Social Science, Social Policy and the Poor in Twentieth-Century U.S. History*. Princeton, NJ: Princeton University Press.

O'Connor, Julia, Ann Orloff, & Sheila Shaver 1999 *States, Markets, Families: Gender, Liberalism and Social Policy in Australia, Canada, Great Britain, and the United States*. Cambridge: Cambridge University Press.

O'Reilly, Marc 2008 *Unexceptional: America's Empire in the Persian Gulf, 1941–2007*. Lanham, MD: Lexington Books.

O'Rourke Kevin & Jeffrey Williamson 1999 *Globalization and History: The Evolution of a Nineteenth-Century Atlantic Economy*. Cambridge, MA: MIT Press.

Oatley, Thomas & Jason Yackee. 2004 "American Interests and IMF Lending," *International Politics*, 41, 415–29.

Odom William 1998 *The Collapse of the Soviet Military*. New Haven, CT: Yale University Press.

OECD 2008 *Growing Unequal? Income Distribution and Poverty in OECD Countries*. Paris: OECD.

2010 *Economic Policy Reforms: Going for Growth 2011*. Paris: OECD.

Offe, Claus & V. Ronge 1974 "Theses on the Theory of the State." In Anthony Giddens & David Held (eds.), *Classes, Power and Conflict*. Berkeley and Los Angeles: University of California Press.

Oh, John Kie-chiang 1999 *Korean Politics: The Quest for Democratization and Economic Development*, Ithaca, NY: Cornell University Press.

Oi, Jean & Andrew G. Walder (eds.) 1999 "Introduction." In *Property Rights and Economic Reform in China*. Stanford, CA: Stanford University Press.

Olson, Laura 2006 "The Religion Gap," *Political Science & Politics*, 39, 455–9.

Omi, Michael & Winant, Howard 1994 "The Art of Reframing Political Debates." In *Racial Formation in the United States: From the 1960s to the 1980s*. 2nd ed., Vol. 5: pp. 13–18. New York: Routledge, 1994.

Opinion Research Business 2008 "More than 1,000,000 Iraqis Murdered." Author. Updated version.

Orenstein, Mitchell 2008 "Postcommunist Welfare States," *Journal of Democracy*, 19, 80–94.

Oreskes, Naomi 2004 "Beyond the Ivory Tower: The Scientific Consensus on Climate Change," *Science*, 306(5702), 1686.

Orloff, Ann 1988 "The Political Origins of America's Belated Welfare State." In *Margaret* Weir, Ann Shola Orloff, and Theda Skocpol (eds.), *The Politics of Social Policy in the United States*. Princeton: Princeton University Press.

Osberg, Lars & Timothy Smeeding 2006 "Fair" Inequality? An International Comparison of Attitudes to Pay Differentials," *American Sociological Review*, 70, 949–67.

Osterhammel Jürgen & Niels Petersson 2005 Globalization: A Short History. Princeton, NJ: Princeton University Press, 2005.

Ozler, Ilgu & Brian Obach 2009 "Capitalism, State Economic Policy and Ecological Footprint: An International Comparative Analysis," *Global Environmental Politics*, 9, 79–108.

Packer, George 2005 *The Assassin's Gate: America in Iraq*. New York: Farrar, Straus & Giroux.

Page, Benjamin & Lawrence Jacobs 2009 *Class War? What Americans Really Think about Economic Inequality*. Chicago: University of Chicago Press.

Paige, Jeffery 1975 *Agrarian Revolution*. New York: Free Press.

    1997 *Coffee and Power: Revolution and the Rise of Democracy in Central America*. Cambridge, MA: Harvard University Press.

Palier, Bruno 2005 "Ambiguous Agreement, Cumulative Change: French Social Policy in the 1990s.'" In Streeck & Thelen, *Beyond Continuity: Institutional Change in Advanced Political Economies*. Oxford: Oxford University Press.

Palier, Bruno (ed.) 2010 *A Long Goodbye to Bismarck? The Politics of Welfare Reform in Continental Europe*. Amsterdam: Amsterdam University Press.

Panic, M. 2007 "Does Europe Need Neoliberal Reforms?" *Cambridge Journal of Economics*, 31, 145–69.

Pape, Robert 2005 *Dying to Win*. New York: Random House.

    2010 "It's the Occupation, Stupid," *Foreign Policy Magazine*, November 14.

Park, James 1995 *Latin American Underdevelopment: A History of Perspectives in the United States, 1870–1965*. Baton Rouge: Louisiana State University Press.

Parsa, Misagh 1989 *Social Origins of the Iranian Revolution*. New Brunswick, NJ: Rutgers University Press.

Patterson, James 2001 *Brown v. Board of Education: A Civil Rights Milestone and its Troubled Legacy*. New York: Oxford University Press.

Payne, Charles 1995 *I've Got the Light of Freedom: The Organizing Tradition and the Mississippi Freedom Struggle*. Berkeley: University of California Press.

Pearson, Raymond 1998 *The Rise and Fall of the Soviet Empire*. New York: St. Martin's Press.

Peceny, Mark 1999 *Democracy at the Point of Bayonets*. University Park: Pennsylvania State University Press.

Peck, Jamie & Adam Tickell 2002 "Neoliberalizing Space," *Antipode*, 34, 380–404.

2001 *Workfare States*. New York: Guilford Press.

Pedersen, Susan 1993 *Family, Dependence and the Origins of the Welfare State*. Cambridge: Cambridge University Press.

Pei, Minxin 1994 *From Reform to Revolution: The Demise of Communism in China and the Soviet Union*. Cambridge, MA: Harvard University Press.

2006 *China's Trapped Transition: The Limits of Developmental Autocracy*. Cambridge, MA: Harvard University Press.

Pierson, Paul 1998 "Irresistible Forces, Immovable Objects: Post-Industrial Welfare States Confront Permanent Austerity," *Journal of European Public Policy*, 5(4), 539–60.

(Ed.) 2001 *The New Politics of the Welfare State*. Oxford University Press.

Pietersee, Jan Nederven 1995 "Globalization as Hybridization." In Mike Featherstone, Scott Lash, & Roland Robertson (eds.), *Global Modernities*, pp. 45–68. London: Sage.

Piketty, Thomas & Emmanuel Saez 2003 "Income Inequality in the United States, 1913–1998," *Quarterly Journal of Economics*, 118, 1–39.

Piven, Frances & Cloward, Richard 1977 *Poor People's Movements*. New York: Vintage.

Pleshakov, Constantine 2009 *No Freedom Without Bread: 1989 and the Civil War That Brought Down Communism*. New York: Farrar, Straus & Giroux.

Plotke, David 1996 *Building a Democratic Political Order: Reshaping American Liberalism in the 1930s and 1940s*. New York: Cambridge University Press.

Polanyi, Karl 1957 [1944] *The Great Transformation: The Political and Economic Origins of Our Time*. Boston: Beacon Press.

Pomer, Marshall 2001 "Introduction." In Lawrence Klein & Marshall Pomer (eds.), *The New Russia: Transition Gone Awry*. Stanford, CA: Stanford University Press.

Pontusson, Jonas 2005 *Inequality and Prosperity: Social Europe vs. Liberal America*. Ithica, NY: Cornell University Press.

Porter, Bernard 2006 *Empire and Superempire: Britain, America and the World*. New Haven, CT: Yale University Press.

Prasad, Eswar 2007 et al. "Foreign Capital and Economic Growth," *Brookings Papers on Economic Activity* 1, 153–230.

Prasad, Monica 2006 *The Politics of Free Markets*. Chicago: University of Chicago Press.

2009 "Bryan's revenge: the credit/welfare state tradeoff and the crisis of 2008–2009," unpublished paper.

Prechel, Harland & Theresa Morris 2010 "The Effects of Organizational and Political Embeddedness on Financial Malfeasance in the Largest U.S. Corporations," *American Sociological Review*, 75, 331–54.

Precht, Henry (interview with) 2004 "The Iranian Revolution: An Oral History with Henry Precht, then State Department Desk Officer," *Middle East Journal*, 58, 9–31.

Putzel, James 2000 "Land Reforms in Asia: Lessons from the Past for the 21st Century," London School of Economics, Destan Working Paper No. 00–04.

Quadagno, Jill 1994 *The Color of Welfare*. New York: Oxford University Press.

Rabe, Stephen 1988 *Eisenhower and Latin America. The Foreign Policy of Anti-Communism*. Chapel Hill, NC: University of North Carolina Press.

1999 *The Most Dangerous Area in the World: John F. Kennedy Confronts Communist Revolution in Latin America*. Chapel Hill, NC: University of North Carolina Press.

Rabinovitch, Eyal 2004 "The Making of the Global Public." Ph.D. dissertation, Department of Sociology, UCLA.

Race, Jeffrey 1972 *War Comes to Long An: Revolutionary Conflict in a Vietnamese Province*. Berkeley: University of California Press.

Radkau, Joachim 2008 *Nature and Power: A Global History of the Environment*. New York: Cambridge University Press.

Raskin, Paul et al. 2002 *Great Transition: The Promise and Lure of the Times Ahead*. Boston: Stockholm Environment Institute, http://www.gsg.org

Reinhart, Carmen & Kenneth Rogoff 2009 *This Time Is Different: Eight Centuries of Financial Folly*. Princeton, NJ: Princeton University Press

Repetto, Robert 2007 "Best Practice in Internal Oversight of Lobbying Practice," http://envirocenter.research.yale.edu

Reynolds, Lloyd 1985 *Economic Growth in the Third World*. New Haven, CT: Yale University Press.

Roberts, J. Timmons & Bradley C. Parks 2007 *A Climate of Injustice: Global Inequality, North–South Politics, and Climate Policy*. Cambridge, MA: MIT Press.

Robertson, Roland 1992 *Globalization: Social Theory and Global Culture*. London: Sage.

Robinson, William & Jerry Harris 2000 "Towards a Global Ruling Class? Globalization and the Transnational Capitalist Class," *Science & Society*, 64, 11–54.

Robnett, Belinda 1997 *How Long? How Long? African-American Women in the Struggle for Civil Rights*. New York: Oxford University Press.

Rockoff, Hugh 1998 "The United States: From Ploughshares to Swords." In Mark Harrison (ed.), *The Economics of World War II: Six Great Powers in International Comparison*. Cambridge: Cambridge University Press.

Rodrik, Dani 2011 "Growth after the Crisis." In Craig Calhoun & Georgi Derluguian (eds.), *Aftermath: A New Global Economic Order?* New York: Social Science Research Council and New York University Press.

Rodrik, Dani & Arvind Subramanian 2008 "Why Did Financial Globalization Disappoint," unpublished paper available on Rodrik's web-site.

Romano, Renee 2003 *Race Mixing: Black-White Marriage in Postwar America*. Cambridge: Harvard University Press.

Roorda, Eric 1998 *The Dictator Next Door: The Good Neighbor Policy and the Trujillo Regime in the Dominican Republic, 1930–1945*. Durham, NC: Duke University Press.

Rosen, Nir 2010 *Aftermath: Following the Bloodshed of America's Wars in the Muslim. World* New York: Avalon.

Rosenberg, Samuel 2003 *American Economic Development since 1945: Growth, Decline and Rejuvenation*. New York: Palgrave Macmillan.

Rotter, Andrew 1987 *The Path to Vietnam: Origins of the American Commitment to Southeast Asia*. Ithaca, NY; Cornell University Press.

Rouquié, Alain 1987 *The Military and the State in Latin America*. Berkeley and Los Angeles: University of California Press.

Rueschemeyer, D. et al. 1992 *Capitalist Development and Democracy*. Chicago: University of Chicago Press.

Ruggie, John 1982. "International Regimes, Transactions, and Change: Embedded Liberalism in the Postwar Economic Order," *International Organization*, Vol. 36.

Runciman W. G. 1966 *Relative Deprivation and Social Justice*. London: Routledge.

Ryan, Charlotte & Gamson, William 2006 "The Art of Reframing Political Debates," *Contexts*, 5, 13–18.

Saez, Emmanuel 2009 "Striking It Richer: The Evolution of Top Incomes in the United States (update with 2007 estimates)" http://elsa.berkeley.edu/~saez/

Sainsbury, Diane 1996 *Gender, Equality and Welfare States*. Cambridge: Cambridge University Press

Sarotte, Mary 2009 *The Struggle to Create Post-Cold War Europe*. Princeton, NJ: Princeton University Press.

Sassen, Saskia 2010 "The Return of Primitive Accumulation." In Lawson, *The Global 1989: Continuity and Change in World Politics*. Cambridge: Cambridge University Press.

Sato, Hiroshi 2003 *The Growth of Market Relations in Post-Reform Rural China*. London: Routledge.

Schaller, Michael 1985 *The American Occupation of Japan: The Origins of the Cold War in Asia*. New York, Oxford University Press.

Schild, George 1995 *Bretton Woods and Dumbarton Oaks*. New York: St. Martin's Press.

Schmitter, Philippe 1974 "Still the Century of Corporatism?" *Review of Politics*, 36, 85–131.

Scholte, Jan Aart 2000 *Globalization: A Critical Introduction*. New York: St. Martins Press.

Schrecker, Ellen 1998 *Many Are the Crimes: McCarthyism in America*. Boston: Little, Brown.

Schulzinger, Robert 1997 *A Time for War: The United States and Vietnam, 1941–1975*. New York: Oxford University Press.

Schumpeter, Joseph 1957 (1942) *Capitalism, Socialism and Democracy*. New York: Harper.

1961 (1911) *The Theory of Economic Development*. New York: Oxford University Press.

1982 (1939) *Business Cycles*, 2 vols. Philadelphia: Porcupine Press.

Schwartz, Herman 2009 *Subprime Nation: American Power, Global Capital, and the Housing Bubble*. Ithaca, NY: Cornell University Press.

Schwartzberg, Steven 2003 *Democracy and U.S. Policy in Latin America during the Truman Years*. Gainesville: University Press of Florida.

Scott, James 1976 *The Moral Economy of the Peasant: Rebellion and Subsistence in South East Asia*. New Haven, CT: Yale University Press.

Scruggs, Lyle & Peter Lange 2002 "Where Have All the Members Gone? Globalization, Institutions and Union Density," *Journal of Politics*, 64, 126–53.

2003 *Sustaining Abundance: Environmental Performance in Industrial Democracies*. New York: Cambridge University Press.

Service, Robert 1997 *A History of Twentieth-Century Russia*. London: Allen Lane, Penguin.

Shadid Anthony 2005 *Night Draws Near: Iraq's People in the Shadow of America's War*. New York: Henry Holt.

Shafer, J. 1995 "Experience with Controls on International Capital Movements in OECD Countries: Solution or Problem for Monetary Policy?" In S. Edwards (ed.), *Capital Controls, Exchange Rates, and Monetary Policy in the World Economy*, pp. 119–56. Cambridge: Cambridge University Press.

Shanin, Theodor (ed.) 1971 *Peasants and Peasant Societies*. Harmondsworth, UK: Penguin.

Shapiro, Judith 2001 *Mao's War against Nature: Politics and the Environment in Revolutionary China*. New York: Cambridge University Press.

Sharkey, Heather 2003 *Living with Colonialism: Nationalism and Culture in the Anglo-Egyptian Sudan*. Berkeley and Los Angeles: University of California Press.

Shaw, Martin 2006 *The New Western Way of War*. Cambridge: Polity.

Sherry, Michael 1995 *In the Shadow of War: The United States since the 1930s*. New Haven, CT: Yale University Press.

Sheshinski, Eytan & Luis López-Calva 2003 "Privatization and Its Benefits: Theory and Evidence," *CESifo Economic Studies*, 49, 429–59.

Shirk, Susan 1993 *The Political Logic of Economic Reform in China*. Berkeley: University of California Press.

Shoichi, Koseki 1998 *The Birth of Japan's Postwar Constitution*. Boulder, CO: Westview Press.

Sides, Josh 2004 *L.A. City Limits: African American Los Angeles from the Great Depression to the Present*. Berkeley: University of California Press.

Silver, Beverly 2003 *Forces of Labor: Workers' Movements and Globalization since 1870*. Cambridge: Cambridge University Press.

Skjærseth, John & Jorgen Wettestad, 2009 "The Origin, Evolution and Consequences of the EU Emissions Trading System," *Global Environmental Politics*. 9, 101–22.

Skidelsky, Robert. 1983 *John Maynard Keynes: Hopes Betrayed*. London: Macmillan.

    2000 *John Maynard Keynes*. Vol III, *Fighting for Britain*. London: Macmillan.

Skidmore, David 1996 *Reversing Course: Carter's Foreign Policy and the Failure of Reform*. Nashville, Tenn: Vanderbilt University Press.

Sklair, Leslie 2000 *The Transnational Capitalist Class*. Oxford: Blackwell,.

Skocpol, Theda 1979 *States and Social Revolutions*. Cambridge: Cambridge University Press.

    1994 *Social Revolution in the Modern World*. New York: Cambridge University Press.

Skocpol, Theda & John Ikenberry 1983 "The Political Formation of the American Welfare State in Historical and Comparative Perspective." *Comparative Social Research*, 6, 84–147.

Skrede, Kristian & Michael D. Ward 1999 "A Revised List of Independent States since 1816," *International Interactions*, 25, 393–413.

Smeeding, Timothy 2002 "Globalisation, Inequality, and the Rich Countries of the G-20: Evidence from the Luxembourg Income Study (LIS)." In D. Gruen, T. O'Brien, and J. Lawson (eds.), *Globalisation, Living Standards, and Inequality, Recent Progress and Continuing Challenges*. Australia: J. S. McMillian.

Smith, Gaddis 1986 *Morality, Reason and Power: American Diplomacy in the Carter Years*. New York: Hill & Wang.

Smith, Neil 2003 *American Empire: Roosevelt's Geographer and the Prelude to Globalization*. Berkeley: University of California Press.

Smith, Peter 2000 *Talons of the Eagle: Dynamics of U.S.–Latin American Relations*. New York: Oxford University Press.

Smith, Tony 1991 "The Alliance for Progress: The 1960s." In Abraham F. Lowenthal, (Ed.), *Exporting Democracy: The United States and Latin America*. Baltimore: Johns Hopkins University Press.

Soederberg, Susanne 2004 *The Politics of the New International Financial Architecture*. London: Zed.

Solnick, Steven 1996 "The Breakdown of Hierarchies in the Soviet Union and China: A Neoinstitutional Perspective," *World Politics*, 48, 209–38.

Sparrow, Bartholomew 1996 *From the Outside In: World War II and the American State*. Princeton, NJ: Princeton University Press.

Speth, James Gustave 2004 *Red Sky at Morning: America and the Crisis of the Global Environment*. New Haven, CT: Yale University Press.

2008 *The Bridge at the Edge of the World*. New Haven, CT: Yale University Press.

Starke, Peter 2008 *Radical Welfare State Retrenchment: A Comparative Analysis*. Houndsmill: Palgrave Macmillan.

Steinmo Sven 1993 *Taxation and Democracy: Swedish, British and American Approaches to Financing the Modern State*. New Haven, CT: Yale University Press.

2010 *The Evolution of Modern States: Sweden, Japan and the United States*. Cambridge: Cambridge University Press.

Stepan-Norris, Judith & Maurice Zeitlin 2003 *Left Out: Reds and America's Industrial Unions*. Cambridge: Cambridge University Press.

Stephens, John 1980 *The Transition from Capitalism to Socialism*. London: Macmillan.

Stern Team, 2008 "Additional Papers and Presentations by Lord Stern." UK Office of Climate Change. http://www.occ.gov.uk/activities/stern_additional.htm

Stern, Nicholas 2007 *The Stern Review on the Economics of Climate Change*. London: UK Office of Climate Change.

Stern, Sheldon M. 2003 *Averting "The Final Failure": John F. Kennedy and the Secret Cuban Missile Crisis Meetings*. Stanford, CA: Stanford University Press.

Stiglitz, Joseph 1998 " More Instruments and Broader Goals: Moving toward the Post-Washington Consensus," *World Institute for Development Economics Research* (WIDER) annual lecture, January 1998.

1999 *Whither Reform? Ten Years of Transition*, Washington, DC World Bank.

Stone, Geoffrey 2004 *Perilous Times: Free Speech in Wartime, from the Sedition Act of 1798 to the War on Terrorism*. New York: Norton.

Stone, Randall 2004. "The Political Economy of IMF Lending in Africa," *American Political Science Review*, Vol. 98.

Strayer, Robert 2001 "Decolonization, Democratization, and Democratic Reform: The Soviet Collapse in Comparative Perspective," *Journal of World History*, 12, 375–406.

Streeck, Wolfgang 2009 *Re-Forming Capitalism: Institutional Change in the German Political Economy*. Oxford: Oxford University Press.

2011 "The Crises of Democratic Capitalism," *New Left Review*, 71, 5–29

Streeck, Wolfgang & Kathleen Thelen 2005 *Beyond Continuity: Institutional Change in Advanced Political Economies*. Oxford: Oxford University Press.

Streeter. Stephen 2000 *Managing the Counterrevolution: The United States and Guatemala, 1954–1961*. Athens: Ohio University Press.

Stuckler, David et al. 2009 "Mass Privatisation and the Post-Communist Mortality Crisis: A Cross-National Analysis," *The Lancet*, Jan 15.

Stueck, William 1995 *The Korean War: An International History*. Princeton, NJ: Princeton University Press, 1995.

ed. 2004 *The Korean War in World History*. Lexington: University of Kentucky.

Sugihara, Kaoru 2000 "The East Asian Path of Economic Development: A Long-Term Perspective," *Discussion Papers in Economics and Business, 00–17, Graduate School of Economics, Osaka University*.

Sugrue, Thomas 1996 *The Origins of the Urban Race Crisis: Race and Inequality in Postwar Detroit*. Princeton, NJ: Princeton University Press.

Suny, Ronald 1993 *The Revenge of the Past: Nationalism, Revolution and the Collapse of the Soviet Union*. Stanford, CA: Stanford University Press.

1998 *The Soviet Experiment*. Oxford: Oxford University Press.

Suskind, Ron 2004 *The Price of Loyalty. George W. Bush, the White House, and the Education of Paul O'Neill*. New York: Simon & Schuster.

2006 *The One Percent Doctrine: Deep inside America's Pursuit of Its Enemies since 9/11*. New York, Simon & Schuster.

Swank, Duane 1992 "Politics and the Structural Dependence of the State in Democratic Capitalist Nations." *American Political Science Review*, 86, 38–54.

2002 *Global Capital, Political Institutions, and Policy Change in Developed Welfare States*. New York: Cambridge University Press.

Swyngedouw, Erik. 1997. "Neither Global nor Local: 'Glocalization' and the Politics of Scale." In Kevin R. Cox (ed.), *Spaces of Globalization: Reasserting the Power of the Local*, pp. 137–66. New York: Guilford Press.

Syklos, Pierre 2002 *The Changing Face of Central Banking: Evolutionary Trends since World War II*. New York: Cambridge University Press.

Talbott, Strobe 2002 *The Russia Hand: A Memoir of Presidential Diplomacy*. New York: Random House.

Tanzi, Vito 1969 *The Individual Income Tax and Economic Growth*. Baltimore: Johns Hopkins University Press.

Taylor, Bill et al. 2003 *Industrial Relations in China*. Cheltenham: Edward Elgar.

Taylor, Bron 1995 "Popular Ecological Resistance and Radical Environmentalism." In Taylor (ed.), *Ecological Resistance Movements*. Albany: State University of New York Press, pp 334–54.

Temin, Peter 2010 "The Great Recession and the Great Depression," *NBER Working Paper* No. 15645.

Tenet, George 2007 *At the Center of the Storm: My Years at the C.I.A.* New York: Harper-Collins.

Thornton, Mills III 2002 *Dividing Lines: Municipal Politics and the Struggle for Civil Rights in Montgomery, Birmingham, and Selma*. Tuscaloosa: University of Alabama Press.

Tikhomirov, Vladimir 2000 *The Political Economy of Post-Soviet Russia*. London: MacMillan.

Tilly, Charles 1993 *European Revolutions 1492–1992*. Oxford: Blackwell.

Tomlinson, John 1999 *Globalization and Culture*. Chicago: University of Chicago Press.

Tridico, Pasquale 2009 "Trajectories of Socio-Economic Models and Development in Transition Economies in the 20 Years since the Fall of the Berlin Wall," unpublished paper, Department of Economics, University of Rome 3.

Trubowitz, Peter 1998 *Defining the National Interest: Conflict and Change in American Foreign Policy*. Chicago: University of Chicago Press.

Tucker, Aviezer 2010 "Restoration and Convergence: Russia and China since 1989." In Lawson et al., *The Global 1989: Continuity and Change in World Politics*. Cambridge: Cambridge University Press.

Tucker, Robert (ed.) 1978 *The Marx-Engels Reader*. 1978 ed. New York: Norton.

Tuminez, Astrid 2003 "Nationalism, Ethnic Pressures, and the Breakup of the Soviet Union," *Journal of Cold War Studies*, 5, 81–136.

Tyler, Patrick 2009 *A World of Trouble: The White House and the Middle East – from the Cold War to the War on Terror*. New York: Farrar, Straus, & Giroux.

Ulvila, Marko & Jarna Pasanen 2009 *Sustainable Futures*. Helsinki: Ministry of Foreign Affairs.

UNEP 2007 Global Environmental Outlook: GEO4.

United Nations Development Program 2009 World Development Report.

United Nations Environmental Program (UNEP) 2007 "GEO4 Report," Global Environmental Outlook.

United Nations Human Development Report 2007/2008 *Fighting Climate Change: Human Solidarity in a Divided World.* Geneva: United Nations.

U.S. Department of State 2003 *Foreign Relations of the United States, 1952–1954: Guatemala.* Washington, DC: U.S. Government Printing Office.

Van Zanden et al. 2011 "The Changing Shape of Global Inequality 1820–2000: Exploring a New Data-Set," *Universiteit Utrecht, CGEH Working Paper Series,* No. 1.

Vandervort, Bruce 1998 *Wars of Imperial Conquest in Africa, 1830–1914.* Bloomington: Indiana University Press.

Visser, Jelle 2006 "Union Membership Statistics in 24 Countries," *Monthly Labor Review,* Vol. 129.

Voigt, Peter & Heinrich Hockmann 2008 "Russia's Transition Process in the Light of a Rising Economy," *European Journal of Comparative Economics,* 5, 251–67.

Vreeland, James 2003 *The IMF and Economic Development.* Cambridge: Cambridge University Press.

Wacquant, Loic 2002 *Prisons of Poverty.* Minneapolis: University of Minnesota Press.

2009 *Punishing the Poor: The Neoliberal Government of Social Insecurity.* Durham, NC: Duke University Press.

Waddell, Brian 2001 *The War against the New Deal: World War II and American Democracy.* DeKalb: Northern Illinois University Press.

Wade, Robert 1990 *Governing the Market.* Princeton, NJ: Princeton University Press.

Walker, Thomas 1997 *Nicaragua without Illusions: Regime Transition and Structural Adjustment in the 1990s.* Wilmington, DE: SR Books.

Wallace, Michael et al. 1988 "American Labor Law: Its Impact on Working-Class Militancy, 1901–1980," *Social Science History,* 12, 1–29.

Wallander, Celeste 2003 "Western Policy and the Demise of the Soviet Union," *Journal of Cold War Studies,* 5, 137–177.

Wallerstein, Immanuel 1974a *The Modern World-System.* Vol. I, *Capitalist Agriculture and the Origins of the European World-Economy in the Sixteenth Century.* New York/London: Academic Press.

1974b "The Rise and Future Demise of the of the World-Capitalist System: Concepts for Comparative Analysis." *Comparative Studies in Society and History,* 16, 387–415.

2003 *The Decline of American Power: The U.S. in a Chaotic World.* New York: New Press.

2012 "Structural Crisis, or Why Capitalists No Longer Find Capitalism Rewarding." In Georgi Derleugian (ed.), *Does Capitalism Have a Future? A Sociological Polemic.* New Haven, CT: Yale University Press.

Walter, Carl & Fraser Howie 2003 *Privatizing China: The Stock Markets and Their Role in Corporate Reform.* Singapore: John Wiley.

Warner, Roger 1996 *Shooting at the Moon: The Story of America's Clandestine War in Laos.* South Royalton, VT: Steerforth Press.

Waters, Malcolm 1995 *Globalization.* New York: Routledge.

Weathersby, Kathryn 1998 "Stalin, Mao, and the End of the Korean War." in Westad (ed.), *Brothers in Arms: The Rise and Fall of the Sino-Soviet Alliance, 1945–1963.* Washington, DC: Woodrow Wilson Center Press.

Weaver, R. K. 1986 "The Politics of Blame Avoidance," *Journal of Public Policy,* 6, 371–98.

Weber, Max 1978 ed. *Economy and Society*. 2 vols. Edited by Gunther Roth & Claus Wittich. Berkeley and Los Angeles: University of California Press.

Wedeman, Andrew 2003 *From Mao to the Market: Rent Seeking, Local Protectionism and Marketization in China*. New York: Cambridge University Press.

Weintraub, Stanley 1999 *MacArthur's War: Korea and the Undoing of an American Hero*. New York: Free Press.

Weiss, Linda 1999 "Globalization and National Governance: Antinomy or Interdependence?" *Review of International Studies*, 25, 59–88.

    2008 "Crossing the Divide: From the Military-Industrial to the Development-Procurement Complex," unpublished paper, Department of Government and International Relations, University of Sydney.

    2009 "The State in the Economy: Neoliberal or Neoactivist? In Glenn Morgan et al. (eds.), *Oxford Handbook of Comparative Institutional Analysis*. Oxford: Oxford University Press.

Weller, Robert 2006 *Discovering Nature: Globalization and Environmental Culture in China and Taiwan*. New York: Cambridge University Press.

Welch, Richard 1985 *Response to Revolution: The United States and the Cuban Revolution, 1959–1961*. Chapel Hill: University of North Carolina Press.

Westad, Odd 1998 " The Sino-Soviet Alliance and the United States." in Odd Westad (ed.), *Brothers in Arms: The Rise and Fall of the Sino-Soviet Alliance, 1945–1963*. Washington, DC: Woodrow Wilson Center Press.

    2006 *The Global Cold War: Third World Interventions and the Making of Our Times*. Cambridge: Cambridge University Press.

Western, Bruce 1993 "Postwar Unionization in 18 Advanced Capitalist Countries." *American Sociological Review*, 58, 266–82.

    2006 *Punishment and Inequality in America*. New York, Russell Sage.

White, John Kenneth 1997 *Still Seeing Red: How the Cold War Shapes the New American Politics*. Boulder, CO: Westview Press.

White, Nicholas 1999 *Decolonisation: The British Experience since 1945*. London and New York: Longman.

White, Stephen 1996 *Russia Goes Dry: Alcohol, State and Society*. Cambridge: Cambridge University Press.

Whitfield, Stephen 1996 *The Culture of the Cold War*. 2nd ed. Baltimore: Johns Hopkins University Press.

Whiting, Susan 2001 *Power and Wealth in Rural China: The Political Economy of Institutional Change*. New York: Cambridge University Press.

Wiarda, Howard 1995 *Democracy and Its Discontents. Development, Interdependence and U.S. Policy in Latin America*. Lanham, MA: Rowman & Littlefield.

Wickham-Crowley, Timothy 2001 "Winners, Losers and Also-Rans: Toward a Comparative Sociology of Latin American Guerilla Movements." In Susan Eckstein (ed.), *Power and Popular Protest: Latin American Social Movements*. Berkeley & Los Angeles: University of California Press.

Wilensky, Harold 2002 *Rich Democracies: Political Economy, Public Policy, and Performance*. Berkeley and Los Angeles: University of California Press.

Wilentz, Sean 2009 *The Age of Reagan: A History, 1974–2008*. New York: HarperCollins.

Willbanks, James 2004 *Abandoning Vietnam: How America Left and South Vietnam Lost Its War*. Lawrence: University of Kansas Press.

Wilson, H. S. 1994 *African Decolonization*. London: Edward Arnold.

Wimmer, Andreas & Brian Min 2006 "From Empire to Nation-State: Explaining Wars in the Modern World, 1816–2001," *American Sociological Review*, 71, 867–97.

Wimmer, Andreas & Yuval Feinstein 2010 "The Rise of the Nation-State across the World, 1816 to 2001," *American Sociological Review*, 75, 764–90.

Wittkopf Eugene & James McCormick 1990 "The Cold War Consensus: Did It Exist?" *Polity*, XXII, 627–53.

Wong, Joseph 2004 *Healthy Democracies: Welfare Politics in Taiwan and South Korea* Ithaca, NY: Cornell University Press.

Woodward, Bob 2004 *Plan of Attack*. New York: Simon & Schuster.

World Bank 1997 *World Development Report: The State in a Changing World*. New York: Oxford University Press.

2007 *World Development Indicators*. Washington, DC: World Bank.

Wright, Donald & Colonel Timothy Reese 2008 *On Point II: Transition to the New Campaign: The United States Army in Operation Freedom, May 2003 to January, 2005*. Fort Leavenworth, KS: Combat Studies Institute Press.

Wu, Yanrui 2004 *China's Economic Growth: A Miracle with Chinese Characteristics*. London: Routledge.

Yang, Dali 1996 *Calamity and Reform in China: State, Rural Society, and Institutional Change since the Great Leap Famine*. Stanford, CA: Stanford University Press.

2004 *Remaking the Chinese Leviathan: Market Transition and the Politics of Governance in China*, Stanford, CA: Stanford University Press.

Yaqub, Salim 2003 *Containing Arab Nationalism: The Eisenhower Doctrine and the Middle East*. Chapel Hill: University of North Carolina Press.

Young, Crawford 1994 *The African Colonial State in Comparative Perspective*. New Haven, CT: Yale University Press.

Zakaria F. 2003 *The Future of Freedom: Illiberal Democracy at Home and Abroad*. New York: Norton.

Zeitlin, Maurice 1980 "On Classes, Class Conflict and the State: an Introductory Note." In Zeitlin (ed.), *Classes, Class Conflict and the State*. Cambridge, MA: Winthrop.

Zelizer, Julian 2009 "The Winds of Congressional Change," *The Forum*, 7, 1–8.

Zhang, Shu Guang 1995 *Mao's Military Romanticism: China and the Korean War, 1950–1953*. Lawrence: University Press of Kansas.

Zieger, Robert 1995 *The CIO, 1935–1955*. Chapel Hill: University of North Carolina Press.

Zubkova, Elena 1998 *Russia after the War: Hopes, Illusions, and Disappointments, 1945–1957*. Armonk, NY: M. E. Sharpe.

Zubok, Vladislav & Constantine Pleshakov. 1996 *Inside the Kremlin's Cold War: From Stalin to Khrushchev*. Cambridge, MA: Harvard University Press.

Zweig, David 2002 *Internationalizing China: Domestic Interests and Global Linkages*. Ithaca, NY: Cornell University Press.

Index